Beyond Westminster
and Whitehall

Beyond Westminster and Whitehall

The Sub-Central Governments of Britain

R. A. W. RHODES

University of Essex

UNWIN

HYMAN

LONDON SYDNEY WELLINGTON

Published by the Academic Division of
Unwin Hyman Ltd
15/17 Broadwick Street, London W1V 1FP

Allen & Unwin Inc.,
8 Winchester Place, Winchester, Mass. 01890, USA

Allen & Unwin (Australia) Ltd,
8 Napier Street, North Sydney, NSW 2060, Australia

Allen & Unwin (New Zealand) Ltd in association with the
Port Nicholson Press Ltd,
60 Cambridge Terrace, Wellington, New Zealand

First published in 1988

British Library Cataloguing in Publication Data

Rhodes, R. A. W.
  Beyond Westminster and Whitehall: the sub-central governments of
Britain.
  1. Local government — Great Britain
  I. Title
  352.041 JS3111
  ISBN 0-04-352222-X
  ISBN 0-04-445128-8 Pbk

Library of Congress Cataloging in Publication Data

Rhodes, R. A. W.
  Beyond Westminster and Whitehall: the sub-central governments of
Britain/R. A. W. Rhodes.
  p. cm.
  Bibliography: p. 414
  Includes index.
  ISBN 0-04-352222-X (alk. paper).
  ISBN 0-04-445128-8 (pbk.)
  1. Local government — Great Britain.
  2. Great Britain — Politics and government.
  I. Title. 87-30651 CIP
  JS3137.R479 1988
  320.8'0941 — dc 19

Typeset in 10 on 11 point Times by Computape (Pickering) Ltd,
North Yorkshire and printed in Great Britain by
Billing and Sons Ltd, London and Worcester

Contents: an Overview

For my Parents, Keith and Irene

Analytical Contents

Tables and Figures

Tables

Figures

Abbreviations

ACAS	Advisory, Conciliation and Arbitration Service
ACC	Association of County Councils
ACCE	Association of County Chief Executives
ADC	Association of District Councils
ADSS	Association of Directors of Social Services
AEA	Atomic Energy Authority
AHA	Area Health Authority
ALA	Association of London Authorities
ALACE	Association of Local Authority Chief Executives
ALANI	Association of Local Authorities of Northern Ireland
ALC	Association of Liberal Councillors
AMA	Association of Metropolitan Authorities
AMC	Association of Municipal Corporations
ASTMS	Association of Scientific, Technical and Managerial Staffs
BA	British Airways
BASW	British Association of Social Workers
BBC	British Broadcasting Corporation
BL	British Leyland
BMA	British Medical Association
BNOC	British National Oil Corporation
BRB	British Railways Board
BSC	British Steel Corporation
CASE	Confederation for the Advancement of State Education
CBI	Confederation of British Industry
CCA	County Councils Association
CCLGF	Consultative Council on Local Government Finance
CCP	Comprehensive Community Programme
CDP	Community Development Project
CEGB	Central Electricity Generating Board
CEO	Chief education officer
CHAC	Central Housing Advisory Council
CHC	Community Health Council
CIPFA	Chartered Institute of Public Finance and Accountancy
COHSE	Confederation of Health Service Employees
CoSIRA	Council for Small Industries in Rural Areas
COSLA	Convention of Scottish Local Authorities
CPRS	Central Policy Review Staff
CSD	Civil Service Department
CSS	County Surveyors' Society
DEA	Department of Economic Affairs
DEmp	Department of Employment
DEn	Department of Energy
DES	Department of Education and Science
DFP	Department of Finance and Personnel (Northern Ireland)

DHA	District Health Authority
DHSS	Department of Health and Social Security
DHSS (NI)	Department of Health and Social Security (Northern Ireland)
DLO	Direct Labour Organization
DoE	Department of the Environment
DoE (NI)	Department of the Environment (Northern Ireland)
DoI	Department of Industry
DT	Department of Trade
DTp	Department of Transport
DUP	Democratic Unionist Party
EEC	European Economic Community
EFL	External financing limit
EIEC	English Industrial Estates Corporation
EPA	Educational Priority Area
ESG (E)	Expenditure Steering Group (Education)
ESRC	Economic and Social Research Council
EZ	Enterprise Zone
FE	Further education
FIG	Financial Institutions Group
FMI	Financial Management Initiative
GB	Great Britain (the UK excluding Northern Ireland)
GDP	Gross Domestic Product
GIA	General Improvement Area
GLC	Greater London Council
GREA	Grant-related expenditure assessment
HIDB	Highlands and Islands Development Board
HIP	Housing Investment Programme
HMI	Her Majesty's Inspectorate
HMSO	Her Majesty's Stationery Office
HSC	Health and Safety Commission
IBA	Independent Broadcasting Authority
ICL	International Computers Ltd
ICPP	Inner Cities Partnerships and Programmes
IEA	Institute of Economic Affairs
IGR	Intergovernmental relations
IHE	Institution of Highway Engineers
ILEA	Inner London Education Authority
IMF	International Monetary Fund
IoH	Institute of Housing
IRC	Industrial Reorganization Corporation
ITB	Industrial Training Board
JCP	Job Creation Programme
JNC/NJC	Joint national council/national joint council
LACSAB	Local Authorities' Conditions of Service Advisory Board
LAMSAC	Local Authorities Management Services and Computer Committee
LBA	London Boroughs Association
LEA	Local education authority
LGTB	Local Government Training Board
MAFF	Ministry of Agriculture, Fisheries and Food
MCC	Metropolitan County Council

MHLG	Ministry of Housing and Local Government
MMC	Monopolies and Mergers Commission
MoD	Ministry of Defence
MP	Member of Parliament
MPO	Management and Personnel Office (of the Cabinet Office)
MRA	Multiple regression analysis
MSC	Manpower Services Commission
MTFS	Medium-term financial strategy
NACLG	National Advisory Committee on Local Government (Conservative Party)
NAHA	National Association of Health Authorities
NALGO	National Association of Local Government Officers
NBPI	National Board for Prices and Incomes
NCB	National Coal Board
NDT	National Development Team
NEB	National Enterprise Board
NEC	National Executive Committee (Labour Party)
NEDC	National Economic Development Council
NEDO	National Economic Development Office
NHS	National Health Service
NICG	Nationalized Industries Chairmen's Group
NIHE	Northern Ireland Housing Executive
NIO	Northern Ireland Office
NRDC	National Research Development Corporation
NUM	National Union of Mineworkers
OECD	Organization for Economic Co-operation and Development
OFTEL	Office of Telecommunications
OPCS	Office of Population Censuses and Surveys
PAR	Programme Analysis and Review
PES	Public expenditure survey
PPBS	Planning Programming Budgeting System
PPS	Policy planning system
PSBR	Public Sector Borrowing Requirement
PSS	Personal social services
Quango	Quasi-autonomous non-governmental organization
Quelgo	Quasi-elected local government organization
RAWP	Resource Allocation Working Party
RCU	Road Construction Unit
RDCA	Rural District Councils Association
REPB	Regional Economic Planning Board
REPC	Regional Economic Planning Council
RIPA	Royal Institute of Public Administration
RLGSC	Regional and Local Government Subcommittee (of the Labour Party NEC)
RSG	Rate Support Grant
RWA	Regional Water Authority
SCG	Sub-central government
SCT	Society of County Treasurers
SDA	Scottish Development Agency *or* Special Development Area
SDD	Scottish Development Department
SDLP	Social Democratic and Labour Party

SDP	Social Democratic Party
SED	Scottish Education Department
SEPD	Scottish Economic Planning Department
SET	Selective Employment Tax
SHHD	Scottish Home and Health Department
SMT	Society of Metropolitan Treasurers
SNP	Scottish National Party
SOLACE	Society of Local Authority Chief Executives
SSRC	Social Science Research Council
STOPP	Society of Teachers Opposed to Physical Punishment
STUC	Scottish Trades Union Congress
TINA	'There is no alternative'
TPP	Transport Policies and Programmes
TSG	Transport Supplementary Grant
TUC	Trades Union Congress
TVEI	Technical and Vocational Education Initiative
UDC	Urban Development Corporation
UDCA	Urban District Councils Association
UK	United Kingdom of Great Britain and Northern Ireland ('Britain' is an alternative short version of the above; see also GB)
UKAEA	United Kingdom Atomic Energy Authority
UP	Urban Programme
WEP	Work Experience Programme
WRVS	Women's Royal Voluntary Service
YOP	Youth Opportunities Programme
YTS	Youth Training Scheme

Acknowledgements

I began work on intergovernmental relations in Britain in 1978 and over the past decade I have incurred innumerable debts. Pride of place must go to the Economic and Social Research Council for providing invaluable financial support. Not only did it fund the research initiative on central–local government relationships, which provided the bulk of the research data drawn on here, but it also awarded me a Personal Research Grant without which this book would have been stillborn. The freedom to spend a whole year reading and writing is priceless, and I am duly grateful.

The work of my fellow researchers on the central–local relations initiative constitutes the heart of this book. I acknowledge the specific contribution of each at the appropriate point in the text. Here, I simply thank them for their help and exonerate each and every one of them from any errors of facts and interpretation in my paraphrase of their work.

In the case of officials in central and local government, convention discourages their acknowledgement by name, and I defer to their natural caution. Without their help, often frank and unstinting, any merits this book may possess would have been reduced immeasurably.

In the case of academic colleagues, convention encourages (to the point of obligation) their acknowledgement. If I named everyone who had been good enough to comment on papers over the past few years, the list would be endless. Consequently, I trust all who showed me the error of my ways at seminars and conferences will accept this general acknowledgement of their help. A few colleagues have helped me to such an extent, however, that they must be identified. Michael Goldsmith (Salford) criticized and, much more important, encouraged me throughout. A simple 'thank-you' must suffice. Brian Hardy (Loughborough) was a model senior research officer who continued to provide concrete assistance and to comment on all my work long after he left Essex. Pat Dunleavy (London School of Economics) and Ed Page (Hull) have worked with me on articles and provided cogent criticisms of some of my earlier work. Both reshaped significantly various themes and arguments presented here. In all probability, neither will agree with my interpretation but they helped to improve it. David Marsh (Essex) never ceased to marvel at my interest in sub-central governments. If underwhelmed with enthusiasm, none the less he challenged continually my interpretation of British government and thereby helped to clarify the argument. John Stewart (Birmingham) and George Jones (London School of Economics) continue to advise and criticize as they have done throughout my academic career. No doubt I should have paid more attention to each and all. The responsibility for all remaining defects remains mine.

All the foregoing are aware of their contribution. Two other people have made unwitting contributions. David Heald's (Glasgow) work on public expenditure in general, and on the nationalized industries (and privatization) in particular, was invaluable. Richard Rose (Strathclyde) has not only made a significant contribution in numerous books and articles to the study of UK politics but he is the guiding light of the Political Studies Association's 'UK Politics Group' and the founder of the Centre for the Study of Public Policy. The conference and occasional papers from these sources have been of great assistance over the years. Without Rose's pioneering endeavours, the obstacles to writing this book would have been formidable. For both authors, I hope this acknowledgement is a pleasant surprise because their work was a pleasing discovery for myself.

For any substantial book, various people play a key supporting role. Austin Baines, Jane Brooks, Sandra Coulter and Terry Tostevin of Essex University's library must have become sick of the sight of me. They obtained inordinate amounts of material on my behalf and even allowed me to visit, unescorted, the inner sanctums! Noel Finney and Carol Snape once again typed and retyped the manuscript promptly and accurately. Each expedited the preparation of the book and all no doubt hope there will be a long gap before the next one.

R. A. W. Rhodes
August 1986

CHAPTER 1

Introduction

The objectives. The structure of the book. Sources.

1.1 The Objectives

The study of British government is too often the study of Westminster and Whitehall. The pictures of senior politicians on television have the all too obvious implication that what they think and do matters for ordinary citizens; but does it? From the standpoint of a consumer of public services, the gallery of national figures with which we are so frequently regaled is less important than might seem to be the case. The house in which 'Henry Dubb' lives, the heating and other energy demands he makes, the school in which his children are educated, the hospital in which they were born, the roads on which he drives, even the tap he turns and the toilet he flushes are not provided by Westminster and Whitehall. Central government may pass a law, provide money, inspect and, on occasion, directly provide a service but, for the most part, it needs the co-operation of other bodies in order to meet its electoral promises. Its influence lies in its ability to cajole, bully and persuade (but not command), and even this ability may not call forth the desired degree of compliance.

This book rejects the fixation on Westminster and Whitehall. The antics of the Opposition as reported in *Parliament Today*, the prospects of a schism in the Labour Party, the aura of doom surrounding an impending Cabinet reshuffle may provide good copy but they have limited effects on the hard question of 'Who gets what public services when and how?' In their place, the focus falls on functional differentiation in British government; on the complex of organizations which are the warp and weft of a modern polity. But if sub-central government (SCG) is the prime vehicle for delivering services, it does not do so in total isolation from the centre. Westminster and Whitehall remain part of the analysis, only this time they are examined from the standpoint of SCG as one set of actors in the web of relationships. To employ Luhmann's (1982, pp. 353–5, xv) provocative phrase, my concern is not with the centre but with the 'centreless society': the differentiated polity with no single centre.

Of course, it would be foolish to argue that the centre in British government could not intervene effectively. It can and does enact laws which are implemented in a manner consistent with the avowed intentions of the government of the day. Its relations with the other governments of Britain are not relations between equals; they are asymmetric, and the centre has a nigh total monopoly of legal resources. But the image of the directive, all-pervasive centre is widespread; it is said that we live in a unitary state in which the government of the day has the right to govern. Perhaps the work of Richard Rose is of greatest significance here. In a series of books and articles (see, for example, Rose, 1976 and 1982; Madgwick and Rose 1982; Rose and McAllister, 1982; McAllister and Rose, 1984) he has recognized the multinational, multiform character of the United Kingdom and yet insisted on the dominance of the centre or 'Mace':

> To write a book about Scottish Nationalism . . . or Welsh Nationalism . . . is to focus upon only one part of the United Kingdom, and upon a minority party within that nation. Similarly, to write a book about the Scottish political system . . . is to assume what remains to be proven, namely that the things differentiating Scotland from England are politically *more* important than what Scotland and England have in common, such as government by Westminster. It is more accurate to speak about British government in Scotland or British government in Wales, *leaving open to empirical investigation* whether, and in what ways, politics in one part of the United Kingdom differs from another . . . Only in Northern Ireland can one properly start from the assumption that government and politics are in fundamental respects *un-British*.
>
> (McAllister and Rose, 1984, p. 8, my emphasis)

The problems with this interpretation lie in the italicized passages. It is not necessary to demonstrate that the periphery is *more* important, only that it is important and cannot be omitted from any account of British government. It is impossible to leave that importance open to empirical investigation if it is assumed that the institutions of, and policies in, Scotland are manifestations of British government in Scotland. This assumption necessarily presupposes the unity and integration of the UK, not its differentiation. Finally, the importance of sub-central government cannot be restricted to the question of nationality. Few if any would argue that local government threatens the national integrity of the UK, but it can and does pose severe obstacles to the policies of the government of the day. For all its pioneering nature, Rose's work presents a fundamentally centralist, integrationist, or, in his word, 'Unionist' picture of the UK. As with so much work on British government, reality is obscured by a focus on the centre.

Behind the easy maxims of the unitary state lie some uncomfortable truths. Central policies fail and are subverted by SCG which develops and implements policies unbeknown or unwelcome to the centre. To understand these features of British government it is necessary to reject the usual centralist perspective and to focus on the constraints both in and on the centre. The constraints in the centre reside in its fragmentation. There is no single centre but multiple centres or policy networks. Paradoxically, fragmentation and centralization can coexist. Each policy network can be centralized, but the weakness of the centre resides in its inability to co-ordinate these multiple centres. The constraints on the centres reside in their non-executant nature; they do not deliver services but are dependent on a variety of other governmental units. This book deliberately rejects the centralist perspective in an attempt to correct a persistent imbalance. It confronts the image of the unitary state with the image of the differentiated polity. The resulting argument may seem one-sided, the image of the strong centre may dissolve, but the picture is no more inaccurate than conventional portraits of British government. To comprehend British government, it is necessary to examine the contradiction of a strong executive dependent on SCG; of authority versus interdependence. My objective is to stake a claim for sub-central government, differentiation and interdependence as characteristics of British government of equivalent importance to the study of the Prime Minister, the Cabinet and Parliament.

Of course, there have been some concessions to this view of British government. It has long been recognized that local government has an important role to play in providing services – hence the preoccupation since the mid-1970s with restraining local expenditure. But this concession is scarcely an improvement. It leads to discussions of central–local relations in education, housing, etc., which imply that this phrase encompasses the relevant policy-makers; to provide 'better' education it is necessary to 'improve' the relationship between the Department of Education and Science (DES) and local education authorities (LEAs). An alternative conception of policy-making in local government emphasizes that local authorities are local political systems with the capacity to initiate and maintain distinct policies (see, for example, Dearlove, 1973, pp. 20–1). The problem with this emphasis is that it tends to underestimate the importance of 'non-local sources of policy change' (Dunleavy, 1980a, p. 98). This phrase does not refer solely to the influence of the centre but also to the gamut of governmental institutions, professions and the corporate economy. In short, local authorities are located in networks of organizations, both public and private (including central actors), and the gestation and implementation of policy cannot be explained by reference to the actions of any one organization. Just as this book focuses on the constraints in and on the centre, it also rejects a focus on the local political system as the source of policy innovation. In place of these foci, it seeks to establish the validity of *networks* of organizations as the most revealing unit of analysis. Policy-making in British government encompasses a wide variety of public sector organizations. A poor family requiring government assistance may need help with gas bills, electricity bills, housing and rate rebates (housing benefit), social work, unemployment and supplementary benefit; and although this list covers five different government bodies, it is incomplete. A thoroughgoing account of British government requires an analysis of networks and of the role of the sub-central level of government within them; a prominence warranted by their undoubted importance for citizens. There is no existing account of the British system of sub-central government in all its network configurations.[1]

Invoking the interests of citizens imbues the argument for the study of sub-central government with noble sentiments. More prosaic grounds support the case. Obviously, citizens should not find their government incomprehensible, but equally the governments of the day should comprehend their 'machine'; they should know its strengths and weaknesses, its capabilities and their capacity to manipulate it. Such knowledge is in short supply. British politicians have a bureaucratic or hierarchy model of the government machine. They expect their interventions to have the intended results. Too frequently, the converse is the case. Judged by their actions, the national political élite has not grasped that the British policy-making system is fragmented and disaggregated, that problems are factorized and that the interdependence of structures and problems requires bargaining between the affected interests and generates multifarious unintended consequences in response to unilateral action. Confronted by the varieties of sub-central government, the metaphor of the government 'machine' is inappropriate – unless the mental image is one bequeathed by W. Heath Robinson. A maze or labyrinth is a far more apposite image (and the minatory connotations seem highly pertinent). To describe and explain sub-central government is not simply to fill a lacuna in the literature but to confront directly a major problem. The problem of sub-central government – whether it is defined as local autonomy, overspending, or inadequate service provision – is equally the problem of central government: the failure to devise or adapt policy instruments for negotiating a maze. The basic objective of this book is to provide a map of the maze that is British sub-central government.

To talk of a maze is to introduce a synonym for complexity and, it is alleged, to so describe British government is both 'trite' and a 'cop-out' (Hood, 1982b, p. 369). The focus on complexity can suggest, however, a number of hypotheses about British government. Thus, increasing scale and interdependence – i.e. complexity – generate decision-making by experts, increasing problems of co-ordination and control, a range of unintended consequences and a decline in policy effectiveness. For all their generality, these suggestions make it clear that mapping the maze is not merely to describe complexity but to focus attention on a facet of British government with manifold consequences for its operation. The following account of SCG will have a considerable amount to say on precisely these kinds of outcome.

Whatever its intrinsic merits, and however necessary, a basic description of the system will be inadequate. The system in 1945 was very different from the system in 1983. These transformations have to be documented. There are three reasons for adopting a historical perspective for even so short a period as 1945–83 (Bulpitt, 1983, pp. 54–5). First, contemporary events have to be located historically if cause and effect, continuities and discontinuities, are to be distinguished accurately. Second, interpretations of the past are part of the stuff of contemporary political debates and such interpretations need to be tested and contested. Finally, many theoretical issues require a historical perspective; for example, no analysis of the changing functions of government would be possible unless it spanned a number of decades. Incorporating a historical perspective into the study of sub-central government could take two forms: synoptic surveys of trends or detailed analyses of critical junctures – i.e. turning-points in the development of sub-central government. The second objective of this book is to provide a synoptic survey of British sub-central government in the postwar period.[2]

Cataloguing change is all well and good, but it is also essential that the development and crises of the system be explained. The third objective, therefore, is to explain the changing pattern of sub-central government. This aspiration is more easily stated than realized. The available theories of British government are numerous and certainly give off an air of mutual incompatibility. To interpret and explain sub-central government requires an explicit model of the system and an awareness of the potential contribution of competing models. This task has been made more difficult in recent years by a rapid increase in the theoretical literature. It is now possible to identify several models concerned specifically with central–local relations, and the major axioms and hypotheses of these models have to be appraised and their strengths and weaknesses for the study of sub-central government have to be assessed.

An alliance of description, history and theory is sufficiently daunting, but the prospectus remains incomplete. The phrase 'sub-central government' suggests that the focus of the study is government organizations. But it will not be possible to determine who gets what public services when and how by limiting the analysis to organizations. This perspective has to be complemented with an analysis of policies. And it is important to stress that the analyses of organizations and of policies are complementary. Policy may be shaped by numerous factors, but the types and activities of government organizations and the procedures shaping their relationships remain an important variable. Accordingly, after exploring the types of sub-central governmental organizations, these organizations are revisited in an analysis of policy-making for such services as education and social work and for such problems as structural reorganizations and intergovernmental financial transfers.

To focus on the policy *process* begs an important question: what difference does it make? Telling stories about bureaucratic politics can be amusing, but how does bureaucratic wheeling and dealing affect the services provided for citizens? In other words, it is necessary to explore the distributional consequences of central dependence on SCG. There can be no pretence that institutional factors provide a complete explanation of the outcomes of the policy process, but they are an important component of any such explanation. In consequence, the case studies of the various policies will examine the extent to which the interactions between the centre and SCG reflect, reinforce, or accentuate the pre-existing inequalities in the distribution of goods and services.

Finally, there is the question of evaluating SCG. In recent years, the air has been rent by the competing cries of those commentators who decry the erosion of local autonomy and the lack of accountability and those who bemoan local 'overspending' and the Leviathan of government. This books forswears evaluations rooted in political philosophy for an examination of the theory(ies) which underpin(s) policies for SCG. It will be argued that such policies must recognize that complexity, indeterminacy and interdependence are defining characteristics of the system. Government interventions will be judged by their strategic flexibility, procedures for institutionalizing indeterminacy and openness of communication. Bureaucratic or hierarchy models of the relationship are both widespread and inappropriate, proliferating policies distinguished by the range of unintended consequences as a result. The criteria employed here for evaluating SCG extend the discussion of accountability beyond the normal preoccupations of representative democracy to encompass accountability systems appropriate to policies rather than institutions. Obviously, they are not the only relevant criteria but they are important and conspicuous primarily for their absence in the continuing debate on SCG.

For a project of such scope, some sacrifice of depth is inevitable. The analysis of educational policy-making would comfortably fill a volume on its own. There are other costs. The study of central–local relations has burgeoned in the past decade, whilst the politics of the nationalized industries have been virtually untouched for an equivalent span of years. The restrictions on the depth of analysis coupled with the unevenness of existing coverage make it particularly important to stress that an overriding objective is to provide a synoptic account of sub-central government. A major part of British government has lingered in the nether world of academic public administration. Inchoate and incoherent, the prime need is for an integrated interpretative account of the whole system. Defects of detail and coverage take a distant second place to this need.

In short, therefore, this book has six objectives:

- to provide a map of SCG;
- to survey the development of SCG in the postwar period;
- to explain the changes in the system;
- to explore the role of SCG in the policy-making process;
- to determine the effect of SCG on policy outcomes; and
- to evaluate policy-making for and by SCG.

1.2 The Structure of the Book

The book has four major sections. The first section (Chapter 2) reviews the various theories of intergovernmental relations (IGR), including public administration, the New Right, centre–periphery relations and neo-Marxist theory. A broad definition of sub-central government is employed covering relations between central political institutions in the capital city and those sub-central political organizations and governmental bodies within the accepted boundaries of the state (cf. Bulpitt, 1983, p. 1). It concludes with a model of IGR which builds upon Rhodes (1981a, 1986a and b) and is described as 'intergovernmental theory'. This model has three levels of analysis: the national government environment (macro), policy networks (meso) and organizations (micro). Its distinctiveness lies in the emphasis on the role of policy networks in shaping the policy process and policy outcomes. These structures of resource-dependent organizations are stable, focused on specific services and the responsible central department, but they incorporate local authorities, the professions and a select few interest groups.

The second section (Chapter 3) describes the variety of actors and relationships in the policy networks. British central government is non-executant; it is dependent upon other bodies in the public sector to provide services. The section focuses on these other bodies (or SCG) and describes the interests, resources and relationships of territorial ministries (e.g. the Northern Ireland Office); intermediate institutions (e.g. the 'regional' offices of the DoE); non-departmental public bodies, a term which covers public corporations, the NHS and the plethora of fringe bodies (executive, advisory and judicial bodies as well as quangos proper); local government, including the new joint boards and committees; and sub-central political organizations (e.g.

8 *Beyond Westminster and Whitehall*

'nationalist' political parties, local interest groups and the professions). Although lengthy, this list vividly demonstrates that British
government is disaggregated; that is, the parts are not drawn together
to form a whole. Moreover, by describing the changing pattern of
relationships for each type of SCG, it is possible to demonstrate that
British government has grown by a process of elaboration and
specialization and that the institutionalization of the professions in this
process of differentiation has become both a distinct feature of British
policy-making and a key central strategy.

The third section (Chapter 4) examines the ways in which policy
networks create continuity and order in the complex maze of SCG.
These networks differ in various ways including their degree of
integration, membership, distribution of ˙ resources and central
dependence on sub-central bodies. It is possible, therefore, to identify
six types of policy networks, and a case study is provided of each type
'in action'. Table 1.1 lists the networks, the corresponding case studies
and the ESRC-funded research projects which provided the data. In
short, there is order in the complex world of SCG, and the concept of
policy network is an invaluable tool for unearthing it.

The final section (Chapter 5) draws together the preceding description and analysis providing an explanation of the development of SCG
in the postwar period and a discussion of the consequences and
contradictions which arise from an interpretation of British government as a centreless society. More specifically, I will suggest that the
centre has increasingly resorted to bureaucratic strategies at odds with
a differentiated and disaggregated polity. As a result, unintended
consequences have multiplied, and relations with SCG have been
politicized. Three contradictions have been paramount. The tradition
of a strong executive and the unilateral exercise of authority has been
confounded by the 'hands-off' nature of central departments and their
dependence on SCG for service delivery. The bureaucratic model of
relations between levels of government – of a co-ordinated centre at
the top of a line hierarchy – foundered on differentiation, on the
fragmentation of the centre and the disaggregation of service delivery
systems. Finally, the factorizing of territorial problems conflicted with
the nationalization of service standards, a process accelerated by the
professionalization of policy systems. Since 1979 in particular, central
intervention has exacerbated the tensions between authority and
interdependence, bureaucracy and differentiation, and territory and
functions, engendering a policy mess in which no level of government
could attain its objectives. The past decade cannot be interpreted as
an era of centralization. It is better described as an era of central
decline in that the centre's capacity to achieve its aims deteriorated.
The answer to the question of who gets what public services when and
how became ever more complex and the distribution of the services
ever more unequal. The contradictions of the differentiated polity

Table 1.1 Policy Networks, Case Studies and Types of Sub-Central Government

Networks	Types of SCG[a]	Case Studies	Sources[b]
Policy communities	Local education authorities and non-departmental public bodies (MSC)	(1) Reforming the grant system (2) Education provision for 16–19-year-olds	E. M. Davies et al., 1983 Ranson, 1982; Crispin and Marslen-Wilson, 1984
Territorial communities	Territorial ministries and local government	As for (1) above, but focused on Scotland	Midwinter, 1984
Intergovernmental networks	Local government	The reorganization of local government	Rhodes, 1986a
Professionalized networks	NHS and local government (personal social services)	Joint funding and care in the community	Webb, Wistow and Hardy, 1986
Producer networks	Nationalized industries and non-departmental public bodies	Contraction and redundancies	T. Davies, Mason and Davies, 1984
Issue networks	Intermediate institutions, non-departmental public bodies and local government	Inner cities policy	Leach, 1982a. Parkinson and Wilks, 1983a; Stewart, Whitting and Underwood, 1983

Notes
[a] All the case studies involve all types of SCG. This column identifies that type of SCG which figures most prominently in the case study.
[b] This list of sources is illustrative, not comprehensive. For a complete listing see Goldsmith and Rhodes (1986).

constitute a daunting challenge for the government of Britain over the next decade.

Given that each of these chapters is substantial, I have adopted a number of devices to guide the reader through the book. First, in common with most academic books, I provide a short statement of the organization and contents of each chapter in its introduction as well as a summary of the ground covered. The summaries occur at the end of each major subsection rather that at the end of the chapter. Second, in addition to the usual contents list, I have provided a detailed analytical contents list: in effect, it is the Ordnance Survey map of the book which should prevent readers getting lost. Third, I have employed tables and figures to summarize both the theoretical and descriptive material. Fourth, at the head of each chapter, I reproduce the relevant portion of the analytical contents list, without the section numbers, to provide both an at-a-glance synopsis of the chapter and a convenient signpost *en route*. Finally, the Subject Index will help the interested reader follow through his/her interest in either a specific institution or policy. Hopefully, these various devices will ensure a clear and comfortable passage through the book in spite of the vast amount of ground covered.

1.3 Sources

This book was conceived as a review and synthesis of *existing* research. The most important sources of data were the research reports of the Economic and Social Research Council (ESRC) initiative on central–local relations. The initiative began in 1978 and explored variations in central–local government relations depending on policy, function and area. It aimed to develop an understanding of intergovernmental relationships, policy-making, implementation and accountability. Since inception, a vast amount of material has been published, and illustrations of this output are provided in Table 1.1 (and for a full listing see Goldsmith and Rhodes, 1986).

The ESRC's initiative, not to mention frenzied government activity, stimulated interest within the academic community over and beyond the commissioned research. The study of central–local relations became a 'mini-industry', and this study has drawn extensively from the range of available material. The References and Bibliography provide a guide to it. Its length and the frequent citations in the text are, of course, a typical academic style of writing. Whether or not such a style has any intrinsic merits, it has three specific purposes here. First, there is no tradition of studying sub-central government as a whole. The literature, although considerable, is diffuse and often specialized, and the book draws it together in order to foster future work in the area. Second, my perspective on British government, is somewhat unusual if not entirely novel. It is more important than usual, therefore, to marshal the available evidence to support the interpretation. Third, at least some of the ground covered will be unfamiliar to all readers, and I have provided more detail than is common for a general essay on British government to aid comprehension. In addition, the detail reflects my conviction that an adequate understanding of how British government operates is positively handicapped not only by the fixation on the centre but also by the tendency to avoid the details of institutional operation and the specifics of policy processes. The hoary chestnuts of the constitution are the worst possible guide to who gets what public services when and how, and, in my judgement, the degree of detail which follows errs on the side of generality.

Unfortunately the governments of the day since 1979 have preferred a few simple *idées fixes* to a comprehensive knowledge of SCG and legislative activity to reflections upon past experience. The survey of existing research had to be supplemented, therefore, by the regular consultation of primary sources, including some interviewing, simply to keep pace with the changes in the system. However, no attempt has been made to provide a detailed account of developments during the Conservatives' second term of office. The bulk of the study covers the years 1945 to 1983. Developments up to 1985 have been covered, but the emphasis has remained firmly on trends throughout the postwar period. Current affairs are described only in as far as they are relevant to understanding the *evolution* of relations, and changes since 1983 have served to consolidate pre-existing trends rather than to introduce any major new transformations. On this occasion, detailed policy changes must come second to a description of the overall pattern.

Notes

1 The major texts on SCG in the postwar period include: Robson, 1948; Chester, 1951; West Midlands Study Group, 1956; Griffith, 1966. More recently see Rhodes, 1986a. Rhodes, 1981a contains an extensive bibliography. However, these references cover only central–local relations. A somewhat broader compass can be found in Rose, 1982 and Bulpitt, 1983, and they can be supplemented by the articles in Madgwick and Rose, 1982, and the data collated in Rose and McAllister, 1982. However, the major concern of these references is territorial politics, and considerably less attention is given to either central–local or interorganizational relations. A useful bibliography on UK territorial politics is Pollock and McAllister, 1980. Finally, the literature on inter-organizational relations is fragmentary. There is no single comprehensive review, but Pryke, 1981, and Curwen, 1986, on the nationalized industries; Hogwood and Keating, 1982, and Saunders, 1983, on intermediate institutions; and Hague, Mackenzie and Barker, 1975, and Barker, 1982a, on non-departmental public bodies all provide useful surveys.

2 Important though the historical context of SCG may be, it is necessary to enter immediately a disclaimer; this book is not, and will not provide, a history of SCG. It concentrates on the operation of the system, in particular on its institutions and policy processes. It will sketch briefly the context to these operations but it will not provide, for example, a history of the Northern Ireland 'problem'. Such an exercise is beyond both the remit of the book and the competence of the author.

CHAPTER 2

Concepts and Models in the Analysis of Sub-Central Government

Introduction. Defining sub-central government. Models of sub-central government: public administration, the 'New Right', centre–periphery relations, the 'radical' model, intergovernmental theory. Towards a theoretical reconstruction: defining the unit of analysis, levels of analysis, criteria of evaluation, objects of study. Explaining the changing pattern of sub-central government – a model of SCG: national government environment, policy networks, organizations and actors. Conclusions.

2.1 Introduction

For the bulk of the postwar period sub-central government (SCG) could be described as the government of Britain 'beyond Whitehall'. This phrase captures the mutual insulation of central and local government. But with the public expenditure crisis of the mid-1970s, the relationship was to be transformed. The politics of SCG were to become part and parcel of the politics of both Westminster and Whitehall. Consequently, central–local relations emerged from the obscurity of scholarly monographs and the confines of courses on public administration. The recurrent conflicts of the past decade have figured prominently in the popular dailies and on the peak viewing television news programmes.

It is all too obvious that this dramatic change has its roots in the declining fortunes of the British economy. With the onset of economic retrenchment, successive governments have sought to control the expenditure of local authorities to further the cause of economic revival. Important though this simple fact may be, it advances our understanding of the changes to only a limited degree. It is as important to understand the form of government intervention and to explain both the consequences of its actions and the multiform reaction of local authorities. And as ever, interpreting British politics, whether the topic is the respective roles of Parliament and the executive, the relative influence of business and trade unions, or, as in this case, the ostensibly mundane topic of sub-central government, is a highly contentious matter. The 'spectacles' which can be worn for viewing events may not be as florid as those of Elton John but they are as numerous. This chapter explores the available range and provides an assessment of their strengths and weaknesses before describing the particular 'pair' which will be used in the remainder of the book for 'viewing' SCG.

2.2 Defining Sub-Central Government

The phrase 'sub-central government' (SCG) is itself somewhat unusual in the context of British government; the most common term employed is that of 'central–local relations'. However, a broader appellation is necessary if only to draw attention to the fact that links between the centre and sub-central units of government are *not* restricted to the relationship between central departments and local authorities. It is also necessary to take into account the decentralized structures of central departments, the nationalized industries and other types of *ad hoc* bodies (otherwise known as 'quangos'), and the different systems of local government within the UK each with its own 'centre'. Extending the study of central–local relations to the study of the relationships between the centre and all types of sub-central units of government is only a first step in the direction of an appropriate definition of the subject-matter. The limitations of this definition of SCG are starkly identified by Tarrow (1978, pp. 1–2):

> How central governments and their territorial subunits are linked politically is not only a problem of intergovernmental relations but also one of managing the class and interest conflicts of modern societies. No more can intergovernmental relations be separated from political sociology than can the current fiscal crisis be separated from the inner logic of the economic system. Both take territorial forms, but both are ultimately related to conflicts of interest and ideology that emerge from the functional cleavages of a modern society.

In short, SCG cannot be limited to the study of the 'pirouettes of pettyfogging bureaucrats', whichever units of government enter into the account; it must also encompass 'territorial politics'. This injunction is not without its problems, most noticeably the elusive nature of any discrete definition of the term 'territorial politics'.

Bulpitt (1983, p. 1) defines territorial politics broadly as:

> that area of political activity concerned with the relations between central political institutions in the capital city and those interests, communities, political organizations and governmental bodies outside the central institutional complex but within the accepted boundaries of the state which possess, or are commonly perceived to possess, a significant geographical or local/regional character.

This definition avoids a concentration on relations between central and local government but at the cost of so broadening the field of study that it becomes difficult 'to separate central–local relations from the wider workings of the political system' (Bulpitt, 1983, p. 53). 'Everything will appear to be connected ... the distinctiveness of the territorial political arena will be obscured' (Bulpitt, 1983, p. 54). This problem arises from the inclusion of *any* interest or communities 'commonly perceived to possess a significant geographical or local/regional character' in the definition.

Tarrow (1978, pp. 3–4) presents a more modest prospectus. He quotes with approval Ashford's (1976, p. 2) distinction between 'territorial influence based on political representation and party organizations' and the 'functional powers of central governments and the changing functional relationships between the center and the sub-units'. In contrast to Bulpitt, Tarrow focuses, therefore, on territorial units of representation and political organization, emphasizing the links between local and national political élites.

Merging the concern with the varieties of governmental institutions with this concentration on the channels for articulating territorial interests, SCG can now be defined as 'the arena of political activity concerned with the relations between central political institutions in the capital city and those sub-central political organizations and governmental bodies within the accepted boundaries of the state'. This conception has a broad focus, but the subject remains distinguishable from the wider political system. In addition, it becomes possible to specify the components of the British system of SCG (see Figure 2.1).

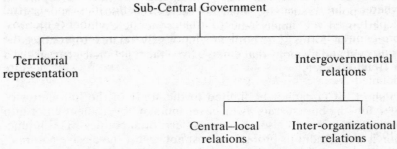

Figure 2.1   *The scope of sub-central government.*

Thus, *territorial representation* refers to the representation of ethnic-territorial units (e.g. Scotland, Wales and Northern Ireland) at the centre and the activities of territorially based political organizations. *Intergovernmental relations* (IGR) refers to the relations between all forms of governmental organizations. It is sub-divided into *central–local relations* or the links between central departments and local authorities and *inter-organizational* relations, which encompass other types of sub-central governmental bodies (e.g. nationalized industries, non-departmental public bodies and the decentralized units of central departments).

No definition or typology is without its fuzzy edges. Here, the definition presupposes that the public sector can be distinguished from the private sector; that we know which organizations are governmental.[1] Of course this distinction has become blurred as government has come to intervene in all aspects of modern Britain (Dunsire, 1973, ch. 10). Equally, local authorities are territorial units with representatives and political organizations active at the centre. However, such qualifications (and additional complications) are the subject-matter of the book. The definition and typology provide the baseline for subsequent exploration. With such a wide-ranging definition of SCG, the potential for divergent interpretations of the crises and developments of the postwar period is considerably enhanced. A review of some of the more common models will serve both to illustrate this diversity and to identify some of the requirements essential to any theory of SCG.

2.3 Models of Sub-Central Government

The explicitly theoretical treatment of SCG is a relatively recent phenomenon. For the bulk of the postwar period, any discussion was limited not only to the relationship between central departments and local authorities but also to the 'agent' and 'partnership' versions of this relationship. Thus, in the agent model, local authorities implement national policies under the supervision of central departments, whereas, in the partnership model, local authorities and central departments are coequals under Parliament. For a number of reasons, pre-eminently the financial dependence of local government on the centre, the relationship has shifted from one of partnership to agency: a trend condemned as an erosion of local autonomy (for a more detailed discussion see Rhodes, 1981a, ch. 2). It was all too easy to point to the descriptive and analytical inadequacies of these models, and since 1979 a considerably more sophisticated range of theories have provided the currency for academic exchange. Thus, Dunleavy (1984, pp. 56–65) distinguishes between conventional public administration, intergovernmental theory, public choice and local state theory. Alternatively, Bulpitt (1983, ch. 1) discusses territorial systems analysis, the centralization/decentralization dichotomy and centre–periphery relations, especially the internal colonization thesis. It will be useful to review briefly these different approaches *and* relate them to the study of territorial representation and IGR in the UK.[2]

2.3.1 Public Administration

For Dunleavy (1982a, p. 215), public administration focuses

> on the institutions, organizational structures and decision/ implementation processes of government. It is a largely 'formal' field, concerned with arrangements and procedures for making decisions, rather than with the substance or impacts of these decisions. It is also a relatively micro-level subject, often concerned with description rather than macro-themes or large scale theorizing. Finally it is an area which is quite largely 'applied' and closely linked with practical problems and practised solutions.

In the study of SCG, the emphasis has fallen on describing the arrangements and procedures for regulating the relationship between central and local government. Accounts are provided of the variety of control mechanisms available to the centre and of the mechanics of the grant system. For Bulpitt (1983, pp. 19–34), the most distinctive feature of this model is its 'centralization paradigm', involving three assumptions: that key decision-making functions are located in the capital city; that it is possible to identify and measure the extent of centralization; and that centralization is 'bad' whereas decentralization (or local autonomy) is 'good'. Moreover, the degree of centralization in British government has increased because of: the transfer of functions from local government to either central government or *ad hoc* bodies; local authority dependence on central grant; and close supervision of local authorities by central departments. As a result, local autonomy has been eroded. Government has become remote, inefficient and unresponsive to local needs. Local government has ceased to be a partner of the centre; it has become a mere agent.

Stated in this form, the public administration model takes on the character of a 'straw man'. None the less, this brief statement indicates the content and scope of the model and the following criticisms should serve to dispel some of the more erroneous (and surprisingly common) assertions and beliefs about central–local relations.

First, central–local relations are not a zero-sum game. The loss of functions by local government to other bodies does not necessarily betoken an erosion of local autonomy. All levels of government could have increased their responsibilities, and the postwar period has seen a considerable expansion in the functions of local government, e.g. social work, planning.

Second, functions are not intrinsically 'local' or 'national' in character. As Dunleavy (1984, p. 57) points out, 'very few functions can be unequivocably classified in this simple way leaving the vast bulk of "welfare state" activities in an uneasy no man's land'.

Third, there is little empirical support for the proposition that 'he who pays the piper calls the tune'. Central grants do not necessarily increase central control of local authorities. (See Rhodes, 1981a, pp. 14–21.)

Fourth, the term 'central–local relations' is misleading in two ways. It implies that IGR is limited to central departments and local authorities, omitting all other types of sub-central units of government. It also implies that central government is homogeneous when, in reality, it is composed of a multitude of discrete, conflicting interests – as indeed is the individual local authority.

Fifth, as Bulpitt (1983, p. 28) points out, it is assumed that 'central dominance of local government is easy' and, additionally, that the centre's intentions are to increase its control of local authorities. But the close supervision of a multitude of local authorities is a task of such daunting proportions that it is of doubtful practicability. Whether or not it is administratively feasible, there is precious little evidence that for the bulk of the postwar period, the centre sought such powers.

Sixth, the merits of local government are asserted rather than demonstrated. In an ideal world, local government may be responsive to local needs, evoke popular interest and enthusiasm, deliver services efficiently and be clearly and directly accountable to the local electorate. In the real world, such characteristics all too frequently take on an air of naïve utopianism. Conversely, it is not self-evident that centralization inevitably breeds remoteness and inefficiency. And the key point here is not that centralization is good (or bad) but that its merits (or demerits) should be *explicitly documented*.

From this brief survey, it might seem that the public administration model had little or nothing to offer in the analysis of IGR. Certainly, it has major limitations as a description of the system, and its capacity for explaining the nature and form of change is equally limited. But it would be a mistake to attempt an overall assessment at this stage. Recently, the model has been restated in more cogent form.

The revival of the public administration model can be most conveniently dated from the publication of the report of the Committee of Inquiry into Local Government Finance (Layfield Committee, 1976). Subsequently, two members of the committee have developed its arguments into a broad ranging defence of local government (Jones and Stewart, 1983) which addresses the issues of centralization and local autonomy. This defence avoids complacency, stressing the *potential* of local government, and explicitly argues the merits of local autonomy.

Autonomy is seen as 'an essential element in achieving more responsible, responsive and accountable government' (Jones and Stewart, 1982, p. 13). If these objectives are to be attained, then local government must be autonomous: that is, 'involved in substantial activities over which it has a considerable degree of choice' (Jones and Stewart, 1982, p. 14). The specific merits of local government are that it has the potential for: the diffusion of power; diversity of response to both variations in local need and the aims and wishes of local inhabitants; social learning through the variations in provision and experiments of different local authorities; and, by its very local-ness, accessibility to citizens and responsiveness from local authori-ties. However, if these advantages are to be realized, and the objec-tives of responsible, responsive and accountable government attained, several reforms are required, not just in central–local rela-tions but also in the structure and functioning of local government. Thus, they argue that: Parliament should enact a charter for local government which would specify the principles guiding central inter-vention (p. 109); there should be a clear separation of expenditure for which the centre is responsible and that for which local govern-ment is responsible and the introduction of local income tax (p. 108); the functions and powers of local authorities should be increased (p. 149); proportional representation should be introduced; and the two tier system should be replaced with unitary authorities (p. 159). Even this highly selective summary demonstrates the swingeing reforms required to create responsible, responsive and accountable government.

The distinctive feature of Jones and Stewart's approach is its nor-mative nature. They specify the merits of local autonomy and the characteristics of an ideal local government system and use them to diagnose and criticize the existing system of centre–local relations. Describing the existing system is a necessary but incidental part of the larger goal of reform, and explanations of the origins of the 'crisis' tend to be at best cursory and often implicit. In short, as Page (1982, p. 26) points out, local autonomy is used both as an evaluative criter-ion and as a prescriptive framework. Ultimately, therefore, any criti-cisms of Jones and Stewart will involve personal beliefs about the 'trade-offs' between such values as, for example, local democracy and territorial justice: an 'essentially contestable' exercise. Without entering the realms of ideology, however, a number of more prosaic points can be noted.

First, the use of some evaluative criterion is inevitable in the study of territorial politics. Although widely used, the concept of local autonomy has remained elusive and it has been used in a highly selec-tive manner. None the less Jones and Stewart attempt an explicit and clear version of this evaluative criterion. Even if it is rejected, the need for explicit criteria remains.

However, and second, there are problems with employing a single criterion. As Page (1982, p. 29) argues, the focus on local autonomy reduces political conflicts to a single dimension: 'When the relevant actors are defined as central and local government, who gains and loses from a set of central government policies can only be central or local government. Which social groups within the local authority gain or lose is ruled outside the debate.'

Third, the evidence for the benefits of local autonomy is unsatisfactory. Local issues are relatively unimportant predictors of local election results. Turn-out in particular and public interest in general are low. And whether the topic is participation or local interest groups, the influence of citizens on local decision-making is unequal and limited. Nor is it clear that local reforms such as proportional representation would generate substantial change. As part of a national political system and political culture, the locus of effective political reform may lie well beyond the confines of local politics. The merits of local autonomy as the sole evaluative and prescriptive criterion are by no means self-evident.

Fourth, the combination of local autonomy as the evaluative criterion with a focus on central–local relations unduly constrains the analysis. Jones and Stewart advocate the reallocation of functions from some *ad hoc* bodies to local government, but otherwise the reforms concentrate on local government and central–local relations. inter-organizational relations and sub-central political organizations receive nary a mention. Extra-local constraints on local autonomy which do not emanate from central government do not form part of the analysis.

Finally, the range of values relevant to the revitalization of local government is potentially enormous. At the very least the incommensurable nature of the values of diversity and uniformity in service provision should be considered. Assuming that clients expect some minimal degree of uniform treatment, the key issue becomes how much diversity in service provision can be tolerated: when should the national government intervene to set a national framework? As noted earlier, it is impossible, on a priori grounds, to distinguish between national and local functions (roles); and, if national frameworks are an expression of political choice which will vary over time with the political process (Jones and Stewart, 1982, p. 11), then the factors which helped to create the current crisis are accorded a key role in its resolution. Rarely are the causes of a problem simultaneously its solution.

For all the estimable clarity of their evaluative criterion, Jones and Stewart remain within the confines of the public administration model. Their analysis is formal, emphasizing structures and procedures, 'linked with practical problems' and having the 'centralization paradigm' at its core. In contrast to earlier contributions, no easy assumptions are made about the effects of financial dependence or the vitality of local democracy. But the focus remains central–local government rather than sub-central government. However, these comments and criticisms do not support the conclusion that the model should be consigned to the dustbin. There are three elements in the model which require continuing attention:

- the need for explicit evaluative criteria;
- the assumption that institutional forms (and reforms) affect both the process and the substance of policy-making; and
- the assumption that local government is the pre-eminent institution of territorial politics in the UK.

2.3.2   The 'New Right'

The dilemma facing anyone providing a short survey of the 'New Right' literature is its diversity. As Jackson (1985b, p. 27) notes, there is no single monetarist model, and many monetarists object to the broadening of the term to include libertarian ideals. None the less, this broadening has occurred, and for the purposes of exposition it will be useful to break the model into three component parts: the arguments from economics (monetarism), from politics (liberalism) and from bureaucracy (public choice). Inevitably, there are overlaps, but this division highlights the central tenets of the 'New Right'.

2.3.2(i)   THE ARGUMENT FROM ECONOMICS: MONETARISM

The shorthand label 'monetarism' could scarcely be less helpful. Beyond denoting that individual contributors share a belief in the importance of the stock of money for macro-economic relationships, it serves only to obscure a diversity of views which has proliferated as the theory has become more influential. For present purposes, Heald's (1983, pp. 35–6) summary will suffice:

(1) Changes in the money stock are the dominant determinants of changes in money income (quantity theory of money).
(2) Changes in the quantity of money will induce portfolio substitution by individuals, across a wide range of assets, not just financial ones but also physical assets such as property and consumer durables (the monetarist transmission process).
(3) Left to itself, the market economy has a self-correcting mechanism in the long run which limits macroeconomic instability (the inherent stability of the private sector).
(4) Irrespective of the initial source of change in the money supply, it will have given predictable effects, even if knowledge about the

structure of this process and the lags involved is imperfect (the irrelevance of allocative detail and belief in the fluid capital market).

These propositions are seen as central. There are also eight supplementary propositions including: the 'use of the monetary stock as the proper target of monetary policy'; rejection of any trade offs between unemployment and inflation; 'a relatively greater concern about inflation than about unemployment compared to other economists'; and 'dislike of government intervention'. Of some importance for the understanding of British economic policy since 1979 are the monetarist beliefs linking the money supply with inflation, and increases in public expenditure with growth of the money supply. The stability of markets is contrasted with the destabilizing effects of government intervention.

The consequences of this model for the public sector in general and territorial politics in particular will be considered under the headings of 'cuts' and 'crowding out'. In spite of their different emphases, it is important to stress that both these arguments conclude that a reduction in the size of the public sector is essential for the economic health of the country.

Cuts Monetarists believe that inflation is caused by growth in the money supply and can be controlled by setting targets for growth in the money supply. The link between such controls and the level of public expenditure lies in the Public Sector Borrowing Requirement (PSBR) or the shortfall of government income over expenditure. It is argued that any borrowing by government to finance its budget deficit will contribute to the growth in the money supply and hence inflation. Cuts in the level of public expenditure, particularly capital expenditure, help to reduce, therefore, growth in the money supply. Thus local authorities have faced severe cuts in their capital expenditure as part of the government's strategy of restricting the size of the PSBR.

Crowding out This argument focuses directly on the size of the public sector, claiming that its growth – i.e. as a proportion of GDP – pre-empts resources which would otherwise be available to the 'productive' private sector. It takes two forms: direct (or physical) and indirect (or financial) crowding out. Bacon and Eltis (1978) argue that the growth in public employment has been at the expense of the private sector – physical crowding out. The argument about indirect crowding out claims that increases in public expenditure finance by borrowing will increase interest rates (if money supply targets are to be met). As a result, consumption will be depressed, the exchange rate will appreciate, and the international competitiveness of British industry will be adversely affected. Again, it is concluded that the size of public sector should be curtailed.

2.3.2(ii) THE ARGUMENT FROM POLITICS: LIBERALISM

This argument has at its heart the link between markets and freedom. The ills of government intervention have already been touched upon. It weakens the productive private sector and fuels inflation. Additionally bureaucratic means of resource allocation are seen as inefficient; politicians are said to 'over-expand' the public sector to maximize votes (and their re-election); and government is said to foster and protect sectional interests, e.g. trade unions, professions. Thus:

> *Government is more and more seen as the protector of powerful vested interests rather than the promoter of efficiency for the benefit of the country as a whole.* It is increasingly recognized that prosperity and freedom in Britain depend crucially upon the survival of the market economy, which must be protected *from* government if it is to survive.
>
> (Littlechild, 1979, p. 12, original emphasis)

Accordingly, the 'minimal state' is seen as a prerequisite of prosperity and freedom. Its functions would be limited to the protection of property rights and external defence: to preserving 'negative liberty' – at its simplest, freedom from the arbitrary will of others, especially public authority (Hayek, 1960, ch. 1; but see Berlin, 1969; Goodin, 1982a).

If the state is a threat to negative liberty, then markets positively enhance such freedoms which are

> inextricably linked to the exercise of individual choice within markets . . . Freedom exists whenever individuals may, unhindered by the state, exploit whatever market opportunities lay open to them . . . The polity's role is to sustain the framework which both facilitates the operation of the market economy and also insulates the economy from direct intervention by the polity. Public expenditure thereby diminishes freedom because it substitutes judgements emanating from the state about the composition of output for unconstrained market outcomes.
>
> (Heald, 1983, p. 73)

The implications of this view for the public sector are dramatic. It requires a substantial reduction in the functions of government and it provides a substantial part of the rationale for 'privatization'.

Heald (1983, p. 299) distinguishes four components of privatization: privatizing the finances of a service by increasing the role of charges; privatizing the production of a service by contracting out work to the private sector; denationalization by either selling off public enterprises or transferring activities to the private sector; and liberalization or the relaxation of statutory monopolies. Such disparate activities share common concerns with limiting state provision and reinforcing the position of the private sector and/or the individual consumer. Privatization can seem one of the more modest implications of the 'New Right' views on freedom. Rowley's (1979, pp. 114–17) proposals for curtailing the power of vested interests – e.g. public bureaucracies, professions and trade unions – include buying individual employees out of their unions and removing the right to strike and picket of all public sector employees: proposals which imply an actively coercive role for government.

2.3.2(iii) THE ARGUMENT FROM BUREAUCRACY: PUBLIC CHOICE

If the defects of market allocations tend to be ignored, the ills of bureaucracy are a bottomless pit of spleen for the 'New Right'. Ignoring the diatribes, Niskanen's (1971 and 1973) analysis of bureaucratic 'over-supply' and the Institute of Economic Affairs' analysis of public services (see, for example, Harris and Seldon, 1976; Anderson *et al.*, 1980) should adequately convey the flavour of the approach.

The distinctive feature of the public choice literature is the deductive form of analysis derived from micro-economics; i.e. it advances a limited number of propositions, deduces their consequences under varying conditions, compares these deductions with empirical observation and thereby evaluates the theoretical constructs. Four propositions recur (see, for example, Bish, 1971; Mueller, 1979, ch. 8; Jackson, 1982a, ch. 5).

- *Scarcity* – individuals want more goods and services than are available and it is necessary to explore, therefore, the efficiency of the several mechanisms for allocating goods and services, most notably markets.
- *Methodological individualism* – the individual is the basic unit of analysis.
- *Self-interest* – individuals take actions because they stand to benefit from them.
- *Individual rationality* – in making choices the individual chooses that course of action which will give him/her the greatest satisfaction.

Studies within this idiom demonstrate a marked normative preference for markets (or quasi-markets) in the allocation of resources. Thus, individuals are the best judge of the quantity and 'mix' of services they want, and allocation through markets not only reflects such preferences more accurately than bureaucratic allocations but also provides a more 'efficient' solution to the problem of scarcity. There are now a number of studies of the behaviour of bureaucrats as rational, self-interested actors and of bureaucratic inefficiency.

Niskanen's analysis of bureaucratic behaviour posits two self-interested and rational actors: the bureaucrat and the politician. The former is the sole supplier of public goods and services and aims to maximize the agency budget in order to obtain greater status, discretion and emoluments. The latter is the sole buyer of bureaucratic outputs and aims to maximize the votes cast for him in the next election. Bargaining in this kind of bilateral monopoly has a number of special features which lead to the *oversupply* of public goods. Thus, on the supply side, there is a monopoly of information on costs; i.e. the politician cannot know whether he/she can get more for less or even more for the same level of expenditure. On the demand side, budget requests are considered by specialist committees with a disproportionate number of representatives from constituencies with a known and high demand for the public good in question. With no information to challenge the costing of services and strong disincentives against pruning budgets, oversupply can, according to Niskanen, be as great as twice the optimum in terms of citizen preferences. Moreover, costs increase as the costs of any alternative source of supply increases. Niskanen's solution to the problem of oversupply is to institute competitive bidding between agencies. In this process of competing for contracts, tasks would be allocated to the lowest bidder, and the bureaucrats would have to release information on costs.

The IEA's various publications similarly illustrate the public choice approach to bureaucracy. Its policy proposals invariably stress the substitution of private for public provision, charging for services which the public sector *has* to provide or, where this is impractical, introducing voucher schemes. The rationale for these proposals lies in the belief that individual choice should inform the allocation of public goods. And as a logical corollary, they argue that 'X-efficiency' or minimizing inputs for a given output (Leibenstein, 1966) is low in public bureaucracies. Thus, where services are provided free, output will be expanded beyond the level at which consumers remain willing to pay. Charging for services and the introduction of vouchers both provide incentives for X-efficiency. Note that again the analysis points to a reduction in the scope of government and an extension for the role of the market.

Although described separately, these strands of 'New Right' thinking are interwoven. The assumptions of rational self-interested actors and methodological individualism in public choice theory are entirely compatible with the stress on markets in libertarian political philosophy and monetarism. The analysis of bureaucratic inefficiency is an important strand in libertarian arguments for the minimal state. The adverse effects of government intervention diagnosed by monetarists serve the same purpose. All paths lead from rational man to a market economy, the minimal state and hence freedom. The weave is not perfect, however, and some of the threads would fail Marks & Spencer's quality control standards.

2.3.2(iv)   A CRITIQUE

A thoroughgoing critique of the *mélange* which constitutes the 'New Right' would lead to a book-length study. Here it will be possible to note only some of the major problems (see Jackson, 1984, for a detailed critique of monetarism).

First, 'government policy making needs to recognize that the world is a highly complex and uncertain place. Policies based upon simple axioms and maxims, therefore, run a high risk of resulting in catastrophe' (Jackson, 1985c, p. 61). The problem with monetarist economies lies less in their belief that monetary impulses are an important factor accounting for variations in output, employment and prices, and more in the unqualified assertion that they are the predominant factor, allied to the failure to specify the transmission process – i.e. why and how do changes in the quantity of money alter decisions about production and employment? The inability of monetarist axioms to provide adequate guidance for the management of small open economies is demonstrated by the mixed fortunes of the avowedly monetarist policies of the post-1979 Conservative government (see Jackson, 1985a).

Second, and an essential prerequisite to the analysis of recent British economic policy, the postulated link between money supply targets and the PSBR is not well founded. As Milton Friedman has commented:

> The key role assigned to targets for the PSBR . . . seems to me unwise for several reasons. (1) These numbers are highly misleading because of the failure to adjust for the effect of inflation. (2) There is no necessary relation between the size of the PSBR and monetary growth. There is currently such a relation, though even then a loose one, only because of the undesirable techniques used to control the money supply . . . (3) The size of the PSBR does affect the level of interest rates. However given monetary growth, the major effect on interest rates is exerted by the real (i.e. inflation adjusted) PSBR not the nominal PSBR . . . (4) Emphasis on the PSBR diverts attention from the really important aspects of government fiscal policy: the fraction of the nation's output that is diverted to uses determined by government officials.
>
> (Cited in Heald, 1983, p. 51)

Third, while direct 100% crowding out is a theoretical possibility, there is no strong empirical evidence to support its existence in practice' (Jackson, 1984, p. 2.31). Thus, Karram, (1984, p. 55) concludes that the expansion of public employment was less than Bacon and Eltis's (1978) crude head-count allows and that there was a low degree of labour substitutability between the public and private sectors (see also Wilkinson and Jackson, 1981; Jackson, 1983).

Fourth, the primacy of markets is assumed rather than demonstrated. As Lindblom (1977, pp. 78–85) argues, there are a substantial number of market defects, including the assumption of no or few transaction costs (e.g. the administrative and other costs of market exchanges); the disregard of negative and positive externalities (or the uncounted costs and/or benefits of transactions for third parties); the assumption of complete information (when no consumer is competent across the range of purchases); the existence of monopolies; inability to provide public goods (i.e. goods which if provided for one person – e.g. defence, a lighthouse – are necessarily available to all without paying); the failure of market incentives to draw voluntary responses and consequent need for coercion; the generation of insecurity and instability (for example, unemployment); and the moral objections to the pre-eminence of individual preferences (and to some kinds of exchange) in market systems. All mechanisms for resource allocation have strengths and weaknesses, and markets (and quasi-markets) are no exception. The 'New Right' displays a keen interest in the defects of bureaucratic mechanisms but far less in the imperfections of markets. To show that government action to remedy market defects can exacerbate the problem (Littlechild, 1979) still leaves the defects which prompted that action. Evaluating the relative efficacy of markets and hierarchies, and identifying the conditions under which they are effective, is a more daunting and important task than the easy assertion of virtue for any one resource-allocation mechanism.

Fifth, the libertarian political philosophy not only presents a narrow conception of liberty but also disregards a range of relevant values, most notably (and wilfully) that of equality. Thus, it can be objected that markets (and most important the ownership of private property) generate unfreedoms; that poverty created by a particular set of social and economic arrangements (rather than individual motivation or incapacity) is a form of coercion; and that no one value is absolute but must be traded off against other values. Above all, the concept of liberty can be extended to include freedom to realize individual potentialities and to admit that redistributive policies are not an unwarranted interference with property rights but a justifiable means towards self-realization through the removal of economic constraints. And it is this narrowness of vision which is the most objectionable feature of the libertarian philosophy. As Goodin (1982a, p. 152) argues, the distinction between negative and positive freedom 'is dangerously misleading ... because it poses the issue far too starkly. Positive and negative freedoms are not, as the labels imply, absolutely contradictory notions. Indeed, they are not two different notions at all but only incomplete references to the same underlying conception of freedom.' He distinguishes between agents, constraints and end states (whether they be actions, circumstances, or conditions of character), arguing that freedom exists when an agent is free *from* constraints *to* act, etc. Whether or not negative liberty is seen as a prime value (cf. Goodin, 1982b, ch. 5), it has been elevated to such a position of dominance by the 'New Right' as to impoverish political debate and analysis.

Sixth, the equation that capitalism promotes freedom is not as self-evident as its repetitious assertion might suggest. The 'New Right' focuses on market freedoms, ignoring their relationship to such political freedoms as universal suffrage and freedom of speech and of assembly. After all, the mass of property-less citizens could vote for a more egalitarian distribution of property. Either the potential for conflict when an inegalitarian distribution of property coexists with the widespread conferment of political rights is ignored; or the 'strong state' is invoked to protect property rights; or limitations upon political freedoms are canvassed. Thus bureaucrats are to be disenfranchised to prevent them voting for greater public expenditure (Tullock, 1979, p. 38). As Heald (1983, p. 76) comments: 'The dangers which universal suffrage posed for the established order were well recognized in nineteenth-century debates. Much of the recent advocacy of constitutional reform to limit the activities of the state has been a semi-conscious echo of such fears about democracy.'

Finally, the analysis of bureaucratic behaviour founders on its unrealistic assumptions about the motivations of bureaucrats; the lack of supporting data; the unrealist reform proposals; and the inaccurate specifications of the context of behaviour. It is commonly argued that the 'realism' of the assumptions in the public choice literature is irrelevant provided that the model generates testable hypotheses supported by empirical work. There is marked absence of such empirical work, and where it does exist it is at best inconclusive and more commonly fails to support the hypotheses. Moreover, as Goodin (1982c, pp. 31–2) has pointed out, the bureaucrats are not just budget-maximizers. For example, they are also 'mission committed', that is, motivated by the content of policies. Ignoring the particular conditions of United States executive–legislative relations, it is also inaccurate to suggest either that bureaucrats necessarily restrict the supply of information or that politicians have no mechanisms for acquiring it. Finally, it is implausible to argue that agencies will compete and that this competition will generate information. Even on Niskanen's assumption, the rational self-interested bureaucrats will collude with each other to protect their budgets.

The 'New Right' model has been considered at some length because of its influence on developments in British sub-central government. At the theoretical level, the implications of the model for sub-central bodies are clear, including cuts in public expenditure and manpower, divesting sub-central authorities of functions, central intervention to impose the minimum state and protect and enhance individual choice and liberties and restrictions on bureaucratic power. And although developed and applied to the public sector as a whole, all of these themes have been specifically applied to local government.

Thus, Walker (1983, p. 4) asserts that 'the entire central–local debate is a spurious one' and he continues (p. 5) with a rejection of local autonomy: 'they keep up the forms, pretences and inefficiencies of autonomous governing bodies. The key has become not the existence of independent local councils, but the nature and extent of the "services", which they exist to provide.' The same theme pervades Henney's (1984) critique of local government. Indeed, the cover of his book shows money from the town hall going down the drain: a succinct depiction of his views (see also Anderson *et al.*, 1980). The system of central–local relations and the fiscal crisis are *not* the problem: 'Rather, we should be considering how we can improve the performance of the services that local government presently provides in order to make them: *more responsive to consumer requirements, more cost effective, and more democratic and accountable*' (Henney, 1984, p. 389, original emphasis). The book recounts numerous examples of local government's 'persistently poor record' in housing, planning and financial management; it is part of 'the flaccid corporate state'. The causes of this waste of money are as numerous as they are familiar, including: the lack of consumer influence; professionalism with its tradition 'that nobody outside the professional group should have the right to manage them' (p. 349); aggressive and political public sector unions; weak management arising from the lack of performance standards; fragmentation of the management structure; the range of activities of councils and the lack of ability and appropriate (e.g. commercial) experience of councillors and officers; political considerations overriding concern with costs and the consumer; the absence of external constraints, including the lack of dismissals for incompetence, 'gentle' adults, limited public scrutiny and 'little perception of the importance of money'; and encouragement to spend by central government with no effort to increase cost-effectiveness. The indictment is total:

> local government ... has become too big, too distant, too politicized too subject to pressure from vested interests, and too complicated for ordinary people to understand, let alone control.
>
> (p. 380)

Local government has become part of the corporate state, an arrangement for the institutionalized exercise of political and

economic power by – and for – the real and imagined interests of
large sectors of society.

(p. 380)

Each sector of the corporate state has its own 'cultural cocoon' of
values providing a rationalisation that the interests of the sector are
congruent with the greater good ... the vested interests ... have
monopoly power and, where they do not, they often prefer to seek
to limit competition and change ... The corporate state minimises
accountability; indeed in the worst cases it *institutionalizes irrespon-
sibility*.

(p. 381, original emphasis)

If the diagnosis has a familiar ring, then the prescription will evoke a
similar sense of *déjà vu*. It covers: disbanding the metropolitan
counties and the GLC; transferring the bulk of municipal housing to
the control of occupants; funding higher education through central
grants to students rather than funding colleges; transferring primary
and secondary education to a social market system; simplifying the
planning system; limiting local government's functions to genuine
public goods and its services to those with 'serious needs'; and making
the residue more democratic (e.g. introduce proportional representation), accountable (e.g. make the ombudsman's decisions enforc-
able at law) and efficient (e.g. place officers on three- to four-year
contracts, not tenure; and lay a statutory fiduciary duty on councillors). In sum, the functions of local government should be reduced
substantially, and the remaining activities should be subject to market
and quasi-market constraints. The fiscal crisis will disappear; the
remaining services could be funded from the rates (with some limited
central resource equalization).

Henney not only provides a clear example of 'New Right' political
and economic ideology; he also displays its weaknesses. The possible
weaknesses of social market solutions are simply not considered: a
touching example of faith but a poor basis for major reforms. The
social consequences of his analysis for low income groups are not
considered. His analysis of local politics is jaundiced by his dislike of
the Left in London politics. It is simply assumed that the interests of
public sector unions are not valid, whereas those of the ratepayer are
merely 'common sense'. The virtues if any of professionalism reside
primarily in the protection of jobs: a cocoon against challenge. The list
of means for improving cost-effectiveness is meagre and cursorily
argued and pays little or no attention to the problems of institutionalizing cost-effective procedures and checks. If Henney identifies *some*
of the defects of local government, his analysis is unduly narrow and
his nostrums are a product of fashionable ideological reflexes.

However, the ideology of the 'New Right' can obscure its potential contribution to the analysis of territorial politics. It is important, therefore, to note the *range* of issues to which it directs attention:

- the relationship between public expenditure and inflation;
- the mechanisms (and targets) for the control of public expenditure (and of growth in money supply) and their effectiveness;
- the 'proper' functions of government, the size of the public sector and the scope for divesting it of functions;
- the strengths and weaknesses of markets and bureaucracies for the allocation of resources and the conditions under which each strategy is effective;
- the determinants of public expenditure, especially the influence of professions, bureaucrats and public sector unions;
- the effects of government intervention;
- the incidence of 'X-efficiency' in public bureaucracies and the means for improving cost-effectiveness.

Most of these questions are of such importance that further discussion is inevitable, although the answers may lack the appealing simplicity of the 'New Right's' solutions.

2.3.3 *Centre–Periphery Relations*

At its simplest there are three major variants in the study of centre–periphery relations: diffusion theory, internal colonialism (or dependency theory) and theories of administrative and political brokerage (Tarrow, 1977, pp. 18–35; Bulpitt, 1983, chs. 1 and 2). The latter variant is indistinguishable from intergovernmental theory and is discussed under this heading below.

Diffusion theory at its most general is concerned with the study of development: with the process of differentiation in social roles. When applied to relations within states, the theory explores the persistence and/or erosion of territorially based (commonly ethnic) cleavages in the process of modernization (Rokkan, 1970). For example, the integration of peripheries to a central value system is seen as a key facet of nation-building, with the diffusion of knowledge, skills, etc. producing national homogeneity. At its simplest, the interaction of centre and periphery erodes the bases of separate ethnic identification and produces commonality (but see Page, 1978a, pp. 297–300, for important qualifications).

The internal colonialism thesis, to be equally simplistic, argues that an economically advanced centre colonizes, i.e. dominates and exploits, less advanced areas (Hechter, 1975, pp. 17–22 and 39–43, from which the following summary is paraphrased). This model of the relationship between centre and periphery has five key propositions.

- Uneven industrialization creates territorially based advanced and less advanced groups.
- The dominant core seeks to perpetuate its advantage by policies which institutionalize the existing system of stratification, reserving high-status social roles to its members.
- This cultural division of labour contributes to the development of distinctive ethnic identities.
- The political position of peripheral groups is weak because they lack resources.
- Economic and political inequalities are counter-productive, generating ethnic solidarity and a reaction against core dominance.

These economic, cultural and political bases to core domination and exploitation frustrate political integration.[3]

There are a number of general problems with the literature on centre–periphery relations as well as the specific problems of diffusion and dependency theory.

First, the language is extremely loose, with definitions of the key terms 'centre' and 'periphery' demonstrating an inordinate degree of variety. They encompass central and local government, central and peripheral regions and urban and rural areas.

Second, the scope of the theory is imprecise. At times, the distinction between centre and periphery is seen as part of the structure of territorial politics in all countries. At other times, it exists in only some countries.

Third, for the UK alone, the literature covers the persistence of nationalism, the rise and fall of nationalist parties, the demise of local government, the modernization of territorial institutions, the evolution of British 'Union' and central–local relations. The distinctiveness of the model evaporates in its diffuse objects of inquiry.

Fourth, and paradoxically, the theory suffers from arbitrary limitations. There is a tendency to assume a single national or internal centre when, in fact, there can be multiple centres, some of which can be external to the polity under examination.

Fifth, both diffusion and dependency theory have a number of specific limitations. For example, Hechter's account of the Celtic fringe in British politics is methodologically unsound (Page, 1978a, pp. 303–12), presents a one-sided account of the historical development of the UK (Birch, 1977, pp. 33–4) and disregards both the impact of external forces on the British centre and the mechanisms of central control (Bulpitt, 1983, pp. 42–4). Equally, diffusion theory presents an ambiguous account of the causes of territorial conflicts and the persistence of peripheral sectionalism. However, these two theories will not be explored in detail. Rather I will briefly summarize and comment upon Bulpitt's 'dual polity' theory – the most stimulating contribution to the analysis of centre–periphery relations in the UK.[4]

Bulpitt's analysis begins with a broad ranging definition of territorial politics (see above, page 14), and he argues that, in order to avoid the problems of other approaches to centre–periphery relations, any analytical framework must focus on the politics of centre–periphery relations, viewed historically, and on the strategies of the centre for managing the periphery. This general orientation points to a number of specific problems requiring analysis (Bulpitt, 1983, pp. 52–66):

- the location and nature of the centre;
- identification of the centre's 'operational code' (or the rules of statecraft employed over time by political élites);
- the political linkages between centre and periphery, especially central penetration of the periphery and the assimilation of local élites;
- the external support system (or central efforts to minimize the impact of external forces on domestic politics);
- the intentions of the centre and its strategies for influencing (including the control of) peripheral actors;
- the resources of the centre;
- central autonomy or the capacity of a centre to gain autonomy from peripheral forces to concentrate on 'high politics', allowing peripheral governments and political organizations considerable operational autonomy in 'low politics': the 'dual polity'.

Bulpitt then surveys the evolution of the Union of the United Kingdom. Of particular interest is his argument that between 1926 and the early 1960s the territorial politics of the UK took the form of a 'dual polity':

> a state of affairs in which national and local *polities* were largely divorced from one another. Those contacts which existed ... were ... bureaucratic and depoliticized. In this period the Centre achieved what it had always desired – relative autonomy from peripheral forces to pursue its 'High Politics' preoccupations.
>
> (pp. 235–6)

This central operating code came under threat with the weakening of the external support system. Thus, since 1979 the onset of 'hard times' has led to an alteration of the code with the emphasis falling on 'the Centre's ultimate responsibility for macro-economic policies and hence the legitimacy of its attempts to increase its control over local authority expenditure' (p. 236). Bulpitt concludes that the UK is an example of a system with a single predominant centre located in

London; England has never been the centre. The location of the centre within London has varied – the court, the Cabinet, the political-administrative community of senior ministers and civil servants – but it has always retained its 'court ethic'. Union confronted the centre with intractable problems: its 'difficult estate'. Ireland is the obvious case, but, as important, the dominant English have never taken Union seriously and have 'trivialized' or exhibited a 'strong distaste' for peripheral government. The centre's intentions have been to distance itself from the periphery. Preoccupied with 'high politics' and a weakening external support system, it has sought autonomy, rejected territorial ideologies and a bureaucratic machine to rule the estate and relied on indirect rule; it has been an archetypal 'absentee landlord'. There was the court and the country and a predominant bias insulating central élites from 'low politics'.

Inevitably such a sweeping analysis poses problems, many of which are acknowledged by Bulpitt. First, 'territory' is an ambiguous concept. As Bulpitt (1983, p. 53) notes: 'social scientists are unable to differentiate territorial attributes from non-territorial ones in any systematic way . . . Even more confusing, some political issues may be fought out *across* territory but not be, at root, *about* territory' (original emphasis). These problems are compounded by Bulpitt's own definition of territorial politics, which is so extended as to become difficult to separate from the wider polity (see above, page 14).

Second, the drawback of all macro-political studies is that 'The supporting data for many of these arguments is much less than perfect. And, of course, the central autonomy/collaboration theses are untestable, they cannot be disproved' (Bulpitt, 1983, p. 239).

Third, the distinction between 'high' and 'low' politics has a tautological flavour; i.e. because the policy or function is a local government responsibility, it must be 'low politics'. Certainly it is inordinately difficult to distinguish empirically between 'high' and 'low' politics. The centre's interest in such 'low' matters as public health or education is long-standing (see, for example, Finer, 1957; Chester, 1981, ch. 8).

Fourth, the focus on the centre's intentions and its operating code poses severe research problems. Not only is evidence scarce because of government secrecy, but the code is implicit and ill-articulated if ever made public. Imputing intentions and assumptions to the behaviour of central élites is an equally unsatisfactory source of data.

Finally, there is the misleading implication in Bulpitt's analysis that local government is but one of a series of equally important territorial institutions. In the UK context, local government is the foremost of such institutions and cannot be equated with, for example, the territorial structures of nationalized industries. It cannot be relegated to the status of just another territorial structure.

The debit side of the balance sheet is, however, substantial. The topics that Bulpitt's analysis draws attention to include:

- the definition of territorial politics to include all sub-central governmental and political organizations;
- the importance of a historical perspective;
- the analysis of the *centre's* location, intentions, operating code and strategies;
- the variegated political linkages between centre and periphery.

In essence, Bulpitt turns over the usual coin of the realm, rejecting the concern with local government – its structure, politics and problems – for a focus on the centre's problems. Any resulting overstatement does not detract from his central message: the restrictive definition of problems within conventional studies of SCG.

2.3.4   The 'Radical' Model

The invasion of Marxist theory into the study of urban politics (and eventually local government and central–local relations) had a substantial impact. Being the height of fashion exacts a penalty, however; the initial model becomes imitated, plundered and diluted. If, at the outset, 'the state' was said to preserve a basic unity in spite of its various institutional manifestations and 'All its parts work fundamentally as one' in order to 'reproduce the conditions within which capitalist accumulation can take place' (Cockburn, 1979, pp. 47 and 51), within a short space of time the focus of debate had shifted to the relative autonomy of the state (and its constituent units) and to include variants of a Weberian rather than Marxist inspiration. Accordingly, it is more accurate (if less revealing) to talk of a 'radical model' and of 'local state theory'.

The radical model (Dunleavy, 1982a, pp. 217–20) has five components. First, it rejects explanations couched in terms of the motives and behaviour of individual actors, arguing that these actions are either determined or constrained by structural factors.

Second, the model explores the relationship between IGR and social classes and interests. For example, the reorganization of local government in 1974 is not seen as a response to problems of functional effectiveness but as a means of limiting working-class control of local authorities (Dearlove, 1979).

Third, the model focuses on 'crises' or periods of enforced and concentrated change. Emphasizing crises helps to identify the social roots of administrative problems and directs attention to the displacement of conflicts. Thus ameliorative action to deal with administrative problems is said to create tensions elsewhere in the system.

Fourth, the model is based on functional explanation; that is, events are 'explained' by the functions they serve within the political system. Thus the state intervenes in industry because it has to maintain the conditions of capital accumulation.

Finally, the radical model espouses the value of public participation, emphasizing not simply 'the inherent value to be placed on autonomous decision-making' but the systematically distorted communication fostered by technocratic government which 'negates fundamentally human qualities and inevitably induces a loss of common purpose . . . in society' (Dunleavy, 1982a, pp. 219–20).

It is argued that this model has particular merits for the analysis of budgeting, professionalization and government organization (including the local state). A brief look at the application of the model to the local state will illustrate its potential. Two broad interpretations of the local state can be identified: the mobilization (or optimist) and inertia (or pessimist) schools of thought. The mobilization school emphasizes the potential of local government as a vehicle for working-class mobilization, action and control. Thus local government persists because of its legitimating function; the state is responding to local needs. But the existence of a fragmented state structure coupled with divisions within the ruling class mean that the working class can win concessions. For Duncan and Goodwin (1982, pp. 159, 172 and 175–6) the local state form is 'vulnerable to replacement by class relations'; 'social relations and social consciousness (especially class relations and class consciousness) are unevenly developed' and 'take place in – and change their form in' – local state institutions. 'Local state power is open to class conscious working-class groups', disturbing 'the class compromise so delicately assembled'.

The inertia school stresses that, even if the working class can capture local institutions and use them to press for reform, the fragmented, decentralized structure of government dilutes this action, facilitating the continued dominance of ruling-class interests. Participation in local government is skewed in favour of certain groups (e.g. the petty bourgeoisie), the social roots of conflicts are disguised, and, as a result, local institutions are both a major obstacle for a reforming, national 'socialist' government and a weak vehicle for reform (see, for example, Dunleavy, 1980a, ch. 5).

Even these brief summaries should bring out both the prominence of functional explanation and the stress on the social roots and consequences of state action in the radical model. The major problem is the distinctiveness of these emphases; indeed none of the central tenets of the radical model seem particularly distinctive (O'Leary, 1985a). Any 'virtue' is a product of an overly sharp and ultimately unrealistic view of conventional public administration. Public administration may be conventional and have many defects but it has never been myopic to the point of blindness. For example, the managerial and practical orientation of organization theory has been criticized frequently (Albrow, 1968), and a variety of studies have explored the social consequences of inequalities in the distribution of organizational power (e.g. Clegg, 1975, Salaman, 1979). Equally, the radical model has no monopoly of critiques of professional power, and its emphasis on the displacement of conflict bears a marked affinity with the commonplace analysis of 'unintended consequences'; indeed, such functional analysis is endemic within the social sciences.

Second, the model is not internally consistent. Neither the analysis of crises nor the value of participation is logically required. Routine activities can be as revealing of underlying power structures as a crisis, as the now extensive studies of the mobilization of bias and non-decision-making have demonstrated (for a short summary see Lukes, 1974). And the discussion of participation is unrelated not only to all the earlier propositions but also to the topics to which the radical model can (allegedly) contribute distinctive analyses (O'Leary, 1985a).

Third, functional analysis provides a redescription not an explanation of events (Barry, 1970), and the conditions under which it constitutes explanation are difficult even to approximate (Elster, 1979, pp. 28–35, and 1983, pp. 55–68). To say that an event or outcome occurred because it was functional, it is necessary to specify the mechanism which produced the result. This condition is elusive because such mechanisms are not just difficult to identify but also are rare. Moreover, the radical literature provides too many examples of tautological 'explanation' for comfort. Not only is the need to identify the mechanism producing functional results ignored, but the argument is circular and admits of no counter-factual statements (Saunders, 1980, pp. 180–9, and 1981, pp. 279–86).

Third, the existing literature does not remotely constitute a theory of sub-central government. The dominant characteristic is the critique of conventional approaches (variously defined). The supporting empirical material is conspicuous primarily for its absence. However, there is one important exception to this point: Saunders's 'dual-state' thesis. The potential of the radical model can be more accurately assessed after a consideration of this, perhaps the major, application of the radical model to SCG.[5]

At its simplest the dual-state thesis argues that there are three significant dimensions along which national and local political processes differ: economic function, mode of interest mediation and affinitive ideology. The state has two major economic functions: social investment and social consumption. Social investment refers to those aspects of state provision which constitute constant capital for the private sector (e.g. physical infrastructure) and it functions primarily in the interests of capital. Social consumption refers to those aspects of state provision which are consumed individually by the population as a whole or by sections of it (e.g. health care, public housing) and it functions primarily in the interests of sections of the population other than capital, although it may well benefit the latter. There is a tension between these two economic functions because increases in social consumption via increased taxation may adversely affect private sector profitability – referred to as a 'rationality problem'. There are three decision-making strategies that the state can employ to confront this problem: bureaucratic intervention, pluralist competition, or corporatism. Saunders argues that 'there has developed a bifurcation of British politics, for while social consumption policies are still by and large resolved in the competitive arena of democratic politics, social investment has been insulated by means of the corporate bias' (Saunders, 1982, p. 60). However, this development creates tensions between rational planning and democratic accountability, manifested, for example, in overload in the demand for services which impairs the government's ability to manage the economy. Allied to this rationality problem there is also a legitimation crisis as state intervention and a belief in the needs and rights of citizens undermine both private property and the market principle.

Saunders (1982, p. 61) relates the foregoing distinctions to the levels of the state apparatus. Thus:

> local government in Britain is typically concerned with the provision of social consumption through competitive modes of political mediation and organized around the principle of citizenship rights and social need. Central and regional levels of government, on the other hand, are typically the agencies through which social investment and fiscal policies are developed within a relatively exclusive corporate sector of politics organized around the principle of private property rights and the need to maintain private sector profitability.

There are, however, many problems with this ideal-typical schema. First, the distinction between the economic functions of the state poses intractable classification problems. State expenditures do not fit neatly into one or other category. As Clegg (1982, p. 5) notes: 'the variety of interests involved, the special case of commuting, the fact that means of transport in urban areas are generally *an indivisible form of support for both production and consumption* activities create intractable problems for analysis' (original emphasis). And as Dunleavy (1984, pp. 71–2) points out, education can be classified as a means of legitimation, as social investment in human capital, or as a type of collective consumption; and, as a result, state expenditure will be socially contingent, varying from society to society and over time. Nor is the problem simply one of a priori classification. It also 'undermines the causal sequence of the dual state model by suggesting that institutional allocations are logically and causally prior to the differentiation of state activities into social investment or consumption categories' (ibid., p. 71–2).

Second, functions cannot be unequivocally allocated to the different levels of the state apparatus. The functions of local government encompass both social investment and consumption. For example, Goodwin (1982) concluded from his study of Sheffield that the local authority actively sustained capital accumulation. Similarly, Martlew's (1983) review of central–local financial relationships stresses the interdependence and shared interests of central and local spending departments.

Third, corporatist modes of political mediation are not specific to the central/regional level. As Houlihan (1983b, pp. 14–15) has argued, the existence of corporatist structures at the local level weakens the dual-state thesis, and the work of Flynn (1983) and King (1983) clearly demonstrates the existence of such structures.

Fourth, the range of decision-making strategies considered is unnecessarily restrictive, omitting policy systems dominated by professions. Dunleavy (1984, p. 77) has argued that we need to focus on the role of professions in originating, disseminating and implementing new ideas and suggests that professionalized policy systems should be seen as a fourth decision-making strategy. And if the professions are accorded importance, it raises the further problem that policy initiation in local government is *not* a response to local political inputs – pluralism – but is heavily influenced 'by professionally promoted "fashions" which are nationally produced'.

Finally, the dual-state thesis is fundamentally a functionalist theory; that is, policy-making is 'explained' in terms of a set of predetermined functions of the state in capitalist society. And as Saunders (1980, pp. 180–9) recognizes, this raises a number of problems. Thus all state interventions must presumably serve the functions of either legitimation, or investment, or consumption, or some combination of these three; and, *pace* his earlier critiques of neo-Marxist theory, Saunders's current formulation denies that the state has distinct interests and acts to promote its own needs for growth and power. Such an 'autonomous' conception of the role of government may have its weaknesses, but the scope for such action should surely be a matter for empirical investigation, not definition, as should the range of functions performed by the state.

The 'dual-state' thesis has been discussed in some detail because it is virtually the only neo-Marxist-influenced theory which has directly addressed the topic of sub-central government. But even in the most developed form to date, theories of the local state seem flawed. As Saunders (1984, p. 26) concedes:

There *is* a bifurcation of politics at the regional level but it reflects not the distinction between different types of agencies (e.g. RWAs and RHAs) discharging different types of 'functions' (production/ consumption), but rather that between different types of interests (producers and consumers) operating in relation to any given agency.

Indisputably Saunders's theory has an empirically sharper cutting edge than more grandiloquent theories of the state. But because his research revealed a situation 'more complex and muddled than a straightforward application of the thesis would lead one to expect', the resulting generalizations 'are tentative and are hedged around with many exceptions and conditions' (p. 50). Saunders's shift towards an exploration of the dynamics of policy formation within state agencies, especially the professionalization of policy systems, coupled with the analysis of the constellations of interests interacting with the agencies, represent both a major concession to his critics and a significant reformulation of the thesis.

There are, however, a number of important points which emerge from this account of the dual-state thesis:

- the importance of an explicit theory of the role (and functions) of government;
- the need to identify and explore the conflicts between the range of governmental functions, e.g. regulatory, allocative and legitimation;
- the analysis of the strategies of intervention of government;
- the analysis of the distributive consequences of public services;
- the need to extend analysis beyond the institutions of IGR to incorporate government functions, interest mediation and ideology.

In sum, there are valuable lessons to be learnt from the thrust of Saunders's analysis even after the bifurcated functional allocation at the heart of the theory has been discarded.

2.3.5 *Intergovernmental Theory*

Anderson (1960, p. 3) defines intergovernmental relations (IGR) as 'an important body of activities or interactions occurring between governmental units of all types and levels within ... the federal system'. This general definition has been elaborated by Wright (1974, pp. 1–16), who identifies five distinct characteristics. First, IGR recognizes the multiplicity of relationships between all types of government. Second, it emphasizes the interactions between individuals, especially public officials. Third, these relationships are continuous, day-to-day and informal. Fourth, IGR insists on the important role played by all public officials, be they politicians or

administrators. Finally, it emphasizes the political nature of relationships and focuses on substantive policies, especially financial
issues such as who raises what amount and who shall spend it for
whose benefit with what results. In summary, Wright (1974, p. 4)
claims that 'The term IGR alerts one to the multiple, behavioural,
continuous and dynamic exchanges occurring between various
officials in the political system. It may be compared to a different,
novel and visual filter or concept that can be laid on the American
political landscape.' This 'visual filter' if novel does not constitute a
theory. It is more a check-list for collecting data. However, Beer
(1973, 1976 and 1978) does provide an explanation of some recent
changes in United States federalism.

Beer (1978, p. 17) argues that two types of influence have become
prominent in United States IGR:

> One results from functional specialization in the modern state. I
> call it the professional bureaucratic complex ... The other results
> from territorial specialization and I call it the intergovernmental
> lobby. The action and interaction of the professional bureaucratic
> complex and the intergovernmental lobby constitute the new form
> taken by representational federalism.

The emergence of the professional bureaucratic complex reflects the
scientific advances of the postwar period. Professional specialisms
have abounded and developed a new role in policy-making. In alliance with the interested legislators and affected interest groups, the
professions have become key actors in the 'iron triangles' which have
exercised decisive influence in fields such as health, housing, urban
renewal, transportation, education and energy. Moreover, as these
programmes have not been implemented by the federal government,
vertical bureaucratic hierarchies have emerged facilitated by the
shared discipline of professionals.

The outcome of this rise of technocracy is not dictatorship by men
in white coats: 'one of the more interesting features of this new
influence is the way in which it has promoted the rise of a countervailing power in the form of the intergovernmental lobby' (Beer,
1978, p. 18). This 'topocratic' influence (from *topos* meaning 'place'
and *kratos* meaning 'authority') has challenged the pre-eminence of
the technocrats. Thus:

> As the mayors and other executives of the governments through
> which these programs were carried became aware of their value –
> their political value and their problem-solving promise – they
> developed a heightened interest in and increasing contact with
> federal policy-making and administration.
>
> (Beer, 1978, p. 18)

The result of this development has been a complex pattern of both centralization and decentralization. The process has been centralizing because the programmes were formed by federal technocrats but decentralizing in that they were adopted at the sub-central level. It has drawn state and local officials into the federal government but it has also exposed the federal government to the topocratic perspective.

Intergovernmental theory has not been confined to the study of United States federalism. The impact of professional influence, the logic of technical rationality and the complex interdependencies within decentralized governmental structure have been themes explored for a number of advanced industrial liberal democracies. Thus, Hanf (1978, pp. 1–2) argues that the characteristic problem of such countries is that

> the problem-solving capacity of governments is disaggregated into a collection of sub-systems with limited tasks, competences and resources ... At the same time governments are more and more confronted with tasks where both the problems and their solution tend to cut across the boundaries of separate authorities and functional jurisdictions ...
>
> A major task confronting political systems in any advanced industrial country is therefore that of securing co-ordinated policy actions through networks of separate but interdependent organizations.

Intergovernmental theory emphasizes the limits to rational policy-making, the factorizing and professionalization of policy systems, the interdependence of governmental organizations and the emergence of policy from network interactions. However, for all its sophistication, it has a number of limitations. First, as Tarrow (1978, pp. 1–2) points out, intergovernmental theory fails to relate the networks and their policy outcomes to conflicts of interest and ideology (see also Dunleavy, 1984, p. 60). The question of who benefits is ignored.

Second, the focus on technological and organizational imperatives provides an incomplete account of the role of government. Its role is seen as benign, and, if it is not seen as the referee of group conflicts, equally its relationships with particular interests are not explored.

Finally, the focus on the similarities between advanced industrial societies (i.e. on the emergence of disaggregated policy networks) diverts attention away from the differences between networks. Whether the causes of variation are the type of policy area or the social interests affected, intergovernmental theory tends to disregard quite overt differences between, for example, economic and social welfare policy-making.

Rhodes (1981a, esp. chs. 1 and 5) provided an explicit application of intergovernmental theory to British central–local relations. His framework was based on five propositions:

(a) Any organization is *dependent* upon other organizations for *resources*.
(b) In order to achieve their *goals*, the organizations have to exchange resources.
(c) Although decision-making within the organization is constrained by other organizations, the *dominant coalition* retains some discretion. The *appreciative system* of the dominant coalition influences which relationships are seen as a problem and which resources will be sought.
(d) The dominant coalition employs *strategies* within known *rules of the game* to regulate *the process of exchange*.
(e) Variations in the degree of *discretion* are a product of the goals and the relative power potential of interacting organizations. This relative power potential is a product of the resources of each organization, of the rules of the game and of the process of exchange between organizations.

(p. 98, original emphases)

Central–local relations take on the aspects of a 'game' in which both central and local participants manoeuvre for advantage, deploying the resources they control to maximize their influence over outcomes and trying to avoid becoming dependent on the other 'players'. The relevant resources include: constitutional-legal, hierarchical, financial, political and informational resources. They are illustrated in Figure 2.2.

Central government	Local government
• control over legislation and delegated powers	• employs all personnel in local services
• provides a large part of local service finance under block grant	• local knowledge and expertise
• control of capital expenditure	• control of policy implementation and key knowledge about how to administer policy
• sets standards for and inspects some services	• independent power to raise taxes (rates) to finance services
• national electoral mandate	• local electoral mandate

Figure 2.2 *The resources of centre and locality.*
Source: Dunleavy and Rhodes, 1983, pp. 113–14.

The resources of an organization constitute a potential for the exercise of power. Whether that potential is realized depends upon the effective deployment of resources: on the rules of the game and the choice of strategies. The rules of the game are the less formal or conventional rules which 'largely define the institutions of society . . . they set the approximate limits within which discretionary behaviour may take place' (Truman, 1951, pp. 343–4). Strategies are the means for imposing upon other organizations an organization's preferences concerning the time of, conditions for and extent of the exchange of resources. An organization which effectively deploys its resources will maximize its scope for decisional manoeuvre (or discretion) and be able to choose amongst various courses of action or inaction. Examples of rules of the game include the need for trust and secrecy in negotiations, the 'government's right to govern' and territoriality or non-intervention in other people's policy area. Examples of strategies include bargaining, incorporation, confrontation, persuasion and the use of incentives.

This game is treated as the 'figure' or the micro-level of analysis. It is also necessary to explain changes in the distribution of resources and the rules of the game: to contextualize the patterns of interaction. This context or 'ground' is explored using Schmitter's (1979) concept of corporatism. It is argued that central–local relations are moving away from competition and bargaining between local authorities and central departments towards a system in which organizations are aggregated in policy communities limited to the accredited spokespersons for local government (Rhodes, 1981a, pp. 111–25). Competition is limited, and a system of interest intermediation – literally the group 'comes between' its members and government – is created in which the membership is regulated in return for influence over government policy. And this shift to corporatism is said to be related to the changing economic context of government.

In short, central–local relations are seen as a complex game in which the various levels of government are interdependent but which is shifting from pluralistic bargaining to corporatism. This framework is clearly within the intergovernmental tradition and it has been subject to a range of criticisms (for a summary, citations and commentary see Rhodes, 1986b).

Perhaps the most significant failing of the power-dependence model is its failure to distinguish clearly between the levels of analysis, and consequently it does not adequately explore the relationship between them. Many of these problems stem from the use of corporatist theory to analyse the 'ground'. Without reviewing the corporatist literature in detail (see Jessop, 1978; Panitch, 1980; Cox, 1981; Jordan, 1981), some of the major problems should be noted.

It is important to distinguish between corporatism as a form of government–interest-group relations and as a theory of the state (Marsh, 1983, p. 1), and it is as a form of government–interest-group relations that corporatism is relevant in the study of SCG. The concept obviously has its roots in the analysis of economic functional group-ings but it has been extended to other types of groups and sub-central government (Cawson, 1978 and 1982; Foster, Jackman and Perlman, 1980). Rhodes (1985b and c) argues both that corporatism provides a rigid metaphor of government–interest group relations and that it cannot be extended to sub-central government. The characteristics of corporatism such as the aggregation of interests, licensing of groups, monopoly of representation and regulation of members are rarely found in unsullied form. This state of affairs has prompted adjectival proliferation, e.g. 'neo-corporatism', 'liberal corporatism', 'bargained corporatism'. Indeed, Jordan (1981, p. 110) objects to this 'trick' of 'altering the definition to make it fit', argues that it is 'merely pluralism in a new environment' and concludes that

> The nature of British politics has certainly changed – but not towards anything which could be identified with any rigorous definition of the corporate state. If one looks at the major works which have popularized the corporatist tag one finds surprising reluctance to apply the term without reservation ... The order that they see in British politics is the order of segmentation, inter-sectoral bargaining, limited access, voluntary groups: is there a need to conjure up corporatism with its distinctive associ-ations? ...
>
> Corporatism suggests hierarchy and unambiguous relations. Its vocabulary is of command, order, discipline, authority. In contrast the more useful kind of image would appear to be the network.
>
> (Jordan, 1981, pp. 113 and 121)

Given these weaknesses in corporatist theory,[6] it is hardly surpris-ing that the power-dependence model contained an inadequate formulation of the 'ground' and, consequently, of the changing role of government.

There are a number of other weaknesses in the framework which should also be noted, although more briefly:

- At the micro-level, the model does not present an adequate account of intra-organizational political processes and of the ways in which they are related to inter-organizational processes. Moreover, the conception of resources under-emphasized their subjective, volatile, transmutable nature.
- The conception of the role of central government does not reflect the centre's hegemonic or structural power.
- At the macro-level, the explanation of the changing role of government was implicit and ambiguous.
- The model lacked a historical dimension.
- The model failed to explain variations between policy areas.

- The model, although it employed a broad definition of IGR, paid limited attention to territorial representation.

On the face of it, local state theory is all ground and no figure, whereas intergovernmental theory is all figure and no ground. It is the complementarity and/or incompatibility of these several models which remains to be considered.

2.4 Towards a Theoretical Reconstruction

At first glance, the several models seem to be essentially incompatible. They espouse different values, focus on different facets of SCG and put forward highly varied explanations. The 'New Right's' libertarian values, preoccupation with efficiency and reducing the scope of government and stress on the power of interest groups and bureaucrats contrasts markedly with the radical model's participatory/humanitarian values, preoccupation with the social origins and consequences of state action and functional explanation rooted in the state's role in maintaining capital accumulation. But behind this apparent diversity lie some important general lessons for the description, analysis and explanation of SCG. These lessons cover: defining the *unit* of analysis, specifying the *levels* of analysis and identifying the *criteria* of evaluation. In addition, there is a recurrent concern with particular *objects of study* including the power of professionals and bureaucrats, the scope (and means) of central interventions and the distributional consequences of state action. It is this common ground which warrants brief elaboration.

2.4.1 Defining the Unit of Analysis

At the outset, this chapter defined SCG in broad terms. Of all the models considered, only the literature on centre–periphery relations consistently employs an equally wide ranging definition. Hopefully, it is now clear that limiting the subject to central–local relations is both arbitrary and misleading. Accepting this simple point is only a partial improvement. Thus, for all its broad-brush treatment of British government, the radical model still focuses on central–local relations. Such tunnel vision is nigh inevitable in the study of British SCG because local government is the pre-eminent territorial institution. Perhaps in consequence, there are few studies of inter-organizational relations in the public sector. It is necessary, therefore, both to redress the current imbalance in the study of SCG by 'rescuing' inter-organizational relations from partial obscurity and to accord central–local relations their deserved primacy. In addition, this focus on IGR has to be wedded to the analysis of territorial representation, recognizing that each territorial unit has its own system of IGR.

2.4.2　Levels of Analysis

In part, the apparently irreconcilable nature of the models stems from differences in the level of analysis. It is important to distinguish between:

- *the micro-level* – interactions within and between individual sub-central units of government;
- *the meso-level* – patterns of interaction between sub-central and central units of government; and
- *the macro-level* – the national socioeconomic and political context of meso- and micro-level interactions.

The differences between, for example, Bulpitt's analysis of centre–periphery relations and intergovernmental theory lie in the macro-level analysis of the former and the meso-level analysis of the latter, whilst the 'New Right' is preoccupied with the micro-level analysis of bureaucratic power and inefficiency. Further differences (and confusions) flow from the failure to state explicitly the relationship between the levels of analysis: a failing prominent in, but not limited to, the intergovernmental model.

2.4.3　Criteria of Evaluation

The list of normative criteria contained within the models is dauntingly long, including local autonomy, individual (negative) liberty, territorial justice (or equality) and accountable, responsive and responsible government. The tasks of describing the range of relevant values and exploring their implications both for each other and for the system of SCG would require a political philosophy of SCG. The prime objectives of this book are, however, description and explanation. Whilst this book makes no pretence to 'the pristine purity of total detachment' associated with 'value-free' research, it strives to be objective (if not neutral) in that the arguments are cast in form amenable to error-correction (or control) procedures (Landau, 1979, p. 44).

It is particularly difficult to remain neutral when exploring SCG; it illuminates graphically the problems of government in an advanced industrial liberal democracy. The criteria of evaluation deployed in this book are not drawn from political philosophy, however, but are internally generated. Thus, policies are judged not by their effects on, for example, local autonomy, but by the adequacy of their underlying theory. As Wildavksy (1980, pp. 35–6) argues, all policies are theories; they promise that if X is done Y will result and Y will be 'good'. Consequently policies for SCG must be rooted in an adequate, or at least plausible, description and understanding of the system. To the extent that they ignore the central characteristics of SCG, the policies can be found wanting.

2.4.4   Objects of Study

For all their diversity, the models share common preoccupations. Foremost amongst these concerns is the influence of the profession. Whether the professions are seen as monopolies perpetuating public waste and inefficiency (the 'New Right'), or key actors integrating central and sub-central levels in 'closed' policy systems (intergovernmental theory), or the controllers and distributors of public services (radical model), they are deemed to be key actors in SCG. Equally, there has been a growing concern with the centre's intentions and strategies. This concern is manifested in several ways: in the analysis of its 'operating code' (centre–periphery relations); in the critique of its mechanisms of control (public administration); and in the exploration of the range of, and conflicts between, government functions and strategies (radical model). In addition, both intergovernmental theory and the radical model have stressed the need to analyse policy and its consequences. There are two related points behind this injunction. Both models are rejecting a focus on institutions in favour of the analysis of the policy-making process. Although the institutional framework of SCG shapes the perceptions and behaviour of actors, it is not the only, nor even necessarily the major, determinant of action. By analysing the policy process, it becomes possible to assess the importance of institutional factors relative to other influences such as the professions. However, describing how policy is made is only a first step. Such descriptions assume that differences in the policy process matter; that the distribution of services and resources is affected by variations in policy-making. 'Who benefits?' thus becomes a central and shared question, even if the answers of the two schools of thought can differ greatly.

To this point the chapter has identified several models of SCG, each with strengths and weaknesses. In spite of many differences, these models point to some general lessons, and identify some specific topics, which any model of SCG must take into account. Dunleavy (1980b, p. 131) has argued that 'research into central–local relations should not only be theoretically based ... but should be multi-theoretical, i.e. it should draw on *several* or all of the theories relevant to the empirical questions examined, using them as sources of competing hypotheses and interpretations to guide the research' (original emphasis). Whilst sharing Dunleavy's enthusiasm for theoretically based research, I do not share his pessimism about the prospects for integrating the insights of the several theories. The following sections present a model of SCG which, although it has its roots in intergovernmental theory, attempts to incorporate hypotheses and interpretations suggested by the other approaches.

2.5 Explaining the Changing Pattern of Sub-Central Government: a Model of SCG

The politics of sub-central government have become part and parcel of the politics of Westminster and Whitehall, and any model of SCG must attempt to explain this transformation. It is not the objective of this book to provide an account of the changes in British government during the postwar period, and yet no account of SCG can disregard them. Accordingly, those features of the *national government environment* which directly impact on the sub-central system must be identified and their effects described. This task constitutes the macro-level of analysis.

The number of governmental and political organizations at the sub-central level is enormous, and the range of relationships is probably infinite. It is necessary to look for regularities in these relationships, and the concept of *policy networks* is a particularly useful tool for ordering the profusion of links. The analysis of policy networks forms the meso-level of analysis.

The search for order may be an essential step, but it is as important to recognize variety. The behaviour of particular *actors*, be it individuals or organizations, is not simply a product of their environment. Actors can also shape that environment to greater or lesser degrees. This micro-level of analysis involves exploring relationships within and between individual organizations.

The major objective of the rest of this chapter is to explain each level of analysis. Inevitably, this exercise involves the definition of key terms, and to defend myself against the charge of aridity which such discussions can engender, it is important to stress that an interpretative map is required for the remainder of the book; it is essential to set out the major themes and issues. Subsequent chapters will unpack these abstractions and generalizations, and the qualifications necessitated by the messy confusion of the practice of SCG will come into focus.[7]

2.5.1 National Government Environment

The phrase 'national government environment' (Stewart, 1983, pp. 11–12 and 65–8) refers to central government institutions and their socio-economic environment as they impact on SCG. Because the study of SCG cannot be divorced from the study of British government, it is necessary to identify the processes within this larger environment which are of greatest relevance. But the act of selection will imply necessarily a 'general theory' of British government, a model of the distribution of power in British society. It would take us too far afield to discuss the several models of power in Britain. Suffice it to record that a variant of neo-pluralist theory of industrial society will be employed.[8] As with any theory, it has its blind spots but it meets both the requirements listed in Chapter 1 and, as the remainder of the book attempts to demonstrate, is particularly well suited to the analysis of SCG. This approach suggests that the following processes within the national government environment are central to understanding SCG: an unstable external support system; the decline of the mixed economy; the growth of the welfare state; the extension of the allied processes of functional differentiation and professionalization; the development of a social structure characterized by multiple (non-class) cleavages; and the continuing stability of a political tradition characterized by a two-party system, a unitary institutional structure and a central élite ideology defending the mixed economy welfare state. The discussion of these features will provide a brief exposition of neo-pluralist theory and, more important, it will specify in some detail its relevance to SCG.

2.5.1(i) AN UNSTABLE EXTERNAL SUPPORT SYSTEM[9]

In one sense, Britain can be described as an 'open polity'; politically and economically, it has become vulnerable to external forces. Bulpitt (1983, p. 59) argues that any centre 'will attempt to minimize the impact of external forces on domestic politics'. The distinctive feature of the British national government environment in the postwar period has been the inability of the centre to maintain an external support system which did minimize the impact of external forces. Thus, at the end of the Second World War, the external forces were integrative. Britain had

> 'won' the war, established the welfare state, 'the envy of the world', and subtly transformed the Empire into a self-governing Commonwealth association, with the United Kingdom at its head. In addition, the 'special relationship' with the United States provided both a wealthy benign protector and continued front-rank status in international politics.
>
> (Bulpitt, 1983, p. 137)

By the 1970s this system had collapsed:

> The most obvious manifestations of this were the lost potential for major independent military action . . . the UK economy was one of the weakest in the western world . . . Moreover, many of the old regime's most important external supports, the Commonwealth, the Sterling Area . . . and the special relationship with the United States, had apparently lost their effectiveness . . . As well as membership of the European Community, United Kingdom sovereignty was now seemingly heavily qualified by the actions of multi-national companies, the United States Treasury and State

Departments, NATO, the International Monetary Fund and the
Organization of Petroleum Exporting Countries.
(Bulpitt, 1983, p. 167)

Britain had lost an empire, and a new role seemed ever more distant.

The importance of this transition for SCG lies, first, in the direct
impact of external events on domestic events. The most obvious
examples are membership of the EEC and the rise in world commodity prices in the mid-1970s. Thus membership of the EEC not only
provoked domestic conflict but it also changed the law affecting SCG,
created direct links between the Community and SCG and centralized
some functions, e.g. environmental pollution (Hull and Rhodes, 1977;
Haigh, 1984; Rhodes, 1986d). The increase in world commodity prices
was instrumental in creating the 'fiscal crisis' of SCG in the 1970s.
There are, however, other indirect effects of equal importance. The
magic escape route of 'high politics' or international adventures was
now denied to the centre. Its apparent weakness in the face of external
forces led to dissensus at home on Britain's role in the world and
opened up the prospect of separate national development within a
supra-national framework. It encouraged territorial dissent. Crucially, it also bred an inward looking centre, which sought to resolve its
problems by domestic interventions. Nowhere was this more evident
than in the management of the economy.

2.5.1(ii)   THE DECLINE OF THE MIXED ECONOMY

The term 'mixed economy' is used more often than it is defined.
Rogow and Shore (1955, pp. 10–11) suggest that

> the term 'mixed economy' refers to an economy characterized by
> (1) public and private enterprise, but with nationalization confined
> to the basic public utilities and industries which occupy a crucial
> power position within the economy; and (2) state regulation and
> control of the private industrial sector, particularly with regard to
> investment, prices, exports, imports and other supply and demand
> factors.

Another, somewhat vaguer term used to characterize the British
economy for the bulk of the postwar period was 'Butskellism', which
encompassed government ownership of 'key' industries, intervention
to manage the economy and the welfare state (Brittan, 1969,
pp. 112–14; Dearlove and Saunders, 1984, pp. 272–3). Indeed: 'No
succinct or pithy definition of the mixed economy is possible and, even
if it were, it would not be very useful. The mixed economy as a
prevailing paradigm was, not surprisingly, a melange of diverse not
readily mixable elements' (Smith, 1979, p. 100). Accordingly, a broad
definition, encompassing government ownership, intervention and

the welfare state, is inevitable. The latter two components are discussed below (see sections 2.5.1(iii) and 2.5.1(vi) below). At this juncture, the emphasis falls on the general topics of the economic functions of government and the problems generated by economic change.[10]

A key point about the 'mixed economy' is the range and scale of the government's economic functions. It is responsible for a diverse range of public corporations including not just the well-known cases of gas, electricity, coal and the railways but also, amongst many others, Rolls-Royce, British Leyland, British Aerospace and the National Freight Corporation. In addition, in varying forms and for varying periods of time the government has been an investor and shareholder in private industry through such bodies as the National Enterprise Board. The economic functions of government are not limited, therefore, to fiscal and monetary policies for managing the economy; it is directly involved in industry as employer, investor and manager.

Moreover, its responsibilities for production and investment have to be reconciled with its responsibility for the welfare state. In an era of economic growth, such a reconciliation can be effected. However, in a recession, welfare expenditures can be maintained or improved only by increases in taxation. Such increases erode the productivity of the private sector by reducing profits and hence investment. The economic and welfare functions can conflict, and this 'resource squeeze' (Newton, 1980, pp. 12–13) has become acute in Britain with the intensification of economic decline.

Diagnoses of the problems of the British economy abound, and disagreements over the causes are as frequent as they are acrimonious. Until the 1970s, however, the problems did not seem intractable, and before the 1960s the claim that 'you've never had it so good' contained at least a grain of truth:

> Measured by almost any of the available economic indicators, the fifties was a decade of economic progress for the British economy. The vigorous recovery of 1945–50 had already restored pre-war average levels of consumption, and in the next ten years production and consumption rose, and in durable goods there was an extension to mass consumption of enjoyments still the privilege of a minority in 1939. Apart from two short spells around 1952 and 1958, there was full employment.
>
> (Worswick, 1962, p. 68)

Thereafter, Britain's vulnerability as an open economy became more and more marked:

> Policy makers in Britain have been faced with the problem of trying to compensate for the fact that Britain has a long history of a

relative lack of success as an industrial society. In a world where trade barriers have been falling, British industry has not competed successfully in world trade in manufactures: imports have risen very fast and Britain's share in world exports has fallen year by year. In consequence, it has proved increasingly difficult to combine full employment with an adequate balance of payments.

(Blackaby, 1978b, p. 653)

The era of 'stop-go' economic policy-making, in retrospect, takes on the aura of a golden age. Thus: 'the picture that emerges up to 1973 is of an economy which was rather stable, had a controllable inflation rate, fairly low unemployment, and moderate rate of real growth' (Peston, 1984, p. 142). With the escalation of world commodity prices, most notably oil, the underlying weaknesses of the British economy could no longer be disguised or ignored; it had entered the era of 'stagflation' – the combination of nil growth and high inflation – and deindustrialization. This latter term has been variously defined. For Cairncross (1979, p. 10) it refers to the 'progressive failure to achieve a sufficient surplus of exports over imports to keep the economy in external balance'. Or, somewhat more precisely, Singh (1977, p. 128) refers to 'an efficient manufacturing sector . . . which, currently as well as potentially, not only satisfies the demands of consumers at home but is also able to sell enough of its products abroad to pay for the nation's requirements'. More vividly, commentators discuss, 'the British disease' of 'low productivity, resistance to change, failure to adapt to more advanced technologies and to the fastest growing markets' (Keegan and Pennant-Rea, 1979, p. 34).

By the 1980s the problems of the British economy were compounded of an aged and ageing industrial base, a declining productive (especially manufacturing) capacity, a lack of international competitiveness, high inflation, high unemployment, an unreformed pay bargaining structure, a large and expanding public sector and, in consequence of some combination of these factors, a low growth rate. If there was some agreement that the manufacturing sector was relatively inefficient, there was intense disagreement about the contribution of public expenditure (and pay bargaining structures) to such weakness. The advent of 'monetarist' economic policies simply fuelled the debate. If diagnosis was contentious, the symptoms were plain for all to see: recession and mass unemployment. Such a dramatic decline could not fail to affect SCG.

But economic decline is not the only significant trend. The combination of technological change and the decline of the old manufacturing industries has led to a significant growth in the service industries and in non-manual occupations. In Bell's (1976, p. 14) terms there has been a shift from a goods-producing to a service-producing economy, and the professional and technological classes have become pre-eminent.

The facts of economic decline and economic restructuring have pervaded all facets of SCG and its relationship with the centre.

To a significant degree SCG's problems have become an epiphenomenon of national economic management. Thus, the centre has 'off-loaded to the periphery'; that is, it sought to resolve its economic problems initially by modernizing the institutions of SCG to make them more efficient and subsequently by directly regulating their expenditure. This strategy reflects the position of SCG within the 'mixed economy'. It has been the prime vehicle for the expansion of the welfare state (see section 2.5.1(iii), below) and it accounts for a substantial proportion of both total public expenditure and GDP. The most frequently cited example of this trend is local government expenditure, which during the 1970s accounted for some 30 per cent of total public expenditure and 14 per cent of GDP. Reliable statistics are not available for all non-departmental public bodies but their expenditure has also increased rapidly – e.g. the National Health Service, the nationalized industries.

The scale of SCG can be seen in the numbers of people employed (see Parry, 1980). Not only was public employment a large proportion of the total workforce but it has grown rapidly throughout the postwar period. For example, total local authority full-time employment grew by 16.4 per cent between 1952–62 and by 26.4 per cent between 1962–72 (Newton and Karran, 1985, p. 28). This pattern was repeated throughout the public sector. Thus, public enterprise accounts for 12.7 per cent of GDP, 9.4 per cent of total employment and 22.6 per cent of gross domestic fixed capital investment (Pryke, 1981, table 1.1, p. 2). The NHS accounted for 6.2 per cent of GDP and 4.8 per cent of total employment, spending some £16.9 million in 1984. Between 1949–84 its costs increased threefold in real terms and it accounted for 12.6 per cent of total public expenditure (Merrison Commission, 1979, pp. 431–3; Klein, 1983, p. 67; Ham, 1985, pp. 38–9). Even the resources commanded by the smaller non-departmental public bodies can be considerable. Thus, the water authorities had a combined revenue and capital expenditure of some £1,234 million in 1979-80 compared to £13,536 million for local authorities (both 1975 prices) (Gray, 1982, p. 162). For other non-departmental public bodies there is a paucity of reliable data. Bowen (1978, pp. 26–7) calculated that the bodies in his survey accounted for £2,367 million (1974–5) and employed 184,000 people. Pliatzky (1980, pp. 1–18) calculated that 489 executive bodies spent some £5.8 billion, employed some 217,000 people and accounted for 86 per cent of all expenditure by non-departmental public bodies. The largest non-departmental public bodies included the Regional Water Authorities, Manpower Services Commission, New Towns Development Corporations, UKAEA, the Civil Aviation Authority and the Research Councils. In short, the overwhelming majority of the bodies spent very little, and their total expenditure was smaller than either total local authority expenditure or the £24 billion turnover and 1.6 million employees of nationalized industries.

The sheer size of SCG as a proportion of public sector expenditure made it vulnerable to retrenchment in an era of economic decline. This vulnerability was accentuated by the resurgence of ideological politics. Cuts in sub-central expenditure ceased to be a question of practical politics and became a component of a larger debate about the role of government. Whether or not the scale of public expenditure was a factor in Britain's economic decline, the ideology of central élites now emphasized that the balance between the public and private sectors was wrong (see section 2.3.2, above, and section 2.5.1(vi), below). The former had expanded at the expense of the latter, and the balance had to be redressed. In this climate, SCG was no longer vulnerable to 'cuts'; they were now inevitable. The ideological debate was not limited, however, to the size of the public sector. The scope of its activities was also under threat; in theory, the welfare state was to be dismantled.

Economic restructuring also affected SCG through its impact on social structure. With the decline in manual workers and the expansion of the non-manual, service industries, the basis of class politics was eroded, and other cleavages emerged as the basis of political alignments. Thus, between 1959–83, the ratio of non-manual to manual workers shifted from 40:60 to 45:55 (Crewe, 1983, table 5 and pp. 193–4). The saliency of other social cleavages, including religious, national and sectoral cleavages, became more pronounced, and SCG became a locus within which social conflicts were enacted and resolved. The combination of economic decline and a changing social structure played a significant part in politicizing SCG (see section 2.5.2(ii), below). The other key factor influencing the politics of SCG, in a manner which both complemented and contradicted the consequences of economic and social change, was the expansion of the welfare state.

2.5.1(iii)   THE GROWTH OF THE WELFARE STATE

Whilst the boom in the world economy generated growth in the UK economy and disguised its underlying weaknesses, governments used SCG as the vehicle for building the welfare state. If local government lost some functions, others were expanded greatly, whilst the era of 'quangocracy' was ushered in. A variety of specialized, even uni-functional non-departmental organizations were created. As well as fragmenting governmental structures and factorizing problems (see section 2.5.1(iv) below), the creation and expansion of the welfare state fuelled the massive expansions of SCG expenditure (see Table 2.1 and the comparative statistics on the growth of welfare state programmes in Rose, 1984, table A7.1, p. 213).

Table 2.1 The Growth of Local Government Welfare Spending, 1945–75 (% Total Current or Capital Expenditure)

	1945		1950		1955		1960		1965		1970		1975	
	Cu	Cp	Cu	Cp	Cu	Cp	Cu	Cp	Cu	Cp	Cu	Cp	Cu	Cp
Welfare services														
Education	17.6	1.7	30.3	8.5	33.4	11.4	37.3	5.1	37.9	11.0	35.1	12.9	35.9	10.2
Housing	6.6	32.9	9.5	70.9	13.4	68.5	15.0	56.9	15.0	59.0	14.7	48.4	16.6	65.9
Poor relief	4.1	0.4	—	—	—	—	—	—	—	—	—	—	—	—
Hospitals	5.9	0.8	—	—	—	—	—	—	—	—	—	—	—	—
Local health services	—	—	3.8	—	3.7	0.3	3.7	0.4	3.6	0.7	3.1	0.8	—	—
Welfare services (social services)	—	—	2.9	0.9	3.3	0.6	3.1	1.2	3.2	1.3	3.0	1.2	6.1	1.8
Other services														
Highways and lighting	5.8	5.9	8.4	1.6	7.9	2.0	7.0	5.4	6.9	6.4	5.3	9.9	4.0	7.6
Police	4.8	0.4	5.7	0.7	5.9	1.2	5.8	0.6	6.1	0.7	5.6	1.0	5.4	0.9
Sewerage	1.9	1.7	2.1	2.9	1.9	3.7	2.1	6.2	2.3	5.1	2.4	6.7	—	—
Refuse	1.8	—	2.4	0.2	2.3	0.1	2.0	0.2	1.9	0.2	1.8	0.7	1.9	0.5
Parks	1.0	0.4	1.6	0.4	1.5	0.4	1.5	0.5	1.3	0.8	1.2	0.7	1.3	1.8
Fire	0.7	—	1.6	0.1	1.6	0.3	1.5	0.4	1.5	0.3	1.2	0.3	1.3	0.2
Libraries and museums	0.6	—	1.0	0.1	1.0	0.1	1.1	0.3	1.1	0.3	1.1	0.4	1.1	0.5
Trading services	30.2	44.1	15.8	9.3	13.3	6.9	11.3	8.0	9.5	6.5	7.2	8.9	2.4	2.9

Abbreviations: Cu: current expenditure; Cp: capital expenditure.
Sources: Foster, Jackman and Perlman, 1980, pp. 102–26; Jackman, 1985, pp. 150–1.

The use of SCG rather than central departments to develop welfare services had a number of important repercussions for policy-making in British government. First, it created a set of vertical, function-specific linkages between centre and SCG. For example, the channels of communication between the centre and local authorities were not based on territorial representation but on service-specific professional-bureaucratic complexes or policy networks (see section 2.5.2, below). Functional politics supplanted territorial representation as the well-spring of policy-making in SCG. It also created tensions. To quote Sharpe (1979a, p. 20, original emphasis):

> the decentralist trends in the politics of the West are, paradoxically, also a product of the centralization of society and the state machine. That is to say, they are a *reaction* to centralization and not a mere epiphenomenon of it ... we must acknowledge the possibility that the very centralizing socio-economic forces generate a *political* reaction among the putatively integrated.

Thus the resurgence of nationalism in Britain in the 1970s can be seen, in part, as a reaction to the centralizing, homogenizing effects of functional politics. This tension between territorial and functional politics has recurred in the history of SCG in the postwar period.

Second, it has been argued that the emergence of distinct welfare policy networks has bifurcated patterns of policy-making. Thus, on the grand economic issues involving, for example, the distribution of income and wealth and the prerogatives of private industry, there is limited conflict and pressure group activity. Policy-making is characterized by a high degree of consensus, and participation is limited to key functional (or producer) groups.[11] In contrast, welfare politics is more open; conflict is more prevalent, and there is competition between affected groups (see, for example, Lindblom 1977 and 1979). Rhodes (1986a, pp. 389–90) has argued that it is nigh impossible to distinguish consistently between grand economic issues and the rest but has suggested that any established policy area, both economic and welfare, has stable constellations of interest which act to limit conflict and the number of participants. Consequently, the emergence of the welfare state has created a kind of political oligopoly, or government by policy networks in which conflict, competition and participation are minimized. SCG is integrated to these networks, and, in consequence, the tension between territory and function is re-enacted on a smaller scale. Within particular policy areas, the politics of place – of local diversity and needs – is subordinated to the politics of service provision – of national standards and best professional practice.

Finally, the expansion of the welfare state increased the vulnerability of SCG to central attempts to curtail expenditure. In Britain, and throughout Western Europe, service expansion was not matched by the expansion of SCG's resources. Rather, it was financed by central subventions, primarily various grants-in-aid. The functions and resources were not commensurable at the sub-central level (Sharpe, 1981, p. 6). With the onset of economic decline, the centre had to hand the means for regulating sub-central expenditure; the grants used previously to pay for the welfare state. Reducing grant was a simple way of imposing financial stringency on both wholly grant-funded non-departmental bodies and local authorities which had an inelastic local tax base. Both scale of expenditure and source of income rendered SCG a prime target for expenditure reductions.

2.5.1(iv) THE EXTENSION OF FUNCTIONAL DIFFERENTIATION

Previous sections have referred to the key role of professional-bureaucratic complexes or policy networks in the policy-making of the welfare state. They are a product of the process of bureaucratic functional differentiation.

Division of labour is, of course, as much a feature of public as of private sector organizations. None the less, the scale of the process is impressive. Any head-count is fraught with danger; for example, there is no agreed definition of quangos, and the available statistics are incomplete. Bowen (1978, p. 1) estimates that the number of such bodies increased by 78.5 per cent between 1950 and 1965, a trend continued into the 1970s. However, this survey excludes the nationalized industries, and, as Hogwood (1979a, p. 12) notes, this and other exclusions are arbitrary. Pliatzky (1980, p. 5) puts the figure at 2,117, excluding the NHS and nationalized industries, whereas Hogwood (1979a, p. 22) lists 661 such bodies for Scotland alone. Whatever the 'real' number, there is a clear trend towards increasing functional differentiation in British government, and by the mid-1970s the administrative pattern was complex. Rhodes and Page (1983, p. 111) estimate the total number of public sector organizations at 14,074 *excluding* all delegated levels of administration. Hogwood and Lindley (1982, pp. 48–9) have identified 315 regional units of administration for 37 central departments. To this number it is possible to add, for example, the regional levels of non-departmental public bodies. To seek an accurate figure for the number of sub-central governments is probably an illusionary exercise; boundaries are ever changing. One conclusion should be obvious, however; the welfare state was (and remains) administered by disaggregated policy systems.

However, to point out that government has become complex is a truism. The more important issues concern the causes and consequences of this process. The causes of functional differentiation lie in the increasing scale of government activities and interventions to manage the mixed economy and the associated ideology of central élites. The key consequence is the emergence of policy networks.

A defining characteristic of bureaucracy is that it is based on the knowledge and expertise of officials with the consequent danger that the power of the political head of the organization is eroded. And as expertise becomes the basis of power, policy-making becomes private, removed from public scrutiny (Page, 1984). The apogee of such power occurs when professional groupings become institutionalized in government bureaucracy. Dunleavy (1980a, pp. 113–14, and 1982b, p. 194) discusses the various forms of relationship between professions and bureaucracy, including contractual relationship with the professions in private practice (e.g. consultants); direct employment by the government of a minor part of the profession (e.g. architects); direct employment of the bulk of the profession by government (eg. town planning, medicine); and employment of virtually all the profession by government (e.g. social work, teaching). And the professionalization of bureaucracies reinforces the trend towards functional differentiation. Dependence upon expertise fosters functional differentiation and the employment (even creation) of professions, which in turn accelerates the fragmentation (and complexity) of government.

It is not solely the structure of government which is fragmented; the problems that this structure manages are increasingly 'factorized'; that is, problems are decomposed into their semi-independent component parts (Simon, 1969, p. 73). When fragmented structures are coterminous with factorized problems, the disaggregated policy system becomes the cause of its own policies. Wildavsky (1980, pp. 62–83) argues that, as policies proliferate, they generate reciprocal effects on each other. Interdependence amongst policies increases faster than our knowledge, and unanticipated consequences proliferate. Consequently: 'public agencies are ever more involved in making adjustments to past programs, creating new ones to overcome difficulties and responding to forces in other sectors or in society' (Wildavsky, 1980, p. 81). Policies 'feed on each other', and 'sectoral symbiosis reigns supreme'. Policy is ever changing in response to the internal logic of policy sectors, not the stimulus of party manifestos, public opinion or pressure group politics (unless, of course, such groups are incorporated to the sector).

This process has provoked a reaction. In Beer's (1978, p. 18) terms it has called forth the countervailing power of the 'topocrats'. In Britain, the clearest topocratic challenges were the putative rise of corporate planning and the several attempts to strengthen the national community of local government. The former involved the creation of new management structures and processes within local authorities to counter departmentalism or professionalism (Stewart, 1971; Rhodes, 1979). The changes served to increase the power of the majority party leadership, the chief executive and the director of finance (i.e. the topocrats) at the expense of committee chairmen and service chiefs (i.e. the technocrats); or, to be precise, they would have done so had the technocratic rearguard action been less effective.

The phrase 'the national community of local government' refers to the set of organizations at the national level representing the interests of local government (Rhodes, 1986a, pp. 11–16). During the 1970s the (then) Labour government incorporated the national community to the Consultative Council on Local Government Finance (CCLGF) as part of its policy for curtailing local expenditure. The national community was to act as a counterweight to the expensive proclivities of the technocrats (see Chapter 4, section 4.2.1). And even here, the professions remain prominent, with the national organizations of chief executives and finance directors acting both in support of the national community and in their own right.

The extension of functional differentiation may have entrenched professional expertise in government, but it should not be thought that it heralded the era of 'rational' policy-making. This phrase refers to that species of procedural rationality which stresses the setting of objectives and establishing the economic costs and benefits of alternative means for achieving them. Whatever the strengths and weaknesses of this approach to policy-making, the complexity generated by the fragmentation and factorizing of structures and problems, coupled with the uncertainties of an open polity with a fragile external support system, renders nugatory the aspiration towards such synoptic analysis (Cohen and Lindblom, 1979). The professionalization of policy systems is an alternative strategy. It places a premium on expertise, substitutes professional ethics for other forms of accountability and, therefore, insulates the policy process from party political pressures. Moreover, when coupled with fragmentation, it encourages bargaining between administrative agencies and enhances a redundancy wherein overlapping jurisdictions generate multiple solutions to problems and increase of effectiveness.

The emphases placed upon rationalization and professionalization (expertise) are the distinct emphases of neo-pluralist theory, and two implications of the analysis require further comment. First, Dunleavy (1982b, pp. 185–6) has criticized neo-pluralist theory for assuming that administrative pluralism and professionalization are beneficial for Western liberal democracies. Not all species of neo-pluralist theory are so optimistic, but, setting this reservation to one side, these normative implications are not a *necessary* component of the analysis. The consequences of rationalization and professionalization can be determined by empirical investigation rather than by stipulation. The assumption which underpins the analysis here is that the relationships between functional differentiation, professionalization and fragmentation are multifarious, varying between policy areas, and have contradictory implications for liberal democracies.

In general terms, functional differentiation is said to be beneficial for liberal democracies because it promotes specialized expertise in policy-making; fragments administrative jurisdictions, thereby requiring bargaining and negotiation between agencies; deconcentrates governmental functions, thereby reducing the degree of centralization; and supplements accountability to elected assemblies with control by professional peer groups and their ethic of 'social responsibility'. Such outcomes are possible but only if a number of other conditions are met; administrative pluralism is a necessary but insufficient condition. In particular, the consequences of administrative pluralism depend on the degree of closure/indeterminacy of policy networks and the extent to which communication within and between policy networks is open/closed. Thus, any policy network is indeterminate to the extent that its boundaries are vague and the outcomes of its policies are not fixed. When the network's domain is determinate and its policy outcomes are predictable, it has achieved closure. All policy networks are indeterminate to some degree, and the capacity to cope with change and the unintended consequences of change will depend on the openness of communication. As problems succeed problems and problem definitions change, the network should become more elaborate, i.e. differentiated, in response to the new information about its policies and their consequences. In this ideal world, administrative pluralism increases the degree of decentralization and improves accountability when there are procedures for institutionalizing indeterminacy and open communication within (and between) the network and its domain (including the clients of the service).

In reality, policy networks practise premature closure. The professions monopolize skills and knowledge. 'The organized few consult the disorganized many', and the professions practise a form of 'exclusionary social closure' through restrictions in labour supply and protection of members from external judgement (Parkin, 1979, pp. 54–8). Equally, the networks respond to problem succession by 'capture'; that is, multi-network treaties are negotiated:

> if elements (like departments) are related, so that a change in one mandates a corresponding chain of changes in others, the interaction costs would be prohibitive and the uncertainty boundless. If it were possible, however, to decouple linkages between departments and substitute a division of labour involving their respective spheres of responsibility, a minimum of interaction and a maximum of predictability could thus be maintained.

> These treaties internalize externalities by creating even larger departments so that a subject formerly outside of several is now internal to the one.

(Wildavsky, 1980, p. 74)

Indeterminacy and openness of communication are essential attributes of networks if administrative pluralism is not to become the basis for the monopoly of policy-making by circumscribed networks and exclusionary professions. In Luhmann's (1982, pp. 147–8) terms:

> a high internal complexity entails allowing alternatives, possibilities of variation, dissent, and conflicts in the system. For that to be possible, the structure of the system must be, to a certain degree, indeterminate, contradictory and institutionalized in a flexible way. Against the natural tendency toward simplification and the removal of all uncertainties, it must be kept artificially open and remain under-specified.

Accountability in British government focuses on the relationship between public sector organizations and elected assemblies (Smith, 1981; Heald, 1983), reflecting nineteenth-century preoccupations with representative democracy (e.g. Mill, 1910, p. 239). In governmental systems with a high degree of internal differentiation, accountability cannot be limited to single organizations but must encompass the network, its relationships *and the policies*: 'the best guarantee of control is designing accountability systems which are appropriate to the policy, rather than specific to the institution' (Gray, 1978, p. 170). Equally, considerations of procedural correctness must take second place to network procedures for institutionalizing indeterminacy and guaranteeing open communication. These considerations are not the only relevant criteria for evaluating policy networks but, given their nigh total omission from the discussion of accountability in SCG, they can safely be emphasized here.

Second, the picture of government which emerges from the foregoing analysis is far removed from the Leviathan of the 'New Right'. It neither acts in the interests of a particular class (or factions of capital) nor umpires the competing claims of pressure groups in the public interest. Without denying that government can and does act to sustain the socioeconomic structure, it also has other functions – e.g. regulation, production, allocation, redistribution, legitimation – amongst which are the interests of the professional-bureaucratic complexes with their own needs for maintenance, growth and power. Government is, therefore, an independent entity not an epiphenomenon of class relations. The question of whose interests are served by government assumes, therefore, central importance.

2.5.1(v) THE DEVELOPMENT OF NON-CLASS CLEAVAGES

The effects of class on British politics have been extensively described and analysed. The sub-heading for this section is not intended to suggest that class has become unimportant, provided that the concept encompasses both the control of property *and* power in the labour market. Rather the intention is to draw attention to the persistence, and extension, of non-class cleavages in Britain. It is the existence of the separate but related systems of domination of class, status and parties (Weber, 1947, pp. 424–9, and 1948, ch. 7) which is of most concern for the analysis of SCG.

The Weberian analysis of class has been developed usefully by Parkin's (1979, esp. chs. 4–6) analysis of 'social closure' or 'the process by which social collectivities seek to maximize rewards by restricting access to resources and opportunities to a limited circle of eligibles' (p. 44). Closure strategies fall into two main categories: exclusionary and usurpatory. The former refers to 'the attempt by one group to secure for itself a privileged position at the expense of some other group through a process of subordination'; it 'represents the use of power in a "downward" direction because it necessarily entails the creation of a group, class, or stratum of legally defined inferiors'. The latter is 'the type of social closure mounted by a group in response to outsider status and the collective experiences of exclusion'; it represents the use of power in an upward direction, 'biting into the resources and benefits accruing to dominant groups' and employing distinctively 'the public mobilization of members and supporters, as in the use of strikes, demonstrations, sit-ins, marches, picketing' in order to attain civic, social and economic rights (p. 74).

This formulation has a number of advantages for the study of social cleavages in SCG. First, it does not polarize society into two main classes (in, of course, the ubiquitous final instance) but recognizes that 'racial, ethnic and religious conflicts have moved towards the centre of the political stage' and, consequently, that 'any general model of class or stratification that does not fully incorporate this fact must forfeit all credibility' (p. 9).

Second, whilst the exclusionary rights of property figure prominently in Parkin's analysis, he also treats the professions, and the use of credentials for closure, as of equal importance for analysing the distributive system of power (or stratification). Thus: 'Professionalization ... may be understood as a strategy designed ... to limit and control the supply of entrants to an occupation in order to safeguard or enhance its market value' (p. 54). Credentialism ranks with property, race and gender as a base of social closure.

Third, the combination of 'usurpationary activities against employers and state' with 'exclusionary activities against other less organized groups of workers' – referred to as 'dual closure' (p. 9) – provides a valuable tool for exploring the behaviour of 'semi-professions' or the 'failed professions' of teacher, nurse and social worker. These groups 'have been unable to secure full professional closure by establishing a legal monopoly or control over the number and quality of entrants and consequently resort to 'acting in a "trade-union" capacity' (pp. 102–3).

Finally, his analysis accords the 'state' a key role in social closure. It is 'through the action of the state that cultural groups become hierarchically ranked', and 'exclusion . . . follows upon the state's own negative treatment of the target group' (p. 96). The state endorses the exclusionary rules and institutions supporting the formal system of distributive justice. Indeed, in the case of the semi-professions, they are 'virtually the *creation* of bureaucracy, having been set up as government agencies for the administration of the welfare state' (p. 106, original emphasis). And in the case of usurpatory activities which occur on the borderline between lawful and unlawful, the state continuously redraws the boundaries for legitimate actions (pp. 74–5). The bureaucracy is seen as a 'powerful stratum distinct from social classes' which provides the base for the state as 'a separate and possibly competing basis of power to that of social classes' (pp. 126–7). The key questions concern who controls this instrument of social domination and control; the state is 'an agency that buttresses and consolidates the rules and institutions of exclusion governing all relations of domination and subjection' (p. 138).

In short, Parkin's analysis of social closure demonstrates vividly the paucity of the attempt to reduce the study of the social context of SCG to the capture of the local state by the working class. To the enduring and pervasive effects of class it is necessary to add the cleavages based on ethnicity, religion, gender and nationalism as well as the sectoral cleavages engendered by government intervention and the provision of public services. A thorough review of all the cleavages would be inordinately lengthy and repetitive. To demonstrate the importance of non-class cleavages, this section reviews briefly class de-alignment and religious, national and sectoral cleavages. Later sections will discuss the professions and semi-professions in more detail (see Chapter 3, sections 3.6.1(iii) and 3.7.2).

The roots of class de-alignment lie in the changing social structure of Britain, and its political ramifications are clearly revealed by changes in voting behaviour. The class basis of electoral behaviour has weakened, reflecting an increasingly differentiated social structure. In brief, there has been a growth in the numbers and in the proportions of males and females in employment in the professional and intermediate social classes and decline in the manual social classes (Goldthorpe, 1980). This trend continued in the 1970s. Between 1971 and 1981 the proportion in the professional and intermediate classes increased to 29 per cent for men and 22 per cent for women, whereas the proportion in the manual social classes declined to 56 per cent for men and 36 per cent for women (*Social Trends*, 1985, p. 22).

Crewe (1983, p. 183) characterizes the years 1945–70 as the era of stable two-party voting. Its main characteristics included two-party dominance, votes cast primarily along class lines, limited regional differences in party support and consistent ideological differences between the parties and their respective supporters. Thus the bulk of Conservative support came from white-collar or middle-class support-ers, whereas the bulk of Labour support came from blue-collar or working-class supporters. Class was 'the basis of British party politics: all else is embellishment and detail' (Pulzer, 1972, p. 102). However, 1970 onwards is seen as the era of partisan de-alignment in which electoral allegiance to the two main parties declined, votes were decreasingly cast along class lines, regional differences in party support widened, and ideological differences emerged between potential Labour supporters as the electorate moved to the right (Crewe, 1983, p. 183). Thus, turn-out fell, the electorate became more volatile, and the proportion of the electorate voting for the two main parties declined consistently. From a high of 80 per cent, the main parties share of the vote fell to 54.7 per cent in 1974 and, after recovering slightly in 1979, fell again to 50.8 per cent in 1983 (Crewe, Särlvik and Alt, 1977, table 1, p. 130; Crewe, 1983, table 1, p. 196). This shift of allegiance away from class politics represents both an erosion of party identification and the increasing saliency of other social cleavages: 'Alternative bases of partisanship emerged (or re-emerged after decades) in some areas: language and culture in rural Wales, national identity in Scotland, race in a few cities' (Crewe, 1983, pp. 192–3). Although the interpretation of these trends continues to give rise to debate (see Dunleavy, 1979 and 1980c and d; Crewe, 1983; Franklin and Page, 1984; Dunleavy and Husbands, 1985), the key points are not disputed; de-alignment has occurred, and non-class cleavages have become potentially important for understanding poli-tical behaviour. The next step is to explore, therefore, the importance of such cleavages in the UK and to broaden the discussion beyond the confines of electoral behaviour.

Even the most cursory comparison of the four nations of the UK reveals that they are culturally distinct; that is, they differ markedly in their religious affiliations and nationalities (Rose, 1982, pp. 13–20 and 24–5). The political importance of such differences is more varied. Thus, the majority of English identify with the Church of England, whereas the majority of Scots identify with the Presbyterian Church of Scotland. This difference has only a limited effect on voting behaviour. Both established churches tend to be pro-Conservative and anti-Labour. The differences within Scotland are far more sig-nificant, with Catholics strongly pro-Labour. The echoes of Northern Ireland recur with the conflict over the issue of Roman Catholic schools (Miller, 1981, pp. 88 and 144–6). And it is in Northern Ireland that the salience of religious cleavages is greatest, with 99 per cent of the support for the Ulster Unionists and the Democratic Unionist Party coming from Protestants, whilst 99 per cent of the SDLP's supporters are Catholic. Moreover, some two-thirds of the support for each bloc is drawn from the working class. Religion cross-cuts and supplants class as the primary cleavage. With these two important exceptions, although religious differences persist, class alignments remain a major determinant of voting behaviour, and if the class politics of the major parties is a diminished influence, none the less it remains prominent.

If anything, national identity distinguishes more sharply between the four nations than religion. Thus, 57 per cent of the English think of themselves as English, 52 per cent of the Scots think of themselves as Scottish, and 57 per cent of the Welsh think of themselves as Welsh. Approximately one-third of each nationality think of themselves as British. The exception is Northern Ireland, where 67 per cent of the Protestants think of themselves as British, whereas 69 per cent of the Roman Catholics think of themselves as Irish (Rose, 1982, table 1.1, p. 14). The political saliency of national identity varies between the four nations. In England nationalism is taken for granted and no consistent distinction is drawn between England and Britain. In Scotland and Northern Ireland (and to a lesser extent Wales) national identity is the bedrock of support for minority, national parties. Thus, throughout the 1970s (four elections), nationalist parties averaged 20 per cent of the total vote in Scotland, 10 per cent in Wales and 29 per cent in Northern Ireland (Rose and McAllister, 1982, pp. 86–90). Moreover, the issue of 'devolution' sharply distinguished Scotland and Wales from England where there was no equivalent issue. As Miller (1981, p. 227) demonstrates, attitudes towards devolution 'had a strong effect on SNP voting and every other variable that influenced SNP support did so only in interactive combination with devolution'. National identity is related, therefore, to distinct patterns of voting and specific issues and, in the case of Northern Ireland, to a marked lack of consensus on the country's constitution. A substantial Catholic minority perceives itself as Irish and votes for parties advocating a united Ireland.

The expression of political differences arising from religious and national cleavages is not confined to patterns of voting behaviour. As Miller (1983, p. 110) notes, 'the re-emergence of the periphery has been largely non-electoral and its success is obscured if we restrict attention to voting patterns'. Language nationalism in Wales has prospered not through the ballot box but through lobbying central élites, direct action and protest and even, at times, outright violence. In consequence, although only 21 per cent of the Welsh are bilingual, government policy seeks to preserve the language in schools, public administration and the mass media.

The importance of these cleavages has been recognized in many ways by the UK government. First and foremost, there are the distinct institutions of government and administration in the peripheral nations, ranging from the devolved government of Stormont to the more limited administrative functions of the Welsh Office; their very

Table 2.2 *Identifiable Public Expenditure in Scotland, England, Wales and Northern Ireland 1960–80*

Per head: United Kingdom = 100	Scotland	England	Wales	N. Ireland
1960–1	112	99		99
1961–2	114	98		99
1962–3	114	98		103
1963–4	115	98	113	101
1964–5	113	98	114	100
1965–6	111	98	112	105
1966–7	112	98	113	105
1967–8	118	97	110	106
1968–9	124	96	113	119
1969–70	126	96	111	113
1970–1	117	97	104	118
1971–2	119	97	108	122
1972–3	127	95	110	127
1973–4	118	97	104	124
1974–5	117	97	104	134
1975–6	119	96	110	136
1976–7	120	96	112	144
1977–8	120	95	115	147
1978–9	119	95	112	150
1979–80	121	96	111	142
1980–1	121	95	125	138

Sources: Before 1970, King, 1973, Table 22; after 1970, Parry, 1982, p. 100.

existence is political recognition of social differences. Perhaps more important, religious and national differences affect the provision of public services. The discriminatory allocation of council housing in Northern Ireland is only one obvious example. Scotland's educational system differs markedly from the rest of UK, and religious issues such as denominational schools remain alive. Similarly, the peripheral nations have a higher level of public expenditure than England (see Table 2.2).

Thus, per capita expenditure in Northern Ireland was £1,111 in 1976, compared to £949 in Wales, £875 in Scotland and £754 in England. And whilst total public expenditure in England fell by 3 per cent between 1964–76, it rose in Scotland and Wales. In short, religious and national differences continue to exert an influence on elections, institutions and public policy.

The term 'sectoral cleavage' refers to 'those who are dependent on the public sector for their employment or for the provision of their consumption requirements, and those who rely on the private sector' (Dearlove and Saunders, 1984, p. 196). Logically, therefore, 'consumption cleavages' refers to cleavages 'created by the existence of public and private (broadly speaking collective and individualized, and often also service and commodity) modes of consumption' (Dunleavy, 1980a, pp. 70–1). The relevant collective services include housing, transport, education and health. It is argued that, for example, the working class is split into two: manual workers in the public sector, relying on public transport and living in council houses and voting Labour; and those in the private sector who own a car, buy their own house and vote Conservative. Sectoral cleavages cross-cut class cleavages and, in the example given, weaken the traditional allegiance of the working class to the Labour Party. The importance of sectoral cleavages for voting behaviour is currently a matter of keen debate (cf. Franklin and Page, 1984). But whether or not a rational interest in the enhanced provision of public services affects voting behaviour, sectoral cleavages are important for understanding the politics of service provision by SCG.[12] The major political consequences of sectoral cleavages for service provision can be summarized as: the tactics of mobilization (of client support), the dynamics of inertia and exclusion and the fragmentation of dissent both between social groups and units of SCG.

Created by government action, sectoral cleavages serve to maintain that action. Clients can be mobilized to resist threatened reductions in expenditure or to highlight gaps in service provision. Such support is a resource for the policy networks in their competition for finance and manpower. For example, the indignation of middle-class parents at both the reduction in places at universities, the reduction of student grants and the corresponding increase in cost to themselves of such education has been a constraint on attempts to reform the financing of higher education. Conversely, sectoral support for the compulsory sale of council houses has facilitated government action to the discomfort of a Labour Opposition prepared to entertain discretionary sales and then only with reluctance. Services lacking substantial client support, e.g. leisure and recreation, are at a marked disadvantage and vulnerable to cuts in expenditure.

Client support can be mobilized, but the policy networks at the heart of public service provision are not locations for pluralistic, competitive politics. As Dunleavy (1980a, p. 74) argues, they are

> powerful national ideological structures ... socially created and sustained by dominant classes, groups or institutions ... [which] make available to individuals in different social locations particular perceptions of their interests *vis-à-vis* state policies and the interests of other groups.

In other words, the policy networks determine the framework within which any debate about the service takes place. In addition, they control the agenda of items to be discussed; decide who can discuss these items by regulating access; and, of course, identify when external support is required. Such restrictions, coupled with the need to maintain consensus within the complex, sustain an incremental pattern of policy-making in which policy is indeed its own cause (see section 2.5.1(iv), above).

The 'closed' nature of policy networks means that they can regulate and exclude demands from citizens. It also means that they are a major constraint on the government of the day. The institutionalization of interests in governmental policy networks is a source of inertia; or, in Lowi's (1969, p. 89) phrase, 'Government by and through interest groups is in its impact conservative in almost every sense of that term.' Thus, the putative dismantling of the welfare state since 1979 has encountered major obstacles not simply in the form of public protest but also in the resistance of policy networks. The attempt to create 'the minimal state' has had to surmount the obstacle of vested interests entrenched within the machinery of government. The 'centre' is an abstraction compounded of multiple interests and inter-network competition, resistant to co-ordination and determined to the point of recalcitrance in defence of their 'turf'. The threat to the welfare state is real enough, but its dismantling is some way off. The Grand National is a canter for novices in comparison.

The degree of dissent is further limited by social and governmental fragmentation:

> political struggles around issues of consumption cut across class lines. Sometimes, this results in the formation of new and strange alliances . . . Middle class teachers join with working class parents to fight school closures . . .
> At other times, however, this redrawing of political alignments results in a hopeless fragmentation among people who more often find themselves on the same side . . . The politics of consumption . . . are often divisive and involve struggles and conflicts between sectors of the population which cut across social classes.
>
> (Dearlove and Saunders, 1984, p. 328)

Allied to a governmental structure in which welfare provision is divided between centre and SCG and the same function can be split between SCGs, conflict is spread, dampened and ultimately dissipated. SCG, as a prime vehicle for the delivery of welfare services, is simultaneously a locus for the conflict generated by sectoral cleavages, a means for dissipating that conflict and an additional point of access for the middle class.

The objective behind this brief discussion of the social context of SCG is to make explicit the assumption that it is characterized by multiple cleavages and to illustrate the contention that non-class cleavages are a significant influence on SCG. The obvious conclusion is that SCG is a locus for conflict rooted in a range of cleavages. Defining the local state as a condensate of local class relations is to exclude, by stipulative definition, a multiplicity of conflicts based on gender, ethnicity, religion, nationality and sectors. It remains possible that class is the all-pervasive cleavage. If so, the matter can be resolved empirically. However, the persistence of class de-alignment within the national government environment suggests that the most salient feature of the social context of SCG is its fragmentation.

2.5.1(vi) A STABLE POLITICAL TRADITION

The UK political tradition will be discussed under three subheadings: the unitary institutional structure, the party system and the ideology of central élites. It will be argued that the continuing stability of this tradition limits the capacity of the centre to respond to the changes discussed in earlier sections; constrains its ability to manage complexity; and shapes decisively the form of any central response.

A unitary institutional structure It is a commonplace to refer to Britain as a unitary state because 'the power to delegate or revoke delegated power remains in the hands of the central authority' (Rose, 1982, p. 50). Such a general characterization tells us precious little about Britain. It is more revealing to describe the central authority as 'a stateless Crown of indefinite domain without a uniform set of institutions for governing the United Kingdom' (Rose, 1982, p. 6). This statement draws attention to the multinational, multiform character of the British unitary state; it begins to tell us what kind of unitary state is being analysed. Unitarism comes in as many guises as the more widely documented species of federalism. The characteristics of this specimen can be best appreciated by examining the Union, the Mace and the Maze.

Lacking both a codified constitution and the European conception of the state as a separate entity superior to citizens, the Crown acts as a substitute because 'it is both sovereign and singular, incorporating in it the sum total of governmental powers'. The Crown in Parliament conjoins executive authority with representative institutions and is symbolized by the 'Mace' (Rose, 1982, p. 50). In somewhat florid terms, Rose is pointing to parliamentary sovereignty as a central characteristic of the UK institutional structure; what Parliament has joined together it can indeed cast asunder – it is legally supreme. If the centre is dependent on SCG, the relationship is asymmetric. The centre monopolizes legislative resources.

This supremacy is at the heart of a multinational governmental system. As Rose (1976) argues, the theses of cultural and political homogeneity must be rejected for the UK. Union there may be, but cultural diversity has persisted (see section 2.5.1(v), above), as have separate educational and legal systems: 'union without uniformity' (Rose, 1982, p. 35). UK governments have not tried to create a single nation. Union rests not on a shared nationality but on the acceptance by the distinct nations of parliamentary sovereignty.

Paralleling this diversity are the institutions of government. In addition to the Scottish, Welsh and Northern Ireland Offices there are the distinct local government systems of Scotland, Northern Ireland and England. Add to this structure the intermediate institutions of the regional offices of central departments, the water and health authorities, the nationalized industries and quangos and one key feature of British government becomes clear; the central authorities are non-executant bodies (Sharpe, 1977). Services are not delivered by London-based ministries but by a plethora of other organizations, the constitutions and functions of which differ between the constituent nations of the UK. Determinant authority remains with the Mace but it is dependent upon the 'Maze' – the multiform institutions of UK government – for the execution of its policies.

The party system   The main features of the UK party system seem transparently obvious: a two-party system based on a simple plurality electoral system. Consequently, there is much debate about the inequities of the electoral system for third parties and a great deal of criticism of adversarial politics wherein ideologically extreme parties are said to reverse each other's policies when in office, disregarding the national interest. This 'Westminster-centred' view disregards one of the major functions of the party system: integration of the constituent nations of the UK. Competition between UK-wide parties focusing on functional issues dominates election. Nationalist parties exist, their electoral strength is, at times, impressive, but they have remained *minority* parties within their territorial units. Neither class de-alignment, nor the upsurge of nationalist parties in the 1970s, nor the emergence of the Alliance in the 1980s has yet affected permanently the capacity of the major parties to sustain unionist values.

Arguing from a UK perspective that the two-party system integrates the constituent nations does not stamp out either differences between the nations or fluctuations in the fortunes of the major parties. The internal politics of Northern Ireland is a sharp reminder that integration cannot be equated with homegeneity. The erosion of electoral support for the major parties in the 1970s led to a minority, quasi-coalition government between 1976–9; to a weak government dependent for its continued existence on the support of minority (including nationalist) parties. Curiously these 'fluctuations' are not a modern phenomenon. The 'Irish problem' has complicated UK domestic politics for all the twentieth century (and beyond). And for only fifty-six of the eighty-five years of this century has the UK had government by a party with an overall majority in Parliament. The problem to be explained, therefore, is not the territorial instabilities of the 1970s but the persistence of territorial issues and cleavages for the bulk of this century.

The first point to note is, of course, that the stability of the twentieth century is a chimera of selective memory. For example, the creation of the Republic of Ireland, in itself a traumatic event, was part of 'Home Rule All Round', and between 1910 and 1926 'devolution' was firmly on the political agenda and a source of divisive conflict. Concurrently, the Labour Party saw local authorities as a vehicle of social change and a means to national power. Popularism and Home Rule were twin threats to Unionism. That, for the bulk of this century, the impact of such sub-central instability on the centre has been so limited stems in part from a second key feature of the party system: the insulation of the national political élite from local élites. Local parties were poorly organized and, in many local authorities, virtually non-existent, dominated by 'a culture of apolitisme' (Bulpitt, 1983, pp. 148–52). Sub-central interests were weakly represented at the centre, and MPs became divorced from local politics. If local parties had national party labels then it was, to overstate the argument, the only point of contact. In sharp contrast to France, there was no practice of *cumul des mandats* whereby local interests were directly voiced in the centre by politicians holding office at many (if not all) levels of government. Lacking such access, centre and its sub-central units were insulated from each other, divorced by the failure of national parties to penetrate sub-central arenas.

The ideology of central élites   The phrase 'ideology of central élites' immediately suggests that the shift to social-market liberalism under Margaret Thatcher's government will be the topic under discussion. But the pre-existing ideology requires exploration: an ideology which encompasses both economic intervention and the centre's territorial operating code.

The phrase 'Keynesian demand management' is commonly used to describe intervention to promote economic growth and thereby ensure full employment. As Bulpitt (1986, p. 26) points out, government policy between 1945 and the 1960s was not 'wholeheartedly Keynesian', and a phrase such as 'economic intervention' is sufficiently vague to capture both the ill-defined nature of the consensus and its divergent emphases – on types of planning and on the priority accorded to welfare policies. Indeed, imprecision was essential for it to survive recurrent balance of payments crises. The resultant 'stop-go' policies barely dented the consensus. To introduce a mild note of precision, the consensus covered action to stabilize the economy and a preference for 'automatic pilots' (Bulpitt, 1986, p. 28), such as fiscal policies, for achieving this objective. Fiscal policy varied in both content and the enthusiasm with which it was adopted, but numbered among its components were changes in the level of taxation, the scale of public expenditure and the size of the budget deficit in order to influence the level of aggregate demand in the economy or, to be more precise, to maintain full employment. It was argued that fiscal policies would keep the economy at full capacity because they would stimulate private investment and the output of the private sector. If the increase in demand generated inflation because the increase in production lagged behind the increase in money and stimulated a rise in imports and a balance of payments crisis, then the government should 'fine-tune' the economy by depressing or stimulating demand as appropriate. Moreover, to minimize the various uncertainties and to co-ordinate the activities of individual companies (and trade unions) in the private sector, prices and income policies and national economic planning (in one guise or another) were increasingly seen as essential adjuncts of fiscal policy (for a succinct history of these ideas see Smith, 1979, chs. 5–7).

In this period, there was a distinct territorial operating code described by Bulpitt (1983, pp. 64–5) as the central autonomy, dual polity model; that is, the centre sought to insulate itself from sub-central politics in order to enhance its autonomy in matters of 'high politics'. The insulation was political, however, not bureaucratic. There were extensive bureaucratic-professional linkages; they were the engine of the welfare state. But with ever-increasing intervention to manage the economy and extend the welfare state, the political isolation of sub-central institutions was under threat; they were to be modernized.

Thus, intermediate institutions were in favour, and regional economic planning councils and boards were created (see Wright and Young, 1975; Lindley, 1982). More important, from the mid-1960s local government reform was high on the political agenda. As Isaac-Henry (1975, p. 8) suggests:

> The 1940s and 1950s were periods of great social reforms in the fields of education, housing and social services. Whilst this was going on it might be thought inappropriate to embark on extensive reform since the resulting upheaval could have caused delay and might have affected the quality of these services. Furthermore in order to carry out these new measures successfully the enthusiasm and goodwill of local authorities would be essential.

The time was ripe after the establishment of social welfare programmes when the disruption of political routines would be minimized.

One indicator of the potential for future conflict emerged with the first elections of the reorganized local authorities. The modernization of local government in 1974 gave expression to the demand for improved functional effectiveness in SCG. But it also politicized local government. To an unprecedented degree, the new councils were party controlled. In 1970, 15 out of 58 English and Welsh county councils were either non-party or controlled by Independents. By 1974 only two councils had Independent majorities. By 1977 the two major parties had 70 per cent of all the seats on English and Welsh local authorities and controlled 79 per cent of all councils. The local parties had been nationalized, at least in name (Rhodes, 1975a; Gyford, 1985a). The politicization of individual local authorities was soon to spill over into relations between centre and locality (see pages 84–5).

Less widely noted is the stronger link between local government and Parliament. In 1945, 32.7 per cent of all MPs had experience in local government, 43.5 per cent in the case of Labour, whereas the same was true for only 14.1 per cent of Conservative MPs. By 1974, 38.6 per cent of all MPs had local government experience, and whilst the Labour proportion had risen only slightly to 46.4 per cent, the Conservative proportion had more than doubled to 31.0 per cent. Moreover, three-quarters of the MPs were elected to Parliament whilst serving as councillors, and just under half represented constituencies geographically related to their local government ward (Mellors, 1978, pp. 90–9). And the proportion continued to rise, standing at 44.4 per cent in 1979 (Gyford and James, 1983, p. 103). If such MPs did not become national figures as in the USA or France, if the link between parliamentary and local government experience had limited apparent effect on their behaviour, none the less the link existed. It could, and would, be activated as SCG moved to the centre of the political stage.

The interventionism of the mixed economy welfare state conflicted with the insulation of the territorial operating code, raising the prospects of both a substantial redefinition of the role of sub-central government and an increase in the centre's problems in managing territorial conflict. This potential for conflict was realized only slowly. The insulation of centre and SCG hampered its expression, and the expectation of incremental growth 'bought off' opposition. The fact that expenditure on the welfare services had grown created an expectation of continuing growth. In theory at least, problems and conflicts could be resolved by additional expenditure. This 'ideology of growth' was pervasive (Stewart, 1980).

Economic intervention, the dual polity and the ideology of growth were threatened by the deterioration of the British economy. It was clear that 'fine-tuning' the economy was neither closing the ever-increasing gap between Britain and its major competitors nor containing inflation within acceptable bounds. Experiments with planning scarcely left the drawing-board, prices and incomes policies bought short-term stability at the cost of storing up substantial wage increases, and the modernization of government institutions in general and SCG in particular bore few of the claimed fruits in efficiency. Such problems heralded the so-called era of corporatism (Middlemas, 1979; Cawson,1982): a transitional phase, built on cosmetic rather than remedial surgery. However, it had three important implications for SCG. (On the concept of corporatism see pages 43–4, above, and on 'corporatism' in SCG see Chapter 4, section 4.2.1).

First, central intervention increased in scope. Previously, the centre had provided grants to sustain the expansion of the welfare state. When public expenditure had to be controlled in order to 'fine-tune' the economy, grant had been regulated. After the IMF crisis of 1976 central attention was no longer limited to the level and rate of increase of grant. It was now concerned to limit total local expenditure, i.e. grant plus expenditure paid for out of local taxes (rates). Government public expenditure White Papers became increasingly explicit on both the desired total of local expenditure and its distribution between services.[13] Changes in the level of grant were seen as a means for influencing the total, and ministers, although reluctant to specify the size of rate increases, none the less urged moderation. Local expenditure had become the target of central intervention.

Second, the increasing scope of central intervention had some marked effects on the politics of SCG. In the dual polity, local élites had been marginalized; they had few channels of communication and limited contact with national political élites. But if local expenditure was to be controlled, the compliance of local élites was essential. Some means was required to guarantee support for the target reductions in local expenditure. The chosen means can be described as a strategy of incorporation; that is, the centre co-opted local political leaders in England to a national consultative forum known as the Consultative Council on Local Government Finance (CCLGF). For the first time, national and local political leaders met regularly to discuss common problems. If consultation with local political leaders was to be a practical proposition, then the multiplicity of interests in SCG had to be aggregated. This aggregation was based on the national representative organizations of local government and elevated the topocrats to prominence. The intergovernmental lobby was an ally of the centre in the fight to curtail the expenditure demands of the technocrats and their policy networks. Coupled with the politicization of local government following reorganization, the interventions of the centre were contributing actively to the erosion of the dual polity.

At the same time, the centre pursued a strategy of factorizing the 'problem' of local expenditure by splitting it into manageable 'bits'. Thus, the functions of the Welsh Office were extended, whilst Scotland developed its own, less formal consultative mechanisms: each nation developing its preferred channels of political communication.

Paradoxically, the tension between the centre's territorial operating code and politicization was masked in the short term by devolution and changes in local political control. The devolution debate was seen as a specific problem – nationalism – to be dealt with by *ad hoc* measures. No attempt was made to reconstitute the territorial code, nor could it be when England was omitted from the debate to all intents and purposes. The victory of the Conservatives in the mid-term local elections effectively supplanted the ideology of incremental service growth. Local authorities complied with central demands for restraint and the (then) Labour government benefited from local Conservatives' ideology of retrenchment: a transition which anticipates changes in central élite ideology. This compliance delayed conflict. With the election of a national Conservative government in 1979 the consequences of politicization were thrown into sharp relief by that government's brand of ideological politics.

In brief, the Thatcher government believed that public expenditure contributed to inflation, and, in addition to cuts in that expenditure, the role of government had to be limited drastically (see section 2.3.2, above). SCG was to conform to central policy on expenditure, irrespective of whether that expenditure was grant or rate borne. The centre was to intervene more systematically and on a grander scale than in the recent past to control the income and expenditure of individual organizations, be it local authority or nationalized industry. Attempts at direct control and political subordination replaced insulation. Retrenchment was the order of the day.

It is important to recognize that the term 'retrenchment' does not necessarily imply that the expenditure on particular services was reduced. The term encompasses actual reduction in expenditure but, most important, changes in the expectations of, and aspirations to, incremental service expansion (Stewart, 1980). The belief that SCG expenditure should be curtailed, that the centre's views on the management of the economy should prevail, has become a pervasive component of local government's 'responsibility ethic' (Bramley and Stewart, 1981, p. 60). It has been articulated most cogently by the topocrats. The ideology of growth has been supplanted.

If central élite ideology has rejected economic intervention and the ideology of growth, other facets of its ideology have remained constant. Indeed, advocates of 'the minimal state' have provided the clearest assertion for more than a decade of the centre's belief in its right to govern (Birch, 1964, pp. 243–4). The unilateral exercise of executive authority has been central to the attempt to bring limited government into being.

Executive authority is one of the 'chestnuts of the constitution' (Heclo and Wildavsky, 1974, p. 341), and the various arguments about the power of the Prime Minister, etc. will not be rehearsed here. Three points are relevant for the analysis of SCG. First, this assertion of central autonomy had been common, historically, in the field of 'high politics' – in, for example, international affairs. With an unstable external support system and economic decline, matters of domestic politics became the target. The centre had always had the capacity to so intervene; now, it was exercised.

Second, with the ever-increasing functional differentiation of British government, the tradition that 'leaders know best' was not supplanted but increasingly constrained by dependence on SCG. There is a tension between executive authority and the inter-dependence of centre and SCG for the implementation of policy. If bureaucratic directive strategies are adopted, then governments have to confront unintended consequences, recalcitrance, instability, ambiguity and confusion. If compliance is sought, and a more concilia-tory mix of strategies preferred, then the governments have to confront 'slippage' or the adaptation, at times substantial, of policies in the process of implementation. And yet it is precisely such slippage which provides the incentive for unilateral action. This tension has plagued all governments in the postwar period – it induces ministerial 'schizophrenia' (Anthony Crosland in Kogan, 1971, p. 171) – and has been a recurrent feature of relationships between the centre and SCG.

Third, executive authority is neither the sole preserve of prime ministers nor exclusive to political leaders. As the earlier discussion makes clear, decision-making is fragmented between policy networks with sporadic prime ministerial interventions. Ministers responsible for domestic departments are, to a substantial degree, sovereign in their own turf. Co-ordination is achieved (if at all) and conflicts resolved (or at least suppressed) in and by the Cabinet *and* its multifarious committees, supplemented by bureaucratic mechanisms. The means of bureaucratic co-ordination include the Treasury and the public expenditure survey, interdepartmental committees, the Cabinet Office and the official committees which 'shadow' ministerial Cabinet committees. Fragmentation of policy-making has generated, therefore, a variety of co-ordinating mechanisms and networks: a complex 'central executive territory' (Madgwick, 1986, p. 32). Indeed the continuous growth of, and change in, the central executive territory attests to the elusive nature of the goal of effective central co-ordination.

Finally, the tension between executive authority and inter-dependence has its roots not only in the fragmentation of the differentiated polity but also in the development of non-class clea-vages. Beer (1982, p. 147) points to the decline of the civic culture – a combination of rational political participation and deference to auth-ority – as 'an unintended and dysfunctional effect – a contradiction – of the collectivist polity itself'. This 'romantic revolt' was 'a response to the elitist and corporatist pretensions of the system'. Not only did the civic culture decline but there was 'the rise of the new populism' (p. 209). Beer is correct in pointing to the importance of the new populism, especially for the Labour Party (see section 2.5.2(ii), below) but unhelpfully focuses on values as the well-spring of change rather than its structural locus in sectoral cleavages. The challenge to executive authority was not simply a response to pluralist stagnation but was generated by governments whose services created the vested interests 'in revolt'. Sectoral cleavages, not a decline in the civic culture, and the creation of interests dependent on public service provision, not changing values, underpin the new populism.

The discussion of the processes within the national government environment has covered a lot of ground rapidly. It has introduced some unusual terminology; identified a number of tensions within the system of SCG, including territory versus function and executive authority versus interdependence; and suggested a number of explanations for changes in the system. But before drawing these several strands together, it is necessary to explore in more detail the concept of 'policy networks'. This shadowy presence in the analysis of the national government environment must be brought into sharper definition.

2.5.2 Policy Networks

2.5.2(i) VARIETIES OF NETWORK

Following Benson (1982, p. 148), a policy network can be defined as a 'complex of organizations connected to each other by resource dependencies and distinguished from other . . . complexes by breaks in the structure of resource dependencies'.

Rhodes (1981a, ch. 5, 1985a and 1986a, ch. 2) elaborates this definition, arguing that networks have different structures of dependencies, structures which vary along five key dimensions:

- *Constellation of interests* – the interests of participants in a network vary by service/economic function, territory, client group and common expertise (and most commonly some combination of the foregoing).
- *Membership* – membership differs in terms of the balance between public and private sector; and between political-administrative élites, professions, trade unions and clients.
- *Vertical interdependence* – intra-network relationships vary in their degree of interdependence, especially of central or subcentral actors for the implementation of policies for which, none the less, they have service delivery responsibilites.
- *Horizontal interdependence* – relationships *between* the networks vary in their degree of horizontal articulation: that is, in the extent

to which a network is insulated from, or in conflict with, other networks.
- *The distribution of resources* – actors control different types and amounts of resources, and such variations in the distribution of resources affect the patterns of vertical and horizontal inter-dependence (see section 2.5.3(i) below).

Although the available research on British policy networks is limited, none the less it is possible to identify some of the main varieties in SCG.[14] Thus, it is possible to distinguish, at a minimum, between policy and territorial *communities* on the one hand and issue, pro-fessionalized, intergovernmental and producer *networks* on the other.

Policy communities are networks characterized by stability of relationships, continuity of a highly restrictive membership, vertical interdependence based on shared service delivery responsibilities and insulation from other networks and invariably from the general public (including Parliament). They have a high degree of vertical inter-dependence and limited horizontal articulation. They are highly integrated. The distinction between policy and *territorial communities* refers, rather obviously, to differences in their constellation of inter-ests. Policy communities are based on the major functional interests in and of government – e.g. education, fire (Richardson and Jordan, 1979; Rhodes, 1986a, ch. 8) – whereas territorial communities encom-pass the major territorial interests – e.g. in Scotland, Wales and Northern Ireland (Keating and Midwinter, 1983; Rhodes, 1986a, ch. 7).

Other networks differ in that they are less integrated. The least integrated form is the *issue network*. The distinctive features of this kind of network are its large number of participants and their limited degree of interdependence. Stability and continuity are at a premium, and the structure tends to be atomistic (Heclo, 1978). Commonly, there is no single focal point at the centre with which other actors need to bargain for resources. The prime example in British government seems to be the field of leisure and recreation. Seven central depart-ments have responsibilities in this area, and at the sub-central level there are many non-departmental and intermediate organizations as well as all the tiers of local government (see Travis *et al.*, 1978, esp. p. 27a).

Professionalized networks are characterized by the pre-eminence of one class of participant in policy-making: the profession. The most cited example of a professionalized policy network is the National Health Service, wherein the power of the medical profession is substantial (see Chapter 4, section 4.4). The water service provides a further example wherein the constraints on water engineers seem particularly weak (Keating and Rhodes, 1981; Gray, 1982; Saunders, 1983, pp. 34–7). In short, professionalized networks express the interests of a particular profession and manifest a substantial degree of vertical independence whilst insulating themselves from other networks.

The analysis of the influence of professions cannot be confined to the distribution of resources but must also cover ideology. Dunleavy (1981a, p. 10) suggests that professions with operational control in peripheral agencies will develop a national level ideological system. Consequently, trends in national professional opinion constrain or influence the centre, and the national professional association will both periodically formalize professional opinion and continuously disseminate information on best professional practice. Peripheral agencies see the national level system as a source of ideas; it sets the parameters to their decision-making. Finally, the rotation of professions between peripheral agencies coupled with the usual traits of a profession, e.g. training and qualifications, serve to reinforce the national level ideology: to present a unified 'view of the world' based on common ideas, values and knowledge. And Dunleavy's (1981b) case study of high-rise housing illustrates the operation of one such national level ideological structure. Professional influence is exercised in traditional interest group activities (e.g. lobbying) it is institutionalized in policy networks; and it sets the parameters to decision-making through national level ideological structures.

Intergovernmental networks or, in the case of England, the 'national community of local government' (Rhodes, 1986a, pp. 11–16 and ch. 3) are the networks based on the representative organizations of local authorities. Their distinctive characteristics are topocratic membership (and the explicit exclusion of all public sector unions); an extensive constellation of interests encompassing all the services (and associated expertise and clients) of local authorities; limited vertical interdependence because they have no service delivery responsibilities but extensive horizontal articulation or ability to penetrate a range of other networks. The intergovernmental networks differ between the four nations. In England, there are a large number of organizations acting on behalf of local authorities in some capacity. This set of organizations speaks for disparate interests but manifests a high degree of interdependence, hence the appellation 'national community'. However, their links with individual local authorities – their members – are sporadic. In Scotland, Wales and Northern Ireland there is no equivalent to the English national community. Local authorities in each nation have their representative organizations, and only in Wales is there more than one such body. Moreover, the reduced scale of the networks means that they operate informally with far less reliance on explicit consultative mechanisms and far greater exchange with their members (James, 1982; Connolly, 1983; Rhodes, 1986a, pp. 256–67).

Given its topocratic membership, it might be anticipated that the national community of local government would conflict with the technocratic policy communities. However, national level ideological structures are not limited to the service specific policy communities and their associated professions. There is a 'national local government system' – which incorporates not only the national community and the policy communities for local government services but also the territorial intergovernmental networks – and this set of organizations defines the national role and state of opinion in local government as a whole (Dunleavy, 1981b, p. 105; Dunleavy and Rhodes, 1983, pp. 121–2; Rhodes 1986a, pp. 31–2, 36 and 416). It is a key means by which local government can convey a wide variety of different views to Whitehall and it also provides a framework within which any individual local authority can situate its problems, concerns and strategies. Local authority actors do not decide policies for their area in isolation; they look to the national local government system for guidance about what standard of service to provide, for ideas to imitate or avoid, for ways of tackling common problems and for justifications or philosophies of particular strategies. Some councils are innovators across a wide field of policy, but they are rather exceptional. Most councils most of the time follow national trends in the local government world, or national trends in their kind of authority facing their kind of general problem under their kind of political control. Each of them will innovate from time to time in one issue area or another, adding their own small contribution to the national picture. But most of the time local decisions are made within nationally defined parameters of what counts as good policy, rather than helping to redefine those parameters. If policy networks represent the all-pervasive functionalism in the organization of British government, then the national local government system is a mechanism of ideological integration.

Producer networks are distinguished by the prominent role of economic interests (both the public and the private sector) in policymaking; their fluctuating membership; the dependence of the centre on industrial organizations for delivering the desired goods and for expertise; and the limited interdependence amongst the economic interests. Thus Tivey (1982a) describes the development of the Nationalized Industries Chairmen's Group, its links with the Treasury and how it uses its knowledge of its industries to compete with the private sector for government resources. However, the effectiveness of the Group is constrained by competition between its members: competition which extends beyond the distribution of public money between the industries to the market-place and the sale of their respective products. Similarly, Dunleavy (1982b, p. 191 and fig. 11.2, p. 192) suggests that private industry has been a major influence on the development of policy in the nuclear network – a network in which, for example, GEC is firmly embedded.

Of late, the analysis of economic producer groups has been dominated by corporatist theory. Apart from the conceptual inadequacies of this theory, it has not fared well when applied to policy-making in British government. Leaving aside the bi-partite 'Social Contract' – the archetypical case which has been over-cited and remains a bad example – the case of industrial policy offers little solace. Thus, Hogwood (1979c) and Grant (1982) argue that an industrial policy community exists but its boundaries are imprecise and, in spite of a degree of informal contact, it remains loosely integrated. Clarity is served if this network is distinguished from the highly integrated policy communities, but it is clear that producer networks have few if any corporatist characteristics. It is possible that the concept of corporatism could retain some utility but only if limited to government-imposed integration/regulation: 'state corporatism' in Schmitter's (1979, p. 20) formulation. When so restricted, it does at least refer to a specific type of network relationship.

The distinction between the public and private sector does not refer solely to industry; it is also relevant in the analysis of professions. Dunleavy (1982b, pp. 193–5) argues that, when a profession is split between the public and the private sector, the latter tends to have a higher status within a unified profession. When the public and private sectors work together, for example in research and development, the flow of influence will be from the professionals in the private sector to those in the public sector. A profession can be a key channel of influence for the private sector. Thus:

> the concentration of nuclear engineers in these governmental bodies (i.e. UK Atomic Energy Authority, Atomic Energy Commission of America) working very closely with nuclear power plant manufacturers, has distorted their conceptions of the public interest on nuclear power.
>
> (Dunleavy, 1982b, p. 197)

In yet another form, professional influence emerges as a key element in policy networks.

The variety of networks is potentially much greater than the examples discussed above. However, the most important conclusion to be drawn from the examples concerns the need to compare networks. There is no one pattern of relationships for all policy areas. The definition of networks and the discussion of characteristics and types have suggested a basis for such comparison and illustrated the known variety. Two topics remain to be explored: the relationship between networks and the national government environment and relationships within and between networks. To this point, the analysis of networks has been static, an exercise in definition and typology. It is also necessary to explain changes in the context and in the relationships of policy networks.

2.5.2(ii)   POLICY NETWORKS AND THE NATIONAL GOVERNMENT ENVIRONMENT

Within a unitary institutional structure, the centre is the fulcrum of policy networks. Allied to the tradition of executive authority, central government cannot be treated as one more group; its role is constitutive. It can specify unilaterally substantive policies, control access to the networks, set the agenda of issues, specify the rules of the game surrounding consultation, determine the timing and scope of consultation, even call a network into being. Whilst it may prefer, and on occasion be constrained, 'to create a nexus of interests so that co-operation flows from a sense of mutual advantage' (Richardson and Jordan, 1979, p. 105), it retains the option of coercion. Through the substantial resource it controls, the centre has the luxury of choice between the many available strategies. Policy networks are not necessarily a constraint on government but can be manipulated by government in its own interest; the relationship is asymmetric.

This general point to one side, it is necessary to recognize that the centre has a multiplicity of interests. Policy networks may be based on a department or even a section of a department, each of which can have a distinct policy style. Relationships within a network are shaped by the 'departmental philosophy' or the 'store of knowledge and experience in the subjects handled, something which eventually takes shape as a practical philosophy' (Bridges, 1971, p. 50). This observation is unremarkable, but it is difficult to explain variations in style if the central department is treated as a unitary. If the era of the 'giant department' (Clarke, 1971) has passed, none the less large, multi-functional departments persist. Thus, the Department of the Environment (DoE) is composed of major divisions including (at various times during the 1970s) water, transport, local government, housing, planning and construction. By no means all of these divisions are at the heart of a function-specific network, but equally there is no single DoE policy network. It is inadequate, therefore, to search for *a* departmental philosophy. It is also necessary to search for variations within departments to determine whether or not a single department has several distinct styles: a possibility rendered all the more probable when it has been created from several previously separate departments. The separate organizational arrangements devised for transport and construction during the 1970s attest to their distinctiveness. The terms 'central government' and 'the centre' have to be understood, therefore, as shorthand for a diverse collection of departments *and* divisions.

It is only to be expected that this diversity is matched by the range of interests within central government. At its simplest, it is possible to distinguish between the 'guardians', or the Treasury, concerned to restrain public expenditure, and 'advocates' or the service spending departments (Wildavsky, 1975, p. 7). However, a further two distinctions are necessary. The 'advocates' comprise those departments (and policy networks) which have a direct involvement with the services of SCG and those which have no such involvement. The latter will be at least neutral in, for example, any argument with the Treasury involving local expenditure, and more probably they will have a healthy interest in local authorities bearing the brunt of any reductions in expenditure. Last but by no means least is the DoE, which, as the areal department responsible for local government, acts both as 'guardian' in the negotiations about government grant and as 'advocate' for spending on those services for which it has responsibility. And this characterization of the interests within central government is general, omitting the particular interests associated with, for example, a specific policy initiative. To the range of policy networks, therefore, it is necessary to add a parallel and profuse range of interests.

Second, the analysis of policy networks presupposes that they have a key impact on policy content. However, as Lowi (1972) has argued, the 'politics determines policy' axiom can be turned on its head; 'policies determine politics'. It is no mere coincidence that the Home Office, responsible for policies on police, fire and prisons, should be repeatedly characterized as authoritarian, secretive and directive. Lowi's reversal of conventional axioms has the virtue of pungent argument but the problem of overstatement; policy is both a dependent and an independent variable. But leaving such complexities to one side, it is clear that the analysis of policy networks cannot be limited to an analysis of process; it must encompass policy content.

The second feature of the British political tradition which conditions the operation of policy networks is the two-party system. Ministers face in two directions. They are the heads of the bureaucracies at the heart of policy networks but they are also the leaders of the majority party. Policy networks have not supplanted party political channels of communication and influence. Party is at times a complementary and at other times a rival channel of influence. The effects of party are pervasive. It spans levels of government and communicates a range of interests. Most important, it spans the policy network. If policy networks are closed, then party is one of the means for prising them open. Rhodes (1986a, pp. 387–9) concluded from his study of the national community of local government that party was the grit in the molluscs of Whitehall-based policy networks, capable of stimulating change. Of course, British government cannot be reduced to the simplistic duality of party versus bureaucracy. But the fluctuating relationship between the two is central to understanding the sources of inertia and innovation in the policy process.

The relationship between policy networks and economic growth/ decline, the conflict between functional politics and territorial representation and the interaction of functional politics and sectoral cleavages were all discussed earlier (see section 2.5.1, above). But the emphasis throughout has fallen on the extension of functional politics at the expense of territorial representation. The dual polity was created, local élites were marginalized, and uniform service provision prevailed over regional/national differences. These developments are only half the story. Paradoxically, the extension of functional politics also served to politicize SCG. Policy networks may reflect many features of the national government environment but they also changed that environment.

The most obvious reactions to the extension of functional politics were the re-emergence of nationalism and the emergence of the topocratic professions and the intergovernmental lobby to counter the influence of the technocrats and the function-specific policy networks. An intermediate tier of representation supplanted direct contact with local political élites but functional politics also led to the modernization of SCG and the attendant spread of party politics. It generated sectoral cleavages and contributed to class de-alignment. SCG became the locus of conflicts rooted in multiple social cleavages, and the politicization of local government began to pervade central–local relations with the onset of economic decline. SCG politics became the politics of Westminster and Whitehall. The extension of functional politics was an important factor in the erosion of the dual polity and the politicization of SCG.

A number of features of this trend warrant further comment. First, local government witnessed the revival of municpal socialism in new clothes.[15] The 'new urban Left' (Gyford, 1983a, 1983b, 1984 and 1985b) rejected the legacy of a centralized, reformist socialism. As Beer (1982, p. 167) notes, the Labour Party was 'wholeheartedly democratic, but the democracy to which it adhered in theory and practice was not participatory, but deferential, representative, indirect and centralized. Populism was as foreign to it as localism and individualism.' The romantic radicalism of the new urban Left rejected the responsibility ethic as but deference in a different guise. Rather local government was to be the means for resisting the 'cuts' but also an example of what socialism could achieve. The bases of support for this programme of radical activism were diverse, encompassing party and community activists, radical elements in the local government professions and socialist councillors. The 'new alliance' embraced the women's movement, black organizations, environmentalists and CND: indeed, the spectrum of social movements with their origins in the 1960s (Boddy and Fudge, 1984, pp. 7–9). And local government's 'responsibility ethic' was an anathema to the new urban Left. The politics of confrontation saw new stars in the firmament with Ken Livingstone and David Blunkett becoming national figures. Conflict over the GLC's 'fare's fair' policy and the Liverpool budget were not isolated incidents but illustrations of the new style in SCG.

Furthermore, the landscape of local politics has changed markedly with the rise of the SDP/Liberal Alliance. After the 1985 shire county council elections, twenty-five out of forty-six English and Welsh parties had no overall control. The Alliance was the largest single party on two councils and formed the minority administration on five councils. As yet this change has had its most marked effects on council procedures; but, with the onset of the budgetary process:

> The newly hung counties can certainly expect a new period of uncertainty, with protracted negotiations, an increasingly delicate officer role in terms of confidential briefings and information distribution, and committee and council meetings of quite unprecedented length.
>
> (Leach and Stewart, 1986, p. 15)

The rise of the Alliance in local government not only fosters its parliamentary aspirations but destabilizes local politics at a time of unprecedented instability and holds out the prospect of complex coalition politics.

Third, politicization was not a feature of local government alone. Public sector unions, disillusioned by fifteen years of pay policy, reacted angrily to the 'cuts' in public expenditure, privatization and a government which sought to limit drastically union power. The ever-present threat of unemployment may have exercised a restraining influence on some unions, but militancy was the order of the day in the NHS, the nationalized industries and the civil service.

The government confronted, therefore, an increasingly turbulent sub-central system, but the policy networks, as part of the national government environment, now constrained the ability of the centre to respond to the changes in SCG. The very existence of the networks caused certain policy-making processes and outcomes. A product of the welfare state, they had a vested interest in, and helped to fuel, its continued expansion. In an era of economic decline, they resisted political pressure for cuts: a bulwark of inertia. As the centre sought to control SCG, its bureaucratic strategies foundered on the disaggregation of policy systems, politicization and the multiplicity of interests in and of the centre. Thus, local government current expenditure rose in real terms between 1979–83 (see HMSO, 1983a). Nor was this pattern exceptional. Total public expenditure continued to rise and in spite of repeated cries of anguish, NHS expenditure rose by 14 per cent in real terms in the same period (*Social Trends*, 1985, p. 122). Indeed, as Ward (1984, p. 26) demonstrates, only housing of the major welfare services experienced a 'cut' in expenditure in real terms (see Table 2.3), although a focus on resources is unable to demonstrate whether or not there has been a marked deterioration in service levels. Thus, although the NHS had a 17 per cent increase in volume

Table 2.3 *Growth of Public Expenditure by Programme in Cost Terms*

	% changes 1980–81 to 1983–84
Defence	14.2
Overseas aid and services	4.4
Net payments to EEC	83.9
Agriculture	23.9
Industry, etc.	−3.8
Arts	6.0
Transport	−5.1
Housing	−49.3
Other environmental services	0.6
Law and order	19.0
Education	0.0
Health	5.8
Social security	25.5
Other public services	−16.1
Common services	29.9
Scotland	3.3
Wales	0.0
N. Ireland	7.9
Asset sales	−63.5
Planning total	7.0
Planning total, excl. asset sales	7.7
Planning total, excl. asset sales and net sales of land and buildings	8.4
Net interest	26.7
Total expenditure, incl. interest	9.2

Note: Figures are adjusted for reduction in National Insurance surcharge and changes in treatment of housing and sickness benefits and of Property Services Agency.
Source: Ward, 1984, table 7, p. 6.

expenditure (1979–84), this figure reduced to 7.2 per cent (4 per cent for hospitals, etc.) when the relative price effect (or higher costs of the NHS) was taken into account. It was further estimated by the Department of Health and Social Security that demographic and technological pressures required an increase in expenditure of approximately 6 per cent. Consequently, the hospital and community health sector experienced problems in meeting demands (Social Services Committee, 1984, pp. x–xi). As the committee commented, the NHS needs to live at the same rates of pay and price inflation as the rest of us. None the less the alleged dismantling of the welfare state remains some way off.

Policy networks have become as central a feature of the national government environment as some of the hoary old chestnuts of constitution, less prominent and debated but a more determinant influence. They lie at the heart of one of the major problems of British government: policy messes, or the non-correspondence of policy systems and policy problems. The failure to appreciate that service delivery systems are complex, disaggregated and indeterminate has led to the failure of policies. The process of differentiation in government requires not only policies on substantive problems but also policies on the procedures for managing differentiation (or institutionalizing indeterminacy). Moreover, these comments are a critique not of functional differentiation in itself but of the failure to recognize that it is a central feature of the policy process; substance and procedure have to be endlessly traded off in the internally differentiated or pluralized system of SCG.

Policy networks in all their variety are a defining characteristic of SCG. Exploring this variety requires an examination of relationships within networks, of the process of exchange and the rules and strategies governing resource transactions. This task of micro-level analysis is undertaken in the next section.

2.5.3 Organizations and Actors

Rhodes (1981a, ch. 5) presents a 'power-dependence' framework for the analysis of relationships between central departments and local authorities. With its emphasis on the game-like quality of the links – on the resources of participants and the rules of the game, strategies and appreciative systems conditioning their exchange – this framework is equally applicable to intra- and inter-network relationships (see pages 41–5, above).

Before exploring the central concepts of power-dependence theory, it will be helpful to classify the organizations and actors in SCG (see Table 2.4).

'The centre' refers to the institutions of Westminster and Whitehall. These terms are synonyms for the Mace or the Cabinet, Parliament and central departments, but the geographic association is important; the centre refers to governmental institutions in the capital city. Consequently, all other governmental organizations belong to sub-central government, thereby generating some highly contentious categories. Thus, the territorial ministries of Scotland, Wales and Northern Ireland, although not located in the capital city, are conventionally treated as part of the centre. However, this classification emphasizes their distinct geographical location in order to pose the important question of whether they are central or territorial institutions. The selfsame rationale applies to the treatment of 'intermediate institutions' or the deconcentrated units of central departments (Keating and Rhodes, 1982, p. 67) as SCG. Rose (1982, pp. 107–8) points out that

Table 2.4   *The Types of Public Sector Organization*

---

(1) The centre
    Functional departments
(2) Sub-central government
    (a) Territorial ministries
    (b) Intermediate institutions
    (c) Non-departmental public bodies
        (i)   Public corporations
        (ii)   National Health Service
        (iii) Fringe bodies: • Executive
                               • Advisory
                               • Tribunals
                               • Quangos
    (d) Local government (including 'quelgos')
    (e) Sub-central political organizations
        (i)   Political parties
        (ii)   Interest groups
        (iii) Professions

'Every government must be organized in both functional and territorial terms', and 'the government of the United Kingdom is not
organized strictly along unitary lines'. This classification emphasized
the territorial dimension in order to explore the extent to which territory and function conflict rather than assuming that they are complementary.

There are fewer problems with 'non-departmental public bodies'
(Smith and Stanyer, 1976, p. 15; Pliatzky Report, 1980, p. 1).
Deliberately created to distance the centre from the function or
activity – to operate 'to a greater or lesser extent at arm's length from
Ministers' (Cabinet Office and H.M. Treasury, 1985, p. 1) – they have
to be treated as apart from it. In addition, these bodies often have
elaborate territorial organization. The problem here is not their
classification as SCG but classifying the throng which fall into the category.[16] They have a number of shared characteristics, most notably
the fact that they are non-elected but are distinguished primarily by
their heterogeneity. On the pragmatic grounds that it facilitates the
collation of official statistics, a modified version of the classificatory
schema in the Pliatzky Report (1980, pp. 132–3) has been adopted;
that is, I have included the several bodies specifically excluded by
Pliatzky (e.g. the NHS, the nationalized industries). Thus, 'public corporations' (including the nationalized industries) are defined as

a legal entity established normally by Parliament and always by
legal authority (usually in the form of a special statute) charged with

the duty of carrying out specified Governmental functions (more or less precisely defined) in the national interest, those functions being confined to a comparatively restricted field, and subjected to some degree of control by the executive, while the corporation remains juristically an independent entity not directly responsible to Parliament.

(J. F. Garner, 1970, pp. 4–5)

M. R. Garner (1985, appendix 1) adds four constitutional characteristics to these legal characteristics:

(i)   the public corporation is generally exempt from the forms of parliamentary financial control applicable to government departments;
(ii) its employees are not normally civil servants . . .;
(iii) it would raise its capital finance by borrowing, normally from the public but occasionally from the Treasury, and not by the issue of shares;
(iv) it would cover its revenue expenses from the proceeds of the sale of its goods and services.

The National Health Service is *sui generis*, being an admixture of 'direct administration and decentralization' (Sharpe, 1977, p. 60), best described as 'discontinuous hierarchy' (Webb, Wistow and Hardy, 1986, p. 38), and it is treated as a separate category here. The remaining bodies could be referred to as 'the rest' but the term 'fringe bodies' seems marginally more precise. The term 'quango' is used in its original restrictive sense to refer to semi-private bodies (Barker, 1982a), whilst the term 'fringe' covers bodies 'which are not Government Departments or part of a Government Department' with 'executive, administrative and regulatory functions'; with 'functions of judicial kind'; and 'bodies whose principal function is to advise Ministers and their Departments' (Pliatzky Report, 1980, pp. 1 and 132–3). Although scarcely precise, this classification does at least capture some of the heterogeneity. The rest of the book will provide illustrations of the variety; but to keep the exercise within manageable proportions, the discussion of public corporations will focus on the nationalized industries, and that of fringe bodies will focus on the executive category, most commonly the Regional Water Authorities (RWAs) and the Manpower Services Commission (MSC).

The only undisputed 'territorial institution' in Britain is local government. Local authorities share the characteristics of an elected executive, independent taxing powers and multiple functions as well as a limited geographical jurisdiction. Again, this category poses questions. Obviously, local councillors are elected to represent 'their' area; but for example, given the strong vertical links between the officials and professionals of equivalent central and local departments, it can be argued that local authorities are loose federations of single-function organizations: that they are predominantly functional organizations. To further complicate matters, the Local Government Act 1985 created both a directly elected, uni-functional body in the Inner London Education Authority and a series of indirectly elected boards to run specific services for London and the major conurbations. Such 'quelgos' or quasi-elected local government organizations (Dunleavy and Rhodes, 1986, pp. 115–6) further compound the fragmentation of British government and the problems of labelling and classification.

Finally, the term 'sub-central political organizations' covers non-governmental organizations. It refers to territorially specific interest groups and political parties, including the major producer groups. It also encompasses the national–local linkages within, for example, political parties and professions.

It is possible to elaborate this classification. For example, the Kilbrandon Commission (1973, p. 226) identifies five types of non-departmental public body; executive bodies, industrial or commercial boards, advisory bodies, appellate bodies and consumer protection. Rhodes and Page (1983, p. 118 and table 5.7) identify eleven different local government systems within the UK. Such detail is not necessary here (but see Chapter 3 in its entirety). It is sufficient to demonstrate that there is a range of organizations, falling into five broad groupings. The remainder of the book will explore the utility of classifying public sector organizations by territory, by degree of decentralization, by range of functions and by election/non-election. Sufficient has been said to make it clear that the potential membership of policy networks is both diverse and numerous, as are the resources each organization commands.

2.5.3(i) RESOURCES

Rhodes (1986a, p. 17) suggests that five resources, or means for supplying the needs of public sector organizations, are central to exchange within SCG.

- *Authority* refers to the mandatory and discretionary rights to carry out functions or services commonly vested in and between public sector organizations by statute or other constitutional means.
- *Money* refers to the funds raised by a public sector/political organization from taxes (or precept), service charges or fees, borrowing, or some combination thereof.
- *Legitimacy* refers to access to public decision-making structures and the right to build public support conferred either by the legitimacy deriving from election or by other accepted means.

- *Information* refers to the possession of data and to control over either its collection or its dissemination or both.
- *Organization* refers to the possession of people, skills, land, building materials and equipment and hence the ability to act directly rather than through intermediaries. (This list draws upon Benson, 1975, p. 232; Rhodes, 1981, pp. 100–1; Hood, 1983, pp. 5–6.)

The definition of resources by actors in SCG is subjective; resources are variable, depending on the perceptions of actors, and their usefulness is relative over time and to issues (Simeon, 1972, p. 201). Any list must be seen as a starting-point and assessed by its subsequent utility. This list is not comprehensive but it has proved useful in the past (Rhodes, 1986a, esp. ch. 3). Resources are not only variable and transmutable. Their effect on relationships also depends upon both the rules governing exchange and the skill with which they are deployed, i.e. the strategies of actors.

2.5.3(ii) RULES OF THE GAME AND STRATEGIES

Rhodes (1986a, pp. 391–2) has identified the following rules of the game (see also Lijphart, 1968; Heclo and Wildavsky, 1974, pp. 14–21; Richardson and Jordan, 1979, pp. 103–5):

1 *Pragmatism* doctrinal, especially party, disputes should not prevent the work being done.
2 *Consensus* agreed settlements are preferable to imposed solutions.
3 *Fairness* the parties affected by proposed policies, even known opponents, should have the opportunity to state their case.
4 *Accommodation* where agreement is not possible, the 'loser' is not antagonized, a special case of the British love of the under-dog, and pains will be taken – through consultation over the details – to minimize losing over the principles of policy.
5 *Territoriality* actors do not extend their demands beyond their known remit. Thus, there is a 'lead' department for issues, and other central departments (for example, Treasury) should not intervene. Similarly the national community is constrained in its interventions in policy communities.
6 *Secrecy* discussions should be private and limited to the affected parties and not open to wider public scrutiny.
7 *Depoliticization* issues should be subject to technical rather than political criteria as in the case of grant distribution.
8 *'Summit diplomacy'* decisions should be taken by élites, meeting in secret, and be a product of direct, face-to-face discussion. Thus, Tony Crosland met the political leaders of the associations.
9 *Local democracy* local authorities as elected units of government

have a legitimate sphere of competence which is 'out of bounds' to central departments.

10 *'The right to govern'* certain matters are in the national interest, and the centre has both the right to intervene to preserve that interest and a monopoly of legitimate coercion to impose its definition of the national interest.

11 *'Trust'* access to discussions, secret and otherwise, and effectiveness in these discussions hinges on assessments of reliability. If and only if a group is deemed reliable, as in the case of the associations, will it command an entrée and attention.

These rules are 'conventional' and are not immutable. Not all rules were operative for all the postwar period and they varied in their relative importance.

In exactly the same manner, Rhodes (1986a, pp. 392–3) specifies the range strategies available to the participants (see also Elkin, 1975; Offe, 1975; Saunders, 1980 and 1981; Cawson and Saunders, 1983; Fox, 1983; Dunleavy, 1984):

1 *Bureaucratic* through its command of resources, especially legal resources, government can authoritatively determine relationships between public sector organizations. Such actions can be positive – requiring local authorities to undertake certain activities (that is, direction) – or negative – preventing particular actions (control).

2 *Incorporation* the co-option of local government into central decision-making processes, a strategy which can generate 'clientelism' or the identification of departments with the interests of groups and shared priorities.

3 *Consultation* central government initiates discussion of its proposals with local government without committing itself to any modifications.

4 *Bargaining* each unit of government commands resources required by another or others and they attempt to agree the terms of any exchange.

5 *Confrontation* local authorities defy central government either by breaking the law and refusing to terminate an illegal policy or by failing to implement a statutorily prescribed policy or by adopting policies expressly (if not legally) rejected by the centre.

6 *Penetration* the reverse of incorporation, and the attempt by local authorities to find allies amongst one or more central departments for their view of a policy, weakening central determination to adopt the policy by a process of divide and rule.

7 *Avoidance* the units of government cannot agree on policy, so each deploys its own resources to achieve its own ends, ignoring or vetoing the other party or parties.

8 *Incentives* the offer of financial or other inducements to foster the adoption and implementation of policy.

9 *Persuasion* literally, to cause actors to accept that the facts are as stated by a variety of means including rational arguments, lobbying, advice and the promotion of ideas in good currency, that is, 'best professional practice'.

10 *Professionalization* the creation of single-issue policy areas (not necessarily by unilateral central action) wherein professional criteria, interests and values dominate conventional political processes.

11 *Factorizing* the simplification of problems by subdivision and allocation to sub-central, appointed units of government (for example, quangos, regional institutions).

The strategies are not equally available. Bureaucratic, factorizing, consultation, incorporation and incentive strategies are means open to central departments. Confrontation, penetration and avoidance strategies are means commonly employed by local authorities. The centre has, therefore, the luxury of extended choice in its means for managing SCG, choices which are conditioned by its appreciative system.

2.5.3(iii) APPRECIATIVE SYSTEMS

This concept refers to 'that combination of factual and value judgements which describe the "state of the world" or "reality"' (Vickers, 1965, ch. 2; Rhodes, 1981a, p. 104). It is the accumulated wisdom or map of the world of a central or local department which enables it to steer a course through its environment. For example, Rhodes (1986a, pp. 386–7) concluded from his study of the national community of local government that the topocratic professions espoused the 'responsibility ethic' (i.e. the belief that local government should accept the centre's views on local expenditure in the interests of national economic management), whereas the technocratic profession espoused 'functionalism' (i.e. the belief in the economies of scale associated with large local authorities for improving service delivery). Similarly, particular services had a clear appreciative system which, in the case of education, has been described as the 'logic of the arithmetic'; i.e. policy was determined by the numbers of pupils in each education sector (Lodge and Blackstone, 1982, pp. 34–5; see also Rhodes, 1986a, pp. 326–7, for a more detailed description and citations).

Of all the appreciative systems within SCG, however, it is perhaps the centre's territorial operating code which is of greatest importance.[17] Initially this code took the form of the dual polity wherein the centre's preoccupations were with 'high politics' and its own autonomy from peripheral forces, and any difficulties over the respective roles of central and sub-central government were avoided with vague invocations of 'partnership'. Subsequently, the emphasis switched to central autonomy in the management of the economy and central interventions to regulate and, if possible, directly control sub-central expenditure. Tentatively, the government has experimented with a populist operating code of bypassing sub-central governments, appealing direct to citizens and vesting them with legal rights *vis-à-vis* local authorities. Primarily, however, government was seen as a bureaucracy in which the centre's wishes were transmitted down to the lowest levels. Bureaucracy was to be reduced by bureaucratic means. Unfortunately, this map of British government is faulty. The command code confronted the messy reality of the disaggregated, differentiated polity, and, rather than simplifying the state apparatus, the government made it more complex, confused and ambiguous. As yet it has not found a coherent code to replace either the unwanted dual polity or the faulty command code. This transformation was major and remains a continuing source of problems *for the centre* in the management of SCG.

For all its opaque qualities and associated research problems (Young and Mills, 1980), the concept of appreciative system is invaluable for drawing attention to the systematic way in which patterns of organizational (including the political parties') values influence, for example, the choice of strategies and set the limits to the range of options considered by policy-makers. It is the glue holding together potentially conflicting interests within a profession or, to be more specific, the disparate organizations which constitute the national local government system. For all the problems it poses, it is essential to grapple with the influence of patterned values on the SCG policy process.

2.6   Conclusions

This chapter has concentrated on defining in some detail the levels of analysis (and associated concepts) necessary for understanding the development of the system of SCG. They are summarized in Table 2.5. It has been argued that an adequate model of SCG must encompass the multiplicity of governmental bodies and requires three levels of analysis. Several objects of study have also been identified including the professions, the strategies and operating code(s) of the centre and the distributional and social consequences of policy networks. Subsequently, I presented a model which incorporates these elements within a broadly neo-pluralist framework.

The distinctive feature of such a framework is its emphasis on economic, social and political differentiation. Consequently, SCG has been described as a system with a high degree of internal

Table 2.5   *The Framework of Analysis: A Summary of Key Concepts*

	Micro-level	Meso-level	Macro-level
UNIT OF ANALYSIS	Public sector organizations: (1) 'The centre' (2) Territorial ministries (3) Intermediate institutions (4) Non-departmental public bodies (5) Local government (6) Sub-central political organizations	Policy networks: (1) Policy/territorial communities (2) Issue networks (3) Professionalized networks (4) Intergovernmental networks (5) Producer networks	National government environment
KEY CONCEPTS	Resources: authority money legitimacy information organization Rules of the game Strategies Appreciative systems	Structures of dependence: constellation of interests membership vertical interdependence horizontal interdependence distribution of resources	Processes: external support system mixed economy welfare state rationalization/professionalization class de-alignment stable political tradition – multiform institutions – two-party system – central élite ideology

differentiation. The pluralization of policy networks has created a complex, disaggregated and indeterminate structure. The institutionalization of interests within networks, most notably professional interests, allied to particularistic ideologies (or appreciate systems) act as integrative mechanisms, but the system remains complex. It has become the locus of conflicts rooted in multiple social cleavages, both absorbing and diffusing such conflict, as well as the source of sectoral cleavages. And as a component of an open polity it has been subject to the destabilizing influence of an unstable external support system and changes within the national government environment. The temptation for the centre has been to seek simple means to reduce complexity rather than employ selective, variegated strategies to stabilize it. In consequence, central interventions have accelerated the destabilization of SCG and generated policy messes.

This picture of SCG will be elaborated in two ways. In Chapter 3, I will describe the interests, resources and relationships of the multifarious actors in SCG. In Chapter 4, I analyse the role(s) of the several types of policy network. In effect, SCG is broken up into its constituent organizations and then reassembled in the form of functional networks. In the course of these exercises, the themes of this chapter will be revisited, revised and restated. Consequently, I will return repeatedly to the effect of a changing context on patterns of relationships in the postwar period; the fluctuating conflict between territorial and functional politics; the extension of functional differentiation, its effects and the countervailing influence of party and party ideology; the centre's changing strategies and territorial operating code, especially the recurrent tensions between interdependence and executive authority; the power of professions in the disaggregated service delivery systems of the welfare state; the politicization of IGR; and the distributional effects of SCG in a differentiated polity. And amidst this plethora of themes, it is important to repeat that the grandiloquent objective is to replace the conventional notion of Britain as a unitary state with that of the centreless society or differentiated polity characterized by interdependence, non-local policy-making, otiose forms of accountability and ambiguous and confused relationships in which fragmentation and centralization coexist.

There are, however, two important omissions from the framework. First, I have not attempted to draw together the three levels of analysis and provide an explanation of the changes in SCG. This task has been reserved for Chapter 5. However, as will become clear from the description of organizations, actors and networks in Chapters 3 and 4, the postwar years have been divided into four periods and they are central to any explanation of the development of SCG. In brief, 1945–61 was the era of stability in the external support system, economic growth and *apolitisme* in SCG; 1961–74 was the era of 'stop-go', modernization and territorial protest; 1974–9 was an era of economic decline in the UK, exacerbated by an unstable external support system, in which local élites were incorporated into central decision processes; 1979–85 was the era of sustained economic recession, repeated central interventions to control sub-central institutions (and expenditure) and the politicization of territorial politics. Each phase will be described in more detail subsequently; it is sufficient to note the divisions at this juncture. Chapter 5 will utilize them to provide a summary explanation of crisis and change in SCG.

Second, I have ignored the normative concerns so prominent in other models of SCG, whether that concern be for local autonomy, efficiency, or participation. Evaluations rooted in political philosophy, although they are relevant and important, are eschewed in favour of an internally generated appraisal; policies are appraised for the adequacy of their underlying theory of SCG. They must recognize that complexity, indeterminacy and interdependence are defining characteristics of the system. The plurality of organizations and the indeterminacy of the system's structure cannot be assumed away as political inconveniences. Strategic flexibility is an essential prerequisite of effective intervention. Complex structures require a high degree of tolerance for indeterminacy and an openness to strategic possibilities. Equally, flexibility requires openness of communication. The following analysis of SCG will suggest that many central policies are based on a wholly inadequate conceptualization of the system. The resulting policy failures and plethora of unintended consequences were, therefore, inevitable. This kind of evaluation has a more restricted scope than that rooted in political philosophy; it provides no 'ideal' system of SCG. But it will provide the analytical foundations for such 'grand illusions', delineating the potentialities and the constraints inherent in the current system and, most important, the contingent, permeable character of that system through its relationships with national government and that government's external environment.

Notes

1 It is increasingly common to distinguish between 'government' and 'state'. The latter term is said to be preferable because it encompasses the non-elected components of the polity (e.g. Dearlove and Saunders, 1984, p. 163). However, it is inaccurate to suggest that the term 'government' excludes such non-elected components as the police, judiciary and military (cf. Budge *et al.*, 1983). Moreover, British politics has never had the continental tradition of the state (Dyson, 1980, pp. 36–44 and 186–201). To use the term 'state' is potentially misleading, asserting either the comparability of British and continental traditions or the superiority of a Marxian epistemology. Here, the term 'state' is used only in conjunction with the radical model; the term 'government' is employed as the general description; and it is defined, following Nordlinger, 1981 (p. 9), as 'a complex set of institutional arrangements for rule operating through continuous and regulated activities of

individuals acting as occupants of offices'. This definition explicitly (pp. 9–10) encompasses 'elected and appointed, at high and low levels, at the center and the peripheries – who are involved in the making of public policy'.

2 Almost invariably, brief summaries and critiques of approaches with many adherents provoke the accusation that one is constructing and attacking a 'straw man'. To guard against this danger, I present a general characterization of each model *and* a more detailed discussion of one of its more influential proponents. Moreover, my aim is not simply to demolish shibboleths but to identify those elements of each model which are of continuing *utility*.

3 For an *explicitly* Marxist explanation of centre–periphery relations in terms of 'uneven development' see Nairn, 1977 (rev. 2nd edn 1981). On the special case of Northern Ireland see Farrell, 1976.

4 This summary is drawn from Bulpitt, 1983. The book incorporates some previously published material but omits, in whole or in part, Bulpitt, 1975, 1976, 1980 and 1982. These papers usefully expand upon his basic thesis.

5 With the exception of Marxist literature on centre–periphery relations, the radical model has focused, in common with conventional public administration, on central–local relations. Important exceptions to this generalization include Pat Dunleavy's work on quangos (Dunleavy, 1980a, pp. 102–3 and 108–9, and, more important, 1982b) and some recent, and at the time of writing unpublished, work by Saunders, 1983 and 1984, which is briefly surveyed in Dearlove and Saunders, 1984 (pp. 392–402).

6 In response to the many criticisms of corporatist theory, Cawson distinguishes between macro-, meso- and micro-corporatism. He considers policy networks to be 'competing labels for the same concepts' (Cawson, 1986a, p. 158; see also Cawson, 1986b). There is a great deal of common ground between my use of policy networks and Cawson's meso-corporatism, but two notes of caution are in order. First, the concept of corporatism has acquired multiple, contiguous and contradictory meanings, and it is doubtful that it can ever be used without some degree of ambiguity creeping into the discussion. If an equivalent label is available, pragmatism would seem to dictate its use. Second, the equivalence between the labels is more apparent than real at present. Although there is said to be a continuum from pluralism to corporatism, there is little agreement about the variables along which these two 'systems' vary. Cawson's nominee of 'concentration in the structure of interests' is of such generality that it is unlikely to assist in the comparison of policy areas. It would seem a matter of some urgency for corporatist theory to specify the dimensions (plural) of corporatism and the conditions under which they develop. Such a statement can hardly be premature after some ten years of theory and case studies.

7 In order to simplify the presentation, the bulk of the examples in the following section are taken from local government. As a result, it should not be thought that the argument applies only to local government. The various propositions will be applied to other species of SCG in Chapter 3. I have selected local government as the source of examples because it is the premier territorial institution in British government. Chapter 3 will demonstrate that it is not the only such institution.

8 It seems impossible to avoid wearing a label; to be without an academic pigeonhole is not to exist. I can live with the appellation 'neo-pluralist', provided the roots of my formulation in the Weberian theory of bureaucracy are recognized! A useful if 'potted' account of much of the theorizing I have drawn upon is provided in Alford and Friedland, 1985 (II) under the tendentious label of 'the managerial perspective'; tendentious because it implies a narrowness akin to 'business management' when the bulk of the authors reviewed explicitly locate themselves in the Weberian bureaucratic tradition. Given the vague nature of 'my' label, and the diffuse literature thereby alluded to, the following (recent) authors have been drawn upon (to differing degrees): Lowi, 1969; Bell, 1976; Lindblom, 1977; Wildavsky, 1980; Nordlinger, 1981; and Luhmann, 1982. The 'bureaucratic tradition' is cogently reviewed in Perrow, 1979, and I owe a large, if imprecise, intellectual debt to the

work of Sir Geoffrey Vickers, 1965, and Herbert Simon and the 'Carnegie School' which is alive and well (and not merely a footnote in the history of organization theory) in the work of James March; for a recent, highly relevant example see March and Olsen (1984). There are few explicitly 'neo-pluralist' accounts of British government, but see Richardson and Jordan, 1979; Rose, 1982; Budge *et al.*, 1983; Rhodes, 1986a and b. Finally Gray and Jenkins, 1985, provide a view of British government through bureaucratic spectacles which usefully supplements Heclo and Wildavsky's, 1974, seminal account.

9 Strictly speaking the external support system is not a process within the national government environment but an influence upon it. However, whilst it is important to note the instabilities originating in the external support system, it is not necessary to explore them in any detail for the analysis of SCG. Accordingly, this section focuses on the centre's ability to manage its external support system, which can be treated plausibly as a process within the national government environment.

10 On British economic policy since 1945 see Worswick and Ady, 1962; Dow, 1964; Brittan, 1969; Stewart, M. 1977; Blackaby, 1978a; Keegan and Pennant-Rea, 1979; Peston, 1984.

11 The word 'function' has acquired so many specific meanings that some care has to be exercised in its use. It is used in an economic sense to refer to the functional groupings of trade unions and industry. It is used in a Marxist, teleological sense to refer to the functions of the state in capitalist states. It can refer to the services provided by government and even to any activities of an office-holder or government body. Doubtless, there are other meanings. Here, it is used primarily to refer to the services of government. Any other usage will be indicated by the inclusion of a qualifying adjective.

12 The theory of sectoral cleavages has its roots in 'a definition of urban politics in terms of the study of decision-making on collective consumption processes'. Collective consumption refers to 'consumption processes whose organization and management cannot be other than collective given the nature and size of the problems' (Dunleavy, 1980a, pp. 45 and 50). However, as Franklin and Page, 1984 (pp. 524–5), point out, there is little consistency in defining collective consumption; the criteria for identifying the relevant services are intuitive; and the definition would seem to exclude housing because it is a commodity not a service. Furthermore, consumption locations are both cumulative and not additive (cf. Cawson and Saunders, 1983, p. 24; Dunleavy and Husbands, 1985, p. 140).

Although the analysis of collective consumption has its roots in neo-Marxist theory, these underpinnings are not necessary. To return to the discussion of social closure (pages 62–3, above), the government sustains (and, on occasion, creates) the rules and institutions supporting the formal system of distributive justice (in this case, the distribution of services). Thus, criteria of eligibility for receipt of a service are an exclusionary device, creating 'have's' and 'have-nots', and equally are the cause of usurpatory behaviour by those deemed ineligible. Consequently, the structural underpinnings of sectoral cleavages lie in the simple facts that public services are an element of the distributive system; that access to and dependence on the services are differentially distributed; and that a material interest in the services can influence political behaviour independent of other influences.

For the analysis of SCG it is not necessary to specify, theoretically, the form of political behaviour. For the study of electoral behaviour it is essential that the several bases of sectoral cleavages be cumulative to exercise an effect on aggregate, national voting patterns. Although Crewe, 1983 and Franklin and Page, 1984, concede that sectoral cleavages explain some proportion of the variance in electoral behaviour, the disputes over definitions and methodology continue unabated. Such minefields should be entered only in dire necessity. At the disaggregated, local level there is ample case study evidence on the proliferation of micro-politics (e.g. Donnison, 1973; Pickvance, 1976; Darke and Walker, 1977; Dunleavy, 1977) supporting the contention that closure processes over access to, and dependence on, public services are translated into political action. Dangerous minefields can be forsworn, therefore, in favour of a focus on the interrelationships between class de-alignment, the growth of the welfare state and sectoral cleavages and an empirical investigation of the function of SCG, as a locus of sectoral conflicts, in regulating these relationships.

13 This point is easily demonstrated by comparing public expenditure White Papers pre- and post-1975. Neither *Public Expenditure to 1977–78* (Cmnd 5519, HMSO, 1973) nor *Public Expenditure to 1978–79* (Cmnd 5879, HMSO, 1975) mentions local authorities in its 'General Review', and the data on local expenditure are relegated to the appendices. However, *Public Expenditure to 1979–80* (Cmnd 6393, HMSO, 1976) has two pages on local authorities in the 'General Review' (pp. 12–13), and the text contains 'plans ... for the development of individual local authority services'. These 'plans' were even more fully laid out in *The Government's Expenditure Plans* (Cmnd 6721, HMSO, 1977), which reconciled, for the first time, White Paper and Rate Support Grant figures for local authority current expenditure.

14 This classification is an empirical one, restricted to SCG. Benson, 1982, pp. 154–8, distinguishes between all governmental networks in terms of their 'types of structural interests': i.e. demand (or client) groups; support groups (which provide needed resources for the public sector organizations); administrative groups (or those occupying positions of administrative control); provider groups (which deliver services); and co-ordinating groups (or those responsible for rationalization within and between programmes). Networks will vary, therefore, as the configuration of interests varies. There are a number of problems with this approach. First, the constellation of interests is only one relevant dimension of network structure. Second, in the context of British SCG, it is difficult to distinguish demand from support groups and administrative groups from provider groups. Third, economic functional groups are omitted as such, forming part of (presumably) support or provider groups. Equating manfacturing industry with either environmental groups on the one hand or the medical profession on the other seems unhelpful. However, given the current state of research on networks any classification must be treated with caution. The listing employed here is tentative.

15 Although space precludes a detailed discussion, my survey of the available theories omits a large but diffuse socialist literature. A useful preliminary survey is provided by Sancton, 1976, and some more recent contributions are summarized and evaluated in Gyford, 1985b. Not only is there a need for a historical account of socialist thinking on decentralization, the areal division of powers and local government, but there are also a number of more specific gaps – for example, Herbert Morrison and Harold Laski's democratic centralism and its implications for local government. The liberal theory of local government has been better served by commentators than the socialist theory, and it is time that the inequity was redressed. My thanks to Peter Richards (Southampton) for prompting these reflections.

16 The terminology in this area is incredibly vague. The acronym 'quango' referred initially to 'quasi autonomous *non-governmental* organizations', i.e. private bodies with public functions (e.g. the Jockey Club). Subsequently, it has been extended to include everything that is not a central department or a local authority (Barker, 1982a). Alternatively, there have been attempts to classify the throng of organizations, e.g. G (government); QG (quasi-government); QNG (quasi non-governmental) and NG (non-governmental) (see Hague, Mackenzie and Barker, 1975, pp. 9–15). It is far simpler, in the absence of any satisfactory criteria for classification, to refer to these bodies as 'non-departmental public bodies'. It is at least clear that they are not central departments or local authorities. Similarly, the decentralized arms of central government are referred to as the regional level of government or, more ambitiously, 'the regional state' (Saunders, 1983). The description 'intermediate institution' or meeting place of bodies representing

diverse interests is preferred because it makes only minimal claims for the significance of this level. The functions and status of intermediate institutions cannot be a matter of stipulative definition. They are explored in Chapter 3.

17 The terminology on this topic is diverse, including: 'cognitive maps' (Axelrod, 1976); 'assumptive worlds' (Young, 1977); 'operating ideology' (Sharpe, 1976 and 1985); 'guiding philosophy' (Webb and Wistow, 1982a); 'operating code' (Bulpitt, 1983); 'departmental philosophy' (Bridges, 1971); and 'ideological corporatism' (Dunleavy, 1981a). Vickers's, 1965, discussion of 'appreciation' remains one of the first attempts to explore the effects of such maps of the world on the policy process and it remains one of the best. My comments were prompted by reading Vickers, and therefore I have retained his concept.

It is perhaps worth emphasizing, given the neo-pluralist roots of my approach, that I do not embrace the associated thesis of the 'end of ideology'. There has been a decline in traditional class (total) ideologies, but with changing social structures/social cleavages new (particularistic) ideologies have emerged (Kleinberg, 1973, pp. 16–23 and n. 37). The analysis of appreciative systems is central to understanding the influence of particularistic ideologies although, because my focus is the policy networks of SCG, it represents only a partial analysis of the rise of such ideologies.

CHAPTER 3

Organizations and Actors

Introduction: interests, resources and relationships. The centre and its functional organization: the interests of functional departments, relationships within the centre, the resources of the functional departments, relationships with SCG – the instruments of control, summary. The territorial ministries: summary. Intermediate institutions: the interests of intermediate institutions, the resources of intermediate institutions, the relationships of intermediate institutions, summary. Non-departmental public bodies: the interests of non-departmental public bodies, the resources of non-departmental public bodies, the relationships of non-departmental public bodies, summary. Local government: the interest of local government, the resources of local government, the relationships of local government, summary. Sub-central political organizations: central–local relationships within the political parties, central–local relationships and the professions, sub-central political environments, summary. Conclusions.

3.1 Introduction: Interests, Resources and Relationships

Institutional description is the heart and soul of public administration; it is only the musculature of this account. To describe the structure and functions of all species of SCG would produce an encyclopaedia of British government. Not only would it be tedious to compile and boring to read but, more important, it would also obscure the focus on networks and their policies. Accordingly, this chapter provides only a brief description of the major organizations and actors as an essential prerequisite to the analysis of policy networks.

To insist that institutional description is but one part of the analysis of SCG is not to consign the topic to the status of an afterthought. Organizational form affects the behaviour of actors in networks, and the allocation of functions to particular organizations has a crucial influence on the membership of networks. Organizations guarantee some continuity and stability of performance as individual actors come and go. They are one of the important influences on policy-making. It is essential to classify, therefore, the various forms of organization, to compare them and to determine their effects on policy-making. In Chapter 2, Table 2.4 and section 2.5.3 distinguished between the centre, territorial ministries, intermediate institutions, non-departmental public bodies, local government and sub-central political organizations. This chapter describes and compares these types of SCG. The main objective is to introduce the major actors and their policy networks, because the characteristics of the networks and of individual constituent organizations exercise together a major influence on policy-making. The analysis of policy outputs and impacts is reserved for later chapters. A subsidiary objective is to provide a sketch map of the terrain that is SCG.

The simple fact that institutional variations are treated here as part of the analysis of networks means that this comparison of public sector organizations has a number of distinctive features. It is necessary to go beyond such conventional topics as the distribution of functions and examine the resources, interests and relationships of each type of SCG. Accordingly, this account is structured around the classification of *resources* in Chapter 2, section 2.5.3(i). It compares the authority, money, legitimacy, organization and information controlled by each type of SCG. It describes the *interests* of each type of SCG within the networks and, more specifically, it explores the *relationships* between the public sector organizations. The chapter presents a formal picture of SCG. The resources and relationships described are those prescribed in legislation or which arise from long-standing convention. With such a thumbnail sketch of the major participants and their relationships, it will then be possible to focus explicitly on policy and explore SCG 'in action'. At this juncture, it will be possible to determine whether or not variations in the distribution of resources affect policy outcomes and if the formal pattern of relationships can be found in the day-to-day interactions within networks.

3.2   The Centre and its Functional Organization

In common parlance, 'central government' is monolithic. The reality is vastly different. There is continual tension between the forces of integration, most notably the Cabinet and the Treasury, and the special interests of the spending departments. It is more accurate, therefore, to talk of the interests of the centre: a phrase which at least recognizes the divergent aims and fragmentary character of central institutions. Equally, the 'centre' does not have *a* relationship with SCG; there are a wide variety of relationships involving a diverse set of instruments of influence, persuasion and control.

3.2.1   The interests of functional departments

The interests of functional departments *vis-à-vis* SCG fall into four main types: area, service, guardianship and rival.

3.2.1(i)   AREAL INTERESTS

Areal interest refers to the responsibility of central departments for elected local authorities. The most obvious example is the Department of the Environment (DoE), which is the 'voice' of English local government interests within the centre. It plays a key role in negotiating the annual block grant settlement with the Treasury and then allocating it between local authorities. Most important, the DoE's interest is not confined to a single service. It is local government's friend at court, ostensibly looking after its interests 'in the round'.

The areal interest of the DoE is not unique. The territorial ministries of Scotland, Wales and Northern Ireland speak both for their territory and for 'their' local authorities. However, all these central departments wear several hats. They are also service departments with direct responsibility for particular functions; guardian departments responsible for overseeing the financial (and service) performance of their SCG; and rivals competing for resources for 'their' type of SCG and 'their' functions. Departments will accord each of these roles a different priority for different policies at different times with considerable potential for conflict between the interests within a department.

3.2.1(ii)   SERVICE INTERESTS

The service interests reside in departments responsible for national policy-making on functions implemented by local authorities. The most obvious examples are education (DES), personal social services (DHSS), transport and highways (DTp) and police, fire and civil defence (Home Office). Each department is responsible for the legislation on, and the supervision of, services provided by local authorities. In some cases, the service may be funded by a specific grant, and the service department will negotiate directly with the Treasury and allocate the money to local authorities, e.g. the Home Office and the specific grant for police. Up to 1980 the service departments were also responsible for loan sanctions or the approval of specific capital projects. For the most part, however, service departments seek to protect 'their' notional share of the grant negotiated between the Treasury and the DoE. Moreover, the defining characteristic of a block grant is that it is unhypothecated; it is not divided into fixed amounts for each service. The service departments attempt to persuade local authorities to spend the appropriate share of the grant on their service. Indeed, the service departments are probably the best friends of local government at the centre because their interests coincide either in seeking an increase in funds or in resisting 'cuts'.

3.2.1(iii) GUARDIANSHIP

The 'guardian' interest is enshrined in the Treasury. It negotiates with the service and lead departments the level of central funding of current expenditure through grants and the total ceiling on capital expenditure. In the words of a senior local government official (and former civil servant):

> people get it wrong by thinking that there is a national chasm between central and local government. The clash comes between our point of view and that of the Treasury, and these clashes occur within central government between the promoters of services and the controllers of finance.
>
> (cited in Rhodes, 1986a, p. 139)

And the Treasury's rise to pre-eminence in the area of SCG – an area where it had no direct contact and in which it had displayed a spasmodic interest up to the 1970s – is one of the most dramatic changes in the postwar period (see Chapter 4, section 4.2.1). However, guardianship is not its sole preserve. With the increasing pressure to restrain public expenditure, guardianship has emerged to prominence in the DoE and territorial ministries. One former Secretary of State for the Environment described his role as that of a 'mini-chancellor', alluding to his responsibility for the overall level of local expenditure. Indeed one of the motives behind the creation of the DoE was to improve central co-ordination for a range of local government services and to counter the claims on resources of the service departments. The DoE has the potentially conflicting interests, therefore, of arguing for resources for local government and, at the same time, restraining their expenditure. In a similar fashion, the DTp has to oversee the financial targets of its nationalized industries, and the DHSS has to contain the growth in NHS expenditure within central targets and promote cost reduction.

3.2.1(iv) RIVAL INTERESTS

The 'rival' interest resides in the domestic service ministries with functions administered by SCG but not by local authorities. Consequently, they have no interest in defending the funding of local authority services and every interest in competing for resources for their services and their type of SCG. Thus, the Department of Health and Social Security (DHSS) is responsible for the NHS, and the Departments of Industry (DoI), Transport (DTp) and Energy (DEn) are responsible for their respective nationalized industries. Indeed, virtually every domestic ministry has some form of sub-central organization. Perhaps the major example of such rivalry in recent years has been the success of the Manpower Services Commission (MSC) and Department of Employment (DEmp) in wresting the initiative (and funds) from the DES and LEAs for vocational training for the 16–19-year-olds.

Quite obviously, all spending departments compete for resources. The distinctive feature of this interest is that the competition extends beyond function or service interests to encompass rivalry between different types of SCG. Thus, there is the competition within DHSS between the health service and the personal social services. Because these services involve different SCGs, there is a marked difference in the constellation of interests for each policy network. Similarly the DoE has to contain the rivalry between water and local government services (e.g. housing).

Indeed, the DoE provides a graphic illustration of the diversity of roles and interests within the centre. It is the areal department for local government, the 'guardian' of local expenditure, the defender of particular service interests (housing), and contains rivals for public funding (water). There is the danger that this summary will suggest a picture of continuous internecine warfare. In fact, the centre is accurately described as a 'federation of departments' or as 'a series of planets circling round the central spine' (Armstrong, 1971, pp. 315 and 320). As an antidote to the description of diversity, therefore, it would be wise to look at the ways in which relationships within the centre are regulated: to examine the central spine.

3.2.2 Relationships within the Centre

The major means of bureaucratic and political co-ordination with the centre are the Treasury and the public expenditure survey (PES) and the Cabinet and Cabinet Office (including the official committees which parallel Cabinet committees). In addition, there is a plethora of bilateral meetings and interdepartmental committees as well as the famous, even notorious, informal Whitehall grapevine-cum-club. For the obvious reason that resource allocation decisions are at the heart of relationships within the centre, this section concentrates on the integrative function of the expenditure process.[1]

The main features of the PES up to 1979 were forecasts of expenditure of existing policies at constant prices; a survey of all expenditure by the public sector over a period of five years; and the analysis of expenditure by function and economic category. The system's objectives have been described as follows by HM Treasury (1971, p. 20):

The expenditure surveys . . . do not try to agree upon any particular level of Government expenditure to be recommended to Ministers, nor upon its allocation. They confine themselves to the task of agreeing a factual report showing where present policies are likely to lead in terms of public expenditure at constant prices. . . . if they remain unchanged over the ensuing five years. The main purpose of the exercise is to enable Ministers to see where present policies will lead so that, considering this against the economic prospect, they may decide whether the forecast demand upon resources by the public sector needs to be increased, ought to be left unchanged or should be diminished; and whether the allocation of these both now and as it will be over the five year period . . . is in accordance with their own view of economic, social and political priorities.

Potentially, therefore, 'power is shifted to the centre, that is, to the Treasury', and the PES can be seen as 'an attempt to find a basis on which the Treasury would not be defeated' (Treasury officials, cited in Heclo and Wildavsky, 1974, p. 202).

The PES could be seen, therefore, as one of the major counter-weights to the divergent roles and interests within the centre. It was a set of ostensibly rational planning and control procedures, with the Treasury at their heart, which constrained the natural proclivities of spending departments. However, as Heclo and Wildavsky (1974, p. 238) point out, the PES

enshrined incrementalism with a vengeance. It is incrementalism to the *n*th power. If PESC helps prevent departments from going beyond established bounds, it also commits the Treasury in public to keeping their expenditures going at the projected rate. Both sides find it more difficult to depart from the historical base. If PESC makes it less likely that new monetary programmes with large spending implications will be introduced inadvertently, it also helps to assure departments that their on-going programmes will not suddenly be disrupted.

Moreover, with the onset of double-figure inflation, the ability of the Treasury, through the PES, to regulate the spending departments was further eroded: 'I think that the planning system called PESC, which was very noble and imaginatively conceived, has not in fact produced any of the advantages that it was supposed to be going to produce' (Godley, 1975, p. 215).

Thus, the out-turn figures for 1974–5 exceeded the 1971 projections for that year by some £5.8 billion, and 70 per cent of this increase was *not* a consequence of announced policy changes (Wright, 1977). As a result, there was a shotgun marriage between the PES and cash limits or 'an administrative limit on the amount of cash that the government propose to spend on certain services, or blocks of services' for a year ahead (HMSO, 1976, para. 8). There was now a monetary cost (and ceiling) for a given volume of services. The emphasis had switched from planning to control and from real resources to the financing of programmes. This trend was strongly reaffirmed by the 1979–83 Conservative government:

> [It] has gone further than its predecessor in bringing revenue raising considerations to bear on public expenditure decisions. In contrast to the pre-1976 situation in which public expenditure decisions were taken without too much regard for their implications for taxation and borrowing, the [Conservative] government seems to have started from its desired taxation levels and borrowing targets and attempted to scale down public expenditure plans to fit accordingly.
>
> (Else and Marshall, 1981, p. 273)

The medium-term financial strategy (MTFS) has come to the fore as *the* government planning document. The key indicators of economic performance became the money supply and the Public Sector Borrowing Requirement (PSBR). And to confirm this trend, the figures in the annual public expenditure White Paper were presented in cash not volume terms.

There was no evident decline in the Treasury's influence as a result of these changes. It had pressed for cash limits well before their eventual adoption and the 'Spanish Inquisition' component of its guardianship role was reinforced. Departments were now confronted by sustained pressure to cut programmes, and the base of past expenditure was to be challenged. But if the PES had made the base inviolate, the new cash-based system was to demonstrate that it was relatively invulnerable. Conflicts over priorities became increasingly difficult to resolve and were referred to a new Cabinet subcommittee – the 'Star Chamber' – to forestall the flood of appeals to full Cabinet (Jenkins, 1985). Through successive PES White Papers, plans were continually adjusted upwards as public expenditure rose inexorably. If the cash-based presentation of these figures reflected the new priorities, it also served the none too subsidiary purpose of masking the real increase in expenditure: a political convenience not to be spurned lightly! The Treasury was a formidable champion of restraint by the spending departments, but they were worthy challengers, inured to temporary setbacks and ever willing to come out for the next round.

It is a mistake to imply that the conflicts between the Treasury and spending departments are purely bureaucratic conflicts. Ministers are the prime advocates for their departments. The expenditure process is inextricably entwined with ministerial infighting and co-ordination through the Cabinet and its committees:

> At heart, British Cabinet government retains, with a devilish twist or two, all the characteristics of government by committee. The major

twist in British Cabinet government arises from the fact that most committeemen are also the chief executives of their own departmental empires, empires where their individual reputations are made and/or unmade. They are on their own, but they are not alone. They may not always stand but they do fall together ... Everyone knows they serve themselves by serving their departments. The ardour of each in performing his assigned role is (or is supposed to be) checked by others doing the same.

(Heclo and Wildavsky, 1974, p. 369)

And the ardour of ministers has been well described by Joel Barnett, former Chief Secretary to the Treasury. He describes an essentially three-stage political process. First, the Cabinet, and crucially the Chancellor of the Exchequer and the Prime Minister, agree the broad strategy. Second, the various cuts are negotiated in 'bilaterals' between the Treasury and the spending department's ministers. Third, any continuing disagreements are referred back to Cabinet or Cabinet committee (Barnett, 1982, chs. 6 and 10). There are a number of features of this process worthy of note.

Without accepting the prime ministerial government thesis, the Prime Minister's influence on macro-economic policy in general, and public expenditure in particular, is considerable. Thus, 'Denis Healey was more than just influenced by the Prime Minister ... Jim Callaghan ... literally decided, or at least concurred in, the policy ... Denis ... had to work very hard to convince the Prime Minister' (Barnett, 1982, p. 63). And Denis Healey was widely perceived to be a strong Chancellor. The Cabinet is consulted, and the discussions may be both long and heated, but the determinant influence will be the alliance of Prime Minister and Chancellor, with the Cabinet being as 'unrealistic as ever' (Barnett, 1982, p. 102). There are no grounds for believing that Mrs Thatcher is any more reticent than Mr Callaghan.

However, agreement on the broad strategy tends to be submerged by subsequent detailed and very extensive (Barnett, 1982, pp. 65 and 67) discussions on its application. To overstate the case somewhat, every programme in every department is an exception. Of course, all ministers agree on the need for restraint, but in their particular case any cuts would be disastrous, run counter to electoral promises, etc. Thus, whilst the Thatcher government's policy to cut public expenditure was a clear commitment, (apparently) pursued with determination by the Prime Minister, it foundered in the bilaterals where John Biffen, the (then) Chief Secretary to the Treasury, 'was too easy-going in his ... discussions with spending ministers' (Riddell, 1983, p. 117). Similarly, Barnett (1982, p. 65) reports that for Barbara Castle, Secretary of State for Health and Social Security, 'it was almost a matter of principle not to concede anything in bilaterals but to go down fighting in Cabinet'. And not all ministers 'go down'. Peter

Shore, Secretary of State for the Environment, was so 'touchy', 'ill-tempered', 'passionate' and 'prickly' that he 'got away' with a much reduced cut in housing expenditure (Barnett, 1982, p. 94). Even determined chief secretaries to the Treasury lose some of the battles, 'at least for the time being'. As Barnett (1982, p. 96) concludes, the cuts depend 'on the strengths and frailties of particular Ministers', and the judicious appeal to Cabinet can preserve departmental interests.

On paper, the Treasury (through the PES and latterly the MTFS) and the Prime Minister/Cabinet would seem to be potent counter-weights to the centrifugal forces of departmentalism in the centre. In practice all attempts at co-ordination have to confront, and are regularly confounded by, the divergence of interests within the centre. As Heclo and Wildavsky (1974, p. 371) conclude: 'The weakness at the centre of British government is struggled against manfully by the Treasury, CSD, Cabinet office and CPRS. *But it is a debility all the same*' (my emphasis). The ebb and flow of relationships within the centre in the competition for resources condition relations between the centre and SCG.

3.2.3   The Resources of the Functional Departments

3.2.3(i)   AUTHORITY

Authority refers to the mandatory and discretionary right to carry out functions or services commonly vested in and between public sector organizations by statute or constitutional convention. From the stand-point of the centre, the key prop of its authority in law is the absolute sovereignty of Parliament; it is 'hierarchically superior to any other legislative body in the state' (Elliott, 1981, p. 25). A number of consequences follow from this simple fact of British political life. First, there is 'no higher legal authority than the Queen in Parliament, and the Queen in Parliament alone can change the law'. Second, 'it is not legally possible for any body or power in the state to question the enactment of the Queen in Parliament'. Third, 'there is no limit on the legislative powers of the Queen in Parliament' (Garner, 1974, pp. 15–17). SCG, in all its forms, is a creature of statute; con-sequently, its organization, functions, finance, even its very existence, depend on the grant of powers by the Queen in Parliament. To describe the relationship between centre and SCG as asymmetric is to draw attention to the former's monopoly of legislative powers.

That being said, the statutes governing SCG only rarely prescribe the form of its relationship to the centre: 'The number of statutes which speak of the Minister's role in relation to local authorities in . . . general terms is small. Most concentrate only on his specific powers of approval or oversight' (Griffith, 1966, p. 51). The most notable exception to this assessment is the Education Act 1944. Section 1 lays down that the duty of the Minister:

shall be to promote the education of the people of England and Wales and the progressive development of institutions devoted to that purpose, and to secure the effective execution by local authorities, under his control and direction, of the national policy for providing a varied and comprehensive educational service in every area.

The powers of the minister are reinforced by section 68:

If the Minister is satisfied . . . that any local education authority . . . have acted or are proposing to act unreasonably with respect to the exercise of any power conferred or the performance of any duty he may give such directions as to the exercise of the power or performance of the duty as appear to him to be expedient.

The relative clarity of this example is in marked contrast to the case of the fire service. There is a longstanding dispute between the Home Office and the local authority associations on the Home Office's view that the Home Secretary has a general responsibility to Parliament for the fire service (Home Office, 1978, p. 1). It is the view of the associations that the Fire Services Act 1947 lays 'responsibility for securing an efficient fire service . . . directly in the local fire authorities and that the Home Secretary has certain carefully defined if extensive powers' (Roberts and Hodgson, 1978, p. 232).

The Holroyd Committee's (1970, p. 72) recommendations support this interpretation of the Act, namely, 'that the Home Secretary and the Secretary of State for Scotland be given a specific statutory responsibility for promoting the efficiency of the fire service throughout Great Britain . . . for the guidance of local authorites in the performance of their statutory functions'. If the Home Office was already responsible for securing an efficient fire service, there would seem to be little point in recommending that the Home Secretary be given such a responsibility. This example demonstrates that, even when there is a general statement of the centre's responsibilities, it is often vague and may not be enforceable at law (Garner, 1974, p. 435). Generally, statutes vest powers in local authorities *and* include a variety of *specific* central controls over local authorities (Elliott, 1981, p. 32). These controls are discussed in the next section. The most apt conclusion for this discussion of the centre's authority over local government is Elliott's (1981, p. 100) succinct statement that 'Local government is absolutely subject to the will of Parliament on national matters; no legislative capacity of local government may take precedence over such an expression of Parliamentary will.'

Other types of SCG are subject to the will of Parliament in exactly the same way. However, general statements of the centre's role are more prevalent. For the nationalized industries created before 1945, it was rare for the minister to be given general powers of direction. After 1945 such general powers were increasingly common. Thus, for the National Coal Board (NCB):

> The Minister may, after consultation with the Board, give to the Board directions of a general character as to the exercise and performance by the Board of these functions in relation to matters appearing to the Minister to affect the national interest, and the Board shall give effect to any such directions.

In theory at least, the industries were to be free to run their day-to-day affairs on a commercial basis, whilst the minister remained answerable to Parliament for general policy (Robson, 1962, ch. 6; Morrison, 1964, ch. 12). As might be expected from the looseness of the phraseology, it proved difficult to draw a clear line between managerial/commercial judgements and general policy (see pages 120–4, below). In addition, ministers were vested with a number of specific powers which vary from industry to industry but invariably included the borrowing powers and pricing policy of the industry as well as the appointment of chairmen and members of the board.

Similar statutory provisions govern the NHS and the water service. The 1946 Act setting up the NHS vests responsibility in the minister

> to promote the establishment in England and Wales of a comprehensive health service designed to secure improvements in the physical and mental health of the people of England and Wales and the prevention, diagnosis and treatment of illness, and for that purpose to provide or secure the effective provision of services.

The Water Act 1973 lays a duty on the Secretary of State for the Environment and the Minister of Agriculture, Fisheries and Food to promote jointly a national policy for water in England and Wales. The Minister of Agriculture can give directions to the Regional Water Authorities (RWAs) on their fisheries and land drainage functions whilst the secretary of state can issue directions for the RWAs' remaining functions. Even before they were formally classified as nationalized industries, the RWAs constituted a 'quasi-nationalized industry' (Gray, 1982, p. 146), and, as one might expect, the secretary of state could issue directions on the rates of return on net assets and water charges as well as approving RWAs' borrowing. In short, for the nationalized industries, the NHS and the RWAs, ministers have both extensive general powers of direction and specific powers of control.

The position of the remaining miscellany of fringe bodies is varied. Bowen (1978, p. 33) suggests that:

A fringe body is responsible to a Minister for carrying out the designated function. It is free to do this in its own way within the limits set by its terms of reference and by the resources conditionally allocated to it. A Minister is generally answerable to Parliament for terms of reference of a fringe body and any statement of its functions as well as for the financial provision made for Exchequer funds for its work. He is not however answerable for particular acts of a fringe body nor does he normally concern himself with its day to day operations.

Of the 252 bodies in his survey, 174 were set up by Act of Parliament, 112 were financed by grants in aid, 140 had chairman appointed by a minister, and 158 submitted annual accounts to the minister/Parliament. Beyond these data, Bowen provides little information on the extent to which they are subject to ministerial direction. Even with the same sponsoring department, the position can vary greatly. Thus, the MSC is subject to direction by the Secretary of State for Employment on specific matters under the Employment Protection Act 1975, whereas the Advisory, Conciliation and Arbitration Service (ACAS) is statutorily free from ministerial direction. With this cautionary example in mind, Bowen's summary will suffice for present purposes. For all types of SCG, the key question now concerns the way in which the statutory powers are exercised. It matters little that the minister has extensive general powers if they have never been employed. The lack of explicit powers may be remedied by the use of other forms of influence. And of these other influences, none has commanded so much attention as the role of financial resources in the relationship between centre and SCG.

3.2.3(ii) FINANCIAL RESOURCES

Financial resources refer to the funds raised by public sector organizations from taxes (or precept), from service charges and from borrowing. The financial resources of British central government have four distinctive features. First, the centre monopolizes all the buoyant or income-elastic taxes; as prices rise, so does the centre's tax yield (Sharpe, 1981, p. 7). Only local government has its own tax, and that is subject to 'fiscal strain':

> revenue can be increased only by increasing tax rates. There is no automatic expansion of the tax base with rising general price levels, and certainly no fiscal dividend. But since increasing the tax rate is an overt and visible political act it is likely therefore to meet more tax payer resistance than a similar increase in an income-elastic tax system, although the tax levied is the same. This greater visibility inhibits politicians from increasing revenue as rapidly as they might if the tax were buoyant. Hence fiscal strain or resource squeeze.
>
> (Sharpe, 1981, p. 9)

Second, it confers the power to tax, charge, or borrow on SCG and it can amend or abolish those powers at will. Thus, it can refuse to revalue property so that the rates keep pace with inflation, specify the prices to be charged by nationalized industries and set ceilings upon the borrowing powers of all SCGs. Third, it can employ 'money-moving' strategies to influence the policies of SCG. In particular, it decides the total and distribution of grants between SCGs. Thus, in the postwar period, local authorities have obtained on average 46 per cent of their total income from central grants. And a large number of non-departmental bodies are virtually dependent on central grant, including the NHS, which receives only a minor proportion of its income from fee-paying patients. Only the nationalized industries are an exception, raising the bulk of their funds through charges for their goods and services, although even here government subsidies can be the key to continued economic viability. Finally, the centre has a series of specific powers to regulate the disbursement of funds by SCG. There have been dramatic changes in the controls of SCG. All types of SCG have experienced a tightening of the screw and a variety of radical new departures. They can be most conveniently described in the discussion of the centre's instruments of control.

In short, the centre has a formidable arsenal of financial weapons to hand coupled with the capacity to modify or enhance such armaments at will. A word of caution is now in order. The possession of financial resources does not mean that they are employed to gain SCG's compliance or that, if they are employed, they have the intended effects or that they are the centre's most potent weapon. Chapter 4 will explore the relative importance, and the actual consequences, of the centre's financial resources.

3.2.3(iii) POLITICAL LEGITIMACY

Political legitimacy refers to access to public decision-making structures and the right to build public support conferred on representatives by the legitimacy deriving from election. And once defined, the centre would seem to have a surfeit of this resource. The elected government of the day is at the head of public decision-making structures and has widespread access to, and in some circumstances control of, the national media to build, maintain and manipulate public support. Above all, it has a monopoly of legitimate violence and a range of instruments for its exercise. Whoever wins an election has the right to govern, and British government is no stranger to the unilateral exercise of authority. However, it does not have a monopoly of political resources, and election is not the only legitimating basis for political action.

Only one unit of SCG has an equivalent claim to political legitimacy: local authorities. They too are directly elected and can claim to speak, not for the nation, but for the inhabitants of their area. The conflict between the centre and local authorities is, therefore, qualitatively different from that between, for example, the centre and a non-departmental body. The former case can be described as a clash of electoral mandates, whereas the latter involves narrower, sectional interest.

All species of SCG can claim to speak with authority on the operational problems of their service(s). The Nationalized Industries Chairmen's Group and the Water Authorities' Association can claim to understand the commercial and managerial problems of their industries, if not uniquely, then at least with a detailed knowledge commanded by few others. And when such expertise is allied to professional organization, as in the case of the medical profession and the NHS, expertise and professional values can rival political values as the basis for decisions; the policy system becomes professionalized and insulated from the political system.

In short, the centre is the pre-eminent, if not the exclusive, political authority in the UK, and, given the earlier discussions of the unitary state, executive authority and parliamentary sovereignty (Chapter 2, section 2.5.1(vi)), no other conclusion is possible. Stating the obvious should be avoided whenever possible. Here, it is important to stress the formal pre-eminence of the centre because this study focuses on the constraints imposed on it by SCG. The legal, financial and political resources commanded by the centre lead ineluctably to the conclusion of a determinant central authority. And yet the practice of SCG suggests a centre hemmed in on all sides by binding constraints. To explore this apparent paradox it is necessary to identify, in the first instance, the bases of central pre-eminence. Subsequently, the limits to that power can be specified. A first step to specifying the limits (and to resolving the paradox) is the analysis of the informational and organizational resources of the centre.

3.2.3(iv) INFORMATIONAL RESOURCES

Informational resources refer to the possession of data and to control over either their collection or their dissemination or both. The distinctive feature of the centre's informational resources can be described, following Hood (1983, p. 6), as 'nodality' or

> the ability to traffic in information on the basis of 'figureheadedness' or of having the 'whole picture' ... Nodality equips government with a strategic position from which to dispense information, and likewise enables government to draw in information for no other reason than that it *is* a centre or clearing house.

Consequently, the centre has data on all local authorities or all nationalized industries and can form an overall judgement on, for example, their financial performance.

The opposite side of this particular coin, however, is that the centre is collating information from SCG. The data are collected and disseminated by SCG; the centre depends on their co-operation. It has a number of means for acquiring data, ranging from passively waiting for them to cross someone's desk through mutually beneficial exchanges to actively ferreting out information by sending out inspectors (see Hood, 1983, ch. 6). Thus, data arrive in the form of complaints about punctuality and rolling stock, alerting both the centre and British Rail to the need for modernization in a particular region. Data on declining standards of medical care are provided because these help doctors, health authorities and the DHSS in the competition for resources. DES inspectors visit school and report on the standards of teaching and equipment. Overwhelmingly, however, the centre adopts a relatively passive posture.

Compulsion and active data collection by the centre take second place to mutually beneficial exchange rooted in the self-interest of participants and the voluntary completion of returns. To a significant degree, therefore, SCG controls information needed by the centre. Moreover, the centre does not have the organizational resources to acquire the information in its own right.

3.2.3(v) ORGANIZATIONAL RESOURCES

Organizational resources refer to the possession of people, skills, land, buildings, material and equipment and hence the ability to act directly rather than through intermediaries. And as Sharpe (1977, pp. 60–1) points out:

> one of the primary characteristics of British central government is that it is not itself an executant of policies . . . the 'coal face' role is performed by executant agencies . . . Central departments usually confine themselves . . . to controlling, financing, inspecting, advising, guiding and broad policy-making roles.

The major exceptions to this statement are the line functions of employment and social security and the special case of defence. Thereafter, the people, skills, land, buildings, material and equipment are in the possession of SCG, and the centre acts through intermediaries. The dependence on SCG may be 'unique among Western democracies' (Sharpe, 1977, p. 61) but it is certainly a key constraint on the pre-eminence of the centre. The centre's relative lack of control over informational and organizational resources has to be weighed against its relatively predominant (but not total) control of legal, political and financial resources. The informational and organizational resources controlled by the various types of SCG will be described below. It is now necessary to turn from the resources of the centre to the means at its disposal for influencing SCG. The possession of resources is a necessary but not sufficient condition of influence; they have also to be deployed effectively. To examine the instruments of control is to explore how the centre uses its resources.

3.2.4   Relationships with SCG: the Instruments of Control

The relationship between the centre and SCG is multifaceted and highly variable. To introduce a topic which will be explored in far more detail in the case studies, this section examines the instruments of control which, formally, the centre can deploy to regulate its relationships with SCG.

It possesses a formidable array. Griffith (1966, pp. 54–62) identifies the following: statutory provisions (including by-laws), circulars, confirmatory and appellate functions, adjudicatory functions, inspection, default powers, audit, control over officers and controls over local bills. In addition, he discusses separately central controls over grants and borrowing. In a similar vein, Garner (1974, ch. 15) distinguishes between financial, approval, directory and advisory controls. The only major omission in these listings is control through policy planning systems (PPSs), which did not emerge to prominence until the 1970s. This section provides a brief description of each of the centre's instruments of control under the headings of financial, non-financial and judicial controls, distinguishing between formal provisions and practice. The application of particular controls will be described briefly, and these introductory remarks will be expanded in Chapter 4 and its analysis of particular policy areas.

3.2.4(i)   FINANCIAL CONTROLS

Financial controls can be subdivided into loans, grants and audit, and for each type of control there have been substantial changes in the postwar period. It will be possible to describe only the most important of these changes. In the first instance the financial controls over local authorities will be described, followed by a briefer discussion for other types of SCG.

Financial controls over local authorities
Loans   For the bulk of the postwar period, local authorities had a general power to raise a loan subject to the consent of, for the most part, the Secretary of State for the Environment (see Local Government Act 1933, s. 195, and Local Government Act 1972, s. 172). The DoE (formerly MHLG) gave consent not only for its own services but also for other central departments. Thus, a project would be approved by the appropriate department and then the DoE (MHLG) would grant loan sanction (Griffith, 1966, p. 90). Introduced initially to ensure the financial propriety of local authorities, loan sanction became a major instrument for influencing both local policy decisions

and total local expenditure (Layfield Committee, 1976, p. 242). In addition, under the Borrowing (Control and Guarantee) Act 1946, the Treasury controlled the source of local borrowing. There was some flexibility in the system. Thus, the secretary of state fixed a total borrowing limit for the 'locally determined sector': i.e. a mix of projects which individually cost less than £0.5 million. Within this total, an authority could set its own priorities. Moreover, the controls applied to borrowing, not capital expenditure, and a local authority could fund capital expenditure from revenue and/or from receipts on sale of assets. This discretion was removed by the Local Government, Planning and Land Act 1980, s. 72, which gave the secretary of state the power 'to specify in relation to any authority ... an amount of prescribed expenditure for each year'. Expenditure is prescribed in five main blocks: education, housing, transport, social services and other services. Within each block, a local authority can determine its own priorities; but now total capital expenditure is regulated strictly, with few opportunities to carry forward unspent allocations and the 'adjustment' of future allocations to take account of any 'overspend'.

Grants   During the postwar period, the grant system has been ever-changing. Thus, the Exchequer Equalization Grant (1948) gave way to Rate Deficiency Grant (1958), which in its turn was succeeded by Rate Support Grant (1966), itself modified in 1974. The maelstrom of the Conservative government then gave us Block Grant (1980), itself substantially modified in 1982 and supplemented with Draconian teeth by the Rates Act 1984 and the introduction of 'rate-capping'. Jones and Stewart (1983, p. 37) argue that there were seven different grant systems between 1979–83, and that figure had risen to nine by 1985. Quite clearly, a description of all these changes would be inordinately lengthy (but see Drummond, 1952; Drummond and Kitching, 1962; Hepworth, 1970 and 1984; G. Rhodes, 1976). Consequently, this account concentrates on, first, the major transformations and, second, the current system.

    The development of the grant system up to 1966 had two key characteristics: resource equalization and consolidation. Thus, the Exchequer Equalization Grant was designed to provide some parity of resources between local authorities by relating grant to the rateable value and population of each authority. The Local Government Act 1958 abolished specific grants to, *inter alia*, education, local health services, the fire service and child care. The new general grant, based on the estimated or 'relevant' expenditure of the consolidated services, was distributed by a formula including a basic amount per head of population and supplementary, prescribed amounts for various demographic features (e.g. children under 5, persons over 65). The Exchequer Equalization Grant continued as the Rate Deficiency Grant and it still aimed to bring the rateable resources of each local authority up to a national average. Martlew (1983, pp. 140–1) comments that the shift from specific to block grant was favoured by the Treasury, which argued that specific percentage grants encouraged extravagance. Block Grant would enable the centre's contribution to local expenditure to be fixed in advance. This aspiration to control central funding of local services foundered virtually at inception on central and local pressure to increase service spending. Local expenditure growth, not control, was the order of the day, and the past decade's focus on resource equalization and consolidation now took second place to needs and distribution (see also G. Rhodes, 1976).

The year 1966 saw the merger of earlier grants into a Rate Support Grant (RSG) and the distinction between the resources, needs and domestic elements. The resources element was payable to any local authority with rateable resources less than a national average. The domestic element was, in essence, a subsidy to domestic ratepayers or, more technically, a partial de-rating of domestic hereditaments. The needs element aimed to equalize 'between authorities in the amount they need to spend per head of population' (Layfield Committee, 1976, p. 217 and annex 27). It accounted for the bulk of RSG, and it was particularly important, therefore, that variations in spending needs were measured accurately and grant was distributed accordingly. The Local Government Act 1974 introduced (ostensibly) technical changes to the system in order to improve the measurement of need/distribution of grant. Controversy surrounded it until its abolition in 1980 (see Chapter 4, section 4.2.1).

The Conservative government elected in 1979 not only wished to control public expenditure but also objected to the RSG system, which was considered inordinately complex and said to favour high-spending local authorities. The government introduced Block Grant, which merged the resources and needs elements of RSG. From 1980 the Secretary of State for the Environment assessed how much each local authority needed to spend for each major group of services. Crucially, if a local authority spent more than this grant-related expenditure assessment (GREA), it lost grant at an increasing penalty rate. The secretary of state had taken powers to control, therefore, not just total central grant to local authorities, but also the expenditure of individual local authorities. Unfortunately, the new system did not deliver expenditure cuts on the anticipated scale. Spending targets, separate from GREA, were introduced and under the Local Government Finance Act 1982 supplementary rates were abolished. However, local authorities compensated for loss of grant by raising the rates. The 'cuts' still did not materialize, and so the secretary of state now took powers to set the rate for 'overspending local authorities': 'rate capping'. Now he can determine the income of selected local authorities. The postwar period has witnessed, therefore, the imposition of substantial limitations upon the revenue-raising and spending discretion of local authorities. (On the different developments in Scotland and Northern Ireland, see Chapter 4, section 4.3.1 and 4.3.2.).

Audit Between 1972 and 1982 the accounts of local authorities were audited either by central government inspectors, known as district auditors, or by professional auditors 'approved' by the secretary of state. If the district auditor considered that any expenditure was *ultra vires* (or contrary to law), he could apply to the courts for a direction that the expenditure was illegal. For sums in excess of £2,000, councillors were liable to repay the money ('surcharge') and to disqualification as a member of the local authority. These powers have been highly controversial (Keith-Lucas, 1962; Minns, 1974; Skinner and Langdon 1974) and have given rise to a number of widely known cases – for example, Poplar (see Keith-Lucas and Richards, 1978, ch. 4, for a summary).

Following the Layfield Committee Report in 1976, the (then) Labour government set up the Advisory Committee on Local Government Audit. Between 1979–82 this body commented upon the annual report of the Chief Inspector of Audit and suggested ways of increasing value for money in local government. A toothless watchdog, it was abolished in 1982 and replaced in January 1983 by the Audit Commission, which took over the District Audit Service from the DoE. There are three significant features to this change. First, the commission can be given directions by the secretary of state. He had no such power *vis-à-vis* the District Audit Service. Second, the commission appoints the auditors, and local authorities no longer have the right to choose private approved auditors, although the commission still approves private auditors and would not normally override the wishes of a local authority. Finally, the commission can 'make recommendations for improving economy, efficiency and effectiveness in the provision of local government services'. The commission retains all the powers of the 'old' district audit, but its remit is no longer limited to the legality of expenditure. The *potential* for central interference exists if, in its early years, the commission wore the mantle of critic of the centre (Audit Commission, 1984).

In short, the centre has always had a powerful set of financial controls over local authorities but, in recent years, it has added more potent weapons to its arsenal. The actual effects of these controls will be discussed in Chapter 4. However, all other types of SCG are subject to specific financial controls. In recent years they too have experienced both a tightening of the financial screw and and at times dramatic transformation in the nature of the controls.

Financial controls over non-departmental public bodies Upon nationalization the several industries were required to cover costs 'taking one year with another': the break-even principle (Robson, 1962, pp. 282–3). On the one hand they were not to abuse their position as monopoly suppliers to make 'excessive' profits but, on the other hand, they were not to make a loss and act as a drain on the Exchequer. In addition, the industries were subject to a number of specific requirements including, for example, the production of audited annual accounts and an annual report to be laid before Parliament.[2]

From the outset, a number of industries found it difficult to meet the break-even requirement – for example, British Railways, the National Coal Board, BOAC. Throughout the postwar period, governments have simultaneously asserted the virtues of planning the industries on a sound commercial basis and intervened continuously in their pricing policy on grounds of social cost, political ideology and management of the national economy. As subsidies mounted (Jones, 1978, p. 488) so the debate on pricing rules continued unabated, between economists on the merits of marginal cost pricing, between political parties on the social responsibilities of the industries and between government and the industries on the former's interventions to set prices. The 'commercial' view of the industries was most urgently argued by the Herbert Committee (1956, p. 97): 'We state our view without any qualification that the governing factor in the minds of those running the Boards should be that it is their duty to run them as economic concerns and to make them pay.' The government equivocated. The White Paper *The Financial and Economic Obligations of the Nationalized Industries* (HMSO, 1961) required the industries to break even over a five-year period, instituted targets for internally generated investment and endorsed the existing practice of ministers agreeing plans for overall capital investment. Such changes introduced a welcome air of precision into the finances of the nationalized industries. However, government interventions on pricing policy were to continue, and noncommercial activities were not to be subsidized by the Exchequer, although they would be taken into account in setting financial targets. Government support for a 'commercial' approach to the industries was only a qualified support. In the main, it wanted to increase the ability of the industries to finance their own capital investment. A further White Paper, *Nationalized Industries: a review of economic and financial control* (HMSO, 1967), continued the search for a more sophisticated system of financial appraisal. It introduced discounted cash flow techniques for the appraisal of investments, amended pricing policy by requiring that prices be related to marginal costs and accelerated the development of performance indicators. Described as 'an intellectually impressive document', primarily because it focused on the economic rather than the financial appraisal of investments and prices, the new system was never fully implemented; for example, a large proportion of the industries' investment programmes were not evaluated because the expenditure was categorized as 'replacement' or 'necessary' (Heald, 1980a, pp. 243 and 246). Indeed, the White

Paper was strongly criticized for failing to clarify the relationship between its three components: the test discount rate for investment, long-run marginal cost pricing and the financial targets (see Foster, 1971). As Pryke (1981, pp. 257 and 258) comments, the 'relatively favourable performance during the 1960s' of the nationalized industries meant that government interest had largely evaporated, and the White Paper had 'little effect': an outcome anticipated by Foster (1971, p. 43) in his assessment that 'all arguments are qualified to the point of equivocation'.

If by 1970 'the public corporations' finances were no longer a cause for anxiety' (Pryke, 1981, p. 259); then four years later they were in chaos. The industries were required to moderate or freeze price increases under the various stages of prices and incomes policy, and subsidies for non-commercial activities escalated. In 1974–5 they received £1,725 million in revenue support and £2,750 million in capital expenditure. As in the case of local government, economic crisis stimulated a reassessment of relationships, and, again as for local government, the new era was heralded by a Labour government.

In December 1973 the Select Committee on Nationalized Industries had reported on *Capital Investment Procedures* (HC65), calling for a thorough review of 'the role of the nationalized industries in the economy and the way they are to be controlled in future'. In June 1975, reminded by the oil crisis and the IMF, the government responded to this call by asking the National Economic Development Office (NEDO) to conduct such a review (*Capital Investment Procedures*, HMSO, 1975). The NEDO report was scathingly critical, pointing to 'a lack of trust and mutual understanding', 'confusion over the respective roles', 'no systematic framework for ... long term objectives and strategy' and 'no effective system for measuring ... performance' (NEDO, 1976, p. 8). Such a diagnosis was familiar. The solution was more novel. The NEDO report rejected the hands-off, or separation of roles philosophy in favour of a concerted approach. A Policy Council composed of the range of interests within the industry would be responsible for strategy, and the minister would have to get its agreement to a change in policy; if he failed, then he could issue specific directives. The government was not persuaded of the need for such innovations.

The White Paper *The Nationalized Industries* (HMSO, 1978) marked a retreat to the 1960s in its use of financial targets for maintaining a hands-off relationship. It was to provide the financial framework for the early 1980s. The White Paper announced that the government would seek amendments to the nationalization statutes to allow ministers to give specific directions to boards. Each industry was to prepare a corporate plan, embodying long-term strategy, which would have a 'central place' in the relationship, setting the framework for annual reviews. The Treasury was to set financial targets which, subsequently, assumed a variety of forms including an average annual rate of return on net assets (Gas) or as profits in relation to turnover (Post Office) or as a requirement to break even (Railways) (Treasury and Civil Service Committee, 1981, p. xii; a summary of the (then) current financial targets is provided by Heald and Steel, 1981, p. 15). In an era of rapid inflation, it was to be expected that cash limits would be a prominent part of the new controls. The White Paper confirmed that estimates of the nationalized industries' external financing requirements (i.e. loans, public dividend capital and grants) would be treated as an external financing *limit* (EFL). The annual review of investment plans was also to continue, although each industry would now be required to achieve a 5 per cent rate of return on new investment. Performance indicators were to be introduced (again) in order to promote both improvements in the standard of service and reductions in cost. Finally, the 'commercial view' was given forceful support; each industry was to set its prices with regard to its market and its overall objectives, including financial targets. There were, however, no specific pricing rules, and, in effect, the policy was to abandon marginal cost pricing.

With its stress on financial objectives, this White Paper marks a return to the preoccupations of 1961 (see, for example, HMSO, 1978, p. 25), a focus entirely congenial to the new Conservative administration. The Conservative manifesto wanted 'to see those industries that remain nationalized running more successfully and we will therefore interfere less with their management and set them a clearer financial discipline in which to work' (Conservative Party, 1979, p. 5). Initially, therefore, the operating framework for the industries comprised its EFL, a financial target, a cost reduction objective and performance (or quality of service) standards. The Conservatives emphasized the commercial or 'hands-off' view of the role of nationalized industries, with EFLs becoming the single most important target. However, the industries borrowed more than expected and, in response to their financial targets, increased their prices faster than the rate of inflation. There were also disputes over investment plans and the large deficits of such industries as BSC and BL. Relationships between the government and the nationalized industries deteriorated, and Mrs Thatcher was said to think that the responsible ministers had 'gone native' and scarcely disguised her impatience with some chairmen – for example, Sir Peter Parker of BRB, Lord Ezra of NCB (Riddell, 1983, pp. 48 and 173). The Central Policy Review Staff was asked to review the relationship in 1981. It recommended, *inter alia*, setting the industries clear objectives, the formation of an advisory group in sponsoring departments to provide analysis on the industries' plans and performance, breaking up the industries into profit centres, revising board composition and regular external efficiency audits (cited in Committee of Public Accounts, 1983, p. viii). The report succeeded only in accelerating the deterioration in relationships, infuriating both chairmen and sponsoring departments.

The 'success' of the 1978 financial control regime was limited, however. For example, the Committee of Public Accounts (1983, pp. viii–xii) found that both the BRB and NCB had had problems in submitting full corporate plans; that there had been shortcomings in the monitoring information supplied to departments; that neither the NCB or the BRB had met its targets for grant finance; that performance information was supplied to departments, but in two out of three cases it had not been possible to agree indicators. Four industries – the NCB, the BRB, British Steel and British Transport Docks – exceeded their original or revised EFL, and the committee commented that the EFL system as a whole operated with 'considerable flexibility'. Finally, the committee doubted that the investment appraisal system was the basis for investment decisions. It concluded that because 'the White Paper system is not working as intended . . . departments have been forced into a situation where they exercise continuous intervention, with a daily dialogue, leading to blurring of responsibilities and possible resentment' (Committee of Public Accounts, 1983, p. xvii).

This diagnosis was supported by the industries' chairmen, who were particularly scathing about EFLs and financial targets. Sir William Barlow (Post Office) considered that 'current cash limit policy is detrimental to the efficient management of a profitable public sector industry', and the Treasury and Civil Service Committee 'could scarcely conceal its incredulity' about the 'optimistic assumption' of the government about nationalized industry finances, regarding the targets as 'questionable' (cited in Heald and Steel, 1981, p. 16). As Curwen (1986, p. 91) points out, the industries had to obey rules covering different time periods. EFLs apply to one year, financial targets cover three to five years, and investment targets were specific to each project (for a summary of these several targets for selected industries in 1983 see Curwen, 1986, pp. 109–18). Most important, 'the short-term tail' wagged 'the long-term dog' and the EFL figure could vary inexplicably; for example, the NCB's EFL for 1981–2 was £882 million but was said to have been £1,225 million in the 1983 public expenditure White Paper (Curwen, 1986, p. 92).

Up to 1981, therefore, government policy was 'more of the same'. Indeed, the modifications to the system in 1982 reinforce this interpretation. It was announced that, in future, each industry would have agreed strategic objectives; business experience in Whitehall would be strengthened, and a new system of monitoring the industries' plans and performance would be introduced. The commercial view of the nationalized industries prevailed, but from here on it was not to be 'more of the same'.

First, there were a number of ostensibly minor developments which carried great hopes. Riddell (1983, p. 173) argues that Conservative policy focused on changing the chairmen of the industries – on getting the right people – and such people had a proven track record in the private sector: e.g. Ian MacGregor (NCB), Sir John King (BA). The Monopolies and Mergers Commission (MMC) was to be the stick prodding the industries to be more efficient. Under the Competition Act 1980, s. 11, the terms of reference of the MMC had been extended to include the nationalized industries, and the government announced that it would be increasing the number of references to the MMC (Garner, 1982). The government also continued to intervene on pricing policy. Indirectly the financial targets ensured some degree of influence on prices, but the government was prepared to issue directions. For example, British Gas was told to increase its prices to cover marginal costs. And such directions were issued to achieve non-commercial or broad national economic management objectives, the price increases being, in effect, a form of indirect taxation. All of these changes, allied to the revised financial control system, reveal a government casting about for some solution to its policy problems.

Second, the government took a far less sympathetic view than its predecessors of the social responsibilites of the industries. It was prepared to countenance closures and redundancies to make the industries profitable. The NCB, British Leyland (BL) and the British Steel Corporation (BSC) have been encouraged to rationalize their activities, i.e. reduce their capacity and labour force. It has also refused to intervene in pay disputes (in the sense of agreeing to increases and, subsequently bailing out the industry). This lack of sympathy for 'social responsibility' cannot be equated with non-intervention. As with all previous governments, the Conservatives intervened regularly and most spectacularly in the case of the miners' strike where they gave the NCB a blank cheque to outface the NUM.

Third, and most important, privatization came to the fore. Riddell (1983, p. 170) argues that the Thatcher government developed a 'passionate aversion to nationalized industries, partly through frustration'. Before 1981 privatization was still known as denationalization, and the 1979 election manifesto referred only to aerospace and shipbuilding. But as frustrations grew, denationalization was broadened into privatization. As a whole, the industries exceeded their planned borrowing limit by some £1.75 billion (in real terms) between 1979–83. In response, the defects in the financial control system identified by the Committee of Public Accounts were to be expunged by removing the industries from the public sector.

The origins of the policy cannot be limited to the specific problems of the nationalized industries. First, this development had been anticipated in the Ridley Report (*The Economist*, 27 May 1978), a Conservative Party research group report. Although the leaking of its proposals embarrassed the party leadership, no doubt prompting the more modest manifesto proposals, events after 1982 bear a marked similarity to it. It was removed from the shelves and dusted off not because of the failure of the 'commercial policy' but because of the larger failure of public expenditure policy in general and local expenditure policy in particular. As Dunleavy and Rhodes (1986, pp. 135–6) argue, experience with the hidden taxation of enforced price increases demonstrated to ministers the revenue-raising potential of the profit-making industries. The lesson was not lost on a government beleagured by an ever-expanding public sector and the perpetual frustration of its control measures. Privatization was born of opportunism, not principled policy development, and this conclusion is borne out by the absence of any official statement of the government's philosophy (both Curwen, 1986, pp. 164–72, and Heald and Steel, 1982, attempt to repair the omission).

The term 'privatization' is opaque, covering a variety of policies and serving a range of objectives (see Chapter 2, section 2.3.2(ii). However, for the nationalized industries, it covers two broad strands of policy: liberalization and denationalization (Heald and Steel, 1982, p. 334). The former refers to the relaxation of statutory monopolies. Thus, the Transport Act 1980 deregulated express coach services, and the monopoly of British Telecom on the supply, installation and maintenance of equipment has been loosened. The latter refers to the sale of an enterprises' assets. Thus, entire enterprises have been sold, e.g. Radiochemical Centre (now Amersham International) and the National Enterprise Board's subsidiary companies such as International Computers (ICL) and Fairey Holdings. More commonly, public corporations have been converted into companies, and the government has sold a proportion of the shares. Examples include British Aerospace, Cable & Wireless and British Telecom. Between 1979–83 twenty-five public enterprises were privatized in whole or in part. However, several of the undertakings are of minor importance (e.g. Amersham International, British Sugar Corporation); major industries were affected only marginally (e.g. the Post Office's letter monopoly, British Rail subsidiary activities); and the actual sale of shares was much delayed in many cases (e.g. British Airways). In consequence, the revenue raised from asset sales was much lower than expected. The government raised only £1,147 million (Steel and Heald, 1985, pp. 82–3) and it came near its targets only by manipulating the figures and including, for example, the forward sales of BNOC's oil and the premiums on North Sea oil licences.

Government plans were not aided by opposition – most notably from British Gas, which resisted privatization in part and delayed the sale of Wytch Farm oilfield and its offshore oil interests – and by the poor financial state of some industries. Finally, the management of the sales created many problems. The sales of several enterprises were notably oversubscribed, suggesting that the price was too low. For many observers, the sales were an example of asset-stripping – the unacceptable face of capitalism for the previous Conservative Prime Minister, Mr Heath. By 1983, therefore, privatization had 'developed in a rather piecemeal and *ad hoc* manner', and 'the public enterprise heartland such as coal, electricity, gas and railways, remained largely unscathed' (Steel and Heald, 1985, pp. 75 and 81). Thereafter the pace of change intensified.

If 1983–4 saw more of the same with the sale of government shareholdings in British Petroleum and Cable & Wireless, of greater significance was the sale of 50 per cent of the shares in British Telecom. The sale was massively oversubscribed; the government raised £1.5 billion, whilst investors saw a rapid appreciation in the price of their stock. And to come was the first major incursion into the heartland of public enterprise: the sale of British Gas. Government receipts already exceed massively those from the period 1979–83, standing at some £1,168 million for 1983–84 and £2,444 million for 1984–5, and will continue to increase for the forseeable future (for a list of asset sales to 1985–6 see Curwen, 1986, pp. 174–5). But the form of privatization – the sale of shares in a public company – raises as many questions as it answers about government control of the industries (see section 3.2.4(ii), pages 137–8, below).

If rapid progress has been made since 1983 in the privatization programme, liberalization has remained piecemeal and *ad hoc*, evoking little or no private sector interest. There were few takers for the privately produced supply of electricity to the national grid introduced in 1981. The attempt by the Mercury Company to introduce a business-oriented telephone network was much delayed and characterized by regular visits to the courts. The deregulation of bus licensing produced little private sector competition as municipally owned companies aggressively outpriced new entrants. Further attempts to introduce private sector competition were introduced in 1985 with the banning of municipal subsidies, but the consequences of this legislation remain to be seen. Only in the deregulation of express coach services was there any appreciable degree of success. In fact, using the terminology of deregulation to describe these developments is an inappropriate United States import. If anything, they amount to the *re*-regulation of industry (see section 3.2.4(ii), pages 137–8 below).

Privatization represents one response to the failure of the government's public expenditure policy; it was not the only one. As well as seeking to centralize local expenditure control and to privatize the public corporations, it also promoted indirect centralization in the guises of 'efficiency drives' and 'bypassing'. The former refer to the several measures aimed at reducing the costs of public sector service provision, of which contracting-out is the most notable example. The latter refers to the use of non-departmental bodies for the delivery of services in preference to local authorities. If local expenditure could not be controlled, if local authorities could not be trusted with new services, then they would be allocated to other agencies which, at least in theory, were more amenable to central direction.

The NHS is financed through general taxation, and this source has never amounted to less than 77 per cent of total income, standing in 1984 at 86 per cent. National Insurance contributions account for a further 11 per cent and can be viewed as tax revenue in different guise. Other sources of revenue include charging users (for example, prescription charges, pay beds), which accounts for 3 per cent of income and funds raised through subscriptions, donations and legacies. Neither amount to a significant proportion of total income (Merrison Commission 1979, ch. 21; Ham, 1985, p. 40; Klein, 1983, pp. 38–9, 72 and 139). The centre can limit, therefore, the total resources of the NHS. Its capacity to influence the distribution of resources, between areas and specialisms, is considerably less effective, however.

The most recent attempt to improve the geographical allocation of resources stemmed from the work of the *ad hoc* Resource Allocation Working Party (DHSS, 1976a). From 1977–8 resources were allocated on the basis of each region's population, weighted to take account of the groups that make the greatest demands on the service (e.g. children, the elderly) and of morbidity. The RAWP formula gives each region its target share of resources, and growth money has been distributed so as to close the gap between actual and target resources. Thus, regions above their target have received no increase in allocations, whereas regions below target have had increases up to 1.9 per cent. Although the gap between the above- and below-target regions has narrowed slightly, progress has been slow in the era of resource squeeze and the system has been criticized for its concentration on financial inputs rather than service outputs, the exclusion of measures of social deprivation from the formula and its adverse impact at the sub-regional level (Buxton and Klein, 1978). Moreover, such distributive goals have increasingly taken second place to detailed intervention to reduce costs, especially since 1979.

With the advent of the Conservatives, government determination to constrain expenditure was reasserted, cash limits on current expenditure and tight controls over capital expenditure remained the norm, and real term increases in expenditure barely kept pace with demographic and technical change. In addition, privatization has had an impact. Charges for prescriptions and dental and ophthalmic services have been increased regularly. Liberalization has had an effect, with the opticians' monopoly on the supply, replacement and repair of spectacles (but not sight-testing) being opened up. More important has been the centrally enforced increase in contracting-out.

The origins of contracting-out lie in 1969 when the Wilson Labour government decided to reduce the number of civil servants by putting out the cleaning work of central departments to private firms (Ascher,

1987, pp. 24–5). Initially, the Thatcher government also focused on central departments, especially the MoD, but a vocal lobby of MPs, some of them financially linked to major contract cleaning firms, pressed ministers to do the same thing in the NHS (Ascher, 1987, pp. 38–40 and 72–5). Although a DHSS study group found little potential for savings in the NHS, the government pressed ahead in 1983 with circulars compelling district authorities to put cleaning, catering and laundry work out to tender. The procedures to be followed were laid down by the centre, which, on occasion, intervened to direct District Health Authorities to accept private, rather than 'in-house', bids. At first contractors seemed to be making major inroads to NHS work, but a feature of such 'privatization booms' is artificially low pricing by firms anxious to gain a market share. As the defects of some of the early contracts emerged, as the health service unions became better organized, so NHS 'in-house' bids became more successful. DHSS claims that some £19 million per annum have been saved have to be interpreted with some caution. Ascher (1987, p. 189) points out that only 222 out of an expected 2,000 tendering exercises had been carried out; half of all health authorities had put no service out to tender; the savings represent under 2 per cent of the £958 million spent on the ancillary services; and one-third of the total saving is accounted for by in-house units. The assessment that progress has been disappointing seems justified.

Finally, the NHS has been subject to more conventional forms of efficiency drive. The structure has been simplified with the abolition of Area Health Authorities. The internal management structure has been reorganized, and the previous system of collegial control by representatives of the medical and nursing professions has been replaced by general managers in each district and hospital akin to chief executives in private firms (Griffiths Report, 1983). A national package of performance indicators was issued in 1983 (and again in a revised form in 1985) covering such matters as the costs and adequacy of the service. Annual efficiency savings of between 0.2 and 0.5 per cent were imposed on health authorities. And these forms of cost consciousness have not, as in the case of contracting-out, been the reflex actions of an ideologically committed government but have commanded support from less partial sources such as Parliament's Committee of Public Accounts (1981). (For further details see Klein, 1982; Pollitt, 1985.)

The financial position of fringe bodies is almost infinitely varied. They are funded by grants-in-aid (e.g. MSC), statutory levy (e.g. Horserace Betting Levy Board, Industrial Training Boards); annual grant (e.g. Race Relations Board, Health Education Council); departmental vote (e.g. British Museum, Central Council for Education and Training in Social Work); drawing on the National Loan Fund (e.g. New Town Corporations); and charges for services (e.g.

Agricultural Marketing Boards). The most common form of finance is grants-in-aid: 112 bodies out of 252 (Bowen, 1978, pp. 27–9, 34 and table xiv). For all these forms of finance, the centre has considerable powers. Thus, the statutory levies are usually determined by ministers and approved by statutory instrument. For the various grants and departmental votes, ministerial approval is, of course, mandatory. And as ever, fringe bodies are subject to specific regulations on the publication and audit of their accounts and their presentation to Parliament (158 out of 252), although it is significant that a substantial minority do not so account for their expenditure.

Initially the attitude of the Conservative government to fringe bodies was distinctly hostile. 'Hunting the Quango' (Holland, 1979, p. 3) became a favoured blood sport, and Sir Leo Pliatzky conducted a review for the Prime Minister with the object of effecting a substantial reduction in their numbers and expenditure. This *Report on Non-Departmental Public Bodies* (Pliatzky Report, 1980) recommended that 30 (out of 489) executive bodies, 211 (out of 1,561) advisory bodies and 5 (out of 17) tribunals be wound up. This 12 per cent reduction in numbers gave an estimated saving of £11.6 million. Since executive bodies alone spent £5,800 million, the hunt found no pot of gold. It was also anticipated that further savings would materialize through expenditure cuts, the sale of assets and *ad hoc* reviews of particular bodies. By November 1984 it was reported by the Prime Minister that 700 bodies had either been wound up or had their expenditure reduced, giving a total saving of £118 million per annum (Hansard, 19 November 1984, written answer, pp. 57–8). However, these (inflated) figures were more than offset by the increased expenditure of selected fringe bodies. Indeed, to discuss savings in this context is to focus on a peripheral issue, because government policy underwent a complete volte-face.

Confronted by a recalcitrant local government system, the government bypassed it and, rather than 'hunting the quango', actually increased the number and size of fringe bodies. A major beneficiary of this desire to bypass local authorities was the MSC (see Chapter 4, section 4.2.2(ii)), but the same pattern emerged for the inner cities with the creation of enterprise zones, Urban Development Corporations and the substitution of task forces for inner-city partnerships (see Chapter 4, section 4.7). The abolition of the GLC and the metropolitan county councils proliferated bodies – 'Quelgos' or quasi-elected local government organizations – for such services as fire, police, waste disposal and transport (see Chapter 4, section 4.5.3).

If fringe bodies 'benefited' from the centre's strategy of bypassing local government, they were not to be spared from the other major component of indirect centralization: the efficiency drive. Thus the government also acted to clarify and tighten up the accountability of fringe bodies (and non-departmental bodies in general). The Civil Service Department (CSD, 1981, revised as Cabinet Office (MPO) and HM Treasury, 1985) published a guide for departments which recommended *inter alia* that bodies dependent on the government for 50 per cent of their funds should be subject to detailed financial control covering scrutiny and monitoring of performance, checking on staff numbers and grading and approval of rates of pay and conditions of service. In short, the bodies were to be subject to a far more stringent regime.

The major change in financing the water service occurred in 1973 and not after 1979. Prior to 1973 the service had been funded through the water rate and the general grant to local authorities. Post-reorganization, grant could no longer be used to subsidize charges, and the major source of income has become charges to consumers, a change which led to substantial price increases. The system of loan sanction for capital expenditure was also abolished and replaced by cash limits. Within its limit, each RWA can borrow from the National Loans Fund (or overseas) and self-finance expenditure, for example, from its surplus on revenue account. The government can influence not only total capital expenditure but, through the imposition of self-financing requirements, the pricing policy of the industry. Indeed, it has been prepared to require price increases in order to limit the industry's borrowing requirement and to accelerate the repayment of outstanding debt. And, as in the case of the other profitable public utilities, the scope for offsetting increases in public expenditure was not limited to such indirect taxation. Thus, the water industry was reclassified as a nationalized industry, and in 1986 it was announced that the individual RWAs would be sold off (HMSO, 1986a), a decision deferred pending a third term in office.

For all types of SCG, therefore, the picture is one of a set of interdependent yet *ad hoc* initiatives geared to reducing public expenditure. With the failure to control local expenditure in particular, the government bypassed local government, proliferated fringe bodies and privatized public corporations. However, it is important to guard against imputing too clear a logic to the development of government policy. It was born out of failure by way of opportunism, with only limited success in most of its guises. There may have been no single 'U-turn' but there has been much 'zigzagging'. Hands-on control of local authorities, 'hands-off' controls of public corporations and financial regulation of fringe bodies are not logically related but contradictory components of a policy given unity only by vague ideological pronouncements on turning back the frontiers of the state and good management.

3.2.4(ii)   NON-FINANCIAL CONTROLS

Non-financial controls are as multifarious as they are diverse and nowhere more so than in local government. As before, this account distinguishes between local government and other units of SCG.

Non-financial controls over local authorities   These controls fall into five broad groupings: legislative, executive, advisory, monitoring and political. They are considered *seriatim*.

Legislative controls   In addition to the general statutory powers vested in ministers, the centre also has many specific statutory powers. Of these powers, probably the most important is the power to make subordinate legislation and it abounds in, for example, land use planning. In addition, ministers can control subordinate legislation enacted by local authorities. Thus, if a local authority wishes to do something, its actions have to be approved, and its scheme confirmed by the minister. Examples include compulsory purchase orders, development schemes (coastal protection, highways) and by-laws. The latter usually have to conform to DoE model by-laws.

Executive   Statutory provisions regularly accord central decision-making primacy over local decision-making. The major forms of such control are consents and directions, appeals, inquiries and default powers.

   Consents are particularly common in financial matters, and the most notable example in the postwar period was, of course, loan sanction. However, there are also many examples in housing and planning. A minister can issue *directions* or instructions to a specific local authority; e.g. he can require that an application for planning permission be sent to him for decision. He can also hear *appeals* against the decisions of a local authority on, for example, payment of pensions to local government officers, refusal of planning permission and the replacement of protected trees. Although described as quasi-judicial such appeals are administrative appeals concerned with matters of fact and policy and not the law. *Inquiries* are fact-finding missions to ensure that the minister is fully informed when reaching a decision. In housing, highways and planning, the minister can appoint an inspector to hold a local public inquiry, report on the facts of the case and make recommendations. The minister decides the policy, however, and he need not accept the inspector's recommendations (for a detailed description of the planning appeal and inquiry systems see Barker and Couper, 1984). *Default powers* are the centre's ultimate deterrent; they involve the minister taking direct responsibility for the function by, for example, appointing his own commissioner (e.g. housing, civil defence) and are rarely used.

Advisory   Advice is issued in many forms – circulars, departmental letters, technical bulletins and handbooks – and of these, circulars are best known. They serve many purposes: collection of statistical information, explanation of new statutes and/or delegated legislation, detailed technical guidance, general policy guidance, instructions on action to be taken and translating UK legislation into the administrative context of the peripheral nations. Indeed, the territorial ministries issue circulars to their own local authorities. Although circulars can have express statutory backing, it is far more common for them to proffer advice which is variously seen as meddling, paternalistic and irrelevant. On occasion, such advice is even seen as helpful and is read before filing. The formal numbering of circulars facilitates this last activity, and they can penetrate no further than the chief executive's secretary!

Monitoring (1): inspection   The classic form of monitoring is inspection, and British government has a plethora of inspectorates of various types. Gerald Rhodes (1981, ch. 1) distinguishes between enforcement and efficiency inspectorates. The former exist to see that specific statutory requirements are met, particularly for protecting the individual at work or in other economic transactions. Contravention of the law is a criminal matter, and action is taken through the courts. Efficiency inspectorates exist so that Whitehall can supervise local government to ensure administrative efficiency. They operate through administrative action and have few if any sanctions, although some can refuse to sanction the payment of grant to local authorities. There are thirty-four enforcement inspectorates employing some 17,300 inspectors. There are only three efficiency inspectorates – six of the Scottish inspectorates are counted separately – employing a mere 600 inspectors and they are concentrated in three services: education, fire and police (G. Rhodes, 1981, appendix 2, p. 234). There are, however, a number of other candidates for inclusion. The Social Work Service of the DHSS always had an inspecting function but it was not transformed into an inspectorate until 1983–4. The probation inspectorate of the Home Office is an efficiency inspectorate in Scotland, where probation is a local authority function. In England and Wales, the service is provided by local magistrates working with local authorities. Finally, the Audit Commission, as it extends its activities into the area of value for money, could develop into the foremost efficiency inspectorate. As of 1985, its work is more accurately described as audit rather than inspection. (This section draws on G. Rhodes, 1981, pp. 196–7 and 272–4.)

To further compound the problem of identifying the inspectorates, advice is a major part of all their work. Only the police inspectorate still retains the right to sanction the award of grant. Respect and persuasion are the remaining coin for the others, although, of course, they have a right to visit premises, inspect documents and interview staff.

In Scotland, Raab (1982, p. 94) argues that the executive, regulatory and advisory functions of the education HMIs exercised a strong centralizing influence. None the less, as G. Rhodes (1981, p. 197) concludes, for the most part 'formal inspecting powers seem to play a limited part in the promotion of efficiency by central government'. Inspecting powers are 'simply a historical survival', and the key to their survival lies in their capacity 'to gather systematic information about the way in which central government policies are being carried out' (G. Rhodes, 1981, p. 199). In short, they help to repair the deficit in the informational resources of the centre. But if the acquisition of information is an indirect benefit of inspectorates, it formed a central part of the rationale for introducing policy planning systems (PPSs).

Monitoring (2): policy planning systems   By the end of the 1970s, the School for Advanced Urban Studies (1977) was able to identify twenty-two policy planning systems. The best known examples are Transport Policies and Programmes (TPP) set up in 1974 and Housing Investment Programmes (HIP) established in 1977. At the outset the PPSs shared five features (Leach *et al.*, 1983, pp. 25–6). They were comprehensive, emphasizing the interconnected nature of the problems. They were rooted in the rational model of policy-making with its emphasis on objectives, the analysis of alternatives and the evaluation of actions taken. They planned the use of resource for a number of years ahead. They were introduced as a means of increasing local autonomy; they were to be flexible, freeing local authorities from detailed project control. However, within a short space of time, three additional features became prominent. They became a means for central departments to safeguard their policy priorities. They provided substantial amounts of data for the departments. They were used as bidding documents by local authorities. If all eight features were mentioned in the various documents setting up the PPSs, the shift of emphasis was significant. The transformation is summarized as follows by Leach *et al.*, (1983, pp. 26–7, original emphasis):

> The move from an emphasis on *strategy* to an emphasis on *programmes*; from a concern with the *rationality of the process* to a concern with the *content of programmes*; from a *broad policy focus* to a (relatively) *narrow* one; from an attempt at *medium-term resource planning* to an overriding concern with *next year's programme* and with *financial control* aspects thereof; from an emphasis on *joint planning* to a form of *bidding system*; and finally from an explicit concern with *local knowledge/autonomy* to an implicit *central dominance*.

PPSs were planning documents expressing the functional interests of central departments and, in a time of resource squeeze, buying local compliance through the prospect of an enhanced capital expenditure allocation. The information thus acquired by the departments helped them to sustain their policy priorities.

In contrast with the inspectorates, PPSs have an organizational dimension. The systems increased the dependence of local authorities on the regional offices of the DoE. On their inception, the regional DoEs advised local authorities on how to do their PPSs. With the onset of 'cuts' after 1979, they advised over possible future developments and helped local authorities dress up their proposals in a context where DoE ministers were willing to veto 'unacceptable' projects. The DoE's regional offices acted, therefore, 'as a two-way channel of advocacy and advice' and played 'a crucial mediatory role' (Leach *et al.*, 1983, p. 34). PPSs served to strengthen the organizational resources of the centre. The centre's instruments of control are not simply a means of mobilizing resources to influence local authorities. They are also a means of repairing resource deficits: of undermining the centre's dependence on resources controlled by local government.

Political controls The phrase 'political controls' does *not* refer to political party or partisan controls of local authorities but to the way in which the local authority conducts its affairs. In a liberal democracy, control through the ballot box needs to be supplemented by the provision of information to the public and by means for the citizen to obtain redress for his/her grievances. Thus the Public Bodies (Admission to Meetings) Act 1960 as amended by the Local Government Act 1972 ensures that the meetings of the council and its committees are open to the press and public. Other similar provisions include the right to make objections to the district auditor and to inspect copies of the minutes, abstracts of the accounts and registers of various kinds (e.g. planning applications). More recently, Part II of the Local Government, Planning and Land Act 1980 gives the secretary of state the power to issue a 'code of recommended practice as to the publication of information . . . about the discharge of functions' and to make regulations requiring local authorities to publish that information. Finally, concerned about the incidence of 'political advertising' funded from the rates and the effects of partisanship on councillor–officer relationships, the government appointed the Widdicombe Committee to investigate the practices and procedures of local authority business. Empowered to make any necessary recommendations for strengthening the democratic process, the committee's initial deliberations focused on 'political advertising'; and following an interim report, the government introduced the Local Government Act 1986, which restricts local authority publicity to general information about council functions. In addition, the government supported a private member's bill which, as the Local Government (Access to Information) Act 1985, allows public and press access to information relating to committee and subcommittee agendas. With the final report of the Widdicombe Committee (1986a) further legislation seems probable.

The creation of two independent Commissions for Local Administration under the Local Government Act 1974, Part III, means that citizens can now seek redress for grievances arising from maladministration by a local authority. The local commissioner acts on a complaint received through a member of the local authority, although he can accept a complaint directly if a member refuses to act. The commissioners' reports are published, but they have no powers to enforce their findings (Justice, 1980).

Non-financial controls over non-departmental bodies   The range of non-financial controls over local authorities is extensive. The equivalent controls for non-departmental bodies are less comprehensive, although they can be equally specific, and they differ in several respects from those over local authorities. There are no controls over the powers of non-departmental bodies to make subordinate legislation; with few exceptions they have none (e.g. Transport Boards). And their non-elected constitution means that they are subject to a different set of political controls. This survey of the centre's non-financial controls over non-departmental bodies concentrates on such differences.

For all the nationalized industries, the sponsoring minister can issue general directions but, in practice, rarely does so. The miscellany of specific powers includes approval of programmes of reorganization and of training, education and research functions. Perhaps most significant, the minister can appoint and dismiss the chairman and members of the board, although the conditions governing his actions vary greatly. For example, he can be required to consult the chairman before appointing board members, choose from a specified profession or group, declare a seat on a board vacant because of the member's prolonged absence and appoint for a fixed term with no power of dismissal. The power to dismiss has been rarely exercised, but the appointment of chairmen in particular is seen as an opportunity to install an individual with talents and aspirations acceptable to the government.

The industries are required to provide their sponsoring departments with information and, it is alleged, are advised by the departments on a day-to-day basis on virtually all aspects of their operations. There is, however, no formal system of circulars. As with all industry, the nationalized industries fall within the jurisdiction of the enforcement inspectorates. Several industry specific inspectorates now form part of the Health and Safety Executive: e.g. mines and quarries, railways. In addition, some specialized inspectorates remain. The Department of Energy (DEn) employs gas examiners, gas meter examiners and gas engineers. Thus, gas examiners test gas at terminals to ensure that it is of the appropriate quality, whilst gas engineers inspect installations on consumers' premises and investigate serious incidents. Other examples include the electricity engineering inspectorate (DEn) and the accidents investigation branch of the civil aviation safety inspectorates (DT). The corporate plans instituted by the White Paper (HMSO, 1978) have a marked affinity with PPSs in local government, providing both information for the centre and the context for decisions.

The political controls over nationalized industries, and all non-departmental bodies, are distinctive. In sharp contrast to local authorities, none are directly elected, and consequently various substitute forms of control exist, including direct central political control. For the nationalized industries, political controls exist in the form of parliamentary debates and questions, provided, of course, they are matters within the responsibility of the minister – for example, a ministerial direction, financial assistance. In addition, up to 1979 the Select Committee on Nationalized Industries conducted investigations both on individual industries and, more comprehensively, on matters affecting several industries – for example, ministerial control, finance. Since 1979 such investigations have been split between the appropriate 'departmental' select committee. A second form of political controls are the consumer councils, pre-eminently for gas and electricity. There are also user councils for post, transport, coal and civil aviation. In theory at least, the consumer councils exist as a check on the monopoly power of the nationalized industries. Their numbers have increased throughout the postwar period, and the Pliatzky Report (1980, p. 175) gives a total of forty-three councils. Their main functions are to comment on prices and to make 'representations' about consumer complaints. The councils have experienced some difficulty in developing their adversarial, consumer role. As Tivey (1982b, p. 147) comments, 'The balance of expertise and experience will always be on the side of the industries.' In practice, therefore, their impact has been limited, and there have been several calls for their position to be strengthened (for example, Redwood and Hatch, 1982). It is misleading, however, to focus on the formal non-financial control on nationalized industries.

On the one hand, compared for example to local authorities, ministers appear to have sweeping general controls over the nationalized industries. On the other hand, the battery of detailed controls seems *relatively* empty. And yet neither of these points is crucial. As Robson (1962, p. 142) points out: 'the power to issue directions and other legal means of control possessed by Ministers are of far less importance in the relations between the government and nationalized industries than the influence exercised informally through discussion, negotiation and pressure'. Little has changed over the years. Thus, Curwen (1986, pp. 56–7) concludes that 'intervention has been piecemeal and unsystematic' and opines that 'the concept of the public interest is very troublesome'; in consequence, 'governments generally prefer to keep it as ambiguous as possible so that any choices are compatible with it'. Nor is it clear that denationalization will alter the relationship substantially. The government has limited individual shareholdings and it remains the largest, if not the majority, shareholder in the new 'hybrids' (Heald, 1985); it has the means to intervene. The desire to do so may emerge should the companies run into financial difficulties; the sales to date have been limited to profitable concerns, but that 'state of grace' is impermanent. There is also a tendency to confound denationalization with competition. It is quite possible that the sale of shares will create a private sector monopoly with attendant temptations for government to regulate its affairs (e.g. gas). 'Hands-off' policies such as denationalization could foster efficiency and minimize government interference but not necessarily so. Perhaps the most glaring uncertainty surrounding the newly privatized industries concerns the capacity for central intervention. In the case of British Telecom, the government has created the Office of Telecommunications (OFTEL) to protect the 'public interest', that is, to provide safeguards against monopoly power. It has extensive policing powers covering prices, the terms on which it connects services to the system, the way it treats bids to 'license' parts of the system for alternative systems, equipment purchasing policy and the provision of 'social' services such as call-boxes. Such detailed controls were never necessary in the past. Privatization includes both liberalization and *re*-regulation, therefore, and there will be new regulatory bodies in the future (see, for example, Littlechild, 1986). Allied to continued government shareholding, this regulation points to ambiguities if not contradictions in government policy. Heald (1985, p. 20) argues that a new regulatory body could be 'captured' by its industry, thereby negating any safeguards; or the lack of any formal separation between regulators and government could make it easier for the latter to exert pressure and gain compliance for current policy; or the regulatory body could exert its stringent controls over its industry, providing the kind of conflict so common since the 1940s. In other words, the balance of public and private interests remains to be struck; commercial interests versus public policy will remain a recurrent agenda item after the privatization designed to resolve it.

Both the RHAs and RWAs can be given directions by the respective secretaries of state, who can and do make regulations on a variety of matters and review the decisions of the authorities. Circulars are issued aplenty, and if there are no efficiency inspectorates there is one anatomy inspector (DHSS) who regulates the use of donated bodies for teaching anatomy in medical schools, and there are eleven drugs inspectors (Home Office) who check, *inter alia*, the records of medical practitioners and other authorities handling dangerous drugs for their possible misuse (G. Rhodes, 1981, p. 237 and 253–4). Following the 1973 reorganization of the NHS, there was even an attempt to introduce a rational planning cycle equivalent to the PPSs in local government (DHSS, 1972, ch. 3), but, as Klein (1983, p. 128) concludes, 'planning could not be carried out in terms of imposing centrally determined norms and standards'. Rather, and inevitably, it 'became a process of negotiation' between centre and periphery. Since 1982 a simplified planning and review system focused on the District Health Authorities (DHAs) has been in operation. DHAs prepare short-term (two years) operational programmes, including a programme for cost reductions which is then the subject of a two-stage annual review. First, ministers and senior DHSS officials visit each Regional Health Authority for a performance review of its strategic plan. Second, the region has a similar meeting with each DHA (see Ham, 1985, ch. 5; Webb, Wistow and Hardy, 1986, pp. 215–20).

The non-elected constitution of the NHS and RWAs has led to rather elaborate attempts to construct political controls. As with local government, there is an ombudsman or Health Service Commissioner to investigate maladministration but not, of course, the merits of policy nor, significantly, clinical judgements. The sharpest contrasts with local government lie, however, in the role of nominated lay representatives on the Regional and Area Health Authorities (RHAs and AHAs) and of parliamentary select committees.

Initially members of the RHAs were all ministerial appointments but included four local authority nominees. Similarly, the larger AHAs had four local authority nominees, increased subsequently for both levels to one-third. However, with the replacement of the AHAs with District Health Authorities (DHAs) in 1982, it was reduced to four once again. In addition, Community Health Councils (CHCs) were created in 1974 to give consumers a voice in the NHS. Half their members are appointed by local authorities, one-third represented local voluntary groups, and the balance were appointed by the RHAs. In Klein's (1983, p. 116) opinion the CHCs can 'throw grit into the normal machinery of NHS decision-making' but they can only protest and cause delay; 'they could not compel action'.

Initially the boards of the RWAs had a majority of local authority members, but the Water Act 1983 abolished all local authority partici-pation. The boards now have nine to fifteen members, all of whom are appointed by ministers. With the cessation of indirect representation, the only 'outside' interests with an effective voice in the water indus-try are the nominees of the National Farmers' Union and county councils on the Regional Drainage Committees. None of the pro-visions for representing the public either directly through CHCs or indirectly through local authority nominees have proved effective constraints on the avowedly managerial and professional organization of health and water. The voice of the expert remains paramount. Indeed, the potentially most effective control lies in the ministerial appointment of lay members; the minister can dismiss his nominees.

The final element of political control is via ministerial accountability to Parliament. As with the nationalized industries, the minister faces questions on the policies and finances of the NHS and water services; and for the former such questions cover a wide range of administrative matters. Both services are investigated by select committees. Lay membership, indirect representation, consultative/advisory bodies, the ombudsman and ministerial accountability to Parliament all substitute for control by direct election, giving a variegated, spasmodic and often ineffective pattern of political controls.

A patchwork quilt of controls exists for fringe bodies. For example, the Minister of Housing and Local Government issued a direction to the Welwyn Garden City and Hatfield New Town Development Corporation on its restrictive definition of the term 'family' in its long-term leases (Garner, 1974, p. 330)! However, the overall position is best described as one of 'blurred and spasmodic' control (Johnson, 1979, p. 388). Indeed, given that this form of organization is chosen to provide some measure of independence from executive control, any other conclusion would be surprising (for example, see Hood and Bradshaw, 1977, p. 456). Equally, parliamentary scrutiny can be only highly selective. A select committee can investigate a particular body or class of bodies, but it is 'beyond their scope to exercise anything like a comprehensive oversight' (Johnson, 1979, p. 390). The alliance of vague legislative standards and a measure of both operational and policy independence is a sure-fire recipe for ministerial actions that do not achieve the stated purpose.

3.2.4(iii) JUDICIAL CONTROLS

Judicial controls fall into the category of central instruments of control although they are not an instrument controlled by the government of the day. Judicial review cannot be discussed in any detail (see de Smith, 1980), but, in the most general terms, the courts will exercise control where an agency has exceeded its powers and it will review the exercise of discretion by them. Thus, they will intervene to declare an action *ultra vires* when the principles of natural justice have been breached; when statutory powers have been exceeded (substantive *ultra vires*); when the procedures laid down by statute have not been followed (procedural *ultra vires*); when there has been an error of law; where an agency fails to carry out its statutory duties; and when an agency has acted in 'bad faith' or 'abused its power' (Garner, 1974, pp. 113–14). In theory, the doctrine of *ultra vires* is the cardinal feature of British administrative law and it applies to all types of SCG.

There are, however, a number of caveats to this statement. First, the Local Government Act 1972, s. 137, gives local authorities the power to spend the product of a 2p rate on anything which 'in their opinion is in the interests of their area or any part of it or all or some of its inhabitants'. The power is limited, but this exercise of discretion cannot be controlled by the courts. Second, 'the statutory powers of public corporations are so widely drawn that it becomes virtually impossible even to visualize circumstances in which any court could hold any particular act of such a corporation to be *ultra vires*' (Garner, 1974, p. 327). Finally, as Elliott (1981, pp. 67–70) points out, appeals by individuals to the courts and actions against local authorities in breach of contract or of duty (tort) have been 'unjustifiably ignored' as a means of judicial control in favour of a concern with *ultra vires* and prerogative writs. In fact, the 'knock-on' effect of individual decisions on appeal can be considerable because the 'defeat' can be used as a resource by local authorities to gain action or concessions from the centre.

The importance of judicial control has become glaringly obvious over the past five years. The courts have been called upon, in a nigh unprecedented manner, to regulate the conflicts between central and local government. There have been a striking number of key court cases (for a survey see Lomas, 1985; Loughlin, 1986), and they have had three important consequences. First, as Grant (1984, p. 5) notes, the increased risk of litigation has led to 'greater legalism'; 'the relatively loose manner' with which local government legislation was drafted has given way to 'a tight style of draftsmanship'. Lawyers are brought in more frequently 'to provide insurance against challenge in the courts' and to make policies 'judge-proof'. The effects of recent developments are manifest in 'the display of meticulous legalism' and the 'artificially constructed wall of procedure' for blocking judicial review. The objective is 'to transform local government into a more rule-bound organization by structuring discretionary powers, laying down detailed statutory procedures, imposing specific duties and giving formal rights to third parties' (Loughlin, 1985, p. 69).

Second, as Lomas (1985, p. 96) concludes, an ideological pattern emerges from recent court cases with the judiciary protecting and furthering the interests of private property and private rights (see more generally Griffith, 1981). For example in *Norwich CC* v *Secretary of State for the Environment* (1982, 1 All E. R., p. 747) the judge commented: 'The concern of the court, as always, is to protect the individual from the misuse or abuse of power by those in authority. The individual here is the tenant.' (cited in Lomas, 1985, pp. 90 and 96.)

Finally, as a logical corollary of the previous point, the courts have been impervious to the values of local government – 'to the nature and functions of local government . . . the needs of public administration' – displaying an 'antipathy to public service provision and to local state intervention' (Lomas, 1985, p. 96). In *Bromley London Borough Council* v *GLC Greater London Council* (1982, 1 All E. R., p. 165) the court re-invented the concept of fiduciary duty whereby the GLC was said to have a duty 'not to expend . . . money thriftlessly but to deploy the full financial resources available to the best advantage'. In consequence, any local authority exercising its discretionary power and providing services above the statutory minimum could be said to be breaching its fiduciary duty to ratepayers (Loughlin, 1986, p. 42–3; Lomas, 1985, pp. 92–4). In sum, therefore, 'law does not even recognize the institutions of local *government*' (Loughlin, 1985, p. 59), and yet judicial control has come, or perhaps been dragged, to the forefront of the conflict between central and local government with deleterious consequences for the latter.

3.2.5   Summary

The centre has been described as a diverse federation, with departments playing a variety of roles, including the lead, service, guardian and rival roles. The centrifugal forces in the centre are restrained by the Treasury, initially through the PES and subsequently the MTFS and cash limits, and the Cabinet and its committees. But the alliance of bureaucratic and ministerial interests is a formidable obstacle to central co-ordination, creating weakness at the centre of British government. In its relationship with SCG, the centre has a monopoly of legal resources and, if not a monopoly, then the preponderant share of financial and political resources. The tradition of 'hands-off' or non-executant central departments means, however, that the centre is dependent upon SCG for informational and organizational resources. The possession of resources does not guarantee influence; they have to be deployed effectively. The centre has an impressive arsenal of instruments of control. It has financial controls over loans, grant and audit of all types of SCG, and in the case of local authorities the centre has sought ever more Draconian means to regulate current expenditure. The non-financial controls of the centre are multifarious, encompassing general statutory powers; specific powers of confirmation, approval, regulation, direction, default and decision-making; advice and monitoring through circulars, etc., inspection and policy planning systems; and political controls over the way SCG conducts its affairs. Judicial controls are not exercised by central government but they are controlled from the centre. Although the courts have been reluctant to intervene and adopted a limited construction of their powers of judicial review, none the less litigation and detailed legalism have become characteristics of central–SCG relations. In short, the potential for influence of the centre seems boundless. But this section has focused on the *formal* powers of the centre. The ability of the centre to translate its formal pre-eminence into effective action is the central theme of the case studies of the policy networks. And a formal analysis begins to suggest limits to the centre's influence. Its interests are both diverse and conflicting. SCG may lack legal, financial and political resources but it has some *and* it has the preponderant share of informational and organizational resources – a dependence acknowledged by the centre in its attempts to repair the deficits through the inspectorates and PPSs.

3.3   The Territorial Ministries

In every political sense, the territorial ministries are much more part of Whitehall than they are part of Scotland, Wales or Northern Ireland (Rose, 1982, p. 105).[3] They cannot be described as the governments of the peripheral nations. Thus, the Secretary of State for Scotland is not Scotland's Prime Minister but a member of the British Cabinet. In the words of the first permanent under secretary of the Welsh Office:

> the position of the Secretary of State is almost exactly the same as the position of any other department or any other minister. We have a constitutional situation in which government operates collectively. Therefore, on any big issues ministers sitting together in the Cabinet may decide to overrule a departmental minister and insist on a particular policy.
>
> (Cited in Rose, 1982, p. 103)

Conventionally, therefore, the national offices are considered part of that diverse federation known as the centre. They will not be so viewed here. In order to pose as sharply as possible the question of whether or not they exercise policy-making discretion, they have been classified as a species of sub-central government (see Chapter 2, Table 2.4 and section 2.5.3). The preceding quotation answers the question without providing any assessment of the degree of discretion or the conditions under which it occurs. In fact, there are three good reasons for separating the national offices from the centre.

First, the national offices are organized on a territorial, not functional, basis; they are located in the periphery, not Whitehall and are responsible for a wide range of functions; they articulate both territorial and functional interests. Consequently, for local authorities and a variety of non-departmental bodies, they are not just one of many central departments with responsibilities for SCG but the prime port of call: 'their centre'.

Second, the national offices have additional roles; the responsibilities of a central department and of intermediate institutions (see section 3.4, below) are fused in the one unit. Thus, as Smith and Stanyer (1976, pp. 92–3) point out, they cannot be treated as an example of field administration, i.e. administrative deconcentration. In addition to the roles common to functional departments, they also adapt UK policies for implementation in the periphery; promote

Table 3.1   *The Functional Jurisdiction of Territorial Departments*

Functional departments (England)	Territorial ministry has some functional jurisdiction		
	Scotland	Wales	Northern Ireland
Agriculture	Yes	Yes	Yes
Civil Service	No	No	Yes
Defence	No	No	No
Education and Science	Yes	Yes	Yes
Employment	Yes	Yes	Yes
Energy	Yes	No	Yes
Environment	Yes	Yes	Yes
Foreign and Commonwealth	No	No	No
Health and Social Security	Yes	Yes	Yes
Home Office	Yes	No	Yes
Industry	Yes	Yes	Yes
Law Officers	Yes[a]	No	Yes
Trade	Yes	Yes	Yes
Transport	Yes	Yes	Yes
Treasury	No	No	Yes
Totals	11	8	13

Note:
[a] The Lord Advocate's Department is separate from the Scottish Office, but it is very much a territorial department with functional jurisdiction.
Source: Rose, 1982, p. 118.

policies in response to national differences and needs; and lobby for resources not only for particular services but also for the nation as a whole.

Finally, the national offices operate within dual political environments: the shared environment of UK politics and the individual political environments of each constituent nation with its own distinct ethnic identity, sub-central political organizations, legal, educational and religious institutions. For these reasons, government within the peripheral nations has been bestowed with a variety of labels: e.g. the Scottish political system, decentralized government, administrative devolution, devolved government and pro-consular government. The problem with each and every such label is that they imply a high degree of separateness from the centre. It will be argued here that the key feature of the offices is their *dual* character; they are simultaneously in the centre and for a territory. This fusion of territorial and central responsibilities is best captured in the expression 'territorial ministries'.

The territorial ministries, as Whitehall departments, express the areal, service, guardianship and rival interests like their counterparts in London with the complication that *all* these roles are played both within the national offices and between the national offices and other Whitehall departments. The major functions of the national offices are shown in Table 3.1.

The territorial ministries speak not only for local authorities within their area but, more intangibly, they represent the interests of their area as a whole; they are territorial organizations with their definition of the territory's interest as well as spokespersons for local authorities with their own definitions of territorial interests. An account of the areal interests of the national offices has to distinguish between these general and specific interests.

The national offices have the usual areal role of negotiating grant to their local authorities but, at first sight, they would seem to have a more all-embracing remit than the DoE for English local authorities. The national offices are multi-functional and they could speak for SCG not just on grant but for all its services. In theory at least, each is a single Whitehall department with its own minister of Cabinet rank. They should be able to develop, therefore, considered and co-ordinated positions towards both their own SCGs and Whitehall: to be more 'corporate'. For example the Layfield Committee (1976, p. 345) opined that the Scottish Office was 'in a position . . . to ensure that the actions of its own functional departments are co-ordinated' (see also citations in Page, 1978b, p. 55). Internally, Scottish Office co-ordination should have been facilitated by the creation of Central Services, in effect a new department, and of the Management Group, composed of departmental heads. Similarly, the Department of Finance in the Northern Ireland Office is charged with a co-ordinating role similar to that of the Treasury. Allied to the much smaller scale of administration in the periphery, the potential for a corporate approach seems substantial.

However, internal cohesion is under constant strain from functional pressures. Fragmentation and departmentalism persist in the Scottish Office, with agriculture and education particularly resistant to the calls for co-ordination (Parry, 1981). Consequently, Keating and Mid-winter (1983, p. 17) conclude: 'Departmental secretaries . . . retain considerable autonomy, and departmental interaction resembles the independence of Whitehall ministers.' Birrell and Murie (1980, p. 141) also concluded that co-ordination between departments in the Northern Ireland Office was 'inadequate'; 'departmental isolationa-lism' was the norm. The national offices have to be seen, therefore, as federations of departments: as Whitehall writ small. The multi-functionalism of territorial ministries breeds fragmentation, defeating (or at least severely constraining) the various attempts to develop corporate approaches. And the explanation of this feature of the national offices lies in the call of Whitehall-based functional departments; function overrides territory within the offices and in their relations with Whitehall. Consequently, their areal role remains confined to the interests of local authorities: to grant, boundaries, organization and administrative procedures. Or more succinctly, it covers the 'how' rather than the 'what' of government. Thus, Rose (1982, p. 103) argues that the Scottish Education Department (SED) is not concerned with *Scottish* education policies but with education and with problems shared throughout the UK. The point is over-stated, betraying a centralist perspective. Indisputably the 'grand' issues of education – that is, its compulsory nature, school-leaving age, etc. – are decided at the UK level for the UK. But a wide range of issues – for example, curricula, supply and training of teachers – are *not* matters of UK policy. The distinctive feature of educational policy-making in Scotland is not that the SED moves in step with the DES but that it both moves in step *and* develops distinctive policies. Functional and territorial interests coexist, at times uneasily, and the SED can use the DES as a court of appeal should it find its service interests compromised. If the UK ministry is the 'lead' department on the grand issues, then the territorial ministry has its own distinctive range of issues and responsibilities.

There are, of course, variations between the departments of terri-torial ministries in their capacity for independent policy initiatives. For example, the DoI is the lead department on all matters of policy, interpreting guidelines and ensuring consistency in the treatment of applications. It 'takes responsibility for *negotiating* changes on policy' and it negotiates with the territorial departments with concurrent responsibilities' (Hogwood, 1982a, pp. 45–6 original emphasis). Ministers think first about functions and second about the territorial dimension. As Birrell and Murie (1980, p. 141) argue, functionalism is inherent within the system:

> The practice of setting up separate departments with their ministries and permanent secretaries tended to reproduce on a lesser scale some of the same difficulties implicit in a very much larger adminis-trative system. Departmental isolationism was encouraged in some departments by the policy of 'step-by-step' with Westminister.

After the suspension of Stormont in 1972, the mechanisms for co-ordinating the Northern Ireland departments were strengthened, but creation of the Northern Ireland Office also led to a closer integration with Westminster and Whitehall.

Given the all-pervasive effects of functionalism, the national offices are cast frequently into the role of supporting Whitehall departments:

> A sort of 'log-rolling' can develop in which the Scottish Secretary backs up the Minister for Agriculture or Education or Transport, in the knowledge that increased expenditure for these departments will not penalize but help him in securing more for Scotland. He

thus has many potential allies in the Cabinet, who will not resent Scotland getting perhaps more than its share of housing subsidies, schools, and roads in return for support for their policies.

(Kellas, 1984, p. 46; see also 1st edn 1973, p. 50).

Or, more pungently, the tactics employed by departments of the territorial ministries in their service role can be summarized as 'more means better' (Rose, 1982, p. 100). Indeed, the position of the territorial ministries within public expenditure process reflects the pre-eminence of functional politics. Although the territorial ministries now receive a block allocation, it is built up functionally and parallels the budget allocations of the corresponding Whitehall department. The secretaries of state can increase their allocation only by supporting their functional colleagues (Keating and Midwinter, 1983, p. 21). None the less, they inject a 'national' dimension into discussions of UK functional policies by the tactics of judicious support.

This pre-eminence of functional departments and policies is reflected in the standing of territorial ministers. Both the Scottish Office and the Welsh Office 'have developed into established, that is, settled and accepted, legitimate, parts of British government. They are still obviously quite low in the Whitehall pecking order, but they are known, tolerated, at least no longer disdained' (Kellas and Madgwick, 1982, p. 16). Similarly, the secretaries of state are 'second division'. Scottish and Welsh affairs are rarely high on the Cabinet agenda, most being considered in Cabinet committees. The territorial ministers will sit on those committees concerned with, for example, social, industrial and agricultural policy but they are far less likely to sit on the major committees concerned with defence, foreign affairs and management of the economy. The Northern Ireland Secretary does not chair *ad hoc* committees on the province's troubles; that position will be occupied by a senior minister.

If the territorial ministries appear in support of functional departments in Whitehall, it does not mean they fail to inject territorial considerations into the UK policy process or that they are ineffective in lobbying for resources (see below). It does mean that relationships with Whitehall are dominated by functional politics. And within their territories, relationships with local government are similarly dominated. Each department of the territorial ministries seeks to ensure that local authorities spend the appropriate share of central grant on its service: 'Policy is a matter for them. My concern is with the maximum uptake of resources in my particular area. They know what local needs are, and I can't judge them' (Scottish Office official, cited in Midwinter, 1980, p. 42). Since 1979, oversight by the Scottish and Welsh offices has become tougher. Sporadic intervention on functional lines has been overlaid with a set of directive controls. Within their areas, the territorial ministries are the 'centre' for local government, and, as in the capital city, areal interests vie with service interests in the ever-oscillating competition for resources. The conflict of interests has been intensified by the revival of guardianship. Thus, the Scottish Office negotiates with the Treasury for public expenditure in Scotland and with local authorities over the total and distribution of central grant, *and* it regulates local income and expenditure to keep them within UK determined ceilings. Guardianship has generated political conflict and local recalcitrance and eroded the consensual style which prevailed for the bulk of the postwar period.

There are, however, some marked differences between the territorial ministries. Thus, Scotland has been a testing ground for the new financial controls over local authorities of the post-1979 Conservative governments, whereas since 1973 the major 'local government' services in Northern Ireland have been the responsibility of non-departmental bodies (for example, education, housing), and local government proper has remained responsible for minor functions (for example, recreation, cleaning and sanitation). Central grant to Scottish local authorities has fallen, whilst the (small) grant to district councils in Northern Ireland has risen (Connolly, 1983). Overall, however, like the DoE, the territorial ministries have the potentially conflicting roles of arguing for resources for their territory and its SCG and of regulating SCG expenditure (for a more detailed discussion see Chapter 4, section 4.3.1).

In sum, the territorial ministries contain all the interests found in Whitehall. The tension between areal and service interests is manifest both in internal relationships and in relationships with Whitehall. The scope for policy leadership would seem to be severely constrained by the pre-eminence of functional politics in British government. Such a conclusion would be premature. A range of factors influence the scope for policy leadership. If functional politics are a constraint, the legal, organizational, informational and political resources of the territorial ministries provide opportunities for independent action.

The first factor influencing the scope for independent action of the territorial ministries is their legal resources. The statutory responsibilities of the territorial ministries vary, with the Welsh Office, for example, acquiring a comparable range of functions to the Scottish Office only recently. They also vary between services – with the Scottish Office having considerable powers in education but limited responsibilities for energy – and over time, with the Northern Ireland Office's responsibilities increasing greatly with the imposition of Direct Rule and the reorganizations of the 1970s. Even where the ministries' responsibilities are limited, such legal resources provide access to the appropriate Whitehall network.

The second factor is the indeterminacy of the territorial communities; i.e. the greater the spill-over effects of any policy for the rest of the UK, the greater the limits on policy leadership. Where, however, the effects of the policy are confined to the nation concerned and especially when a territorial ministry has evolved a distinct tradition of autonomy, as in the case of the Northern Ireland Civil Service before 1972, the scope for policy leadership can be considerable. Thus, teacher training and teacher supply in Scotland are seen as a matter for the Scottish Office because the policy area is insulated from the rest of the UK and there is a long-standing tradition of autonomy in education. Similarly, Birrell and Murie (1980, chs. 9 and 10) argue that Stormont developed distinct policies in housing, education, health and social services.

In the case of the Welsh Office, its relatively recent creation and even more recent extension in functions mean that it lacks a tradition of autonomy. It

> rarely puts a *Welsh* dimension into its local policies and services. Indeed, it is very difficult to see what there is that is specifically Welsh, except perhaps the issue of language, in much of central–local relations, and the Welsh Office appears largely unwilling and perhaps unable to transmit the *Welsh* dimension upwards into imperial policy debates. Hence there is a marked tendency for the Welsh Office to accept core policy initiatives and to adopt them with little variation, though the informal processes by which they come to be adopted may be distinctive in themselves.
>
> (Goldsmith, 1984, p. 9, original emphasis)

None the less there is evidence that the Welsh Office is spreading its wings. Webb, Wistow and Hardy (1986, pp. 77–9 and 97–100) argue that the Welsh Office is implementing 'a radically different pattern of services' for the mentally handicapped. Irrespective of their longevity, therefore, the territorial ministries have the capacity to develop distinct policies, and this capacity is sustained by their organizational and informational resources. They fuse the interests of Whitehall departments with the managerial and service (implementation) interests of intermediate organizations (see section 3.4, below, for a more detailed description). Consequently, they have direct contact with their SCG rather than indirect contact through regional offices, and data can be collated across a range of functions and organizations within a single ministry. If the benefits of nodality are not always realized, none the less the territorial ministries are the experts for their areas. As Oliver (1978, p. 108) noted, after the imposition of Direct Rule, he experienced difficulties with Westminster because of the latter's unfamiliarity with the differences in law and administration. The Northern Ireland Civil Service had become an 'independent and autonomous body' and, after Direct Rule, it 'maintained its separate structure and identity' (Birrell and Murie, 1980, pp. 153–4). Such expertise is an important element in legitimating the claim for distinctive treatment; the ministries can speak with authority on the needs of their territory and in the knowledge that they have a proven capacity to administer such policies.

The political resources of the territorial ministries are as intangible as they are important. As ministers of Cabinet rank their secretaries of state command access at the highest levels of British government but they are also subject to the same political pressures as the UK government. An issue of high political and especially party saliency can drive out all consideration of distinct territorial needs – for example, pay beds in the NHS, protection of children in care (Keating and Midwinter, 1983, pp. 21–2). Conversely, the relative importance of issues varies between centre and periphery. The salience of policies on water supply (Wales) or fisheries (Scotland) may be greater for the territorial ministries than for the corresponding UK department. In these circumstances, the territorial ministries can take the lead in getting the issue on the political agenda and may even become the lead department in Whitehall for that issue. Thus, the revaluation of property in Scotland in 1985 and the attendant outcry led the Secretary of State for Scotland to force yet another reconsideration of alternative sources of local revenue on to the Cabinet.

If access is the major political resource of the territorial ministries, the ability of the secretary of state to act as the 'voice' for territorial interests can be enhanced by his political environment. There is a 'relatively coherent community' of MPs and sub-central political organizations. Their activities can be evidence of discontent and a weapon to be wielded in inter-ministerial and interdepartmental negotiations as well as support for secretaries of state as the lobby for territorial interests. In the 1970s the hand of Labour Secretaries of State for Scotland was strengthened by the electoral position of the government of the day. Successive Labour governments depended on Scottish seats, and the threat posed to them by the rise of the SNP gave the Secretary of State for Scotland added political muscle in his fight for additional resources. And in the course of such negotiations, the personal qualities and skills of the minister can be crucial. William Ross was seen as a 'separatist' Secretary of State for Scotland, and his determined fight to keep the Chrysler car plant open at Linwood was decisive. He argued that, in a context of high unemployment and a strong SNP vote, failure to fund Scottish industry may mean that the 'UK may have to say farewell to its share of North Sea Oil' (*World in Action*, 1976, p. 22). And a strong minister reinforces the hand of his civil servants in the Whitehall policy networks (Keating and Midwinter, 1983, p. 23). Conversely, a Conservative secretary of state in an otherwise Labour Scotland runs the risk of alienating the Scottish electorate. He has no mandate and 'he runs the risk of damaging not only his party but the Union itself' (Miller, 1981, p. 262).

To counterbalance this discussion of the legal, organizational, informational and political resources of the territorial ministries, it is important to remember, that they are but a constituent unit of the centre. Rose (1982, pp. 110–12) distinguishes between uniform, concurrent and exceptional policies. He estimates that exceptional (i.e. territorially specific) policies account for 0.1 per cent of public expenditure and 1.3 per cent of public employment. Concurrent policies account for the overwhelming bulk of expenditure and employment.

Developing this point, Keating and Midwinter (1983, pp. 23–4 and 25–6) argue that education and social work are 'largely self-contained' and 'policy on local government is handled separately'. For agriculture and fisheries 'joint policy making is the norm', whilst for law reform, criminal justice and administration uniformity in policy is preferred with wide variations in administrative practice. They conclude that autonomy is greatest for organizational and administrative matters and weakest for functional policy with, consequently, a high degree of policy uniformity. In a similar vein Parry (1981, pp. 1–2) identifies several recent policy *innovations* – for example, the reorganization of local government, the health service and social work, and urban renewal. He also cites numerous historical examples of such innovation: for example, education authorities operating labour exchanges (1908), public housing provision (1917) and comprehensive land use planning (1963). He sees considerable scope for autonomous action in some fields, notably personal social services, but argues that the amount of activity fluctuates, with the period 1965–75 being distinctive for the amount of innovation (pp. 32–3). More commonly, both the Scottish and Welsh Offices 'are engaged in the humdrum business of implementing policies decided elsewhere and introducing modest variations where they can suit the conditions, needs and idiosyncrasies of the two countries' (Kellas and Madgwick, 1982, p. 29). The degree of discretion ranges from autonomy to dependence and varies between policy areas and overtime, with the former demonstrating greater capacity to place territorial matters on the central agenda.

For much of the postwar period, the Northern Ireland Office was unique in the autonomy it enjoyed. The financial arrangements of the 1920 Act were designed to make Northern Ireland self-financing, and, if this aspiration was quickly nullified, the resulting financial subsidies 'still left Northern Ireland with a large measure of discretion over public expenditure' (Birrell and Murie, 1980, p. 28 and also pp. 15–22 for a description of the financial arrangements). Indeed, Birrell and Murie (1980, pp. 28–9) conclude that

> While remaining firmly within the United Kingdom, Northern Ireland ... developed with many characteristics of an independent state ... it is arguable that in practice the status of Stormont government was closer to the federal model than the devolution

model – that is, the two governments were almost co-ordinate in powers with each other . . .

Direct Rule brought Northern Ireland 'into the mainstream'. Northern Ireland legislation has been modified to bring it into line with the mainland. But continuity rather than innovation has been the order of the day, and the combination of one-party dominance, conservative ideology and a civil service with a long-standing tradition of autonomy has contributed to the persisting variations in policy. Birrell and Murie (1980, p. 10) estimate that, between 1965 and 1970, 40 per cent of legislation was peculiar to Northern Ireland (that is, exceptional legislation) and they explicitly reject Rose's (1971, p. 97) contention that Northern Ireland's policy developed in step with the rest of the UK. They argue that the general principle of parity in welfare programmes was very general and left considerable room for interpretation. Consequently, 'policies . . . concerning the major social services, education, housing and children's welfare were markedly different from those obtaining in the rest of the United Kingdom' (p. 11). In a similar vein, Goldsmith (1984, p. 10) concludes that the Northern Ireland Civil Service departments have 'considerable autonomy' (see also Connolly, 1983):

Northern Ireland political networks . . . have successfully ensured its place on the Imperial political agenda, not only over the last fifteen years, but for centuries. The result is considerable process and network variations, and some policy differences, and underlying each of which is the sectarian differences and rivalries at all times.

If the differences between territorial ministries are now less marked, the Northern Ireland Office remains the most autonomous: a legacy of devolution and insulation from Westminster and Whitehall.

It is difficult to demur from Goldsmith's (1984, p. 21) conclusion that the other territorial ministries exercise discretion when the centre sees fit, with occasional concessions won in the Cabinet. First and foremost, the ministries are part of the UK with appropriate loyalties. Policies are predominantly concurrent and apply to all parts of the UK. The ministries manage 'low politics', and the centre both supports this role and encourages territorial variations when and where they ease its management problems. But whenever crucial political issues are involved, the centre will resort to direct and unilateral action. Any and all territorial discretion has a fragile base, but equally, the centre's has the power to intervene, not necessarily to control.

3.3.1 Summary

With their fusion of the interests of central departments and intermediate institutions, geographical location in the periphery and distinct sub-central political environments, the 'national' offices are a major voice of territorial interests in British government. Functional politics and policy remain paramount; the territorial ministries commonly appear in support of UK functional departments, but they do inject an areal dimension into UK policy-making, establishing autonomy in some policy areas. Even within the unitary state that is Britain, the exercise of executive authority is constrained by central–SCG interdependence. Territorial and functional politics vie with each other within the centre. Interdependence is manifest in the day-to-day interactions of networks but is discernible even in the formal analysis of interests, resources and relationships.

3.4 Intermediate Institutions

The territorial ministries articulate territorial interests *in* the centre but they are not the only form of territorial organization *of* the centre. All central departments have some form of sub-central structure. The term 'intermediate institutions' refers to these deconcentrated structures.[4] However, they do not exist to articulate territorial interests. The sheer diversity of structures within and between central departments demonstrates that functional and administrative criteria dominated decisions on boundaries. Intermediate institutions express the interests of functional departments, and the resulting organizational pattern can be described as a maze only at the cost of some simplification. As Rose (1982, pp. 116–17) has shown, the territorial organization of a function can cover part of one nation, one nation, more than one nation and the whole of the UK. Central departments are, therefore, internally heterogeneous, and the structure of territorial administration is a complex mosaic.

In the postwar period, such administrative deconcentration has had a chequered history. After the war, the majority of central departments dismantled or contracted their regional machinery (see Mackenzie and Grove, 1957, pp. 263–72; Smith, 1964, ch. 1). Thus, the Ministries of Education and of Housing and Local Government both closed their regional offices. Between 1953 and 1962 total staff in intermediate institutions fell by some 30,000 or 7 per cent, although the remaining 361,834 staff accounted for 35 per cent, of all civil servants (Smith, 1964, pp. 25–6). After the Labour election victory in 1964, however, regionalism was in vogue in the guise of regional planning within the framework of a national economic plan. Consequently, in 1965, the Regional Economic Planning Councils (REPCs) and Boards (REPBs) were created. The demise of national planning and abolition of the Department of Economic Affairs were but a temporary disruption. Responsibility for the REPCs and REPBs was transferred to an enlarged MHLG and in 1970 to the 'giant' DoE

Table 3.2   *Variations in Regional Boundaries: Names of Units and Use of Regions, 1979*

	Geographical coverage	Number of unit regions in England	Number of standard regions inc. minor modifications
Departmental units			
Department of Employment (Unemployment Benefit)	GB	7	4
Department of Industry Regional Offices[a]	E	8	6
Department of Industry Regional Development Grant Offices	GB	3	0
Department of Industry/Trade Export Services[a]	E	8	6
Export Credit Guarantee Department	UK	8	0
Regional Economic Planning Boards[a]	UK	8	8
Departments of Environment/Transport Regional Directors[a]	E	8	6
Department of Environment Housing Regions[a]	E	9	6
Department of Environment Planning Regions[a]	E	9	6
Department of Environment Rent Assessment Panel Areas	E	15	4
Department of Environment Ancient Monuments Works Areas	GB	7	2
Department of Environment Audit Districts	E & W	11	1
Property Services Agency[a]	UK	8	0
Department of Transport Roads and Transport Controllers[a]	E	9	6
Department of Transport Road Construction Units	E	7	1
Department of Transport Traffic Areas	E & W	9	3
Home Office: Prison Service Regions	E & W	4	0
Home Office: Fire Inspectorate Regions	E & W	4	0
Home Office: HM Inspectorate of Constabulary	E & W	6	0
Home Defence Regions	E & W	9	4
Lord Chancellor's Office: Court Circuits	E & W	6	0
Ministry of Agriculture, Fisheries and Food: Regions[a]	E	7	2
Ministry of Agriculture, Fisheries and Food: Agricultural Development and Advisory Service	E & W	7	2
HM Land Registry	E & W	11	0
Department of Education and Science: HM Inspectors Divisions[a]	E & W	7	2
DHSS: Social Work	E	9	5
DHSS: Social Security	GB	10	4
Ministry of Defence: TAVRA Regions	UK	10	3
Ministry of Defence: Army Districts	UK	7	2

Ministry of Defence: Naval Flag Officers	UK	4	0
Civil Service Department			
Regional Offices	UK	8	5
HMSO	UK	3	0
Inland Revenue: Tax Organization	UK	12	0
Inland Revenue: Valuation Office Regions	E & W	23	0
Customs and Excise: Collections	UK	23	0
Central Office of Information[a]	E	9	5
Charity Commission	E & W	2	0

Note:
[a] Unit represented on the Regional Economic Planning Boards.
Source: Hogwood and Lindley, 1982, pp. 48–9.

combining physical planning, transport and housing. Dispersal of civil servants to the regions was the order of the day, and the DoE acquired the largest regional presence (Parry, 1980, pp. 33–40) along with the responsibility for co-ordinating the centre beyond Whitehall. But the momentum was dissipating. The REPCs became part of tripartite teams, with local authorities and central departments charged with devising regional strategies. The scope of regional planning became broader, the number of affected government departments became legion, and the centre's interest declined (Skelcher, 1980): a trend accelerated by the distrust of central departments of the DoE's incursions on their turf and by the ever more obvious implications of the regional plans for national economic management. Inaction ceased in 1979 when the REPCs (but not the REPBs, now renamed interdepartmental Regional Boards) were abolished by the new Conservative government. Economies were the order of the day again – staff in the regional offices of the DoE has been reduced by 20 per cent since 1979 (Houlihan, 1984, p. 415) – and regional strategic planning assumed a low priority with the DEmp and DoI withdrawing from joint work with the DoE on such strategies. (For a more detailed account see Wright and Young, 1975; Lindley, 1982.) For all these fads and fashions, the inert mass of intermediate institutions remained unseen and unsung.

The diverse nature of this type of SCG can be seen in Table 3.2. Thus, regional organization varies not only between departments but also within departments. The REPCs/REPBs provided England with a set of eight standard regional boundaries. Disregarding minor boundary differences, no department, not even the sponsoring DoE, uses the standard boundaries for all its functions, and some departments (e.g. Inland Revenue) use none. Indeed, the DoE has seven functions each with a regional organization, only one of which – the REPBs! – uses all eight standard regions, and for two functions the number of regions is significantly greater, e.g. rent assessment (fifteen). And a simple perusal of Table 3.2 shows that the diversity of boundaries is matched by the variety of functions. Saunders

(1983, p. 1) has pointed out that the intermediate institutions are characterized by 'their functional diversity, their non-contiguous boundaries and their relative political invisibility'. Such a daunting set of characteristics poses problems for any classification.

However, the 'problem' with intermediate institutions is not to provide an adequate taxonomy but to identify and explain variations in their roles within policy networks and the consequences which follow for the distribution of public services. Switching from institutional taxonomy to interests, resources and relationships substantially reduces the problem of describing intermediate institutions.

3.4.1 The Interests of Intermediate Institutions

The interests of intermediate institutions[5] fall into three main categories: managerial, service and areal (for alternative classifications see Leach *et al.*, 1983: Houlihan, 1984). Managerial interest refers to the tasks deconcentrated by the central departments to facilitate the execution and integration (or co-ordination) of administrative tasks (and other affected organizations). Service interest does not on this occasion refer to the competition for resources, but to the implementation of central departmental policy. Thus intermediate institutions collect information on their area and the department's policies, monitoring its progress and reporting back on inadequacies and possible reforms. They also intervene at the sub-central level to promote departmental policies. Finally, areal interest refers to lobbying by intermediate institutions on behalf of their area and its other sub-central governments.

3.4.1(i) MANAGERIAL INTERESTS

Execution Execution refers to the specific tasks delegated to an intermediate organization by the central department. Listing the tasks would be as endless as it is pointless. The simple point is that regional offices enable central departments to operate more effectively; there are few farms in Central London! Simply to illustrate the range of tasks, the MAFF provides technical advice to individual farmers and to RWA engineers on land drainage/sea defence; the DTp administers TPPs; the DoE has a large range of tasks ranging from administering HIPs to visiting buildings of historic/conservation merit; the DoI both sifts applications for industrial assistance and provides small grants to industry; the Exports Credits Guarantee Department (DT) provides export advice and sells insurance; and so on. The degree of discretion permitted varies greatly (see pages 161–3, below).

Integration refers to both the formal co-ordination of intermediate institutions (and non-departmental public bodies) and the informal bringing together of a range of other sub-central interests. Commonly described as the policeman or oversight role, it will be referred to here as reticulist activity – literally, arranging a network (see Friend, Power and Yewlett, 1974). Formal co-ordination is a prime role of the DoE. It chaired the REPB and it acts as a clearing-house whenever the reaction of intermediate institutions is required to the plans and programmes of other agencies. As Young (1982, p. 78) comments: 'The DoE ... attempts to co-ordinate different policies. In so far as any point in central governments exists which provides some sort of corporate link to local authorities, it is the regional DoE that most approximates to it.' However, although the formal co-ordination role has attracted more attention, it is less important than the reticulist activity of individual organizations (including the DoE). To begin with, co-ordination across departments, even at the sub-central levels, runs counter to the entrenched functionalism of British government, acting as a catalyst to the ever-present fear of turf invasion. Reticulist activity has its roots in the self-interest of participants, most commonly in shared administrative and service delivery problems. Thus, intermediate institutions build bridges between clients – in this context, local authorities and firms and industries in both public and private sectors – to foster the implementation of policy. It acts to sustain the policy network, not to co-ordinate the actions of several networks. The exact form of reticulist activity can vary greatly. The intermediate institution can attempt to resolve conflicts between other members of the network (arbitration); it can provide information and advice (consultancy); it can smooth the administrative path of both clients and other network members unfamiliar, for example, with a new central initiative (diplomacy); and it acts to protect the network from the depredations of other organizations (turf protection) (for example, see Hambleton, 1983; Leach *et al.*, 1983; Houlihan, 1984). These specific activities share one common feature: the desire to maintain the integrity of the network.

3.4.1(ii) SERVICE INTERESTS

Information and monitoring refer, self-evidently, to the acquisition of data for the centre and to the review of central policy initiatives. As noted at several junctures, the centre has 'hands-off' controls of SCG. Information and organization are the prime resources of SCG. Intermediate institutions are one means of repairing these resource deficits. Thus, they administer PPSs, one of the centre's major instruments for acquiring information. In Young's (1982, p. 90) words, intermediate institutions are the 'eyes and ears' of Whitehall in which role they follow Harold Geneen's (President, ITT) maxim of 'no surprises' (Sampson, 1974, p. 68). Thus, the regional offices of the DoE meet regularly with senior local government officers and visit local authorities to develop relations within them. The need for such contacts is clear; Marsham Street expects to be briefed about, for example, delegations from local authorities to see the secretary of state. Similarly, the DoI monitors the assistance given to firms. Often such monitoring involves only compiling statistical reviews, but for 'difficult' cases, there will be regular visits by regional officials (Hogwood, 1982a, p. 42). Indeed, Hogwood concludes that this activity is 'one of the main "administrative convenience" reasons for the existence of regional offices'. However, over and beyond convenience, this role alleviates the dependence of the centre on other organizations be they firm or unit of SCG.

With the growth of PPSs, professional officers have carved out a central role for themselves. The technical process of acquiring information has become professionalized. As Houlihan (1984, p. 410) notes:

> the region is not simply a passive recipient of information, a task which the headquarters could easily fulfil, rather it is involved in checking the veracity of information, identifying new information requirements and evaluating the information supplied . . . much of the data needs to be professionally checked and decoded. The result is a strengthening of the professional role at the regional level.

He concludes that professional linkages are 'dominant' in the HIPs process; that the introduction of HIPs accentuated the trend towards professionalization (see also Houlihan, 1983b); and that this trend served to build a mystique around HIPs which minimized political interference.

Intervention   refers to the promotion of central policies and policy networks, initiating actions by other network members and direct involvement in the decision-making process of other network members. The ability of intermediate institutions to persuade firms, local authorities, etc. to adopt government policy is an important supplement to other forms of advice such as circulars. Promotional activities cannot be equated, however, with the provision of advice and information. Within an established network, such activity scarcely deserves comment. It is more revealing to view promotional activity as an extension of the centre's constitutive power: of its ability to create networks. Thus, promotional activity involves network building and the development of a shared appreciative system. The conflict between the Treasury and DoE at the centre on whether the Community Land Act should be 'planning-led' (i.e. the organization of land by local authorities should be consistent with their development plans) or 'finance-led' (i.e. the scheme should be self-financing in the short term) led to twists and turns of policy which handicapped regional offices of the DoE in its efforts to build shared understandings on the operation of the policy (Barrett, 1981). In this case, there was no coherent network, and for this and other reasons the scheme was never effectively implemented, judging by the centre's stated intentions.

Over and beyond network building, intermediate institutions can initiate action by members of the network. Preston (1984) shows that the regional offices of the DoE have encouraged applications for European Regional Development Fund loans and have provided not simply information and advice but also expertise in the preparation of applications. Young (1982, p. 81) notes similar initiatives in the preparation of General Improvement Area (GIA) schemes and for applications for Derelict Land Grants.

There is a difficult line to be drawn between these examples of participation in local authority initiatives and directly influencing the decision-making process of local authorities (or other network members). Young (1982, pp. 83–8) argues, however, that the regional DoE has had such direct influence in, for example, the preparation of Structure Plans. His contention is borne out by Bridges and Vielba (1976, p. 80), who demonstrate the extensive involvement of the DoE in the Staffordshire Structure Plan Inquiry; the inquiry panel was appointed by the DoE and included local DoE officials; the DoE selected the issues to be examined and the participants at the examination; it provided the pre-examination briefing and it directly intervened in the public proceedings. Moreover, the regional DoE was intermittently but frequently consulted whilst the plan was being prepared and had considerable opportunity to influence its contents. Similarly, Leach *et al.* (1983, p. 34) concluded that the regional offices of the DTp and DoE had considerable influence on the projects submitted for approval in the ICPPs of local authorities and that 'close and positive working relationships' existed for HIPs and TPPs also. Hogwood (1982a, p. 41) notes that the DoI encourages its regional offices to play a promotional role. They also 'steer' industry within and between regions; act as 'brokers' pointing firms towards the best source of assistance; and process applications with discretion to make a grant up to £2m under the Industry Act 1972, s. 7. Such activities clearly amount to promotion and initiation, although it is not clear that they add up to direct influence on a firm's decision-making.

3.4.1(iii) AREAL INTERESTS

Lobbying refers to the activities of intermediate institutions on behalf of network members within 'their' region. If the interests discussed above betray a centralist perspective – they were in the interests of the centre – the lobbying role indicates that these organizations can 'go native' or be 'captured' by interests within their area. The point has been well made by Young (1982, p. 89): 'The regional office . . . plays a classic middleman role having loyalties to the centre while developing loyalties to the region.' He also cites the examples of DoE and DoI antipathy frustrating the lobbying activities of districts in the western part of West Yorkshire County Council whilst North-East Lancashire benefited greatly from regional office support in Manchester. Consequently, a highly distinctive role of intermediate institutions is that of fighting the centre on behalf of network members. However, it must be remembered that it is *a* role, not *the* role: 'The regional offices are . . . in an ambivalent position. They represent the region's interests to the centre, but try to retain a sense of balance and objectivity when arguing Marsham Street's views and ministers' arguments in the region' (Young, 1982, p. 90).

The contrast with the territorial ministries is particularly sharp at this point. They share a common interest in execution, integration, monitoring and intervention, but the ministries have an explicit and legitimated interest in articulating territorial interests. Intermediate institutions' territorial interest can be described only as incipient: expressed in the breach not the observance of their legitimated managerial and service interests. They are territorial organizations of the centre, not channels for expressing territorial interests in the centre; that is, they remain functional organizations at root. There is no Secretary of State for England to represent territorial interests in Cabinet/interdepartmental discussions. Omitting embellishment and detail for the moment, the overly harsh conclusion is that the 'regional' level of 'government' in England has neither a constituency nor a political head.

In virtually all respects, the interests of intermediate institutions reflect this position as agents of central departments. They are part of a bureaucratic hierarchy, following goals and tasks determined at the centre; their activities are an extension of the responsibilities of their head office. Similarly, the extent of their integrative and interventionist roles is limited to the turf of head office; where the centre leads, the region intervenes. The rivalry between central departments is mirrored sub-centrally in the problems of the DoE in formally co-ordinating the centre's regional presence. There is no direct parallel to the guardianship role of the Treasury, or even of the DoE, although the possibility that, inexorably, the logic of rate capping will drag the regional DoE into the 'vetting' of local budgets cannot be dismissed.

3.4.2   The Resources of Intermediate Institutions

Strictly speaking, the intermediate level is an informational and organizational resource of the centre. The resources controlled by intermediate institutions in their relations with either the centre or other units of SCG are limited. None the less, some resources can be identified. First, some intermediate institutions have discretion in the allocation of financial resources. The Regional Development Boards of the Agricultural Development and Advisory Service (MAFF) have virement powers, i.e. can transfer funds between those of its activities funded by block grant (Keating and Rhodes, 1982, p. 64). The regional offices of the DoI also have financial discretion. The Industry Act 1972 created two types of regions for the DoI: those with 'assisted areas' within their region and those with none. Regional Development Grants are payable to firms in the former regions. Within national guidelines, the regional offices can approve grants up to £2m and appraise projects up to £10m. Moreover, there is no fixed budget for such assistance, and no application has been rejected because of shortage of funds (Hogwood, 1982a, pp. 39–41).

The regional offices of the DoE/DTp have some control over financial resources sought by local authorities through the HIPs and TPP planning systems. Thus, the DTp has substantial discretion in financing trunk road improvements up to £1¼m, and its recommendations on Transport Supplementary Grant (TSG) are influential in head office decision-making. Rather exceptionally, the DoE/DTp have some political resources in the sense that they have a distinct constituency: the local authorities. In no sense of the word do they 'represent' local authorities, nor do they have any political muscle comparable to the territorial ministers, but their relatively close contact with local authorities enables the regional office to speak with a degree of authority on the needs and problems of their area. Allied to the information acquired formally through the PPSs and informally through visits and other forms of personal contact, the regional DoEs can be seen as a 'voice at court' rather than mere agents of head office. Young (1982, p. 91) reports that the regulations governing the implementation of the Community Land Act were relaxed 'more swiftly' because of feedback from the regional offices on the problems experienced by local authorities. As noted earlier, this 'eyes and ears' role is central to the existence of the regional offices, and all of them, not just the DoE, play it. If the DoE's regional offices seem to have more clout, the point should not be exaggerated. Not only do individual regional offices vary in seeking to extend the opportunities for 'independent' action but they also remain in a hierarchical relationship to the centre.

3.4.3 The Relationships of Intermediate Institutions

Page (1985, pp. 3–4) distinguishes between 'street-level discretion' or the capacity to interpret the rules and guidelines issued by head office and 'institutional discretion' or the capacity to determine whether a service should be provided, to whom, how and at what level. 'Street-level discretion' is universal in all formal organizations (Hill, 1972, ch. 4; Lipsky, 1978) and exists for intermediate institutions in executing their multifarious tasks. 'Institutional discretion' is far more limited and, in so far as it exists, is tightly constrained. Intermediate institutions are one of the centre's instruments of control and have no instruments in their own right, only such discretion in the operation of the instruments as head office chooses to grant. From this baseline, however, four important caveats can be entered.

First, intermediate institutions are embedded in a set of linkages between centre and locality. No account of intermediate institutions can claim to be accurate if it focuses on bureaucratic linkages to the exclusion of all others.

Second, to the extent that they have a distinct constituency, intermediate institutions can speak for their area (and its SCG) and, by lobbying, help to shape the rules and guidelines which (ostensibly) limit them to the exercise of 'street-level discretion'. There is considerable variation between both departments and areas in this respect. The scope for lobbying hinges on such factors as the personal qualities of regional civil servants, the extent of 'corridor politics' or informal contact, a shared appreciation of the 'legacy of decline' within a region and the degree of control exercised by headquarters (Young, 1982, pp. 93–4).

Third, their reticulist activity may not have a great effect on whether or not a service is provided, to whom and at what level but it is an important influence on how a service is delivered. Network integration and maintenance may seem an uninspiring activity, but its importance to the workings of disaggregated policy systems should not be underestimated.

Fourth, some 'regional' offices have been granted substantial discretion in the execution of specific tasks. Allied to lobbying and reticulist activities, they can occupy, therefore, a grey area between administrative deconcentration and decentralization. The label 'intermediate' is fitting in two senses. Not only are the regional offices in between central and local government, they are also neither bureaucratic agents nor decentralized bodies.

Finally, the discretion of intermediate institutions has varied over time. Hogwood (1982a, p. 59) argues that 'the trend has been towards greater (though still relatively limited) discretion to deconcentrated units' in England. For example, the regional offices of the DoE enjoyed a high degree of discretion in the late 1960s, and early 1970s when it had a distinct planning function. It is, however, the only major example of such discretion over a substantial period of time. Moreover, just as the centre's relationships with the SCG have shifted over time, so the regional offices of the DoE have moved from agency to an intermediate role and back to agency again under the post-1979 Conservative governments. The heyday of the 'active' regional office coincided with the period of institutional modernization, and the attempt to create a strong regional presence was as abortive as the hope of economic regeneration through reform of the machinery of government was naïve.

Table 3.3 *Variations in the Regional Boundaries of Non-Departmental Organizations*

	Geographical coverages	Number of unit regions in England	Number of standard regions inc. minor modifications
Units of bodies listed in 'Civil Service Year Book'.			
Manpower Services Commission:			
Regional Manpower Services Directors[a]	GB	7	4
Employment Services Division	GB	15	2
Training Services Division	GB	7	4
Special Programmes Division	GB	7	4
Advisory, Conciliation and Arbitration Service	GB	7	4
Health and Safety Executive	GB	18	0
Price Commission	UK	10	2
Countryside Commission	E & W	9	6
Nature Conservancy Council	GB	8	0
Sports Council	E	9	6
Forestry Commission	GB	5	0
Units of selected other public bodies			
Tourist Board Regions	E	12	3
Post Office: Postal Regions	UK	8	0
Post Office: Telecommunications Regions	E & W	9	1
Regional Water Authorities	E & W	9	1
Housing Corporation Regions	GB	8	3
British Rail Regions	E & W	4	0
National Bus Company Regions	E & W	3	0
Electricity Boards	E & W	11	0
Gas Regions	GB	10	0
BBC Regions	UK	9	1
IBA Regions	UK	10	0
Regional Health Authorities	E	14	3

Note:
[a] Unit represented on the Regional Planning Boards.
Source: Hogwood and Lindley, 1982, p. 49.

3.4.4 Summary

The territorial organization of central departments forms a complex mosaic and is as heterogeneous within a department as it is between departments. At heart, intermediate institutions are an expression of the dominance of functional politics in British government, serving the managerial and service-implementation interests of their Whitehall headquarters. They are a resource of the centre, embedded in multiple linkages, but with some limited resources of their own which enable them to mediate between centre and locality. The degree of discretion varies within and between departments over time, but they warrant the label 'intermediate institutions' because they are neither bureaucratic agents nor decentralized bodies. Like Topsy 'they growed' and epitomize not the principled homogeneity of a centralized, unitary state but the *ad hoc* heterogeneity of the differentiated advanced industrial society.

3.5 Non-Departmental Public Bodies

By design non-departmental public bodies are at arm's length from central political institutions. In addition, they have their own regional level organization. Accordingly, this section considers relationships both within the centre and within a non-departmental organization between headquarters and the regional organizations. More so than with any other organizational type, this section explores virgin territory, although as for all other types of SCG it focuses on interests, resources and relationships. However, it is not possible to present a comprehensive review of all species of non-departmental bodies.

Table 3.3 illustrates the scale of the exercise. This highly selective list of non-departmental public bodies shows the range of organizations involved and their heterogeneous sub-central structures, again within a single organization (for example, the MSC) as well as across all organizations. Moreover, the listing excludes territorially specific non-departmental public bodies. Scotland, Wales and Northern Ireland also have a large number of non-departmental public bodies. Some selectivity is unavoidable, therefore. This section focuses on the nationalized industries and the NHS. When possible (and where relevant) it also includes material on other bodies.

3.5.1 The Interests of Non-Departmental Public Bodies

The interests of non-departmental public bodies are as heterogeneous as their origins are diverse (Hood, 1978). At its simplest, it is possible to identify the following interests: economic, managerial, service, areal and professional. They will be considered *seriatim*.

3.5.1(i) ECONOMIC INTERESTS

Economic interests are an obvious category for all public trading bodies but one which requires unpacking. The phrase refers to commercial viability or the financial obligations laid upon, for example, the nationalized industries by the centre, whether expressed as breaking even or a rate of return. Such interests foster competition between industries as in the case of the energy industries wherein electricity, gas and coal all attempt to increase their market share. In addition, the industries have to demonstrate that they are efficient, and the recurrent concern with marginal cost pricing, X-efficiency and value for money are all specific manifestations of their economic interests.

Of course, such interests are not the sole preserve of nationalized industries. They are ever-present for all public sector trading bodies and can be found in such diverse bodies as the BBC, the Forestry Commission and the RWAs. Moreover, many non-departmental public bodies have links with the private sector although they are not trading bodies. Examples include the Agrément Board, which assesses new products used in the construction industry, and the National Research and Development Corporation, but any comprehensive listing would be of inordinate length.

There is a second meaning to the phrase 'economic interests' which is relevant in this context; it can refer to the private sector. Thus private sector economic interests are co-opted on to non-departmental public bodies, e.g. the HSC, MSC and NEDO. In addition, private sector economic interests have key roles within particular agencies, as in the case of the AEA. Similarly, the Land Drainage Committees of the RWAs are composed of the nominees of the minister and county councils, and their Local Committees are dominated by farmers and landowners (Parker and Penning-Rowsell, 1980, pp. 205–6). Although the reorganization of 1973 purported to create organizations which encompassed the complete water cycle, land drainage remained a 'structural anomaly', a concession to agricultural interests (Jordan, Richardson and Kimber, 1977, p. 331). Parker and Penning-Rowsell (1980, p. 242) conclude that such sectional interests 'have a dominant influence on water planning', although the evidence on the influence of industry is 'skimpy' and is not reflected in the structure and organization of the RWAs (Saunders, 1983, p. 45).

3.5.1(ii) MANAGERIAL INTERESTS

Managerial interests refer, as in the case of intermediate institutions, to the deconcentration of tasks by central departments (and by the headquarters of non-departmental public bodies) with the concomitant requirement to administer those tasks effectively. Whatever the centre's reason for hiving off the activity – be it to promote efficiency, to conceal government growth, or to govern by stealth – non-departmental public bodies have to provide an executive, regulatory, or advisory service within some financial constraint, co-ordinate their own activities and liaise with other organizations. And reticulist activity is a prominent component of managerial interests. Not only do they have their own sub-central structure to regulate but they also have to expend considerable time and attention on other inter-organizational linkages. (See Friend, Power and Yewlett, 1974; also articles in the occasional journal *Linkage*.) For example, Cousins (1982, pp. 156–8) illustrates the range of bodies linked to both the Greater London Council and the London Borough of Bromley, commenting on the complexity and confusion of accountability thereby engendered. In a similar vein, Hood (1982a, pp. 59–61) suggests that the focus of analysis needs to switch from bilateral relationships to organization sets or 'congeries of quasi-independent agencies'. Multiplex, multilateral relationships are an ever-present feature of the management of non-departmental public bodies (for further examples see the case studies of individual organizations in Hague, Mackenzie and Barker, 1975 and Barker, 1982a, especially the discussions of accountability). And in seeking to manage their sets or congeries, many non-departmental public bodies confront the problem of an indeterminate domain. They operate in the interstices of pre-existing jurisdictions and they seek to establish 'domain consensus': that is, agreement amongst the affected organizations that each other's goals, in terms of services provided and population served, are legitimate (Thompson, 1967, pp. 27–98; Rhodes, 1981a, pp. 45–6). For example, economic policy provides many examples of jurisdictional invasions and disputes amongst non-departmental public bodies. Thus, Smith (1975, p. 59) describes the conflicts between the Economic Development Councils, Industrial Training Boards, Industrial Reorganization Corporation, REPCs, National Board for Prices and Income, Monopolies Commission and Commission on Industrial Relations in the rush to become 'the custodian of the nation's economic conscience'.

3.5.1(iii) SERVICE INTERESTS

Service interests are common to all functionally based organizations within British government, and non-departmental public bodies are no exception. In contrast to central departments, non-departmental public bodies are not concerned to protect their notional share of local authority expenditure. They are, to employ the earlier category, rivals to local authorities. But they are equally concerned to maintain (and increase) their allocation of resources and their jurisdictions or domains. Thus, the Nationalized Industries Chairmen's Group lobbies the Treasury about its EFLs, and the health policy community competes for its share of public expenditure within the DHSS and in the broader expenditure policy community.

The functions of non-departmental public bodies are enormously varied. Although manifestly unhappy with the analysis, Bowen (1978, pp. 32–3) reports that 48 bodies in his survey were industrial, 54 economic and financial, 28 agricultural, 91 educational and 59 social welfare bodies. Exact numbers probably count for little; the important point is the vast range of activities (see also Pliatzky Report, 1980, pt II, which classifies the bodies by their sponsoring functional/territorial department).

Inevitably, there are conflicts of interests within non-departmental bodies, and this is very evident in the case of the nationalized industries. Their economic and service interests are not coterminous because of the industries' social obligations. Thus, they provide services which are unremunerative – e.g. electricity to rural areas, air services to the Scottish Highlands and Islands. The Select Committee on Nationalized Industries (1968a, p. 153) argued that

> Ministers, as the custodians of social and public interests should be responsible for deciding the nature and extent of the industries' social obligations, and that the industries should be primarily guided by commercial considerations except in so far as they are required by Ministers to fulfil or have regard to social obligations ... Boards should usually receive some form of financial compensation for social obligations they undertake.

If compensation has been paid, no clear demarcation of social and economic responsibilities has occurred.

Recent years have also seen a major challenge to the domain of non-departmental public bodies over and beyond that inherent to a differentiated, disaggregated polity. Privatization and 'hunting the quango' were both policies designed not simply to alter and challenge but also to abolish their jurisdictions (see section 3.2.4(i), pages 129–31, above). Consequently, protecting service interests is no longer confined to the competition for resources but extends to the very existence of the service/organization.

3.5.1(iv)   AREAL INTERESTS

Areal interests exist in two forms for non-departmental public bodies: the territorially specific bodies in Scotland, Wales and Northern Ireland, and the 'regional' structures of particular bodies.

The nether world of non-departmental public bodies in Scotland, Wales and Northern Ireland is heavily populated. Of all central departments, the Scottish Office has the largest number of executive fringe bodies, with eighty-four (Pliatzky Report, 1980, p. 5). Hogwood (1982b, p. 75) estimates that there are 16 nationalized industries, 45 quasi-judicial bodies, 37 educational bodies, 7 marketing boards and 556 other governmental bodies in Scotland. All these bodies can be said to have an areal interest in that they are concerned with either territorially specific problems or territorially specific aspects of a UK-wide problem. The Highlands and Islands Development Board is an example of the former, and the Scottish Consumer Council and the Scottish region of the MSC of the latter. Hogwood (1979a, pp. 22 and 24) estimates that a third of all fringe bodies in Scotland are exclusively Scottish. Health is also a Scottish Office responsibility, and the service is provided through fifteen area boards, ten of which decentralize to districts.

The Welsh Office is a relative newcomer, and the number of

Table 3.4 *The Allocation of Functions in Northern Ireland: by Organizational Type*

	Centralized boards	Area boards	Government departments	District councils
Health services		*		
Personal social services		*		
Education		*		
Housing	*			
Town and country planning			*	
Libraries		*		
Roads			*	
Water and sewerage			*	
Police	*			
Vehicle registration and licensing			*	
Fire services	*			
Registration of births, marriages and deaths				*
Electricity	*			
Gas				*
Recreational facilities				*
Car-parks			*	
Cleaning and sanitation				*
Markets and abattoirs				*

Source: Birrell and Murie, 1980, p. 174.

non-departmental public bodies in Wales is less than in Scotland, comprising sixteen executive and twelve advisory bodies plus three tribunal systems. The list of bodies has marked similarities with Scotland, including the Welsh Development Agency, the Sports Council for Wales and the National Library for Wales, although there are the obvious differences in the organization of, for example, water, which is a non-departmental function in Wales and a local government function in Scotland.

As ever, the position in Northern Ireland is more complex. Excluding the nationalized industries and the NHS, there were 59 executive, 58 advisory and 15 tribunals in the province. Moreover, the executive bodies are responsible for the major local government services (see Table 3.4).

Thus, housing is governed by the Northern Ireland Housing Executive comprised of six ministerial appointments and three nominees from the Housing Council. This council comprises one representative from each district council and it advises the Executive. For administrative purposes, the executive has divided the province into three regions, ten areas and thirty-nine districts (Birrell and Murie, 1980, p. 172).

For health and social services there are four area boards, appointed by the minister, with 30 per cent of the nominees coming from the district councils, 30 per cent from the professions and the remainder from business, trade unions, the universities and voluntary organizations. For administrative purposes there are seventeen districts with boundaries coterminous with (one or more) local authority areas. There are five education and library area boards. Other local authority services, e.g. planning, were allocated to the DoE(NI). This structure was a response to sectarian conflict and, in particular, discrimination in the distribution of public services. Shaped by territorial problems, the operation of this structure continues to reflect the local political environment (see page 78, below).

The organization of the nationalized industries varies between the three peripheral nations. In Scotland, electricity is under the Scottish Office. The North of Scotland Hydro-Electric Board and the South of Scotland Electricity Board have an autonomous pricing policy. Gas and coal are the responsibility of the UK ministry, although there is some decentralization. The pattern for transport is particularly variegated, with British Rail sponsored by the DTp, whereas road transport is a Scottish Office responsibility. Broadly speaking, the position in Wales is roughly equivalent to that in Scotland with the major exception that the Welsh Office has no responsibility for the energy industries.

In Northern Ireland the various utilities are *not* part of the mainland's nationalized industries. As early as 1935 road transport and the railways were nationalized, and up to 1964 the Ulster Transport Authority had a monopoly of all public transport. Water and gas were administered by local authorities (and commonly by joint local authority boards) before the reorganization of 1972, and electricity was the responsibility of the Electricity Board of Northern Ireland, the Joint Electricity Council, the Belfast Corporation Electricity Department and the Londonderry Commission Electricity Department. The parallels with English local government in the interwar period is striking. Since 1972 either central departments or the centralized *ad hoc* board have become the preferred forms for the utilities: in part because they provide 'a method of taking contentious areas of responsibility . . . out of local political influence and control' (Birrell and Murie, 1980, p. 158). Thus, electricity is now centralized in the Electricity Board of Northern Ireland, whilst roads and water are the responsibility of the DoE(NI). Gas remains, however, a local government function, primarily because the province is not linked to the North Sea gas distribution grid, and this fuel is not widely used.

As Table 3.3 indicates, the deconcentrated structures of nondepartmental public bodies are highly varied. The simple conclusion to be drawn from this table is that the structures exist for functional reasons: for administrative convenience and not in response to areal interests. However, once created, they become a point of access to, and a vehicle for, such interests (see pages 176–7, below).

3.5.1(v) PROFESSIONAL INTERESTS

Professional interests refer to those groups of employees who monopolize skills and expertise to control the supply of labour – exclusionary closure through 'credentialism' (Parkin, 1979; and see Chapter 2, section 2.5.1(v)). In the case of the so-called semi-professions, their interests are advanced by a combination of credentialism and strikes and the other methods associated with trade unions: dual closure. As Dunleavy (1982b) argues, professionalization and the growth of non-departmental public bodies have advanced hand in hand, in part because these bodies are insulated from public and political scrutiny and provide few effective checks to professional influence. Consequently, a major set of interests articulated in and through non-departmental public bodies belong to professional groups. Their influence is particularly marked in the RWAs and the NHS. It is sufficient to note the importance of these interests here, given the extensive discussion below.

3.5.2 *The Resources of Non-Departmental Public Bodies*

In his analysis of Scottish fringe bodies, Hogwood (1979a, pp. 30–3, and 1982b, pp. 81–6) presents virtually the only analysis to date of the resources of non-departmental public bodies, and it forms the basis of this section.

Underpinning the activities of all non-departmental public bodies is the authority vested in them commonly by statute but also by administrative act (Design Council), Treasury minute (National Gallery), royal charters (BBC, British Council), royal warrant (standing commissions), Companies Act registration (Health Education Council, National Consumer Council) and charitable trust registration (Commonwealth Institute). However acquired, such legal authority sets the parameters to the bodies' activities, although, as in the case of the nationalized industries, the vesting instrument may be vague on the powers of the respective parties. Most distinctive when compared to local authorities, the bodies are uni-functional. Each and every local authority performs a range of disparate functions. No matter how complex their activities, non-departmental public bodies do not have an equivalent range; they are specialized instruments of government.

The financial resources of non-departmental public bodies are equally varied (see section 3.2.4(i), pages, 120–31, above); but, with with the exception of the trading bodies, they are dependent on the centre. However, the result is not the heavy hand of central control because of differences in the centre's ability to control the distribution of resources between both particular activities and areas. For example, the DHSS has experienced considerable difficulty in redistributing expenditure from acute medicine to the 'Cinderella services' and between regions (see Chapter 4, section 4.4).

The political resources of non-departmental public bodies are limited; they are non-elected bodies with no distinct constituency. This relative weakness can be offset to a degree by the nature of the appointments to governing boards and committees. The lower the proportion of the board appointed by ministers, the greater the number of ministerial nominations from other organizations (e.g. local government), and the greater the extent to which members represent affected interests then the greater the constraints on ministerial influence. In a similar vein, full-time tenured appointments can be expected to foster independence to a greater degree than part-time, *ad hoc* appointments. Political resources can also be enhanced by overlapping membership with other organizations, past memberships of other offices (with access to their networks of political contacts) and, of course, the political and negotiating skills of chairmen and board members. Finally, as in the case of local authorities, non-departmental public bodies have formed national associations to present their views. Examples of such associations include the RHA chairmen, the National Association of Health Authorities (NAHA), the Association of Community Health Councils, the Nationalized Industries Chairmen's Group (NICG) and the Water Authorities' Association. With the exception of these associations, the list of *potential* political resources illustrates above all else the relative weakness of non-departmental public bodies: they compensate for a lack of such resources, whereas, for central departments and local authorities, they are a supplement – even a luxury – to be called upon if necessary.

Non-departmental public bodies have, for the most part, a restricted grant of authority, no independent source of finance and a limited arsenal of political resources. They do have, however, organizational and informational resources aplenty. In what should by now be seen as classic fashion, the non-executant style of British government vests hands-on controls in sub-central organizations. Thus, non-departmental public bodies implement central policy, adjusting it to local circumstances, own and manage the buildings and equipment, employ the staff and monopolize data on the operation of their services. They can decide the balance of operating activities, the timing and sequencing of activities and, on many occasions, the relative priority of various central policies. The ostensibly mundane activity of implementation can decisively shape policy. Obviously, some non-departmental public bodies have relatively few staff, have been established recently and depend themselves upon other organizations to perform the relevant activities. Their capacity to shape policy is consequently more

Table 3.5   *The Size of Selected Non-Departmental Public Bodies*

		Expenditure in 1978–9 (£m)	Number of employees 1978–9 ('000s)
Regional Water Authorities (England and Wales) (10)	Department of the Environment and Welsh Office[b]	1,721[a]	70.4
New Town Development Corporations (England and Wales) (17)		527	9.2
Housing Corporation		405	0.6
Manpower Services Commission	Department of Employment	548[c]	26.3
Industrial Training Boards (24)		201	4.4
Health and Safety Commission and Executive		46	4.3
Remploy Ltd		52	10.6
Research Councils (5)	Department of Education and Science	342	11.6
National Enterprise Board	Department of Industry	206	0.1
English Industrial Estates Corporation		29	0.3
National Research Development Corporation		28	0.2
Scottish New Town Development Corporations (5)	Scottish Office	107	2.9
Scottish Development Agency		65	0.7
Scottish Special Housing Association		86	3.1
Atomic Energy Authority	Department of Energy	213	13.5
Civil Aviation Authority	Department of Trade	109	7.5
British Council	Foreign and Commonwealth Office	91	4.5
Commonwealth Development Corporation		56[d]	0.4
Arts Council	Office of Arts and Libraries	50	0.4
Welsh Development Agency	Welsh Office	49	0.5

Nationalized industries

	Turnover (£m)	
British Aerospace	894	70.2
British Airports Authority	162	7.3
British Airways Board	1,640	57.7
British Gas Corporation	2,972	102.9
British National Oil Corporation	432	1.0
British Railways Board	1,979	182.2
British Shipbuilders	810	84.0
British Transport Docks Board	120	11.6

British Steel Corporation	3,288	186.0
British Waterways Board	12	3.4
Electricity Council and Boards	5,116	159.8
National Bus Company	437	64.3
National Coal Board	271	234.9
National Freight Corporation	394	36.9
North of Scotland Hydro-Electric Board	173	4.1
Post Office	4,619	411.0
Scottish Transport Group	106	13.8
South of Scotland Electricity Board	443	13.7
Total	23,868	1,644.8

Notes:
[a] Includes National Water Council.
[b] The Scottish Office are also concerned with Housing Corporation expenditure in Scotland.
[c] The MSC figure excludes grants of £93 million from the MSC to the Industrial Training Board.
[d] Calendar Year 1978.
Source: Pliatzky Report 1980, pp. 14 and 182, and appropriate departmental entries.

limited than for the large, well-established body. Table 3.5 gives the total staff and expenditure for the 'top twenty' non-departmental bodies and major nationalized industries, thereby illustrating their potential influence on policy.

Such simple indicators obscure one key characteristic of the informational and organizational resources of non-departmental public bodies: the influence of professions. Organizational specialization and insulation from political control provide a culture for their breeding, as evidenced by their 'success' in the water industry and the NHS. The capacity of non-departmental public bodies to shape policy is rooted in their command of organizational and informational resources and in the power of the professions. To a significant degree they epitomize the professionalized policy system of the differentiated polity.

3.5.3 The Relationships of Non-Departmental Public Bodies

The discussion of the various interests of non-departmental public bodies implies that they will be embedded in a complex of relationships. In brief, bodies with economic interests have distinctive relationships with, and are influenced in many ways by, the private sector; managerial interests generate extensive reticulist activity between organizations and a reliance on rational planning techniques for resolving conflicts within and between non-departmental public bodies; service interests have led to bureaucratized, deconcentrated structures within non-departmental public bodies which permit only 'street-level discretion'; areal interests have generated variegated structures, a confusion of functional and geographic administration, conflicts over domain and a degree of responsiveness to particular territorial needs, although in England the regional structures of the majority of non-departmental public bodies have limited power bases and few regional interests to represent; and, finally, they are a locus of professional interests which exercise a determinant influence on policy. Quite clearly, there is no uniformity, and any one non-departmental public body can have multiplex relationships. In addition, the discussion of the centre's instruments of control described the varied pattern of formal relationships (see sections 3.2.4(i), pages 120–31, and 3.2.4(ii), pages, 136–40). This section simply provides a brief categorization of the varieties of relationship.

Perhaps the most significant aspect of non-departmental public bodies with economic interests is their relationship with the private sector. At its simplest the relationship can be competitive, as between rail freight and road haulage or between public and private bus companies, especially since the deregulation of routes. However, the influence of private economic interests is more pervasive than competition for customers. As Miliband (1973, p. 54) argues, nationalization did not remove an important area of economic activity from private sector influence:

> the exceedingly conventional, bureaucratic and 'business-like' manner in which the government envisaged the administration of the nationalized industries, combined with its appointment of men drawn from large-scale enterprises to their boards, helped to ensure that the enlarged 'public sector', far from proving in any sense an embarrassment – let alone a threat – to the private sector, would in fact become a useful adjunct to it.
>
> (Miliband, 1973, p. 98)

All notions of joint control by trade unions and government (see Tivey, 1978, ch. 4) were jettisoned for ministerial control. From today's vantage-point it is difficult to view or imbue nationalized industries with the passion or revolutionary potential they once bore. For good or ill, they are industries to be run in as 'business-like' a manner as possible: an adjunct to the private sector. Against this context, there is an air of inevitability about the discussion of commercial viability and even privatization.

Following Garner (1985, p. 10), the balance of relationships between government and the industries from 1945 to 1982 can be characterized as a shift from *devolution* (the Morrisonian concept of wide autonomy for the industries with limited political accountability) through *separation* (the Herbert Committee's notion of commercial freedom for the industries and ministerial responsibility for public policy) to *collaboration* (the NEDO proposals for joint corporate/ strategic planning). Subsequent years could be described as *divestment* (the government shedding both commercial and policy responsibility), but it would be more accurate to talk of *re-regulation* (the search for means of preserving the public interest for privatized services). And the common thread running through all these changes in the relationship is the inability of the centre to establish an enduring, or even an effective, framework of accountability. As Johnson (1978, p. 133) concludes, 'In theory it ought to have been possible to establish a stable division of responsibilities, but in practice this has not happened!'

As noted earlier, the influence of the private sector can be enhanced by the role of professions, as in the case of scientists in the nuclear industry or construction engineers and architects in public housing (see Chapter 2, sections 2.5.1(iv) and 2.5.2(i)). They bridge the gap between the public and private sectors create unified policy systems and provide yet another avenue of influence for private industry (Dunleavy, 1982b, p. 205).

All such links with the private sector imbue policy networks with distinct characteristics (see Chapter 4, section 4.6) and give rise to such concerns as 'privata opulentia et publica egestas', to quote Tawney ([1931] 1964, p. 116), rather than Galbraith's (1962, p. 211) oft-cited aphorism of 'private opulence and public squalor'.

The effect of managerial interests on relationships was very clear in the several reorganizations of the 1970s. As Jordan, Richardson and Kimber (1977, p. 318) note, the reorganization of water in 1973 was management-oriented, implying 'a belief in planning, a preference for efficiency rather than participation: it presents a system designed to meet technical rather than political criteria'. This orientation was reinforced by the Ogden Report (1973), which 'clearly reflected a bias towards officers' (Gray, 1982, p. 146) in its advocacy of corporate planning. In a similar vein, Klein (1983) calls his chapter on the reorganization of the NHS 'the politics of technocratic change', and the most casual perusal of the Grey Book (DHSS, 1972) on the new management arrangements reveals a touching faith in the capacity of rational planning and decision-making to resolve conflicts between the centre and RHAs and between the different interests in the NHS.

Reforms can exist on paper only, but the importance of managerial interests has, if anything, increased with the intensified resource squeeze. Thus, Saunders (1984, p. 6) suggests that 'The key post in the management team today is less likely to be the Chief Engineer than the Director of Finance, and the first question asked today about any proposed scheme is not whether it is needed (still less how it can be constructed) but whether it can be afforded.' In a similar vein,, relations with the centre have become dominated by financial considerations. Thus Saunders (1984, p. 9) concludes that RWAs determine their own priorities within tight financial constraints laid down by central government. Autonomy on priorities is conceded, whereas financial management is stipulated.

For the nationalized industries, managerial and financial

considerations dominate relations between headquarters and regions/ areas. Indeed, Pryke (1981, p. 22) ignores all the separate administrative arrangements for electricity production and supply and refers to the British Electricity Boards 'as if they were a single organization'. In 1973 the Gas Council and twelve area boards were replaced by the British Gas Corporation. Previously the minister/Treasury negotiated, for example, the investment programme for each board. Now, as has always been the case for the NCB, there is one account and one investment programme (Select Committee on Nationalized Industries, 1968b, pp. 262–4 and 347–8). However, some qualifications are necessary for the industries in the peripheral nations (see pages 177–8, below).

It was noted earlier that reticulist activity was prominent in the behaviour of non-departmental public bodies. The search for domain consensus, or the indeterminacy in their jurisdictions, is the motivational well-spring of much of their reticulist activity and it also reflects the pervasive effect of differentiation in the politics of advanced industrial societies; it is an inevitable product of bureaucratization. Growth through elaboration is a response to turbulent environments or the proliferation of policy problems and their lack of fit with existing policy systems. This logic of adaptation through differentiation does not lead inevitably to non-departmental forms of organization, although it minimizes the disruption to the 'plurality of social systems' (Burns, 1966) which would attend any internal reform of a central department or local authority. Ironically, 'crowding out' is a distinctive feature of British government, not in the economic sense, but as a description of network relationships in which policy spaces become congested and organizations compete for domain legitimacy.

As with central departments and intermediate institutions, deconcentration within non-departmental public bodies serves the interests of the centre. The following description of the regional structure of the MSC by Davies, Mason and Davies (1984, p. 49) applies with equal force to many non-departmental public bodies:

> The regional role . . . was autonomous in one sense only, they knew more about the market at regional level than anyone else, and the Centre gave them autonomy to glean that information, and to make responses on the basis of that information. However, the autonomy was severely constrained, and closely monitored by the Centre.

In short, the regions had 'street-level' but not 'institutional' discretion; they advised on and promoted central policies. Similarly, the divisions of RWAs 'are basically insignificant' (Saunders, 1984, p. 8). They are 'entirely subordinate' to the region and 'enjoy precious little autonomy', although they recommend schemes to the region, and, according to Parker and Penning-Rowsell (1980), p. 35), water authority planning is 'extremely "bottom-up" in character'. To an equal and probably greater degree than intermediate institutions, the regions/ areas of non-departmental public bodies remained in a hierarchic relationship with their headquarters.

The major exception to this conclusion is the NHS. Relationships within the NHS have been characterized by Elcock and Haywood (1980, p. 51) as 'the politics of the pork barrel', and they argue (p. 47) that

> accountability is not a hierarchical relationship between a superior and a subordinate but a multi-dimensional process in which super- iors attempt to instruct or guide subordinates, subordinates accept, evade or resist such attempts at instruction, and third parties become involved in supporting one side or the other, usually the subordinate. Accountability is upwards, downwards and outwards.

They then provide examples of the AHAs' strategies of resistance to regional attempts to redistribute resources (Elcock and Haywood, 1980, ch. 3; see also Haywood and Alaszewski, 1980). Following the reorganization of 1982, the power of the 'new' district authorities was, if anything, increased. They can develop their own policies and have discretion in the implementation of regional initiatives (Saunders, 1984, p. 35). Consequently, relationships within the NHS cannot be characterized as hierarchical or bureaucratic but as multilateral and negotiated (see Chapter 4, section 4.4).

The area organization of non-departmental public bodies does not exist solely for functional reasons. Kellas (1973, p. 59) sums up the overall picture as 'a confusion of functional and geographic admin- istration', and Rose (1982, p. 119) concludes that 'The only generali- zation is negative: there is no uniformity.' Quite clearly, functional considerations are dominant. *But* jurisdictions are adjusted in response to territorial pressures, areas/regions can articulate terri- torial interests, and within the peripheral nations the relationships between the non-departmental public bodies and their territorial ministry can reflect the push and pull of service and areal interets.

For the nationalized industries, commercial considerations may be ever-present irrespective of location, but their organization in the peripheral nations means that decisions can be obtained from the territorial ministry without referring back to Whitehall and that distinctive territorial needs can be taken into account in judging the industries' social obligations. For other non-departmental public bodies, territorial interests are of greater concern. For example, the Highlands and Islands Development Board (HIDB) argues for the interests of its particular geographic area but has to compete for resources with the service interests of both 'central' departments (i.e. the Scottish Economic Planning Department (SEPD)) and non-departmental public bodies (e.g. the Scottish Development Agency (SDA)). The HIDB's jurisdiction and policies have been redefined as a result of such conflicts. Thus, it has withdrawn from transport investment but it has a 'concordat' with the SDA whereby the HIDB looks after small businesses and the SDA and SEPD are responsibile for major projects (Keating and Midwinter, 1983, p. 39).

The clearest example of the effects of territorial interests on non-departmental bodies can be found in Northern Ireland. Thus, Birrell and Murie (1980, p. 217) argue that the Northern Ireland Housing Executive (NIHE) 'has been overwhelmed by the politico-religious influences on it'. Consequently, its new building programme has 'extended religious segregation'. And relations between the NIHE and the NIO are 'ambiguous'. The NIHE sees itself as a source of expertise, capable of developing policies; in short, it is a comprehensive housing agency. However, the DoE(NI) is responsible for approving its pro-gramme in a context where matters of detail can be politically sensitive. Consequently, the relationship is 'a negotiated one', and the per-manent secretary DoE(NI) has complained that he is 'at one remove' from the NIHE with corresponding control problems. The NIHE clearly 'has to take on board various conflicting pressure'. (This section is paraphrased from Connolly, 1983, pp. 117–37.) Functional politics may be all-pervasive in UK government but it is continually circums-cribed by territorial pressures: by the distinct political environments of territorial ministries and non-departmental public bodies.

The problems of generalization become particularly acute when examining the sub-central linkages *within* the organizational structure of an English non-departmental public body. If intermediate institu-tions can 'go native', their scope for lobbying is restricted by the absence of a clear constituency. This constraint is even more acute for the majority of non-departmental public bodies. Thus, Keating and Rhodes (1982, p. 60) conclude for the RWAs that 'In terms of constituency, their position is certainly confused' and for the MSC that 'the constituency is national' (p. 62). The 'regional' structures of non-departmental public bodies have limited power bases and little or no vested *regional* interests to represent. Intermediate institutions' links with local authorities provide some vestiges of legitimacy for a lobbying role. The sub-central units of non-departmental public bodies lack even this rudimentary vestment.

Last but by no means least, relationships within non-departmental public bodies are shaped, often decisively, by the degree of pro-fessionalization of the body and its policy area. For the water industry, Parker and Penning-Rowsell (1980, p. 48) argue that the water agencies, both central and sub-central, are 'dominated by engineers', who tend to be 'intensely technical', 'reluctant to involve others in problem solving' and have 'a strong allegiance to the established agency's goals'. It is important to note that these remarks are *not* confined to the RWAs. '[T]he professional staffs of national advisory agencies ... are certainly dominated by engineers and scientists' (p. 49), and national professional associations 'exert a strong influence on overall water policy' (p. 50); see also Jordan, Richardson and Kimber, 1977; Richardson, Jordan and Kimber 1978). The key central–local linkage is, therefore, a professional one, with water policy a prime example of technocratic control and of legitimacy rooted in expertise (see also Keating and Rhodes, 1981; Gray, 1982, p. 146; Saunders,1983, pp. 34–5).

In a similar vein, Elcock and Haywood (1980, p. 139) argue that RHAs are 'extensions of interests within the NHS rather than the representatives of central policy'. Where there is a conflict with the centre, the interests of powerful staff in the region prevail. And pre-eminent among such interests are the medical profession. Haywood and Alaszewski (1980, pp. 134–40) argue that medical practitioners have power in three senses: they are free from managerial control and have clinical autonomy; at the local level, they control the agenda of decision-making; and, more generally, the medical model of disease (i.e. as the treatment of clinically defined ill health) defines the purpose of the health service. Klein (1983, pp. 56–7) provides a remarkably similar analysis and, in addition, notes how the profession 'permeated the institutional decision-making machinery of the NHS'. However, he enters two important qualifications. First, the medical profession had a right of veto over policy but it did not necessarily get what it wanted in a positive sense. Second, the resource squeeze of the 1970s led other groups within the NHS to challenge medical control, prompted central efforts to limit resources and provoked splits within the profession (Klein, 1983, pp. 115–16). As Saunders (1984, p. 45) concludes, the medical profession remains 'very powerful' but it is not 'hegemonic': 'they can be and have been confronted and policies (e.g. the move to community care, the transfer of waiting-list patients to other districts for treatment, the introduction of a performance review system) have been introduced even against their resistance' (p. 46). Saunders's conclusion is drawn from a case study of an area authority, but few commentators would demur for either the regional or the national level (see, for example, Ham, 1985).

Professional influence is, therefore, the basis of autonomy for some non-departmental public bodies. Any analysis of the policy process must encompass relationships between professions and the centre and within the profession between the national associations and non-departmental public bodies.

3.5.4 Summary

Of all the units of SCG considered in this chapter, non-departmental public bodies come in most colours. Functional and geographical jurisdictions compound complexity and confusion, creating a veritable maze of bodies and relationships. The only permissible generalization does seem to be that there is no uniformity. However, it is possible to identify some recurrent interests among non-departmental bodies: namely, economic, managerial, service, areal and professional interests. Equally, it is clear that the capacity of non-departmental public bodies for independent action is rooted in their command of organizational and informational resources. Nor is the variation in relationships wholly random. First, in the peripheral nations, the sub-central structures of non-departmental public bodies are a means of adapting functional policies to territorial interests and providing a point of access for such interests. Second, non-departmental public bodies bridge the gap between public and private sectors by, for example, incorporating the latter to the machinery of government. Their economic interests are distinctive if not unique in SCG. Third, they are a locus for professional influence. The relative weakness of political and public controls, coupled with the specialized nature of the policy area, provides a context which fosters the development of professionalism. For all their variety, therefore, it is possible to generalize about non-departmental public bodies. They provide a nigh perfect example of government growth by elaboration: of bureaucratic differentiation in the advanced industrial polity.

3.6   Local Government

By this point, one of the major themes of this book should be transparently obvious: that the SCG of Britian is inordinately complex. And yet it is only now that the major type of sub-central unit of government enters into the account. If the discretion available to other units can, at times, seem considerable, the degree of discretion (and capacity for resistance) of the only directly elected territorial institution in the UK has frequently proved a major obstacle for a centre determined on local compliance with central objectives. Nor should the theme of this section hold any surprises; there is no UK local government system, but several distinct systems. The structure of local government has changed markedly in the postwar period, most notably with the reorganizations of the 1970s. There are also the differences between the systems in the constituent nations of the UK. In England, there is the additional complication of different systems for the conurbations. These areas were not only treated differently in the reorganization of 1974 but they were reformed yet again in 1985 with the abolition of the GLC and the MCCs. In order to provide an economical description of local government, this section concentrates on the systems as they were in the 1970s (and as they remain in the peripheral nations and the counties). The changes in the conurbations

Table 3.6 *The Major Types of Local Authority: Area and Numbers*

	England			Wales	Scotland	Northern Ireland
	London	*Conurbations*	*Shires*			
Top-tier authorities	Greater London Council	Metropolitan counties (6)	County councils (39)	County councils (8)	Regions (9)	Districts (26)
Bottom-tier authorities	London boroughs (32) City of London Inner London Education Authority	Metropolitan districts (36)	County districts (296) Parishes (7947)	County districts (37) Parishes (682)	Districts (53) Islands (3) Community councils (1343)	

Key:

NMC = Non-metropolitan county
NMD = Non-metropolitan district
MC = Metropolitan county
MD = Metropolitan district
GLC = Greater London Council

ILB = Inner-London boroughs
OLB = Outer-London boroughs
COL = City of London
NPR = Non-peripheral regions
NPD = Non-peripheral districts

PR = Peripheral regions
PD = Peripheral districts
ISL = Scottish islands
NID = Northern Ireland districts
SCILL = Scilly Isles

A = Reserve powers to provide housing subject to a request by a district council and/or the approval of the secretary of state.
B = Certain transport functions such as provision and maintenance of footways. For more detailed breakdown for England and Wales see Layfield Committee (1976, p. 372).
C = Education in inner London is provided by the Inner London Education Authority, which is a special independent committee of the Greater London Council.
D = The Greater London Council maintains housing stock inherited from the London County Council.
E = Certain minor powers.
F = Police and fire in the Scilly Isles are administered by Devon and Cornwall.
G = No expenditure on burial grounds 1977–80.
O = Not a function of local government.

Source: Budge *et al.*, 1983, pp. 116–17.

Table 3.7 Allocation of Functions in UK Local Government

	England				London				Wales		Scotland						
Function	NMC	NMD	MC	MD	GLC	ILB	OLB	COL	NMC	NMD	NPR	NPD	PR	PD	ISL	NID	SCILL
Education	✓	A		✓	C	✓	✓	✓	✓		✓		✓		✓	O	✓
Housing	✓	✓	✓	✓	D	✓	✓	✓	✓	✓	✓	✓	✓	✓	✓	O	✓
Libraries	✓		✓	✓		✓	✓	✓	✓	✓		✓	✓		✓	O	✓
Transport	B	B	✓	B	✓	B	B	B	B	B	✓	✓		✓	✓	O	✓
Refuse collection	✓	✓	✓	✓	✓	✓	✓	✓		✓				✓	✓	✓	✓
Refuse disposal	✓		✓	✓	✓	✓	✓	✓	✓	✓	✓	✓	✓		✓	✓	✓
Social work	✓	✓	✓	✓	✓	✓	✓	✓	✓	✓	✓	✓	✓	✓	✓	O	✓
Leisure, recreation and museums	✓	✓	✓	✓	O	O	O	✓	✓	✓	✓	✓	✓		✓	✓	✓
Police		✓	✓		✓	✓	✓	✓	✓		✓	✓	✓		✓	O	F
Fire	✓		✓	✓	✓	✓	✓	✓	✓	✓	E	✓	✓	✓	✓	O	F
Burial grounds											E				✓	E	G
Consumer protection	O	O	O	O	O	O	O	O	O	O	O	O	O	O	✓	✓	✓
Environmental health	O	O	O	O	O	O	O	O	O	O	✓	✓	✓	O	O	O	✓
Water and sewerage	O	O	✓	✓	✓	✓	✓	✓	✓	✓	✓		✓		✓	✓	O
Gas															O	✓	✓
Planning	✓	✓	✓	✓	✓	✓	✓	✓	✓	✓	✓	✓	✓		✓	✓	✓
Building regulations	✓	✓	✓	✓	✓	✓	✓	✓	✓	✓	✓	✓	✓		✓	✓	✓

Table 3.8   *The Groups and Systems of Local Government in the UK*

Group/system	1976 population (000s)	% of the UK population	Expenditure per head 1976–7 (£)
English and Welsh group	42,015	75	257.63
(1) Non-metropolitan English system	27,675	49	241.69
(2) Metropolitan English system	11,664	21	287.81
(3) Welsh system	2,766	5	290.41
London group	7,112	13	371.80
(4) Outer London system	4,559	8	310.80
(5) Inner London system	2,548	5	470.18
(6) City of London system	5	a	5,822.63
Scottish group	5,206	9	326.87
(7) Scottish mainland non-peripheral system	4,715	8	326.98
(8) Scottish mainland peripheral system	425	1	316.12
(9) Scottish island system	66	a	388.78
Northern Ireland	1,538	3	22.37
(10) Northern Ireland system	1,538	3	22.37
Scilly Isles	2	a	290.28
(11) Scilly Isles	2	a	290.28
Whole United Kingdom	55,873	100	272.03

Note:
a Indicates less than one per cent.
Source: Budge *et al*., 1983, p. 119.

are described in Chapter 4 (see section 4.5.3). As before, this section provides a comparative analysis of the interests, resources and relationships of the several systems.[6]

3.6.1   The Interests of Local Government

The interests of local government can be classified by type of authority, service, profession, political party and area.

3.6.1(i)   THE INTERESTS OF TYPES OF LOCAL AUTHORITY

With each constituent nation of the UK, there are several types of local authority. They differ in number of functions, size (of population and expenditure as well as, rather obviously, geographical area) and degree of urbanness, and each type acts to preserve its distinctive identity. The major types of local authority are shown in Table 3.6. And this structure represents a drastic simplification of that which existed for the bulk of the postwar period (see Redcliffe-Maud Commission, 1969; Wheatley Commission, 1969; Macrory Report, 1970).

The allocation of functions within and between the several systems of local government is shown in Table 3.7. This table shows the number of functions for each type of authority. Clearly, the most distinctive type is the district council in Northern Ireland, which has only residual local government functions compared to the mainland systems.

The systems of local government also differ in the distribution of functions between the levels of local government. Thus, in England, the distribution of functions between county and districts in the conurbations distinguishes these authorities from their namesakes in the shires.

In theory, and as shown in Table 3.8, there are seventeen different types of local authority. In practice, combining the range and distribution of functions, there are eleven local government systems, and the importance of these distinctions is shown in Table 3.8. Thus, the largest single system is the English shires, and the smallest system is in the Scilly Isles. In fact, the easiest way to assess the importance of a local government system is to examine its functions. Thus, the Scottish regions spend more than the English and Welsh districts because they have more functions – for example, education, social services.

With the exceptions of Scotland, where there is a single association, and Northern Ireland, where there is only one type of authority, each type of local authority has its own national representative body – or local authority association – which lobbies on its behalf. Any proposed alteration to the boundaries or functions of local authorities evokes a defensive response from these associations and provides the clearest example of the importance of type of authority as an interest in local government. It is by no means the only example. Both before and after the reorganization of 1974, disputes between the types of local authority remained common. Thus, the GLC and the London boroughs had a series of disputes over planning after 1965 (Self, 1971). Cities which became district councils on reorganization have lobbied incessantly for the return of functions (Rhodes, 1986a, ch. 6). As Alexander (1982, p. 66) concludes:

> It is clear that district councils, as a class, are perceived as having interests that conflict with those of the counties. This is a damning indictment of a major institutional reform that was intended to end uncertainty and bring to a conclusion the wrangles ... that had characterized the old system.

The existence of shared functions (known as concurrent powers) and of joint arrangements for carrying out a function (known as agency agreements) simply exacerbates the conflicts between types of authority.

3.6.1(ii) SERVICE INTERESTS

To a substantial degree, the interest of type of local authority overlaps with service interests; all types of local authority wish to retain or enhance their range of functions. However, the two interests are analytically distinct, and the service interests generate a distinct set of alliances and conflicts: between centre and locality, between departments within a local authority, between technocrats and topocrats and with other units of SCG as well as between types of local authority.

First, local authorities seek to win central support for local services either directly through increased grant, legislation and amendments to subordinate legislation or indirectly by 'clearing' proposed actions, seeking 'clarification' of powers or 'moral support' in departmental letters, circulars, etc. In this process, the central service departments can become important allies in resisting the guardianship interests of the Treasury and the DoE. Demands for greater authority and/or more financial resources do not necessarily affect the interests of other types of authority and can generate alliances across local authorities to foster a common service interest. If local authorities are the prime territorial institution of British government, the functional linkages, or vertical alliance of service interests between centre and locality, are strong and an ever-present source of tension within local government, for example in the education service.

Second, the abstraction 'local government' conceals, as in the case of 'central government', the variety of interests within local authorities. Departmentalism or weakness at the centre is as much a feature of local authorities as it is of the centre, to the extent that Regan (1980, p. 8) describes local authorities as 'a headless state'. And the competition between departments is the most striking instance of service interests 'at work'. Kogan and Van der Eyken (1973, pp. 48–51) note the 'increasing intrusion' of other departments into education's turf, and one of their chief education officers reports losing a substantial capital allocation from the DES because the proposal conflicted with local housing priorities (p. 160). Examples of bureaucratic politics in local government are rife (see, for example, Lee, 1963; Dennis, 1972; Rhodes, 1975b; Rosenberg, 1984), and at their heart is the competition between service departments for resources.

Third, although the centre may have weaknesses, the rivalry between guardians and service interests is re-enacted at the local level, with chief executives and directors of finance prominent in the former camp. The most concerted effort to strengthen 'the central capability' of local authorities lies in the introduction of corporate planning. Thus, the internal organization of local authorities was revamped, and central, integrative mechanisms were introduced for both leading elected members (e.g. policy and resources committees) and paid officials (e.g. management teams, the appointment of chief executives as the head of the official 'side' of the authority). In theory at least, these innovations were to be wedded to a rational planning cycle through which individual departments and the authority as a whole were to set objectives and monitor their effectiveness in achieving these explicit goals (see Rhodes, 1979, for a fuller summary of this ideology; Greenwood *et al.*, 1980, for a survey of the extent of change). The chief beneficiaries of these changes were topocratic professions, and the conflict between them and the technocratic departments became acute on occasion, evoking screams of pain from some education departments.

Finally, local government interacts with a variety of other sub-central units of government, and the competitive relationship between rival and service interests at the centre recurs in the localities. For example, the policy of community care, whereby long-stay hospital patients such as the elderly and the mentally ill are cared for in the community, has been floundering. Although 'joint finance' may have helped to 'pump-prime' local authority action, it did nothing about the long-term costs of such care. Without a long-term transfer of resources from the NHS to local government, local authorities drew back from community care; the policy is foundering because neither the NHS nor local government can or will forgo resources (see Chapter 4, section 4.4). A more explosive example is the 'invasion' of the MSC into further education. Its enhanced responsibility for vocational training has provoked conflict at national and local levels and resulted in the diversion of funds from local authorities to a non-departmental public body (see Chapter 4, section 4.2.2(ii)).

The strength of the service interests in local government bears testament to the pervasive influence of functional politics in British SCG. Local government may express uniquely territorial politics but it is riven with functional cleavages which span levels of government. And again professional interests figure prominently, on this occasion articulating functional interests within local government.

3.6.1(iii) PROFESSIONAL INTERESTS

Professional interests are institutionalized in the departmental structure of local government; professional and managerial organization are virtually coterminous. This combination underpins the power of professionals and led the West Midlands Study Group to comment as early as 1956 (p. 244) that local autonomy was being eroded by

a service professionalism divorced from the old conception of a local government service and finding its strongest links with the central government departments and, through it, with colleagues in other areas all over the country, rather than with councils and committees and colleagues in other departments.

The roots of this professionalism lie in the interwar years. Page (1985, pp. 23–8) describes how local government officers lobbied for a system of national negotiating councils for recruitment, pay and conditions of service rather than seeking regulation by central government. Professionalism sprang from the demands of staff

> and first expressed itself in a movement by the various categories of local government officers to establish their own institutes for conferring qualifications by examination. The desire to abolish patronage and to improve the status of the various grades by eliminating the untrained . . . (was) . . . the chief motive compelling the members of practically all the brain-working grades in local administration to set up barriers against haphazard entry into the various vocations.
>
> (Warren, 1952, p. 61)

Self-regulation has remained a distinct characteristic of local government officers and it is, of course, a defining characteristic of professionalism as a mechanism of exclusionary closure. With the expansion of the welfare state, the range of professions has broadened considerably, but self-regulation remains the defining attribute.

Whilst the interests of the professions reside in the protection and development of 'their service', they are by no means identical to the service interests. The particularistic ideologies of the professions are not confined to the scale of funding nor to the service needs of the locality. For example, Foley (1960, pp. 76–8) argues that the ideology of British town planning has three potentially contradictory strands:

1　Town planning's main task is to reconcile competing claims for the use of limited land so as to provide a consistent, balanced and orderly arrangement of land uses . . .
2　Town planning's central function is to provide a good (or better) physical environment; a physical environment of such good quality is essential for the promotion of a healthy and civilized life . . .
3　Town planning, as part of a broader social programme, is responsible for providing the physical basis for better urban community life; the main ideals toward which town planning is to strive are (a) the provision of low-density residential areas (b) the fostering of local community life and (c) the control of conurban growth.

The selfsame visionary streak is derided by Davies (1972, ch. 12 and 13) and espoused in Faludi (1973), pp. 39–45). In a similar vein Hollis (1967, p. 38) has characterized social work ideology as beginning with:

acceptance, the dispassionate commitment to the well-being of the person we are trying to help. We make positive use of the individual's capacity for self-direction by jealously guarding his freedom of choice. We are guided in the help we offer by our value assumptions that man and his fulfillment are intrinsically valuable, that men are mutually dependent and bear responsibility for each other, that men are equal in their essential value and rights, that man's destructive tendencies must be held in leash and overbalanced by the strength of his love, as he moves in the direction of love turned outward rather than inward. We use in our work the scientific method and its assumptions that there is lawfulness in human affairs and that painstaking study, illuminated by intuitions, can bring us a progressively clearer appreciation of truth.

If such messianic loquacity seems as awesome as it is naïve, Halmos's (1965 and 1970) characterization of the 'counselling ideology' provides a similar picture in a more analytic vein. He argues that the ideology – the 'socially determined belief-system about the nature of human relationships' (1970, p. 21) – contains five propositions. First, 'the positive – loving, compassionate, sympathetic, co-operative, creative or what you will – polarity has an edge over the negative polarity of our strivings' (p. 15). Second, 'all socially relevant human behaviour is learnt in intimate social relationships', and 'the only procedures through which this social learning can be effectively modified is in intimate social relationships' (p. 16). Third, 'it is professional to use tested science, and tried skill, and it is unprofessional to use the total, and certainly unmeasurable "mix" of one's personality. Yet to maintain his effectiveness the professional has not only tried to make use of his personality, but also explicitly prescribed to the acolytes its use as a professional resource of the greatest magnitude' (p. 16). Fourth, 'In an era of liberalism ... professional practitioners most often and publicly show that they don't go beyond the brief either society or their clients have given them, and that they don't meddle with other people's lives' (p. 17). Finally, 'Counsellors will construe their work as analogous to the healing work of medicine with clearly identifiable terminal cures as ends' (p. 17). From wholly different viewpoints, Hollis and Halmos point to love, the individual, science, intuition and truth as components of social work ideology, and these components are echoed in the Seebohm Report (1968) with its references to, for example, learning through intimate social relationships (Halmos, 1970, p. 113). Similarly the British Association of Social Workers (BASW) included in its draft code of ethics the injunction to recognize

the value and dignity of every individual human being, irrespective of origin, status, sex, age, belief or contribution to society. The profession accepts a responsibility to encourage and facilitate the self-realization of the individual person with due regard for the interests of others.

(BASW, n.d., p. 6)

For all the debate about the role and tasks of social workers (Barclay Report, 1982; BASW, 1983), Halmos's 'client-centred', counselling psychology, curative model of social work remains a 'cogent' analysis (Hunt, 1978), and its pervasiveness is reflected in the pejorative appellation of social workers as the 'bleeding hearts brigade'. (On architects see Malpass, 1975; Dunleavy, 1981b, pp. 53–5 and 133–8; on housing see Kirby, 1979; Laffin, 1982, ch. 5; on treasurers see Rosenberg, 1984; on engineers see Laffin, 1982, ch. 4; on education see Rhodes, 1986a, and citations therein.)

The pervasiveness of these ideologies is reflected in stereotyping within local authorities. Remarks like 'the iceman cometh' reflect a recognition of the treasurer's concern with financial probity and restraint. Or, in a more sardonic vein, one councillor asked (rhetorically), 'Why are officers in planning departments called Justin and Quentin and officers in housing Bill and Harry?' – a reaction to the 'trendy' nature of planning and the prosaic nature of housing management.

The significance of such particularistic ideologies lies in their impact on local authority decisions and in the non-local nature of such influences. For example, Muchnick (1970, p. 65) argues that the failure of urban renewal in Liverpool stemmed 'from the organizational needs of the actors themselves (i.e. the Housing and Planning Departments), their orientations and preferences'. Malpass (1975) demonstrates how the design and character of two housing estates in Newcastle were changed drastically on several occasions by a combination of architects' decisions and interdepartmental disputes. But perhaps even more important, the professions create a national climate of opinion which constitutes the guidelines on best professional practice for individual local authority departments. Thus, Dunleavy (1981b, pp. 105–6) documents the emergence of high-rise housing in Britain, arguing that the design professions generated 'powerful feedback processes' which created 'cumulative endorsement of high flats' (see the discussion of the national local government system in Chapter 2, section 2.5.2(ii)). Professional interests can and do shape the definition of service interests (locally and nationally).

In sharp contrast to non-departmental public bodies however, professional interests in local government do not reign supreme. Not only is there extensive competition between the professions in multi-functional local authorities, but the expertise and status of the professions have been challenged. Generally the 'New Right' is intensely critical of professional 'monopolies'; client deference has been eroded; and the claim to professional competence has been undermined by a series of welfare scandals. More specifically, resource squeeze has increased competition between professional groups and restricted the opportunities for developing new forms of service provision; and most important, the interests of the political parties vie with professional definitions of problems and their priority: a challenge which has intensified with the politicization of local government (see Pollitt, 1984; Laffin and Young, 1985).

3.6.1(iv) PARTY POLITICAL INTERESTS

Up to reorganization, the colonization of local government by political parties was remarkably incomplete (see Chapter 2, section 2.5.1(vi), pages 71 and 72–3). The all-purpose, urban county boroughs were the heartland of party activity. None the less, there were some marked differences between Conservative- and Labour-controlled local authorities. Boaden (1971, p. 112) concluded:

> Labour councils were more active in services with a significant impact on the overall role of government. They were bigger spenders on the bigger services. In addition, they were more active where the service appeared to benefit sections of the community supporting them.

Party affected priority within and between services (see also Alt, 1971; Ashford, 1975). The most thorough study of this topic concluded not only that party control affected expenditure patterns, but 'the larger the majority the party enjoys the greater party ideology shows itself' (Sharpe and Newton, 1984, p. 200). The more competitive the party system, the greater the similarity in the expenditure patterns of the parties. In addition, some of the differences between the parties do not have large expenditure effects; for example, the abolition of corporal punishment in schools has no expenditure effect, and the decision to cancel an urban motorway actually reduces expenditure. Decentralization and participation are low-cost policies (Sharpe, 1980; Sharpe and Newton, 1984, ch. 1).

Since reorganization, the politicization of local government has become marked. Not only have the two major parties colonized the bulk of local authorities, but the 1980s have witnessed the rise of the 'new urban Left' within the Labour Party and of the Alliance (see Chapter 2, section 2.5.2(ii)). There are no analyses of the expenditure patterns of the post-reorganization local authorities available equivalent to those just discussed. However, it is clear that important differences remain. Labour councils have incurred the wrath of central government for spending more than government targets as they have sought to protect their level of expenditure. The policies of some new urban Left councils have provoked controversy, even outrage, to such an extent that the government appointed the Widdicombe Committee to examine political conduct in local government. Their policies were also a factor in the decision to abolish the GLC and the metropolitan counties (see Boddy and Fudge, 1984; Forrester, Lansley and Pawley, 1985, ch. 3).

The rise of the Alliance in local politics is too recent to allow for a complete assessment. However, the claim that 'hung councils' will be a force for moderation must be viewed critically. Leach and Stewart's (1986) survey demonstrates that a significant number of 'hung councils' experience heightened internal political polarization, delay, uncertainty and demise of forward planning (especially budgetary planning) (see also Blowers, 1982).

Party interests receive their clearest expression in the differences in policies (and associated levels of expenditure), but such a conclusion begs the question of whether or not the interests so expressed are those of the local or national parties. The 'nationalization of local politics' thesis suggests that the spread of the national parties and concomitant decline of purely local parties will limit local variations within any one party (Grant, 1977, p. 1; Young, 1975, pp. 29–33; Ashford, 1982, pp. 156–8), but national party labels have not suffocated local party policies (see section 3.7.1, below).

3.6.1(v)   AREAL INTERESTS

Rhodes (1986a, pp. 404–5) concluded that one of the problems for the national community of local government and especially the local authority associations was the simple fact

> that local government is *local* government. Its actions are legitimate because they are taken by locally elected councillors on issues of local concern. A national community of local government *is* a contradiction in terms. The Associations have to generalize when their defence of local government lies in diversity. They have to develop a perspective on national issues whereas their main concern is local problems (original emphasis).

If the areal interests of local government have been left until last, it is not because they are unimportant. Just as the specific areal interests of their members are a major problem for the associations, so area pervades all aspects of local government, reappearing in the tension between national and local parties, between the allegiance of the officer to his profession and to his employer, between national standards of service provision and local needs and between the interests of local government as a whole and of particular types of local authority. It could not be otherwise; areal interests are ubiquitous, lying at the heart of the rationale for the only elected territorial institution in the UK and the pre-eminent unit of SCG.

If local definitions of needs, problems and policies – adopting purely local policies and adapting national legislation to local conditions – are a pervasive feature of local government, areal interests also take on a more specific form. Thus, the regional location of local authorities affects their response to central initiatives. Obviously, such differences will be most marked in the peripheral regions, to the extent that they have their own representative bodies to deal with their 'centre': namely, the Convention of Scottish Local Authorities (COSLA), the Association of Local Authorities of Northern Ireland (ALANI) up to 1985 and the Council for the Principality. In addition, there are regional groupings within the English associations: for example, the North of England County Councils' Association within the ACC and the London Boroughs' Association within the AMA. These several organizations exist to protect the distinct interest of their area (for a more detailed discussion see Rhodes, 1986a, ch. 7).

Areal interests are also articulated by the professions. Topocrats exist to defend the interests of the area as a whole. They are yet another counterweight to the influence of the technocratic professions, to the dominance of functional politics. Thus the Society of Local Authority Chief Executives (SOLACE) and the various professional organizations of treasurers (Chartered Institute of Public Finance and Accountancy (CIPFA), Society of County Treasurers) express the 'interests of local government' – the politics of place – rather than service interests.

Part of the problem of discussing the areal interests lies in the fact that their specific manifestation varies so greatly from local authority to local authority. The socioeconomic environments of local authorities can differ greatly, and even broadly similar authorities can have distinct problems. Both West Yorkshire and South Yorkshire may have an ageing industrial base, but the former has a declining textile industry whereas the latter has a declining coal and steel industry with corresponding differences in the aid available; for example, the European Coal and Steel Community makes funds available for declining coal and steel areas. To further compound the problem of describing areal interests, they are interwoven with all the other interests in local government. Type of authority, area, service, party and profession can all espouse an increase in central funds for education or even object to the removal of education from local government (albeit with less unanimity). For all its ubiquity, however, area remains analytically distinct from other interests, at the heart of the several local government systems and the major bastion against the ever-present challenge of functional politics.

3.6.2   The Resources of Local Government

The resources of local government have been described briefly in Chapter 2, section 2.3.5, Figure 2.2, and section 2.5.3(i). This section concentrates, therefore, on comparing the several local government systems and providing statistical information on the scale of these resources.

3.6.2(i)   AUTHORITY

Table 3.7 above, not only illustrates the differences between the local government system but also describes, given that all local service provision has to be authorized by statute, the distribution of authority between centre and locality and between types of local government. The allocation of a function to local government is also a grant of authority.

Thereafter, it becomes more difficult to generalize. First, as the Layfield Committee (1976, pp. 403–5) discovered, it is difficult to distinguish between mandatory legislation which imposes a duty on local authorities and permissive legislation which allows, but does not require, them to act:

> the bulk of local government expenditure falls somewhere between the two extremes, being determined not by formal requirements alone nor by free local choice alone but by a complex mixture of pressures and influences. Informal advice and exhortation from government departments, inspection, nationally accepted standards, accumulated past practice, professional attitudes, political influences and actions by various pressure groups, national and local, all play a part in determining local expenditure, along with the statutory provisons.

Examples of services with little local discretion include electoral registration and mandatory awards to students. Services with considerable discretion include parks, swimming-baths, museums and art galleries and the development of industrial estates. For the major services such as education, however, it is difficult to find mandatory requirements; the bulk of the activities collectively known as education are open to local variation. Indeed, the duties imposed for some services are so minimal, as in the case of public libraries, that local authorities have substantial discretion.

Second, the several local government systems vary not only in the range and distribution of functions but also in the scope and content of this legislation. There is a large amount of territorially specific legislation in Scotland and Northern Ireland. Budge *et al.* (1983, p. 120) calculate that 72 per cent of the legislation on Northern Ireland's local government and 47 per cent of the legislation on

Table 3.9 Sources of Revenue Income of Local Authorities, 1974-5 to 1984-5 (%, by nation)

	1974-5	1975-6	1976-7	1977-8	1978-9	1979-80	1980-1	1981-2	1982-3	1983-4	1984-5
Fees, etc.											
England and Wales	18.8	19.4	20.3	20.6	21.4	21.6	21.2	21.4	21.3	20.8	21.2
Northern Ireland	15.0	15.2	14.7	16.2	16.3	16.9	16.2	15.9	15.1	15.9	17.6
Scotland	n.a.	15.0	16.6	17.8	18.8	18.2	17.3	18.5	19.4	19.3	19.5
Grants											
England and Wales	51.8	53.6	51.9	50	48.6	47.3	46.4	44.6	42	41.9	41
Northern Ireland	26	24.1	22.9	23	21.9	21.4	20.6	21.0	22.5	24.2	24.6
Scotland	n.a.	58.0	58.9	56.5	55.4	56.1	55.3	49.8	48	50.6	50
Rates											
England and Wales	29.4	27.0	27.8	29.4	30	31.1	32.4	34.0	36.7	37.3	34.3
Northern Ireland	59	60.7	62.4	60.8	61.8	59.7	62	63.1	62.3	59.9	57.8
Scotland	n.a.	27.0	24.5	25.7	25.8	25.7	27.4	31.7	32.6	30.1	30.5

Note: The percentages for each nation do not always total 100 because changes in balances have been omitted.

Sources: Connolly, 1983; Local Government Trends; Scottish Abstract of Statistics; and private correspondence.

Scottish local government is territorially specific. If children in Scotland have to remain in school until they are 16 under UK legislation, the supply and training of their teachers, the curriculum and the examinations are a product of purely Scottish legislation.

Finally, although local authorities have both considerable grants of authority and substantial discretion in its exercise, it is important to remember that this grant is made by Parliament and can be revoked at any time.

3.6.2(ii) MONEY

It is often argued that local discretion is undercut by the dependence of local authorities on central grant; 'he who pays the piper calls the tune'. The argument is overstated. As Table 3.9 demonstrates, local authorities have various sources of income, and grant has declined as a source of income at the very time that worries about centralization have peaked.

In addition, individual local authorities (and systems) vary greatly in their dependence on grant. Thus, local authorities in peripheral Scotland receive the highest proportion of grant and the City of London the lowest proportion. Of all systems, Northern Ireland is least dependent on grant primarily because it is no longer responsible for the major local government function (for detailed figures see Budge *et al.*, 1983, table 5.9, p. 123). In short, there are enormous variations between local authorities and between the local government systems. Caution is necessary, therefore, in generalizing about the consequences of dependence on central grant. Indeed, it is the directly contrary point that should be emphasized; all local authorities have independent tax powers. Although rates have to be raised disproportionately to meet reductions in grant ('known as the 'gearing effect') and although since 1984 the government has powers to limit rate increases (known as 'rate capping') none the less local authorities remain the only unit of SCG with an independent tax-raising capacity.[7] In consequence, they can finance their own decisions about the level of expenditure on individual services and about the relative priority accorded to services. This capacity is a corner-stone of local discretion.

3.6.2(iii) POLITICAL RESOURCES

The political resources of local government are diverse. For example, local authorities in the peripheral nations have their own centre with a minister of Cabinet rank. These territorial centres have a distinctive political environment, and its relative compactness arguably facilitates contact. There is an identifiable sub-central political system which provides easier, more frequent and more effective access for local authorities. In addition, the secretary of state can articulate their interests at the highest levels of government. In this respect, the DoE

Table 3.10 *Political Control of UK local authorities, 1976 and 1985*

	C '76	C '85	L '76	L '85	A '76	A '85	I '76	I '85	NOC '76	NOC '85	Other '76	Other '85	Total
England													
Non-metropolitan districts	163	139	30	54	n.a.	3	53	25	49	67	1	8	296
Non-metropolitan counties	20	10	6	5	n.a.	1	1	0	12	23	0	0	39
Metropolitan counties	2	0	4	6	n.a.	0	0	0	0	0	0	0	6
Metropolitan districts	13	5	20	24	n.a.	0	0	0	3	7	0	0	36
GLC	0	0	1	1	n.a.	0	0	0	0	0	0	0	1
London boroughs	13	13	18	15	n.a.	0	0	0	1	4	0	0	32
City of London	0	0	0	0	n.a.	0	1	1	0	0	0	0	1
Scilly Islands	0	0	0	0	n.a.	0	1	1	0	0	0	0	1
Northern Ireland													
Districts	n.a.		n.a.		n.a.		n.a.		6	1	20	25	26
Scotland													
Regions	1	1	2	3	n.a.	0	2	2	4	3	0	0	9
Districts	4	3	17	25	n.a.	1	18	16	13	5	1	3	53
Islands	0	0	0	0	n.a.	0	3	3	0	0	0	0	3
Wales													
Counties	0	0	4	4	n.a.	0	3	2	1	2	0	0	8
Districts	4	3	11	16	n.a.	0	13	9	8	4	1	5	37

C = Conservative, L = Labour, A = Alliance (includes Liberal and Social Democratic Party controlled councils), I = Independent (including non party), NOC = no overall control, n.a. = not applicable.

Note:
[a] In 1977, 17 councils had a Unionist majority, 3 had an anti-Unionist majority, and 6 councils were deadlocked. In 1985 the figures were 16, 9 and 1 respectively, with Sinn Fein gaining 59 seats overall.

Sources: *Local Government Trends*, 1976; *Municipal Year Book*, 1977 and 1986; Birrell and Murie, 1980, p. 188; Connolly and Knox, 1986, p. 27.

is but a pale shadow of the territorial ministries. English local authorities have no equivalent voice or friends at court.

Perhaps more important, the political control of local authorities varies greatly, influencing their access to their centre. Table 3.10 shows the number of authorities controlled by the various parties, both after reorganization and in 1985, demonstrating a number of the salient features of local political systems. First, in England, the Labour Party had the upper hand in the conurbations and London, whereas the Conservatives were strongest in the counties. However, and second, Conservative ascendancy in the counties has been challenged by the rise of the Alliance. By the 1985 county council elections the Alliances's electoral intervention in England had created twenty-three (out of thirty-nine) 'hung councils' wherein no party had an absolute majority.

Third, the pattern of political control is different in the peripheral nations. The Conservatives are weak in Scotland and Wales, with political control shared by the Labour Party and Independents. Local political control in Northern Ireland is *sui generis*. The 'other' column in Table 3.10 encompasses Unionist, Unionist/Loyalist, SDLP/ Nationalist/Independent councils, with Sinn Fein coming to electoral prominence in 1985.

Fourth, such aggregate figures do not reveal variations in the type and extent of party influence. Jones (1975, pp. 19–22) identified several kinds of political system; simplifying his typology, the following major types of local party system can be identified:

- *The non-party*: predominantly in the hands of non-partisan independents although the council may contain some (or one) small minority parties.
- *The partially party*: the parties contest the elections, but, once elected, members behave as independents
- *The emergent party*: both independents and parties contest the election, and members on the council are organized into socialist and anti-socialist groups.
- *The wholly party*: parties both control elections and form the basis of organization within the council. This category can be further subdivided into:
  – the one-party monopolistic;
  – the two-year party competitive; and
  – the multi-party.

Whilst the first three types of party system persist, especially in the shire districts, the history of the postwar period is one of ever more widespread partisan elections and ever more disciplined party organization within councils (see also Stanyer, 1976, pp. 152–6).

Finally, the discussion of types of local party system still obscures some of the variety because it continues to rely on national party labels. For example, there are some sharp contrasts between Conservatives in urban authorities with their group meetings, whips and party patronage and Conservatives in the shire counties and districts, who still retain an air of squirearchy and abjure the paraphernalia of modern party organization. Most important, the new urban Left within the Labour Party challenges the centralizing Fabian tradition of the national party, rendering any neat identity of national and local party as implausible as it is misleading (see also section 3.7.1, below; Widdicombe Committee, 1986b).

A number of consequences follow from this variety. First, local elections regularly produce a swing against the government, and no national government can rely on the support of like-minded local politicians, even when they are of the same party. The local party will have its own views on local problems and priorities and be willing to debate the merits of a policy, in public as well as private. Local government is littered with examples of councils ignoring central policy preferences, actively opposing them and pursuing policies of which the centre disapproves (see Rhodes, 1976, pp. 183–91). Second, party is another channel of communication with the centre. Whether through the local government committee of the party, the national conference and its resolutions, or informal contact, local politicians can seek the ear of national political figures (Rhodes, 1986a, ch. 6). If the links between national and local élites are weak compared, for example, to France, none the less they exist, and the recurrent furore over grant and its distribution has increased their importance. Party provides both the motives and the means to influence the centre and a rival channel of influence to the professional-bureaucratic policy networks.

The final political resource of local authorities is their national representative bodies, collectively termed the intergovernmental network. The English local authority associations constitute a national community of local government, which has been described as 'part of the constitution' of the country (Duncan Sandys, cited in Griffith, 1966, p. 33); but Rhodes (1986a, p. 415) concluded that

> The national community is not ineffectual . . . but equally it is not a decisive or determinate force: it is a legitimized consultative channel with neither the resources nor, in many instances, the desire to challenge government . . . [it] can be seen as a constraint on central departments. The description 'post offices' seems to underestimate the effectiveness of the national community just as the description 'part of the constitution' overestimates it. The truth is far more prosaic: it is a domesticated pressure group.

Thus, they are consulted over the implementation of legislation and they do advise on the drafting of Bills but, once the government has decided to act, they are unable to change the principles of that legislation.

It is a mistake, however, to view the national community as but the pressure group for local government. It is the flawed institutional network at the heart of central–local relations. It is flawed in two senses. First, given the weak links between national and local political élites, the national community emerged after 1974 as an intermediate tier of representation, attempting to aggregate the interests of all types of local government. It was actively supported in this aspiration by the centre and, in consequence, it came to speak with two voices; it articulated the interests of local government *and* explained central policies to local government. Involvement with centre spilled over into incorporation and apologia: into too sensitive an appreciation of

the centre's problem. Second, the national community was flawed by
the range of interests it encompassed. It had to reconcile the interests
of type of authority, party, services, area and profession (see Rhodes,
1983). On the controversial issues such as grant, reconciliation
became a mere figment of the imagination, generating conflicts within
as well as between associations. Any and all pretence of speaking for
local government was swamped by the reality of irreconcilable interests within local government, prompting Rhodes (1986a, p. 416) to
conclude that the survival of the national community was 'a miracle of
the imperfections of government'. That it did survive suggests that it
served the interests of the centre as much as those of local authorities.

The remainder of the intergovernmental network comprises the
local authority associations in the peripheral nations. Apart from the
obvious differences that their 'centre' is the territorial ministry and
that local authorities are represented by a single association (except in
Wales), the most notable feature of this element of the intergovernmental network is that ALANI and COSLA also have problems
reconciling the multifarious interests of their constituent authorities.
Thus, ALANI refused to recognize the change in name of Londonderry to Derry City Council. Councils with nationalist majorities,
most notably the SDLP, saw this refusal as yet another example of
misuse of the association by Unionists and walked out. Thereupon the
DoE(NI) withdrew recognition of ALANI as the voice of local
government (Connolly and Knox, 1986, p. 19). Similarly, Craig
(1980, p. 128) reports that COSLA had three main divisions –
urban/rural, region/district and party political – which fuelled a
constitutional controversy within the association and 'endangered the
very existence of COSLA'. She concludes (p. 137) that the associations' weakness was the need to 'reconcile the views of competing
authorities', an exercise which both generated uncertainty and
'diverted energy from COSLA's other business'. The existence of a
single association 'does not put an end to the conflicts'.

The political resources of local government have been discussed at
greater length than the other resources for the simplest of simple
reasons; it is the only unit of SCG cloaked with electoral legitimacy. It
is unique in its range of political resources. The discussion of the
'national' political subsystems, types of political control and the
national community of local government should not be allowed to
obscure local government's accountability to local electorates rather
than, as in the case of all other units of SCG, accountability to
Parliament through a minister.

3.6.2(iv)   ORGANIZATIONAL RESOURCES

Local government controls far more organizational resources than the
centre. The partial exception is Northern Ireland, where local government services have been transferred to the centre. The consequences

of this imbalance are equally obvious. Local government has 'hands-on' controls of services and the capacity to modify central policy in the process of implementation. Conversely, the centre depends on local authorities to translate intentions into acts. However, organizational resources do not necessarily reinforce local discretion because they are inextricably interwoven with informational resources dominated by professionalism.

3.6.2(v) INFORMATIONAL RESOURCES

The 'hands-on' control of services by local authorities is reinforced by their control of information about these services. The centre depends upon local authorities for 'feedback' on implementation. However, the departments of local government are highly professionalized; organizational and informational resources are coterminous.

The available data on the local government professions are limited. Some indication of the degree of professionalism can be gleaned by looking at the distribution of employment by services (this section is paraphrased from Budge *et al.*, 1983, p. 128). Thus, 48 per cent of local government employment is accounted for by the education service, 27.1 per cent of whose employees are teachers. 9.5 per cent are in the social services, and 12.9 per cent are in 'miscellaneous services' which includes senior management. Only a small proportion of total employment is accounted for by services with a high proportion of manual workers (see also Karram, 1984), and this pattern is repeated in the peripheral nations.

The consequences of this control of informational resources are contradictory. On the one hand, it increases the dependence of the centre on local government, but, on the other hand, the professions exercise a nationalizing influence by, for example, promulgating shared notions of best professional practice through their national associations. Whether or not this kind of influence can be treated as 'local', or even as supporting the interests of local government rather than the sectional interests of the profession, will be explored below.

In sum, therefore, local government controls a range of resources and is unique among SCG in its political resources. Its status as the pre-eminent territorial institution of British government is reflected in the variety and complexity of its relationships.

3.6.3 The Relationships of Local Government

Houlihan (1984, p. 404) provides a convenient summary of the variety of relationships between centre and locality. The overwhelming majority of categories in Table 3.11 are self-explanatory, and each will be illustrated briefly rather than discussed at length.

Bureaucratic relationships are widespread, having their roots in legislation, especially delegated legislation. They are particularly

Table 3.11 *Relationships between Central and Local Government*

Form of linkage	Basis of relationship	Key characteristics of relationship
Bureaucratic	Legislation, convention	Relatively clearly defined, predictable, regular, frequent
Technical	Requirements of the plan	Periodic, cyclical, financial
Professional	Shared expertise	Continuous, narrowly-based
Personal	Shared interests/problems	Irregular, very frequent
Informal consultative	Information transmission	Political, irregular, infrequent
Formal consultative	Information exchange	Overtly political, regular
Party political	Broadly common ideology	Infrequent, not always consensual, excludes officers

Source: Houlihan, 1984, p. 404.

common in the control of expenditure (see Chapter 4, section 4.2.1) but by no means limited to it: for example, the sale of council houses. Technical relationships emerged to prominence with the introduction of PPSs in the 1970s and their requirements for supporting information and planning documents (see section 3.2.4(ii), pages 134–5, above). Professional relationships are almost a defining characteristic of central–local relations and occur between all levels of government formally in advisory bodies and informally through individual contact as well as through common membership of professional bodies (see section 3.7.2, below). Personal contact at the officer level occurs at both middle management level, for example over the interpretation of rules and regulations governing the exercise of compulsory purchase powers, and at chief officer level, for example national discussions of shared problems such as the repair of system-built houses (Houlihan, 1984, p. 406). Informal consultative relationships involve elected members and are less frequent than the personal contacts of officers but more structured. These involve delegations to central departments and Parliament as well as parties aboard yachts on the Thames (Crossman, 1975, pp. 39, 60–1, 352–3, 391, 410, 429, 525, 563, 598 and 612). Formal consultative relationships are a characteristic device of British government, and central–local relations are no exception. The most publicized example in recent years is the CCLGF (Rhodes, 1986a, ch. 4). Finally, party political relationships have become more prominent since reorganization in 1974. Such relationships are episodic and not confined to internal party committees or annual conferences. Indeed, the local government committees of the parties are the tip of an iceberg, serving to direct attention away from periods of intense intra-party activity (Gyford and James, 1983, pp. 138–47; Rhodes, 1986a, ch. 6; see section 3.7.1, below).

This classification of relationships covers both central departments and their regional offices. There are a number of important qualifications to this general picture. First, local authorities are embedded in networks composed of a range of public and private bodies. These relationships are discontinuous and multiplex, admitting of no neat characterization. As with all sub-central bodies, local authorities indulge in continuous reticulist activity, and relationships vary from outright conflict to incorporation to council committees (see, for example, Flynn, 1983; King, 1983).

The scale of this activity is indicated by Cousin's (1982) analysis of the London Borough of Bromley's network of contacts. His admittedly incomplete listing includes 56 unofficial and quasi-official bodies in Bromley and 27 similar bodies connected to the GLC but operating in Bromley (see also Friend, Power and Yewlett, 1974; Hogwood, 1982b, p. 76). Moreover, the number of official bodies was increased by the abolition of the GLC and metropolitan counties. These local authorities were replaced by joint boards and joint committees – collectively termed 'quelgos' or quasi-elected local government organizations (Dunleavy and Rhodes, 1986, pp. 115–6). Such services as fire, police, waste disposal, highways and traffic management, arts and recreation, trading standards and consumer protection and the funding of voluntary organizations are all the object of some form of joint action by district councils/London boroughs, a pattern that can only be described as 'extremely complex' (see pp. 247–9 and 308–9 below; Flynn and Leach, 1984, p. 1; see also Flynn, Leach and Vielba, 1985).

Second, the pattern of relationships in the peripheral nations is distinguished by the relatively lower incidence of formal consultation and the greater reliance on personal contact and informal consultation (see, for example, Kellas, 1973, pp. 211–12; Birrell and Murie, 1980, p. 130; Madgwick and James, 1980; Kellas and Madgwick, 1982, pp. 27–8; Keating and Midwinter, 1983, p. 76).

Third, since 1979 the pattern of relationships has moved sharply away from formal consultation in favour of bureaucratic relationships (see Chapter 2, section 2.5.2(ii)). This transition should not be overemphasised. For example, technical relationships in the PPSs were also strengthened (see section 3.2.4(ii), pages 134–5, above), and party political channels had periods of intense activity (Rhodes, 1986a).

Fourth, the government did not rely exclusively on 'hands-on' controls. It also extolled the virtues of privatization for local government, primarily in the forms of increased charges for services and contracting-out. In addition, the government enforced the sale of council houses, restricted the activities of direct labour organizations (see Flynn, 1985) and encouraged the injection of private sector capital into local authority urban development projects. By comparison with both changes in the grant system and denationalization/liberalization for non-departmental public bodies, 'hands-off' controls in local government developed slowly. Primarily concerned with refuse collecting, cleaning services, catering and public cleansing services, contracting-out has been rejected by many local authorities. For example, Ascher (1987, pp. 221–2) reports that only eleven councils awarded contracts worth more than £50,000 between 1982–3, and thereafter there was 'a significant decline in the volume and value of major service work put out' (p. 223). By 1985 'only two dozen councils had privatized street cleaning or refuse collection and only about half a dozen county councils or metropolitan boroughs had contracted out school cleaning or the provision of school meals' (p. 227). The push for contracting-out did not come from an ideologically committed centre as happened to the NHS but from local initiatives to remove inefficiencies generated by a strong trade union presence (p. 243). The selective adoption of contracting-out was unwelcome both to contractors and to the centre. In February 1985, therefore, the DoE issued a consultative document on mandatory contracting-out, and legislation is inevitable (DoE, 1985). To date, 'hands-off' controls have remained in their infancy for local government (for detailed surveys of contracting-out in local government see the annual survey conducted by the *Local Government Chronicle*, e.g. Hardingham, 1983 and 1984).

Fifth, categorizing relationships in this way draws attention away from the mix of relationships in a given policy area. Thus, Houlihan (1984, p. 408) suggests that the relationship between the DHSS and local authorities is bureaucratic and technical, and the relationship between its regional offices and local authorities is professional (for example, social work) and bureaucratic (for example, housing benefit). The Home Office's relationship with fire and police authorities is predominantly bureaucratic. The DoE has the most complex mix encompassing the full range of relationships. These variations in the mix of relationships will be described and analysed in more detail in the discussion of the networks in action.

Finally, the emphasis on the diversity of relationships has to be counterbalanced with the recognition that there are pressures for, and means of attaining, integration. The pressures for integration reside in the fragmentation of the centre and consequent imperatives for co-ordination. The means of integration are not limited to PES and other measures for reinforcing the internal co-ordination of the centre. They extend also to the range of national level organizations representing local government. These organizations form the national community of local government (Rhodes, 1986a, p. 54) within which the political parties and topocratic professions play a key interlocking role. In turn, the national community is linked to a range of service-specific policy networks through its membership of central advisory and consultative bodies. Together these networks constitute the national local government system (see Chapter 2, section 2.5.1(iv), pp. 58–61 and 79–80) which has its own distinct institutions, most notably the Audit Commission and the Commission for Local Administration. These bodies are focal points or 'bounding institutions' (J. D. Stewart, 1983, p. 67), spanning services and types of authority, which help to sustain, and even to create, national-level ideological structures. In other words, they create 'values, beliefs and assumptions about how local authorities should conduct their affairs. They lay down best practice in terms that can become standard practice' (J. D. Stewart, 1983, p. 67). The Audit Commission's proselytizing for the 'three Es' of economy, efficiency and effectiveness is perhaps the best example of such influence in recent years. Thus Webb, Wistow and Hardy (1986, pp. 187–8 and 213–4) conclude that the 'value-for-money' ethos fostered by the commission had 'hastened ... power drifting into the hands of finance staff', a trend summarized by social service professionals as 'the money-men are in the ascendancy'. If the influence of the national local government system is diffuse, none the less it is an important restraint on the centrifugal forces generated by local government's diverse interests, its range of resources (and the corresponding dependence of a non-executant centre) and the mix of relationships in and between policy areas.

The single most important consequence of local government's diverse relationships is the inertia thereby engendered. Central decisions are not translated into action in any straightforward manner. On occasion, local authorities can simply reject central policy. The resulting conflict can be intractable. For example, Clay Cross refused to implement the Conservative government's Housing Finance Act. Whatever the merits of the case, the law had clearly been broken, and it would seem reasonable to presume that the authority could and would be brought to heel. However, as Mitchell (1974, p. 177) argues, Clay Cross demonstrates the ineffectiveness of central control. Or in the words of one senior official, it 'opened my eyes to just how much a council can get away with if it sets its mind to it'. If there are problems in controlling outright defiance, they multiply when the centre faces a council set on policy maintenance rather than innovation. Thus, Hartley (1971, p. 450) suggests that the easiest authorities to control are those that want to do something. Deliberately inactive local authorities which, for example, do not wish to build council houses in spite of central subsidies are difficult to handle. Equally, the determined authority can act in the face of central opposition (Blackstone, 1971, pp. 133–4).

All of these examples are pre-1979. It might be thought that the post-1979 Conservative government would have found ways and means of containing recalcitrant local authorities. In fact, its record is mixed. On the sale of council houses, it has imposed its policy on local authorities and it has also effected a dramatic reduction in local capital expenditure. But central attempts to contain local expenditure have taken on the character of a boxing match as each side throws punch and counter-punch to defeat the other's policy. After five years, local expenditure had not been contained, and the combatants had entered into the 'rate capping' rounds with no end in sight to the contest.

If local authorities can resist central policy, it should not be thought that such conflict is the norm. Relationships remain predominantly consensual and consultative even after 1979. The recalcitrance of recent years is noteworthy but it has not replaced local government's 'responsibility ethic'. The degree of compliance remains substantial if beset by tensions. The purpose of this discussion is to demonstrate that local authorities have the capacity to resist central interventions, not that they invariably do so. And awareness of this potential for recalcitrance reinforces the organization and informational dependence of centre on locality. The centre may be the senior partner but it is a partner in a relationship of interdependence. To turn a blind eye to this interdependence is to adopt a faulty territorial operating code, to provoke recalcitrance and to generate policy messes. As the pre-eminent territorial institution in British government, local government can exact a price for its compliance and impose costs should its legitimated policy preferences be overridden. No other unit of SCG has a comparable capacity.

3.6.4 Summary

Local government may be the pre-eminent territorial institution, but this pre-eminence does not bespeak unity. The several types of local authority, their range of service interests, the entrenched professionalism of local authority departments, the ever more pervasive party political differences and the markedly different needs of areas serve to guarantee that local government speaks with many voices. The 'interests of local government' as a whole are as elusive as the phrase is grandiloquent. In pursuit of their several interests, however, local authorities have a range of resources. Inevitably, there are marked variations in their distribution. Most distinctively, local authorities are elected units of government subject to variations in political control and with very different local political systems. Most important, they have hands-on control of services through their command of organizational and informational resources. Whatever the variations between the several local government systems in authority and money, all share the capacity to modify central policy in the process of implementation. In consequence, local authorities are embedded in complex networks of interdependence. Their relationships with the centre are bureaucratic, technical, professional, personal, informal consultative, formal consultative and party political. And the mix of relationships extends to non-departmental public bodies and the private sector, varying from policy area to policy area. The most important consequence of the diverse interests, resources and relationships of local government is the inertia thereby engendered. Local government's responsibility ethic may sustain a high degree of compliance with central policy, but such policy is not implemented in a straightforward fashion. Indifference, recalcitrance and conflict have become ever more prominent features of central–local relations. Local authorities have legitimated interests different from those of the centre and the resources to support opposition to central policy. The diversity which is seen as enabling the centre to divide and rule local government is also the major stumbling block to effective central intervention. The costs of bureaucratic controls can be high, and the capacity of local government to impose such costs on the centre makes it unique amongst SCG.

3.7   Sub-Central Political Organizations

The universe of political organizations is vast if not limitless, rendering any attempt to provide a comprehensive account nugatory. The problem of describing them is compounded secondly by the non-local nature of much of their activity. Many pressure groups have a local base but gravitate towards the centre for their lobbying and other activities. Thus, the regional branches of the CBI can be considered only marginal sub-central pressure groups. Even on ostensibly local issues such as the non-domestic rate, the bulk of lobbying occurs at the national level. Third, the bulk of the available literature focuses on either the local or the national dimension to pressure group activities. It ignores the central–local dimension. Finally, at the purely local level, an encyclopaedia would not suffice to describe the micro-politics of, for example, the inner cities. Consequently, this section is subject to a number of arbitrary constraints.

Earlier sections of this chapter have emphasized the importance of political parties and the professions. These earlier discussions did not cover central–local relationships within the parties and the professions. The distinct political environment of the territorial ministries was also stressed, but their distinct political organizations were not described. The first task of this section will be to repair these omissions. In addition, it will conclude with a general account of sub-central parties and pressure groups if only to convey the flavour of this element in territorial politics.

3.7.1   Central–Local Relationships within the Political Parties

The structure of British political parties has been described as fragmented rather than centralized and as characterized by 'bargaining among barons' (Rose, 1974, p. 165).[8] Most accounts of the parties omit links between the national and local levels. In so far as this topic is covered, local parties are said to have become 'nationalized'. The parties are seen as unitary and the local level as a pale reflection of the centre, useful for aiding the electoral machinery. An essential first step is to determine, therefore, whether the parties are unitary or 'stratarchies'; that is, they have a 'hierarchical pattern of stratified devolution of responsibility for the settlement of conflicts'. Conflicts are not resolved by the party leadership. In addition, the parties have to 'cope with widely varying local milieus of opinion, tradition, and social structure, and this encourages the recognition and acceptance of local leadership, local strategy, local power' (Eldersveld, 1964, p. 9, cited in Gyford and James, 1983, p. 4). It will be argued here that the parties are 'stratarchies' and that there are several dimensions to intra-party linkages. The linkages in Figure 3.1 lettered A, B and C are not covered here (see Rose, 1974). Linkage 1 has been described

Centre

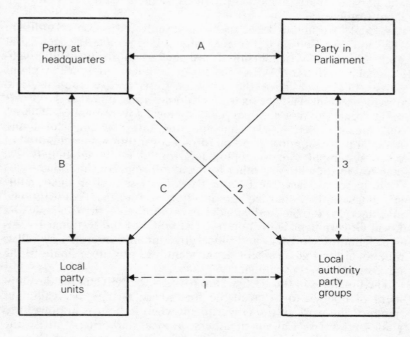

Figure 3.1   *Party linkages.*
Source: Gyford and James, 1983, p. 7.

in a number of case studies (for example, Jones, 1969; Newton, 1976). This section concentrates on linkages 2 and 3.

Both major parties make provision for local party groups in their national organizational structure (linkage 2). Within the Conservative Party, the National Union of Conservative and Unionist Associations, the membership wing of the party, has its National Advisory Committee on Local Government (NACLG) and Conservative Central Office, the administrative wing of the party, has a local government department. The NACLG is primarily composed of Conservative leaders in local government (60 per cent), but there are places for up to six MPs, and the link with the party in Parliament is reinforced in the Policy Liaison Group, in effect a subcommittee of the NACLG. The NACLG acts as a link between the party leader and all branches of the party 'on the problems concerned with local government, and on any proposed legislation' (cited in Gyford and James, 1983, p. 34). However, its role is only advisory, its influence resides in persuasion, and its main activity is to air views. A further opportunity to air views and persuade party leaders is provided by the annual Local Government Conference.

A local government department was established in Central Office in 1946 and, like Central Office generally, is best seen as the secretariat of the Conservative leadership. It provides administrative and organizational help to the NACLG and for the annual conference; explains party policy; publicizes the work of Conservative councils, and provides technical advice on local electioneering. It has no direct role in the formulation of national policy on local government. As Gyford and James (1983, p. 43) conclude, the links between local and national party do not depend on formal constitutional machinery but on a 'system of internal diplomacy' rooted in shared beliefs and manifest in soundings or other forms of informal consultation.

On paper at least, the Labour Party has less faith in tacit understandings and a marked predilection for formal constitutional machinery. It too has both an advisory committee – the Regional and Local Government Subcommittee (RLGSC) of the National Executive Committee (NEC) – and a local government conference as well as a national local government department. All are subordinate to the NEC and the party's annual conference.

The functions of the RLGSC are to assist the NEC 'in the development of policy'; to be available for 'advice on specific issues'; to 'monitor the work of the Government when Labour is in power'; to guide and advise Labour members on local authorities; advise the 'Home Policy Committee on local elections'; and arrange 'the annual Local Government Conference, meetings of Labour Group representatives on Local Authority Associations, and relations with Labour Groups' (cited in Gyford and James, 1983, p. 53).

The membership of the RLGSC has grown from 14 in 1955–6 to 46 in 1979–80. In the same period the balance of membership has shifted from numerical domination by MPs and NEC members to encompass a wider range of interests, especially representatives from the party's regions and the local authority associations. Similarly, the Local Government Conference has become a more elaborate affair, including delegates from the local party organizations as well as councillors and working groups on particular issues as well as rallying speeches by the front bench. Gyford and James (1983, p. 63) conclude that the RLGSC and annual conference, when able to speak for a substantial body of opinion on a subject', can 'claim a place, albeit a modest one, in the process of party policy-making' (see also Rhodes, 1986a, ch. 6).

The Local Government Section was established in 1936 and it has remained small. The local government officer acts as secretary to the RLGSC, producing background briefs for the committee. In conjunction with the Research Department, the section provides information and advice for the party on local government matters (most notably, the estimable *Local Government Handbook*). In effect the section acts as civil servants to the NEC and RLGSC and, in the preparation of initial policy papers, it can 'impart a political overtone to the work they do' (Gyford and James, 1983, p. 65).

The organization of the other parties is nowhere near as elaborate. Up to 1977 the Liberals had a full-time local government officer at headquarters, a task now carried out by the Association of Liberal Councillors (ALC). The ALC is a constituent body of the party, like the Young Liberals, with its own members and a direct role in policy-making. It is not part of the central organization. Initially, its main function was to win more local elections. It now advises on a range of local government matters. In contrast to the Conservative and Labour parties, responsibility for local government has remained with the grass roots, and in this organizational sense there are no central–local linkages. The advance of the SDP in local government is recent and has affinities with the Liberal emphasis on community politics, but the form of future central–local linkages remains to be seen. (On the Ecology Party – now the Green Party – see Gyford and James, 1983, pp. 84–6; and on ratepayers' associations and other 'purely local parties' see Grant, 1977.)

As measured by the number of MPs with a local government background, the links between local government and Parliament (linkage 3 in Figure 3.1, above) have become stronger. Following the 1979 election the proportion of such MPs had risen to 44.4 per cent overall, and the figure for new MPs of 56.4 per cent was the highest in the postwar period (Gyford and James, 1983, table 5.1, p. 103; see also Chapter 2, section 2.5.1(vi), page 73). The problem with such data is that they are a poor indicator of the extent to which such MPs articulate local interests, because, on acquiring parliamentary status, MPs tend to forsake local government.

There is one other important party political linkage of more recent origins: contact via party groups on the local authority associations. The politicization of the associations lies not, as one might assume, with the Labour Party but with the decision by the Conservatives on the (then) Association of Municipal Corporations (AMC) to oust its Labour chairmen after their sweeping gains in the local elections of 1967: a decision taken with the active support and encouragement of the local government officer at Conservative Central Office. The future pattern for both parties of party organization within the associations and closer liaison with party headquarters had been established. The trend was to be accentuated by the reorganization of 1974 and, after 1979, by the policies of the Conservative Party. Consequently, the political leaders of the associations have become figures on the national stage. Perversely this trend has created rifts with party headquarters. The association groups may have 'been the creation of the parties headquarters' but 'they could no longer be called their creatures, nor the creatures of parliamentary leaderships, for they contained politicians with interests, and goals, of their own' (Gyford and James, 1983, p. 125).

The foregoing account is limited to the formal relationship within the parties. In reality, intra-party relationships vary greatly, ranging from detachment through co-operation to antagonism. Detachment does not mean that the levels within the party are disaffected but that there is a clear division of labour. In the words of the Labour group leader on Ipswich District Council, 'we row our own boat'. Local councils know what is best for their area; 'self-sufficiency' is the key word and insulation the dominant characteristic of the spasmodic relationships. Sir John Grugeon, the leader of Kent County Council, illustrates co-operative relationships: 'He is one of the leading figures of the Conservative local government world and has been involved in, if not influential in, all the major policy decisions on local government by the present [1979–83] Conservative government' (Gyford and James, 1983, p. 127).

Antagonism is dramatically illustrated by the clash over South Yorkshire County Council's policy of subsidizing bus fares. The (then) Labour government's policy was that fares should rise in line with inflation, and in addition it had to reduce public expenditure as a condition of the IMF loan. Consequently, there was impasse. In the 1977–8 Transport Supplementary Grant (TSG) settlement, the Secretary of State for Transport, William Rodgers, withheld some £4 million from South Yorkshire, allocating it a mere £291,000. Protests through the AMA and in bilaterals between the county and the department were to no avail. The key channel of influence was internal to the Labour Party. Thus, the local Labour MPs met the minister; the NEC through the RLGSC supported South Yorkshire; and critical resolutions were approved at the local government conference. South Yorkshire, in the words of the minister's political adviser, was 'being a right bloody pain' through party channels (Gyford and James, 1983, p. 146). Its war of attrition was to prove successful. For the 1978–9 TSG settlement, the council 'lost' a portion of the transport subsidy elsewhere in the budget; only a proportion of its total revenue support was declared in the TSG submission. This bid for £2.5 million was accepted by the minister, who was fully aware of the real level of subsidy. He concluded that 'on the whole they probably got what they wanted' (Gyford and James, 1983, p. 146). Lacking allies within the party, with multiple demands on his time and confronted by an opponent who commanded considerable ideological legitimacy within the party and gave the matter single-minded attention, the minister gave way with as much grace as he could muster. As Gyford and James (1983, p. 151) put it, 'the political parties are by no means monolithic as far as their internal central–local relations are concerned' (see also Rhodes, 1986a, ch. 6).

In short, therefore, the political parties are 'stratarchies'; they are not unitary. If parliamentary channels of influence are relatively unimportant and ineffective, then intra-party channels of communication are important for local government as a means of influencing central policy and they can be supplemented with pressure from party groups on the associations. The nationalization of local politics is a nationalization of electoral labels. Heterogeneity extending to intra-party, central–local conflict is the lot of both major parties. The Conservative Party's internal relationships are of lower visibility than those of the Labour Party, but whether the mechanism for resolving conflicts is 'internal diplomacy' or 'adversarial', both parties have to manage central–local conflicts. Rhodes (1986a, p. 389) has described party as 'the grit in the molluscs of Whitehall-based policy networks'. Local parties have a similar irritant value within the national party.

To this point, the discussion has focused on relationships and has disregarded the interests and resources of local parties. Until it had been shown that the parties were not unitary and that local politics had not been nationalized, an exploration of the bases of heterogeneity was unnecessary. It is now time to repair these omissions.

The interests of local parties are as diverse as the localities in which they are active and at times they are indistinguishable from such areal interests. Two aspects of these interests warrant further comment. First, in the Labour Party, local interests are interwoven with larger ideological debates, epitomized currently by the new urban Left's belief in using local government to demonstrate what socialism can achieve. Its goal of mobilizing citizens to fight the cuts in expenditure and to 'promote radical social change through political action at the grass roots' (Gyford, 1985, p. 66) conflicts with, for example, the party's long-standing commitment to central action for national standards of service; it is a clash of territorial operating codes (Keating, 1984, p. 76). In these circumstances, national and local interests become indistinguishable. Local socialism becomes the banner for reforming the national party (for a more detailed discussion see Gyford, 1985b, esp. ch. 4).

Second, within both parties, an ever-prominent interest is expressed in the call for loyalty. It is particularly marked in the Conservative Party, where 'there is an implicit assumption that everyone is on the same side' and 'an emphasis on discussion and consensus building' (Gyford and James, 1983, p. 20). Indeed, the stresses and strains within the party attendant on the 1979–83 Conservative government's policies on local government arose in part from the refusal to discuss: to countenance alternatives. In the Labour Party, solidarity is not an implicit assumption but the subject of argument. None the less it can be invoked to override local party interests. To describe intra-party central–local relations and to identify local party interests is not to deny that national party views can prevail. It is to insist that such views do not prevail as a matter of course; they have to be negotiated. And such negotiations are affected by the resources of the participants.

A major constraint on the ability of the national parties to impose their views lies in the simple fact that 'Constitutionally none of the parties possess any mechanisms whereby local politicians can be forced to comply with the wishes of the party at the centre' (Gyford and James, 1983, p. 195). The financial and organizational resources of the party at the centre are equally modest whilst it remains dependent on local parties for information on what is going on in local government. Political resources in this context are elusive, depending upon the personality and skills of the individual and on his or her reception in the various courts of appeal within the parties. Overall, 'the distribution of resources is such that neither national nor local politicians can command the loyalty and obedience of their party colleagues at the other level of government' (Gyford and James, 1983, p. 200).

In sum, therefore, the parties are 'stratarchies'; intra-party channels of communication are an important route for influencing central policy, and neither level has the resources to control the other. But, if they are not unitary, 'their historic orientation towards achieving their goals through the established unitary state has prevented them from defining a distinctive role for local government' (Gyford and James, 1983, p. 210).

3.7.2   Central–Local Relationships and the Professions

To examine central–local relations and the professions is to revisit the policy networks because the most distinctive feature of the professions compared to other sectional groups is their institutionalization in the structure of government.[9] The professions, in local government in particular but also in government more generally, are 'organizational professions', and the locus of their activity in central–local and inter-organizational relations is the appropriate, function-specific policy community. It is necessary to examine, therefore, the distinct patterns of institutionalization of the topocratic and technocratic professions. Apart from their involvement in government, the professions are organized as 'learned societies', in which capacity they recruit and train personnel, organize conferences and seminars, produce research and publications and, as with any other organized group, proselytize and lobby for their interests. Finally, the organizational professions are also trade unions and practise 'dual closure'; that is, they deploy both exclusionary and usurpatory strategies (see Chapter 2, section 2.5.1(v), and section 3.6.1(iii), above). Thus, they can use working to rule and strikes as a means of influencing the government. In effect, therefore, the professions can have three bites at the cherry of political influence. This section will discuss professional influence under the three headings of networks, societies and trade unions for both technocrats and topocrats. As in the preceding section, the focus will be on relationships. There is, however, one major difference. Professional influence is not peculiar to local government but is a pervasive feature of non-departmental public bodies – for example, the NHS and the water industry. Consequently, the discussion of the technocratic professions is subdivided to cover both local government and other public sector bodies.

3.7.2(i) THE TOPOCRATIC PROFESSIONS

A concern with the range of services within a particular geographical area is not the only distinctive characteristic of the topocratic professions. They are also peculiar to local government, involved in a range of policy networks and eschew usurpatory strategies. The major topocrats are the Society of Local Authority Chief Executives (SOLACE) and the accountancy profession, variously organized as the Chartered Institute of Public Finance and Accountancy (CIPFA) and in societies specific to the particular type of authority (for example, the Society of County Treasurers).

The constitution of SOLACE speaks of it taking a lead 'in matters of fundamental importance to the health and future of local government'; of playing 'its part in defending the concept of local democracy'; and of providing 'leadership and commitment to the ideals of local government'. Such statements reflect the topocratic orientation of the society. The constitution also speaks of fostering the interests of chief executives, but all trade union matters are entrusted to a separate organization, the Association of Local Authority Chief Executives (ALACE). SOLACE's relationship with the local government policy community – the national community of local government – is particularly close. Indeed, SOLACE's honorary secretary felt that it was 'desperately important that there should be a good relationship'; 'we have got to work with the local authority associations'. The society nominates advisers to all the committees of all the associations, and the two topocratic professions are unique in this respect. Thus in 1979 they accounted for 32 per cent (ACC), 42 per cent (ADC) and 35 per cent (AMA) of all advisers in each association. In sharp contrast, it is exceptional for the technocratic professions to provide advisers for any committee other than that which is directly concerned with their field of expertise (Rhodes, 1986a, pp. 84–5).

There are, of course, different interests within SOLACE; this is inevitable, given that its membership is drawn from all types of local authority in the UK. The clearest example of such differences is the existence of the Association of County Chief Executives (ACCE). It was formed in 1974 to continue the relationship of the Society of **County Clerks with the pre-reorganization County Councils'**

Association (CCA). Thus, the ACCE and not SOLACE nominates officer advisers to the ACC. Membership of the ACCE is conditional upon membership of SOLACE, and the former studiously avoids raising an independent voice.

The organization of the accountancy profession is considerably more complex. Membership of the CIPFA is accorded to all who attain the requisite professional qualification, as determined by the institute, and irrespective of type of employing authority or their position in that authority. Neither SOLACE nor any technocratic profession in local government confers professional qualifications, and all are restricted to chief officers (and in some cases their deputies). The *raison d'être* of the CIPFA is to advance the standing of, and standards in, accountancy and financial management in the public sector; consequently, to foster this general professional interest, it undertakes a wide range of activities: for example, professional training, statistical advisory services and research and publication. Indeed, the standing of the CIPFA is enhanced not only by its extensive services but also by the range of organizations which benefit from them, including central departments.

To cater for the interests of the several types of local authority, treasurers are also organized in local government societies: the Society of County Treasurers (SCT), the Society of Metropolitan Treasurers (SMT) and the Association of District Council Treasurers in England, and there are separate societies in the peripheral nations, e.g. in Scotland the Society of Directors of Finance. The members of these societies are chief officers (and their deputies) all of whom are members of the CIPFA, and their *raison d'être* is to provide advisers for the association. Otherwise the two types of treasurers' organization are virtually indistinguishable.

For both SOLACE and the treasurers, advisers are appointed as individuals on the basis of their expertise, experience and integrity. They are expected to reflect the problems of their type of local authority and best professional practice. They are not mandated by their societies, a state of affairs officially accepted by the societies themselves. They are not required (or even expected) to accept and forward any recommendations their societies may make. At most they report back, although even here experience is mixed, with the SCT expecting no such reports and the SMT expecting but not getting them.

Both the CIPFA and SOLACE have elaborate regional activities, which in the CIPFA's case are primarily concerned with relatively narrow professional activities (for example, seminars for accountancy students). SOLACE has sixty-four branches (based on the counties) combined into twelve territorial divisions. The latter produce their own working papers, comparable to the work of the society's *ad hoc* national working parties, and arrange their own seminars. Neither topocratic society has any formal policy-making structure below its central machinery.

This description of SOLACE and the CIPFA makes them seem unprepossessing bodies, and their influence does not reside in spectacular campaigns or intensive lobbying. They are part of the air that is breathed; their influence resides in continuous involvement and the ideologies articulated. The ideology of the topocratic professions can be most succinctly summarized with the phrases 'the interests of local government' and 'local government's responsibility ethic'. Thus, they are concerned to preserve the status and roles of local authorities in British government and to ensure that, in carrying out these roles, local authorities respect the centre's right to manage the economy and to determine the appropriate level of public expenditure. The alternative phrases 'protect the status quo' and 'extol the virtues of sound financial management' may sound conservative (with a small 'c'), and to some ears derogatory, but they are uncomfortably close to capturing the heart of topocratic ideology. For example, Flynn (1985, pp. 122 and 132–3) points out that government legislation on Direct Labour Organizations (DLOs) was facilitated by the work of the CIPFA, which provided an accounting code of practice and helped to draft the regulations: 'Without the detailed work of the CIPFA, the legislation could not have been implemented. The shift of role of the CIPFA was a significant one: from offering guidelines to individual treasurers on how to keep accounts to the imposition of an accounting system.' The CIPFA 'was seen by local government as an important source of support for the government'. Similarly, in the era of the CCLGF, the topocratic professions were key supporters of this centrally inspired attempt to restrain local expenditure through persuasion and incorporation. It is not that these professions are well placed to air their views – as indeed they are – but that it is virtually impossible to avoid hearing their expression. Whether the forum is an association or an advisory/consultative body, they will be present. If precise attributions of influence are elusive, the presupposition of influence through continuous involvement is irresistible.

In reaching this conclusion, it is important to remember that the topocratic professions have a priceless resource: the legitimacy of expertise. No technocratic profession is of higher standing in the world of local government, and, in the era of cuts, financial expertise is highly valued. And if chief executives are a new breed, they are heirs to the town and county clerks and the mystique of the law. Upon reorganization in 1974, 84 per cent were solicitors by profession and 10.5 per cent were treasurers. The proportion of treasurers has risen slightly in the intervening years, but the position remains the virtually exclusive province of solicitors and treasurers (Lomer, 1977). The chief executive and treasurer may be specific to local government but both have ties to professions of high standing in other sectors of British life. This alliance of status, professional expertise and knowledge of local government may not guarantee a respectful audience for their views but it goes some considerable distance towards it.

The topocratic professions are key actors in the national community of local government and, as its advisers, they have access to the range of local government policy networks. Commanding the legitimacy of expertise, they exercise influence through continous involvement, eschewing the more overt forms of pressure group activity. Few technocratic professions command equal status or are as well placed to exercise influence over an equivalent range of issues.

3.7.2(ii)   THE TECHNOCRATIC PROFESSIONS

The discussion of the topocratic professions implies that professional influence is monolithic. The picture which will emerge from even the briefest portrait of the technocratic professions is one of disparities of influence. Whereas the water engineers seem indomitable, the history of housing is of a profession struggling for recognition. The medical profession seems a constant in the history of the NHS, whereas the rise and 'fall' of the highway engineers illustrates that professional power cannot be treated as a given. Moreover, no matter how established, the capacity of a profession to exert influence varies with the particular issue, the prevailing economic conditions and the salience of the policy for the government of the day. To accord the professions an important role in territorial politics is essential given that they have been accorded serious attention in the literature only recently. However, care must be taken to recognize the limits to professional influence. The professions described below have been chosen to illustrate such variations in a range of governmental settings. The theme is a simple one: technocratic professions are ever-present to variable effect.

As an immediate antidote to the topocratic professions, and to continue for the moment with local government examples, the rise and fall of highway engineers is instructive. Engineering is one of the oldest professions in local government; and in terms of finance, highway engineering has been the single most important area of engineering in local government for the bulk of the postwar period. Its roots lie in the work of Edwin Chadwick on sanitary conditions which led to the Public Health Act 1848 and the appointment of sanitary engineers and surveyors. In parallel, pioneering civil engineers like Thomas Telford and John Loudon Macadam called for improvements in the calibre and training of road engineers. By the end of the nineteenth century engineers were established first in the town and then, after their reform, in the counties. The Association of Municipal and Sanitary Engineers, for senior officers only, was established in 1873 and by 1885 had begun to develop a certification function. The Institution of Civil Engineers was established in 1818 and the County Surveyors' Society (CSS) in 1885.

With the arrival of the motor car, the impetus for road improvements gathered momentum. In 1910 a Road Board was established, and for the first time engineers were appointed in central government. The chief engineer was a former county surveyor, a pattern continued with the creation of the Ministry of Transport in 1919 and its divisional road engineers. Between the wars the main preoccupation was road improvements and maintenance, but the Trunk Roads Act 1936 introduced the concept of central responsibility for a national system, and, following its foundation in 1930, the Institution of Highway Engineers (IHE) lobbied for a national system modelled on the German autobahn. These ideas were adopted by the CSS, the majority of whose members belonged to the IHE, and its plans, with the support of the CCA, formed the basis of the modest motorway programme announced by the Labour government in 1946.

The period of economic reconstruction following the war saw major road construction accorded a relatively low priority. The turning-point was the mid-1950s when expenditure began to grow rapidly with the ministry responsible for the new system of motorways and the counties acting as construction agents. Above all the assumptions, promulgated by the CSS and the IHE, that roads should be built to accommodate expanding traffic became the cornerstone of policy and was not to be seriously challenged for twenty years.

With the extension of road construction, highway engineers, both at the centre and in the locality, became more deeply institutionalized in government. Within the Ministry of Transport, a new post of Director of Highway Engineering was created as joint head of the highways organization, and professional and administrative staff were more closely integrated throughout the organization: in effect giving the engineers a direct input to policy in place of their previous advisory role (Regan, 1966). Moreover, these organizational changes enabled the ministry to deflect calls for more delegation to local authorities. In keeping with the times, the benefits of economies of scale pervaded the discussion of reorganization. New Road Construction Units (RCUs) were to be inserted between centre and locality, and motorway work was concentrated in just sixteen counties. The proposal divided the CSS – a 'flashy idea' – but it enhanced the influence over the roads programmes of those county surveyors in the sixteen participating counties. The RCUs were staffed by engineers from both centre and locality, and their overall effect was to create a strong roads policy community or, to employ Painter's (1980, p. 183) description, 'an extreme case of sectoral self-containment'. They even created a new career ladder, from county surveyor to RCU director.

An an example of a professionalized policy community, roads could be seen as an archetypal policy network in British government:

immovable, immutable and inertial. But then came the reorganization of local government and the environmentalists, followed by economic decline.

The creation of the RCUs had created the 'haves' and 'have-nots' amongst highway engineers. The reorganization of local government in 1974 created the 'have-nothings'. Former county borough and district engineers found themselves in new district authorities with virtually no engineering functions other than those conferred through agency agreements with the counties. If organization had initially bolstered the rise of the profession, reorganization was dividing and undermining it.

Moreover, cherished assumptions about roads were under threat from an unanticipated quarter, the environmental movement: 'the "slippage" problem was changing from a "technical" one of lengthy procedures, and inefficiency in scheme preparation, to a "political" one of the growth of intransigence' (Painter, 1980, p. 178).

There had always been statutory procedures for hearing objections to, for example, the line of a motorway. Such local and public inquiries had always been seen as a source of delay (see, for example, Gregory, 1967) but now they were seen in a sinister light, as an ideal vehicle for politically motivated obstruction (see, for example, Levin, 1979). The anti-roads lobby was in full swing, disrupting two major inquiries in 1976 at Aire Valley and Winchester. (On the tactics of the various environmental groups see Kimber and Richardson, 1974.) Such 'slippage' coincided with reductions in public expenditure, making roads vulnerable to cuts (Painter, 1980, p. 182). They were not long in coming as the minister announced a switch to a selective programme of construction because the national motorway network was nearing completion. And as road construction declined, the future of the RCUs became uncertain, and, with much havering, they were run down. With the advent of the Conservative government in 1979, the run-down ceased to be a relatively simple, if tortuous to negotiate, matter of redeploying RCU staff. Privatization in the guise of handing over road construction to private sector consultants became the order of the day with only localized schemes going to the counties. Opposition from the CSS, ACC and AMA was to no avail, and there was nothing for the engineers to do but to return to the concerns of their founding fathers, highway maintenance. However, with the decline of the roads programme, 'the integrity of internal logics and political arrangements within policy sectors was not directly challenged'. the policy community remained intact, and the 'reappraisal' simply meant that the roads men 'for the most part merely lowered their ambitions' (Painter, 1980, p. 184).

If the rise of engineers as the first technical profession was spectacular, its decline has been a more sedate affair. From the apogee of motorway construction it has returned to the plateau of highway maintenance. Perhaps the most noteworthy feature of this trend is the intimidating combination of circumstances necessary to bring it about. The restriction of opportunities for sections of the profession brought about by the reorganizations in 1967 and 1974; the scale and intensity of the environmental lobby; past success so that ministers could argue the national network was complete; and the economic decline of Britain were all required. The hoary old analogy with the phoenix may yet be appropriate, and the example of the autobahn may return to fuel another escape from recession (Dudley, 1983).

More briefly, the case of housing management illustrates not the heights of professional influence but the long drawn out struggle of a quasi-profession to scale the foothills. For the bulk of the interwar years, housing management was predominantly if not exclusively the responsibility of treasurers, town clerks, engineers, or surveyors. The forerunner of what would become the Institute of Housing (IoH) was established in 1931, but progress was slow.

The postwar commitment to housing accelerated not only the number of units built but also concern with their management. Progress towards the development of a housing profession was slow, however. Thus, in 1965 just over half of the housing authorities employed a housing manager, and only 418 out of 1,135 had a housing department. Consequently, the ministry, the associations and IoH met to discuss ways and means of improving training.

At the same time, the climate surrounding housing policy was changing. The stress on building to meet the demand for housing, on numbers of units, gave way to an area-based approach: to a conception of housing policy as a series of local problems. The implications of this change for housing management were spelt out in a report by Professor Barry Cullingworth for the Central Housing Advisory Council (CHAC, 1969). It advocated expanded responsibilities for local authorities: a comprehensive housing service and unified housing departments which moved beyond the landlord–tenant relationship to encompass social welfare and the corporate management ideas current in local government. These ideas were enthusiastically adopted by housing officials and were given an enormous boost by the reorganization of local government in 1974. Thus, the Bains Report (1972) advocated the appointment of a director of housing responsible for the total housing function. As so often in the past, central initiatives and promptings were instrumental to the development of the housing profession.

The IoH did not spurn the opportunity presented by reorganization. It pressed for a comprehensive housing service. In 1975 a survey by the IoH found that fifty-one out of fifty-four local authorities with over 150,000 population had housing departments with chief officers, forty of whom were also members of the management team. However, some housing functions remained outside the new housing departments – for example, rent collection – especially in the smaller district councils. The housing profession was, at last, acquiring a substantial institutional base in the localities.

At the centre, the progress of the housing profession was equally slow. The first central adviser on housing management was appointed in 1944, but real development did not occur until the Labour government of 1974–9. From proselytizing by individual advisers, the (then) ministerial team at the DoE, Anthony Crosland and Reg Freeson, set in motion a review of housing policy, instituted HIPs and proposed in 1977 the establishment of a Housing Services Advisory Unit, which came into being in 1979, only to be abolished by the Conservative government.

In tandem with these developments, which provided the housing profession with a central organizational base, albeit a restricted one, there was a strong push to improve training. At the time a mere 3.5 per cent of the non-manual staff in housing departments were qualified. Considerable controversy surrounded the proposal for a central training council, but as the dust settled the LGTB emerged with a Housing Service Training Committee, which contributed funds to the training of senior management. The IoH remained disgruntled with this arrangement, but in spite of encouraging noises the post-1979 Conservative government has taken no steps to establish a central training council.

By the end of the 1970s, therefore, the housing profession had begun to establish itself. Central initiatives and corporate management in local government meant that the shackles of indifference and rival professions could be shaken off. Unified housing management was the order of the day: the wave of fashion to be ridden to the goal of an institutionalized and, therefore, recognized profession. Compared to social workers, the rise to prominence may not have been spectacular, but rise it was. The route march over the foothills was complete; the peaks remained to be scaled.

If housing illustrates the slow struggle for recognition, it also illustrates that policy communities and professionalism are *not* synonyms. As Dunleavy (1981b, p. 18, esp. fig. 1.2) demonstrates, there is a 'unified' consultative network at the national level in which the IoH is a participant; but the key actors, for example on housing construction, were the National Consultative Council for Building and Civil Engineering, the Building Economic Development Committee and the Building Research Station, all of which had significant private sector representation. Amongst the professions, architects and planners were the most prominent, but Dunleavy (1981b, p. 20) concludes that the trend has been to consolidate industry influence; producer interests have squeezed out the consumer. In a similar vein, Laffin (1986, p. 217) concludes that:

in highway engineering the professional community made a major contribution towards creating the modern policy community in the roads sector ... the professional community provided the problem definitions and the policy response as well as most of the leading participants in the policy community. In contrast, the housing professional community had very limited influence within the housing policy community. That community was dominated not by professional accounts of policy but by politicians' accounts and, to a lesser extent, civil servants' concerns with the orderly local administration of public housing.

Moreover, the housing profession remained insufficiently integrated and organized to deploy usurpatory strategies. Exclusionary strategies prevailed and are manifested in the current attempt to improve training and establish a professional qualification. There is not only a sharp contrast with established professions such as engineering but with other emergent professions in the postwar period such as social work and education, which vigorously employed dual closure.

Thus, the social work dispute of 1979 over the implementation of regrading schemes for social workers covered fourteen local authorities and involved some 2,600 social workers going on strike, most notably in Tower Hamlets. Moreover, it followed hot on the heels of the Birch Report (1979), which can be seen as the high point of social work credentialism, proposing target dates after which untrained people could not be employed as social workers. The protracted teachers' dispute over pay in 1985–6 similarly illustrates the operation of the strategy of dual closure and it reflects also the widespread discontents of the organizational professionals in an era of resource squeeze. Teachers had not simply seen their salaries eroded by inflation and 'cash limits as public sector pay policy' but were witnessing the contraction of the profession (and the service generally) under the impact of falling school rolls and a challenge to their competence, with the several measures and proposals to evaluate the performance not only of individual schools but also of individual teachers. Allied to proposals to alter conditions of service, pay was the focus of discontent but by no means its root cause.

The discontent of the organizational professions is mirrored in the militancy of public sector unionism. Laffin (1985, pp. 19–20) suggests that, although unionization (usurpation) and professionalization (exclusion) have been complementary strategies historically, unionization became the primary defence mechanism in the 1970s, with important implications for professional solidarity. For example, the National Association of Local Government Officers (NALGO) provided the negotiators on the chief officers' joint national council (JNC) up to 1984. However, since its first official strike in 1970, NALGO's new-found militancy placed chief officers in no-man's land during disputes, their loyalty compromised in the eyes of elected members. Consequently in 1984 the Federation of Management and Professional Officers' Union was formed, replacing NALGO representatives on the JNC.

These examples demonstrate both the variations in professional influence within local government and the stresses and strains of recent years. However, the archetypal examples of professionalized policy networks lie in non-departmental bodies. Their non-elected character has proved an ideal growth culture for the professions whether the particular case is water engineers or the medical profession.

The history of the medical profession in general and the British Medical Association (BMA) in particular has been oft told (see Eckstein, 1958 and 1960; Stevens, 1966; Forsythe, 1973). The extent to which the profession has become embedded both in the national policy network and in the management of the NHS can be gauged from its representation at every level in the NHS (see Brown, 1979, p. 35). As Saunders (1983, p. 58) concludes, 'doctors enjoy a degree of formal influence ... which is probably unparalled in any other industry or public sector service in Britain'.

Before accepting that the medical profession exerts monolithic and determinant influence, it is as well to note the degree of heterogeneity within it. The Hospital Doctors' Association, the Hospital Consultants' and Specialists' Association, the Medical Practitioners' Union and the Royal College of Physicians and Surgeons exist as potential rivals to the BMA. And within the NHS, the unions – most notably COHSE and ASTMS – and other professions (for example, nursing) – represent interests which can conflict sharply with those of the doctors' organizations. None the less, in spite of challenges during the 1970s, the BMA has remained pre-eminent amongst the organizations representing the medical profession. Its 'insider group' status has reinforced its position *vis-à-vis* other associations; for example, it has sole negotiating rights with the DHSS. At the most fundamental level, the BMA has the doctors and the DHSS wants them (Willcocks, 1967, p. 105). As Jones (1983, pp. 96 and 99–100) argues, government intervention in medicine has served to reinforce the position of the BMA; the reciprocal, intimate interdependence 'was secured by the arrival of state medicine'. Consequently, there is 'no serious challenge to the British Medical Association as the representative of the British doctor' (Forsythe, 1973, p. 7), and policy-making in the NHS reflects 'a continuing medical hegemony' (Haywood and Alaszewski, 1980, p. 135).

The involvement of engineers in the water industry is not as formally elaborate as the NHS machinery for representing doctors but it is as pervasive. Thus, Parker and Penning-Rowsell (1980, pp. 47–9) conclude that the executive, advisory and research agencies of the water industry are dominated by engineers and scientists. Moreover, there are no countervailling agencies (and professions) articulating the social and economic aspects of water planning. Professional organizations like the Institution of Water Engineers and Scientists, the Institution of Public Health Engineers and the Institution of Civil Engineers exert a strong overall influence in the policy network, particularly with their bias towards a 'supply-fix approach': that is, an emphasis on increasing supply capacity to meet shortfalls on the assumption that benefits of increased capacity will exceed the costs of its provision. Schemes favoured large engineering projects with low unit costs and ignored marginal cost, environmental and social considerations (Parker and Penning-Rowsell, 1980, ch. 3). Even in Scotland where water is a local government function, engineers dominate the water planning process. Scottish policy is the responsibility of a chief engineer in the SDD, and in regional councils engineers remain paramount after the budget has been agreed. The absence of formal machinery has proved no obstacle to professional influence.

In sum, therefore, the impact of professional groups on policy-making, although variable, is often considerable, particularly in non-departmental public bodies insulated from elected representatives (see also Massey, 1986). But if central–local relations within the political parties provided evidence of local diversity, this discussion of the professions provides evidence of nationalization. The consequence of professional influence is the promotion of homogeneous standards, not local diversity. Their locus in policy networks places them in, if by origin they are not of, the centre. The outcome is centralization by aggregation of interests and nationalization of standards; the source is the professionals employed by sub-central organizations.

3.7.3 Sub-Central Political Environments

3.7.3(i) THE PERIPHERAL NATIONS

The most obvious and distinct feature of the political environments of the peripheral nations is the existence of nationalist parties. The Scottish National Party (SNP), Plaid Cymru, the Ulster Unionists, the Democratic Unionist Party (DUP), the Social Democratic and Labour Party (SDLP) and, most recently, Sinn Fein all share some common characteristics. They concentrate their electoral activities in the appropriate nation and do not aspire to a majority of seats in the House of Commons. However, they do seek to win the majority of seats within their nation, and their appeal is across class: to territorial and not to functional allegiance. These essentially minimal characteristics apart, the nationalist parties are *sui generis* to their territory.

The present-day SNP was formed in 1934, but its parliamentary ambitions did not come to the fore until the 1960s. In 1967 it won the Hamilton by-election, since when it has fought virtually every seat in Scotland, peaking in the October 1974 election with 11 seats and 30.4 per cent of the vote. Its aim, as expressed in the party's constitution, is 'self-government for Scotland – that is, restoration of Scottish national sovereignty by the establishment of a democratic Scottish Parliament within the Commonwealth' (cited in Rose and McAllister, 1982, p. 70). It is not the only nationalist party of recent times. The Scottish Labour Party was formed in 1976 at the height of the devolution debate. Its objective was a Scottish Parliament 'capable of applying socialist solutions to the problems of Scotland'. It fared ill at the polls and disappeared after the 1979 election.

Plaid Cymru (the Welsh Party) was formed in 1925. Its electoral success has always been less impressive than that of the SNP. It too peaked in October 1974 with 3 seats and 10.8 per cent of the vote. Its aims differ significantly from those of the SNP. Although they share a commitment to self-government for their respective nations, Plaid Cymru also aims 'to promote the culture, language, traditions and economic life of Wales' (cited in Rose and McAllister, 1982, p. 74). This cultural component of Welsh nationalism is a distinct emphasis, translated into a variety of policy demands on, for example, Welsh language teaching, the use of Welsh as an 'official' language and a fourth Welsh-language television station.

In Northern Ireland there is no one nationalist party; all are territorial parties fighting Northern Ireland seats alone. Functional politics is conspicuous by its absence. Moreover, elections are by the single transferable vote system of proportional representation, sustaining intra-party factionalism and a plethora of minor parties. The 'Loyalist' party is, of course, the Ulster Unionist Party, and unionism pervades all aspects of life in Northern Ireland. It is way beyond the remit of this book to discuss its origins and development or even the history of the Ulster Unionist Party. It is important, however, to note the following points. First, unity within the unionist camp has to be perpetually striven for and it has often been elusive, as is evidenced by the variety of splinter groups (see Rose and McAllister, 1982, pp. 77–9). Second, it can call upon the support of the Orange Order, founded in 1795 as a self-defence grouping against Roman Catholicism, which provides the organizational and religious base of the party. Third, the cross-class alliance of protestant working-class and squirearchy political leadership is an 'unhappy and unlikely alliance of people thrown together by what they were fundamentally opposed to rather than by any positive or co-operative principles' (Arthur, 1984, p. 64). Fourth, the unionist ideology has a clear organizational basis, has remained relatively fixed over time and pervades Northern Ireland's policies and politics. Its major components include rejection of a 'United Ireland', continued union with Britain, defence of extant boundaries and the political domination of unionism. Finally, it has a permanent majority. Changes in the electoral system and conflicts within the unionist camp have not dented the size of the Loyalist vote or its capacity to dominate a divided opposition.

These points about the Ulster Unionist Party identify the defining characteristics of the Northern Ireland party system: the close identification of religious and political affiliations and the ideological nature of the system. Nowhere are these characteristics more firmly entrenched than in the DUP. Formed in 1971, it upholds the position of Northern Ireland as an integral part of the UK and argues for the restitution of Stormont and a stronger stance against terrorism. Its very existence bears testimony to the strains within unionism, especially during the 1970s. Ian Paisley's brand of fundamentalism, coupled with an effective 'machine', has enabled him to mount a sustained and credible challenge to the Ulster Unionist Party, and 'as long as constitutional uncertainty reigns and the security question is paramount' he will continue to be a threat (Arthur, 1984, p. 140).

Perhaps the greatest weakness of the opposition parties is the division between those actively hostile to the current system, e.g. Sinn Fein, and those prepared to attempt reform from within , e.g. the SDLP. Thus, Sinn Fein denies the right of the Northern Ireland government to exist and has continuously supported armed struggle. After 1959 it pursued a policy of abstention from Westminster elections but since 1982 has contested Assembly, local government and Westminster elections, winning seats in all and challenging the SDLP for leadership of the Catholic/nationalist minority. The SDLP was founded in 1970 and it has consistently favoured power sharing and improving links with the Irish Republic. Threatened by the electoral success of Sinn Fein, of late it has reverted to a more 'traditional' position, with the call for a United Ireland a more prominent feature of its platform.

The consequences of these features of the Northern Ireland party system are as obvious as they are important. They promote conflict, driving out centre parties, and an ideological style of political debate. The permanent majority has bred a frustrated opposition, and any discussion of the distribution of power in Northern Ireland focuses on the structure of the Ulster Unionist Party. Policies have been distorted in favour of the majority, most notably in education and housing, and any role for the civil service in promoting social (welfare) reforms has been constrained. Unionist dominance and ideological politics have been the past, are the present and remain the foreseeable future for Northern Ireland.

The distinctiveness of the political environments of the peripheral nations extends to pressure groups. Even a brief description needs to distinguish between unified UK-wide groups, UK groups with an organizational presence in the periphery, and peripheral groups. In general, functional politics dictates the organization of business and trade union bodies. At most, they have a regional structure. In the case of the CBI, the Scottish regional council will approach the Scottish Office on purely Scottish matters, but the remainder are passed on to headquarters. Similarly, the Scottish Trades Union Congress (STUC) 'represents UK unions' and 'cannot be seen as the voice of an independent Scottish trade unionism' (Keating and Midwinter, 1983, p. 75). In both these cases, informal contact with the Scottish Office is close, and Keating and Midwinter (1983, p. 73) conclude that 'the small and cohesive nature of the Scottish political and industrial elite' has produced an 'insider network'. Yet groups in Scotland and Wales retain the option of operating at two levels of government, and the attraction of Westminster and Whitehall is strong.

In Northern Ireland, there are some significant variations. Thus, the CBI has a regional council operating on a directly comparable basis to its Scottish counterpart. However, the trade unions have not played a significant role. They were small, up to 1965 strikes could be declared illegal, and the government refused to recognize let alone consult the Northern Ireland Committee of the Irish Congress of Trade Unions. Moreover, the tensions created for the unions between membership of a left-wing all-Ireland body and representing a Loyalist workforce constrained them to concentrate on pay and conditions of work and ignore larger political issues.

Of greater significance are the churches and the Orange Order. Thus the churches – and the government has responded to Roman Catholic demands – have been influential in education. They have also exercised a more general influence on such matters as abortion, divorce and homosexuality. The influence of the Orange Order lies in its integrating role. It has drawn together the several Protestant churches, has close links with the Ulster Unionist Party and, through overlapping membership of a variety of community organizations, has exercised a pervasive influence: to the degree that membership is seen as a prerequisite of candidate selection for elections. The Order is a bastion of sectarian interests and the status quo. Birrell and Murie (1980, pp. 130–1) conclude that the churches, the Orange Order and private business are important conservative groups, whereas 'trade unions, radical movements and "cause" groups have had little influence'. Above all, 'there has been a general lack of pressure group input into the policy process'. On such issues as 'planning, housing and other social issues' the activity of pressure groups was 'minimal'. In this instance, the ease and informality of access supposed to attend legislative devolution did not materialize. Such quiescence does not typify the localities.

3.7.3(ii) THE LOCALITIES

Comparatively, it has been argued that Britain has a low level of pressure group activity in the locality (Gyford, 1976, p. 102 and citations). But at the time these assessments were being essayed, the pattern was changing, or, perhaps more accurately, information began to replace opinion on the subject. Thus, Newton (1976, p. 88) describes 'the politics of the four thousand', concluding that 'the extensive day to day use of administrative channels of communication means that a high proportion of pressure group activity is not immediately visible'. Donnison (1973) argued that the late 1960s witnessed a boom in the micro-politics of the inner city, itemizing the need to defend the environment, the 'rediscovery' of poverty and the growing scale of slum clearance and other redevelopment activity. If indeed pressure groups were quiescent in the 1960s, this label was remarkably inappropriate in the 1970s (for example see Darke and Walker, 1977).

A large proportion of these groups were evanescent, but a number developed both a national and a local presence. For example, Shelter not only campaigned nationally for improved housing and for the homeless but also set up local groups. These groups typically took up individual cases, using them to dramatize the failures of a local authority and, consequently, incurring considerable hostility from them. A similar pattern has emerged for a variety of environmental and social welfare groups; for example, Friends of the Earth has some 250 local groups (Ward, 1983, p. 192). In brief, the 1970s have seen a burgeoning micro-politics and the emergence of groups characterized neither by a concern with transient local 'flashpoints' nor the domestication at the national level but by tactical switching between levels of government (see Lowe and Goyder, 1983, pp. 40, 53 and 83).

A third important feature of sub-national political organizations resides in the distinction between economic function and sectoral cleavages. As argued in Chapter 2, section 2.5.1(v), sectoral cleavages arise from dependence on the public provision of services; for example in education, generating cross-class alliances to fight school-closures. This fragmentation can be interpreted as pluralist competition or the dissipation of conflict. Whichever interpretation is preferred, they share common features: that is, a plurality of groups, the transient nature of protest and conflict, the variable influence of the groups and their manipulation by government. Although some groups become institutionalized, most notably the professional providers of the service along with their voluntary counterparts (e.g. WRVS) rather than its recipients, none the less there is a marked contrast with (economic) functional groupings. Thus, Chambers of Commerce and Trades Councils have become domesticated, with regular, routinized contact with local authorities. Saunders (1980,

p. 321) concludes from his study of Croydon that the Chamber of Commerce occupied a 'quasi-official' position; 'it does not need to be a pressure group'. Hampton (1970, p. 6) records that the Sheffield Trades and Labour Council was 'in effect the borough Labour Party'. In both cases, economic interests had been integrated to the policy-making process. On the other hand, sectoral groups are often classified as 'unhelpful' (Dearlove, 1973), p. 158 and experience difficulty in gaining access both because they are shunned and, more pervasive and pernicious, because their tactics and demands do not fit in with the existing rules of the game.

Fourth, the pull of the centre holds sway over local pressure group activity. For the major welfare services, as well as economic and industrial policy, lobbying on the national stage holds out the promise of effective action. In spite of its elaborate regional structure, the CBI has campaigned for reform of the non-domestic rate at the national level rather than seeking to influence individual local authorities. In consequence, local authorities are now statutorily required to consult local business interests before setting the rate. For many groups, local grievances are seen as requiring national action in the form of either legislation or the provision of funds. A pattern has emerged, there-fore, of pressure groups bypassing the local authority and seeking access to the appropriate national policy community. Local pressure group activity is shaped by the characteristics of the national govern-ment environment.

Fifth, group activity is not restricted to the territorial ministries and local authorities. For example, Friends of the Earth has campaigned against the policy of the Central Electricity Generating Board (CEGB) and the UK Atomic Energy Authority on nuclear energy. And this example also illustrates the privileged position of industry in its relations with all units of SCG, not solely local authorities. As Ward (1983, p. 196) argues, nuclear politics and policy hinge on 'the large corporations in the private sector which dominate nuclear construction'. Examples of both the lobbying of non-departmental public bodies and the role of the private sector are legion. It is sufficient to note here that pressure group politics is a feature of all units of SCG.

Finally, one other characteristic of the national government environment shapes local pressure group activity: the two-party system. If lobbying through administrative channels is a feature of British pressure group activity nationally and locally, none the less groups can either substitute for or supplement this activity with approaches to the political parties. Thus Gyford (1976, p. 107) comments that the issue must 'be plausibly presented in the ideologi-cal language of the party concerned' and cites the links between local teachers, the Socialist Education Association, the Confederation for the Advancement of State Education (CASE) and local Labour parties as an example of effective lobbying focused on a party. Such lobbying is not limited to the local party but also encompasses the national party.

These few comments on local pressure groups do scant justice to the topic and barely illustrate the variegated pattern of sub-central political organizations. However, it is important to recognize the burgeoning micro-politics of local government, the pervasiveness of pressure group activity in SCG, the ways in which this activity is shaped by the national government environment and the differences between economic function and sectoral groups. Yet again, it is clear that the ostensible simplicity of the politics of a unitary system dissolves upon closer examination.

3.7.4 Summary

This section has demonstrated that the plethora of institutions in SCG are matched by varieties of sub-central political organizations. It has examined central–local relationships within the political parties, suggesting that local politics has not been nationalized and that the parties are not unitary. Rather, they are better described as 'stratarchies', and intra-party channels of communications are most accurately seen as a channel of local pressure. Heterogeneity, not homogeneity, persists in spite of the nationalization of party labels.

In sharp contrast, the professions do exercise a nationalizing influence. The topocratic professions are noteworthy for their high status and continuous involvement in the national world of local government. The influence of the technocratic professions is more variable, between professions over time and with the issue. The engineering profession defines policy in the roads policy community, whereas for housing the policy community has sponsored the development of housing management. These organizational professions have adopted exclusionary strategies to bolster their status and influence but they can also adopt, as in the case of social work, usurpatory strategies. The most entrenched professions are found, not in local government, but in non-departmental public bodies. The medical profession in the NHS and engineers in the water industry are archetypal examples of professionalized policy networks. And in all these cases, the consequences of professional influence is the aggregation of interests and the nationalization of standards.

The universe of sub-central political organizations is as vast as it is varied. The peripheral nations have distinct political environments characterized by nationalist political parties and territorial pressure groups. These characteristics are most in evidence in Northern Ireland. In the localities, the late 1960s and 1970s witnessed a rapid growth in the incidence of pressure groups. Too diverse to permit a general description, it is clear, however, that pressure groups have become a pervasive feature of SCG, with important differences between sectoral and economic interest groups. Again, heterogeneity is the only possible summation.

3.8 Conclusions

This chapter has provided an introduction to the range of actors and organizations beyond Westminster and Whitehall. A summary has been provided already at the end of each section. These conclusions will not increase the degree of redundancy.

Any formal analysis courts the danger of describing 'what should be' rather than 'what is'. None the less, it is clear that the centre's relationship with SCG has undergone a number of dramatic transformations. There has been a dual shift with the adoption of 'hands-off' controls for non-departmental public bodies and 'hands-on' controls for local authorities. And these changes have posed numerous problems for both centre and SCG, a conclusion attested by the frequent modifications to policy. The development of the welfare state has also been the development of differentiated, disaggregated policy systems. If this plethora of organizations, interests, resources and relationships marks the dominance of functional politics in British government, the postwar period has seen the periodic reassertion of territorial interests in the guises of nationalism in the periphery and recalcitrance in the localities. If the period has been marked by the influence of the organizational professions, that influence has been challenged by both party political and territorial interests. A non-executant centre with a preponderance of authority, money and political resources none the less remains dependent on SCG, which controls organizational and informational resources. And the failure of the centre to acknowledge either its dependence on or the complexity of SCG illustrates the dominant theme of the past ten years: the centre's faulty territorial operating code. It has persisted with a unitary, bureaucratic, or hierarchic model of intervention almost totally at variance with the existing distribution of resources or known pattern of relationships.

A maze may be complex, but there is an order to its apparent chaos. SCG too has a pattern: that of policy networks. Organizations, actors and their interests are integrated in a variety of networks of interdependence, including policy communities, the topocratic national community of local government and professionalized networks. British government is simultaneously fragmented between networks and centralized within networks. The combination of the national community of local government and function-specific policy communities forms a national local government system which exercises a homogenizing, nationalizing influence. There is an ever-recurrent tension, therefore, between disaggregation and territorial interests on the one hand and the integrating and nationalizing policy networks on the other. But at this juncture, the evidence and arguments of Chapter 4 are being anticipated. The simple conclusion of this chapter is that SCG is heterogeneous and that the centre's capacity to manage heterogeneity is constrained by its territorial operating code. In Chapter 4 I move beyond the formal position to examine the dynamics of SCG: to describe the networks 'in action' and their changing patterns of relationships in the postwar period.

Notes

1 There is an extensive literature on PES. On its origins see Pollitt, 1977. On its operation pre-1975 see Heclo and Wildavsky, 1974. On developments post-1975 see Wright, 1977 and 1980; Else and Marshall, 1979 and 1981. For the views of practitioners see Goldman, 1973; Barnett, 1982; Pliatzky, 1982. This account of relationships within the centre omits some of the much vaunted but shorter-lived innovations of the 1960s and 1970s, namely Programme Analysis and Review (PAR), Central Policy Review Staff (CPRS) and the Civil Service Department (CSD). On these institutions see respectively Gray and Jenkins, 1982 and 1985; Fry, 1985 (pp. 80–93).

2 A useful bibliography on the nationalized industries is provided in Young, 1984 (pp. 444–52). Unfortunately, the political science literature on the industries has been a lacuna from the early 1960s. On recent developments the work of David Heald and David Steel has been particularly helpful. See Heald, 1980a, 1980b, 1984 and 1985, Heald and Steel, 1981 and 1982; Steel and Heald, 1984 and 1985.

   Table 2.4 and section 2.5.1(iii) in Chapter 2 refer to public corporations, a category which covers both the nationalized industries and a miscellany of bodies including the Bank of England, the BBC, the IBA, Cable & Wireless and the Covent Garden Market Authority but excludes companies in which the government has a major share-holding (see Pliatzky Report, 1980, appendices B–D, pp. 182–4). To simplify the description I have focused on the nationalized industries – the largest single category of public corporations – and I describe the other corporations only in passing.

3 This account omits the Crown dependencies and a detailed consideration of the Scottish islands. On the Channel Islands see the Kilbrandon Commission, 1973 (chs. 31–3). On the Isle of Man see Kermode, 1979.

4 The more common terminology is 'regional offices'. However, the term 'regionalism' has multiple connotations. Sharpe (1972) distinguishes between centralist and decentralist regionalism. The former refers to administrative deconcentration and the quest for efficiency. The latter refers to the modernization of local government and the decentralization of power. To avoid any suggestion that the regional offices effect a decentralization of power, coupled with the fact that the term 'region' does not refer to a consistent set of geographical areas, I avoid the term in favour of the neutral 'intermediate institution'. My usage is narrower than that employed by Keating and Rhodes, 1982, who include non-departmental public bodies. Finally, this account excludes the local offices of intermediate organizations, which are numerous, in order to simplify the description.

5 Sections 3.4 and 3.5 draw upon the essays in Hogwood and Keating, 1982; supplemented by Hague, Mackenzie and Barker, 1975; Barker, 1982a; and the two official surveys: Bowen, 1978, and Pliatzky Report, 1980. I have concentrated on the DoE, DoI and DTp because these departments figure prominently in the discussion of networks in Chapter 4.

6 This section draws upon Budge *et al.*, 1983 (ch. 5), and I would like to thank Ed Page (Hull), who collaborated with me in preparing the original chapter.

7 The RWAs levy a water rate which could be seen as a tax but is far more accurately described as a charge. The joint bodies/committees established after the abolition of the GLC and the metropolitan counties have precepting/taxing powers.
8 This section draws heavily upon, and in part paraphrases, Gyford and James, 1983. My grateful thanks to them for permission to so use their research.
9 This section paraphrases Laffin, 1986, for the discussion of highway engineers and housing and Rhodes, 1986a, for the discussion of the topocratic professions. My thanks to Martin Laffin for permission to use his research.

CHAPTER 4

The Policy Networks

Introduction. Policy communities: financing local government, education in an era of retrenchment. Territorial communities: the politics of Scottish local spending, varieties of territorial communities, conclusions – the politics of the pork barrel. Professionalized networks: introduction, providing for the mentally handicapped, 'care in the community' and the mentally handicapped, the relationships, characteristics and consequences of professionalized networks. Intergovernmental networks: introduction, the changing context and relationships, the reorganization of local government – key actors and their roles, the characteristics of intergovernmental networks, conclusions – *cui bono*? Producer networks: the evolution of industrial policy, contraction and redundancies, conclusions – independence, selectivity and privilege. Issue networks: the policy context of the inner city, the rise and fall of institutional complexity, conclusions – partnerships as an issue network. Conclusions.

4.1 Introduction

The term complexity does not mean an absence of order: the organizations and actors are integrated in a variety of policy networks. The objective of this chapter is to describe these networks and the ways in which they have changed in the postwar period. Chapter 2 provided a broad-sweep theoretical account of SCG; this chapter adds the detail necessary for understanding the networks 'in action'. Chapter 3 introduced the major participants and identified the main trends in relationships; this chapter details the fluctuating relationships in a series of case studies.

An essential preliminary step to this exercise is the selection of case studies. A range of criteria are relevant, including type of policy network, types of SCG, availability of data and importance of the policies. Table 1.1 in Chapter 1 shows that the case studies encompass all types of network and SCG. In addition, it lists the sources for each case study. The Economic and Social Research Council's research initiative on central–local relations provides the primary data base for the following analyses. Finally, all the policies are important either in terms of the actors' perceptions or in terms of expenditure (and commonly both). Thus, the changes in the grant system or the reorganization of local government were indisputably major events. Education and the Personal Social Services (PSS) are major local services. Closures, redundancies and rationalization have been a central issue for nationalized industries and lie at the heart of the MSC's activities. The inner cities initiative has been a much vaunted attempt to create a new policy network which explicitly aimed to link the public and private sectors. In short, if the case studies do not constitute a 'representative sample' – whatever that may be – they encompass the range of concerns expressed in the theoretical analysis and are sufficiently diverse to admit competing interpretations and contradictory evidence.

Ideally, the case studies should be 'thick descriptions', that is, encompass the viewpoints of the disparate actors involved and be capable of multiple interpretation. The sheer number of examples precludes even an approximation to this goal. Rather, I present one relatively brief case for each type of network, supplemented by other examples, when available. The reader is referred to the original sources for further detail and, in a number of instances, to competing interpretations. This manner of presentation will enable the reader to form a judgement on the plausibility of an interpretation of SCG rooted in the analysis of networks whilst retaining some detail.

If the case studies are not 'thick descriptions', they are 'theory laden'; that is, they are used to explain policy outcomes. Such explanatory case studies (Yin, 1984) must follow the logic of the theory developed in Chapter 2. Consequently, in general terms, the presentation moves from a discussion of the changing context through a case study focusing on the roles and relationships of particular actors, before concluding with a discussion of the characteristics of the network and the distributional consequences of its particular configuration of interests, resources and relationships.

Finally, the sequence of the case studies is not arbitrary. The discussion proceeds from tightly integrated policy communities to the loosely integrated issue networks. The early examples are particularly supportive of a network interpretation. However, the discussion of producer and issue networks provide a greater challenge to the theory. With their low degree of integration and spasmodic activity, it is important to ask whether or not conceiving of them as networks adds anything to our understanding of policy-making in these policy areas. The selection and sequencing of the case studies does not pre-ordain the conclusions. A subsidiary aim of the presentation is to provide at least some means for the heretic and unbeliever to avoid conversion.

4.2 Policy Communities

4.2.1 Financing Local Government

The context of local government finance has changed from loose-coupling through bargaining and incorporation to directive or bureaucratic relationships and incipient centralization (see Chapter 3, sections 3.2.2 and 3.2.4(i)). Rhodes (1986a, ch. 4) has provided a detailed account of developments in the 1970s. This section summarizes that account but concentrates on the story up to 1985, describing the legislative changes introduced by the Conservative government and exploring their consequences, intended and otherwise. The story unfolds in four stages. First, the macro-economic strategy of the government is briefly summarized. Second, the policies on local government within this strategy are described, and the consequences both for local government as a whole and for the individual local authority are discussed. Third, the changes post-1983 are described and evaluated. Finally, I pose the question of who benefited from these changes.

4.2.1(i) THE ECONOMIC CONTEXT

The sorry story of local government finance could be seen as a spectacular example of government ineptitude: a total failure to comprehend the system it sought to manage. Such a conclusion contains far too large a grain of truth for comfort but it is only part of the study. The 'problem' of controlling local expenditure was compounded by the government's economic strategy.

The corner-stones of this strategy were the MTFS and the PSBR.[1] The MTFS stipulated for four years ahead the government's targets for the money supply, which was to be reduced from 10 per cent in 1979 to 6 per cent in 1983. The PSBR was to be controlled also, and this conjunction of monetary and fiscal policy was to bring inflation under control. This (ostensibly) simple strategy faced severe problems of implementation, illustrating 'Goodhart's law' that 'any statistical regularity will tend to collapse once pressure is placed upon it for control purposes' (Jackson, 1985b, p. 18).

The second corner-stone of government policy was the PSBR, but again Jackson (1985c, p. 67) points out its defects:

> The PSBR is a meaningless target for economic policy ... First, borrowing by the nationalized industries and local authorities which are for capital spending will not have the same consequences as borrowing to pay current spending ... Second, the PSBR contains borrowing used to finance private sector capital spending through the public sector's purchase of private sector assets. Third, unemployment and inflation influence the PSBR. Fourth, the size of

the PSBR has a limited impact on interest rates and its crowding-out effects are of limited importance the further away the economy is from full employment.

Between 1979–83 economic theory and economic reality diverged markedly. £M3 continually exceeded targets in spite of their upwards adjustment. Public expenditure as a proportion of GDP rose from 41 to 44 per cent. Taxes as a proportion of GDP also rose. These development were totally at variance with the government's stated objectives.

The policy exacerbated the problems of the UK economy: 'By responding to increases in the money supply by increasing the interest rates and tightening the PSBR and public spending, the Government unwittingly pushed the economy into a deeper recession' (Jackson, 1985a, p. 146). Although the government insisted that 'there is no alternative' (TINA), its policies were adjusted. £M3 became less prominent, and, no doubt because there was an election in the offing, government expenditure rose by 8 per cent, interests rates fell, and business liquidity was improved by a reduction in National Insurance surcharge. In true Keynesian fashion a small consumer boom ensued, and industrial output began to revive. The MTFS began to perish 'at the hand of a thousand qualifications' (Jackson, 1985a, p. 148). TINA became less strait-laced, elastic replacing whalebone to moderate the degree of deflation.

This brief review of the government's economic strategy has a number of important implications for understanding government policy towards local government. First, the economic rationale for a reduction in local expenditure was non-proven. At best, there is a tenuous relationship between the PSBR, the money supply and inflation. Second, in so far as there is an economic justification, it applies to local government capital expenditure alone and not, belying the overwhelming bulk of legislation, to current expenditure. As Enoch Powell observed: 'By all means limit Exchequer grants and Government loans: but every monetarist knows that rates cannot cause inflation and councils cannot print money. So why set every elected council by the ears from one end of Britain to the other? It doesn't add up' (*Sunday Express*, 11 October 1981, cited in Jones and Stewart, 1983, p. 61). Third, the cuts in capital expenditure are, in effect, cuts on the private sector, especially on the construction industry, and as such contributed to the deflation of the British economy. Fourth, the 'problem' was not local but central overspending. To cope with its own overspending, the centre sought to 'off-load to the periphery' to minimize the rise in public expenditure. Consequently, and finally, there has been no reduction in public expenditure but a redistribution between both levels of government and services. Many of these points may seem obvious, but it is important to recognize that the changes in central policy on local expenditure stem from no imperatives of economic policy. The logic of the government's economic strategy did not require cuts in either local current expenditure or in that proportion of local capital expenditure used to finance private sector capital spending. The centre's 'right to manage the economy' was a shibboleth which also served to disguise the fundamentally party political and ideological nature of its policy initiatives.

4.2.1(ii) CONSERVATIVE POLICY, 1979–83

Between 1979–83 there were seven different systems for distributing grant to local authorities:

(1)   The rate support grant system based on needs and resources elements, inherited from the previous government.
(2)   The system as under (1) above but with the 'transitional arrangements' penalties applied in 1980–1.
(3)   The block grant system based on grant related expenditure introduced under the rate support grant settlement for 1981–2.
(4)   The block grant system with hold-back penalties based on volume targets, introduced in June 1981.
(5)   The block grant system with hold-back penalties based on volume targets, but with exemptions for authorities meeting grant related expenditures, introduced in September 1981.
(6)   The block grant system with holdback provision related to a composite target based on GREs and volume targets and introduced in the rate support grant settlement for 1982–3.
(7)   The block grant system with holdback provision related to composite targets, and the abolition of supplementary rates, under the Local Government Finance Act 1982. (Jones and Stewart, 1983, p. 37).

The reasons for these continual adjustments are clearly shown in Figure 4.1; local expenditure regularly exceeded any and all central targets in spite of the regular upward revision of those targets. The consequences of these changes will be discussed in a moment. At this point, it is important to understand *how* these changes came about: to describe the process of grant determination.[2]

Up to 1979 the PES and the CCLFG were the central mechanisms of the process. Thus, the centre produced its own estimates of public expenditure for the next five years and then discussed the local government component with the national community of local government in the CCLGF. Since 1979 the PES has been replaced by the MTFS as the government's central planning document, and the CCLGF has ceased to be a forum for consultation and become a platform for government statements. There would seem to have been

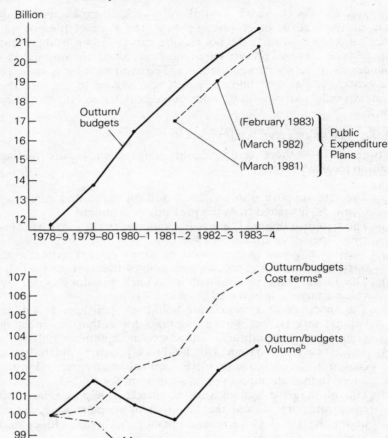

Figure 4.1 *Local authority current expenditure in cash, volume and cost terms, England and Wales.*

Notes:
[a] Current expenditure as defined for Rate Support Grant purposes.
[b] The volume series is the expenditure series in cash adjusted for the effect of pay and price increases specific to the local authority sector. The cost series is the cash expenditure series adjusted for the effect of general inflation as measured by the GDP deflator.
Source: HMSO, 1983a, p. 7.

a dramatic transformation. This characterization requires qualification.

The national community's involvement in the PES had always been
minimal. The desire of the local authority associations for greater
involvement in the PES was first expressed in 1971, and, with the
creation of the CCLGF, they were promised 'participation . . . at the
formative stages of the public expenditure planning process' (Joel
Barnett, cited in Rhodes, 1986a, p. 120). It was not forthcoming. At
best, the associations were invited to comment on the implications of
the figures in public expenditure White Papers. They did not participate in joint forward planning. Indeed, the expectation that they
would do so was always unrealistic. The PES was a structured, internal
and substantially closed review of existing commitments which presented information to ministers for collective decision on the scale,
composition and rate of growth of public expenditure. Local government's involvement never meant more than the provision of information by local government which would be 'considered' by ministers
and civil servants in the next round of PES deliberations. The
expenditure community is closed. It is a tool of central co-ordination
and one of the means for combating the weakness of the centre, of
strengthening the horizontal links. For at least one Treasury official,
the major benefit of the CCLGF was not improved relationships with
local government but improved co-ordination within Whitehall of the
central departments with local government services. Consequently,
the changes post-1979 were less dramatic than might at first appear to
be the case. Involvement in the PES could hardly be further reduced.
It was already minimal.

Although the PES was the major influence on the grant determination process, there still remained some area of manoeuvre and
negotiation. Fractions of 1 per cent involve large sums of money, and
the associations sought to influence the size of grant at the margin and
to alter its distribution between the several types of local authority in
favour of their members. This area of negotiation has been substantially reduced. The proceedings of the CCLGF since 1979 have
been described as follows:

> Consultation has ceased since 1979 . . . it isn't consultation, it's a
> forum where they start telling you what you're going to do . . .

> Now regrettably I don't think Michael Heseltine has ever wanted to
> get a view from anyone except himself . . .

> . . . the Consultative Council now is a statement from the Secretary
> of State, a statement from each of the three Associations and the
> Secretary of State says 'we make a note of your comments, next
> business'.

In as far as consultation exists, it is on party lines: 'They've got a club situation where they all talk in private corners, the Tories almost go to bed with each other they're so close' (all citations from Rhodes, 1986a, pp. 142–3). If the PES set the parameters to consultation before 1979, none the less genuine consultation and even, on occasion, negotiation took place. Subsequently, consultation has been abjured for unilateral central decision, modified at the margin by intra-party lobbying (for examples see Gyford and James, 1983, ch. 8). It is this shift from the 'logic of negotiation' (Jordan and Richardson, 1982, pp. 81 and 85–92) to unilateral imposition which is the most notable transformation and the one with the highest political costs.

Before examining these costs in more detail, it is necessary to unpack the notion of the 'centre' in this particular context. The term refers primarily to the Treasury. The history of local government finance is the story of the Treasury's search for an effective means of incorporating local expenditure into its system for regulating public expenditure. The Treasury was the heart and soul of the PES; the CCLGF was its innovation (Rhodes, 1986a, ch. 4), and it was always made clear that if control by consent was not forthcoming then other means would be sought. With the apogee of the MTFS and PSBR, the 'alphabet soup' changed but not the Treasury's involvement or its primacy (for examples of the Treasury's attitude to local spending see Jones and Stewart, 1983, ch. 7). The expenditure community is distinctive because it has strong horizontal linkages and is closed to even the most respectable insider groups. The Treasury continues its struggle to constrain public expenditure against the function-specific policy networks with their vertical coalitions of interest and, in so doing, has ventured beyond its normal Whitehall confines seeking vertical links of its own through the CCLGF and direct control of individual local authorities. There is no finer testament to the weakness at the centre of British government than this failure of the pre-eminent department to attain the control it has pursued so vigorously for over a decade. The full dimensions of the 'policy mess' that is local government finance remain to be explored.

The consequences of Conservative policy can be summarized under seven main headings: control, privatization, unilateralism, litigation, uncertainty and risk avoidance, unintended consequences and recalcitrance (Rhodes, 1984). Each outcome will be considered *seriatim*. Parenthetically this list is incomplete; the consequences of the post-1983 legislation are discussed below (see section 4.2.1(iii)).

Control To employ Stewart's (1983, p. 61) distinction between intervention and control, government actions impinged on individual local authorities to variable effects, only some of which were related to the centre's intention of cutting local expenditure. The exact nature of the 'cuts' has been described already (see Table 2.3; Chapter 3, section 3.2.4(i); Figure 4.1, above), and the major consequence of the search for control was uncertainty.

Privatization Whichever guise it assumed (see Chapter 2, section 2.3.2(i), the amount of privatization was limited. The important exceptions were the rise in council house rents and the sale of council houses. Instead of freeing resources for the private sector, this strand of Conservative policy served primarily to exacerbate relationships between the two levels of government.

Unilateralism It is difficult to avoid the conclusion that prior agreement on policy was an essential prerequisite of consultation. Corporatist-style arrangements were rejected, the rules of the game were unilaterally abrogated, and the logic of negotiation collapsed. The new directive style served to promote recalcitrance.

Litigation With ever-increasing conflict, there has been frequent resort to the courts to regulate relationships between local authorities as well as centre and locality. There have been an unprecedented number of key cases (see Chapter 3, section 3.2.4(iii)), and the incidence of litigious behaviour has prompted 'legalism' at both levels of government as they sought to check the validity of their own and the other parties' actions.

Uncertainty and risk avoidance The combined effects of an ever-changing grant system, unilateral changes in the rules of the game and legal challenges created a climate of uncertainty in which, to employ Wildavsky's (1975, pp. 11–12) phrase, 'repetitive budgeting' occurs – e.g. mid-year budgetary revisions, the use of large contingency funds and the continuous allocation (and reallocation) of funds from it. In effect, local government did not know what money it had to spend, and the centre did not know what local authorities would spend. Uncertainty has also bred an attitude of 'never do now what you can leave until later' and led to the development of a variety of strategies for avoiding the consequences of ever-changing government policy: 'creative accountancy', an outcome worth considering in a little more detail.

When the government determined the GREAs for individual local authorities and then set local authorities cash-limited volume targets below their GREAs, the incompatible nature of these two targets dictated that local authorities act prudently and minimize the effects of such changes. Even local authorities which had consistently shown restraint in determining their level of expenditure found that they were classified as 'overspenders' and subject to grant penalties, a situation which arose simply because the government's targets were arbitrary. This unpredictability in the grant settlement has meant that the level of grant (and possible penalties) has become a paramount consideration in the budgetary process, and risk avoidance has emerged as the dominant budgetary strategy.

Greenwood (1983, p. 165) concluded after studying the changing patterns of budgeting in twenty English local authorities between 1975–80 that

> the process of resource allocation is becoming more centrally structured, frequently along the lines of the Spanish Inquisition model. That model is characterized by a series of private meetings of elite individuals at officer and member levels, connected to wider constituencies within the authority ... Whatever bureaucratic or rational analysis occurs does so within the bounds of political negotiations and is likely to be the product of the chief executive working to establish the status of his role.

Allied to this centralization, the process of budgetary review has become 'less incremental in terms of preparing estimates. There was a greater willingness at the centre to review existing expenditures' (Greenwood, 1983, p. 161).

Davies *et al.* (1983, p. 179) also confirm this trend. They carried out interviews with members and officers in twenty-two English local authorities, characterizing the broader review of expenditure as the 'financial plan approach' and concluding that it was the commonest form of budgetary review. This approach has four main features: a medium-term forecast of commitments; the separation of committed and uncommitted growth; an expenditure limit set in advance of estimates; and the simultaneous consideration of revenue and capital estimate (Davies *et al.*, 1983, p. 179). However, there was considerable variation in the methods used to determine the expenditure limit. A broad distinction can be drawn between 'expenditure-led' and 'rate-led' authorities. In the early years of the Conservative government 'expenditure-led' authorities adopted the 'guideline approach'; that is, local authorities used the figures laid down in the government's annual White Paper on public expenditure as a more or less precise guide to their level of expenditure. However, with the new era of penalties, the White Paper figures receded in importance to be replaced by the 'target approach' in which the government's announced volume targets and the penalty system formed the basis for limiting expenditure. Allied to late announcements of grant figures, local authorities also found it increasingly difficult to plan more than a year ahead. For some local authorities, however, the targets were seen as totally unrelated to their circumstances, requiring, for example, Draconian service cuts. Such local authorities, not invariably Labour-controlled ones, adopted a 'rate-led approach';

that is, the authorities decided on an acceptable rate increase and worked backwards to the level of expenditure. And it is hardly surprising that the majority of local authorities focused on expenditure rather than income, for one of the latter's major components, central grant, was both unpredictable and known only towards the end of the budgetary cycle. In short, uncertainty over government grant has become the major influence on the budgetary process, generating an increased concern with expenditure limits (however determined). Such concerns as the incidence of local needs and problems take second place to these limits in the majority of local authorities.

If grant had important repercussions for the structure of the budgetary process its effects were by no means limited to the overall process. A number of distinctive budgetary strategies have emerged. Traditionally, a local authority built up its balances to cushion the rate; increases could be minimized, staged and delayed by drawing on accumulated reserves. Now, such balances are essential because local authorities cannot predict the incidence (or size) of penalties. Similarly, the government's estimate of inflation is ignored in favour of the local authority's 'realistic' figure. Both strategies help to minimize uncertainty. There are also some rather more innovative strategies. For example, one county council, anticipating a call to reduce expenditure from the government in the middle of the financial year, created a specific contingency fund of £3 million and rated for it. When it was called upon to revise its budget (as anticipated) it simply 'cut' this item. Similarly, current expenditure is reclassified as capital expenditure to avoid 'overspending', and capital expenditure is deferred to avoid its current expenditure implications. Thus, routine repairs and maintenance become a charge to capital expenditure, specific capital grants are used for revenue purposes, and a home for the mentally handicapped is forsworn because the staff, heating and other running costs necessary to open it would be a charge on current expenditure. All of these stratagems enable an authority to keep its current expenditure down and to avoid grant penalty.

The aura of budgeting in an era of 'cuts' is captured by the following quotes from local government officers and members:

> The most basic problem of the grant system is the inability to plan ... I've become a short term man, I fear, and ... I've got to live from year to year and from hand to mouth ...

> ... one of the most unfortunate points in the whole procedure ... the uncertainty of the thing. The Treasurer can use all the professional expertise at his command, but what he cannot know is what other authorities overall are doing, and with the close ending of the grant, the whole thing is just a gamble ...

The distance between ourselves and the target was too great to make an effort . . .

We've always taken government targets seriously until we got this 5.6% reduction (1981–2) which we didn't take seriously because we don't think anyone could seriously mean it.
(All citations from Davies *et al.*, 1983, pp. 195, 227, 259 and 251)

Grant has made budgeting short-term and unpredictable, generating attitudes of incredulity and indifference. It is tempting to conclude that the harder successive secretaries of state tried, the more they got (of what they didn't want)! Certainly the attempts by local authorities to minimize the uncertainties of the new system led to consequences which were unintended by central government.

Unintended consequences The continuous changes in the grant system and the failure to cut local current expenditure may be the most serious unintended consequences from the government's standpoint but they are not the only ones. Two examples will suffice. First, capital expenditure did not just fall sharply in line with government plans. The tight revenue squeeze on local authorities made them reluctant to incur capital expenditure generally and to use the revenue from capital sales in particular. Moreover, the receipts from such sales were larger than planned. As a result, capital spending fell below the intended levels, prompting (unsuccessful) calls from the centre for increased expenditure! Second, the resource squeeze on local authorities increased the cost of provision in other parts of the public sector. The mentally and physically handicapped remained in the more expensive National Health Service and were not transferred, in accord with government policy, to local authority care because of the resource squeeze on the personal social services. Similarly, a large proportion of the rent increases required for council houses have fallen upon the DHSS.

Recalcitrance As the centre abandoned consultation for unilateralism, so local authorities abandoned co-operation for confrontation. Thus, Labour-controlled authorities increased their rates to compensate for loss of grant, and their expenditure regularly exceeded government targets. The full-blooded adversary response focused on subsidized public transport. Following the House of Lords decision on the GLC's 'fare's fair' policy, the government introduced the Transport Act 1982 to tighten its controls over public transport, especially the level of subsidy. This move was obviously partisan, provoking an antagonistic response and, once again, resort to the courts.

With an election imminent, the Conservatives faced a choice. They could intensify direction in spite of its manifold attendant unintended consequences or search for a more conciliatory mix of strategies. The (then) Secretary of State for the Environment, Tom King, seemed to be extending an olive branch by talking of abolishing volume targets. DoE civil servants cautioned against detailed control of local finance and of dismantling the GLC and the metropolitan county councils (MCCs). The Prime Minister wanted to 'do something' about local government, however (Forrester, Lansley and Pauley, 1985, pp. 64–6, from which the following is paraphrased). No matter that MISC 79 under William Whitelaw's chairmanship had concluded that there was no visible alternative to the rates. Somewhat tentatively, it had suggested abolition of the 'overspending' GLC and the MCCs, but Tom King was known to doubt the wisdom of such a move. Mrs Thatcher was dissatisfied and established a subcommittee of the Economic Committee of the Cabinet, which endorsed the abolition proposals and, once again, reviewed the rates. But now there was an election and a gap in the manifesto waiting to be filled with the local government proposals. Enter the Treasury in the guise of the Chief Secretary, Leon Brittan, with a proposal to limit rate increases. Again no matter that the proposal had been rejected by Cabinet. There was a gap to be filled, and Mrs Thatcher disregarded all known opposition within the government and the party and inserted 'rate capping' and 'abolition' of the GLC/MCCs in the manifesto. TINA applied to local government as well as economic policy; direction remained the chosen path. The Conservatives now had an ill-conceived policy and, on winning the election, no secretary of state. The previous incumbents were unrepentant opponents, and there was no rush of volunteers for the job; enter Patrick Jenkin and 1984, disguised as a comedy of errors.

4.2.1(iii) TO 1984 AND BEYOND

The story of the legislation on rate capping (and incidentally on 'streamlining the cities') could alternatively be described as a 'black comedy', but such entertainment must be abjured for the more prosaic task of describing the outcome of the legislative process and the consequences of that legislation.

The central objective of the Rates Act 1984 is to take away the power of local authorities to determine their own rate level. For this purpose, local authorities fall into two groups: those subject to the selective limitation scheme and the rest, subject to a general limitation scheme to be activated should the need arise by the secretary of state. To date, the latter has not been activated and will not be considered further.

Under the selective limitation scheme, the secretary of state chooses the local authorities to be rate capped. He must specify the criteria for his selection; that is, they must be 'high-spending' authorities. The local authority must exceed its GREA by £10 million for the year and its target by at least 4 per cent. The secretary of state then stipulates a notional level of total expenditure for each selected authority. The authority can appeal against the total, that is, seek a derogation. When the total grant available to local authorities is known, the expenditure limit can be translated into a maximum rate, taking into account the financial reserves of the local authority. If the two sides agree on this rate, it becomes the legal limit. Assuming that the local authority does not agree with this rate level, and that it has not been able to renegotiate it with the secretary of state, the latter can lay an order before the House of Commons or impose, without parliamentary approval, an interim maximum rate. The local authority may not levy a rate which exceeds the maximum stipulated by the secretary of state.

The major lesson of recent years is that what the government wants it doesn't get, and the years 1983–5 were no exception. Normally attention is focused on the fact that the government can control both the income and expenditure of local authorities and has increased sharply, therefore, the degree of centralization in British government. This assessment may seem as obvious as it is inescapable, but there are a number of important caveats to such a bald assessment. Pre-existing features of the financial system remained unchanged (for example, the rise in local expenditure and in the rates, repetitive legislation for unintended consequences and instability and ambiguity), whilst others were dramatically intensified (for example, politicization, technical complexity and inequity).

'Cuts'   Between 1983–5 local current expenditure continued to rise in real terms and to exceed government planning figures: by £770 million in 1983–4 and £850 million in 1984–5. By the government's own admission, local current expenditure rose by 1.5 per cent per annum in real terms throughout the 1980s (HMSO, 1986b, p. 4). Capital expenditure recovered, although it remained at half the levels prevailing for the 1970s, and the pre-existing trend of reducing the proportion of local expenditure funded by grant continued, falling to 41 per cent in 1984–5. The corollary of this trend was a substantial increase in the rates over and beyond the rate of inflation. An age-old means of central control returned to favour: the specific grant. Thus between 1981 and 1985 specific grants rose (as a proportion of grant) from 17.6 per cent to 22.9 per cent (Grant, 1986, p. 20). Controversially, up to one per cent of aggregate LEA expenditure can now be allocated in the form of a specific education support grant.

The contribution of rate capping to the reduction of the 'overspend' by local authorities was marginal. First, the number of councils affected was small: eighteen in 1984–5 and ten reselected (with two new additions) in 1985–6. The government was implementing a marginal reduction in a marginal number of local authorities and could not expect a dramatic reduction in local 'overspending', let alone total local expenditure. Second, there were pressures on other councils to increase their expenditure. High-spending local authorities, worried that they might be future candidates for rate capping, levied rates to increase their reserves to ensure that they were cut back from the highest feasible level with money in the bank. Even 'moderates' found they had to increase their rates to cope with the additional functions inherited from the abolition of the GLC and the MCCs. Rate capping, rather than reducing local expenditure and the rates, may cause both to rise.

Nor is it likely that any 'savings' will arise from the abolition of the GLC and the MCCs. Initially the government was reluctant to specify the savings (HMSO, 1983b, p. 22) but subsequently, in the explanatory and financial memorandum prefacing its Local Government Bill, it put the savings at £100 million annually, although ministers had gone as high as £120 million and 9,000 jobs. In fact the only published detailed analyses of the savings were produced by opponents, who estimated that the increase in costs, assuming limited co-operation between the successor authorities, would be between £36 million and £61 million per annum (Coopers and Lybrand, 1984, p. 14).

Repetitive legislation   The DoE has become locked into a vicious circle of legislating for unintended consequences, and rate capping/ abolition did nothing to break this circle. Because only one of the rate-capped councils was Conservative controlled, the government's action provoked a concerted campaign of opposition from 'victimized' Labour authorities which refused to set or delayed setting a rate. Consequently, the government legislated in the Local Government Act 1986, specifying a date for fixing the rate. The public relations campaign against both rate capping and abolition of the GLC/MCCs was sophisticated and effective. Consequently, the government appointed the Widdicombe Committee to review, amongst other things, 'political' advertising by councils and, anticipating the committee's findings, it introduced with unseemly haste legislation to restrict such activities along with a code of practice of such severity that it had to be modified substantially. The continuing failure to control local expenditure, and the political embarrassment created by the increase in the rateable value of Scottish properties upon their revaluation, prompted another review of local government finance, the publication of the Green Paper, *Paying for Local Government* (HMSO, 1986b), and the 'promise' of a 'community tax' (better known as a poll tax) in the next Parliament. This list by no means exhausts the unintended consequences but it does demonstrate that in two short years the spate of legislative activity abated not one jot; repetitive legislation for

unintended consequences is itself an important unintended consequence.

Instability and ambiguity   Recent developments continue to generate
instability and ambiguity. Attacks on the grant system have been
increasingly vociferous; and, on top of this system, the government
has imposed a plethora of elected and indirectly elected bodies,
subject to a variety of financial controls, in place of the GLC and the
MCCs. To describe the new system as complex is to resort to English
understatement:

> It seems inconceivable to us that the new arrangements will produce
> a system which is more comprehensible and accessible to individual
> citizens. A two-tiered local government certainly has its problems
> but a system consisting of a host of separate joint boards and joint
> committees of dubious accountability, backed up by a new range of
> central government controls, all superimposed upon the existing
> district tier seems to us considerably more confused and problem-
> atical.
>
>   (Flynn and Leach, 1984, p. 42)

Abolition has already had some specific effects. To pay for the
transition, grant has been redistributed from the county councils to
the urban areas, provoking both howls of protest and large rate
increases. Precisely how these transition costs were incorporated into
the grant settlement was a source of delay, of confusion to treasurers
attempting to predict their grant entitlement and of political fudging
as the secretary of state announced that additional grant would be
available to the counties, although how much would be available to
whom by when remained a mystery.

The constant changes have also fed litigious behaviour. For
example, Bradford and Nottingham councils initially won a court
ruling that the guidance issued by the secretary of state on their level
of budgeted expenditure was unlawful because it discriminated
between local authorities (*Times Law Report*, 4 October 1985).
Although overturned on appeal, the case delayed the grant settlement
for 1986–7. The sense of *déjà vu* is overwhelming; stability has become
an anathema.

Politicization   The politicization of central–local relations has
increased apace. Historically, national and local political élites have
been insulated from each other. In sharp contrast to France, for
example, Britain has no tradition of politicians 'collecting' offices at
the national and local level, of holding at the same time a seat in
Parliament and a chairmanship of a local council. The budgetary crisis
in Liverpool heralded a new era. The secretary of state was drawn into

negotiations with the city over its 1983–4 budget and, if in fact the minister made few concessions, he indisputably lost the political battle by appearing to make them (Midwinter, 1985). Rate capping has the potential to suck the minister and the DoE into numerous one-to-one negotiating positions with local authorities willing and able to impose high political costs. Admittedly, this strategy was rejected by the councils rate-capped in 1984–5, which preferred to act as a group and refused to seek a derogation. There are also risks for the local authority seeking a derogation; for example, the secretary of state must be given all the information he wants in order to reach his decision and he can further reduce the permitted rate level. But the united opposition of the Labour councils crumbled as the deadline for making a rate became imminent; and attempts to bargain with the centre now seem a more attractive option. Such bargaining holds perils for the centre. To become embroiled in the budgetary details of eighteen or more councils will strain its organizational resources; will provide opportunities for opponents to publicize errors and inconsistencies; and will lead to the secretary of state imposing requirements to cut services and make redundancies – actions scarcely likely to enhance his popularity or gain him a good press.

Politicization has also affected the national community of local government. After the May 1985 county council elections, the Conservatives lost control of the Association of County Councils for the first time, further weakening the consultative links between centre and locality and pushing the revival of the local authority associations as local government's intermediary tier of representation ever further into the distance.

The foregoing comments are speculative to some degree, but the drift to politicization has not been lost on the government, which has noted 'a worsening of the relationship between central Government and even the moderate and responsible local authorities' (HMSO, 1986b, p. 5). This development may yet generate the most severe unintended consequences for the centre to date.

Technical complexity The defects of the grant system have become increasingly apparent, and, more important, the system has been attacked from unexpected yet authoritative quarters. Both the Audit Commission and the Comptroller and Auditor General have argued that the system is contributing to inefficiency and ineffectiveness in local government (Audit Commission, 1984; Committee of Public Accounts, 1985). Its major defects include a lack of clarity about the principles and objectives underlying GREA; the inadequacy of individual service components of GREA (e.g. transport, housing,); and the use of penalties which have diverted attention away from costs of a common standard and created obstacles for a consensus on the principles of the system (Bramley, *et al.*, 1983, paras. 20.30 to 20.40).

In a similar vein the Audit Commission (1984) criticized 'unnecessary uncertainties', the accumulation of some £1,200 million in reserves to counter uncertainties, 'serious distortions' in the allocation of grant, the complexity of the system and the lack of incentives to improve efficiency and effectiveness. It argued that a potentially sound system based on GREAs was 'being eroded because of, *inter alia*, the distorting effects of penalties and targets' (p. 44). The inadequacies of the system were now so transparent that, for 1985–6, the government abolished targets. At the same time as the GLC and MCCs were abolished and funding arrangments for the new joint bodies came into being, the government generated a new set of uncertainties surrounding the transition to the GREA system – incidentally, a move originally scheduled for 1981–2!

Inequity   One of the more puzzling features of the grant system for its supporters is its random or arbitrary nature. Cost-conscious 'moderates' who have assiduously followed government policy find themselves subject to grant penalties. Some shire district councils find that the combination of grants and housing revenue account surpluses means that they do not have to levy a rate, whilst urban authorities, confronted by major economic and social problems, are starved of funds. Thus one of the most affluent shire counties in England, Buckinghamshire, received virtually the same block grant as the city of Liverpool, which had the same population and some of the worst social problems in the country. The inner-city riots of 1981 and 1985 have seen targets, penalties and rate capping direct resources *away* from the areas of greatest need! The grant system has produced objectively perverse outcomes. This key effect of the grant system will be explored in more detail below (see sections 4.2.1(v) and 4.7).

It would be foolhardy to deny that the thrust of the post-1984 reforms is centralizing but, equally, it would be shortsighted to overestimate the capacity of the centre to realize its objectives. Conservative policies contain the seeds of their own ineffectiveness. If centralization does ensue, it seems certain that the system will be complex, ambiguous, unstable and confused. The resultant policy mess will lead inexorably to a further reorganization of local government, if only for the centre to abolish a system in which its interventions fail to have the stated effect.

4.2.1(iv)   THE EXPENDITURE COMMUNITY AND THE TERRITORIAL OPERATING CODE

The sorry record of Conservative policy can be attributed to personalities, to Mrs Thatcher's determination to 'do something' about local government and to the ineptitude of particular secretaries of state for the environment. Any such explanation would be incomplete at best. A more adequate account must turn to the nature of policy networks, especially the expenditure community, and to the centre's territorial operating code.

The distinctive features of the expenditure community are its exclusive membership and extensive horizontal linkages coupled with diversity of interests of central bureaucratic/political élites and the topocrats. The PES and MTFS and the devices whereby the Treasury challenges the service departments, which in turn seek to protect/ enhance their 'turf'. In so doing, the service departments can call upon the support of the interests institutionalized in their policy networks. The Treasury is the centre within the centre lacking any vertical linkages to marshal in support of its case and dependent upon a co-ordinating committee – the Cabinet – riven by the very conflicts of interest it seeks to regulate. The experiment with the CCLGF sought to repair one of the more obvious weaknesses of the central capability; it provided the Treasury with allies. The national community of local government and the topocratic professions could be expected to see expenditure problems 'in the round' and to support a shift away from service spending towards a more corporate approach and financial soundness. To abandon the CCLGF was to forsake incipient vertical linkages, to adopt hands-on controls at the same time as one abandoned direct links. The hands-off controls of the 1960s were congruent with central insulation and local operational autonomy. To adopt hands-on controls and reinforce central insulation betrays a flawed comprehension of the system of central–local relations. The function-specific policy networks betrayed no equivalent *naïveté*, as evidenced by their capacity to resist the 'cuts'. If the resource squeeze induced stresses and strains within various policy communities, it did not fracture them nor did it emasculate their vertical links and isolate the centre.

There are two components to the centre's rules of statecraft – its territorial operating code – which warrant further comment. First, central interventions were rooted in a macro-economic strategy which, independently of any merits or defects it might have for running an open economy in an unstable international environment, simply did not require control of local current spending. Policies are theories; they promise that X will result in (will cause) Y. But there is limited evidence linking local current expenditure to the PSBR or the latter to inflation. Policies encapsulating a theory of disputed validity can expect to confront problems of implementation. Or, in more florid language, the prisoner will be more resigned to his confinement if he has committed the crime for which he was imprisoned. In the case of local government, there was no agreement as to what crime (if any) had been committed.

Second, the centre abandoned hands-off for hands-on controls. Central autonomy and the dual polity were replaced by a directive or command operating code and bureaucratic relationships. Not only did

Beyond Westminster and Whitehall

the expenditure community reinforce its own insulation from local
government but it seemed unaware of the degree of disaggregation
and interdependence within the function-specific networks. Direct
controls unsupported by an organizational (or network) base confronted established networks in which central interests were dependent on local government. The simple fact that differentiation constrains co-ordination was not part of the territorial operating code.
Thinking the unthinkable and accepting that leaders do know best, it
seems trite to suggest that the omniscient still require the means for
giving effect to their commands. Historically, the dual polity had
obviated the need for such an operating structure. And yet the
centre's actions presupposed that it already had such a structure;
Napoleon without the Napoleonic structure of decentralization strut-
ted and postured to little effect. Whosoever had been at the head of
British government would have been constrained by disaggregation,
differentiation, network structures and the pre-existing territorial
operating code.

In short, a focus on policy networks is crucial to understanding the
failure of Conservative policies on local government. It had a faulty
territorial operating code which denied network efficacy if not their
existence. The closed expenditure community lacked the organizational means to effect control. The function-specific networks had
the means but were the Treasury's rivals not its allies. Hands-on
controls confronted differentiation and created a policy mess.

4.2.1(v) THE POLITICS OF INERTIA AND INEQUITY

The question of who benefited from developments since 1979 admits
of no easy answer. The question has to be broken down into
component parts. It is necessary to distinguish between levels of
government and types of local authority, between services and, most
important, between expenditure and its impact. The impact of expenditure on the several interests and classes in society is best considered
on a service-by-service basis and will be discussed in later sections. At
this point, I review the distribution of total expenditure between levels
and types of government and between services.

In sum, the major beneficiaries were central government and,
amongst the services, agriculture, defence, law and order and social
security (see Table 2.3 in Chapter 2). The services of the welfare state
may have been subject to a resource squeeze, but, housing apart, their
expenditure grew in real terms. The overwhelming impression given
by the aggregate statistics is one of the power of the politics of inertia.
Rhetoric apart, the policy networks protected their turf. This conclusion requires three important caveats.

First, the centre protected itself by off-loading cuts to the private
sector and local government. As Jones and Stewart (1983, pp. 66–7)
demonstrate, central expenditure was planned to grow at the same

time as local authority expenditure *for the same service* was to be cut (for example, arts and libraries, road maintenance).

Second, off-loading penalized some types of local authority more than others. Thus, the distribution of grant favoured county councils at the expense of metropolitan authorities. The shires' (counties and districts) share rose from some 46 per cent in 1979 to 56 per cent in 1984: a complete reversal of the trend under the previous Labour government.

Third, a focus on expenditure totals disregards the need to spend. Even if expenditure grows in real terms, it may not keep pace with the growth in the need for services, especially in a society with high unemployment and an ageing population. In theory, GREAs take account of need in distributing grant. In practice, cash-limited volume targets set below GREAs have limited the extent of redistribution to poor, high-need local authorities (see section 4.7, below).

The distributive consequences of the grant system are mixed. On the one hand, the politics of inertia has limited the extent of any cuts; the policy empires struck back at central control. On the other hand, the resource squeeze has had a disproportionate, adverse effect on urban authorities with a high incidence of need; the most vulnerable were least able to protect themselves in a context where only the strong survive. With declining populations and low rateable values, the use of rates to offset grant reductions meant spectacular increases bound to incur the government's wrath. Off-loading to the periphery by policy networks illustrates the politics of inertia; but, by defending the status quo, they perpetuated and exacerbated pre-existing inequalities. The grant system was inequitable, and the operation of policy networks ensured that it would be so. The full extent of the distributional consequences can be appreciated only if the fortunes and fate of particular services are examined. This general analysis suggests, however, that for both growth and cuts in public expenditure the integrated networks – policy communities – sustain their position at the expense of the least integrated, issue networks. An exploration of the education policy community will show how an integrated network can ride the resource squeeze.

4.2.2   *Education in an Era of Retrenchment*

4.2.2(i)   THE EVOLVING CONTEXT

Policy-making in education has been variously described as 'group sub-government' (Manzer, 1970, p. 3), a 'consensual network' (Kogan, 1975, p. 72) and a 'policy community' (Rhodes, 1986a, pp. 325–45). Within this policy network the role of the Department of Education and Science (DES) has been described as 'vitally impor-tant' (Lodge and Blackstone, 1982, p. 18), 'the most important single force' (OECD, 1975) and the wielder of 'determinant authority' (Kogan, 1975, p. 238). There is said to be a clear departmental view of policy; the DES 'goes where the arithmetic leads' (Lodge and Blackstone, 1982, p. 35) and it is 'promotional' in its relations with local authorities (Griffith, 1966, pp. 522–4). However, it is not the only important actor. The local education authorities (LEAs) through the associations and the teachers' unions are pre-eminent amongst 'the small fraction of the formally defined constituency of educational government' who are consulted (Lodge and Blackstone, 1982, p. 40). Consequently, Regan (1979, p. 35) can argue that 'there are substantial areas of education where no DES control exists' and describe central–local relations in education as a 'partnership'. Provocatively, education has been described as a 'school-based service, occasionally influenced by local authorities and occasionally influenced by central government' (Stewart, 1986, p. 181). These apparently contradictory views of the relationship can be resolved by examining variations between educational policy areas and the phases in central–local relations during the postwar period.[3]

Webb and Wistow (1982a, p. 14) distinguish between governance, resource and service policies. Governance policies concern perceptions of the role of government and the relationships between its constituent units. Resource policies concern the desired level of financial, staffing and capital inputs. Service policies concern the needs of client groups. These distinctions were developed for the analysis of the personal social services but are equally applicable to education. Thus, Sir Toby Weaver (1979, pp. 76–8) argues that teachers have the determinant influence on the curriculum or service policies, whilst for resource policies the DES has considerable influence over finance and LEAs over organization and staffing. Finally, DES influence is greatest on governance policies, especially 'in the sphere of individual and social opportunity' (or access). The controlling voice emanates from a different quarter (or more accurately, third), depending on the characteristics of the particular policy:

> the strength of any policy control exercised by the Secretary of State and his Department will vary with the form of control used, with the educational task involved, with the relationship in which the Department's 'shareholders' stand to it, whether in the capacity of ... clients, subjects or partners.
> (Weaver, 1979, p. 76)

Policy control has also varied throughout the postwar period.

Ranson (1982, pp. 1–13; see also Ranson, 1980) argues that the balance of power within educational policy-making has shifted from central dominance and bureaucratic relationships up to the mid-1950s through local dominance and bargaining relationships until the early

1970s to a period of central regulation and a return to bureaucratic relationships over the past decade.

As shown earlier (see Chapter 3, section 3.2.3(i)), the Education Act 1944 (s. 1 and s. 100) gave the minister extensive powers. Thus, LEAs were required to produce a development plan which, once approved, took the form of a development order which an LEA could vary only with ministerial approval and which was supported by a specific grant. The objective was to transform secondary education, and the minister was given extensive powers to bring this about. If no development orders were made, if no overall plan existed, none the less the department monitored individual LEAs, scrutinized expenditure in detail to the extent of disallowing specific items for grant, gave detailed advice in circulars and issued elaborate codes of guidance. Central direction was enhanced by both a consensus amongst the major actors in the policy community and an equal determination to transform the system on the part of the LEAs and teachers' unions. The pattern of policy-making at this stage has been summarized ably by Bogdanor (1979, p. 161):

> This process of elite accommodation reached its apogee during the post-war period when, so it was believed, many policy decisions in education were taken over lunch at the National Liberal Club by a troika consisting of Sir William Alexander, Secretary of the Association of Education Committees, Sir Ronald Gould, General Secretary of the National Union of Teachers, and the Permanent Secretary at the Department of Education. If these three agreed on some item of educational policy, it would more often than not be implemented.

During the 1960s the balance of power shifted to the LEAs. The specific education grant had been replaced in 1958 by the general grant. Similarly, detailed control of capital expenditure and guidance on other matters were relaxed. On the face of it, the era of comprehensive education might be interpreted as yet another example of central influence. In fact, it illustrates the scope for local discretion in three ways. First, the policy initiative was taken by local authorities (see, for example, Rhodes, 1975b, pp. 164–72). James (1980, p. 33) concluded that the centre delayed local attempts to introduce comprehensive education before 1965. Thereafter, the centre's own plans drew heavily on local experience, in effect promoting local policies. Second, the LEAs were able to negotiate considerable discretion. The DES conceded leeway to the LEAs in designing comprehensive schemes which suited local conditions and resources. Finally, the LEAs resisted and frustrated central interventions. For example, Pattison (1980, p. 63) notes that forty-seven out of ninety-seven LEAs in England have at least one grammar school, and a significant minority (at least eleven) retain selective systems. He provides a case study of Sutton London Borough's resistance to comprehensive reorganization, arguing that the tradition of co-operation and the centre's control of finance were not effective means for controlling local authorities and that there were important restrictions on the use of the major alternative means, legislation. Indeed, he concludes (p. 73) that the national local government system was a key non-local source of influence favouring reorganization. It had a 'self-reinforcing', 'multiplier' effect, and 'the diffusion of innovation process acquires its own momentum and is not necessarily dependent on central government stimuli'.

In short, in common with other welfare state services, the 1960s were an era of expansion for education. Local discretion was facilitated by the abolition of specific grant, leaving the DES only with 'hands-off' controls. The constraints on the centre were reinforced by the militancy of the teachers' unions and the increasingly vociferous voice of clients – e.g. the Confederation for the Advancement of State Education (CASE), Society of Teachers Opposed to Physical Punishment (STOPP), Child Poverty Action Group. But the centre sought and gained the desired expansion of the service, although it arguably never had the means to direct that expansion. Necessarily, it was limited to resource policies, to providing the fuel and exhortation, leaving service policies or the form of growth to local decision.

With the onset of economic decline in the 1970s, relationships were to change yet again. For example, the teaching profession had established extensive control over the curriculum and examinations through the Schools Council. However, from 1975 the DES sought to increase its own influence in precisely these service policies (see, for example, Lawton, 1980). The search for regulation and control was to intensify, reaching into the organization of educational provision – for example, conditions of service and the assessment and promotion of teachers – as well as the more common regulation of financial resources. The remainder of this section focuses on the changing fortunes of the education policy community since 1975. More specifically, it examines changing relationships within the education policy community through a case study of educational provision for 16–19-year-olds, and the effects of the 'cuts' in local expenditure on the education policy community's relationships with other policy networks, most notably the Treasury and the expenditure community, and with individual LEAs.

4.2.2(ii)   RESTRUCTURING THE CURRICULUM: PROVISION FOR 16–19-YEAR-OLDS

One of the more visible consequences of economic recession was the growing number of unemployed school-leavers, a fact which prompted criticism of the schools for preparing young people inadequately for work.[4] Employers complained about young workers' lack of appropriate skills, and more generally there were criticisms of declining standards (Kogan, 1978, ch. 3). To compound the problem, school rolls were falling dramatically. The education service confronted, therefore, turbulent times, and its review of priorities accorded a significant role to education for the 16–19-year-olds.

The great 'rethink' can be conveniently dated from the 'Yellow Book' of 1976, a confidential memorandum on educational standards prepared for the Prime Minister, James Callaghan. It argued that schools did not adequately prepare pupils for their economic roles in society. The vocational relevance of education for 14-plus should be strengthened, and education and training should be planned in a unified way. In a subsequent speech at Ruskin College in October 1976, the Prime Minister stressed the need to improve links between industry and education, and these themes were reiterated in the Green Paper:

> the school system is geared to promote the importance of academic learning and careers with the result that pupils, especially the more able, are prejudiced against working in productive industry and trade . . . teachers lack experience, knowledge and understanding of trade and industry . . . curricula are not related to the realities of most pupils' work after leaving school; and . . . pupils leave school with little or no understanding of the workings, or importance, of the wealth-producing sector of our economy.
>
> (HMSO, 1977a, p. 34)

The Treasury firmly supported the view that 'education could play a much better role in improving industrial performance. The service is inefficient, unproductive and does not concentrate scarce resources in the areas that matter most' (Treasury under secretary, cited in Ranson, 1982, p. 34).

Provision for the 16–19-year-olds was to be the lever for reorienting the education service. The choice of this group seems logical; it was strategically located between secondary school and work. More important, this area had not been accorded any priority in earlier years. The DES priority had been higher education; there was 'a silent conspiracy which allowed 16–19 year olds to "drop out" of the system' (Mason, 1984, p. 66). Consequently, it 'was less hedged around by statutory constraints' (Ranson, 1982, p. 35) and, one might add, professional and institutional limits.

In the words of a Treasury under secretary, there was 'tremendous weariness' about the 'awkwardness' of the education system. No matter that the minister wins additional resources, (s)he is only deciding 'that there will be money in RSG whose allocation is left to the local authorities'. Consequently, 'more central controls are required to direct this great amorphous body' (cited in Ranson, 1982, p. 45). Institutional constraints limited the centre's capacity to reorient the education service. But control was not the only available strategy. Focusing initiatives on unsecured 'policy space' would also facilitate change, and such a space existed in the provision for 16–19-year-olds. The DES adopted precisely this approach to change:

> the 16–19 area is one of the key means of changing the educational system and of achieving the relevance we desire because it sits at the watershed between school and work. If we can achieve things with the new 17+ examination that will give us an important lever to vocationalize or to re-vocationalize the last years of public schooling.
>
> (DES deputy secretary, cited in Ranson, 1982, p. 35)

But by moving into new policy space the DES was extending the boundaries of the policy community. Side-stepping its partners in the troika of the education policy community in this way may facilitate change but it left the DES open to challenge from other policy networks. Domain consensus could not be assumed, it had to be established.

Indeed, 'training' had its own long-standing policy network, and its constituent organizations, especially the DEmp, were ever eager to defend their turf 'against the possible "capture" of training by the Department of Education' (Stringer and Richardson, 1982, p. 24; see also Moon and Richardson, 1985, ch. 4). If the DES was to 're-vocationalize' education and extend its responsibilities in this area, it had to demonstrate that it could implement the desired trans-formation. A brief review of the attempt to rationalize the institutional basis of education provision for 16–19-year-olds will illustrate the problems that the DES had to confront.

Convinced of the need to rationalize existing institutional arrange-ments, the DES undertook a promotional campaign to convince other members of the policy community. A series of speeches by ministers and the permanent secretary launched a campaign for the estab-lishment of sixth-form or tertiary colleges. Small sixth forms in schools offering a limited range of A-level subjects were to be amalgamated into separate colleges, an arrangement which was more economic and enabled the system to offer a broader range of courses, including vocational courses. Schooling was to end at 16. The proposals provoked vociferous criticism, and, to engineer a consensus, the debate moved into formal group settings. A 16–19 Sub-Group was appointed under the auspices of the Expenditure Steering Group (Education) (ESG(E)) of the CCLGF. The ESG(E) existed ostensibly to forecast expenditure for education but it had developed into a wide-ranging forum on educational policy (Rhodes, 1986a, pp. 334–6). The terms of reference of the 16–19 Sub-Group were to consider 'how educational resources for young people above the minimum school-leaving age might be more effectively deployed'.

At an early stage, the extent of the challenge to the assumptions of the education policy community was made clear by the Treasury. It argued that 'the absolute levels of participation desirable for different groups of 16–19 year-olds' need to be determined, and 'the usefulness of FE needs to be proved' (cited in Ranson, 1982, p. 60). It was no longer axiomatic that young people should continue in education as long as they had the necessary qualifications. The sub-group concluded that there was a need for diverse educational provisions to reflect differences amongst young people and that separate provision was required for the vocationally and academically oriented. Under Treasury prompting, provision was to be targeted.

The Secretary of State for Education, Shirley Williams, wanted a prompt response to these deliberations. The ESG(E) prepared a draft circular, but this urgency prompted critical reaction. For example, the ACC argued that the government was not dealing with the problem as a whole. There was a need to review curricula and finance as well as institutional arrangements, and the ACC called for a total review. A consensus did not exist within the policy community. Moreover, Shirley Williams failed to persuade the Cabinet to take prompt action. Consequently, the DES resorted to consultative papers, and a further committee was established, a political counterpart to the officer-composed ESG(E) sub-group. Chaired by a junior minister, Neil Macfarlane, the committee was necessary 'to carry the LEAs with us politically as well as professionally' (DES deputy secretary, cited in Ranson, 1982, p. 66). Or more bluntly, 'for God's sake let's get something decided. For ten years we've been at it and we now need a decision' (p. 67): a sentiment which could be the epitaph of the policy community. The DES was to demonstrate, to Whitehall in particular, that it 'could put its house in order' and 'get something done' (p. 68).

The committee's terms of reference were broad ranging, covering resources and institutions and including relations between the schools and FE and with training agencies, as well as (implicitly) the purposes and role of education in society. However, it was managed in a 'masterly' fashion by the DES (Ranson, 1982, p. 72), and conflict was delayed if not ultimately damped. The major division surfaced at the draft report stage and occurred between supporters of the all-through 11–18 comprehensive school and of the post-16 college, and the disagreements precluded the strong report desired by the DES. It did not come out equivocally for a tertiary system, and the report (Macfarlane, 1980) has been dismissed as irrelevant. However, Ranson (1982, pp. 78–9) argues that the report's lasting contribution was to redefine the nature of educational opportunity as the matching of 'needs and provision to differentiated client groups'. The education

262 *Beyond Westminster and Whitehall*

service was 'to ensure that a range of opportunities is available of a quality that meets the realistic aspirations of young people, parents and society and at a cost which the nation judges it right to pay' (Macfarlane Report, 1980, p. 13). In particular, there should be a greater degree of differentiation at 16 with the majority of young people moving on to vocationally relevant courses. 16–19-year-olds were to be provided for at last, but that provision was to be differentiated and highly structured.

The DES attempt to assert its authority was, at best, a qualified success; it had a policy which commanded support but not a consensus. It now had to be implemented through a combination of persuasion, pressure and control (Ranson, 1985). As in the case of comprehensive education, the initial means was a circular explaining general policy, exhorting action and calling for information from LEAs on their proposed actions. Rather cautiously, Circular 2/81 drew attention to the 'powerful arguments' for educating 16–19-year-olds 'in fairly large groups'. Underpinning these relatively weak policy prescriptions was a strategy of pressure based on the block grant system. Grant was to be calculated on the basis that the LEA had taken reasonable steps to reduce excess capacity. And to keep the pressure on, the DES issued a manual on the costing of educational provision ostensibly to provide a means for LEAs to review options and tacitly to extol the economic advantage of tertiary colleges. The problems of a strategy based on persuasion are illustrated by the example of Manchester.

The LEA had experienced a severe fall in enrolment and, cautiously, it opted for sixth-form colleges. It was a test case, and progress was watched throughout the education world. However, the arrival of Sir Keith Joseph as secretary of state led to the rejection of Manchester's plans on the grounds that it would damage 11–18 schools. This action was based on the Education Act 1980, ss. 12–16, and demonstrated that the DES had effectively extended its potential for bureaucratic control. But if these sections brought 'the Department to centre stage in a crucial policy area' (Ranson, 1985, p. 67), the new controls were negative ones. The DES still could not command the desired changes.

At this juncture, change by persuasion was in disarray. It now seemed to LEAs that the key criterion was to preserve 'good schools', 'a decision to reintroduce grammar schools by stealth' (Ranson, 1982, p. 94). Perhaps more important, it was now clear to the DES that, in order to re-vocationalize education, it needed more direct controls.

The DES was embarrassed: 'we had . . . a serious problem in persuading Whitehall that we could deliver'. In sharp contrast the MSC 'has a big bag of gold, is a centralized bureaucracy and can deliver the goods' (citations from Ranson, 1982, pp. 102 and 103 respectively). The attempt to increase control by hypothecating block grant foundered on local authority *and* DES opposition. Even the attempt to regain some control over curricula experienced difficulty:

> rational planning is very difficult in this area; we are very much in the persuasion game of fixing affairs. My role is one of playing the honest broker . . . and, if necessary, buying them out with a fat purse (e.g. 'if you drop out of this area as we wish we will give you a grant for "curriculum development" elsewhere'): the operation of the network and the mafia is crucial in this field.
>
> (DES assistant secretary, cited in Ranson, 1982, p. 106)

To experience difficulty is not necessarily to fail. If the DES has made less progress less rapidly than it hoped, none the less it has pursued a centralizing strategy. LEAs are under threat:

> the Education Act 1980, the block grant system, the school curriculum initiative and the planned support for education represent, when taken together, an actual or potential diminution of LEA discretion . . . Looking at the education service as a whole, it seems that the DES acting on its own initiative . . . is now in the process of expanding its power and influence at the expense of LEAs.
>
> (Cited in Ranson, 1982, p. 112)

The intention is clear and has been for some time. But as in the case of local government finance, translating the intentions into practice has been a recurrent problem. Most important, if there have been intensifying centralizing pressures, change has not been 'fast enough for it [the DES] to win the game with actors on the boundary of its network' (Ranson, 1982, p. 107). The key relationship in an era of resource squeeze is with the Treasury:

> the Treasury is very critical: education has promised and not delivered. If you give £50m to MSC it will buy you a hard edged reduction in youth unemployment, whereas if you put money in RSG . . . That is why we lose out. The Treasury–Cabinet line is pay money to an organization which will get things done quickly. The Treasury has been a strong controlling influence. The Treasury/MSC link has been a key one. We are trying to gain the same relationship.
>
> (DES under secretary, cited in Ranson, 1982, p. 124)

The DES's attempts to reassert control within its own policy community – to redefine the purposes of education – with its attendant frustrations, has constrained its ability to extend its domain. Into the gap moved the MSC.

To interpret the extended role of the MSC as an incursion of DES turf is only half the story. The DES was a late arrival in the field of training; it experienced problems in redirecting its policy community; and it failed to meet Treasury–Cabinet expectations. The DEmp was already established in training. Since the Industrial Training Act 1964 it had been responsible for improving the quality and effectiveness of training and it had been at the heart of a training policy network based on consultations with employers (CBI), trade unions (TUC) and FE and higher education. The MSC was established in 1974; from its inception it was intended to provide training for young people under the Community Industry scheme, and provision was extended with the Job Creation Programme (JCP), the Recruitment Subsidy for School-Leavers (to be replaced by the Youth Employment Subsidy) and the Work Experience Programme (WEP) – all introduced by 1976. Thereafter the JCP and WEP were combined in the Youth Opportunities Programme (YOP) in 1978. The details of the schemes are less important than the simple fact that a training policy network existed with an established commitment to training young people (for a more detailed history see Stringer and Richardson, 1982; Moon, 1984). Against this backcloth, it is possible to examine the origins of the Technical and Vocational Education Initiative (TVEI).

The MSC's passport into vocational education was provided by the Youth Training Scheme (YTS) and its predecessor programme, the YOP. The YTS was launched in September 1983 and it aimed to provide every school-leaver with a year's work experience and training. From its inception it had a dual role. It was not simply a bridge between school and work – a training programme – but also part of the drive to increase the productivity and competitiveness of British industry (Mason, 1984, p. 67). Thus, in support of the government's avowed strategy of stimulating technological innovation to increase the competitiveness of British industry, the MSC has made provision for training in information technology through the voluntary Computer Services Industry Training Board, which received MSC pump-priming funds and offers a computer services scheme for the YTS; through the Threshold Scheme, which offers computer training for the young unemployed; and through the establishment of Information Technology Centres (Moon and Richardson, 1984). This economic function legitimates MSC involvement in the social policy component of the YTS, and the training link with FE colleges has developed apace. LEAs can act as agents for the MSC, sponsor their own trainees, or mount their own schemes. The success of the scheme depends on local co-operation between employers, the MSC and the LEA, and FE colleges do provide a significant proportion of the training component of the schemes. As Moon and Richardson (1984, p. 27) comment: 'the MSC has, in a short period of time, established itself as the focal point of vocational training and has been tremendously effective in expanding its administrative territory'. It had assumed dominant status in the unemployment policy sector; achieved a degree of closure by separating itself from related policy sectors (i.e. industrial policy, social security); and established close relationships with affected groups (i.e. business, trade unions, local government). These groups had become legitimated, and influenced policy initiatives; and decision-making was characterized by consultation and negotiation (these points are paraphrased from Moon, n.d., p. 10). The MSC's success is reflected in its expenditure, which grew from £727 million in 1979–80 to £1,906 million in 1983–4. Quite clearly, if the education policy community could not 'deliver', then the LEAs were to be bypassed, and there was an established policy community 'waiting in the wings'. Its capacity to 'deliver' was not in doubt, and the strategy of bypassing is illustrated by TVEI.

Moon and Richardson (1984, p. 24) argue that the birth of this initiative 'marked a considerable departure from past practice'. They argue that the typical consultative style of policy-making was abandoned to prevent a radical initiative being amended out of recognition. The TVEI involves the development of a new school curriculum for 14–18-year-olds which combines technical and vocational courses with work experience. It was to be the 'rebirth of technical education' (Norman Tebbitt, *The Times*, 13 November 1982). It was announced by the Prime Minister in November 1982 *without* prior consultation with the education policy community. Subsequently consultation took place to select the participating LEAs, and a National Steering Group was established to agree criteria for submitting schemes and to monitor their progress. But had the MSC mounted a successful raid on the education policy community's 'administrative space' (Moon and Richardson, 1984, pp. 28 and 30)?

First, training was not unequivocally the education policy community's turf; it was a function on the boundaries of the community. Training was indisputably part of the DEmp/MSC empire. Second, *within* both policy communities there had been extensive consultations about the future and form of vocational training, but there had been no negotiations *between* them. Third, consultations within the education policy community on both the organization of and curricula for re-vocationalizing the curriculum (Ranson, 1984) had produced no radical changes. Fourth, the MSC had a proven track record, at least in the sense of delivering a reduction in the number of school-leavers registered as unemployed. Fifth, it is well-proven central strategy to make a radical policy *announcement* and then return to the logic of negotiation. Such a strategy is an indicator of the asymmetric relationships of policy communities wherein the centre has structural power. Evidence is provided by Richard Crossman's announcement in 1966 that local government would be reorganized (Morton, 1970), followed by the appointment of a Royal Commission to explore the form, not the fact, of reorganization. Sixth, the TVEI is a pilot scheme with control of its implementation firmly in the hands of the LEAs. Finally, a money-moving strategy, more especially at a time of resource squeeze, is perhaps the best known and most effective means of inducing compliance.

Consequently, whilst the movement of the training policy network into the design of school curricula is a significant policy shift, it is best interpreted not as a marked departure of policy style but as bypassing: as a demonstration that policy innovation occurs at the interstices of policy communities – a strategy which has underpinned the creation of many a non-departmental public body (Hood, 1978, p. 39). In such circumstances lead status is accorded to (or taken by) those with the proven track record.

However, if bypassing avoids one set of constraints, in this case the LEAs, it is none the less a constrained strategy. As Moon (n.d., pp. 14 and 24) points out in his analysis of the YTS, bargains still had to be struck with a range of interests; the government was locked into a range of new dependencies and had to modify some of its policy intentions as a result. There was a high degree of local discretion because the MSC depends on firms, unions and local authorities to implement its policies, 'making for wide variations in patterns of participation in decision-making and implementation' (p. 23). The same point applies to the TVEI:

> the implementation of the policy depends upon the co-operation of local education authorities, professional organizations, teachers and their unions, and parent–teacher associations ... (t)hese groups have been drawn back into the policy process and we can expect to see the operation of the scheme serving their interests and goals.
>
> (Moon, n.d., p. 32)

In short, the inertia engendered by the logic of negotiation within the education policy community constrained its ability to regulate boundary changes. The characteristics of the education policy community, particularly the high degree of vertical interdependence, are as important a component of any explanation of the outcome on vocational policy as the empire-building proclivities of the MSC. Equally, the long-standing disdain for training meant that there was a policy space awaiting occupation not capture. Given the ideological stance of the government, it is little wonder that one of its architects – the Secretary of State for Education, Sir Keith Joseph – supported the TVEI initiative (Moon and Richardson, 1984, p. 28); his own policy community had manifested little capacity or enthusiasm for so extending its boundaries. And yet these very qualities of inertia were to prove invaluable in resisting the resource squeeze imposed after 1979 by successive Conservative governments.

4.2.2(iii)   EDUCATION AND THE BLOCK GRANT

From the inception of block grant, the DES considered that it would increase its influence over LEA expenditure. It decides on the factors in the education GREA and can, therefore, influence the notional amount of grant allocated to the education service in an individual local authority. As we have seen, the DES attempted to use these powers to re-vocationalize the curriculum. The DES also encouraged the publication of its GREA, believing this would prompt LEAs to follow where it led. And, in line with overall government policy, the DES was calling for a reduction in local expenditure, a call given added urgency by the perceived need for a reduction in 'surplus capacity' as a result of falling school rolls. This section examines the response of LEAs to these pressures.[5]

At the outset, it is important to distinguish GREAs from the system of volume targets introduced in 1980; the latter quickly came to dominate, and the reaction of LEAs differs between these two components of the system. The most obvious consequence of the GREA system was to reinforce the position of the treasurer. The complexity of the system discouraged dissemination of knowledge. For example: 'I don't go out of my way to inform either officers or members ... the latter aren't in any case interested' (treasurer, Metropolitan District, cited in Crispin and Marslen-Wilson, 1984, p. 107). Similar sentiments were expressed by a chief education officer (CEO): 'they [the members] wouldn't know a GRE from a GCE' (cited in Crispin and Marslen-Wilson, 1984, p. 107). The GREA system reinforced the position of the topocratic professions *vis-à-vis* both technocrats and members. It should not be thought that all CEOs remained ill-informed, however, and half of Crispin and Marslen-Wilson's case-study LEAs had made special studies of their education GREA. Most councillors 'know as much as they need to know', that is, very little on the detail of GREA but enough to understand the relationship between GREA, rate level and penalties.

Second, and more important in this context, service GREAs were deemed largely irrelevant: 'it is not relevant to budgetary decisions' (cited in Crispin and Marslen-Wilson, 1984, p. 111). The retort to arguments based on service GREAs was, 'What about the overall priorities?' If the publication of service GREAs served the objective of hypothecating block grant, then it failed. Both members and officers believed they should determine priorities for their area.

Targets and associated penalties had a more substantial impact. Thus, the system stimulated creative accountancy not only at the authority-wide level but also at service level. Thus, small items such as book purchases were charged to capital, thereby reducing current expenditure. Another device was to bring forward expenditure. In March/April 1983 the maximum penalty rate was considerably less than for the following year. Consequently, it was in an authority's interest to spend money immediately, even if this meant simply transferring it to a special fund. Indeed, Crispin and Marslen-Wilson (1984, p. 140) conclude that to the end of 1982–3 'the authorities in our sample were in general able to evade the Government's attempts to bring them into line with public expenditure policy'. When the government intensified its efforts in 1983–4, the attitude was, 'There's no way we're going to get there, so we won't do it', or, in the words of one CEO, the targets were 'demonstrably ridiculous'. The era of cuts 'slowed us down'; 'with no shortage of money, we would be doing broadly the same kinds of things at a slightly higher level'. And if education had been squeezed harder because of 'political perceptions of education as a big spender' none the less there was money for growth in such areas as the YTS and FE. In fact, the system of penalties had an unintended distorting effect. In one sample authority, £400,000 on YTS-related expenditure actually cost £1 million because of penalties: 'to do something the government wants, they penalize us £600,000'. Such outcomes only reinforced the dismissive attitudes of CEOs to GREAs, targets and penalities. In sum, 'the penalty system had not seriously impinged on the education budget, neither in comparison to other services nor in absolute terms' (all previous citations from Crispin and Marslen-Wilson, 1984, pp. 143, 156, 146 and 158 respectively). Between 1979–83 education expenditure remained constant in real terms, and the aggregate effect of the new grant system was to increase the proportion of 'overspenders' (Crispin and Marslen-Wilson, 1984, p. 172).

Within this overall picture, however, the room for manoeuvre hinged on whether or not a programme of school closures or amalgamations had been agreed. Rationalization and 'cuts' were interwoven, and it is important to explore, therefore, the ways in which LEAs managed falling school rolls.

Government policy on the contraction of education has received its clearest expression in its public expenditure White Papers. For example, *The Government's Expenditure Plans 1982/83–1983/84* (Cmnd 8494, HMSO, 1982) projected that the total school population would fall from 8.2 million in 1980–1 to 7.3 million in 1984–5. It planned for a reduction in teacher numbers from 429,000 to 380,000 in the same period. Actual reductions from 1980–1 to 1982–3 amounted to 14,400. Confronted by such divergences, the easiest course of action is to revise the planned total upwards, a course promptly adopted by the government. The 1983 White Paper (HMSO, 1983c) countenanced a high of 395,000 teachers by 1984–5 compared to an establishment of 414,600 in 1982–3. A slightly improved pupil–teacher ratio also replaced the previous tightening of staffing standards. None the less the planned annual rate of reduction in teachers' numbers continued to exceed the rates actually achieved in any preceding year (for a more detailed discussion of the data see Walsh *et al.*, 1984, ch. 2).

The response of LEAs was as varied as government plans were variable, encompassing closures, amalgamations, premature retirement, natural wastage (coupled with no reappointment), temporary and ring-fence appointments, adjusting the curriculum and increasing teaching loads. Walsh *et al.* (1984, pp. 276–80) argue that the overall picture is one of increasing and marked divergences between local authorities. However, policy-making for contraction in LEAs has exhibited a number of common features. First, LEAs have adopted unrealistic policies; for example, cutting appointments whilst adopting natural wastage to reduce numbers serves to reduce wastage levels because new appointments have the highest turnover. Second, short-term solutions with long-term costs have been employed; for example, premature retirement schemes increase financial constraints in the future. Third, present policy determines future policy; for example, authorities continually reduce the qualifying age for early retirement. Fourth, policies tend to reinforce the problems of falling rolls; teacher mobility is reduced by falling rolls and further reduced by 'last-in-first-out' and ring-fence policies. Fifth, policies disadvantage the weakest members of the teaching profession: for example, women returning to teaching. Sixth, action is put off, especially by elected members; for example, 'the policy in effect says that the elections are coming' (Walsh *et al.*, 1984, p. 35). Seventh, school autonomy has declined. Eighth, there has been a growth in formal and written procedures. Ninth, detailed planning has become nigh impossible. The range of interests affected – parents, pupils, teachers, governors, elected members, officials – is so diverse that a consensus cannot be built. Finally, contraction has increased the impact of marginal changes. There is little or no budgetary margin of error, and decisions on a single teacher can have enormous repercussions within a school. As noted earlier in the discussion of local budgeting, planning is short term; LEAs live from hand to mouth. Thus:

> Members are reluctant to consider closure of schools because of the political costs involved. Policy is therefore likely to be piecemeal rather than global. (CEO, metropolitan district)

> The council don't like change, and don't like trouble – they are mild Tories, but the problem of problems not being dealt with is building up. We have no plans at all – it's all *ad hoc*. (CEO, London borough)
>
> (Both quotations from Walsh *et al.*, 1984, p. 45)

The diverse and divergent response of LEAs to contraction illustrates the problems of a non-executant centre. Whatever its pronouncements on either new directions for education or levels of expenditure, its initiative is dissipated in a disaggregated policy system.

4.2.2(iv)   CONCLUSIONS: 'SOME ARE MORE EQUAL THAN OTHERS'

For the bulk of the postwar period, the government of education was characterized by consensus, a high degree of integration of its restricted membership and intensive participation by the technocratic professions rooted in the (vertical) dependence of DES. There was a stable policy-making community based on the troika of DES, LEAs and teachers' unions. Policy-making was incremental. With the intensification of economic decline and then recession, the pressures upon, and the stresses and strains within, the education policy community became greater. Crispin and Marslen-Wilson (1984, pp. 88–91) argue that, in consequence, there is no longer a policy community. They explore the work of the Expenditure Steering Group (Education) of the CCLGF, arguing that it is not a policy community because the DES is a central department before it is a partisan supporter of education; unity amongst the associations is fragile; association representatives argue for more money overall, knowing more grant to local authorities will bring more to education; and the ESG(E) includes topocrats as well as the education interests. They conclude (pp. 175–6) that 'the links between ... the DES and local education authorities did not seem to be mediated through the education policy community as represented by ESG(E)'. This conclusion is as surprising, given their own evidence, as it is misleading.

The simple point about the ESG(E) is that it exists; no other steering group has a comparable remit or acts as a forum on policy generally. Most are limited to assessing the implications of the figures in public expenditure White Papers (Crispin and Marslen-Wilson, 1984, pp. 28–9). Second, the ESG(E) is not, nor has it ever been, a policy community in its own right. It is a component of the education policy community, which includes a number of institutional foci for consultation (Rhodes, 1986a, pp. 325–46). Third, the ESG(E) does not explore the distribution of expenditure between services, the topic most likely to highlight the shared education interests of centre and locality, but between levels (and types) of government and between policies within education, the topics most likely to highlight the different interests of centre and locality. Such discussions assume a shared interest and are designed to foster consensus by airing a range of issues prior to decision. The debate is continued in other forums, which include the teachers' unions, and it is this extensive and systematic process of policy-making by multiple negotiations which characterizes all policy communities.

But if developments since 1979 have not witnessed the demise of the education policy community, Crispin and Marslen-Wilson are correct in identifying the increasing stress on the relations between centre and locality. The DES has attempted to increase its control over the rest of the policy community, and the accompanying resource squeeze has witnessed a struggle to establish a new consensus. The trend since 1979 has been towards greater centralization within both the policy community and individual LEAs. And once again, the results of central action have not matched intentions. The high degree of vertical interdependence within the policy community constrained the centre's ability to redirect policy and relationships. Most significant, the problems of the DES had an adverse effect on its relationships with other policy communities. Its failure to deliver prompted Treasury criticism and weakened its ability to regulate change on the boundary of its domain where the training policy network demonstrated greater capacity.

However, the centre is not without influence. As Taylor and Simon (1981, p. 9) argue:

> That falling rolls constitute a problem rather than an opportunity has much to do with the context of attitudes towards education and the part it plays in the life and growth of capitalist society. The views that we hold about the relations between education and social change, and the directions that might be taken by the latter, powerfully influence the extent to which educational investment is seen as a desirable priority.

The DES, with a strong stimulus applied by the Treasury, has had considerable influence on 'the control of attitudes'; in Ranson's (1984, p. 238) terms it has steered the system towards vocationalism, rationalization and stratification. Thus, education should prepare young people for employment; provision should be targeted on identified client groups (how much opportunity, choice and access to which groups became the key criterion); and in rationalizing provision, the curriculum should be stratified so that the different groups receive provision relevant to their needs and to the 'realistic' expectations of young people. Such a national level of ideological structure can be expected, over time, to exercise a powerful influence on both the policy community and individual LEAs. If the rate of change with regard to 16–19 provision, the level of local education expenditure and the rate and direction of contraction seem slow, hesitant and divergent, none the less:

> The changes seem to embody a conception of future society: 'Education often acts as a kind of metaphor of national destinies. It seems to be a particularly appropriate vehicle for talking about the future of society in general.' In the 1960s the images for young people, as well as for society, were of opportunity, horizons,

mobility and achievement. In the 1980s those images are replaced by ones of realism, localism, place and ascription.

(Ranson, 1984, p. 243, citing CCCS, 1981)

In what ways, therefore, has the education policy community affected the distribution of resources between interests and classes in society? In their analysis of whether education changed British society, Halsey, Heath and Ridge (1980, p. 205) conclude that, judged by the yardstick of equality of access to superior forms and levels of education:

> school inequalities of opportunity have been remarkably stable over the forty years which our study covers. Throughout, the service class has had roughly three times the chance of the working class of getting some kind of selective secondary schooling. Only at 16 has there been any significant reduction in relative class chances, but even here the absolute gains have been greater for the service class. If the hereditary curse upon English education is its organization upon lines of social class, that would seem to be as true in the 1960s as it was in 1931 when Tawney wrote.

The education system has continued to favour the well off, and Britain is no nearer to becoming a meritocracy. The Education Act 1944 aimed to fill places in secondary schools with the ablest candidates. Yet the service classes were allocated consistently more places in some form of selective secondary schooling. Paradoxically, although 'secondary education was made free in order to enable the poor to take more advantage of it ... the ... consequence was to increase subsidies to the affluent' (Halsey, Health and Ridge, 1980, p. 210).

The incremental pattern of policy-making which characterizes the education policy community was a contributory factor to the stability of patterns of education opportunity. Of its very nature, incremental-ism fosters scepticism of radical change, provides a rationalization for inertia and acts as a bulwark for the status quo; it is conservative with a small 'c' (Dror, 1968, pp. 144–6). As Lodge and Blackstone (1982, pp. 33 and 34) argue, the DES is 'pragmatic, conservative and evolutionary', reacting to 'the logic of the education service as it was developing'. Little wonder, therefore, that it failed to develop policies to overcome 'the stubborn resistance of class and class-related culture' (Halsey, Heath and Ridge, 1980, p. 219).

Pessimism is not, however, a wholly accurate response to postwar trends. There was continuous expansion up to the mid-1970s and the key factor influencing class chances of access to selective secondary schooling was the scarcity of places. If the building programme had kept pace with the expanding school population, then the differential between classes might have remained constant (Halsey, Heath and

Ridge, 1980, p. 217). The 'venerable strategy' of increasing levels of education expenditure 'gives no warranty to easy optimism; but neither does it endorse defeatism'. The 'growth and spread of educational qualifications' demonstrates that there is a large pool of educable young people. But 'there is no short cut to equality of class chances', and if increased spending did not necessarily guarantee equality, then the failure to keep pace with the booms in school population unnecessarily limited the effectiveness of the 'venerable strategy' (Halsey, Heath and Ridge, 1980, pp. 216–17).

The onset of public expenditure 'cuts' predictably emphasized class differences. There was no longer an increment of resource to keep such differentials constant. Perversely, the very inertia of the education policy community which, in earlier years, had blunted radical policies now acted as a buffer to increased inequality. The effects of the resource squeeze were ameliorated and slowed. This general point aside, recent trends offer little consolation to those who seek greater equality of opportunity. Change may be slowed but it is change none the less and it is in the direction of a stratified and, therefore more unequal educational system.

This transition has been accentuated by the operation of the block grant system. Although GREAs attempt to measure educational need, the distribution of grant is greatly influenced by the government's system of targets and penalties. Educational GREAs are not redistributive (Bramley, 1984, p. 20). Moreover, inner cities have a high need to spend because of economic decline – which fact is virtually ignored in GREA. In addition, block grant interacts with other policies to produce unintended consequences. Thus, expenditure on the YTS increases the penalties imposed by the government: an 'inconsistency' which has provoked considerable adverse comment. In sum, the grant system exacerbates existing inequalities, and, but for local authorities compensating for grant reductions through rate increases, its consequences for education spending would have been far more severe.

Further sources of support for the education system in resisting the cuts lie in usurpatory strategies and in its capacity either to mobilize its clients or to draw upon their protests. Teaching is a semi-profession, an archetypal example of the organizational professions of the welfare state, and it has failed to secure full professional closure. Without the capacity to control the supply and quality of entrants to the profession, it employs trade union activities to secure its ends: dual closure. Consequently, working to rule and strikes have been an important means for slowing down, if not averting, unwelcome changes, their use distinguishing the education policy community from professionalized networks. Full professional closure rests on exclusionary not usurpatory strategies.

The teachers have not been alone in their fight against contraction.

Sectoral cleavages have been an important source of protest. Thus, individual LEAs have had to confront alliances of the middle and working classes opposed to the closure of particular schools. Sectoral groups are a resource in the fight against cuts, and their effectiveness is demonstrated in the widespread reluctance of LEAs both to close schools and to act before it is essential; in the words of one officer, 'it is difficult to achieve a remit to do anything' (cited in Walsh *et al.*, 1984, p. 35). Sectoral groupings can be composed of cross-class alliances and may also act to mitigate further increases in educational inequality. They are not necessarily so composed, however. Sectoral groupings also serve to increase the points of access for the politically educated and active. Protests about the reduced number of places at universities, the projected scale of parental contributions to both university fees and student grants and the introduction of a loans scheme in place of grants were markedly middle class in origin – the privileged acting to preserve their education subsidies. The campaign against Manchester's proposed tertiary reorganization also illustrates these interests in operation; the call to protect 'good schools' is also a call to protect the interests of those groups with favoured access to them. Sectoral alliances will not necessarily preserve the level of inequality in education at its present level; they may increase it.

The trends to vocationalism, rationalization and stratification can be interpreted, therefore only as steps towards greater educational inequalities. The rebirth of technical education will further limit access to superior forms and levels of secondary education. The educable pool denied access will become larger, and the class differential will become more marked. Central support for private education, selection and the support of 'good schools' are the manifest signs of a new thrust towards educational 'realism' and the rebirth of ascription – the hereditary curse. But the change in the national-level ideological structure poses the most severe challenge to equality of opportunity in education. The educational policy community may not have developed a new consensus because of its multiple interests and disaggregated structure. LEAs may have dissipated central initiatives. Diversity may be the key note of their reaction to contraction and the resource squeeze. But the signposts to the future have been staked out. The asymmetric power of the centre will ensure that its ideological perceptions of the educational imperatives generated by economic decline exercise a pervasive influence over the reorientation of the education system.

4.3 Territorial Communities

The distinguishing feature of territorial communities compared to policy communities is that their constellation of interests encompasses not just functional but also territorial interests. This section explores their distinctive features, focusing on Scotland and, to facilitate comparison, examining policy-making in the field of local government finance.

Given that many of the basic features of this policy area have been described earlier (see Chapter 3, sections, 3.2.2 and 3.2.4(i), and section 4.2.1, above), the case study will be less detailed than the English counterpart. The section also includes additional examples of the territorial communities 'in action' and concludes with a general discussion of their distributional consequences.

4.3.1 The Politics of Scottish Local Spending

Throughout the 1960s and 1970s Scotland improved its share of public expenditure relative to England.[6] This share has been determined since 1978 by the 'Barnett formula' (Heald, 1983, p. 247), which seems to be based on population share and allocates 10/85ths of comparable charges in English expenditure to the Scottish block. Within this total, the Secretary of State for Scotland can determine its allocation to specific programmes. Thus, he determines the level of grant to local authorities.

The Scottish RSG system has differed markedly from the English system and continues to do so. Up to 1979 there was no comparable use of formal techniques – i.e. multiple regression analysis (MRA), the CCLGF – to distribute grant. Rather, the Scottish Office (primarily the SDD, SED and SHHD, with the SDD in the 'lead') consulted the Convention of Scottish Local Authorities (COSLA) to agree a figure for the total 'relevant' expenditure (for grant) of local authorities. After the secretary of state had decided on the proportion of this total which would attract grant – a percentage invariably higher than in England – discussions would then take place on the distribution of aggregate grant to regional, district and island authorities. Grant was divided into resources, domestic and needs, with the latter accounting for a higher proportion of the total in Scotland than in England. It is the distribution of the needs element which involves the use of MRA in England. In Scotland 'the needs formula . . . [is] chosen to "produce" the desired answer'; 'judgement' is exercised to find an '"acceptable" distribution' (Heald, 1980b, p. 33). About 70 per cent is distributed 'by custom and practice' and 'on the basis of total population', and the balance by 'weightings' (D. A. Leitch, Scottish Office, cited in Heald, 1980b, p. 44) which are chosen by the Scottish Office in consultation with COSLA and include such factors as population decline, growth (in new-town population), sparsity and density. Such choices reflect political decisions on the relative share of region/island authorities and of urban/rural areas. Heald (1980b, pp. 41–2) concludes that the 'superficially similar' RSG systems differ in that the Scottish Office has adapted the framework to 'the particular circumstances of Scotland'. Moreover, the Scottish Office can take an overview of public expenditure in Scotland, rendering a consultative council 'superfluous', and there is the flexibility to switch funds between RSG and non-RSG programmes. A 'harmony of interests' exists whereby the Scottish Office secures more funds for Scotland in which local authorities share.

Up to 1979 the trend was for the Scottish Office to seek controls over total expenditure but to resist, and even reduce the amount of, detailed intervention. Consequently, it introduced a range of policy planning systems. They covered housing and roads as in England but, most distinctively, included regional reports and financial plans which covered the range of local services. In Houlihan's (1984, p. 404) terms, relationships were technical-professional; that is, they were periodic, cyclical, continuous and narrowly based on the requirements of the plan. At this time, the secretary of state had four main instruments for controlling current expenditure: alterations to the level of approved relevant expenditure; percentage of grant support; cash limits; and the distribution formula. Control over capital expenditure was achieved under the Local Government (Scotland) Act 1973, s. 94, under which the secretary of state's approval is required for capital expenditure (not borrowing) and the system of financial planning (and allied TPPs and housing plans) introduced in 1977–8, whereby the Scottish Office would make a block allocation for each major programme and local authorities would select projects within the total. If this system of technical relationships met resistance from service departments within the Scottish Office, if the financial planning system operated to limit the scope for local discretion, none the less by 1979 'local spending was clearly under control' (Midwinter, 1984, p. 16). The strategy of incorporation deployed in England was superfluous in Scotland. PPSs had 'delivered the goods'. The policies of the Conservative government seem to suggest otherwise.

'Hands-off' controls were to perish over the next four years, but the differences between England and Scotland were to persist. The Scottish Office had 'to do its bit' within the government's economic policy. Public expenditure in Scotland was to be cut, and so local authorities experienced more of the same. The RSG percentage was reduced, and strict cash limits were deployed. But block grant was rejected, and initially the Scottish Office relied on persuasion, not controls. The honeymoon did not last. By 1980–1 there were a number of specifically Scottish initiatives within the 'old' RSG system.

First, the secretary of state reduced the resources element of grant. To this point, the rateable resources of local authorities had been equalized – that is, brought up to a national standard amount per capita – at a level just below that of the richest local authority. This represented a needs/resources ratio of 4:1, which the Conservative secretary of state, George Younger, increased to 7:1 and then 9:1. The national standard amount fell, and grant was transferred from low-tax-base/high-spending authorities to high-tax-base/low-spending authorities (Heald, 1982, pp. 36–7).

Second, expenditure guidelines were used to enhance control. They had been introduced in 1976–7, at the request of COSLA, and they translated RSG totals into indications for each authority of what it should be spending. They had no statutory authority and have been described as an example of 'indicative planning' (Midwinter, Keating and Taylor, 1984, p. 21). Midwinter and Page (1981, pp. 74–5) concluded that local authorities' budgetary decisions were influenced by the guidelines, but under the Conservatives they have been treated with 'increasing incredulity' by local government (Midwinter, Keating and Taylor, 1984, p. 23). Their method of calculation was changed four times between 1976 and 1982, and COSLA was refused repeatedly an explanation as to how they were constructed. From 1981–2 they were based on the client group method. Expenditure is broken down into services, and the need to spend is assessed according to the number of clients for each service in that authority. The method is fraught with technical problems (Midwinter and Franklin, 1982), but perhaps more damagingly, its results have been adjusted to deter spending (Midwinter, Keating and Taylor, 1984, p. 24). As a result, more and more local authorities appear in excess of their guidelines, and in consequence the guidelines have become a peripheral factor in local budgeting. At one and the same time, however, the secretary of state used them to publicize the overspenders and they assumed a central role in the system of formal control introduced in 1981 (see below). When they were introduced, expenditure guidelines had no counterpart in England and Wales. And even with the introduction of GREAs in England and expenditure ceilings in Scotland the differences continued to outweigh the similarities.

The most distinctive Scottish weapon in the war against local expenditure, and the third change to the grant system, was the introduction of expenditure ceilings. Under the Local Government (Miscellaneous Provisions) (Scotland) Act 1981, s. 14, the secretary of state gained the power to reduce the grant payable to a local authority if its expenditure was 'excessive and unreasonable'. His discretion in so deciding is virtually unfettered; he must have regard to 'the financial and other relevant circumstances of the area of the authority'. He can base his decision on the authority's estimates and, given that Scottish local authorities have no power to levy a supplementary rate or to borrow to offset grant reductions, he is setting an effective ceiling on expenditure. It is at this point that the expenditure guidelines assumed added significance; they were one of the criteria for determining excessive expenditure. They still have no statutory force but they are now a cardinal feature of the grant system.

The fourth modification to the grant system was a form of rate capping under the Local Government and Planning (Scotland) Act 1982. Under the 1981 Act, local authorities were empowered to reduce rates in the course of the year. The government assumed that authorities which had to reduce spending would prefer to reduce rates than return grant to the secretary of state. However, the secretary of state was denied the pleasure of appearing to champion the ratepayer; only one local authority reduced its rate, out of seven against which the secretary of state took selective action. He retaliated by giving himself power under section 1 of the 1982 Act either to reduce grant or to require the authority to reduce its rate or some combination of these two courses of action. Either a local authority subject to selective action 'voluntarily' reduced its rate, or the secretary of state fixed a ceiling on its income.

In short, therefore, SCG in Scotland was subject to the same general pressures to reduce expenditure but the form of its reponse differed markedly from that in England. Rather than employing formal mechanisms, the level and distribution of grant are a matter for the secretary of state's discretion, as are the ceilings on local income and expenditure. But if the form of government action differed, the consequences of its actions bear a marked affinity to the English experience.

Confronted by budgets which exceeded guidelines by some 9 per cent in 1981–2, the secretary of state promptly invoked his new powers. Seven councils were the subject of selective action, most visibly Lothian Regional Council. The responses of the 'hit list' councils varied. Lothian and Stirling favoured a public campaign. For example, Lothian published its Green Book, *Representations to the Secretary of State on the Intention to Reduce Rate Support Grant*, unsolicited copies of which reached as far as the University of Essex. The booklet emphasized the threat to local democracy and in Midwinter's (1984, p. 37) terms 'was the beginning of the election campaign of 1982'. A delegation was sent to Parliament, the GLC provided facilities for press conferences, and a 'day of action' by public sector trade unionists was organized. Other councils were low key and pragmatic. Keating, Midwinter and Taylor (1983, p. 408) describe four tactics: to dispute the factual basis of Scottish Office figures; to demonstrate that expenditure increases were caused by central decisions; to challenge the validity of the government's criteria and analysis; and to demonstrate the real cause of rate increases – e.g. inflation, grant reductions.

There was some scope for manoeuvre. The cuts were announced after the beginning of the financial year. If there were to be no redundancies, and the government did want to avoid them, the cuts would have to be reduced in scale. Consequently, there was a great deal of formal and informal discussion, with officials acting as go-betweens in attempts to find acceptable compromises. At the end of the day, the government got its cuts but not on the scale envisaged. The final reductions totalled £33.7 million out of a total overspend for that year of £180 million. At the outset local expenditure exceeded the RSG figures by 8.9 per cent. At the end, the excess was 8.15 per cent (see Keating, Midwinter and Taylor, 1983, tables 6 and 7, p. 414). Nor was the picture to change dramatically in the next budgetary round.

For 1982–83 the method for calculating the expenditure guidelines was changed to the 'client group' method. Sharp fluctuations in the figures for individual local authorities were avoided by the political decision to include stability factors. As a result, guidelines were brought closer to actual expenditure, and former 'hit list' authorities – e.g. Cumnock, Dundee, East Lothian – received considerable increases in their guidelines, becoming 'normal' authorities (Midwinter, 1984, p. 40). Lothian and Stirling still stuck out like a sore thumb, but, as a result of the 1982 elections, Lothian was a 'hung council' with a Conservative administration. It was keen to negotiate with the Scottish Office and mounted a rigorous defence of its budget, eventually cutting expenditure by £30.7 million and reducing its rate from 116p to 100p with no redundancies and all with Scottish Office agreement. With an impending general election, and an increase in the planned total of local expenditure of some £120 million, 1982–3 was a quiet year, and local expenditure exceeded the planned total by 8.3 per cent.

In 1983–4 the guidelines changed again. The stability factors were removed, and the gap between guidelines and actual budgets widened. However, overall local expenditure exceeded government plans by only 4.5 per cent. Still the government decided on selective action against Lothian and Stirling as in previous years and also against three newcomers: Shetland, Glasgow and Kirkcaldy. The problem for the secretary of state was that his 'objective' definition of 'excessive and unreasonable' expenditure was subject to scathing attack. The guidelines had become the focus of discontent:

> Whilst it has long been recognized that the distribution of grant requires some measure of relative need, the notion of producing precise spending targets for individual authorities is of very recent origin . . . Statistical measures cannot be used to define local needs: these can only be determined through the mechanisms of local democracy which seek to balance local needs against local resources. It must be recognized that the introduction of this approach to central intervention in local affairs, i.e. government by arithmetic, has generated a bureaucratic industry which is engaging considerable resources in the hopeless search for a precise method of centrally quantifying local requirements.
>
> (John Cairns, Chief Executive, Stirling District, cited in Midwinter, 1984, p. 47)

These views can stand as a summary for the views of local government in general, not just of left-wing councils; for example, Highland Region was equally critical. And what of the savings for the local ratepayer? They were marginal; in the case of Glasgow they amounted to 19p per week per ratepayer or 'not even enough to buy a half-pint of Younger's Tartan Special' (Midwinter, 1984, p. 46). Selective cuts amounted to a 1.3 per cent reduction in total Scottish rate-borne expenditure. And if the gap between government plans and actual expenditure was only £144 million, the 'improvement' had come about because of the upward revision of planning totals.

It is scarcely surprising, therefore, that Midwinter, Keating and Taylor (1984, p. 30) conclude that the new powers 'have had only a little impact on expenditure'. They may have 'reduced spending marginally', but the deviation of local spending from guidelines 'has increased since their introduction'. Guidelines remain a 'relatively insignificant influence' on local spending because they are seen as 'unrealistic and unachievable'. Moreover:

> despite ... the new selective controls on local spending, and the continuous fiscal pressure through grant reductions, a surprisingly large degree of discretion remains ... action is possible against only a few councils each year. Thus, an area of uncertainty exists, with scope for manoeuvre and bargaining ...
> ... There is little doubt that if such devices as guidelines or selective action are seen as instruments of central control, they have not succeeded in reducing the level of local spending in line with government plans.

The government's achievement has been to disrupt established patterns without realizing its stated objectives:

> The informal Scottish system of central–local relations depended for its operation on a perception of common interests. It is this which has been sapped, both by the erratic decisions of the Secretary of State, and by the political challenge to his authority by a few radicalized Labour councils. The atmosphere is now one of suspicion and recrimination, with the Secretary of State's victory over Lothian looking hollow. The vast majority of Scottish local authorities are at odds with him.
>
> (Heald, 1982, p. 44)

The differences and similarities between territorial and policy communities should now be relatively obvious. In brief, the territorial organization of the centre provides the focal point for a distinct network which, whilst subject to UK-wide pressures, develops its own distinct policy instruments. To employ Goldsmith's (1986, p. 153) summary:

> The informality and personal nature of the peripheral networks of central–local relations is a reflection of their much smaller size: of differences in the nature of peripheral political communities and in the relationship between local elites and their territorial counter-parts, and the difference in the scale – in finance and service terms – of the issues involved.

Like policy communities, this territorial community has considerable capacity to resist central interventions and to frustrate central objectives. Disaggregation foists vertical dependence on a non-executant centre, and the search for 'hands-on' controls, however distinctive they may be, serves to disrupt consensus. The attempt to replace the informality characteristic of territorial communities with bureaucratic controls and formal mechanisms (of dubious validity) had a haphazard effect.

Again to quote Goldsmith (1986, p. 161), the Scottish Office has had 'only limited success'

> largely because the legislation and its implementation has been uncertain, with the result that space still remains for bargaining and negotiation over expenditure levels between individual authorities and the Scottish Office, something which the small, informal central–local network allows. Scottish local authorities thus continue to retain considerable discretion over expenditure decisions, despite appearances to the contrary.

Arbitrary decisions had variable effect, creating a tension between informal negotiation and 'objective' allocations which generated a policy mess rooted in the centre's faulty territorial operating code. However, before developing this general analysis, it will help to extend the range of examples.

4.3.2   Varieties of Territorial Communities

It is important to explore how the political environments of Scotland, Wales and Northern Ireland influence the characteristics and operation of the network. To talk of varieties of territorial communities is to ask questions about variations in their environment and their domain. This section provides a brief example of policy-making in Northern Ireland, continuing with the example of local government finance. Self-evidently, the example has been chosen to facilitate comparison with the English and Scottish policy communities discussed in the preceding sections.[7]

Negotiations over public expenditure in Northern Ireland have three stages. First, the total expenditure of the Northern Ireland Office is determined in negotiations between the Northern Ireland Department of Finance and Personnel (DFP) and the Treasury and, ultimately, by the secretary of state in discussion with his Cabinet colleagues. In true incrementalist fashion, last year's budget is taken as the base, and negotiations focus on marginal adjustments. The Barnett formula is not explicitly employed (Connolly, 1983, p. 72), although relative population remains a major factor in determining the total. As in the case of Scotland, the ability and determination of the secretary of state in fighting his corner is a major factor in securing expenditure growth. Thus, after cuts in 1979–80 and 1980–1, public expenditure in the Province grew slightly under the tutelage of James Prior.

The second stage is the allocation of total expenditure between the Northern Ireland departments. This allocation is determined by the secretary of state and in bargaining between the DFP and the spending departments which, according to Green (1979), allows significant adjustments to expenditure priorities and patterns.

Finally, the spending departments determine the allocation of grants to SCG. In the case of local government, the general practice of the DoE(NI) has been to hold grant at approximately 21 per cent of net expenditure, although this proportion rose from 20.4 per cent in 1979–80 to 24.1 per cent in 1983–4. The grant system differs from those in England and Scotland. It has two parts: the derating and resources elements. The former compensates local authorities for loss of income through the derating of, primarily, industrial properties. The latter aims to increase the income of poor authorities up to a weighted Northern Ireland average. This grant has grown because total local authority expenditure accounts for a mere 4 per cent of total public expenditure in the province.

The rating system in Northern Ireland is unique. It contains two elements, a normal district council rate and the distinctive regional rate. The latter is a tax on the value of property levied by the DFP throughout the province and it is justified on the grounds that all should contribute to the costs of the services formerly provided by local authorities. It accounts for some two-thirds of the bill for individual ratepayers and is an object of considerable criticism on the grounds that it undermines the principle of local accountability for local expenditure decisions and that the methods of calculating the rate are inequitable. The basis for calculating the regional rate changes constantly, but this rate remains the dominant feature of local taxation.

Further distinctive features of local government finance in Northern Ireland are the continued use of loan sanction for borrowing and the scale of specific capital grants. Out of total capital expenditure in

1981–2 of £24.8 million, such grants accounted for 40 per cent of local authority capital funds. They are used to provide leisure, recreation and community centres. As in the rest of the UK, the total has been cash limited and, in real terms, fell by some 18 per cent between 1979–80 and 1981–2, having grown continuously since the inception of the system in 1975.

If the reorganization of local government in Northern Ireland left local authorities with residual functions, none the less they can still exert some pressure on the centre. Up to 1985 the major channel of communication is the Local Government Consultative Committee, a forum where ALANI, the minister responsible for local government and civil servants from departments with responsibilities for local services meet to discuss central–local relations generally. The Consultative Committee does not attempt to agree a figure for local spending but it does examine figures and developments. Both sides attempt to persuade the other of the error of its ways. The centre also attempts to restrain local expenditure through circulars and, of course, the direct controls of loan sanction, cash limits, specific capital grants and total general grant. However, given an effective informal network of consultation and the small scale of the problem, it has not been necessary to adopt the controls deployed on the mainland. Traditional methods remained adequate.

For the non-departmental public bodies, the financial regime was a great deal stricter. The individual boards prepare their own estimates, which are then agreed by the appropriate department. The resulting budget is cash limited, virement requires departmental approval, and expenditure is subject to monthly and quarterly monitoring. All have had the sanctity of cash limits impressed upon them. Within this general framework, fortunes have varied greatly. The Education and Library Boards have suffered from the conjunction of cuts and falling school rolls, and their expenditure fell by some 6 per cent between 1979–80 and 1983–4. In sharp contrast the Housing Executive, after a short period of cuts, has increased its expenditure by some 3 per cent in real terms, a figure which *excludes* some £100 million of income generated by the sale of council houses which it is free to spend but not to carry over into the next financial year – a luxury denied to housing authorities in England. Housing expenditure has been a priority and it is planned to continue growing. Health and Personal Social Service Boards have had marginal expenditure growth in real terms, but problems have arisen because of the way responsibilities are divided between the boards and the DHSS(NI). The latter is responsible for all major capital expenditure, and boards have argued that the department went ahead with projects but did not provide the revenue to cover the costs when completed and handed over to them. Additionally, the reallocation of funds between boards to foster a more equal distribution of health resources created problems for particular boards at a time when the capital expenditure necessary to increase territorial equality was deferred.

In short, therefore, financial relationships in Northern Ireland illustrate that the peripheral nations employ distinct instruments in the pursuit of UK objectives. Retrenchment may be a common theme, but the means to this end are highly varied. The case of Northern Ireland also demonstrates that there are exceptions to UK objectives. The clearest example is, of course, housing policy, an area of Draconian cuts on the mainland. Moreover, not only do policies differ with the active agreement of the UK government but they are also shaped and, from the standpoint of Westminster and Whitehall, distorted if not subverted by the impact of the province's political environment.

4.3.3 Conclusions: the Politics of the Pork Barrel

Territorial communities, like policy communities, are integrated, stable networks with continuity of membership and a high degree of vertical interdependence. However, membership of the network is informal and inclusive, distinguished by its territorial base and a high degree of horizontal interdependence rooted in shared territorial interests. The degree of integration cannot be judged by the presence or absence of formal co-ordinating mechanisms. Informality characterizes both the vertical and horizontal linkages within territorial communities. Given their size and scale, the networks can encompass all the relevant territorial élite. Interests and membership are not restricted to central bureaucratic and political actors plus the topocratic professions but also include local political élites and the technocratic professions. It is simultaneously restricted and inclusive. As the post-1979 Conservative government has discovered, the resort to formal instruments of control has served to disrupt the existing pattern of relationships without realizing the government's stated objectives.

There are, however, differences between both policy areas and the territorial communities. Rather obviously, the territorial communities have different sets of functions. In addition, the importance of these functions for the UK government varies. Distinctiveness resides in the particularity of the policy or the extent to which territorial variations have UK-wide implications. If teacher training has few such implications, the school-leaving age and secondary reorganization are seen as having substantial spill-over effects. The level of local spending is also deemed to be of UK-wide significance. In such circumstances, the centre determines the broad policy, which is then implemented through distinct territorial instruments. The conclusion that the centre can unilaterally determine policies and priorities cannot be accepted without qualification, however, because territorial political environments are not only a constraint on the territorial community but also on the UK government.

The conflicting ideologies and sectarian structure of Northern Ireland condition government action. Policy on local government, education and housing differs markedly from that on the mainland. Policy in Northern Ireland did not follow UK policies step by step. The mainland's financial inducements to tango prompted the prospective partner to do the quickstep. And if housing policy now reflects the UK government's priorities for Northern Ireland, education policy in the 1970s demonstrated the problems of imposing such priorities (Birrell and Murie, 1980, pp. 238–44). Moreover, in house building the Housing Executive has to take account of the sectarian divides, and its policies thereby reinforce the divisions. Nor are the effects of the political environment limited to substantive policies. Connolly (1983, pp. 27–8) argues that officials try to insulate themselves from sectarian politics: 'to isolate their games of administrative politics from the wider political game'. Allied to the relative sparsity of pressure group activity, a closed and distant territorial community has developed, variously characterized as paternalist, authoritarian and secretive.

Territorial communities, as their name suggests, can and do inject a territorial component into UK government which involves both distinct administrative processes and substantive policy variations. In addition, they have a marked effect on the distribution of government services. There are three main sources of data on the territorial distribution of public expenditure. The identifiable public expenditure series (see Table 2.2, above) shows that public funds were redistributed to Scotland, Wales and Northern Ireland (see also Heald, 1983, p. 245). The Treasury's *Needs Assessment Study* estimated that the incidence of need in the peripheral nations was greater; for example, compared to an English norm of 100 per capita spending, Scotland 'needed' to spend 116 (Treasury, 1979, p. 28). It also calculated that, for the services affected by devolution, Scotland spent 30 per cent above the equivalent English expenditure. Finally, Short (1981) has analysed the regional distribution of public expenditure for the UK. Thus, for the period 1974–5 to 1977–8 he confirms that average regionally relevant public expenditure per capita (UK = 100) consistently favoured Scotland, Wales and Northern Ireland. In short, the territorial communities received preferential treatment in the allocation of public expenditure during the 1970s and, if the data were available, probably during the 1960s as well.

Determining why this pattern of expenditure prevailed is more contentious. Although, as Rose (1982, pp. 136–9) argues, the differential allocations reflect population size, none the less the effect of territorial communities cannot be dismissed as marginal. The territorial communities, through their secretaries of state, inject the needs of their territories into the highest levels of government and protect historic differences in expenditure levels and policy content. It is precisely this ability to play the politics of the pork barrel across a range of functional ministries which makes the territorial communities so distinctive. Their internal horizontal interdependence is complemented by their ability to penetrate a range of networks, a tactic (and an opportunity) denied to functional policy communities. As Kellas and Madgwick (1982, p. 17) note, it is the Scottish Office's job to ensure that its 'finger could usually be in the pie', to support projects for Scotland and, resorting to understatement, 'it is not unusual for the Scottish Office to support the Great Britain department concerned, at official or ministerial level, in seeking the necessary authority' (Kilbrandon Commission, 1970, p. 10).

In short, the territorial communities foster territorial equity, which, it must be added immediately, cannot be treated as equivalent to interpersonal equity in the sense of either the equal treatment of equals or the unequal treatment of unequals (Heald, 1983, p. 239). Thus, although Northern Ireland continues to receive per capita levels of public expenditure well in excess of the rest of the UK, and disparities between it and the mainland have been reduced for a range of services, the distribution of those services within the province continues to sustain sectarian divisions. As Birrell and Murie (1980, pp. 301–2) conclude, 'the adoption of a devolved system itself solves nothing'. It is how devolution operates which is crucial: how, for example, 'social policies and social institutions sustain or challenge inequalities and discriminatory practices'. It is scarcely harsh to suggest that 'Devolution in Northern Ireland too often failed in these respects.' As in the case of the policy communities, territorial communities are but rarely agencies of change. Rather they are the organizational expression of the 'national'-level ideological structures of the peripheries which act both to sustain existing policies and patterns of distribution and to set the boundaries for individual perceptions of their interests in public service provision.

4.4 Professionalized Networks

4.4.1 Introduction

Professionalized networks are distinctive for the pre-eminence of the professions, and this case study compares IGR in the NHS and the personal social services (PSS), focusing on the influence of the medical profession and the social work semi-profession.[8] It does not provide a history of the transition of the NHS from the politics of its creation, through consolidation, to the politics of technocratic change in the 1970s and the onset of disillusionment in the era of resource squeeze

(Klein, 1983). Equally, it does not describe the change in the role of local government from destitution authorities to the promotion of welfare; the emergence of the PSS via the Seebohm Report (1968); the creation of the new unified, generic social work departments, and the subsequent consolidation of the PSS before their progress was also slowed by resource squeeze.

In preference to a general survey of the NHS/PSS, I paraphrase Webb, Wistow and Hardy's (1986) specific study of provision for the mentally handicapped. They identify three reasons for selecting this policy area. First, the mentally handicapped remain one of the priority client groups, and central policy has aimed to redistribute resources from acute, hospital-based specialities towards the 'Cinderella services' or the non-acute, long-stay sector. Second, 'community care' has been a fashionable ragbag of nostrums and policies for two decades, and since 1979, with intensified resource squeeze and the publication of *Care in the Community* (DHSS, 1981), its implementation has acquired a new urgency. A focus on the mentally handicapped facilitates an analysis of the specific successes and failures of a major component of a major policy initiative. Third, both the redistribution of resources and the implementation of 'care in the community' involve collaboration between the NHS and local government. Provision for the mentally handicapped involves, therefore, the study of one attempt to bridge organizational and professional divides. In brief, policies towards the mentally handicapped highlight key issues and relationships both within the NHS and PSS and between them.

4.4.2 Providing for the Mentally Handicapped

In Walker's (1982, p. 16) apt phrase, 'The ... history of community care policies in Britain is one of painfully slow progress towards timid goals'. Commonly the term refers to supportive domiciliary services, but they are *not* an alternative to institutional care. Residential institutions and hospitals are also included, with the DHSS (1977, p. 9) defining the term broadly as covering

a whole range of provision, including community hospitals, hostels, day hospitals, residential homes, day centres and domiciliary support. The term 'community care' embraces primary health care and all the above services, whether provided by health authorities, local authorities, independent contractors, voluntary bodies, community self-help or family and friends.

As Allsop (1984, p. 108) points out, the term covers three broad types of care: services provided in residential settings, services provided by professionals and specialists *in* the community and services provided *by* the community. Equally, there is a range of carers. In addition to the statutory agencies, there is the commercial sector, the voluntary sector and informal care through family and friends. It is scarcely surprising, therefore, that Walker (1982, p. 19) concludes that there is a 'remarkable confusion of aims and a fundamental ambiguity in policy' and speculates that the term's durability derives from its ability to encompass 'the widest possible range of institutions – it is all things to all politicians and policy makers'.

Such a portmanteau concept has attracted a variety of initiatives. The changes prior to 1979 have been summarized by Webb, Wistow and Hardy (1986, pp. 43–4) as

> from exhortations to develop local joint working; to the introduction of national planning processes designed to produce 'parallel planning' . . . in health and local authorities; to the introduction of structural change and local machinery designed to foster systematic local collaborative planning; to the introduction of nationally determined priorities designed to preserve collaborative planning for the priority groups in the face of severe expenditure constraints; to a financial incentive (Joint Finance) for health and local authorities actively to work/plan together.

Or, more briefly, progress took the form of 'a recognition that organizations are "self-interested" and must be paid to work together' (Allsop, 1984, p. 121).

Services for the mentally handicapped have been a central element in all of these initiatives.[9] This client group has been accorded a high priority. In theory, it was to benefit from a redistribution of resources to the Cinderella services and a shift from institutional care to locally based care in the community. These objectives have been embodied in a succession of policy documents, most notably *Better Services for the Mentally Handicapped* (HMSO, 1971). This White Paper was the first comprehensive, national plan for a client group, and a discussion of its fate provides a useful review of the problems of implementing care in the community.

Conditions in Britain's long-stay mental handicap hospitals were exposed as scandalous, and the 1971 White Paper was an attempt to overcome such problems as overcrowding, understaffing, neglect and ill-treatment. It outlined a set of general principles geared to developing care outside hospitals. It was argued that the mentally handicapped should not be segregated from the wider community. Rather each mentally handicapped person should have his/her needs comprehensively assessed, and training and education should be provided so that each could develop to their maximum abilities. Where possible, the mentally handicapped should remain with their family which should be provided not only with general social services but also with appropriate specialist help. Where it was not possible to remain with family, the alternative should be as home-like as possible. Within this overall framework, the White Paper set out five specific objectives: to reduce hospital populations; to provide locally based services from new, smaller hospital units; to improve standards in existing hospitals; to expand local authority residential and day care services; and to promote effective joint planning between health and local authorities. Quantified targets, to be achieved by 1991, were set for these several objectives.

The 'classic' elements of community care can be discerned from even this briefest of summaries. Equally, the limited progress made towards the several objectives illustrates problems of implementation which were to become a 'standard' feature of community care policies. The gap between targets and achievements was considerable (see Webb, Wistow and Hardy, 1986, pp. 53–4), and, as Wistow (1985) documents, a detailed examination of each objective of the 1971 White Paper reveals substantial shortfalls.

First, although the reduction in long-stay patients was accompanied by an increase in short-term admissions, average lengths of stay remained high. Wistow (1985, p. 72) concludes, therefore, that hospitals have remained long-stay institutions and that 'Ironically ... patient death rates rather than active discharge policies appear increasingly to be responsible for the reduction of hospital populations.'

Second, the large, remote hospital was to be replaced by 'mini', 'homely' units offering treatment, not residential care. The proportion of beds in large hospitals did fall. However, this reduction was achieved by scaling down large hospitals and not by building smaller ones. In 1979, 57 per cent of beds were in large units, i.e. hospitals with more than 500 beds. Moreover, the attempt to create 'progressive therapeutic programmes' was handicapped by severe shortages of specialist staffs. In effect, 'residents are not prepared for life in the community', and 'the quality of life inside hospital falls short of that implied by the White Paper's principles' (Wistow, 1985, p. 73).

Third, the DHSS attempt to introduce 'minimum tolerable standards' in existing hospitals ran out of steam by 1975. By 1978 the department considered the number of hospitals which failed to meet minimum standards 'very disturbing'. The examples of Ely and Normansfield stand as permanent reminders that a scandal could erupt at any time (see Martin, 1984, chs. 1–3, for summaries of the numerous inquiries into the conditions in long-stay institutions).

Fourth, the reduction in hospital populations was to be paralleled by the growth in local authority residential services, and between 1970–82 the number of places grew by almost 140 per cent. However, this increase represents only 41 per cent of the target, and the rate of growth between 1980–2 slowed dramatically. 75 per cent of the growth in PSS expenditure on the mentally handicapped had taken place by

1976. 'Unlike the health service', however, 'mental handicap has been accorded high priority in the personal social services', and in consequence its share of total PSS expenditure has continued to grow in the era of resource squeeze from 5.8 per cent in 1975–6 to 6.7 per cent in 1981–2 (Wistow, 1985, p. 75).

Finally, the expansion of local authority services was to be a product of improved co-ordination between local authority and the health service. Such collaboration was to be facilitated by the reorganizations of the NHS and local government which created coterminous areas. In 1974 a statutory duty to collaborate was imposed, and Joint Consultative Committees were established. The problems of effective co-ordination have necessitated repeated initiatives, however, including joint care planning teams, joint finance and, most recently, resource transfer arrangements (see below). The political, administrative and financial obstacles to co-ordination have been considerable and compounded by 'fundamental differences in the philosophies and priorities of the two services . . . In practice, two separate care systems for the mentally handicapped appear to have operated with access to them largely depending upon the point of initial referral' (Wistow, 1985, p. 76).

Although some progress has been made towards the targets in the 1971 White Paper, 'needs continue to be met inappropriately, or not at all, and resources continue to be badly used' (Wistow, 1985, p. 76). It is important to determine, therefore, why policies towards the mentally handicapped have experienced such difficulty.

In short, the policy has encountered three problems: definitional, resources and planning. The DHSS (1980) review commented on the 'absence of consensus both as to what the needs of mentally handicapped really are and as to the nature of help which it is appropriate for particular services to provide'. As Wistow (1985, p. 76) argues, the 1971 White Paper provided no clear guidance. It was a 'timid compromise' which, in the words of a DHSS official associated with its preparation, 'gave some satisfaction to most of the participants in the hospital/no hospital debate' (cited in Webb, Wistow and Hardy, 1986, p. 74). For example, the White Paper states that the mentally handicapped should not be segregated 'unnecessarily'. Whether or not the segregation is 'unnecessary' depends upon the availability of other services and the beliefs of the people implementing the policy. As Webb, Wistow and Hardy (1986, p. 75) conclude: 'In the absence of a definite commitment to change, of an unambiguous set of principles to guide it and of appropriate targets to achieve it, the White Paper was unlikely to be an effective instrument for implementing locally based services.'

The reduction in available resources was dramatic. At the beginning of the period, PSS were planned on the assumption of 10 per cent per annum growth. By 1976 the planning assumption was 2 per cent.

Moreover, many social service departments did not attain even the reduced 2 per cent growth rate. Of 108 social service departments, 27 per cent had a growth rate of less than 2 per cent in 1978–9, and this proportion had grown to 67 per cent in 1981–2 (Webb and Wistow, 1983, p. 27).

Joint financing was the mechanism for providing short-term financial support from the NHS for specific local authority projects. In theory, it should have facilitated the transfer of patients from hospitals to the community. In fact, little progress was made. There was little agreement between the NHS and the PSS on the meaning of community care. Wistow (1983, p. 33) suggests that for the former it meant the provision of residential services for existing patients, whereas for the latter it meant improving domiciliary and day care services and reducing admissions by supporting people who might otherwise require hospital care. In addition, joint finance was costly for local authorities. It provided only temporary support. After seven years the full cost was borne by local authorities. With the onset of resource squeeze there was a clear disincentive for local authorities to use such funds. In effect, for PSS, joint finance has been seen as 'a means of protecting and enhancing their own budgets', and in consequence 'local authority treasurers tended to be suspicious of joint finance, as "back door growth"' (Wistow, 1983, p. 37).

Joint finance is an integral part of the aspiration towards joint planning. Elaborate planning machinery has been established covering the DHSS's favoured priority groups, and joint finance provides the incentive to participate (Booth, 1981; Wistow, 1982). However, the planning system experienced a number of problems, in addition to the problems specific to joint finance. Webb and Wistow (1985a, pp. 215–6) conclude that the system was ineffective because there was no

> systems-wide perception of needs and service interdependencies; ... developed analytical capacity; consensus on the nature of need and on the best ways of meeting it; and ... organizational professional altruism – a willingness to surrender resources and authority in order to achieve a systems-wide objective.

In spite of these defects, the DHSS has remained wedded to its goal of reducing dependence on long-stay hospitals and to extending care in the community. Thus, the 1981 consultative document *Care in the Community* argued that 'Most people who need long term care can and should be looked after in the community. This is what most of them want for themselves and what those responsible for their care believe to be best' (DHSS, 1981, p. 1). Moreover, this initiative gained added impetus from the public expenditure policies of the Conservative government. It was believed that such policies were a 'cheap' alternative to long-stay hospitals and that service improvements could be achieved within existing resources (DHSS, 1981). Government policy was 'to provide succour to the long standing but fading policy of community care' (Webb and Wistow, 1985b, p. 217). The next section focuses on the reaction of health and local authorities to this initiative.

4.4.3 'Care in the Community' and the Mentally Handicapped

After 1981 the explicit objective of the revamped policy was to transfer hospital patients to other forms of care. Under the Health and Social Services and Social Security Adjudication Act 1983 and the DHSS circular HC(83)6, *Health Service Development* (DHSS, 1983), health authorities were empowered to make lump-sum payments to local authorities (and voluntary organizations) for patient transfer schemes. In the long term such schemes would be financed from savings in long-stay hospitals. In the short term 'bridging finance' was required, and joint finance monies were made available; 100 per cent support was available for ten years with a further three years of tapering support – although, in practice, sufficient funds were never available. In order to determine who did and did not respond to this initiative, how and why, this section paraphrases Wistow and Hardy's (1985 and 1986) analysis of the reactions of North Western and Trent RHAs before examining the local response.

4.4.3(i) THE REGIONAL LEVEL

Although joint finance was to provide 'bridging funds' for the 'care in the community' initiative, the scale of available funds was inadequate. Wistow and Fuller (1986, p. 47) estimated that only approximately £20 million per annum was available to fund new revenue schemes. A common problem was to devise financial mechanisms to cover the short-term costs of patient transfers. Wistow and Hardy (1985, pp. 33–6) described how Trent and North Western RHAs established a regional pool from which they made per capita (or 'dowry') payments for each patient transferred to the community. The financial allocations of each DHA are augmented by the dowries, and the districts pay back the supplement from hospital savings. The dowry is equivalent to the average costs per long-stay hospital patient. North Western pays the dowry to all receiving agencies, be it local authority, voluntary organization, or another health authority. In Trent the full dowry is paid only to health authorities because, it is argued, other agencies receive less dependent patients and can claim social security benefits. On the other hand, North Western allows social security payments to be added to the dowry. However, some local authorities consider even this relatively generous amount (totalling £16,000 at

1985 prices) inadequate for the most severely handicapped. Aware that these arrangements provide an incentive to submit schemes for the least dependent patients, all submissions are vetted, and the region insists that accommodation is in ordinary houses and the scheme caters for a mix of patients. Trent has no equivalent criteria, and the RHA allows DHAs considerable latitude. These contrasting features reflect the differing strategies of the two regions.

North-Western RHA has produced a clear and coherent strategy based on the principle of normalization; that is, services should enable each mentally handicapped person to live an independent, full and normal life. Its priority is the development of community provision, not the run-down of hospitals, and it is a firm advocate of residential accommodation in ordinary houses. Trent RHA does not have an explicit service philosophy of this kind. Its objectives are general – e.g. the provision of local services in accordance with individual need – and permit care in existing institutions. In effect, the RHA seeks to encourage local diversity and flexibility of provision.

Although the initiative is relatively recent, Webb, Wistow and Hardy (1986, pp. 101–3) argue that the consequences of these new arrangements can be discerned already. First, 'the number of beds in long stay hospitals for the mentally handicapped will be significantly reduced'. Second, there will be considerable diversity of provision, including the replacement of large institutions with small ones rather than ordinary housing. Third, the effect of resoure squeeze on local authorities has nullified the incentive of joint financing and, as a result, resources will be transferred between health authorities rather than between health and local authorities. For example, the local authority share of joint finance has fallen already from 91.5 per cent in 1981–2 to 77.3 per cent in 1984–5, whilst the health authority share has risen to 19 per cent. Fourth, priorities have switched sharply in favour of patient transfer, whilst needs in the community are not being met adequately. Perhaps most important, the pattern of service provision is being shaped by patients presumed to need some form of institutional care. Webb, Wistow and Hardy (1986, p. 103) suggest that this form of provision is inflexible, ill-suited to mentally handicapped people used to living with their family. And yet this group will make the largest demand on the service in the future.

Quite clearly, the current pattern of service outputs is at odds with the objectives of care in the community. This outcome is the result of several national and local influences on policy-making. First, the shift of resources to services for the mentally handicapped depends upon the demands for resources made by the acute sector. Second, central policy contains important ambiguities, permitting care in many forms. 'Care in the community' is a negative policy; it calls for a reduction in the number of beds in large institutions. It does not tell health authorities what to put in their place and, indeed, permits minimal adjustment of service policies.

Third, the centre's arrangements for financing patient transfers were inadequate. As Wistow and Hardy (1985, p. 32) point out, circular HC(83)6 made no provision for dowries. The RHAs were the only institution in a position to manage cross-boundary transfers by providing financial incentives. The regional systems have had a variable impact. Thus, Trent's dowry discriminates against non-NHS agencies, and local authorities considered the available funds inadequate. Consequently, transfers may be restricted to the NHS and to the less dependent patient. The structure of financial incentives potentially distorts the objectives of care in the community for the mentally handicapped.

Fourth, the degree of negotiation and collaboration between health and local authorities has varied greatly. In Trent, local authorities were consulted *after* a leaflet explaining the financing system had been circulated (Wistow and Hardy, 1986, p. 109). It would seem that consultation meant local authority acceptance of a policy already finalized. In sharp contrast, North Western established a specialist advisory group of health, local authority and voluntary group representatives to devise its scheme. However, the sense of partnership which can be generated by participation at an early stage in the policy process has been conspicuous by its absence in some regions.

Fifth, the operation of, and changes in, the social security system can have marked effects on service delivery; for example, regional perceptions of entitlement to benefit affected the operation of their financing system. In addition, changes in social security benefits had a marked effect on the provision of residential accommodation by the private sector.

Finally, the above problems have been compounded by resource squeeze. Local authorities have been reluctant to negotiate resource transfer in a time of severe financial restriction. In the words of one chairman of a Social Services Committee, 'the climate simply is not there and you can't hope to propagate an atmosphere of trust' (cited in Webb, Wistow and Hardy, 1986, p. 107).

At this juncture, it is important to remember that 'care in the community' is a *national* policy. In reality, because of vagueness about the appropriate form of service provision and inadequate financial incentives, the policy emerged from 'local–local interactions' (Wistow, 1982, pp. 56–7) to a degree which would make it inappropriate to talk of an implementation gap but for the fact that the example reveals yet again the centre's inadequate territorial operating code. In disaggregated and differentiated service delivery systems it is crucial to create a structure of incentives which both promotes interaction and gives the several parties a degree of influence over the others. The structure of incentives actually deployed generated, in some areas, positive inducements for patients to be retained within the NHS (Webb, Wistow and Hardy, 1986, p. 117). The importance of local–local interactions in this outcome can be demonstrated by a more detailed exploration of policy-making at the local level.

4.4.3(ii) THE LOCAL LEVEL

To be cryptic, between the reorganizations of 1974 and 1982 nothing happened to change the pattern of local service provision for the mentally handicapped. There was, however, some planning. In 1978 a 'Ten Year Plan for Services to the Mentally Handicapped' was produced which formed the basis of the (then) AHA's 1979 strategic plan. Its main features were a switch from large to small institutions within the NHS – described as a 'massive transfer from hospital to community' – and 'repatriation' or restrictions upon, and return of, the intake of patients from a neighbouring AHA. In place of four large hospitals, the AHA proposed a service based on 48-bed units (with day places). In addition, there was to be a 75-bed children's unit in the main mental handicap hospital.

In 1979 the national policy context began to exert an influence on the AHA. For example, the Jay Committee (1979) on *Mental Handicap Nursing and Care* unequivocally called for the care of the mentally handicapped in the community, prompting the AHA's nursing and midwifery commitee to claim that the local authority could not improve on its record and to assert that there was no adequate substitute for the existing pattern of care (cited in Webb, Wistow and Hardy, 1986, p. 136). The same year the National Development Team (NDT) – a DHSS 'quango' established in 1976 to visit health and local authorities and advise on the development of services for the mentally handicapped – recommended 24-bed community units for adults, 14-bed units for children, the transfer of low-dependency patients to local authority hostels and homes and the retention of long-stay beds at the main hospital.

The reactions of the AHA and the local authority stressed the problems with the NDT recommendations. The Director of Social Services saw financial restraint as a major impediment, whilst the AHA argued that the NDT had given insufficient attention to the difficulties of an area with a low and dispersed population. It was agreed that a new ten-year strategic plan should be produced.

Plans were overtaken by reorganization, central policy initiatives and potential scandal. In 1982 the AHA was replaced by two DHAs (referred to here as East and West districts), which developed their own strategies. In 1981 the 'care in the community' initiative had brought the candid recognition by the previous AHA of the problem of 'a lack of commitment to ... change by some of the professions, particularly those in the Health Service' who lack 'enthusiasm and drive' and believe 'that hospital-based medicine' is 'of paramount importance'. Consequently, the shift of resources 'will be slow and sometimes painful' (cited in Webb, Wistow and Hardy, 1986, p. 139). Finally, the conditions in one particular hospital were a source of some alarm. Confronted by a potential scandal, West District acted.

Within six months of reorganization, under the prompting of its chairman, who was personally committed to improving services for the mentally handicapped, West District produced an outline strategy which accorded them priority. It also proposed the closure of the 'problem' hospital and its replacement with a combination of new 24-bed units and transfer to the local authority. A planning team was established in 1983 to devise the detailed run-down of the hospitals and to negotiate with the county council. It reported the same year on the means for effecting the closures and transfers within five years. The time scale was short because it was judged that the hospital had the worst patient/nurse ratio in the country, was a bad fire risk, was overcrowded, suffered from poor staff morale and provided a very custodial service. This haste was supported by the region, which, confronted by something bad, was 'so frightened they'll help' (cited in Webb, Wistow and Hardy, 1986, p. 142).

The next step was to negotiate the transfers, a process which to some district officers 'felt as if we were banging our heads against a brick wall' (cited in Webb, Wistow and Hardy, 1986, p. 143). The social services refused to accept the most handicapped persons, to provide day care facilities and to build the group homes preferred by the DHA. Agreement was reached but only because the health authority 'cut our losses and said right, we'll do it', a decision which involved massive amounts of joint finance money. Over five years the total amount was estimated to be £5 million, in effect allocating all joint finance money to the mentally handicapped for a five-year period. The DHA was convinced that without such a transfer of resources the county council would have done 'absolutely nothing, because they have no development money'. And in spite of this transfer of resources, the negotiations were difficult: 'a process not of enthusiasm on their part but of attrition on ours', primarily because 'they honestly didn't believe we would give away money to them' (Webb, Wistow and Hardy, 1986, pp. 143–5). The process was further complicated by the RHA's discriminatory dowry system. Not only was the dowry less than the amount which the DHA proposed to pay the county council, but patient transfers began before the dowry system was introduced. The RHA refused retrospective payment – yet another shock to the DHA. But at least it had a transfer scheme. East District was far from this position.

East District's slow progress had a number of causes. There was no 'problem' hospital to provide impetus. The health authority was building a new district general hospital. It had the first call on funds and, in effect, took up all the DHA's development money. As a result, services for the mentally handicapped could be developed only by shifting resources from the acute sector. If such transfers are difficult, the problem was compounded by the attitude of the professions in the mentally handicapped services, 'who were determined to stick their heels in and remain institutional' (cited in Webb, Wistow and Hardy, 1986, p. 147).

Required by the RHA to produce a strategy for the mentally handicapped, district managers produced a report based on the NDT recommendations, i.e. community care in 24-bed units (with day places). The main hospital was to be retained but reduced in size. These recommendations were welcomed by the region but not within the (then) mental handicap unit.

The opportunity to forestall unit resistance arose in 1984 with the appointment of a new unit administrator and a new director of nursing services, In fact, the boot was quickly on the other foot because the new appointees had a more radical view of community care than DHA management; they preferred small group homes to institutional care. After an educative campaign by the newcomers, the DHA members and managers approved a new strategic plan based on 'a network of housing units to provide domestic type accommodation for four–six patients each'. Patient needs had supplanted institutions; individual-led development had replaced capital-led growth.

If internal negotiations had a satisfactory resolution, external negotiations with the county council were going nowhere fast. Although both parties came to accept the 'normalization principle' as the basis of care, agreement on funding was as contentious as it was elusive. DHA officers became increasingly frustrated. They argued that the county council's existing level of provision was 'sadly lacking' by national standards, and that it should spend more: 'it is about time the County Council stopped mucking about and using us as a crock of gold to avoid them fulfilling their proper responsibilities'. The DHA offered to work with the Social Services Department 'to go and beat hell out the County Council and get yourselves a larger share of the cake'. The offer was rejected. Rather, the department held out for the same deal it had already with West District. This deal was firmly rejected by East District's members and officers. The impasse had yet to be resolved when fieldwork was completed (Webb, Wistow and Hardy, 1986, p. 160).

Given these examples, formal collaboration could be described as a failure if it was expected to produce a county-wide comprehensive plan for a complex, multi-organizational context. Collaboration did produce more modest yet beneficial results. Officers of both districts felt they had persuaded the county council to give greater priority to the mentally handicapped. Within social services, mental handicap had moved 'from the bottom of the heap'. Within the council as a whole, however, social services remained under-funded. Although the health authorities recognized the financial problems of local government, they were convinced that social services were unwilling to make an adequate contribution to service development. Services for the mentally handicapped have been a health-led initiative. Social services tagged along for the ride when and where the health authorities bought the tickets. Circular HC(83)6 was crucial, therefore, in effecting some degree of change. The form, direction and speed of that change were locally initiated and directed. Policy guidance, whether from the DHSS or the RHA, was ambiguous. The region could and did influence district actions and nowhere more clearly than with the dowry system and with its preference for capital-led developments. But it promulgated no clear model of community care. The service actually provided emerged from local–local interactions.

4.4.4   *The Relationships, Characteristics and Consequences of Professionalized Networks*

Although a case study of services for the mentally handicapped in two regions and their districts appears to be a restricted focus, it draws attention to many of the characteristics of professionalized networks. This section draws together and discusses the information on relationships within the NHS. It then compares the relative influence of social workers and the medical profession in order to specify the characteristics of professionalized networks, before exploring the consequences for policy outcomes of these characteristics.

4.4.4(i)   RELATIONSHIPS

In theory at least the constitutional position of health authorities is clear. The NHS is 'provided directly by a minister, who exercises the functions of management in full and is answerable in detail for all acts of omission or commission in the service under his control, unless they can be regarded as individual acts of purely professional judgement' (Powell, 1966, p. 11). However, as the foregoing case study by Webb, Wistow and Hardy (1986) demonstrates, the relationships between centre–region–district cannot be characterized as between principal and agent; in reality, relationships are far more complex, with the formal hierarchic relationship mediated by rules of the game. For region–district relations these rules can be summarized as follows:

> that regions should adequately *consult* districts to ensure the latter's willing acceptance and compliance (even if not wholehearted approval) of regional policies; ... that policies should be '*reasonable*' not only in their own right but in relation to what else is expected of districts (thus it will be possible to negotiate slower implementation of one policy in return for progress on other policies); ... that if 'reasonable' and properly devised, districts have

a *responsibility* ... to carry out such policies; but ... there should still be a degree of *latitude* about how to implement policies.
(Webb, Wistow and Hardy, 1986, pp. 178–9, original emphasis)

Thus, the 'care in the community' initiative allows local discretion in service delivery. Consequently the policy's objective can be, and has been, confounded by the continuation of institutional forms of care. Regions vary in their willingness to direct districts, with Trent RHA adopting an essentially *laissez-faire* approach. Even North Western RHA's directive approach was grounded in extensive consultation with its 'partners'.

The degree of latitude varies, however, with the policy. There was little scope for bargaining over resource policies, nor, for that matter, over contracting-out. In effect, resource policies set the framework within which regions and districts have latitude in the design and delivery of service policies. The rules of the game modify but do not obviate central dominance. Compliance is the norm, and the pattern of relationships varies from 'principal–agent' to 'partnership' to 'bargaining'. The major factors determining the pattern of relationships at any one time are central capacity, professional influence and type of policy (Webb, Wistow and Hardy, 1986, pp. 174–5).

For the DHSS especially, but for the regions also, the heart of the problem of compliance lies in the disjunction between monitoring capacity and differentiated and disaggregated service delivery systems. Superordinate authorities have neither the time, the staff, nor the resources to enforce all policies. Selectivity is the order of the day, and, in consequence, subordinates have opportunities to bargain. Central capacity for peripheral control is finite.

A second major problem for the centre is to square the circle of national accountability with professional autonomy. Compared, for example, to social work the medical profession has an unprecedented degree of autonomy. One of the clearest indicators of this status is the rank of the chief medical officer, who is equivalent in standing to the DHSS permanent secretary and outranks the chief social work services officer. There are suggestions, however, that the era of resource squeeze has enhanced the position of financial managers at the expense of the medical profession (Saunders, 1984). Since care of the mentally handicapped is a relatively low-status medical speciality, one would expect to find evidence of, to employ Alford's terms (1975, pp. 14–15), the challenge of the 'corporate rationalizers' to the 'professional monopolists'. The evidence of Webb, Wistow and Hardy's (1986) case study offers little in support of this hypothesis.

First, 'There is this tendency all the time, in the acute sector, to grow', whereas for the mentally handicapped 'you only get expansion as a result, in the main, of deliberate policy decision' (health authority chairman, cited in Webb, Wistow and Hardy, 1986, p. 182). Second, growth in the services for the mentally handicapped depended upon the prior completion of acute sector projects. Moreover, such growth as did occur did *not* take acute sector resources. Consultants retain the power to veto anything they do not like, and this assessment applies not only to the acute sector but also to mental handicap. For example, one consultant argued that patients could be transferred to the community only if it would improve their quality of life. However, for 90 per cent of this consultant's patients it would not lead to any improvement. Accordingly, 'Perfectly simple, they won't go ... if it isn't going to improve their quality of life I'm not moving them. They can't get round that – no!' (Webb, Wistow and Hardy, 1986, p. 184). Clinical judgement remains a substantial obstacle to accountability; there will be 'a lot of friction in this area of what is managerial responsibility and what is professional responsibility', and 'it remains to be seen whether the general manager function actually will erode the clinician's influence' (unit administrator, cited in Webb, Wistow and Hardy, 1986, p. 185).

The needs of the acute specialities are given priority not simply because of overt acts of professional influence but also because recognition of those needs is culturally ingrained. Thus, West District may have given the mentally handicapped priority and all its joint finance. Other priority groups could have anticipated a share of these funds. But the acute sector had no loss of funds. Moreover, its priority – a new district general hospital – had been completed already. The priority accorded to meeting the needs of the acute sector was not the result of pressure or veto. It was simply accepted by health authority members. As Webb, Wistow and Hardy (1986, p. 187) conclude: 'In effect the acute sector is impervious to outside influences with policies being internally generated. It continues to have the power to structure the debate and therefore to set the parameters of the broad pattern of non-acute services.'

The power of the medical profession resides in its control over service policies. For resource policies, the centre has demonstrated its ability to steer the system through the use of cash limits. Although regions and districts expect to discuss the application of particular aspects of the RAWP formula to their area, and to lobby for specific projects, cash limits and manpower totals are regarded as the sole business of the DHSS: 'the straitjacket within which we operate' (district chairman, cited in Webb, Wistow and Hardy, 1986, p. 195). The DHSS deals predominantly with the regions, and, in sharp contrast to local government, there is no question of its right to limit expenditure. In the words of one participant: 'I've many times sat as chairman of the health authority and wished to God I could put a penny on the rates ... in the health authority you're very much more constrained by your resource allocation' (cited in Webb, Wistow and Hardy, 1986, p. 198).

In short, relationships within the NHS have three distinguishing characteristics: a discontinuous hierarchy (discontinuous because decision-making is by lay, appointed bodies); sub-central units with an independent statutory identity (in spite of their dependence on central funds); and a profession with a unique degree of autonomy encompassing service objectives, consumer interests and the scope of professional judgement (Webb, Wistow and Hardy, 1986, p. 214). The distinctiveness of these relationships can be more clearly appreciated if the NHS is compared with a local government service, the PSS.

4.4.4(ii) CHARACTERISTICS

The defining characteristic of professionalized networks is, of course, the pre-eminence of the professions in policy-making (see Chapter 2, section 2.5.2(i)). The capacity of the medical profession to influence DHSS policy-making has been oft noted and described. It is important to note, however, that the medical profession is the archetypal case. Although, for example, the Association of Directors of Social Services can be influential (Rhodes, 1986a, pp. 385–6) it does not compare with the medical profession's organizations. The latter are included on a wide range of decision-making and advisory bodies. The apogee of this institutionalization of professional influence is the Joint Consultants' Committee. It is composed primarily of representatives from the BMA and the Royal Colleges of England and Scotland. It has quarterly meetings with the DHSS, it is chaired by the Chief Medical Officer, and 'there is nothing that affects medical practice that does not go before the Committee'. Indeed, on clinical matters, any consultative documents 'go to the Joint Consultants Committee even before a draft exists' (cited in Webb, Wistow and Hardy, 1986, pp. 188–9).

The PSS have a discernible network but it is much less integrated and stable. One of the main links between the DHSS and the local authorities is the Social Services Inspectorate. However, in sharp contrast to police and fire, this inspectorate is *not* composed of the most senior members of the profession. Its views are not authoritative within the DHSS, and it is not seen as a source of policy guidance by directors of social services. The main point of contact for the PSS is through the local authority associations, which are not primarily professional bodies. In short, the capacity of the social work semi-profession to influence policy is far more severely constrained than that of the medical profession.

A further sharp contrast between the NHS and local government concerns the topocratic professions. Local authority chief executives and treasurers are the local officials with the highest standing and are disproportionately influential in the local authority associations. There is no equivalent management lobby in the NHS. General managers and administrators do have national associations, but they are ineffectual: 'so far as initiating policy from a standing start, I don't think you could say we ever did that. And I don't think you could ever say we had much impact on government policies with which we did not agree' (district general manager, cited in Webb, Wistow and Hardy, 1986, p. 186). In effect, therefore, medical influence operates at all levels of the NHS hierarchy relatively unchallenged by the topocrats, whereas social work has scaled only the lower peaks of influence and regularly confronts a powerful topocratic rival.

If the PSS confront a situation wherein social workers have relatively low professional standing and face entrenched topocratic professions, they command one advantage by virtue of their position as a *local government* profession: that is, political legitimacy. Thus, local government has resisted overtly central resource policies, whereas such politicized conflict is rare in the NHS. Health authorities have had to accept central expenditure controls. They have no electoral legitimacy to justify conflict between local and national priorities.

The bases of power in local government and the NHS are very different, but both have autonomy. The power of the doctors compensates for the constitutional and political weaknesses of the sub-central units of the NHS. Clinical freedom and professional autonomy have to be respected, requiring that the formal hierarchy be modified by the rules of the game. Consultation, policy ownership, reasonableness and latitude in implementation all attest to the constraints on the constitutional authority of the centre. Control is conditional and limited. The literature on bureaucracy and the professions emphasizes the conflict between the two (see, for example, Parsons, 1947, pp. 58–60; Blau and Scott, 1963, pp. 60–74; Gouldner, 1970). The institutionalization of the medical profession in the NHS demonstrates that bureaucracy, rather than fostering role conflict and divergent commitments, entrenches and enhances professional influence.

To suggest that medical influence underpins sub-central autonomy and constrains central control in the NHS is scarcely novel. To argue that the NHS is an example of a professionalized network is to state a banality. As Ham (1985, pp. 115–16) argues: 'the national health policy community is itself fragmented into a series of sub-communities concerned with specific aspects of policy. These sub-communities are organized around issues such as alcoholism, abortion, policies for elderly people, and so on.' In a similar vein Haywood and Hunter (1982) argue that on some issues (e.g. the elderly) consultation can be characterized as a tightly knit 'iron triangle' whereas on others (e.g. pay beds) it is best characterized as an issue network. The case study of services for the mentally handicapped also suggests that disaggregating the professionalized health network is a fruitful strategy.

First, as ever, it is misleading to talk of 'a centre'. The DHSS has five distinct 'businesses' for which it is responsible: social security, hospital and community health services, family practitioner services, centrally financed services and personal social services. Each of these 'businesses' can be viewed as the core of a network, and the DHSS has often been criticized for the lack of articulation between its constituent parts (Social Services Committee, 1985); indeed, one district chairman wondered 'if people ever speak to one another in the DHSS – the left hand and the right hand' (cited in Webb, Wistow and Hardy, 1986, p. 162).

Second, the earlier discussions of medical influence focused on acute sector consultants. The relatively lower status of consultants in the Cinderella services has been noted, as has the resistance of the nurses in the East DHA to the shift from institutional to community care. In other words, the medical profession is itself differentiated, and there is no necessary homogeneity of interest.

Third, the various policies of the NHS differ sharply in the degree to which they are insulated. A distinctive feature of policies for the mentally handicapped is that they are not confined institutionally either to one of the DHSS 'businesses' or even to the NHS. Where policy effectiveness is related both to the integration of different sections of the DHSS and to dependence on non-NHS actors, network characteristics will differ from policies which are insulated and institution specific.

Finally, the (as yet incipient) conflict between managerial and professional responsibility suggests that appreciative systems within the NHS may be changing. The search for the 'three Es', whether in the guise of contracting-out, performance measurement, or efficiency studies, has led to 'cost consciousness' replacing 'need' as the key decision premiss. The current rationale for community care relies as much on its presumed cost-effectiveness as on the needs of the mentally handicapped (or of any other priority client group). The combination of organizational differentiation, heterogeneity of interests and conflicting values provides strong a priori grounds for believing that the health network is disaggregated. However, Ham (1985, p. 116) concludes that further research is essential 'before the processes occurring in health policy sub-communities can be accurately described', and the analysis of the relationship between the varieties of health networks must await future research.

4.4.4(iii)   CONSEQUENCES

It is possible to identify a number of distinct phases in the evolution of services for the mentally handicapped. Up to the 1971 White Paper, the policy can only be described as *laissez-faire*. Under the impetus of scandals about the conditions in long-stay hospitals and following on the reorganization of the NHS, formalized collaboration became the order of the day, rapidly giving way to an incentives-based system as the machinery of joint planning proved inadequate to the task. With the intensification of resource squeeze, the policy of community care for the mentally handicapped was given a new lease of life because of its presumed cost-effectiveness. Collaboration was replaced by insulation, however, because the disjunction between the NHS structure of incentives and the resource squeeze on local authorities worked against transfers from the NHS to local government. The following discussion of consequences focuses on the last two phases of policy for the mentally handicapped.

Equally any evaluation of the policy has to recognize the constraints on the centre. The major barriers to the implementation of community care for the mentally handicapped can be summarized (paraphrasing Webb, Wistow and Hardy, 1986, pp. 222–5) as follows.

First, control within any one policy stream is limited because service outputs are difficult to specify and because informational and organizational resources are controlled by sub-central units.

Second, coherent policies spanning services and sectors are difficult to initiate and implement because of organizational differentiation within the DHSS and the absence or weakness of mechanisms for pushing innovations at the local level and across sectors, especially across the health/local government divide.

Third, and as a result of the first two factors, policies emerge independently of each other; at best, they coexist uneasily and, at worst, contradict and compete with each other. Policy is 'best understood as contingent and residual: it is not . . . a coherent and efficient application of resources in the pursuit of agreed outcomes; it is more usually the end product – not necessarily intended by any of the key actors – of conflicts and *ad hoc* bargains' (Webb, Wistow and Hardy, 1986, pp. 199–200).

Finally, the attempt to structure local policy environments requires strategies which span policy streams and sectors. Such strategies have been the exception rather than the rule, and the 'care in the community' strategy generated a host of unintended consequences because of inadequate DHSS steerage.

In the light of this summary it is no surprise that the policy of care in the community for the mentally handicapped has led to only a limited transfer of resources either within the NHS from acute to other services or from the NHS to local government. The extent of these transfers has already been described. The key role of the autonomy of the medical profession in limiting transfers within the NHS and of the autonomy of local government in limiting transfers from the NHS has already been discussed. What is perhaps more surprising is the extent to which this case study can be interpreted as an archetypal example of NHS policy-making.

Regional and interpersonal inequalities in the distribution of health services have been well documented (Le Grand, 1982; Townsend and Davidson, 1982; Ham, 1985, ch. 6). For the sake of brevity, the tone of the available research is captured in Tudor-Hart's (1971, p. 412) 'inverse care law', which states that 'the availability of good medical care tends to vary inversely with the need of the population served': a latter-day version of 'to them that hath shall it be given'. In a less flippant vein, regional and interpersonal inequalities in health and in access to health services persist. And numbered amongst the several causes of this outcome is the medical or mechanistic model of health institutionalized in the professionalized health policy network:

> To the extent that a mechanistic model of health holds sway, the health care services will give priority to such matters as surgery, the immunological response to transplanted organs, chemo-therapy and the molecular basis of inheritance. Medicine comes to be structured according to a scale of values associated with such a model. The most sought-after posts will be those at the heart of the model, and medical education and medical careers are similarly influenced . . . once a conception of disease finds embodiment in the structure of a service, major changes become more difficult to introduce. All professions tend to become over-committed to existing practice and their receptivity to the need for change is liable to become weak. The medical, nursing and other professions are no different in this respect.
>
> (Townsend and Davidson, 1982, p. 43; see also
> McKeown, 1976; Ham, 1985, pp. 197–200)

The history of even the very phrase, 'the Cinderella services' attests to the pervasive influence of the mechanistic model. The halting, faltering implementation of care in the community – a policy rooted in a social model of health – and the resistance of the acute sector to resource transfers provide concrete examples of a 'receptivity to change' which is 'weak'. As noted for the function-specific policy communities, the major consequence of an integrated network is that it institutionalizes the status quo, enshrining incrementalism and inertia. More important, the consequences of the health policy network are a direct product of its characteristics. The simple fact that medical interests dominate is crucial to understanding the structure of priorities and hence the inequitable distribution of resources.

Professional influence is visible not solely through overt lobbying. It is at its most pervasive when professional interests and ideology are both institutionalized in the structure of government.[10] As a result, as Jones (1983, p. 99) concludes: 'it is far from clear that either the interests of doctors or the interests of government, or the compromise which is reached as a result of negotiations between government and the BMA, is synonymous with the interests of patients'.

If the power of doctors is a hoary old truth of interest group research, the constraints on the centre are less widely commented upon. Here, it is as important to stress that, contrary to constitutional theory, relationships within the NHS are not those of a principal to an agent; there is substantial slippage in the implementation of service policies. This gap between policy objectives and implementation cannot be explained solely by reference to the power of doctors. Part of the problem lies in the centre's territorial operating code. Policies are designed as if the DHSS were at the apex of a hierarchy when it is but the core of a differentiated, disaggregated network. As Webb, Wistow and Hardy (1986, p. 230) conclude, Whitehall and Westminster operate in 'considerable ignorance' of the complexity they seek to govern: 'key actors in British public administration lack concepts and analytical tools with which to assess the impact of central policies'. Control is not necessarily wrested from the centre by recalcitrant, powerful interests. Because of its faulty operating code, the centre concedes control by default.

4.5 Intergovernmental Networks

4.5.1 Introduction

Intergovernmental networks exist in all four constituent nations of the UK, and whilst there are links between them, at times extensive and intensive ones, this section cannot cover them all. It focuses on the English intergovernmental network, described in Rhodes (1986a) as the national community of local government. This network, in sharp contrast to the other intergovernmental networks, contains a large number of organizations representing local government. The local authority associations include the Association of County Councils (ACC), formerly the County Councils Association (CCA); the Association of Metropolitan Authorities (AMA) and its predecessor body the Association of Municipal Corporations (AMC); the Association of District Councils (ADC) and its predecessors the Rural District Councils Association (RDCA) and the Urban District Councils Association (UDCA). Their major joint bodies include the Local Authorities' Conditions of Service Advisory Board (LACSAB), the Local Government Training Board (LGTB) and the Local Authorities Management Services and Computer Committee (LAMSAC).[11] This section surveys the changing relationships in the postwar period, provides a case study of the role of the English network in the reorganization of local government and concludes with a discussion of the characteristics and consequences of intergovernmental networks.

4.5.2 The Changing Context and Relationships

As Wood (1976, p. 15) stresses, the reform of local government has been on the political agenda for all of the postwar period. Reform did not start with Richard Crossman's announcement in 1966 of a Royal Commission to investigate the 'problem', nor did it end with the arrival of the new local authorities in 1974. In outline, four phases can be identified: 1945–61 was the era of local authority veto and *immobilisme* (see Isaac-Henry, 1975); 1961–74 was an era of bureaucratic relationships and formal consultation (see Brand, 1974; Wood, 1976); 1974–9 was characterized by second thoughts and informal (political) consultation; and 1979 to date can be described only as central unilateralism. At each of these stages the role of the national community of local government changed: from being loosely coupled, to being integrated before its relationships with the centre, and between its own constituents, fissured (see Rhodes, 1986a). The story of reorganization has been told in a number of places, and a chronological account will not be provided here.[12] Rather, I concentrate upon events since 1974. It is important to stress, however, that the 'problem' of local government reorganization spans four decades.

The Local Government Act 1972 created a two-tier system in the metropolitan areas and a two-tier system based on the counties in the rest of England, with the consequent abolition of the county boroughs. As a result, there was a substantial reduction in the total number of local authorities (see Table 3.6).

Given the scale of this reorganization, some respite from further changes might have seemed probable; it was not to be. The county boroughs which remained as district councils resented their loss of status and functions. The new two-tier structure did not remove conflicts between local authorities; indeed, agency agreements and concurrent powers fuelled them. The Labour government was embroiled in the devolution debate and it was canvassing opinion on devolution for England. The Labour Party was seeking to regain lost ground after 'the botched job which the Tories made of local government reorganization' (Labour Party, 1975, p. 8) and was proposing elected regional government for England. The Secretary of State for the Environment, Peter Shore, felt that it was absurd that great cities, such as Bristol and Nottingham, should have been stripped of their powers. All these strands coalesced between 1977 and 1979 into the policy of organic change. At its simplest, organic change involved the redistribution of functions between counties and districts. Thus, education and personal social services would be transferred to the nine largest ex-county boroughs on a case-by-case basis subject to a range of criteria – for example, that the new and old education authorities had adequate resources. Traffic management would be transferred to districts with a population greater than 100,000 and an urban nucleus of more than 50,000. Development control was to be a district function, with only specific categories (for example, mineral workings) reserved for county councils (HMSO, 1979). In short, the proposed adjustments to the new system were the product of irregular, political, informal consultation.

Before the government could legislate, however, it was defeated in Parliament, and a general election was called. Yet the changes did not perish. Organic change had embarrassed Conservative front-bench spokesmen. They saw it as an attack on their reorganization and as opportunism by the Labour government. The Labour Party would control the county councils only rarely but it would control the large districts more regularly. To enhance the powers of these districts was, to Conservative eyes, a partisan move. Unfortunately, these very districts were Conservative controlled and supported organic change. With a general election looming, front-bench spokesmen repaired the breach by promising amendments to the distribution of planning functions and new regulations on agency agreements (a prominent feature of highway and traffic management). The proposals to reallocate education and personal social services were dropped. Organic change was dead, but the price of unity was minor amendments to the allocation of functions, changes which duly occurred in 1980.

Organic change replays many of the themes of the 1972 reorganization with one crucial exception; the policy was never accorded a high priority. The reorganization of 1972 was still fresh in the memory. The government's economic strategy emphasized agreement on the level of local expenditure established in the CCLGF. After 1977 local expenditure was seen to be under control. Organic change was the initiative of a specific secretary of state and not central to the government's overall strategy. Consequently, there was considerably more room for negotiation and manoeuvre, especially given disagreements within the centre. The behaviour of the opponents, notably the DES and the DHSS, can be explained as examples of institutional inertia. Not all policies are a response to macro-economic developments. Indeed, the lack of priority, the irrelevance of organic change for the centre's economic strategy, made it vulnerable to delaying tactics. It would seem that reorganization requires some additional impetus if it is to overcome the multiple obstacles and interests in its path.

For the bulk of its period of office, the Thatcher government displayed little or no interest in institutional reform. Its interest was awoken only when local expenditure was deemed to be out of control and the GLC and MCCs were identified as the worst overspenders. Reorganization was important for the centre's economic strategy and gave the policy an impetus which became irresistible when allied to a degree of partisan conflict which precluded negotiation. Bureaucratic unilateralism was the order of the day.

According to the White Paper *Streamlining the Cities* (HMSO, 1983b), the GLC and Metropolitan County Councils (MCCs) had difficulty establishing a role for themselves and too few real functions.

Their search for a strategic role fostered uncertainty and conflict with the boroughs/districts. In spite of their limited role, however, they consistently exceeded their expenditure targets. It is claimed that the MCCs increased their expenditure by 12 per cent in volume terms compared to no growth by county councils and districts. Consequently, the GLC and the MCCs were to be abolished, with most of their functions becoming the responsibility of the boroughs/districts. Although the government's critique of the GLC and the MCCs does not bear careful scrutiny (see, for example, Coopers and Lybrand, 1984; Flynn, Leach and Vielba, 1985; O'Leary, 1985b) and although the destination of the several functions differed from initial journey plans, none the less the GLC and the MCCs were abolished.

The current distribution of functions in London and the metropolitan county areas admits of no easy summary. For example, Travers (1986, p. 428) calculated that as a London resident he was now paying rates to eighteen bodies (including the borough but excluding voluntary joint arrangements between boroughs). To oversimplify, in the metropolitan county areas, the county has been replaced by a Coordinating Committee of the districts; by joint bodies for fire and civil defence, police and passenger transport; by joint arrangements for waste disposal; and by a Residuary Body (responsible for superannuation and the management of pre-existing debt). Other county functions were allocated to the district councils, although the picture is complicated by voluntary joint arrangements (for example, in planning) and ministerial guidance and reserve powers (for example, in highways). In London, there is also a Co-ordinating Committee and a Residuary Body as well as the retained but reformed ILEA and the pre-existing London Regional Transport and Metropolitan Police arrangements. In addition, there is the joint body for fire and civil defence, four separate joint arrangements for waste disposal and special arrangements for the funding of, for example, voluntary organizations and artistic and cultural institutions. Thereafter the picture becomes more complex, with a variety of joint committees; voluntary arrangements between boroughs; allocation of GLC functions to non-departmental public bodies (for example, land drainage and flood protection to the Thames Water Authority); special arrangements for inner London (for example, the funding of the probation service and magistrates' courts); and the enhanced functions of central departments (for example, DTp and the operation of traffic signals). It is difficult to demur from Forrester, Lansley and Pauley's (1985, p. 162) understated assessment that 'it is not clear that the mixture of joint arrangements and quangos ... is a suitable way forward'.

Paralleling these changes, the relationships of the national community were also transformed. Initially, it was loosely coupled or disconnected, and yet the fluctuating relationships between the network's membership had little effect on the outcomes of the bargaining process. With reorganization, the pressure from the centre was for an integrated national representative presence for local government; it preferred a federation. When this project collapsed, the centre – to all intents and purposes, the Treasury – still sought to strengthen the national community, to aggregate local interests in its own interests. With the election of the Thatcher government this strategy of incorporation was abandoned; the national community was bypassed. Moreover, the government's brand of ideological politics divided the associations on party lines, rendering any and all co-operative action fragile if not futile. It also split individual associations. The English intergovernmental network experienced a dramatic fall from grace. As central–local relations became part and parcel of the politics of Westminster and Whitehall, so politicization fostered one-to-one contact between centre and locality. The dual polity based on the structural separation of centre and locality was collapsing, and with it went the intermediary position of the national community; the bureaucratic command model, the new territorial operating code, left no gap that it could fill.

Amidst all this toing and froing, the dominant impression is of a centre willing and able to change the structure and functions of local government at its merest whim. The decision to reorganize illustrates the structural power of the centre; it can unilaterally set the political agenda. But an analysis of the ensuing policy process and its outcomes reveals the constraints on such action. Turning from chronology to an analysis of actors, processes and outcomes, the nature of these constraints will become apparent, and in the course of this analysis it will be possible to determine the role of the national community in reorganization.

4.5.3 The Reorganization of Local Government – Key Actors and their Roles

4.5.3(i) THE ROLE OF THE NATIONAL COMMUNITY OF LOCAL GOVERNMENT

One point has received more attention than any other in the discussion about the role of the associations in reorganization: the conflicts of interest both within and between them. Although the constitutions of the various associations mention the goal of serving the interests of local government in general, the cold harsh light of reorganization led them to protect the interests of their members. Agreement on boundary changes was possible only when it was clear that no type of authority was under threat (see Brand, 1974, pp. 39, 96–9 and 114).

If type of authority is the main source of cleavage within the national community of local government, it is not the only source.

Brand (1974, p. 129) has argued that 'the leaders of the associations did, in the later years, recognize that change was necessary and were less inclined to defend the indefensible among their members'. For example, the CCA seemed prepared to recognize the advantages of unitary authorities provided arrangements were made to decentralize some services to district committees (Brand, 1974, pp. 125–6).

A further cleavage stems from party allegiance. Usually the AMC/AMA can be controlled by the Labour Party, whilst the CCA/ACC is almost invariably aligned with the Conservatives. As Isaac-Henry (1975, p. 10) has pointed out, however, local government reform was not a policy on which the two parties were diametrically opposed: 'Both of them had a foot in the two main Associations' camps.' Party considerations had a major impact, however, on the reorganization of the national community which followed from the reorganization of its member authorities. The proposed Local Government Federation foundered on the determination of the Labour majority at the AMC 'to have a separate organization for urban areas which they were confident would be controlled by Labour supporters and used to oppose policies of the Conservative Government – especially in relation to housing' (Richards, 1975, p. 170). Conversely, party factors were crucial in the formation of the AMA; the majority of authorities in the AMA – metropolitan counties, metropolitan districts, the London boroughs and the GLC – were Labour controlled, and party identity overrode the county–district conflict (Richards, 1975, p. 171; Keith-Lucas and Richards, 1978, pp. 195–6; Isaac-Henry, 1980a, pp. 36–8).

The 1972 reorganization demonstrates that there are multiple interests and sources of cleavage within the national community. 'Organic change' further demonstrates that the patterns of coalition amongst these interests can be many and varied. Within the ADC, the 'big nine' ex-county boroughs and the 'twenty-two' medium-sized cities lobbied separately and in alliance with the ADC. The ACC strongly opposed the proposed changes, whilst the AMA was a bystander, aware that its involvement could exacerbate tension between the metropolitan counties and districts. More significantly, the active participants cultivated allies elsewhere. Thus, the ADC had frequent consultations with the DoE, providing information on request and supporting the DoE in discussions with other affected parties. The 'big nine' worked through the Labour Party to get the reallocation of functions on the political agenda. The ACC drew widely on the local government professional societies and outside consultants, using its information and expertise to provide ammunition for central departments, most notably the DES, unhappy with the DoE's policy.

For the bulk of the postwar period, therefore, the divergent interests fostered a mosaic of coalitions. After 1979 this pattern was simplified, party became the dominant factor. Thus 'streamlining the cities' was an overwhelmingly partisan proposal, and divisions within the national community reflected party control. The London Boroughs' Association split, and the breakaway Labour-controlled Association of London Authorities vehemently opposed government policy. The ACC and ADC essentially stayed out of the argument since it did not alter the structure and functions of their member authorities, although the ADC did gently remind the government that there was still considerable scope for reallocating functions from counties to the districts. It was a straight fight between the AMA/ ALA/GLC/MCCs and the government, party overriding the long-standing antipathy of counties and districts within the AMA. And perhaps the major legacy of the 1972 reorganization was its catalyst effect in the politicizing of local government: a feature exaggerated after 1979 by the policies of the Conservative government.

If multiple and conflicting interests are a constraint on the effectiveness of the national community, none the less it commands resources of importance to central government. Brand (1974, pp. 91–6) argues that the associations have several resources which make them effective pressure groups. First, they are protective groups and have 'inherent strengths' because they do not have to rely on 'altruistic feelings' but depend on the 'interests of the members themselves'. The interests of members are clearly defined, and local authorities are members of their respective associations. Second, they are the recognized experts: 'They are the people who have knowledge indispensable to central government.' Third, 'pressure groups have power in proportion to the number of times they have previously been consulted', and 'There had been a long tradition of consultation with local government associations.' Moreover, they had access to national decision-making through the party organizations. Fourth, the constitutional position of local authorities makes it seem that, albeit for a small area, 'their legislature had the same validity as the legislature of central government'. Finally, local government is seen as the guardian of certain values in British society, e.g. democratic participation, the counterweight against Whitehall bureaucracy.

There is mixed evidence in support of Brand's analysis. Isaac-Henry (1975, pp. 9–10) explores the extent to which central government is dependent upon the associations for advice, approval and acquiescence. He concludes that the associations had information and expertise which were valued by central government but he doubts that they had any sanctions that could be effectively deployed or that they possessed the power of approval: 'the Association did not seem as formidable as certain ministers made them out to be'. Isaac-Henry (1975, p. 11) quotes with approval the AMC's own assessment of its influence that it acts as an 'advice centre' for government. In a similar vein, Wood (1976, p. 131) comments that:

The value to the Government of the consultative process cannot be over-emphasised ... A good deal of agreement with the Associations ... was reached which meant that the passage of legislation, already certain to be lengthy and tortuous due to the inevitable complexity of the Bill, would not be unnecessarily hindered by lengthy arguments on issues which were not central to the plan.

Turning from academic commentators to the practitioner, opinions are equally varied. In an oft-cited remark, Duncan Sandys described the associations as part of the constitution of the country. For the associations, the CCA stressed that 'local authorities ... will inevitably be controlled by the central government ... In the central/ local relationship local government must inevitably be in the position of a junior partner (cited in Griffith, 1966, p. 507). Any discussion of resources seems inconclusive, therefore.

This lack of agreement can be explained by distinguishing the several stages in the policy process. Most of the comments about the relative weakness of the associations refer to the policy initiation stage. Central government decides upon the policy, at least in broad outline. Thereafter, the informational and organizational resources of the associations make them invaluable and influential in the implementation of that policy. The non-executant role, or hands-off controls, of central departments makes them dependent on local authorities with their substantial store of people, skills and information. Wood (1976, p. 129) records that there were extensive consultations between the DoE and the associations before the Bill was introduced in Parliament. The associations played an important role in the implementation of the 1972 Act, participating in the Study Group on Local Authority Management Practices set up jointly by the associations and the DoE as well as advising on the myriad consultation documents and circulars issued by the department (Richards, 1975, pp. 28–9, 61, 68 and 81). The resources of the associations sustain their role in consultation *after* the broad outlines of the policy have been decided by central government. But this conclusion, whilst appropriate for the 1972 Act, does not explain the role of the associations in organic change.

The events of 1977 to 1979 provide a counterweight to the easy assertions that the centre has structural power and that the influence of the national community is restricted to the implementation stage of the policy process. Quite clearly a determined government with an agreed policy can override any and all objections from local government. But organic change did not have a high political priority, nor was the policy specific to the DoE. Where agreement between several departments is necessary but not forthcoming, then there will be opportunities for influence. If a central department (for example, the DES) becomes an ally of an association (for example, the ACC), the latter's chances of some degree of success are enhanced. The degree of bargaining is a function of the specific policy area.

The simple fact that organic change spanned several departments highlights a characteristic feature of central policy processes: fragmentation. The DES, DHSS, DTp and their associated professions and groups all had serious reservations about the reallocation of their particular function. They accepted that organic change was government policy but bargained intensively with DoE over the terms and conditions of their transfer, succeeding in exacting restrictive terms. The opportunities for the associations to influence central decisions is greater when they can exploit divisions between departments than when the policy is limited to a single policy community.

The ability of the associations to exert influence is fostered by their privileged access. The number of meetings with ministers was large. Both the ACC and the ADC seemed to have unlimited access. The DoE consulted only the main associations in the later stages, suggesting that the associations were seen, to a greater degree than before reorganization, as *the* peak associations of local government. Certainly, no professional society or individual local authority commanded equivalent access, although for less contentious issues there can be greater flexibility about who is consulted and at what stage in the policy process.

However, access and resources do not automatically bestow influence. For example, the ACC had commissioned an appraisal of organic change from Professor J. D. Stewart of the Institute of Local Government Studies (Stewart, Leach and Skelcher, 1978). Although this report, with the DES as its sponsor, penetrated to the highest levels within government, it was enthusiastically sought and used because it supported predetermined positions. Its intrinsic merits were of less importance than the context into which it was introduced. The relationship between central departments and the associations did not, in the case of the DES, spring from their dependence upon the associations for information and expertise. Conversely, the ACC may have had ammunition, but it needed the DES to supply the gun, aim and fire it. The ACC is best seen as a resource of the DES.

These comments are aimed at redressing a balance; they should not be interpreted as arguing that any bargaining is between equals. Peter Shore at the DoE insisted on a policy of reallocating functions and, in a form, attained his objective. The modifications to the policy were won by ministers in Cabinet committees, the existence and discussions of which are 'secret'. But to recognize that national policies are taken by the government is not to deny that the national community and the several policy communities can exert some formative influences. In addition, these comments are also designed to caution against the easy generalization that influence is limited to the implementation stages of policy-making. In many instances this may well be true but it is not an inviolate rule. The national community has the resources to resist central decisions when the centre is divided and has no agreed statement on the principles of a policy.

The associations played a variety of roles during the various reorganizations of local government: ally, lobby, client, veto and bystander. Thus, in 1972 the AMC used its vice-presidents and other sympathetic MPs to ensure that its proposed amendments were heard. The AMA (in 1983–5) and the ACC (between 1977–9) adopted the mantle of aggressive lobbyists. Both have been bystanders, between 1977–9 and in 1983–5 respectively. The ADC was the ally of the DoE on organic change, preparing briefs, attending informal meetings and even submitting evidence to the Royal Commission on the National Health Service at Peter Shore's request. However, rather than providing a detailed description of these various roles, attention will fall on the more distinctive features of the national community's strategic behaviour.

First, there is a danger in equating strategic behaviour with specific forms of action. Severally and jointly the national community of local government is embedded in a network of consultation, both formal and informal. If policy proposals are a matter of concern to the associations, therefore, a considerable amount of preliminary discussion can and will take place at least to clarify the major areas of agreement and disagreement. Such networks serve to replace the more overt forms of strategic behaviour and arise from the privileged position of the associations as part of the structure of British government. A few, and only a few, pressure groups enjoy equivalent status. Peter Walker, Secretary of State for the Environment responsible for the reorganization of local government, said that he had developed 'a healthy contempt for some pressure groups' but he felt that the AMC and the CCA were 'amongst the best he had dealt with', praising the quality of their briefs (cited in Rhodes, Hardy and Pudney, 1983, p. 16). Meetings were frequent on both major and minor matters, and the outcome was usually 'constructive'. Such an assessment would, in all probability, be widely shared amongst government departments and suggests that formal and informal consultation is the dominant strategy of both sides.

Second, although the usual focus of pressure group activity is the Whitehall department and this channel of communication is of considerable importance to the associations, it is by no means the only one. The associations have access also through the party machines. Representatives on the associations have, over the years, built up and consolidated their links with their respective party organizations (Chapter 3, section 3.7.1). As a result, association representatives can influence the policies of would-be governments and they have access to the most senior political levels of government, certainly when their controlling party is also the government of the day but frequently when it forms Her Majesty's Opposition. And as before, this channel of communication is not confined to institutional linkages. There is a political network, and ministers will consult informally with local politicians.

The clearest example of this activity is provided by organic change. Thus, local leaders from the 'big nine' and medium-sized cities assiduously campaigned within the Labour Party, meeting ministers on the RLGSC of the NEC, at annual conferences and at social events. Undoubtedly they were an important factor in getting the reallocation of functions on to the Labour government's political agenda.

Third, the associations can act as conduits for other interested parties. They are the means whereby individual local authorities or professional societies can bring pressure to bear on central departments. For example, a professional society can attempt to influence government policy directly by, for example, written submissions and indirectly through its adviser role to the associations. Similarly, particular classes of authority within one association, most commonly the large urban authorities, can lobby directly, for example by briefing their MP or sending a delegation to ministers, and indirectly by influencing the associations' response, or lack of it, to the government's policy initiative – for example, the GLC between 1983–5. And the ability of individual local authorities to act as 'institutionalized pressure groups' (Scarrow, 1971) can constrain the associations and certainly lead to a proliferation of pressure activity, as was the case over the boundaries for the new local authorities under the 1972 Act (Griffith, 1966, pp. 528–9; Wood, 1976, pp. 155–6).

Fourth, the associations have traditionally been reluctant to adopt the more 'boisterous' forms of strategic behaviour. As Barnhouse (1972, p. 171) notes: 'Apparently, the Associations will first attempt to influence the Government through the private channels open to them, and if this fails they will seek public support for their views.' It is perhaps a tribute to the private channels that the need to seek public support was not more evident up to the 1980s. One achievement of Conservative policy on controlling local expenditure was to stimulate a marked improvement in the lobbying and public relations activities of the national community. These new skills were redeployed to fight reorganization. Campaigns are not new; the RDCA's 'Mr R. E. Mote' campaign during the 1972 reorganization and Rutland County Council's fight for survival are but two examples. Previous examples were not on the scale of the 1984 campaign. Drawing upon academics, business consultants and public relations advisers, national and local campaigns, utilizing the range of the media, were mounted to considerable effect. If the outcome was preordained, the government was moved to rant and rail against 'political advertising' and to appoint the Widdicombe Committee to investigate 'abuses'. The Conservatives were 'Saatchi-d', and the squeals of anguish attest to the effectiveness of the national community's new-found skills. 'Red Ken' found a new status; no longer an anathema, he was transformed from a blot on the British political landscape into a national figure, noted for his articulate and eloquent TV presence. If the AMA, GLC, ALA and MCCs lost, they gave the government's victory a sour taste.

Without denying that bargaining took place or that concessions were obtained in 1972, between 1977–9 and in 1985, it is important to remember that the government remained immovable on the basic principles of its policy *and* it fixed the agenda for consultation. This latter point is stressed by Wood (1976, pp. 95 and 110–11) in his account of the progress of the 1972 Act: 'If the Government was to proceed reasonably quickly it could not afford to include the proposals of any major Association on its consultative agenda ... The White Paper, then, ruled out of order the preferred alternatives of all the main Associations.' Obviously, this ability to control the agenda demonstrates that the relationship between the DoE and the associations was asymmetric. Bargaining there may be but it was not bargaining between equals – a conclusion which is inescapable given the determination of the government to abolish the GLC and the MCCs. The most distinctive feature of the national community is its shifting pattern of coalitions between the major associations. Throughout the period, the associations reacted to government initiatives. The agenda was dictated by the government. The parameters of the debate were not a matter for negotiation. This situation is the common lot of pressure groups in British government and of the associations in all the reorganizations of local government.

4.5.3(ii) THE ROLE OF THE PROFESSIONAL

Wood (1976, pp. 153–4) concludes that other pressure groups such as the local government trade unions (e.g. NALGO), the Police Federation, the Magistrates' Association and the Society of Justices Clerks were unsuccessful in gaining amendments to the Local Government Bill. Individual local authorities and the local authority associations were the major gainers.

For organic change, the local government professional societies had multiple opportunities to make their views known. For example, the Association of Directors of Social Services submitted memoranda to the DHSS, met officials to 'clarify' points, invited the secretary of state to their annual conference, gave their views wider currency through professional journals such as *Social Work Today*, provided advisers to the ACC Social Services Committee and contributed to the ACC's submissions to the DHSS as well as the several general memoranda of observations submitted to the DoE, all of which contained a discrete section on the personal social services. Nor should it be thought that any or all of these activities mark out the ADSS as exceptional. Its role was routine. Every local government professional society of any note has equivalent opportunities to make its views known. The question arises of whether or not these specific activities had a substantial effect on the outcome.

As far as the 1972 reorganization is concerned, Brand (1974, p. 11) strongly argues that 'local government reform became necessary because of the development of certain local government services. Of all these services none was more important than planning.' Crucially: 'The development of a separate profession of planning and the establishment of these planners in Whitehall as well as in local authority planning departments was a crucial ingredient of change' (Brand, 1974, p. 157). In developing this argument, Brand appears to collapse two analytically distinct phenomena. First, there are the specific activities of the planning profession, and second, perhaps more importantly, there is the impact of the idea of planning and the creation of a climate of opinion which favoured large local authorities. As Dunleavy (1981b, pp. 177–8) notes in his study of high-rise building:

> changes in central government policy or the national local govern-ment system cannot be seen as the results of specific professional, industrial, or local authority initiatives aimed at influencing national policy, important though these were. Rather these interests affected policy in much more diffuse ways, by creating and sustain-ing a climate of opinion in the public housing apparatus favourable to high rise, and by constraining Ministry policy change within narrow limits.

Such an interpretation of Brand's argument seems justified when his comments on planning are married to his comments on élite values. He argues (1974, p. 160) that the 'modernization' of local government hinged on the development and acceptance of new values in the provision of social welfare and in economic planning. The symbols used by the Labour Party in the 1964 election legitimized the values of modernization and undermined the legitimacy of those defending the existing institutions.

It is less important, therefore, that particular professions influenced the legislative stage of reorganization – although the planning pro-fession along with the CCA did extract some concessions from the government on the planning clauses – and more important to stress the role of such professions in creating a climate of opinion which limited the range of options considered.

This climate of opinion can be described as the 'functionalist ideology' – a belief in the efficiency and effectiveness of large local government units. It was accorded official recognition in the report of the Redcliffe-Maud Commission (1969) with its fixation on size and was articulated by a range of professions. For example, similar emphases emerge from the evidence to the Redcliffe-Maud Commission (1968, pp. 10, 171–2, 242–3 and 301) by the education and social work professions, although there was disagreement about the exact population size. Moreover, these 'ideas in good currency' received very considerable support from central departments; expertise and authority were wedded. Indeed, the simple fact that the professions were institutionalized in policy communities maximized the impact of their ideas. As actors in such policy networks they were well positioned in terms of both the dissemination of ideas (i.e. they occupied a nodal position) and 'respectability' (i.e. legitimacy, or who is speaking is as important as what is said). The unanimity in favour of large areas is awesome to behold.

In organic change, although the specific activities of particular societies made no discernible difference to the outcome, the professions were a substantial part of the institutional inertia that this policy initiative had to overcome. Their main contribution was negative; their opposition was a concrete problem for the central departments involved – neither the DES nor the DHSS wished to incur needlessly their wrath for another department's policy – and, consequently, it provided further grounds for extended discussions of the practical problems and further impetus in designing safeguards for the transfer of services. With the ACC to the fore, acting as a (willing) conduit for their views, overt lobbying was not required. Opposition to organic change provides a further illustration of one of the major themes of the 1972 reorganization: the need for large local government units. Both the DES and the DHSS were concerned to preserve the gains of the 1972 reorganization, and the same concern was echoed by the professions. 'Functionalism' was the dominant theme in their objections to organic change. The interests of service management still prevailed over the interests of urban areas. In short, the 'technocratic' professions acted to defend their specific service interests.

If precise attributions of influence are elusive, the role of the professions in both 1972 and 1979 was substantial. All the more surprising, therefore, that one of the monuments to the functionalist ideology, the strategic urban authority, should have been dismantled in 1985 whilst the professions stood and watched. To understand this change it is necessary to examine the role of the political parties.

4.5.3(iii)   THE ROLE OF THE POLITICAL PARTIES

One of the more distinctive changes in the process of reorganization between 1966 and 1984 was the emergence of partisan interests as an ever more prominent and determining factor. In the 1972 reorganization, partisan interests were most in evidence in the parties' preferred solutions and in drawing local government boundaries. Thus the Labour Party opted for unitary authorities based on the cities, where their support was greatest. The Conservatives preferred a two-tier system based on the counties, where their support was greatest. It was unsurprising that a Conservative government legislated for a two-tier system; this suited its supporters and at least commanded a measure of support among existing local authorities. To reinforce their advantage, the boundaries of the new local authorities were drawn to protect Conservative electoral fortunes. Steed (1969, p. 952) concluded that the new authorities were 'socially heterogeneous', and consequently there would be 'fewer councils in England which are politically and socially unbalanced'. Dearlove (1979, p. 103) succinctly translates this phrase as a reduction in Labour control (see also Wood, 1976, p. 113). For all their much vaunted importance, the facts of social geography were ignored when they threatened party interests.

There was a similar partisan element to organic change. Michael Heseltine and Keith Speed, Conservative front-bench spokesmen, attempted to blunt the demands of the cities for the return of functions, seeing the attacks on the 1972 Act as 'unwelcome'. Their strategy required united Conservative opposition to organic change, but unity was forthcoming on the eve of a general election only after Michael Heseltine had conceded to Conservative-controlled cities the need to change the allocation of planning responsibilities and to review agency arrangements.

For the Labour Party, the major tension arose not between the party and Conservative-controlled associations, nor between the parties in Parliament, but between the party and the Labour government. The party accepted organic change only reluctantly and with the proviso that it should be seen as a step towards a more fundamental restructuring of local government. Peter Shore had to persuade the NEC and the RLGSC that the two proposals were compatibile: that organic change was the first step on the road to radical reform. Equally important, the Labour party machine was the channel through which organic change was put on the policy-making agenda. Individual local authorities took the initiative, the ADC followed, and the party was seen as the efficacious means for getting government action.

Although organic change does not provide a straightforward illustration of partisan advantage in British policy-making, it none the less demonstrates the manifold impacts of party politics. In addition, there were clear partisan benefits in the positions of the two major parties. The status quo favoured the Conservatives, whereas organic change would have benefited the Labour Party.

The partisan factor in the reorganizations of 1972 and 1979 pales into insignificance compared to 1985. In Forrester, Lansley and Pauley's (1985, p. 66) words, Mrs Thatcher wanted 'to stop the expensive spending of socialist ideologues in the cities'. She was 'to abolish a layer of socialist government' and respond to a 'personal challenge' by removing 'the power base which had enabled Ken

Livingstone to taunt and defy her, to rival and, in some ways, even to better her . . . she would . . . wipe him off the national political map'. Flynn, Leach and Vielba (1985, p. ix) consider this political antagonism thesis 'superficial' and, conceding that the Conservatives were annoyed by the socialist ideologues, argue that the policy was a part of the continuing attempt to control local government.

Abolition or 'streamlining' was a policy born out of failure – failure to abolish the rates, failure to control local spending. It was accorded a high priority because of a pending general election and the need to be seen to be doing something in the manifesto. It was given its 'edge' by the politicization of IGR fostered by Conservative policies. In grant negotiations, any pretence to consultation had been dropped; the CCLGF had been replaced by party channels of influence. Recalcitrance and confrontation challenged the responsibility ethic as the dominant local authority response to central intervention. Not only was the new urban Left flowering in the Brooklyns of Britain, but discontent with central policy was no stranger to the county councils. By 1984, and to an unprecedented degree, central and local relations were in the forefront of the partisan conflict. To personalize the conflict in the form of a confrontation between Mrs Thatcher and Mr Livingstone is misleading. But it is crucial to recognize the partisan context of the proposal. Pleas for a Royal Commission, for a detailed critical appraisal of the problems of governing the metropolitan areas, fly in the face of partisan commitment. And the policy called forth a partisan response. Battle lines had been drawn well before the election, and, with streamlining (and rate capping) at the heart of the Conservative strategy for the control of public expenditure, there was to be no negotiation. Ministerial ineptitude may have protracted the battle, the House of Lords may have inflicted defeats, but there was always an enormous parliamentary majority to overturn any amendments. Streamlining was steamrollered through. The climate was set by the government with its philosophy of retrenchment and the minimalist state, not by the professions. Consultation with the affected associations on either the Bill or its implementation was forgone until the Bill was law; the associations were partisan opponents, a mere adjunct of the Labour opposition. Just as central–local relations had been reduced to the control of local expenditure – a mere epiphenomenon of national economic management – so the reorganization of local government in 1985 was an epiphenomenon of expenditure controls. Party had become the all-pervasive influence.

4.5.4 *The Characteristics of Intergovernmental Networks*

Intergovernmental networks contain an extensive, and at times irreconcilable, range of interests whether or not there is a single representative body at the centre as in Scotland or multiple bodies as in England. The main interests within the national community are type of authority and party, although, quite obviously, its interests do extend to service policies. Defending the structure and functions of local government is its heart.

The interests of the national community also reflect its distinctive nature. The local authority associations cannot be seen as just another pressure group (Stewart, 1958, p. 83; Mackenzie, 1969, p. 274; Isaac-Henry, 1975, p. 9). They are public interest groups because they speak for units of government; they are official and legitimate and command extensive access to the centre (see Rhodes, 1986a, pp. 13–16). They are domesticated or respectable groups which have a vested interest in maintaining that position. Respectability exacts a price. It requires adherence to the centre's rules of the game, places a premium on consultation and negotiation rather than lobbying and campaigns and subjects the associations to the constraints of trust and responsible behaviour. Sustaining the 'responsibility ethic' is a subsidiary but none the less major interest of the national community.

The national community is *topocractic*. 'Topocrats' are not primarily concerned to promote specific policy programmes, as are the 'technocrats'. Their interests are limited only by the geographical area of the government unit from which they are drawn, whereas the interests of the 'technocrat' are narrowly defined by their professional expertise. Topocratic interests span policy of functional areas. And any definition of 'the interests of local government' is as elusive as it is contentious, a point which can be illustrated by considering the membership of the national community.

No local authority association speaks for only one type of local authority, and there are marked differences of interest between associations. Whether the topic is the distribution of functions or of grant between the several types of local authority, the potential for conflict is great. And such tensions have been heightened by the intensification of party politics since 1974. Allied to the long-standing difference of interest between urban and rural local authorities, it is clear that these cleavages can make a consensus on 'the interests of local government' a mirage in the eyes of participants in the national community. And yet, compared to other policy networks, the national community's membership is restricted. For example, trade unions are explicitly excluded, as are the other interest groups concerned with local government. Participation is confined to the associations, the DoE, the topocratic professions and, most distinctively, the political parties. Exclusivity and diversity of interests coexist.

The major difference between the English intergovernmental network and its counterparts in the periphery lies not in its diversity *per se* but in the simple fact that the various interests have separate organizational expression. COSLA's membership includes all types of local government in Scotland. Such federations experience identical conflicts of interest (Craig, 1980), but the basic organizational network and patterns of relationships are greatly simplified. Party political differences can also exact a toll (as in the case of ALANI). A single organization is no guarantee of unity of interest.

Furthermore, membership of an association is voluntary. The national community cannot 'deliver' (or regulate) its members but only persuade or plead with them. It is a set of intermediate organizations with a limited degree of vertical interdependence. Indeed, its links with member local authorities can be described only as distant. The associations are not necessarily the most important channel of communication for individual local authorities. Particular departments can have stronger contacts with their policy community. Large local authorities have their own direct channels of communication with central departments and bypass the national community. In other words, participation in the national community is limited to a few senior members and advisers. Within an individual local authority, the national community can be described as virtually irrelevant for the bulk of members and officers.

These remarks are not heretical. They reflect a basic dilemma for the national community. The point about local government is that it is *local* government. Its actions are legitimate because they are taken by locally elected councillors on issues of local concern. A national community, a *national* local authority association, 'is a contradiction in terms' (Stewart, 1977, p. 35). The associations have to generalize when the defence of local government lies in diversity. They have to develop a perspective on national issues, whereas their members' main concern is local problems. Little wonder, therefore, that the national community can seem to be divorced from its members.

A key feature of SCG in Britain is the existence of policy communities, and they are an important constraint on the national community. Thus, functional allegiances are a source of conflict within individual associations, within the national community and between it and the policy communities – conflicts rooted in the contradictory pressures for both high service standards and sound financial management. The different interests of the national community and the policy communities are paralleled by the differences between the topocratic and technocratic professions, and their role serves to multiply the range of interests to be accommodated.

The topocratic professions provide advisers to *all* association committees, including the most important association committees (e.g. policy, finance), and they are intensively involved in the key policy areas of grant and pay negotiations. The relatively greater pre-eminence of the topocratic professions must not prompt the conclusion that the technocratic professions have restricted access and consultation. The technocratic professions participate in the policy communities. However, interests are not neatly polarized between the associations and the professions. The service committees of the associations are a source of internal stress. The allegiance to 'their' service, coupled with participation in the appropriate policy community, can generate conflicts with the requirements of 'sound' financial management and the interests of topocrats. Functional cleavages are omnipresent.

The national community is extensively and intensively involved in a range of service policies (and their policy communities); it has a high degree of horizontal interdependence. It could be argued that the national community's functions should not encompass service policies; its job is to represent the general interests of local government. This argument points to an important paradox. Any policy initiative will have repercussions for the finance and staffing of local government. Leaving service policy to the technocratic professions would constrain seriously the national community in carrying out its primary functions. But the national community cannot attend to all policy issues if only because of the lack of time and expertise. And the basic problem of defining the 'interests of local government' remains. The broader the definition of these interests the greater the pressure on available resources. But the narrower the definition the greater the probability that the general interests will be compromised.

Finally, it is commonly argued that the associations are constrained by their lack of resources. If advisers and the staff of the joint bodies are added to associations' secretariats, it would seem that the national community is remarkably well endowed with resources. Compared to other pressure groups, it has to be described as large. There are, however, two important qualifications to this comment. The national community has an intensive involvement in a wide range of policy areas. Its resources may be large, but so are its tasks. In addition, a substantial proportion of its staffing resources are 'part-time'. Officer advisers are full-time officials in local authorities. The joint bodies are a shared resource which are not on tap for the use of a particular association. Irrespective of comparisons with other groups, therefore, there is considerable pressure on the resources of the associations.

Second, because the national community cannot commit its members, its negotiating position is weakened. The centre wants the compliance of local authorities, and, whilst the national community can legitimize this demand, it cannot enforce it. It has only the indirect, or hands-off, controls of advice and persuasion. It may point out that voluntary compliance now will forestall legal enforcement later, but any legal sanction will be deployed by the centre not the national community.

Third, a number of constraints arise out of the links between the associations and other members of the national community. The joint bodies are an important resource for the associations, but that potential is not always realized because they have their own constituencies separate from the associations; because they are a shared resource when each association wants advice specific to its own needs; and because the large joint bodies are separate organizations which have, over the years, developed their own appreciation of problems and ways of dealing with them. In sum, the national community has some resources which the centre needs, but its capacity to realize their potential is subject to several constraints, most notably its inability to commit the members who control the needed resources. Moreover, its resources are barely commensurable with its tasks, even when it controls the resources. These characteristics show some sharp contrasts with policy and territorial communities as well as professionalized networks and they have a marked effect on the outcomes of the policy process.

4.5.5 *Conclusions:* Cui Bono?

The effectiveness of, and the extent of integration within, the national community is constrained by the range of cleavages it encompasses. None the less, it is legitimate; it has a recognized right to consultation on a range of issues, most notably grant, pay negotiations and local government reorganization. Its effectiveness varies from policy area to policy area, depending on the issue, the degree of partisan controversy, the stage in the policy process and the range of legitimated competing interests. And, as for any other interest group, it is constrained by the asymmetric nature of its relationship with the centre. Indeed, the constraints can appear so severe that it is important to stress that a substantial proportion of the matters upon which it is consulted are not partisan, controversial issues. The interests of the constituent organizations of the national community are not so continuously divergent that compromises are impossible. The policy-making process emphasizes accommodation and consensus, not conflict, and this characterization applies to relations within the national community as well as with central departments and policy communities.

The national community has had its successes, but the issues which command attention – for example, changes in the structure and functions of local authorities – are the ones by which the national community is judged and they are the very issues upon which agreement is most elusive and where the constraints and cleavages have their greatest impact.

The national community is a legitimized consultative channel; a domesticated pressure group in a governmental system where executive authority and the interdependence of groups and government are in continual tension. The Conservative government's assertions of executive authority highlight the vulnerability of group influences in the short term, until the unintended consequences of

326 Beyond Westminster and Whitehall

imposed policies highlight, in turn, the dependence of government on group compliance.

Nor can the final assessment focus solely on the effects of the national community on central department. It also has an innovative role for members who see the national community as a forum for sharing experience and ideas; it provides a framework for individual local authorities. Together the policy communities and the national community (the national local government system) define the parameters of 'good policy'. Its innovative role may be diffuse, precise attributions of responsibility for specific policies may be elusive, but none the less it plays such a role. As a legitimated part of the structure of government embedded in extensive consultative networks, the national community may not exercise veto powers, it may be vulnerable to the exercise of executive authority, but it has become an established intervening tier of representation capable of influencing, directly and indirectly, both government and its own constituency.

The costs of legitimacy are respectability and responsibility, but they are also its rewards. The advantages of continuous access have to be weighed against the need to play by the centre's rules if the access is to be preserved. The national community of local government is not just a contradiction in terms, it is compounded of multiple contradictions. It is both local government's intermediate tier of representation and the flawed institutional network at the heart of central–local relations. It is the reluctant tool of centre and locality, and yet if governments should seek local compliance rather than control, there would be pressure for some such intermediate tier. Central–local relations over the past two decades have revolved around the tension between executive authority and interdependence, and the national community has mirrored every contradiction and remained *the* legitimated consultative channel for local government.

In many ways the intergovernmental network is an exemplar of the logic of negotiation in British policy-making. Respectable, responsible and institutionalized, it has attained the summit of ambition for the majority of interest groups. Yet its slide from grace in recent years cannot be attributed solely to the intransigence of the centre. The characteristics of the intergovernmental network rendered it vulnerable. The diversity of politicized interests, coupled with limited vertical interdependence, constrained resources and wide-ranging commitments to governance, resource and service policies, limited the capacity of the national community to resist central interventions. Intergovernmental networks contain a greater range of cleavages than policy communities; they are less integrated. Above all, and uniquely, they are partisan networks, and party political conflicts have proved to be an insurmountable obstacle to concerted action. Consequently, the national community's capacity to resist central intervention is constrained; one part of its membership will support the government, committing the 'sin' of placing party interests before 'the interests of local government'. Confronted by a determined centre, therefore, the national community will fare less well than non-partisan, integrated policy communities. Since 1979 it must be counted as a 'loser' with limited ability to mitigate the effects of, let alone modify, central policy.

Whatever the current fortunes of the national community, who gains and loses as a result of its action/inaction? Given that it is not directly responsible for any services, this question admits of no simple answer. The Conservative-controlled ACC and ADC benefited from the redistribution of grant from the cities to counties and districts. On pay negotiations, the national community articulates employers' interest. It may have had to balance incomes policy, cash limits and grant settlements with union pay claims, but it was never part of its remit to outbid the unions on the level of increase. It has always prided itself on following pay norms and/or cash limits; it has been a 'responsible' employer (Rhodes, 1986a, pp. 164–94). The interests of party and professionals are articulated by and through the national community. For example, during reorganization, the functionalist ideology was articulated by the national community. With few exceptions, the national community accepted that the new authorities should be large if its constituent organizations could not agree on the basis of enlargement. As part of the national local government system, the national community helped to sustain the climate of opinion in favour of a functionalist reorganization. More important, however, the national community reflects the pre-existing distribution of power. It is a means for managing the status quo, not for reforming it. It mirrors existing conflicts and interests but it does not transform them. It is 'responsible' and 'respectable', enshrining incrementalism and adding its contribution to the politics of inertia so characteristic of policy-making in British government.

4.6   Producer Networks

All the networks considered so far have had substantial continuity and stability of interests and participants. In turning to examine producer networks, the degree of integration is appreciably lower. The distinguishing characteristics of producer networks are the pre-eminent role of economic interests (both the public and private sector), their fluctuating membership, the dependence of the centre on industrial organizations for delivering the desired goods and for expertise and the limited interdependence amongst economic interests (see Chapter

2, section 2.5.2(1)). This section presents a case study of rationalization and redundancy to illustrate the effects of these several characteristics on the process of policy-making. In the first instance, however, this section surveys the development of relationships in the field of industrial policy to provide the appropriate context for the case study.

Indisputably industrial policy is amorphous. The question of what constitutes industrial policy is contentious. This discussion employs Grant's (1982, p. 2) definition that industrial policy refers to 'a set of measures used by governments to influence the investment decisions of individual enterprises – public and private – so as to promote such objectives as lower unemployment, a healthier balance of payments and a generally more efficient industrial economy'. If the boundaries of industrial policy are imprecise, spilling over into macro-economic and trade policy on the one side and sectoral policies for such fields as energy and agriculture on the other, none the less this definition identifies a distinct area of analysis: the investment decisions of individual enterprises. Equally important, it reflects the range of objectives which industrial policy is expected to serve and recognizes the contribution of the nationalized industries to industrial policy; it is not confined to private sector firms. The case study of rationalization and redundancy is an example both of industrial policy and of the nationalized industries, intermediate organizations and non-departmental public bodies 'in action'. Consequently, this section provides material on a distinctive type of network and on sub-central actors other than local government.

4.6.1   *The Evolution of Industrial Policy*

Modifying Smith (1979, II), the evolution of industrial policy in particular, and economic policy in general, can be characterized as a shift from the 'mixed economy' (1945–61) to the 'managed economy' (1961–70) to the 'regulated economy' (1972–9) and, extending his classification, the 'deregulated economy' (1979 to date). The changing fortunes of the British economy and the evolution of government policy on the nationalized industries have already been described (see Chapter 2, section 2.5.1(ii), and Chapter 3, sections 3.2.4(i) and (ii)). It is necessary by way of introduction, therefore, only to describe the industrial policy of the post-1979 Conservative government.[13]

Although there were three governments between 1972 and 1979 there was, as Grant (1982, p. 49) notes, 'a basic continuity of policy . . . based on a belief in the efficacy of selective intervention'. Industrial policy was based on the Conservatives' 1972 Act. Labour's own Industry Act 1975 had been, at its conception, a radical break with the past. However, although a National Enterprise Board (NEB) was created, its role was emasculated to that of the government's merchant bank, and the proposal that it control the equity of the top twenty-five industrial companies was abandoned (Marsh and Locksley, 1983, pp. 46–8). Similarly the proposed compulsory planning agreements between government and industry became voluntary. Industrial policy was to continue as a variegated pattern of selective assistance, based primarily on section 7 of the Industry Act 1972, which provided interest relief grants to firms that created or safeguarded employment in assisted regions; and on section 8, which provided aid outside assisted areas for particular industrial sectors (for example, wool textiles and red meat slaughterhouses), for new capital-intensive projects and for bailing out particular companies (for further details see Grant, 1982, pp. 51–3). After 1976 total aid to industry fell, not because of a government-imposed resource squeeze in response to the oil crisis and IMF loan, but because 'where selective assistance is concerned, we have been response constrained, not resource constrained' (Sir Peter Carey, Permanent Secretary, DoI, cited in Grant, 1982, p. 52). Quite simply, firms were reluctant to take up the grants.

With the election of the Conservative government in 1979, existing aid programmes under the Industry Act 1972 continued on a reduced scale, employing more restrictive criteria. The regional programme was scaled down and then, as might have been expected, displayed 'creep-back' as the government modified its policy to accommodate particularly hard-hit areas. In brief, selective intervention was replaced by 'constructive intervention' (Grant, 1982, p. 83), a phrase which refers to government support for high-technology industries. To employ the secretary of state's phrase, the government 'was modifying the inheritance' from the Labour government (cited in Grant, 1982, p. 88). Funding was reduced and became more selective, but the continuity of policy was still substantial.

In four respects, however, industrial policy was changed markedly. First, the government introduced Enterprise Zones (EZs) where planning regulations and taxes were relaxed to encourage business to move to depressed areas for a more detailed discussion (see Keating and Midwinter, 1984; Keating, Midwinter and Taylor, 1984). Second, government purchasing policy was modified to encourage public sector organizations to buy and hence showcase new British products. Third, aid was provided to small industries in the form of a guarantee scheme for bank loans. Finally, there was the policy of privatization especially in the forms of liberalization and the sale of public assets (see Chapter 3, section 3.2.4(i)). The problem with this latter policy, of course, was that nobody wanted to buy the lame ducks which continued to breach their cash limits and to act as a drain on the Exchequer. Consequently, and of particular relevance here, the government displayed unusual determination to get the nationalized industries on a commercial footing. It not only insisted on strict financial limits but was prepared to countenance contraction and redundancies to achieve its commercial objectives. The following case study illustrates one attempt to implement this policy in a multi-organizational context.

4.6.2 *Contraction and Redundancies*

The plant in question was nationalized in 1977. Up to 1978 it had made a pre-tax loss of £1.9 million and the nationalized industry (NI) promptly instituted a review of the plant's corporate strategy. The consultant's report was highly critical and recommended a significant reduction in the workforce from 1,400 employees to 921. The NI's policy was to create small strategically located units backed up by larger centres. It decided to close the plant – 'Slimville' – and an announcement to this effect was made by the minister. Initially, the NI argued that the plant was not commercially viable. However, subsidiary companies on the site were to be retained, and the NI decided not to close the plant completely. Redundancy notices were issued in March 1979, calling for 1,107 redundancies, but in May the NI announced that work would continue at the plant, provided manning levels and working practices were changed substantially. The advent of the Conservative government raised the question of the sale of the plant. However, it decided not to sell in the short term but to concentrate on restructuring the entire industry. The option of 12,000 redundancies nationally became policy, and restructuring and redundancies proceeded apace at Slimville. By March 1980 the plant was making a profit with a much reduced workforce of some 175. Davies and Mason (1981a, p. 27) conclude that the decision to close the plant was taken to push through the NI's labour force policy. Market and sales considerations took second place to a reduction of manning levels and flexible working practices. With this brief chronology in mind, the roles of the various actors in the decision to restructure Slimville can be explored.[14]

4.6.2(i) THE CENTRE

Grant (1982, p. 27) argues that there is an industrial policy community, although it is loosely integrated: 'a community of regular meeting attenders'. His description of these attenders provides a useful introduction to the industrial policy producer network. The lead ministry is the DoI, but it is by no means responsible for all British industry. For example, the Department of Energy (DEn) and the DTp are responsible for major nationalized industries. The DoE is responsible for the construction industry. In addition, the territorial ministries have major responsibilities devolved to them. The pre-eminent department up to 1979 was the Treasury, however. Its Industrial Policy Group co-ordinated central action and it even invited industrialists, but not trade unionists, to the Treasury for informal discussion. Since 1979 the Industrial and Commercial Policy divisions within the DoI have adopted the co-ordinating mantle. The sponsorship divisions are the point of contact between government and particular industries. Links between the various central departments with industrial responsibilities vary.

The territorial ministries operate within a UK policy framework and 'may feel cut off from the informal Whitehall information network', especially in the case of 'the more junior of the two ... ministries, the Welsh Office' (Grant, 1982, p. 34). None the less, as noted earlier, the territorial ministries are effective lobbyists, and industrial policy is no exception. Links with the DT are close, and they share a number of common services and a common establishment. '[M]ost conflicts of interest between the two departments can be resolved through the use of the close and extensive bilateral contacts that exist between them' (Grant, 1982, p. 35). Links with other departments vary greatly; some 'see themselves as outposts of Industry', whereas with others the link is 'more tenuous' (Grant, 1982, p. 35).

There are a substantial number of non-departmental public bodies concerned with industrial policy. They include the National Enterprise Board, the Scottish, Welsh and Northern Ireland development agencies, the National Economic Development Council, the Council for Small Industries in Rural Areas (CoSIRA) and the English Industrial Estates Corporation (EIEC).

The most important interest group in industrial policy is the Confederation of British Industry (CBI), advising ministers on all aspects of industrial policy. The trade unions' arrangements for handling industrial policy are not good, and Grant (1982, p. 41) suggests that the TUC does not have an industrial policy. There are, in addition, various specialized groups, including, for example, the Nationalized Industries Chairmen's Group; but, perhaps more important, links with individual firms, or groups of firms in an industry, have been a continual problem. During the 1970s the largest companies developed 'government relations departments', and this trend reflects the increasing importance of contacts with government for them. Beyond such companies, however, government links with firms remain patchy, and knowledge of government financial assistance remains poor.

Even this cursory account of the major actors demonstrates that the producer network focused on industrial policy is loosely integrated. In Grant's (1982, pp. 4–5) terms, there is 'a fluid network of contacts'. Consequently, one would expect the network to be characterized by implementation failures arising from the problem of co-ordinating multiple actors. It is precisely this theme which emerges from an exploration of the closure of Slimville. This section concentrates on relationships at the centre and the policy which emerged from these interactions. Subsequently, relationships between centre and locality will be explored.

Central policy was ostensibly clear: to restructure the industry and increase productivity and international competitiveness. This policy inevitably required large-scale redundancies, and as a result the government had also to take some action to deal with the dislocation, to 'mop-up' unemployment. Potentially there was a conflict between the economic policy of restructuring and the social policy of mopping-up. Initially the Labour government wanted 'to save jobs and to keep as many plants open as possible'. However, this goal was tempered by an insistence that the government could not pump money into non-viable activities. The government could not guarantee jobs, nor could it endorse the 'unbelievably restrictive practices of the workers which they faithfully promised to abandon, but didn't'. Ultimately, therefore, the Labour government's policy was ambiguous. Not so Conservative policy: 'One has to separate commercial decision making from decisions relating to consequences. But we do take into account social consequences, so we have identified blockages to alternative job creation.' The relative priority of economic and social policies seems clear. The position was complicated, however, by the relationship between the DoI and DEmp. The latter was concerned with the employment consequences of restructuring and, in sharper contrast to the DoI, did not stand apart from the NI's commercial decisions: 'we were sensitive to the fact that plants were in high unemployment areas'. Where the redundancies would occur was a matter in which the DEmp attempted to 'guide' the NI. Any ambiguity in policy was further accentuated by the government's relationship with the NI (all preceding quotes from ministers at the DoI and DEmp, cited in Davies, Mason and Davies, 1984, pp. 131–4).

At its simplest, both ministers and the NI manipulated each other. Thus, the NI implied to the unions that closures were government policy, a statement which the minister vehemently denied, whilst admitting they interfered on such matters as pay. Conversely the Conservative government insisted that management decisions were left to management: 'It is not for DoI to intervene in business decisions. Nationalized industries have to have commercial objectives.' This freedom was, however, subject to strict EFLs. Rather oddly, Davies, Mason and Davies (1984, p. 136) insist that the NI was 'an instrument of government policy, an implementing agency'. And yet the NI wanted a reduction in capacity and of the labour force, the unions wanted no redundancies, the Labour government was 'in the middle', wanting to save jobs *and* keep plants open as it restructured the industry, whilst the DoI and DEmp disagreed on where the middle was. With the change of government, economic priorities were firmly endorsed, but the NI's policy remained unchanged. It would seem more accurate to describe the relationship as ambiguous and subject to *ad hoc* interventions – indeed, as typical of relationships between government and the nationalized industries. Moreover, given the collapse of the world market and the long-term decline of the British industry, it is difficult to conceive of any policy that did not require some reduction in capacity; that decision was taken for the British government by the international economic environment. Restructuring was no longer a question of 'is it necessary?' but of where and when. The NI implemented government policy only in the most general sense that it accepted the need for contraction; thereafter the sheer ambiguity of policy left the industry considerable discretion constrained only by random interventions.

These ambiguities of policy and relationship are clearly illustrated by the specific decision to close Slimville. The policy of the NI was to keep the plant open and restructure it. The problem was how to effect that restructuring. The solution was

> to announce its closure, and then stay and oversee the rebuilding of the place. The idea all along was to see whether there were sufficient other activities which would keep the place ticking over, and then when the market opened up, to restructure. They couldn't tolerate the losses any more.
> (Local manager, cited in Davies, Mason and Davies, 1984, p. 139)

The Labour government, concerned about the social impact of the closure, looked for some aid to keep the plant open. The NI refused to reverse its decision, and the search for money failed; indeed, some participants considered it a diversionary tactic. Ministers reviewed each possible closure and, on this occasion, felt that the NI was refusing to play the game of looking for an alternative to closure. One minister went as far as to claim that the NI was asset-stripping the industry and he objected to notional economic criteria being applied strictly to the nationalized industries. Rather, the government should seek to invest in areas of high unemployment. Good intentions quickly evaporated, however, and the minister washed his hands of the affair after the decision on closure had been reaffirmed.

Perhaps surprisingly, the selfsame conclusion can be applied to the role of the unions. The Confederation of Unions' (CU) policy of no compulsory redundancies was reduced to tatters. The pressure to accept such redundancies had grown with the failure to persuade local workers to accept new manning arrangements and voluntary redundancies, consultations over the industry's corporate strategy and the government's arrangements for redundancy. Although the government accepted that some contraction was inevitable and endorsed the objective of maintaining the industry's market share, it did not agree to a reduction in either capacity or the workforce. It was committed to saving as many jobs as possible. However, the Corporate Strategy with its 12,000 redundancies became the basis of the NI's future activities, and the CU opposition to redundancies takes on a symbolic air. In the case of Slimville, the union argued for a maintenance of capacity; in essence it conceded redundancies in order to keep the plant open. The NI was prepared to accept this offer. The consequence locally, however, was that members felt they had been sold down the river. As Davies, Mason and Davies (1984, p. 158) conclude, CU statements on job security were 'bargaining counters'. In the process of bargaining 'the centre plays off the local trade unionists against the [industry's] officers and central government', but the outcome 'does not meet the needs of the workers made redundant'.

Nor did the NI and the CU do a great deal to mop up the unemployment caused by their agreement. A joint working party on the topic seems to have never met. In addition, 'there was little concern at Government level about whether [the NI] was operating a social policy or not' (Davies, Mason and Davies, 1984, p. 161). The government itself enacted a special redundancy payments scheme to top up existing statutory arrangements but otherwise relied on the normal programmes of the MSC – for example, Temporary Employment Subsidy, Special Temporary Employment Programme – to alleviate the problem, in part because of Treasury opposition to the cost. There was one policy initiative; the area was accorded Special Development Area status. In theory, this change should have attracted additional government resources and, steered by Industrial Development Certificates, new industry. In fact, SDA status 'had no impact whatsoever' and 'had a psychological effect only' (Davies, Mason and Davies, 1984, p. 176) – a point explored in more detail in the next section.

4.6.2(ii)   THE LOCALITY

The range of organizations in the industrial policy community is extensive at the national level. When the range of local actors and national–local linkages are included, the picture becomes inordinately complex. This section explores national–local linkages for the NI, the CU and the DoI, as well as the role of non-departmental public bodies, most notably the MSC and the English Industrial Estates Corporation (EIEC), and of the local authorities.

Any generalizations about the role of local management within the NI require considerable caution. Their role will vary with their permanence, attitudes on the future of the industry and their identification with local interests. On this occasion, the General Manager seemed to be bypassed by his HQ and he was a highly visible opponent of closure. Although local management accepted that there had to be restructuring of the labour force, it wanted to keep the plant open. The General Manager sought to encourage new, private initiatives at the yard but saw his idea squashed by the centre. Local management also introduced its own redundancy scheme to foster restructuring, which similarly incurred central wrath: 'a nonsense agreement'. It seemed to place a greater value on the skills of the local labour force than the centre did. None the less, it was prepared to use the closure to get rid of unwanted workers and re-employ the ones it wanted. Opponents of closures and advocates of restructuring, local management's visibility cannot be treated as evidence of its capacity to change central policy. At the very least it managed an ambiguous situation, thereby facilitating central action if not actively encouraging it.

With nationalization, local agreements on task interchangeability and flexibility were superseded by a national agreement. Not only was this a loss of local autonomy, but a union representative on the board of the NI warned the Slimville workforce at a mass meeting that it would have to make greater efforts to return the plant to profitability and that nationalization did not guarantee jobs. In fact, such warnings were commonplace, and the threat of closure was not treated too seriously. When, on this occasion, the threat became a reality, it was a shock which prompted complete rejection of the decision. The union rejected closure and negotiated with management over the numbers to be retained. The workforce agreed to a reduction of 450, but 'utter confusion' reigned at the plant. Negotiations at the national level allegedly yielded an agreement that 175 men would be retained, provided they were selected by the company and there was complete flexibility and a review after three months. The 'agreement' was rejected at a mass meeting but to little effect. For all the negotiations, and 'success' in keeping the plant open, there were large-scale redundancies and a virtually unilateral redefinition of working practices. Negotiation, which was ostensibly the union's route to success, was the means for its defeat. The national level, through its policy of no compulsory redundancy, contained local militancy and conflict. Local interests lost to a national concern with maintaining capacity.

The recriminations called forth by the 'sell-out' were reinforced by a split between CU members still working at the yard and those made redundant. The latter called for denationalization and return of the yard to the private sector, a proposal supported by the local union but rejected nationally. The prevailing climate is pungently described by one union official: 'the industry have "conned us" all the way along the line ... they got away with forced redundancies' (Davies, Mason and Davies, 1984, p. 92). And the national level of the union can be seen only as part of 'the industry'.

All that was left was to mop up the unemployment, and here the roles of the DEmp and MSC are prominent. Thus, the day before the announcement of the closure, the area office of the MSC was informed of the impending redundancies by the regional office. Promptly it opened a job centre at the plant. MSC policy was to direct the workers to skilled jobs in the *national* labour market but it conflicted with the NI's policy of selectively re-employing a proportion of the workforce. Allied to the high earnings expectation of the men, the number aged over 45 and the, at times, highly specialized nature of their skills, 462 were still seeking work ten months after closure. Allied to placement, the MSC also retrains the unemployed. The problem here is the MSC's reactive stance and the importance of mobility for gaining selection. No special training programmes were mounted. Training policy was nationally determined and it required a specific set of skills and a mobile workforce. Local needs had to adapt to the programme, not vice versa.

The provisions for mopping up unemployment saw little recognition of the need for jobs in Slimville. Davies, Mason and Davies (1984, p. 124) conclude that they amounted to no more than 'covert policies for restructuring'. The mopping-up agencies were centrally oriented, had a weak power position and operated inappropriate policies. Even the special redundancy payments scheme, although designed to alleviate hardship, had a restructuring component because it was geared to workers over 40 and was a means of removing them from the labour market. The policies of the local authorities displayed a similar unholy alliance of economic (restructuring) and social (mopping-up) policies.

The county council's development plan emphasized the need for employment growth and for promotional policies to attract industry by the county and the districts. In fact, prior to closure, the level of activity was low. After the closure, the county adopted a more interventionist role. Thus it advocated industrial development through the EIEC and it approached the EEC for funds. This lobbying activity for additional funds was complemented by an attempt to increase the availability of development land; factory building was the preferred solution to the problem of unemployment. The major difficulty was the lack of land in Slimville and its district council and the refusal of the neighbouring district to make sites available. The county had to intervene when the EIEC requested a site and eventually it lodged its own planning application to develop a site against district opposition. For the most part, however, the county was concerned with the economic health of the county as a whole. It wanted the SDA extended, and the emphasis on industrial development was a long-standing county-wide policy.

The range of actors involved at the local level not only guaranteed some conflict but also ensured that there would be problems of co-ordination. Thus the county, and for that matter the DoI, advocated land acquisition, whilst the EIEC insisted that any factory building must be commercially viable. The EIEC was prepared to build up a reserve of land but refused to build the factories on the grounds that empty factories were more embarrassing than inaction. In short, policy depended on the behaviour of individual firms, and the EIEC felt that the demand for its factories was too low to justify building them.

The EIEC's policy illuminates central–local relations within a central department. In theory at least, relationships within the DoI are line management in nature. Thus, policy decisions were taken in Whitehall, whilst the regional office administered section 8 grants under the 1972 Act and advised the centre on policy changes. The DoI's area office was responsible for administering section 7 grants and, along with the EIEC, was seen as the implementer, not adviser, of policy. In reality, perceptions of policy, feasible action and relationships varied at each level. The DoI's view was that Slimville needed small factory units for home-grown firms and that sufficient land was already available. The regional DoI expected the EIEC to acquire more land. It felt 'that land was coming forward but that there were difficulties getting people to use it' (Davies, Mason and Davies, 1984, p. 170). The area office emphasized land acquisition but wanted to attract large firms to the area. It saw its role as primarily promotional, with the county and the EIEC responsible for acquiring land. The role of the EIEC had changed under the Industry Act 1980. Originally, its factory-building and land-allocation programme was determined by the DoI. After the 1980 Act it was required to attract private funds and to develop projects which were commercially viable. Regional expectations that the EIEC would institute an urgent search for land were not, therefore, realized; indeed, the DoI was uncertain about the nature and extent of the EIEC's land search. As Davies, Mason and Davies (1984, p. 164) comment, 'the nature of the "beast" is a complex one', and the contradictory expectation of the several levels within the DoI led to expectations of actions substituting for the real thing.

However, all of these actors did attempt to respond to the 'crisis' of the closure. The Education and Social Work departments of the county might have been expected to develop social policies for the unemployed. In fact, they 'carried out their tasks without responding to changes in the labour market' (Davies, Mason and Davies, 1984, p. 119). The district councils, outside of Slimville and its districts adopted an essentially defensive posture and, even when there was the political will to act, they were constrained by their lack of technical and financial resources. The picture emerges, therefore, of a plethora of organizations which, if they acted, competed with each other and produced contradictory policy outcomes. Their actions were overwhelmingly concerned with restructuring the local economy, and consequently social policies (for the mopping up of unemployment) were totally swamped. Moreover, the restructuring policies depended on the willingness of firms to come to the area, and at no stage was this problem overcome. The plant was restructured with scant regard to the social costs; and subsequent intervention:

> which is justified in terms of those suffering most from the problem, is oriented more and more towards the restructuring of the future local economy. Those who are most affected, however, fall through the holes of a very loosely knit network of agencies.
>
> (Davies, Mason and Davies, 1984, p. 120)

4.6.3 Conclusions: Independence, Selectivity and Privilege

Indisputably producer networks are loosely integrated, but networks do exist; there is continuity of membership and, to a surprising degree, policies. The greatest problem concerns boundaries. As Hogwood (1979b, p. 37) points out, the boundaries become opaque 'where sectoral and regional concerns cross-cut'. Insufficient evidence is available to judge whether or not there is a network which embraces all the policies clustering under the rubric of industrial policy. Examples of discrete networks include nuclear energy and, best documented, agriculture, which is governed by a tightly knit network focused on the Ministry of Agriculture, Fisheries and Food (Self and Storing, 1971). It remains possible, therefore, that there are sectoral producer networks which cannot be subsumed under a generic network such as the 'industrial policy community'. Equally it is clear that there is a producer network focused on the industrial policies of the DoI and the territorial ministries. If the boundaries are opaque, then the core of the network is easier to discern. Most important, all producer networks are subject to common constraints which limit their degree of integration or, at best, make a high degree of integration rare. The case study illustrates both the shared characteristics of producer networks and the constraints on integration.

First, in producer networks the centre is dependent on firms for expertise on a particular industry and its problems and for the implementation of its policies. It has experienced continual problems in acquiring basic, and especially up-to-date, information even on such ostensibly elementary matters as whether or not a firm has a trading deficit and, if so, on what scale. And in implementing its policies, contact with firms has been poor. Individual companies have little knowledge of what government assistance is available, take-up has not been commensurate with available resources, and the lead time for implementation has been long, especially for government harassed by immediate economic problems.

Second, the firms are independent of government. As Young and Lowe remark (1974, p. 205), 'The policies of successive government ... have been based not just on maintaining the commercial independence of the individual firm but on exploiting it.' The aim is to increase competitiveness and profitability, and this affirmation of independence means that 'independent private sector firms cannot be relied on to complete projects partly sponsored by the government'. Because 'most firms ... maintain their independence ... they can frustrate the achievement of the aims of government policy' (Young and Lowe, 1974, p. 207). Thus, the county council's, the EIEC's and the DoI's attempts to attract industry to Slimville foundered on the freedom of firms to ignore government financial and other incentives and move where they want. Similarly, the MSC's retraining policy with its emphasis on mobility was reactive to the demands of firms nation-wide and a recognition that it could not structure or steer their labour requirements.

Third, the competitive relationship between firms and industries constrains the degree of co-operation, and ultimately integration, between economic interests. The government cannot aggregate effectively the interests with which it wishes to negotiate. The major interest group, the CBI, represents primarily if not exclusively the interests of manufacturing industry and only intermittently financial interests. Even in the case of the nationalized industries, co-operation in the NICG is constrained by competition between, for example, the energy industries. The potential conflict is even greater when the government seeks to incorporate trade union interests. Tripartism is the dominant mode of negotiation in the NEDC and other non-departmental public bodies, but, as Marsh and Grant (1982, p. 296) argue, its effectiveness has been greatly reduced by the lack of agreement on economic goals between business and unions. Such problems have been minimized for industrial policy primarily because the TUC has not developed its preferred version of an industrial policy and it has not been party to all the negotiations. Moreover, should negotiations with the TUC and CBI produce an agreement, neither interest group has been able to deliver its members for any sustained period of time. This inability to aggregate interests serves to accentuate government dependence on individual firms.

Fourth, and as a response to the first three constraints, government policy became selective between regions, industries and firms within industries. Selective intervention immediately confronted a paradox; as assistance became targeted, as the government sought to influence decision-making within individual firms, it was in danger of compromising the independence deemed essential to profitability and competitiveness. There were other less fundamental but equally intractable problems. Selective intervention led the government into the monitoring of policy and continuous reappraisal, with 'the overall result ... that governments seem unable to avoid detailed interventionist and industrial policies becoming a series of *ad hoc*, largely uncoordinated responses to individual cases' (Young and Lowe, 1974, p. 197). There were other pressures in this direction (see below), but the logic of selective intervention led to detailed involvement and thence reactions to the specific problems of specific cases. Policy had become its own cause. Maintaining the independence of the firm led to policy slippage, which in turn fostered selective interventions and *ad hoc* responses to particular cases, which, to complete the circle, compounded the problem of policy co-ordination which selectivity sought to solve. Central dependence on independent firms is a defining characteristic of producer networks and a major constraint on integration.

Fifth, the problems of implementing industrial policy are a classic example of 'multi-organizational sub-optimization'; that is, 'the parts of an interconnected system are separately administered in such a way as to render the total administrative effect ineffective or counterproductive' (Hood, 1976, p. 17). Once stated, it is obvious that the several attempts to deal with the social costs of the Slimville closure are an example of this phenomenon. The best single instance of multi-organization sub-optimization is the DoI/EIEC 'policy' on land acquisition. In short, the organizational structure of the network constrained its effectiveness.

Sixth, all the foregoing problems are exacerbated by the uncertain and unstable environment of industrial policy. This instability has a number of dimensions: industrial, political and international. Thus, industry is continually evolving in unpredictable directions, and policy becomes out of date. However, existing commitments mean that it cannot be scrapped, and so it acts as a constraint on new policies. The major political uncertainties lie in the incidence of unemployment, and even the Thatcher government has been reluctant to countenance further increases in, for example, unemployment in Northern Ireland. Fluctuations in the international economy have had severe consequences for manufacturing industry, but that is not the only international constraint. Whether as members of the EEC, party to an international contract, or negotiation with a multinational company, the government is constrained in a range of highly variable ways.

Seventh, the government is constrained by the privileged position of economic interests. Such interests can lobby the government in the usual way, and the CBI has an extensive and intensive involvement in industrial policy even when, as in the case of the Industry Act 1972, its warnings are not heeded. More pervasively, however, business occupies a privileged position:

> Corporate executives in all private enterprise systems . . . decide a nation's industrial technology, the pattern of work organization, location of industry, market structure, resource allocation and, of course, executive compensation and status. They are also the immediate or proximate and discretionary decision makers, though subject to significant consumer control, on what is to be produced and in what quantities.
>
> In short, a large category of major decisions is turned over to businessmen . . . They are taken off the agenda of government.
>
> (Lindblom, 1977, pp. 171–2)

Consequently, for the government, business and its interest groups

> do not appear simply as the representatives of a special interest, as representatives of interest groups do. They appear as functionaries performing functions that government officials regard as indispensable. When a government official asks himself whether business needs a tax reduction, he knows he is asking a question about the welfare of the whole society.
>
> (Lindblom, 1977, p. 175)

A similar point is made about the closure of Slimville by Davies, Mason and Davies (1984, p. 241). The privileged position of economic interests is manifest

> in a series of self-evident 'goods' . . . The idea of economic growth as a 'good', of the selection of those most likely to be productive, of the rejection of those classified as 'low achievers', or of 'low productivity', or 'too old'; these values seemed to pervade the whole structure from centre to locality.

Consequently, 'restructuring' policies are implemented more easily than 'mopping-up' policies. Or, from a different political standpoint:

> In Britain . . . one often gets the impression that people think there is an alternative to technical efficiency and economic profitability, and that somehow the state or 'the community' should be able to get resources from somewhere to permit non-competitive industries to survive.
>
> (Cited in Grant, 1982, p. 147).

However one values technical efficiency and profitability, they exercise a pervasive influence within producer networks and on industrial policy. If economic interests do not invariably win, if there are marked divergences of interest between the various sections of industry, none the less such interests occupy a privileged position. And perhaps the clearest examples of this position lie in the CU's rejection of its policy on no compulsory redundancies in favour of maintaining capacity, in its criticisms of work practices at the Slimville plant and in the internalization of the values of productivity 'by those most vulnerable', namely, the redundant workers and their call for privatization (Davies, Mason and Davies, 1984, p. 242). The question of who benefits could not have a clearer answer – economic interests – just as the losers are transparently obvious: redundant workers.

Finally, the analogy between independent firms and nationalized industries is closer than might be supposed. Successive governments have repeatedly insisted that the managers of nationalized industries are free to make commercial decisions. The industries are expected to be commercially viable, that is, profitable. In short, the industries are subject to the same economic value system as independent firms. There are, of course, important differences, most notably in the scale and frequency of government intervention. However, the industries cannot be seen as mere central implementing agencies, because the yen for commercial independence compromises central intervention. The government may want the industries to serve social policies but the more it intervenes to this end the more it constrains the industries' capacity for independent commercial decisions. And yet the government also wants the industries to be profitable. Consequently, intervention shows a marked tendency to be *ad hoc*, as in the case of firms. For all the government's social conscience over the consequences of the Slimville closure, its haverings and interventions changed neither the decision nor the overall policy on contraction of the NI, which, incidentally, the government had not endorsed.

Given the above range of constraints, it is not surprising that producer networks are loosely integrated. Indeed, the focus on constraints paints a picture of inaction if not impotence. As a corrective to this emphasis, it is important to note that economic interests can be integrated. Where there are relatively few producers and the government is a major if not sole buyer, as in the cases of defence contracting and nuclear energy, the degree of integration can be high. Similarly, industry is aware of the benefits of contact with government. Consensus on a defined range of matters, especially in times of economic crisis, is possible therefore. Finally, the government can force industry to co-operate, a strategy adopted, for example, in time of war. But if integration is possible, it is comparatively rare. Corporatist theory suggests that integration characterizes government relations with economic producer groups. The analysis in this section suggests that such integration is elusive and that the various interests only coalesce around specific problems or specific instruments of government, most commonly involving the disbursement of public funds. Producer networks are not characterized by aggregation, intermediation and consensus but by fluctuating membership, central dependence on firms, limited interdependence amongst economic interests and the privileged position of such interests. In consequence, producer networks are loose-knit networks.

4.7 Issue Networks

Issue networks have been described as loosely integrated, that is, they encompass diverse interests and a large number of participants with a low degree of vertical and horizontal interdependence. The case study of inner cities policies is not, strictly speaking, a study of a network 'in action' but one of central attempts to create a network (and its failure). It provides, therefore, a challenge to the focus on policy networks. As before, the account proceeds from a description of the context of inner cities policy through a case study of the Inner Cities Partnerships and Programmes (ICPP) initiative to a discussion of the characteristics of issue networks. In this particular case, however, I will argue that the focus on network helps to explain why an inner cities policy network was not created (rather than how it operates) and the consequences of this failure for the cities.[15]

4.7.1 The Policy Context of the Inner City

For the bulk of the postwar period, there was no inner cities policy. As McKay and Cox (1979, p. 233) point out, the arrival of inner cities policy 'is evidence of the inadequacy of other urban policies'. These 'other' policies comprised new towns, regional planning, land-use planning and housing and they were directed at such problems as urban sprawl, regional decline and overcrowding. With the 'rediscovery' of poverty, race and the inner city in the mid-1960s, these policies and problems did not disappear but they were supplemented increasingly by policies directed explicitly at the inner city. This section will not describe the broad sweep of urban policy, the role of the planning profession and the rise and fall of such 'spectacular' policies as central area redevelopment and high-rise housing (see, for example, Hall *et al.*, 1973; McKay and Cox, 1979; Dunleavy, 1981b; Cullingworth, 1985). This era of 'technical-professional guidance' has been well documented, and here I focus on the explicit inner city policies.

Concern with the inner cities may have been crystallized by Enoch Powell's 'rivers of blood' speech on 20 April 1968, but there were many tributaries feeding into it. Throughout the 1960s there was a

growing awareness of the persistence of poverty in the midst of the
welfare state and especially of the problems posed by the concentration of immigrants in inner cities. If the debate on race had concentrated on immigration control, there was some recognition of the need
for special measures. Thus, the Local Government Act 1966, s. 11,
provided special grants for teachers in areas with a large immigrant
population. The case for positive discrimination was given a powerful
boost by the Plowden Committee (1967), which proposed the desig-
nation of priority areas for compensatory education and public
expenditure to improve the quality of their substandard schools and
schooling. In consequence the policy experiments known as EPAs
(Educational Priority Areas) were instituted. Five areas were selected
– London, Liverpool, Birmingham, West Riding of Yorkshire and
Dundee – and the experiments were to last three years. The objectives
were to raise the educational performance of children, to improve the
morale of teachers and to increase the involvement of parents in their
children's education. In addition, funds were made available for a
system of special allowances for teachers in EPAs and for a building
programme (for a more detailed account see Halsey, 1972; for a brief
introduction see Halsey, 1978). And as a final example of the diffused
awareness of the problem, the Milner-Holland Committee (1965)
drew attention to housing problems in London and, of particular
relevance in this context, proposed that the worst areas be designated
'areas of special control'. Once again the notion of spatially focused
interventions was in the air. Enoch Powell's speech was to concentrate
the Labour government's mind wonderfully, and the discrete policy
initiatives in education and housing and the distinct policy instrument
of area-based positive discrimination were, in theory at least, to come
together.

The initial response took the form of the Urban Programme (UP),
announced by the (then) Prime Minister, Harold Wilson, to the
'surprise' of officials, whose 'memories differ on whether they had any
prior notice, but it does seem that a few days before the speech
officials were called upon to prepare sketch proposals' (Edwards and
Batley, 1978, pp. 40–1). In some haste, therefore, a package was
prepared, drawing on existing EPA and section 11 experience, in
which additional monies in the form of a 75 per cent specific grant
were to be paid on the costs of projects in areas of multiple deprivation
(Local Government Grants (Social Need) Act 1969). The Home
Office was the 'lead' department, and, although housing was
excluded, the UP spanned service departments, primarily education,
child care and health. By 1975 total expenditure had grown to £55.5
million, and the bulk of the projects had been for nursery schools, play
groups, community centres, advice centres and the like. Quite clearly,
this scale of expenditure made the UP a marginal initiative; it 'topped
up' the mainstream services.

However, no sooner was the UP announced than it was followed by Community Development Projects (CDPs), making it clear that multiple deprivation was to be matched by multiple initiatives. The brainchild of a civil servant, Derek Morrell, chairman of the interdepartmental working party on the UP (Edwards and Batley, 1978, pp. 51–2; McKay and Cox, 1979, pp. 233 and 243), CDPs were considered at the same time as the UP but were not announced until 1969. Funded out of the UP, twelve projects were established between 1969–72 'to assess the community's needs, to improve the responsiveness of the social services to those needs, and to promote the community's self-help' (Edwards and Batley, 1978, p. 51; for a detailed history and evaluation see Loney, 1983).

Both the UP and CDPs were a political response to a perceived crisis. The policies were moulded by civil servants and focused on social welfare, that is, on the problems of the individual and not the economic forces transforming inner cities. As McKay and Cox (1978, p. 505) conclude, the UP was a '"low cost" solution to an imperfectly understood social problem'. Its inability to effect any change is scarcely surprising. Similarly, the expectation that CDPs could improve the local co-ordination of services and make local authorities more responsive to citizens' needs was as unrealistic as it was unrealized. Conflict with local authorities was inevitable. The CDPs did have one important effect; they publicly rejected the social pathology/welfare basis of the UP and CDPs:

> Analyses of the wider context of CDP areas has led us to recognize ... that problems of multiple deprivation have to be redefined and re-interpreted in terms of structural constraints rather than psychological motivations, external rather than internal factors
> (CDP, 1974, p. 8)

With the change of government in 1970, there were signs that the lessons of the experiments were being learnt.

The new Conservative government may have continued the UP and CDPs, but the new Secretary of State for the Environment, Peter Walker, was determined not only to stake the DoE's claims for a prominent, if not the 'lead', role in inner cities policy but also to develop 'a total approach to the urban environment'. He instigated the Inner Areas Studies, comprising three short-term studies of the co-ordination of local services in Oldham, Rotherham and Sunderland, and three long-term policy experiments in Liverpool, Birmingham and Lambeth. The latter retained a small area component but it was allied to an examination of wider economic and demographic changes. It is all too easy to dismiss the initiative as 'more of the same'; it was, but the focus on the economic basis of deprivation in the final reports helped to redirect inner city policy in 1977. In the meantime, it was very much a case of more of the same from the other affected central departments.

Rationalization became the order of the day. In 1972 the Home Office set up the Urban Deprivation Unit to improve the co-ordination of its programme. The Treasury was concerned with the proliferation of projects across departments, and in 1973 an inter-departmental study was set up to rationalize provision (Leach, 1982a, p. 16). It provided another battleground for 'ownership' of inner city policy, which was resolved in favour of the Home Office. For the remainder of the Conservatives' term of office inner cities policy was relatively quiescent.

The years 1965–74 had witnessed the arrival of the inner cities as a 'problem' on the central agenda and a range of policy experiments aimed at finding ways of dealing with it. As McKay and Cox (1979, p 248) conclude, perhaps the most distinctive feature of these experiments was their 'isolation' from the mainstream of urban policies. They also involved marginal increases in expenditure to little or no effect.

With election of a Labour government, experiments were to give way to partnerships, although its early years of office suggested that the dominant theme would remain rationalization under Home Office auspices with further *ad hoc* policies sponsored by other affected departments. Thus the Home Office introduced Comprehensive Community Programmes (CCPs) in 1974, yet another initiative to improve the co-ordination of local services. It involved no extra resources, and only two CCPs were actually launched. Of greater significance was the introduction of Housing Action Areas under the Housing Act 1974, which enabled local authorities to rehabilitate areas of housing stress. Its significance lay in the amalgamation of spatially confined positive discrimination with a major urban policy. This tran-sition from peripheral experiments to action through mainstream urban policies was the key shift in inner cities policy between 1974–9, and the critiques which emerged from the CDPs and, more important, the Inner Area Studies were instrumental in bringing it about.

The immediate stimuli for the revival of inner city policy are not obvious. If anything the 'problem' had receded and it scarcely figured in the Labour Party manifesto. As in the case of 'organic change' (Rhodes, 1986a, pp. 208–10), the birth of ICPP was a 'solo run' by Peter Shore, Secretary of State for the Environment. The UP had lost momentum; CCPs were floundering; the Home Secretary was not particularly interested; the critique of UP by, amongst others, the Inner Area Studies' final reports provided an intellectually respect-able rationale for action (Leach, 1982a, p. 19); it was mid-term initiative directed at Labour's traditional stronghold of support (McKay and Cox, 1979, pp. 255–6); and the new secretary of state was convinced personally of the need to do something about the cities. Whatever the reasons, the time was ripe and the White Paper, *Policy for the Inner Cities* (HMSO, 1977b), was released with considerable *brouhaha*.

The objectives of the new policy were:

(a) strengthening the economies of the inner areas and the prospects of their residents;
(b) improving the physical fabric of the inner areas and making their environment more attractive;
(c) alleviating social problems;
(d) securing a new balance between the inner areas and the rest of the city region in terms of population and jobs.

(HMSO, 1977b, p. 6).

Allied to these objectives were six specific programmes of action:

(1) give a new priority to the main policies and programmes of government so that they can contribute to a better life in the inner areas . . .;
(2) strengthen the economies of inner areas as an immediate priority . . .;
(3) secure a more unified approach to urban problems . . .;
(4) recast the urban programme to cover economic and environmental projects and to increase its size . . .;
(5) review and change policies on population movement . . .;
(6) enter into special partnerships with the authorities – both districts and counties – of certain cities . . .

(HMSO, 1977b, p. 10).

The emphases on economic regeneration, the city region, the redirection of pre-existing major urban policies and funding mechanisms, coupled with a central role for local authorities, were all added to a small-area and positive-discrimination focus to provide a distinctive pot-pourri and, potentially, a substantial realignment of policy, with UP funding increased from £30 million to £125 million. Subsequently seven local authorities were invited to join the partnerships – Liverpool, Manchester/Salford, Birmingham, Lambeth, Docklands, Hackney/Islington and Newcastle/Gateshead – and fifteen were invited to become programme authorities. The former will be the focus of the following discussion. They were designated partnerships because of the scale and intensity of their problems, which, it was argued, required (and justified) both special organizational arrangements and first call on UP funds. Distinctively, the partnerships were to bring together the range of statutory and non-statutory bodies with a role to play in alleviating multiple deprivation. Based on the district council, they would also involve, typically, the county council, the AHA, voluntary bodies and the affected central departments,

348   *Beyond Westminster and Whitehall*

normally the DoE, DTp, DHSS, DoI and DEmp. The programme
authorities did not have equivalent arrangements and can be seen as
'the second division' authorities. Given that extra resources were
promised, 75 per cent financed by the centre, none of the partnership
invitations was refused.

As McKay and Cox (1979, p. 258) conclude:

> If, indeed, Peter Shore's White Paper really does represent a
> reversal of post-war policies and a desire to integrate housing, trans-
> port, planning and economic investment policies in inner cities, then
> the Pandora's Box will truly have been opened, and political and
> bureaucratic battles over resources and jurisdictions will be legion.

The following case study illustrates the prescience of this judgement.
As established networks defended their turf, the incipient issue
network waned without waxing. In the first instance, I describe the
attempt to build a policy network – the partnerships, their organization and funding – followed by an account of the changes in policy
introduced by the Conservative government. Second, I focus on the
fortunes of one partnership, Liverpool, before drawing some general
lessons from the experience of all seven partnerships.

This section has briefly covered the change from an urban policy
rooted in land-use and regional planning and housing to an explicit
inner cities policy, the era of policy experiments and the arrival of the
partnerships or inner cities' issue network. The next section records
the demise of partnerships and the switch of emphasis to economic
development through a deregulated private sector.

4.7.2   The Rise and Fall of Institutional Complexity

4.7.2(i)   THE DESIGN AND EVOLUTION OF PARTNERSHIP,
1977–8 TO 1979–80

For all its length the White Paper said relatively little on the organization and finance of the partnerships or the policies (programmes).
In brief, a multi-tier organizational system was created, comprising a
Partnership Committee, an Officers' Steering Group, *ad hoc* on
working groups and an Inner City Unit to pull the several pieces
together (see Figure 4.2). Each Partnership Committee was composed of one of the DoE ministers, three or four councillors from each
local authority, ministerial representatives from other affected central
departments and the chairmen (or deputies) from the AHAs involved.
It was the fulcrum of the whole exercise, although not formally an
executive body. As Leach (1982a, pp. 41–2) comments, it was an
advisory body, but its decisions 'were invariably implemented by the
other participants'. The Officers' Steering Group serviced the

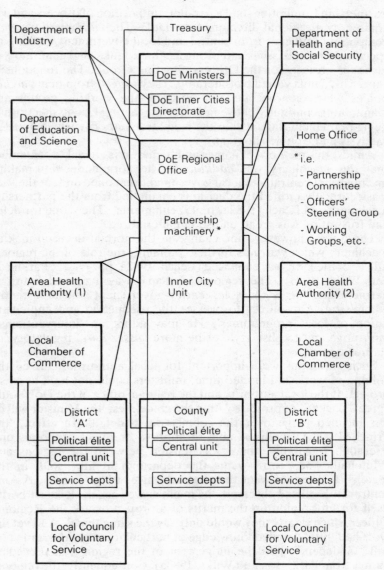

Main links only are shown.

Figure 4.2 *The inter-organizational network of a joint partnership.*
Source: Leach, 1982b, p. 23.

Partnership Committee, had a parallel composition of officers and was chaired by a regional director of the DoE. The *ad hoc* groups were composed of officials from central and local government working on specific topics and issues and acting as 'think-tanks' and generators of ideas for projects for the Officers' Steering Group. The functions of Inner City Units varied considerably. They ranged from being *ad hoc* bodies which concentrated on servicing the working groups and maintaining continuity between Officers' Steering Group meetings to being permanent units within the lead local authority which acted as catalysts and trouble-shooters.

Amidst this plethora of names and bodies, it is crucial to remember that this machinery was *additional*. The normal decision-making machinery of central and local government remained and, at the very least, formally ratified the decisions emanating from the partnership machinery. As Leach (1982a, p. 45) comments, 'The scope for delay and frustration was great, and soon materialized.'

There was, however, one change in the normal decision-making machinery which warrants further comment; the role of the regional offices of the DoE was enhanced (Leach, 1982a, pp. 68–72; Parkinson and Wilks, 1983). The regional principal was a central figure in partnerships: 'he is the sole central government official with the administrative resources to oversee the production and implementation of local programmes'. He may adopt an 'interventionist, innovative and localist' style or be more *laissez-faire*, regulatory, or centralist in style.

Such variations were important for local authorities. Given the volume of work and limited time, ministers could not look at every project. If the local authority and the regional office of the DoE could agree a package of projects within the guidelines, 'the Minister will be less inclined to go over the submission in detail'. In effect, 'the Principal will virtually be able to approve or reject proposals unilaterally'. Inevitably, there was tension between the regions and Whitehall. The centre wants the departmental line 'sold' in the regions. It does not want the regional offices to 'go native'. As one central DoE official observed, 'he might as well ask the local authority itself for an opinion on the merits of a project as ask the Regional Officer, since clearly they would only say the same thing'. And yet the DoE had 'little detailed knowledge of particular authorities and . . . it will . . . depend upon the judgement of the region' (all preceding quotes from Parkinson and Wilks, 1983a). Consequently, the regional offices of the DoE played the range of roles open to intermediate institutions: executive, reticulist, information-gathering, monitoring, intervention and lobbying (see Chapter 3, section 3.4). In effect, for ICPP 'the policy was the regional office's responsibility *unless* a good case can be made for referring it to Whitehall', and the local authorities 'had to rely heavily on the regional office's interpretation of what "the Minister" would or would not find acceptable' (Leach, 1982a, pp. 69 and 72).

The Inner Cities Partnerships and Programmes are another example of PPSs so popular in the 1970s (see Chapter 3, section 3.2.4(ii)). The model was the TPP/TSG system, with the HIPs arrangements being developed within the DoE at the same time. The programme document had a 'firm' first year as part of a rolling programme for three years. Its key function was to draw together the activities of the several organizations involved; it was a symbol of comprehensiveness, co-ordination and long-term commitment. The problem was that their compilation was a formidable task. Leach (1982a, p. 39) suggests that the preparation of a programme required 'a comprehensive inter-corporate strategy for each inner city area linked to an innovative package of relevant projects'. Aspiration and reality were to diverge!

The official starting date was April 1979, and, if the programmes were to be ready, the emphasis had to fall on the feasible plan. Consequently, the 1979–82 programmes described existing problems and activities, and provided a generalized statement of priorities, a balanced set of projects covering economic, social and environment problems and a limited number of innovative projects. Although the DoE resisted attempts by the partnership authorities to revive shelved main programme projects, the authorities rapidly became adept at 'dressing up' submissions; for example, 'rebuilding a branch library' became 'redesignation as a cultural centre' (Leach, 1982a, p. 112). In the time available, little work was carried out on evaluating main programmes and 'bending' them to the new priority.

With the (inevitable) delays in the preparation of the programmes, the first year saw interim financial arrangements. £100 million was allocated for capital projects in 1978–9. This 'construction package' was supplemented by £20 million for specific projects as part of the enhanced UP, and £15 million was made available for environmental improvement in the inner city. Thereafter financial allocations were made by the DoE from a pot of money assembled from contributions by the participating departments from their existing budgets; it was not new money and it was not the subject of negotiation between the DoE and partnership authorities. For the first full year, 1979–80, £125 million was made available and it was distributed roughly in accordance with the severity of the problems in the seven partnerships. In theory at least, the money would increase year by year to prevent commitments pre-empting expenditure on new projects. The centre was to contribute 75 per cent of the cost in the form of a specific grant, whilst the local authority found the balance.

However, enhanced UP expenditure was not the only source of finance for the inner cities. In addition, funds were to be made available through 'the bending of main programmes'. Thus, the centre, not just the DoE (via RSG, HIPs, etc.) but also the DES, DHSS, DoI, DTp and DEmp, was to give the inner city priority and divert resources into this policy and out of existing programmes.

Finally, in order to enhance the range and type of projects which local authorities could fund, the Inner Urban Areas Act 1978 was passed. It gave local authorities powers to encourage economic development, e.g. industrial improvement areas, grants and loans to industry. The official start date was nigh, but the organization had been assembled, the financial mechanism specified, and even programmes had been drawn up and approved with considerable speed by the DoE. The policy was ready for implementation. In May the Conservatives won the general election, and ICPPs were back in the melting-pot.

4.7.2(ii)   POLICY MODIFICATION AFTER 1979–80

Implementation had only just begun, and, in Leach's (1982a, p. 115) phrase, the government was 'not sure whether we like ICPPs or not – convince us'. Uncertainty may have suffused the face of the inner city, but one thing was certain; the 10 per cent increase (in real terms) in resources for 1980–1 was cut, to be followed by a reduction from £211 million to £177 million for 1981–2. Within six months, and to the surprise of many, it was announced that the initiative would continue. There were to be modifications. First, economic development and environmental schemes were to be given priority. Second, capital expenditure was preferred. Third, the organizational arrangements were to be streamlined with both fewer bodies and fewer meetings. Finally, ICPPs were to be the subject of an interdepartmental review. In such circumstances, any notion of a 'strategy for the inner city' went out of the window. The priorities were clear: assemble an acceptable package of economic and environmental capital projects for the year ahead. ICPP were to become a routinized specific grant and the participants preoccupied with project approvals to top up existing programmes.

In February 1981 policy modification gave way to policy change with the announcement that the interdepartmental review had found in favour of the inner cities. The announcement was followed in July by new guidelines from the DoE, which in turn were followed by the riots in Brixton, Southall, Toxteth, Moss Side and several other urban areas. ICCP had moved from uncertainty and mild political indifference to the centre of the political stage in a matter of months and they were to develop a number of new emphases.

First, the DoE guidelines confirmed existing practice – for example, on the priority for economic and environmental projects and on capital expenditure – and in so doing explicitly confirmed that there would be greater central control over the content of projects. The DoE would distribute funds in accordance with the intensity of the problems (an updated version of the existing distributive system), the spending record of the partnerships (in effect, an extension of the block grant system for penalizing 'overspenders') and regional office views on the 'quality' of the submissions. Project approvals were simplified but the DoE reserved the right to reject 'controversial items', as defined by ministers of course. In short, the guidelines rejected the collaborative arrangements for a simpler bid-allocation grant system controlled by the DoE. As might be expected, the role of the regional offices of the DoE changed somewhat under the new government. They remained a key link between local authorities and Whitehall, but their monitoring and control function came to the fore. The scope for innovation and lobbying on behalf of 'their' local authorities was more confined, although their advice on the acceptability of a project, and on ways and means of dressing it up, remained of great value to local authorities.

Second, the original 1977 White Paper's emphasis on economic development was both reinforced and given a distinctive twist. Already the government had sought to involve the private sector in the economic development of urban areas with the creation of Urban Development Corporations (UDCs), Financial Institutions Group (FIG) and Enterprise Zones (EZs). The explicit involvement of the private sector now came to the fore in ICPP. Through local Chambers of Commerce, business interests not only have the technical role of, for example, advising on economic projects but also involvement in specific projects, such as business advice centres and training workshops, and a general consultative role on the programme. The phrase 'economic development' shifted in meaning. Initially it referred to such redistributive goals as reducing levels of unemployment among residents and improving their opportunities. Now it refers to the generation of wealth and to making inner cities attractive to investors. Indeed, ICPP must be seen as a *subsidiary* policy in this respect, playing second fiddle to UDCs, FIG and EZs. Moreover, some local authorities also began to view ICPP as a subsidiary policy, developing their own local economic development strategies and establishing, for example, enterprise boards. At its simplest, the boards provide equity finance for business, rather than loans, and the local authority shares in the profits of the enterprise (Chandler and Lawless, 1985, pp. 228–33). ICCP might remain, but the partners were increasingly travelling on their own.

Third, after the riots, the relevance of ICPP to ethnic minorities were given greater visibility. Thus, the programmes recognized explicitly the need to combat racial discrimination, a junior minister at the DoE was given responsibility for race relations, and projects for or by ethnic minorities were given some priority in the allocation of resources. These changes were marginal in terms of both total ICPP funding and the problem of racial discrimination but, in a simple twist of fate, remind inner cities policy of its roots in race relations.

Finally, political salience was translated into financial priority. For 1982–3 UP expenditure was increased to £270 million, including £55 million for ICPP, the first real increase since 1979–80. There were signs that main programmes were to be 'bent' once again; the 1982–3 HIPs allocation, although still far below 1979 levels, none the less favoured ICPP local authorities. There was also renewed interest in 'strategy' as a prerequisite for drawing together the multiple strands of urban policy and financing. However, the total sums of money involved remain relatively small, and critics have not been slow to dismiss the policy as mere 'symbolism'.

Contrary to expectations, therefore, there was an inner cities policy post-1979, but the ambitions of the 1977 White Paper had receded into the dim and distant past. There was no total approach to the urban environment, only a relatively small specific grant. Parkinson and Wilks (1983a) suggest that ICPP had four broad goals: to create a mechanism for the inter-organizational co-ordination of policy implementation; a forum for interest mediation and conflict resolution; and a more effective institutional capacity; which would be a focus for policy innovation and development. They conclude that none of these goals have been fully realized. Partnerships had *ad hoc* co-ordination; it was dominated by the tensions and conflicts between pre-existing interests and political relationships; it proliferated administrative machinery out of all proportion to both the range of tasks and its capacity (power and resources) to resolve problems; and it generated only a modest degree of innovation (primarily through the centre's commitment to wealth generation). To substantiate this assessment, the experience of partnership in Liverpool will be described, followed by a general survey of the problems of ICPP.

4.7.2(iii) PARTNERSHIP IN LIVERPOOL

Liverpool 'has been the recipient, or victim, of every urban experiment invented' (Parkinson, 1985, p. 16). It was not exempted from ICPP, and the problems which had dogged all earlier experiments promptly beset this latest initiative. Parkinson and Wilks (1983a) identify three features of the local political context which compounded the problems of ICPP. First, Liverpool has an intensely competitive local party system, and between 1974 and 1983 no party was able to command an overall majority; the largest party when in power, be it Liberal or Labour, has adopted an assertive style. Second, the local authority's internal structure has been characterized by a high degree of departmentalism and competition between departments. Moreover, political uncertainty allowed officers considerable scope to shape the ICPP. The problem of bureaucratic politics was further compounded by disputes and by open conflict between Liverpool (the district council) and Merseyside (the county council). Finally, Liverpool had a history of poor relations with its large and vociferous voluntary sector. Neither politicians nor officials welcomed the involvement of the community and the voluntary sector in ICPP, and relations were distant when they were not strained.

The problems emerged at the outset with discussions over the appropriate organizational framework. There were differences of opinion on all sides, between the city and the county, the DoE, the AHA and the voluntary sector. For example, the DoE wanted Liverpool to establish an Inner City Unit. The authority did not want one, arguing that it would be an additional, politically powerless, bureaucratic layer and fearing such a unit would compete with the departments for resources. Equally, the DoE thought that Liverpool's organizational arrangements were too geared to departmental, rather than inner city, issues. Relations between county and district were further strained by the former's claim to be the economic planning authority for the conurbation. An inter-authority committee chaired by a junior DoI minister failed to clarify their respective roles. Eventually the county ceased to play a major role, and the two authorities submitted separate bids to the Partnership Committee. And these disputes occurred even though the issue was depoliticized. The key participants in the ICPP machinery were officials, and there was a clear consensus amongst senior politicians that, if Liverpool was to benefit from the funds, the issue had to be protected from the uncertainty of party politics.

Apart from the Partnership Committee, the organizational structure of Liverpool ICPP was limited. It comprised a special subcommittee of its Policy and Finance Committee along with six departmental working groups co-ordinated by an Officers' Steering Group. This departmental bias was reflected in the programme, which initially lacked a coherent strategy and was a set of bids for funds from the major service departments. However, as it evolved, the economy and the physical environment became the dual focal points of Liverpool's strategy. Consequently, the Treasurer's Department (and its specially created Industrial Development Agency) and the Planning Department (and its Environmental Planning Unit) became the organizational linchpins of Liverpool's ICPP, attracting the bulk of the funds. In 1980 all the working groups, with the exception of an economy group, were abolished, and by 1982 the ICPP had virtually no organizational infrastructure. Bids were made by departments, processed by an *ad hoc* chief officers' group and forwarded to the DoE by the Inner Area Subcommittee. The Partnership Committee met as infrequently as once a year. Participation by any other affected parties was minimal, and the city assiduously resisted pressure from community and voluntary groups to be involved. No other partnership gives so few funds to the voluntary sector.

It is difficult to demur from Parkinson and Wilks's (1983a) conclusion that 'Partnership had been stripped to its bare essentials – and is now a vehicle for spending funds.' With the advent of the Conservative government and the Toxteth riots, the institutions of partnership became 'perhaps even more redundant'. The government's priorities for funding were already the core of Liverpool's strategy; other initiatives such as UDCs, EZs and the Task Force marginalized ICPP and shifted initiatives on to ministers. The current arrangements are '*ad hoc* and incoherent in nature, in many respects sub-optimal' and they have fostered 'local disenchantment'.

For all this disenchantment, however, ICPP account for 10 per cent of the city's budget. The distribution of these funds between projects clearly demonstrates that the priority was to arrest the economic decline of Liverpool. In 1979–80 a broad range of projects was supported, although the bulk of funds, 63 per cent or £7.7 million, were allocated to the economy, housing and the physical environment. By 1982–3, 73 per cent of a total allocation of some £23 million was spent on the economy, the environment and housing. In fact, there had been little new expenditure on social and other projects in earlier years, the bulk of their funds being accounted for by previous commitments. In 1982–3 this expenditure was increased, in part because of 'underspending' on the economy projects. The city provided grants for investment in production, area improvement grants, grants for the development of premises and security grants. The take-up rates on these grants was sluggish as it was for factory units built under the partnership – hence the underspending, to the tune of 50 per cent in 1981–2. Judging from the experience of Liverpool, if inner cities policy was mere symbolism as alleged by many critics, 'the gap between the rhetoric and the reality of inner city policy has become so huge . . . as to cast doubt upon even the symbolic value of the policy for central government' (Parkinson and Wilks, 1983a): a conclusion which immediately poses the question of whether or not the Liverpool experience was unique.

Unfortunately, a survey of the remaining partnerships suggests that the overall assessment must remain essentially pessimistic. Parkinson and Wilks' (1983a) analysis of the spending priorities of the partnerships demonstrates three important points. First, total funding was small. Second, expenditure reflects predictable priorities with the emphasis on capital schemes, physical development, local authority services (rather than the voluntary sector) and, latterly, economic activity. There is little evidence of innovative policies from either central or local government. Finally, given this restricted policy agenda, there is little evidence of conformity to central guidelines. To oversimplify, Newcastle/Gateshead had a dual strategy focused on housing (including housing management) and economic development (through site provision). Liverpool, as we have seen, focused on economy projects and environmental works. Birmingham emphasized private housing improvements and social projects (involving the voluntary sector). Manchester/Salford opted for the voluntary sector and culture/recreation projects. Finally, in London, the two partnerships combined social projects with economic initiatives which emphasized training and employment generation. In short, 'central control' coexisted with local variation in service delivery. But if there was local policy variation, the partnerships are characterized by shared policy problems, especially in the operation of the partnership machinery. Both Parkinson and Wilks (1983a) and Stewart, Whitting and Underwood (1983) have concluded that ICPP generated limited inter-organizational collaboration and co-ordination, had a minimal role as a forum of interest mediation, did not act as a catalyst for institutional change and fostered little policy innovation. At this stage such a broad characterization of the failure of ICPP needs to be broken down into its constituent problems. (The following draws on an excellent summary of ICPP problems in Stewart, 1983a; but see also Stewart, Whitting and Underwood, 1983, s. 6.)

First, ICPP were dominated by administration and repeated the experience of other PPSs (see Chapter 3, section 3.2.4(ii)). Thus, the ambition and complexity of the planning system call to mind Wildavsky's (1969, p. 193) comment on the Planning Programming Budgeting System (PPBS) that 'the main problem with PPBS is that no-one knows how to do it; or rather many know what it should be like in general, but no-one knows what it should be like in any particular case'. ICPP rapidly became a traditional bid-allocation grant system which focused on specific projects rather than policies, procedures rather than strategy and the UP rather than major programmes. In a similar vein Leach (1982a, pp. 147–54) summarizes the defects of the planning system as over-ambition, a lack of coherent strategies, no diagnostic capacity, detailed project control and institutional complexity. He also points to the problems posed by ICPP isolation from main programmes, their marginal status for many departments and inconsistency with other policies and sources of funds. The only merits of the planning system were that it gathered information for the centre and, because the system was flexible and open to multiple interpretation, that it afforded the centre considerable scope to manipulate relations with its partners and placed few constraints on the centre's capacity to change the rules of the game at will. As Stewart, Whitting and Underwood (1983) conclude, 'partnership was merely a new word for central government involvement in inner city affairs'.

Second, ICPP lacked a unified central approach. This problem has two dimensions: bureaucratic politics and political commitment. At the outset, there was token participation by the range of departments but it was rapidly replaced by indifference. As Parkinson and Wilks (1983a) comment, the (then) Secretary of State for the Environment,

Peter Shore, faced considerable political and bureaucratic problems when his department took control of the policy. He had to fight the battle over ICPP twice with the DoI, during the preparation of the 1977 White Paper and during the preparation of the Inner Urban Areas Act 1978. The DoI simply did not believe in concentrating resources on inner cities. In a similar vein, Shore commented that the DES 'just couldn't see it; its contribution was EPAs, and it saw no need for further action. The DHSS had its Resource Allocation Working Party to correct regional resource disparities and did not consider inner cities to be worse off than other areas. With the commitment of central departments so variable, the prospects of improved co-ordination and for bending main programmes were slight indeed. They were non-existent when the political commitment of ministers evaporated. Inner cities policy has been punctuated by short-term surges of narrow political (self-) interest, followed by longer-term indifference. Consequently, there has been no sustained pressure to overcome departmental obstacles at the centre. Short-term political interest has encouraged, if anything, the perception of inner cities policy as mere tokenism and the belief that 'if you keep you head down it will pass you by'. The vaunted cross-departmental evaluation of central government policies on urban deprivation remained a pious hope, exacerbating local authority disillusionment with ICPP.

Third, local authorities reacted conservatively to the initiative, treating it as a source of additional funds for existing departments and policies. The aspiration of selective, redistributive and innovatory policies crumbled under the impact of departmental and professional rivalry. In consequence, local authorities allocated funds to meet pre-existing needs and projects, did not review the contribution of their main programmes to urban deprivation and subordinated the new procedures and structures to existing decision-making processes. The objective of ICPP has become to extract as much money as possible out of the UP.

Fourth, the contribution of a range of other public sector bodies has been marginalized. In Stewart, Whitting and Underwood's (1983) phrase, their role in the partnership was 'analogous to a bring and buy sale'; they came along to see if there was anything of value and then drifted away. AHAs have provided inner city health centres. The MSC has become involved in training and work experience programmes. But even such confined contributions have decreased as the emphasis on economic activity became more prominent.

Fifth, ICCP have had a spasmodic and, at times, unsatisfactory relationship with the non-statutory and private sectors. Involvement of the community did not materialize in some partnerships. Overall, the voluntary sector accounts for some 15 per cent of UP funds, but this relationship is a highly dependent one. Voluntary groups have

tailored projects to local authority guidelines and funding criteria
and are vulnerable to any changes in policy and/or expenditure cuts.
Both voluntary groups and the private sector pose the same
problem: who should be consulted on what and by which means?
The major difference is that the private sector is not dependent on
partnership funding, and the important examples of co-operation are
outside the partnerships (for example, FIG and Urban Development
Grants).

Finally, ICCP have been a policy without content. They are perhaps
best characterized as a 'meta-policy' (Dror, 1968, p. 8) or a policy
about making policies, in this case in housing, education and the
environment, amongst others. In the absence of interdepartmental
co-operation and a review of major programmes, the ensuing vacuum
was filled by an essentially *ad hoc* series of local responses. Latterly, it
has been filled by a narrow concern with local economic development,
with varying degrees of emphasis. But, as Edwards and Batley (1978,
appendix 1) argued before ICPP had got off the ground, inner policy
will not succeed if main programme departments do not change their
priorities and in the absence of any definition of the policy goals for
the inner city. Neither condition is met by ICPP, which remain a policy
without either content or impact on inner city problems. The initiative
has merely succeeded in reinforcing traditional central–local
relationships, and the elaborate partnership machinery has become
unnecessary and/or inconvenient. The response of the Conservative
government has been to bypass, once again, existing instruments and
to diversify the institutions it employs. The proverbial moving finger
'has writ' (small) and moved on. The causes and consequences of this
outcome remain to be considered.

4.7.3   Conclusions: Partnerships as an Issue Network

There are many reasons for the continuing failure of inner city policy.
Perhaps the most fundamental problem concerns problem definition.
As Edwards and Batley (1978, p. 239) conclude, 'the ... social
construction of the social (and physical) problems to which the label
"urban deprivation" has been attached is too inadequate and imprecise to provide a goal or target for clear and *effective* programmes or
policies'. If, as Wildavsky (1980, p. 17) argues, policy analysis is 'an
activity creating problems that can be solved', inner cities policy is an
example of creating solutions to a problem that has never been clearly
defined. The 1977 White Paper shifted the focus from social pathology
to structural factors with its call for economic regeneration of the inner
city but, and crucially, it retained the small area focus. Edwards and
Batley (1978, pp. 249–51) argue that the notion of urban deprivation
needs to be disaggregated into those problems which can be tackled by
national, broad-based policies and those which might be amenable to

an area-based approach. The White Paper fails to make such a discrimination:

> To the extent that effective action on inner cities may require national policies (be it on housing, education, employment etc.), these will not be possible within the partnership arrangements which, by their very nature, continue to conceive of inner-city problems as *local* problems.
>
> (Edwards and Batley, 1978, p. 248)

In a similar vein, Hall and Diamond (1981, p. 132) conclude that SSRC's survey of the inner city and its problems with the categorical assertion that the inner city is *not* 'the most helpful research focus'. Rather, 'Inner cities can best be understood as phenomena resulting from underlying forces in the British economy and society.' None the less, the Conservatives retained the small area focus and, in their preoccupation with local economic development, adopted a narrow definition of the problem which has 'diverted attention from some of the more intransigent problems of inner areas – long term unemployment, poverty, the impact of cuts in public services – and allowed distributional issues to be largely left on one side' (Stewart, Whitting and Underwood, 1983). In sum, from inception to date, inner cities policy has been undermined by the inability of successive governments to state 'precisely what it is that is of social concern' (Edwards and Batley, 1978, p. 249).

A second problem concerns the scale of resources 'thrown' at the problem, however defined. It has been trivial compared to both the size of the problem and the money spent on mainstream programmes. The problem has been exacerbated by the reduction in other sources of financial support. For example, between 1980–1 local authorities generally had a 13 per cent reduction in grant (in constant prices). In partnership authorities the average reduction was 25 per cent (Parkinson and Wilks, 1983b, p. 36). The relatively small amount of money available coupled with cuts in block grant and the imposition of penalties and rate capping all encourage the view that ICPP are a case of symbolic politics and breed disillusionment at the local level.

Third, this disillusionment is fostered also by the variable political commitment of the centre. Be it minister or civil servant, there is little evidence of sustained determination to solve the problem and considerable evidence of political opportunism in the way that inner cities moved up and down the political agenda. It would seem that the centre accepts that there is little chance of regenerating inner city economies (Pahl, 1978) but publicly rejects this 'defeatism' (Leach, 1982a, p. 22) for fear of its political unacceptability and the implications for public order. Moreover, the reluctance of local authorities to review their major programmes, the sporadic nature of community involvement, the depoliticized nature of partnerships and the ease with which departmentalism won the day all suggest that political commitment at the local level was, at best, difficult to sustain.

Finally, and of greatest importance in the present context, inner cities policy floundered around the fringes of the mainstream programmes beset by the vicissitudes of bureaucratic politics. Or, to employ the terminology of policy networks, ICPP were an attempt to create an issue network which failed because they did not have a distinct domain, were isolated from key policy networks and could not integrate the disparate interests involved.

From their inception, ICPP were surrounded by bureaucratic conflicts at both the central and local level, and to describe ICPP as a policy without content is simply to use different words for the failure to establish domain consensus. Moreover, the attempt to build an issue network with its own domain faced a major obstacle; as defined, inner city policy cut across the boundaries of existing, function-specific policy networks. At one and the same time to seek to 'invade' established jurisdictions and to create a multi-functional network was to fly in the face of entrenched features of British government. The necessary pre-conditions for a new network are a discrete function which is not currently part of someone else's domain. It is no surprise, therefore, that ICPP reverted to type, becoming a traditional central–local relationship focused on a DoE-specific grant and isolated from the other networks.

This outcome is totally predictable from the range of interests which, potentially, could have been members of the inner cities issue network. Table 4.1 provides a summary listing and also indicates the potential for conflict between the several parties. Clearly, partnerships were an exercise in institution building, aimed at creating a network, which lacked the necessary convergence of interests or structure of incentives (and sanctions) to generate such convergence. The DoE lacked the allies in the centre necessary to integrate inner cities to the range of public policies, and had active opponents (the DoI). It did not involve agencies in the design of the policy, thereby ignoring one set of potential supporters and creating the impression that it was imposing the policy. Nor was there an established profession, with an integrating ideology, able to straddle the participating organizations. The absence of professional influence provided scope for local variation in defining the new policy. It also handicapped the incipient network as it sought to establish domain consensus, especially when confronted by policy communities and professionalized networks. Finally, the resources available were simply inadequate to buy the compliance of other networks. Without the active co-operation of existing networks, the services of which were central to any strategy to combat urban deprivation, ICPP were doomed to the status of an *ad hoc* marginal initiative. Indeed, it is doubtful that

Table 4.1 *Organizational and Departmental Stances to Inner City Partnerships*

Organizational unit	Orientation to financial resources	Orientation to authority	Political or professional ideology	Other comments
DoE ministers	Maximization of PES allocation for Urban Programme (subject to comparison with competing DoE priorities)	Maximization of influence on (a) partnership strategies (to 1979) (b) programme content (since 1979)	Input of current party political values into programmes	Change in 1979 from major political priority within DoE to minor one
DoE Inner City Directorate	Maximization of PES allocation for Urban Programme; maximization of proportion of allocation actually spent	Maximization of influence on major policy and procedural aspects of programmes	Ensuring that programmes reflect ministerial priorities, and are of a 'high quality' technically	Decrease in priority within ICD since 1979 reflecting above changes
Other central government departments	If providing 'contributions' to UP, ensuring adequate level of UP expenditure on 'appropriate' projects	Protection of departmental policies and programmes from 'outside' evaluation	Input of (professionally based) departmental problem perceptions and solutions into programme	Some departments on balance hostile (e.g. DoI); others 'mildly supportive' (e.g. DES, DHSS)
DoE Regional Office	Maximization of Urban Programme allocation to 'their region' Maximization of proportion of allocation actually spent	Establishment of maximum 'area of discretion' for Regional Offices; exploitation (in both directions) of role as two-way communication channel	Ensuring that programmes reflect ministerial priorities *and* local circumstances and are of a 'high quality' technically	Recent importance of demonstrating a 'regional role' when Regional Office organization is under review
Local political élite (District)	Maximization of UP allocation to their district; ensuring the maintenance of an orderly, predictable flow of resources	Minimization of 'outside' interference in and evaluation of the district part of the programme	Input of current party political values into programme	'Financial resources' provided have become more important as RSG level declines

Local political élite (County)	Securing an adequate level of resources and the maintenance thereof	As above	As above (though values may imply *not* using extra resources provided by UP)	'Financial resources' marginal; protecting programme seen as more important than maximizing resources
Inner City Unit	Maximization of resource allocation to 'their partnership'; maintenance of an orderly predictable flow of UP resources	Establishment of maximum area of discretion for Inner City Unit (esp. *vis-à-vis* service department input)	Development of a high quality, innovative 'corporate' programme document	The only piece of machinery 'speaking for the partnership'; networking ability, and access to local political élites important
'Established' service department	Opportunistic securing of resources for particular projects	Protection of existing programmes and policies against 'outside' evaluation	Input of (professionally based) departmental problem perceptions and solutions into programme	Financial resources relatively unimportant; threats to authority may result in effective withdrawal
'Fringe' service department	Maximization of share of UP allocation within partnership ('the new LDs')	Maximization of influence on relevant content of partnership programme	As above	Financial resources relatively *important*; prepared to concede authority for financial resources
Area Health Authority	Opportunistic securing of resources for particular projects	Protection of existing programme and policies against 'outside' evaluation	As above	Financial resources relatively insignificant; priority given to partnership is *low*
'Private sector' (e.g. Chamber of Commerce)	Opportunistic securing of resources, private investment in appropriate circumstances	Maximization of 'strings attached' to private sector support projects; protection of private interests	Input of 'private enterprise' values into programmes	Doubts about relevance of partnership and competence of local authorities; *low* priority given.
'Voluntary Sector' (e.g. Local CVS)	Maximization of voluntary sector share of UP resources	Establishment of maximum influence on strategy content and resource allocation procedures of programme	Input of 'community self-help' and 'community action' values	weak bargaining position; often internal differences; ultimately money of more significance than authority

any initiative which is not based on the major services and their networks could succeed in transforming the fate of the inner cities.

This discussion of the causes of the failure of ICPP has emphasized the constraints on the centre's ability to build an inner cities issue network and competition with established policy networks. It must be stressed immediately, therefore, that networks are only one component of an adequate explanation. It is the *combination* of inadequate problem definition, lack of resources, intermittent political commitment and network competition which undermined ICPP. The consequences of this failure are all too obvious.

First, the economic and social decline has continued apace. The multiple causes of this trend are not of immediate concern. The central point is that inner cities policy has not succeeded in slowing down, let alone stopping or reversing, the trend because the scale of funding was minimal and because other government policies, most notably on local authority expenditure, diverted resources away from the urban areas at a greater rate than ICPP put them in. It also fostered disillusionment with central policy, breeding the very 'defeatism' it was said to counter, and fuelling the conflict between centre and locality and, in all probability, within the inner cities. If Liverpool is the exemplar of this process (Parkinson, 1985), it is by no means unique.

Second, in response to this failure, the Conservative government has sought to involve the private sector and bypassed existing institutions in the process. The heart of its policy lies not in the partnerships but in UDCs, EZs, FIG and the like. The fate of earlier rounds of *ad hoc* initiatives and bodies – even if concerned, as in this case, with local economic development rather than social pathologies – does not augur well for the future. The most probable outcome is an ever more complex system, characterized by both competition for jurisdiction and contradictory policy effects. Inner cities policy becomes ever more isolated from the mainstream programmes and networks as the instruments purporting to reverse the decline of the cities become ever more diverse.

Finally, the focus on measures to generate wealth and make the cities attractive to investors has been at the expense of distributive policies. ICPP failed to 'bend' the expenditure priorities of the major welfare services, providing only 'topping-up' expenditure in these service areas, and even this contribution has declined progressively with the advent of local economic development. The combination of a net resource loss, bypassing and wealth generation compels the conclusion that ICPP have done nothing to arrest the social inequalities in the inner city and, by diverting attention away from the role of the major welfare state services, in all probability have accelerated the rate of social and economic decline.

4.8 Conclusions

Chapter 3 provided an introduction to the range of actors in SCG. This chapter has identified the trends in central–SCG relations in a range of policy areas and sought to demonstrate the utility of the concept of 'policy networks' for understanding these trends. It has presented a series of case studies of the actors, especially the policy networks, 'in action'. Each of the foregoing sections has its own conclusions, and another summary would be repetitive. It remains to discuss, therefore, the extent to which the data are congruent with the theoretical concerns of Chapter 2. This task is the concern of the final chapter, Chapter 5.

Notes

1 This section draws upon Jackson, 1982b, 1984 and 1985b, and I would like to thank Peter Jackson for allowing me to use his material.

2 This section draws upon Rhodes, 1984 and 1986a, and Davies *et al.*, 1983. I would like to thank John Stewart for allowing me to paraphrase the report.

3 This section draws upon Rhodes, 1986a, and Ranson, 1980 and 1982. My thanks to Stewart Ranson for allowing me to paraphrase his research.

4 This section draws upon Ranson, 1982 and 1984. I would like to thank Stewart Ranson for allowing me to paraphrase his material.

5 This section draws upon Crispin and Marslen-Wilson, 1984 and 1986. My thanks to Alan Crispin for allowing me to use his material.

6 This section draws upon Heald, 1980b, 1982 and 1983, and paraphrases Midwinter, 1984. I would like to thank Arthur Midwinter for allowing me to use his research, and a special thank-you to Arthur Midwinter and Michael Keating for so promptly answering multitudinous requests for information, off-prints and clarification.

7 Ideally this account should have also included Wales, but it had to be excluded because of the lack of data. For *brief* accounts of central–local financial relations in Wales see James, 1982 and 1983; Goldsmith, 1984; Rhodes, 1986a (ch. 7). General accounts of the finances of Northern Ireland can be found in Lawrence, 1965; Kilbrandon Commission, 1973; Birrell and Murie, 1980. On central–local financial relations in Northern Ireland see Connolly, 1983. I would like to thank Michael Connolly for allowing me to use his research and for updating the financial statistics for me.

8 This section is based upon Wistow, 1985; Wistow and Hardy, 1985 and 1986; Webb, Wistow and Hardy, 1986; Wistow and Fuller, 1986; supplemented by Webb and Wistow, 1980, 1981, 1982a and b, 1983 and 1985a and b. I would like to thank Adrian Webb and Gerald Wistow for giving me permission to paraphrase their research and Brian Hardy for answering patiently my many requests for additional information. A version of this section, co-authored with Gerald Wistow, will appear in *Public Administration*, vol. 66 (1988). On the postwar history of the NHS see Eckstein, 1958; Willcocks, 1967; Brown, 1979; Pater, 1981; Klein, 1983. On the postwar history of the PSS see Younghusband, 1978, and Cooper, 1983.

9 For general accounts of these several initiatives see Allsop, 1984, and Levitt and Wall, 1984. On planning see Haywood and Alaszewski, 1980, and Glennerster, 1983. On collaboration and joint finance see Booth, 1981; Norton and Rogers, 1981; Wistow, 1982 and 1983; Wistow and Hardy, 1985.

10 On the face of it, there seems to be a contradiction between the discussion of 'sub-communities' within health and the institutionalization of professional

influence. Although there is a conspicuous lack of evidence, it can be speculated that network disaggregation can be tolerated because there is a consensus around the mechanistic model of health. The health policy network is ideologically integrated, permitting a degree of disaggregation which would undermine other types of policy network.

11 For a more detailed account of all these bodies see Rhodes, 1986a (ch. 3). This book is the major source for the discussion of intergovernmental networks. See also Rhodes, 1983, 1985b and c.

12 The term 'reorganization' means, in practice, alterations to the boundaries of local authorities and the reallocation of functions between local authorities. It is used here in the restricted sense. The major studies of the 1972 reorganization include: Robson, 1966; Brand, 1974; Richards, 1975; Isaac-Henry, 1975 and 1980b; Wood, 1976; Keith-Lucas and Richards, 1978; Dearlove, 1979; Pearce, 1980; Ashford, 1982. On 'organic change' see Rhodes, 1986a (ch. 6); and on abolition of the GLC and the Metropolitan Councils see Forrester, Lansley and Pauley, 1985, and Flynn, Leach and Vielba, 1985.

13 Hogwood, 1979c (p. 18) comments on the lack of literature on industrial policy, and Young 1984 (p. 41), whilst demonstrating that the material on specific industries is voluminous, concludes that 'the political science contribution to the literature is very limited, and there are enormous gaps'. In particular, overviews of the institutions constitute a 'glaring gap' (p. 130), and whilst there are a number of accounts of the development of industrial policy in the postwar period, Young concludes it is a category II topic, i.e. 'limited coverage of the whole subject' (p. 131). See, for example, Grove, 1962; Young and Lowe, 1974; Blackaby, 1978a; M. Stewart, 1977; Hogwood, 1979a; Smith, 1979; Coates, 1980; Grant, 1982. For a more complete list of sources see Young, 1984 (pp. 475–9).

14 This section is based on Davies and Mason, 1981a and 1981b, and Davies, Mason and Davies, 1984. My thanks to Tom Davies, Charlie Mason and Liz Davies for allowing me to paraphrase their research. The case study has been 'anonymized' at the authors' request.

15 The evolution of inner cities policy has been well documented, and useful surveys can be found in Edwards and Batley, 1978; Lawless, 1979; McKay and Cox, 1979; Loney, 1983. Specific quotations apart, section 4.7.1 draws upon Leach, 1982a; sections 4.7.2(i) and (ii) upon Leach, 1982a, and Stewart, Whitting and Underwood, 1983; section 4.7.2(iii) upon Parkinson and Wilks, 1983a; section 4.7.3 upon all three reports. I would like to thank Steve Leach, Michael Parkinson, Murray Stewart, Gil Whitting, Stephen Wilks and Jacky Underwood for allowing me to paraphrase their unpublished work. Parkinson and Wilks, 1983a; and Stewart, Whitting and Underwood, 1983, are not serially paginated, and therefore all page references have been omitted.

CHAPTER 5

The Differentiated Polity: Relationships, Consequences and Contradictions

Introduction. Comparing policy networks. Relationships – explaining the development of SCG: 1945–61 (stability, growth *apolitisme*), 1961–74 ('stop-go', modernization, protest), 1974–9 (instability, economic decline, incorporation), 1979–85 (economic recession, control, politicization). The consequences of differentiation: stability, effectiveness, complexity, equity, accountability. Contradictions in the centreless society – unitary state versus differentiated polity.

5.1 Introduction

Quite obviously, the primary objective of this chapter is to draw strings together. To be precise, it will provide a summary explanation of: the varieties of network, their relationships and their outcomes; and the consequences both of networks and of central policies towards SCG. Finally, I return to the general themes of Chapter 1 and contrast the unitary state and differentiated polity models of British government. Given the volume of material which has been presented on these topics already, a brief summary will be useful, and it is provided in Table 5.1. It covers the types of policy network; the major sub-central actors in each case study/network; their resources; the distinctive characteristics of each network; their changing relationships in the postwar period; and the distinctive policy outcomes associated with each type of network. In short, the table omits all the detail and provides the skeletal structure of the analysis of actors and policy networks. The chapter concentrates on the general task of relating this material to the theoretical discussion. In so doing, the discussion parallels Table 5.1, moving from policy networks to changing relationships and, finally, to the consequences of these changes.

Table 5.1 Policy Networks: Characteristics, Relationships and Outcomes – a Summary

Types of network →	Policy communities		Territorial communities	Professionalized networks	Inter-governmental networks	Producer networks	Issue networks
Case studies →	Finance	Education	Finance	Care in the community	Local government reorganization	Redundancies	Inner city partnerships
Types of SCG							
Territorial ministries							
Intermediate institutions			X			X	X
Non-departmental public bodies							
Public Corporations						X	X
NHS				X			
Fringe (executive)		X				X	X
Local government	X	X	X	X	X	X	X
Network characteristics							
Constellation of interests	Guardian-topocratic	Service-technocratic	Territorial	Service-technocratic	Type of authority-party	Economic	Diverse
Membership	Exclusive (central bureaucratic/political élites)	Restricted (dual closure)	Informal-inclusive	Restricted (professional closure)	Restricted (political parties/public interest groups)	Broad	Broad

Vertical inter-dependence	Low	High	Low	High	Low	High	Low
Horizontal inter-dependence	High	Low	High	Low	High	Low	Low
Resources (of SCG)							
Authority	X						
Money	X	X	X	X		X	
Legitimacy		X	X	X	X		
Information		X			X		
Organization							X
Relationships							
1945–61	Loose-coupling	Bureaucratic	Loose-coupling	*Laissez-faire*	*Immobilisme*	Non-intervention	Technical-professional
1961–74	Bargaining	Bargaining	Bargaining	Formalized collaboration	Bureaucratic-formal consultative	Selective intervention	Experimental
1974–9	Incorporation	Regulatory	Technical	Incentives	Informal consultative	Regulation	Partnership
1979 to date	Bureaucratic	Bureaucratic	Bureaucratic	Insulation	Bureaucratic	Deregulation	Bypassing
Outcomes	Policy mess wherein 'the strong survive'	Inertia protecting institutionalized interests and reinforcing existing class differences	Territorial equity and context-specific policies	Professional dominance and territorial inequity	Aggregation reinforcing technocratic domination	*Ad hoc* interventionism to protect economic interests	Continued economic/social deterioration

Note:
The entries for each category are *not* comprehensive but identify the *distinctive* type of SCG, network characteristics, resources and outcomes.

5.2 Comparing Policy Networks

The key test of the claim made herein for a focus on policy networks lies in the ability of the concept to distinguish systematically between a range of policies. As Table 5.1 demonstrates, it passes the test. The six types of network are clearly distinguished from each other by the five dimensions of constellation of interests, membership, vertical interdependence, horizontal interdependence and resources. In addition, these variations in network characteristics are associated with distinct patterns of relationships and outcomes. Moreover, the 'test cases' of producer and issue networks reinforce, rather than detract from, the claim. They demonstrate that a low degree of integration generates many problems for effective government action. They also point to a conundrum. Effective action presupposes means for involving the interdependent parties. Without such means – the policy network – central intervention is *ad hoc* and ineffective. But creating policy networks imposes a range of constraints on the centre whereby unilateral central action within a network also renders policy ineffective. Helpless with, and hopeless without, policy networks, the centre seeks to avoid being a stranger in a strange land without becoming a prisoner of the very means of assimilation. Like many a migrant before it, the centre has found that establishing peaceful relations and maintaining one's identity are difficult if not impossible goals to reconcile. To forsake similes, the analysis of policy networks identifies a key contradiction of the differentiated polity: executive authority versus interdependence (see section 5.5, below).

The a priori grounds for focusing on networks were identified in Chapter 2, section 2.5.2. The evidence was presented in Chapter 4 and is summarized in Table 5.1. Without repeating an already long discussion, therefore, the case for policy networks must now rest. It will be more productive to switch to the limitations of this focus.

First, the data drawn upon in Chapter 4 was not collected to test explicitly the ideas in Chapter 2. I have reinterpreted research carried out for a variety of reasons. Because all the projects were part of the same ESRC research initiative, there is considerable common ground, and the reinterpretation should not strain credulity, although it may test the patience of my fellow researchers. The procedure remains inherently unsatisfactory, however, and it explains one important omission. With only one exception, the case studies treat central departments as the heart of policy networks. In reality, the heart of a network will be a division of a department, and each department will be part of several networks. Only the case study of the NHS/PSS and the mentally handicapped presented any data on the range of networks associated with a department, but the phenomenon is by no means restricted to the DHSS. Unfortunately no other project explored central departments in the requisite detail. Consequently, the problems of fragmentation and co-ordination within the centre are understated. Future research will need to disaggregate departments into their component networks.

Second, the concept of policy networks was developed for the study of central–local government relations. It continues to display its origins, with the case material having a marked bias towards the welfare state services. It remains probable that the concept has its greatest utility for services in which the organizational professions are influential. In spite of the material on the inner cities and the NI, the utility of policy networks for analysing relationships between economic producer groups and governments remains to be demonstrated.

Third, the data on the national local government system, both its operation and influence, are sporadic. There is some evidence that local authorities follow national trends; that such trends are not determined by the centre; and that bounding institutions, such as the Audit Commission, can be prominent in setting the broad parameters to local action. The existence of a national local government system is a plausible speculation, but considerably more evidence is required before it can be treated as an established feature of IGR. In particular, the influence of the bounding institutions would repay further study.

Finally, and crucially, to claim that the concept of policy networks is an important tool is *not* to claim that it is the only tool. To argue that network characteristics influence relationships and outcomes is *not* to claim that they are the only relevant variable. The concept has been emphasized to establish its utility, not its primacy. It is one of a range of factors which has shaped central–SCG relations in the postwar period. As argued in Chapter 2, policy networks represent the meso-level of analysis. The major defect of this discussion is that it has isolated networks both from the national government environment (the macro-level) and from actors and organizations (the micro-level). When considered in isolation, the analysis of policy networks begs many questions. Most important, it does not explain why and how the rules of the game and patterns of relationships have changed. To confront this issue, it is necessary to place networks in their larger context. The next section explores changes in the national government environment and their effect on relationships with SCG.

5.3 Relationships: Explaining the Development of SCG

Changes in the national government environment fall into four distinct phases in the postwar period: 1945–61 was an era of stable external support system, economic and welfare state growth and *apolitisme*; 1961–74 was an era of 'stop-go', modernization, and territorial protest; 1974–9 was an era of an unstable external support system, economic decline and incorporation; and 1979–85 was an era of economic recession, bureaucratic control and politicization.[1]

5.3.1   *1945–61: Stability, Growth,* Apolitisme

Strictly speaking, the years 1945–51 should be treated as the era of postwar reconstruction and the subsequent decade as one of growth. Any such division on economic grounds masks, however, other substantial continuities; with the benefit of hindsight the era is significant for what did not happen. Nationalist parties were conspicuous only for their electoral weakness. The seeds of civil unrest in Northern Ireland were being sown by the Unionists, but the crop had yet to be reaped. Conflict between central and local government was spasmodic and had a certain novelty value. If any concern was expressed it focused on the loss of functions by local government and the growing dependence of local authorities on central grant; the perennial cry of centralization yet again rent the air (e.g. Robson, 1948). None the less, the era has a number of features of considerable significance.

First, the period was one of external stability, low unemployment, low inflation and relatively high growth rates. This economic surplus provided the means, whilst the central élite ideology provided the motive, to create the welfare state, and local government was to be the prime vehicle for the delivery of its services. Central departments in Britain were and have remained non-executant units of government. They have 'hands-off' control of such major services as housing, education and welfare. Thus, if the period 1961–74 was to see the rate of growth accelerate, this period sees the foundations being dug for that development.

Second, the arrival of government intervention and the welfare state in Northern Ireland sowed further seeds of discontent. Stormont may have been a reluctant interventionist, the welfare state may have failed to redistribute resources to those in greatest need, but both posed in acute form questions of relative deprivation (Arthur, 1984, p. 83) long before the Civil Rights Movement. The contrasting levels of affluence of the mainland and the Province, of Protestant and Catholic, coupled with rising expectations about entitlements, served to emphasize the fragility of devolution.

The third major development was the increasing use by government of *ad hoc* agencies, or non-departmental public bodies. The best known of these agencies is, of course, the National Health Service, but the period also saw the removal of public utilities from local government and the creation of the nationalized industries (e.g. gas, electricity).

Fourth, the period saw the increasing prominence of professionals – not as powerful interest groups lobbying government but as part of the

structure of government; they became institutionalized. The account-
ants, lawyers, engineers and public health inspectors consolidated
their position, and teachers, social workers and planners arrived on
the scene. For the most part, career advancement was solely within
the public sector, and professions, work organization and the departments of local government were identical. The expansion of the
welfare state went hand in hand with the extension of professional
influence (see, for example, Lee, 1963) and the emergence of functional politics.

Fifth, central funding of local services was 'consolidated'. In
1946–7, 24 per cent of central funding was in the form of general
grants: that is, money *not* assigned to specific services. By 1961, this
figure had risen to 68 per cent (G. Rhodes, 1976, p. 155). And yet,
one would expect the central departments with responsibilities for
particular services to resist such an erosion of their influence – and
indeed the (then) Ministry of Education did oppose such consolidation in 1929 (Martlew, 1983, pp. 135–8). Central resistance to block
or general grants evaporated in this period because 'other constraints
on local government emerged in Britain alongside the growth in the
grant system, so that specific grants became less necessary in the
influencing of local service delivery' (Page, 1981, p. 22). These
constraints include the development of the legal framework of services; the vertical coalition of professionals in central and local
government with shared values about (and responses to) service
delivery; and finally the creation of vested interests by the specific
grant so that producers *and* consumers support service expenditure
(Page, 1981, p. 23; Martlew, 1983, pp. 144–5).

Sixth, the period is distinguished by *apolitisme* (Bulpitt, 1983,
p. 150). There are a number of strands to this argument. First, party
colonization of sub-central politics was incomplete, and, for example,
the numerous *ad hoc* agencies were subject to otiose forms of
accountability. Second, a substantial proportion of local councils were
controlled by 'Independents', not the political parties. Third, the
incursion of party politics into local government was resented and
resisted; after all, 'there's only one way to build a road'. Fourth, even
when the parties did control local authorities, there was little difference between them, and control could be purely nominal with little or
no impact over and beyond the election. Decision-making was the
preserve of committee chairmen and chief officers. Above all, IGR
were characterized by professional-bureaucratic brokerage and the
relative weakness of political linkages between centre and periphery.
(For a more detailed discussion see Bulpitt, 1983, pp. 146–55.)

Finally, the interests of the periphery were managed by a strategy of
accommodation. Scottish interests were accommodated by both the
growth of expenditure and the gradual expansion of the functions of
the Scottish Office (Kellas, 1975, pp. 31–40). The same strategy of

economic and administrative growth was applied to local authorities and the Northern Ireland Office, the only exception being Wales. To a significant degree, sub-central and central interests were united in the development of the welfare state and the pursuit of economic growth. The consolidation of functional politics was founded on consensus and quiescence.

5.3.2   1961–74: 'Stop-Go', Modernization, Protest

'The white heat of the technological revolution' did not herald the modernization of the British economy – that lies with the Macmillan-Maudling experiment with planned growth from 1961 – but it provides the era with one of its more potent symbols. Along with the introduction of national planning, regional planning and a new national budgetary process (see Hayward and Watson, 1975; Pollitt, 1977; Blackaby, 1978a) came a more interventionist style of government and extensive reform of the machinery of government at every level. Britain was to be modernized.

And yet consultation and bargaining were the normal style of intergovernmental relations. For most of the period local service spending was buoyant. Central governments of both parties kept an eye out for the electorally damaging implications of any slippage by local government in areas of key importance. For example, slum clearance and rehousing were the major public concerns for most of the 1950s and 1960s, as was the reorganization of secondary schooling from the mid-1960s until the mid-1970s. A whole series of expectations about reasonably consensual dealing between Whitehall and local councils were embodied in the concept of 'partnership'. Ministers often went out of their way to choose modes of implementing policy that maximized voluntary local authority co-operation.

The bargaining phase lasted throughout the Heath government's period of office, despite some selective attempts by the Conservatives to develop more stringent controls. Initially 'lame ducks' were 'to go to the wall' and profitable agencies were 'hived off'. The policies were not long-lived nor did they have a major impact on SCG. With somewhat greater determination, the government forced through changes in council housing finances against strong resistance (including the attempt by the Labour council at Clay Cross in 1972 to refuse implementation of the rent increases imposed). But elsewhere the government was cautious. Sales of council housing were successfully obstructed by all Labour councils. And although a full-scale reorganization of local authorities was put through against much opposition from councils destined to lose many of their powers, the government adopted a two-tier system which was more popular with existing councillors than previous Labour proposals for unitary authorities. Moreover, having decided on the principles of reform, the government was prepared to bargain over such 'details' as the allocation of the planning function. Nowhere is evidence of bargaining clearer than in the determination of the level and allocation of central grant. Through their national representative organizations, local authorities were able to gain small but significant changes in the total and rate of growth of central grant. For local government, therefore, the period witnesses both centrally initiated reform and consultation.

Modernization intensified conflict between central and sub-central units of government. Central intervention provoked confrontations in the fields of education and housing. But given the scale of institutional change, the increase was modest. In part, protest was limited by the pre-existing structure of IGR. Local access to national political élites was relatively weak, whereas professional actors were key advocates of the reform (see Rhodes, 1986a, ch. 6). Perhaps most important, the centre 'factorized' the problem of reform. Thus, there were separate reorganizations of local government in Scotland, England and Wales, London and Northern Ireland: of particular functions (e.g. water, health); and of the centre's decentralized arms (e.g. regional economic planning councils, Welsh Office). At no time was the reform of IGR comprehensively reviewed, and key aspects of the system were ignored altogether (e.g. finance). The central strategy of factorizing encouraged a fragmented response, dampened the level of protest and, in the case of water and health, simply served to reinforce professional dominance. In the case of the nationalized industries, the post-1961 era of commercial freedom had returned many to profitability. The price controls of the Heath government were to return their finances to chaos. The strategy of factorized modernization had few obvious economic benefits.

If this period saw the continued differentiation of functional politics, it also saw major conflicts in the arena of territorial politics. The introduction of direct rule in Northern Ireland in 1972 and the rise of Scottish and Welsh nationalism since 1967 represented a far greater threat to the consensus which had governed territorial politics in Britain.

Explanations of the rise of nationalism abound. The factors which caused the resurgent electoral performance of the SNP include: the decline of the UK economy, loss of confidence in British government, institutional weakness, the relatively greater economic decline of the regions, cultural differences, nationalist feelings and specific issues or grievances – for example, North Sea oil, membership of the EEC. There is corresponding disagreement on the importance of these factors.

Nationalism is not a phenomenon of the 1960s and early 1970s. It is a persistent feature of the British political landscape reinforced by separate educational, legal, religious and governmental systems. Nor can such popular expressions of nationalism as a separate international football team, a national flag and a national anthem be omitted from this list of distinctive characteristics. It is a long-standing phenomenon. However, the strength of Welsh and Scottish nationalism has been overstated. Rose (1982, p. 88) has pointed out that 'By fighting elections, Nationalists register the weakness of their support in their own nation.' The 'problem' to be explained is *not* the rise of nationalism but why the centre in this period took the challenge so seriously. In other words, the issue to be explored is the constraints upon and the weakness of central government. In addition, the increasing salience of nationalism cannot be divorced from the increasing salience of other social cleavages. The combined effects of central weakness and social differentiation were to become marked from 1974 onwards.

Above all, the prominence of nationalism in this period should not obscure the substantial continuities in SCG. The policy networks remained paramount in the expansion of welfare state services; the centre remained politically insulated from local élites; and in Urwin's (1982, p. 68) phrases, 'tolerance and indifference', 'the concern to accommodate demands within the prevailing structure' and 'an *ad hoc* attempt to resolve a specific complaint or demand' continued to characterize central attitudes and actions.

The key feature of intergovernmental relations in this period is instability, no crisis. Economic pressures were mounting, the central strategy of institutional modernization was bearing no obvious fruit, and the incidence of conflict and protest was increasing. The onset of economic decline was to alter the picture markedly.

To this point, the narrative has merely suggested explanations for the changes in SCG between 1945–74. It is now necessary to provide an explicit explanation of the development of SCG in this period. Figure 5.1 provides such a summary. It begins with the assumptions of a stable external support system, economic growth and a central élite ideology based on the mixed economy welfare state. The consequent expansion of the welfare state led to increased functional differentiation and the institutionalization of the professions. The resulting policy networks lie at the heart of a system of functional politics which marginalized local political élites. The dual polity – the insulation of national from local political élites – was supported by both an external support system which still afforded central élites a role in 'high politics' and a two-party system based on functional economic interests which subsumed other social cleavages to class and failed to colonize the localities. In sum, functional politics came to dominate territorial politics.

However, there were stresses and strains within the system of functional politics. Economic growth and the subsequent occupational restructuring fostered class de-alignment. Traditional social cleavages re-emerged (e.g. nationalism), and functional politics

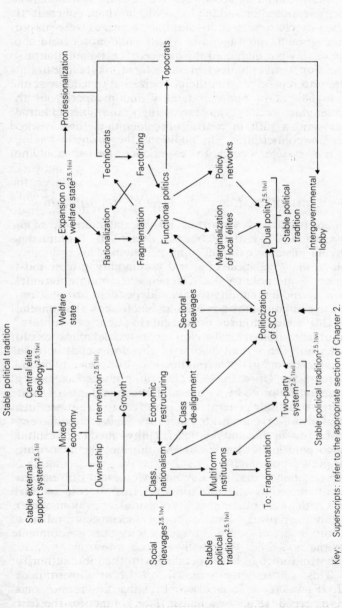

Figure 5.1 *A summary explanation of the politicization of SCG.*

Key: Superscripts: refer to the appropriate section of Chapter 2.
      Arrows: indicate causal relationships.
      Lines: indicate subdivisions of concept.

generated sectoral cleavages. Moreover, Union had established a unitary state with multiform institutions, and the expansion of the welfare state had further fragmented service delivery systems. This complex of organizations became the locus within which the conflicts of a social structure characterized by multiple cleavages were played out. Economic growth and functional politics did not herald the homogeneous society but increased the degree of social and political differentiation. Functional politics fostered a territorial reaction.

It is important to remember that the politicization of local government began in an era of relative stability and prosperity. With deepening economic decline, an increasingly unstable external support system and a shift in central élite ideology, there was a quantum leap in politicization. In addition, the problem-solving capacity of the system began to experience ever-intensifying difficulties.

5.3.3   1974–9: Instability, Economic Decline, Incorporation

Three factors are particularly important for understanding developments in this period. First, the economic decline of the UK was accelerated by an unstable external support system. This instability was economic – the escalation of world commodity prices, most notably oil prices – and political – UK dependence on international bodies and corresponding inability to take independent action. Confronted by massive inflation, the government had to seek a substantial loan from the IMF which required drastic cuts in public expenditure. Second, the reorganization of local government stimulated the spread of party politics and the virtual demise of the 'Independent'. The consequent politicization of local politics was to spread to intergovernmental relations. Third, the 1974 elections produced a minority Labour government followed by an overall Labour majority of four. These knife-edge situations generated imperatives to negotiate with minority parties to preserve a working majority. This conjunction of external economic disruption and political fragility called forth central strategies of incorporation for English local authorities and factorizing for nationalist political demands.

There is clear evidence that the Labour government did make a sustained effort to introduce a kind of top-level, overall 'corporatism' into its dealings with local government. Its essential innovation was to try to incorporate the powerful local authority associations (and their joint bodies) into a sort of 'social contract' about local government spending. For the first time, Whitehall set up a forum in which to discuss the long-run future of local spending with the local authority associations. This Consultative Council on Local Government Finance (CCLGF) was remarkable also in bringing the Treasury and local authority representatives into face-to-face contact for the first time, and in explicitly integrating the planning of local spending into the PES system. The government's hope was that by involving the local authority associations in policy-making affecting local government it would be able to persuade them of the 'realities' of the economic situation, and thus enlist them as allies in the battle to keep down the growth of local spending. In the Treasury's view, the objective of the CCLGF was 'effective control', and if it was not achieved, 'other measures would have to be considered' (Layfield Committee, 1976, p. 327).

How effective the CCLGF was in meeting this aim is difficult to say. Many of its members argue that it was successful in getting the local authority associations to persuade their members to behave with restraint. But, of course, there were other forces working in the same direction: for example, cash limits on central grants to local authorities; the swing in mid-term local elections to Conservative-controlled authorities committed to expenditure restraint. Whatever else it accomplished, however, the CCLGF symbolized a shift of influence within local government away from service-oriented councillors and officers (for example, the education policy community) and towards local politicians and finance directors more concerned with 'corporate planning', increased efficiency and financial soundness. In effect, the CCLGF was a Whitehall attempt to build up the influence of national community of local government, so that it would be better able to control the rest of the local government system in return for consultation and a direct voice in future planning. (This section draws upon Dunleavy and Rhodes, 1983, pp. 125–6; for a full account see Rhodes, 1986a, ch. 4).

Other types of SCG were also 'incorporated' and, in the case of the nationalized industries, they were explicitly part of the 'Social Contract'. Once again their prices were controlled, and, predictably, concern grew over the scale of losses. Ostensibly, the industries had commercial freedom, but this freedom continued to finish a poor second to government views on the needs of the economy. Incorporation was a different label for the continuing failure to evolve a coherent pattern of ministerial intervention and control.

The threat from nationalist politics produced an almost incoherent response from the centre. After the October 1974 election, Labour's majority was slight, and negotiations with third parties (including the SNP) were necessary to maintain a working majority. These elections provided clear evidence of 'partisan de-alignment' (Crewe, Särlvik and Alt, 1977) as the proportion of votes cast for third parties rose, not only in the periphery, but also in England. To remain in office, the Labour government required the support of the Liberals and the SNP, both of which supported devolution.

As if the need to continuously manufacture a working majority was an insufficiently daunting problem, it was compounded by the parlous state of the British economy, which saw the end of economic growth and denied the government the compromises, so typical of functional politics, of marginal improvements in service provision. Both inflation and unemployment rates rose, the former dramatically, and 'stag-flation' replaced 'stop-go' as the curse of the British economy. Under this assault, 'cuts' in public expenditure were the order of the day, and the postwar consensus on the mixed economy welfare state began to crumble. Between 1976–9 the Labour government introduced a species of monetarism, the Conservative opposition was taking a decisive step towards social market liberalism, and the belief in salvation through institutional modernization was collapsing on its transparent failures. Whether these shifts are seen as a loss of confidence in government or the loss of confidence by governing élites, the period was one of reassessment and search for new directions. Moreover, the government was now denied the usual escape route of adventures in 'high politics'. Britain's role in the world had contracted immeasurably and the country was vulnerable to externally generated instability. Attention upon domestic economic ills was not easily distracted, and the Labour government did not have its 'Falklands' to rescue its public esteem. Devolution was, therefore, a policy bred of central weakness rather than nationalist strength. Certainly the policy was much disliked by both ministers and civil servants. The legislation bears all the hallmarks of antagonistic reluctance, being both internally inconsistent and ambiguous (often at the same time).

The first point to note is that the problem of nationalist politics was factorized. Separate policies were pursued in Scotland, Wales and Northern Ireland. Moreover, there was a policy (of sorts) for England. 'Organic change' or the redistribution of functions between the different types of local authority three years after a major reorganization was first mooted in a devolution White Paper and preoccupied the Secretary of State for the Environment between 1977–9. There was still no grand design for the reform of territorial politics, just a series of *ad hoc* responses.

Second, at no stage was the doctrine of the supremacy of Parliament under challenge. Throughout the centre insisted, for example, on the retention of all powers of economic management. However, it is probably a mistake to suggest that constitutional issues were at stake. Political survival was the key consideration for a 'minority' party government; the centre was to concede as little as possible commensurate with the Labour Party retaining power.

Third, although the growth of central intervention took a very poor second place to the devolution debate at the time, the changes in the form of that intervention were particularly significant. The definition of the centre's responsibility for economic management had stressed aggregate control. For local government, this responsibility encompassed the level of central grant to local government. Since 1975–6 this responsibility has been unilaterally redefined. Local *expenditure* (not grant) was explicitly included in the PES, the anticipated level of expenditure for individual local services was identified, and general guidance on the level of rate increases was proffered. In other words, central government was intervening to regulate local expenditure. It had not been so targeted before. Hereafter, the control was to become more specific.

And as ever, finally, there was the sorry plight of Northern Ireland. Direct rule via the Northern Ireland Office prevailed. Public expenditure was increased to offset economic decay. But the most striking facts are the continued insulation of Northern Ireland from mainland politics and the growing indifference of Westminster to maintaining the Union. Governing without a consensus and the failure of the several attempts to find a substitute for direct rule have bred 'contingent commitment' (Rose, 1982, p. 218). Whatever else Northern Ireland may illustrate, it highlights the *ad hoc* and variegated strategies of the centre in managing territorial politics.

Ostensibly a period of dramatic transformations, the years 1974–9 reaffirmed the resilience of the Union. If anything, nationalist politics were weaker in 1979 than at any time in the past decade. But there had been important changes. If the new forms of central interventions in IGR were not newsworthy, they had the potential for transforming the system. That potential was soon to be realized.

5.3.4 1979–85: Economic Recession, Control, Politicization

If one single theme permeates this period, it is the search by central government for more effective instruments of control (not influence) over the expenditures of sub-central government. Control is not, however, the only development of significance. The government has also sought to restrict the size of the public sector by privatization. Although its 'progress' under this head was initially slow, none the less it became a distinctive feature of Conservative policy. Whereas control and privatization can be seen as an attack on the public sector, as a means for curtailing its role in British society, the third feature of proliferating non-departmental public bodies served to expand the public sector and make it more complex.

Certainly local government railed vigorously against both its containment and bypassing in favour of non-departmental public bodies. As relations between the two sides deteriorated, so there were marked changes in behaviour. Successive Secretaries of State for the Environment adopted a unilateral style of decision-making, and the more normal consultative mode was forsaken. Both sides demonstrated an increasing willingness to resort to litigation to resolve their differences. With changes in political control at the local level, recalcitrance replaced consultation, with an increasing number of Labour-controlled local authorities demonstrating a willingness to defy the government's edicts on expenditure. In the vast majority of local authorities risk-avoidance strategies became the dominant characteristic of the budgetary process; that is, local councils sought ways and means for reducing the uncertainties surrounding central grant. In short, the consultation so distinctive of the mid-1970s, was replaced by bureaucratic direction and confrontation.

For central government the results of this new style of central–local relations were a series of unintended consequences amongst which the constant changes in the grant system to gain effective control must be numbered the most serious. The government's explicit objective that *local* income and expenditure conform with *national* decisions proved elusive.

Relations with SCG changed because the Conservative government sought to control public expenditure as part of its monetarist strategy for managing a national economy suffering from high inflation. Local expenditure is a significant proportion of total public expenditure, and as a result its reduction was a prime government objective. Such a reduction may serve economic objectives but it is primarily part of a broader political strategy for restructuring the welfare state. In accordance with its avowed commitment to social market liberalism, the government also sought to expand the role of the market in the provision of services and to reduce government involvement.

The achievements of the new system can be described, at best, as mixed. It is clear that Conservative cuts were not as severe as widely perceived. Between 1979–80 and 1982–3 total public expenditure rose as a proportion of GDP, and central government's expenditure increased sharply. The big spenders were not for the most part local government services, and some local services declined dramatically, e.g. housing. The Conservatives cut substantially the centres contribution to local services; the proportion of net current local expenditure financed by block grant fell from 61 per cent to 56 per cent, whilst the proportion of expenditure financed by specific grants rose. Local government manpower fell by 4 per cent in the same period. Most dramatically, local capital expenditure was subject to stringent regulation and was reduced by some 40 per cent in real terms from an already severely reduced base. And yet, in spite of the 'cuts', local current expenditure *increased* between March 1979 and March 1983 by 9 per cent in real terms.

In short, as with the previous Labour government, the bulk of the 'cuts' fell on local government and on capital expenditure, whilst, ironically, the Conservatives presided over an increase in both total public expenditure and local current expenditure (for a more detailed discussion see Rhodes, 1984).

After four years of direction and control, the Conservatives returned to office in 1983 facing a choice between intensifying bureaucratic direction and a more conciliatory mix of strategies designed to win compliance. It chose to intensify direction. Inter-governmental relations seemed to be entering a new phase of explicit centralization. Thus, the government now limited the rate levels of high-spending local authorities ('rate capping') and abolished both the Greater London Council and the metropolitan counties. Theoreti-cally, local expenditure was to be brought under control by regulating the income as well as the expenditure of local councils and by abolishing the worst 'overspenders'.

The consistency of government is more apparent than real, however. There was no 'U-turn', but government policy in response to the failure of its local government policy bears all the hallmarks of opportunism. It sought to compensate for escalating public expendi-ture by the use of non-departmental public bodies, thereby bypassing local authorities, and by the sale of public assets (otherwise known as privatization), the receipts from which were used to offset expenditure increases. The problems and prospects of these policies continue to unfold. (see Chapter 4, section 4.2.1), but the history of the postwar period suggests the all too obvious outcome; when control is the preferred strategy, the outcome will be unintended consequences, recalcitrance, uncertainty, ambiguity and confusion. To a consider-able degree, the government has been and remains a prisoner of the interests it seeks to regulate, for those interests are part of the structure of government. And in seeking to escape from such con-straints, government policy has ceased to display its much vaunted single-mindedness of purpose.

Strategies towards Scotland, Wales and Northern Ireland in this period are variations on the same themes. Scotland can be seen as the 'test-bed' for English legislation. Most of the grant innovations were introduced in Scotland first; for example, the Secretary of State for Scotland can reduce the grant to an individual local authority if he thinks its expenditure is 'excessive': a power not available to the Secretary of State for the Environment until 1985. In Northern Ireland, grant to local authorities actually rose as the centre pursued strategy of 'more of the same', i.e. proposing (unacceptable) alter-natives to direct rule, using public expenditure to fight economic decay and insulating mainland politics from the problem. In Wales a Welsh Consultative Council on Local Government Finance was introduced to implement the new grant system. Revealingly this innovation had initially been proposed as part of the Labour govern-ment's devolution package. It now reappeared as a means for control, *not* devolution. *Both* cases provide a wonderfully clear example of the centre factorizing problems and using institutional reforms to solve its own problems.

As before, the changes between 1974–85 can be summarized in an

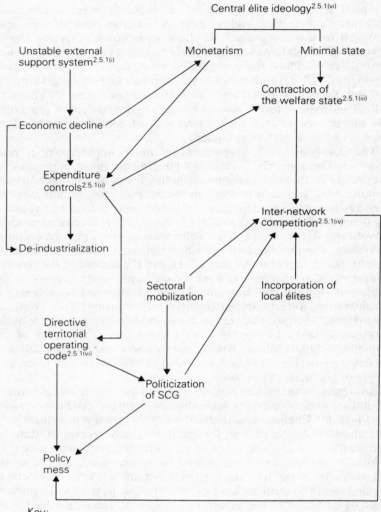

Key:

Superscripts: refer to the appropriate section of Chapter 2.

Arrows: indicate causal relationships.

Lines: indicate sub-divisions of concept.

Figure 5.2   *Economic decline and SCG.*

explicitly explanatory form. Figure 5.2 identifies the major causes of changes in SCG under the exigencies of economic decline.

With the increasingly apparent failure of successive governments to manage the mixed economy successfully, the postwar consensus on intervention, ownership and the welfare state began to founder. In its place, the 'New Right', concerned with the money supply, the PSBR and the minimal state, emphasized reductions in public expenditure and the contraction of the welfare state. This 'resource squeeze' intensified competition between policy networks determined to preserve their turf. Clients were mobilized, and direct contact with local political élites was established. The 'hands-off' character of the dual polity was replaced by a command territorial operating code. Nowhere was this change more obvious than in the changes to the system for distributing grant to local authorities, but it is also evident at an early stage in the efforts to reduce the number of quangos and in the investment and pricing controls over the nationalized industries. But direction was a high-cost strategy. At first, the centre had channelled its political contacts through an intermediate tier of representation based on the national community of local government. Increasingly, this channel was replaced by face-to-face contact between ministers and individual (or small groups of) local authorities. Directive strategies provoked recalcitrance and non-compliance, and ministers were dragged reluctantly into conflict with the 'overspending' local authorities: conflict which spilt over, ever more commonly, into litigation. The politicization of local politics had spilt over into IGR. The costs in time and even loss of political face were mounting. To make matters worse, the policy failed. The planned cuts in total public expenditure did not materialize. The new central élite ideology had not countered economic decline with a reduction in the size of the public sector but it had intensified the politicization of SCG and generated a policy mess wherein nobody achieved their objectives.

Moreover, the changes in SCG began to exert an increasing influence on the national government environment. These feedback effects are summarized in Figure 5.3. Thus, expenditure controls fell largely on local capital expenditure and, in effect, off-loaded public sector cuts on to the private sector, e.g. the construction industry. This simply contributed to the deindustrialization of the British economy and rising unemployment. Government action was intensifying economic decline, which in turn increased the pressure on the welfare state, most notably social security payments to the unemployed. Coupled with the difficulties of making cuts because of the capacity of policy networks to resist the pressure for reduced expenditure and increasingly strident protest from client groups, welfare state expenditures continued to rise. This increase threatened the government's monetary targets, intensified the search for means to control public

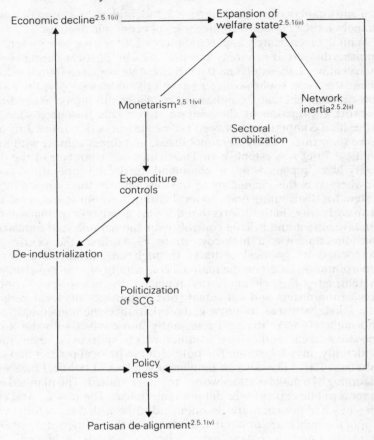

Key:

Superscripts: refer to the appropriate section of
   Chapter 2.

Arrows: indicate causal relationships.

Figure 5.3 *The impact of SCG on the national government environment.*

expenditure and generated yet more recalcitrance in SCG; thus the downward spiral continued. The resultant policy mess casts doubt on the efficacy of the ideology of central élites and thereby contributes to partisan de-alignment. For all the resounding nature of their electoral victory in 1983, the Conservative share of the vote was their lowest winning proportion of the postwar period, and the major parties' share of the total electorate barely exceeded 50 per cent.

This summary explanation of changes in SCG is bald in the extreme. In reality, the sequences of cause and effect are rarely so clear cut. But a simple, even simplistic, presentation provides a sharp analytic cutting edge, all the more necessary when the subject is as complex as SCG and when many of the necessary caveats have been noted already in earlier chapters. The next step is to determine the consequences of these changes in the national government environment for the policy networks, and of the resulting changes in the networks for the various types of SCG and interests and classes.

5.4 The Consequences of Differentiation

Table 5.1 identifies the distinctive outcomes for each type of policy network. However, the discussion of consequences cannot be so limited. It must cover an analysis both of the consequences which arise from the characteristics of SCG and of those which stem from changes in that system. In addition, the changes in the national government environment can be exogenous (i.e. an unstable external support system) or endogenous (i.e. changing central strategies of intervention). Finally, the consequences can be specific to one class or interest, one policy network, one type of SCG, or they can be SCG-wide. A thorough analysis of the consequences of the differentiated policy requires a discussion of this variety of effects. They will be considered under the general heading of stability, effectiveness, complexity, equity and accountability, and under each heading I will specify who is affected, how and by what. The schematic outline of the discussion is given in Table 5.2.

Table 5.2   *The Analysis of Consequences*

Who is affected?	How are they affected?	By what are they affected?
A class/interest	Stability	SCG characteristics
A type of SCG	Effectiveness	
A policy network	Complexity	SCG change:
	Equity	exogenous
	Accountability	endogenous

The first step, however, is to specify in a little more detail the criteria which will be employed in this evaluation.

I argued in Chapter 2, section 2.5, that evaluations rooted in political philosophy would be forsworn in favour of an internally generated appraisal. I suggested that policies towards SCG must be based on an adequate theory of how the system worked and I have presented a theory of SCG which has stressed that complexity, interdependence, differentiation and disaggregation are its defining characteristics. Consequently, the following discussion will be based on the argument that the management of (and in) SCG requires strategic flexibility, tolerance of indeterminacy, openness of communication and the evaluation of policy impact.

Strategic flexibility is essential because no one strategy will be equally effective for all types of network, SCG and policies. Each initiative requires its own means or structure of incentives and sanctions to generate compliance. Indeed, this criterion seems so obvious as to verge on banality, and yet the experience of the past decade can be summarized as 'there is no alternative' (TINA) to a bureaucratic strategy. In such circumstances even the banal warrants repetition. Consensus strategies may have acquired a 'bad reputation' in the era of conviction politics, critics of the government may wish to recreate consensus, but it is not the only alternative to bureaucratic imposition. Compliance strategies involve the deployment of a *structure* of incentives and sanctions wherein, for the majority of actors, the benefits outweigh the costs. It is not used here to refer to the imposition of high costs alone or to the offer of incentives alone. It refers to their combination and to be effective it does not require agreement on ends (or consensus), only that the balance of advantage favours the preferred course of action. Of late such compliance strategies have come a poor second to the imposition of sanctions.

Indeterminacy is probably the most continuous criterion employed, if only because it offends administrative tidiness.[2] The call for better co-ordination is widespread, and its merits seem self-evident. The key question of 'co-ordination of what by whom' is easier to pose than to answer in a differentiated policy. A complex of institutions in an unstable environment means that the 'what' of co-ordination is ever changing. To specify 'who' is responsible for co-ordination is to provoke turf disputes by amending the distribution of power within and between organizations and, most important, to build in rigidities and constrain the capacity to respond to change. Given environmental instability and the search for closure by policy networks, indeterminacy – in the guise of duplication, overlap and competition between functions – enhances the incentives for networks to respond to change. For example, the scope for innovation is enhanced whenever the boundaries of a network are imprecise, and innovation is a means for a network with an indistinct or threatened domain to establish itself by assuming uncontested functions. A toleration of indeterminacy can also counter the ever-present danger of a network monopolizing a function and acting on behalf of its own narrow constellation of interests. The result is likely to be a more complex set of institutions and functions, and the complexity generated by indeterminacy has to be traded off against the dangers of rigidity and closure posed by co-ordination.

To realize the potential of indeterminacy, it has to be allied with openness of communication. The monopolistic tendencies of networks thrive on secrecy. Premature closure restricts information and knowledge of the degree of, and opportunities for, change. For a network, especially its units of SCG, organization and information are power. Open communication within and between networks and between networks and citizens (and their elected representatives) is essential if the system of government is not to become wholly divorced from those it is ostensibly meant to serve.

This criterion could be described as idealistic – who says organization says restricted communication – but there is an important prosaic, even descriptive, component to it. For the networks to be effective, to avoid the vicious circle of bureaucracy and to cope with an unstable environment, they too require open communication, internally and externally. Closure protects the extant constellation of interest at the expense of rigidity or an increasing inability to respond to change. Openness of communication is as necessary to the effectiveness of networks as it is to counter their monopolistic tendencies; it is in the self-interest of its potential opponents.

Self-interest commonly motivates, but incentives to openness still have a role to play. The evaluation of policy impact is a vehicle for both increasing the flow of information and countering the tendency of the responsibility for policies to disappear in the interstices between multiple actors. The key features of such evaluations are that they focus on what policy actually achieves – and not on inputs (for example, finance) or process (for example, the time taken to do something) and span the range of organizations involved. In effect, the networks, rather than any one constituent organization, will be held to account for the consequences, not the amount or form, of their actions. Given that governments should be held to account for their actions, the focus on policy impact incorporates complexity, disaggregation and differentiation into the evaluation of their actions. Nor are such evaluations to be designed for and consumed solely by network members. The focus on impact requires the involvement of the consumers of the services as a major source of relevant information. And such participation also serves to foster openness of communication both through the involvement of consumers and indirectly through their representatives who will receive and comment upon the evaluations. The central elements of this focus on policy impact are the concern with networks *not* institution, specific policies *not* process, impact *not* inputs and openness of communication.

Obviously I have done no more than introduce the criteria of evaluation to be used below. They will be discussed in more detail when reviewing the specific consequences arising from the form of, and the changes in, the system of SCG. Over and beyond trying to provide a clear basis for the following discussion, these remarks are designed to demonstrate that the differentiated polity requires an extension of our evaluative criteria beyond the somewhat restricted notion of local autonomy.

5.4.1   Stability

Stability is a prime characteristic of policy networks, especially policy communities. Based on a limited constellation of interests with restricted membership, the communities routinize relationships by incorporating the major interests to a 'closed' world. Policy communities are a means of creating stability and hence they institutionalize the existing distribution of power. They are also a prime example of 'dynamic conservatism' or of fighting to remain the same (Schon, 1973, p. 31). External change, whether induced by central intervention or other forces, has to overcome the closure practised by policy communities, their capacity to regulate their external relationships (see, for example, Chapter 2, section 4.2.2).

Turning to the consequences of change, three general points about the postwar period are in order; indeed, they are so obvious that they are in danger of being overlooked. Thus, network relations have been stable for the bulk of the postwar period; in response to external instability and economic decline, change has occurred at an accelerating rate since 1974; and it has been resisted by the policy communities. Less obviously, the response of the centre to instability has been to intervene repeatedly in the policy networks; and, in consequence, stable relationships seem to belong to a long-forgotten golden era, and ambiguity, confusion and uncertainty have come to characterize both SCG as a whole and network relations. In spite of protestations and (ostensibly) policies to the contrary, they have remained pre-eminent for over a decade. Exogenous change prompted endogenous changes which accentuated the degree of instability confronting all actors.

The rate and consequences of instability vary between the policy networks. Thus the major welfare state services, education and health, underwent the politics of creation in the immediate postwar period, and the process of network building was characterized by a high rate of flux.

When these services had been established, the time was ripe for institutional modernization. Clearly, change in intergovernmental networks pre-dates the instabilities of the 1970s and 1980s. Again these points are obvious from a cursory inspection of Table 5.1. Their importance lies in the simple facts that many changes for the policy communities were a product of negotiation and that, although the roots of recent instability may lie in economic factors, change is not necessarily a product of economic circumstances. As the account of the development of SCG attempted to demonstrate, any mono-causal or reductionist explanation of current instabilities is doomed to failure. Thus, for all the shifts in the national government environment and government policy, the changes in producer and issue networks were superficial once the wartime controls had been dismantled. Their distinctive network characteristics, particularly the low degree of vertical and horizontal interdependence, served to minimize the consequences of instability. In spite of variations in the incidence of change, however, all networks have been subject to uncertainty, ambiguity and confusion, albeit to differing degrees, since 1979.

The well-spring of change may have been economic recession but it was given a highly distinctive twist by the new central élite ideology. Bureaucratic modes of intervention were the order of the day, and this means for dealing with economically generated uncertainties itself became a source of uncertainty, producing a range of unintended consequences. Again patterns of change were the product of a complex of factors. The consequences for specific actors and organizations of such interventions (*not* control) were often dramatic.

To this point, the term 'stability' has not been defined. Commonsense usage seemed adequate. Schon's (1973, p. 9) definition of stability as a belief in the 'afterlife-within-my-life' or 'in the unchangeability, the constancy of central aspects of our lives' helps to identify some of the less obvious consequences of recent instability.

The individual administrator in SCG has been beset by new legislation, procedures and forms of financial provision. Uncertainty has induced a short-term perspective, a tendency to live from hand to mouth. In principle, it may be undesirable to run services on such an unplanned basis, but this is not the major consequence of instability; that lies in the disruption of appreciative systems. These maps of the world have undergone three significant changes. First, the assumption of incremental growth has been eroded. As Stewart (1980, pp. 17–18) argues, the expectation of continuously increasing resources provides a means for resolving problems, increases the possibility of organizational consensus, enhances the scope for bargaining to resolve conflict and encourages the aspiration that all needs will be met in time. Resource squeeze has the effect of increasing organizational and political conflict, and, when allied to uncertainty over the scale and availability of funds, such conflicts are intensified, consensus becomes elusive, and defensive behaviour prevails.

Second, service priorities have been challenged. There is a marked parallel here with changes in the budgetary process. Thus, it was common for the budgetary base, i.e. last year's expenditure, to be taken for granted and for discussion to focus on the increment. With resource squeeze, the base itself was challenged. In like manner, service chiefs expected new priorities to be discussed, but the challenge to their 'base' priorities was both unexpected and unwelcome. The clearest example lies in the attempts to revocationalize the curriculum, a policy which challenged long-standing assumptions about equality of opportunity in education. Allied to criticism of the quality of education (and the performance of teachers), the result has been to induce a siege mentality in the education service.

Finally, local government's 'responsibility ethic' has had to weather a series of storms and, if it remains intact, it is somewhat battered. Not only have some Labour-controlled councils repudiated the ethic in its entirety, but many other councils have also become disillusioned. The phrase 'we didn't think anyone could seriously mean it' aptly captures the guarded cynicism with which central pronouncements are greeted and suggests why 'creative accountancy', or observing central guidance in letter if not in spirit, has become so widespread.

Simply because the foregoing examples refer to local government it should not be thought that the effects of instability are limited to this type of SCG. For example, the nationalized industries have undergone (variously) contraction, strict EFLs, enforced price increases, liberalization and asset sales – scarcely a combination favouring coherent investment (or corporate) planning. In the NHS, medical domination has suffered a nigh unique if not unthinkable challenge to its priorities from the new general managers and the centre's efficiency regime. In all these cases it is not simply the fact of resource squeeze but also the form it has taken which has bred instability; that is, the continuous recombination of ever-modified financial instruments has created a high degree of uncertainty. This effect has occurred even when there has been no reduction in real resources.

The earlier discussion of indeterminacy suggested clearly that a degree of instability was essential to prevent premature closure by networks and rigidity in the face of environmental change. On these grounds the instabilities of the past decade should be welcomed. However, it is important to distinguish between the conscious manipulation of networks to increase their responsiveness and instability as an unintended consequence of actions which disregarded the characteristics of the system of SCG. Recent government action falls into the latter category, and the irony of the situation is that the instability generated by government policy has fed back to the centre and increased the uncertainties which it confronts. The system of SCG has been destabilized, the consequences of any policy initiative have become less predictable, and a pattern of either repetitive legislation (e.g. local government finance) or bypassing existing institutions (e.g. education, inner cities) has emerged in order to cope with growing uncertainty. In short, the government's response to instability generated further instability which undermined the effectiveness of its policy.

5.4.2 Effectiveness

The reign of efficiency in the guise of the Rayner scrutinies, MINIS or FMI[3] has driven out, to all intents and purposes, a concern with the effectiveness of policy. At its simplest, effectiveness refers to the degree to which stated policy goals are realized, a definition which both presupposes that soluble problems have been created and ignores the substantial problems of measurement.[4] For present purposes, a more sophisticated formulation is not required. The stark conclusion is that over the past decade policies for SCG (endogenous change) have proliferated unintended consequences and created a 'policy mess' for SCG as a whole wherein no individual policy network or type of SCG achieves stated policy goals. This assessment is, of course, too bald; in order to develop a more exact appreciation of the effectiveness of policy-making for and by SCG, it is necessary to examine how the centre managed SCG and to encompass all of the postwar period. These tasks will be accomplished by taking the current state of SCG as a starting-point, examining central strategy since 1979 and then looking back to early periods to identify why the management of SCG has become ineffective.

Indisputably Westminster and Whitehall have the resources to direct SCG. They have the authority, money and political legitimacy to set the framework within which SCG operates. Given that the Conservative government opted for a bureaucratic or directive strategy, the key issue concerns tactics, or how to direct SCG. At first the emphasis fell on centralization, or redefining the framework of SCG, and the major problem concerned the precision with which it stipulated the context within which SCG operates, because 'hands-off' control, or the non-executant nature, of central departments limits the effectiveness of such broad-scope policies. Relatively dependent on SCG for informational and organizational resources, the best the centre can do with broad-scope policies is signpost the direction in which SCG should move. Examples of signposting policies are the reduction in the proportion of local expenditure funded by grant (or, for that matter, the EFLs of nationalized industries) and the use of cash limits to impose a *de facto* incomes policy on the public sector. Neither policy will ever deliver an exact reduction in either local expenditure or public sector pay settlements, but they are a source of continuous pressure restraining the rate of growth. From the centre's viewpoint, therefore, the disadvantage of the signposting tactic is that it allows considerable policy slippage.

An alternative tactic for giving effect to bureaucratic strategies was to 'target' specific problems and/or institutions and throw money and/or sanctions at them. Good examples of this tactic include the sale of council houses, the abolition of the GLC and metropolitan counties and the sale of the assets of a nationalized industry. Targeting is successful precisely because it is focused. It is a tactic which cannot be deployed effectively to regulate complex sets of relationships or multiple problems masquerading as *an* issue. From the centre's viewpoint, therefore, the disadvantages are not only that the incentives/sanctions can be avoided but that relevant targets are missed altogether.

The third tactic was to bypass the recalcitrant institution and/or intractable problem in favour of more controllable institutions and soluble problems – in effect, to break them into manageable, i.e. targetable, pieces. Examples of this tactic include the redefinition of 'inner cities' as a problem of wealth generation, the use of UDCs, EZs and the like to bypass the partnerships and the introduction of the TVEI by the MSC, bypassing both the DES and the LEAs. The disadvantages of this tactic are that the opportunities to employ it are relatively restricted – there is a limit to the number of institutions that can be either created or put to new uses; some degree of co-operation from some units of SCG will still be required; and it faces the ever-present problem of turf disputes.

A final tactic can be described as indirect centralization or attempts to change the processes of policy-making rather than the substance of policy. Examples include the Audit Commission with its remit to promote economy, efficiency and effectiveness, the introduction of competitive tendering in the NHS and the use of performance indicators throughout the public sector. The disadvantage here is that the effects of the tactic are diffuse and the benefits take some considerable time to emerge. For governments pressed to demonstrate their merits, indirect measures of this kind can be only supplementary, never the main means for achieving policy goals.

The Conservative government had other means for attaining its ends – for example, it could have removed powers from local government – but this list covers the major tactics towards SCG. The most obvious point is that governments have to choose strategies and associated tactics. It cannot be assumed that SCG will translate central intentions into practice without the use of some means for ensuring the appropriate action. Central pronouncments, no matter how authoritative, are insufficient by themselves. Moreover, the Conservatives' choices were heavily circumscribed by the commitment to a bureaucratic strategy. The dominant strategy of the postwar period, the 'logic of negotiation', was rejected. The costs of not permitting policy to emerge from the interactions of government and affected interests were high and compounded by a maladroit use of the remaining means.

The failure to appreciate the limits of the chosen tactics confounded the expectation of control. Thus, signposting tactics require clear signals, and the annual grant settlement failed to provide them. As Gibson (1985, pp. 61–3) shows, the settlements placed insufficient financial pressures on local authorities. The government needed to cut grant substantially so that local authorities were faced with large increases in the rate if they were to spend at the planned level. Yet the settlement regularly gave local authorities a 'rate holiday'; for 1981–2 it required a 1 per cent increase in rates and balances, for 1983–4 they could have reduced their rates by 2 per cent. Having conspired to defeat its own objectives, the government then tried to target the expenditure of every local authority, an aspiration of such preposterous proportions that its failure was inevitable but it locked the DoE into a never-ending spiral of legislating for unintended consequences. The government's subsequent resort to bypassing and privatization reveals the same failure to appreciate the limits of its chosen means. Proliferating non-departmental public bodies simply increased expenditure and generated problems of regulation, whereas privatization bred the re-regulation of public utilities.

Self-imposed constraints on the strategic options and a lack of appreciation of the tactical limits do not augur well for effectiveness. The degree to which stated policy goals were not achieved is substantial. Of the early major policies, local expenditure targets have never been met; 'quangos' were not abolished but increased in number and expenditure; the EFLs of the nationalized industries were exceeded massively; and public sector expenditure continuously increased. In addition, there was the chaos surrounding the transfer of housing benefit from the DHSS to local authorities, the continued decline of the inner cities and the struggle to get new policies off the ground, most notably vocational education and community care. Even the relatively successful policies had substantial problems. Thus, the sale of council houses has gone hand in hand with accelerating housing decay, and the control of capital expenditure has induced underspending below even the government's low targets and transferred the cuts from the public sector to the private sector construction industry, thereby contributing to economic recession. Little changed after the 1983 election. The GLC and metropolitan counties have been abolished, but the anticipated savings seem elusory and there are severe doubts about the workability of the new structure. Rate capping has provided no marked reductions in local expenditure at the aggregate level. Privatization is an ideological label for a ragbag of policies. Deregulation evoked little private sector enthusiasm. Contracting-out had minimal impact on local government and produced marginal savings in the NHS. Asset sales provided much valued and substantial sums of money to offset the PSBR but left unresolved the issue of government control.

Finally, these specific failures were compounded by a range of unintended consequences. Several such effects have been discussed in some detail already (see, for example, Chapter 4, section 4.2), but it is important to emphasize that they were not confined within any one policy area. The central sanctions which required substantial council house rent increases had the effect of increasing the expenditure of the DHSS (through payment of rent rebates and the successor system, housing benefit). The squeeze on local authority current expenditure delayed the implementation of care in the community (and the use of joint finance) at the expense of the NHS budget. Perhaps the best symbol of these consequences is that when the government sought a third term of office, its manifesto contained a promise to reform the rating system. Such a delay can only be described as unanticipated.

The conclusion that the record of the 1980s has been one of policy decline seems inescapable: the one certainty in a destabilized world. The government's policies are perceived as centralizing, not because they achieved their stated goals, but because they have intervened frequently if imperfectly. Disruption is not control, and the phrase 'policy mess' encapsulates the period more accurately than 'centralization'. One of the causes of this policy mess was the transition from the dual polity territorial operating code, and its associated strategies, to the command code.

For the bulk of the postwar period, central strategies were characterized by flexibility. The territorial operating code was designed to insulate the centre from local political élites: the dual polity. Consequently, the most contentious of policies continued to display the hallmarks of the 'logic of negotiation', of bargaining between professionals and civil servants in the policy networks. But the heyday of the dual polity had passed. With intensifying economic decline, the centre's strategy was incorporation, which still presupposed that negotiation would generate a consensus. But there are signs of the new command territorial operating code with the centre, in this context the Treasury, taking a view on the appropriate level of local expenditure (rather than on the central contribution to local expenditure). This erosion of the dual polity foreshadows the policy mess of recent years, as, to a lesser degree, do the introduction of cash limits, mid-year budgetary revisions, capital expenditure controls and vague pronouncements on the desirable size of rate increases.

The singular virtue of the dual polity was insulation. Central political élites did not become embroiled in either local issues or the details of implementation. Local authorities complied with central requests and, in return, saw their service expansion fuelled by central funds. The cost for the centre was policy slippage: if local authorities did not want funds to expand services, or preferred different policies, then the centre had few sanctions with which to impose its wishes. The necessary condition for this relationship was economic growth; local conformity was bought by the centre. The 1960s in particular epitomize the deployment of 'hands-off' or indirect controls by the centre, suggesting that it is the most effective strategy for managing the differentiated polity.

Even without the benefit of hindsight, it is clear that the effectiveness of both SCG, and the centre's capacity to manage it has been undermined by the abandonment of the dual polity operating code and strategic flexibility and the introduction of a command code wholly at odds with the reality of a differentiated, disaggregated system. And if this discussion has focused on the policy decline of SCG as a whole, it is because multiple examples of the problems of the networks and types of SCG have been provided already and, rather obviously, are an integral part of the overall decline.

If the government's ability to react to an unstable environment was constrained by the dynamic conservatism of the policy networks, its faulty map of SCG rendered its policies ineffective. The resulting policy mess was further intensified by the increasing complexity of SCG.

5.4.3 Complexity

Given the amount of space devoted to describing the increasing scale and interdependence of British government, it will be sufficient to repeat that this growth characterizes the whole of the postwar period. The Conservative governments post-1979 are no exception, and their policies on, for example, youth unemployment, the inner cities and the GLC and metropolitan counties have, in all probability, accelerated the trend. The consequences of this growth are manifold. Thus, in general terms, Elgin and Bushnell (1977, p. 37) identify the consequences arising from complexity, and the following have already been described for British government at various junctures:

1 Diminishing relative capacity of a given individual to comprehend the overall system.
2 Diminishing level of public participation in decision-making.
3 Declining public access to decision-makers.
4 Growing participation of experts in decision-making.
5 Disproportionate growth in costs of co-ordination and control.
   . . .
8 Increasing challenges to basic value premises.
9 Increasing levels of unexpected and counterintuitive consequences of policy action.
10 Increasing system rigidity.
11 Increasing number and uncertainty of disturbing events.
   . . .
14 Increasing system vulnerability.
15 Declining overall performance of the system.
16 Growing deterioration of the overall system unlikely to be perceived by most participants in that system.

It would be repetitive to illustrate each of these points. Complexity interacts with, and reinforces the effects of, the several problems associated with equity and accountability and will be further considered under these headings. It is sufficient to note, therefore, that complexity continues to increase, has an independent effect on the problems of the differentiated polity and intensifies the problems of stability, effectiveness, equity and accountability.

5.4.4   *Equity*

To this point, the consequences of SCG characteristics and of changes in relationships for interests and classes, as well as the outcomes identified in Table 5.1, have been ignored. The omissions were deliberate because the consequences of instability, policy decline and complexity for interests and classes can be more effectively considered together with the questions of equity and outcomes. This section discusses briefly the concepts of territorial and interpersonal equity and their relationship to SCG characteristics and changing relationships, before examining the consequences for *all* actors in SCG, devoting special attention to the range of effects on classes and interests.

Heald (1983, pp. 239–44) argues that territorial equity involves a complex series of trade-offs between local autonomy and interpersonal equity. He identifies (p. 243) the following paradoxes:

(1)   Territoria: equity (actual outcome version) is:
    – consistent with interpersonal equity;
    – inconsistent with local autonomy.
(2)   Territorial equity (potential outcome version) is:
    – inconsistent with interpersonal equity;
    – consistent with local autonomy.

Thus, the actual outcome version of territorial equity 'requires that there *actually are* equal standards of provision in all areas', whereas the potential outcome version requires that there is the potential for equal standards; in short, the time-worn debate between equality of outcome and equality of opportunity recurs. The former is a centralizing concept of territorial equity; the appropriate level of service is uniform and in accordance with the centre's definition of need. The latter involves both central and local perceptions of need, and the centre's role is confined to equalizing the resources amongst units of SCG. The same distinction between actual and potential outcomes applies to interpersonal equity. Territorial and interpersonal equity will be compatible only when they are both defined in terms of actual outcomes; that is, individuals will receive the same service irrespective of where they live. For potential outcomes, individuals within a particular area will be treated equally, but, because service levels will not be uniform, there will not be equity across areas either for particular services or for the individual's shopping-bag of services.[5]

The potential for conflict and muddle between these different conceptions of territorial and interpersonal equity is considerable. As Heald (1983, p. 252) concludes: 'It is likely that policymakers' preferences are both volatile and ill-defined, thus greatly reducing the chances of there being a coherent and consistent policy.' The mosaic of distributional consequences associated with the various networks and types of SCG attests to the extent of incoherence.

Table 5.1 suggests that the effect of networks is to sustain the existing and unequal distribution of resources as between both areas and persons. The clearest example is the NHS, where the territorial distribution of resources has remained markedly unequal for the whole of the postwar period. Central attempts at redistribution have foundered on the domination of the health network by the medical profession, breaching any and all yardsticks of territorial and interpersonal equity. As in health, equality of access/opportunity (or potential outcomes) has been the dominant view in education, thereby encouraging the exercise of discretion by SCG over the quantity and mix of services. The major exceptions are the territorial communities. Although the available data have a number of weaknesses, none the less the territorial communities have been favourably treated in the allocation of public expenditure. As with the policy communities, the policy of redistribution is based on the potential outcome version of territorial equity. Moreover, the distribution of resources within the territories is seen as the responsibility of SCG, thereby sacrificing interpersonal equity. The Welsh territorial community is a partial exception to this pattern of redistribution, reinforcing the conclusion that an established, integrated network is an important prerequisite of favourable treatment.

The distributional consequences of producer and issue networks are also a product of network characteristics. In the case of the former, the low degree of integration within the network meant that there were few checks and balances on economic interests and that network behaviour and effects reflected their interests (and disinterest). In the case of the latter, the sheer diversity of interests coupled with low integration meant that its policy impact was minimal. This incapacity meant that the economic and social deterioration of the cities continued apace.

The expenditure community through the block grant is, in theory at least, in a position to redress territorial inequalities. Given that there are separate grant systems in England, Scotland, Wales and Northern Ireland, block grant clearly aims at the potential outcome version of territorial equity, precluding interpersonal equity. In addition, block grant is unhypothecated; i.e. the moneys are not earmarked for particular services. A local authority can spend more or less on a service and vary expenditure between services, again breaching interpersonal equity. There are also some specific problems arising from confusion in central objectives. Thus, the redistribution of resources in favour of the inner cities has foundered on the technicalities of the grant system (for example, it does not recognize the 'needs' generated by population decline) and on the conflicting claims of redistribution and reducing local expenditure (for example, as urban programme funds have increased, grant has been withdrawn at a greater rate).

This discussion of territorial and interpersonal equity and the outcomes of policy networks demonstrates not only the complexity of the relationship between them but also that interpersonal equity is invariably sacrificed in any highly disaggregated system. The functional organization of British government in policy networks, the discretion of SCG and the absence of any means for prescribing the functional pattern of expenditure all serve to subordinate interpersonal equity (potential *and* actual outcome versions) to the potential outcome version of territorial equity (imperfectly realized). As Sharpe (1985) has argued, the equation of SCG with inequality and the centre with redistribution and uniform standards undermines the validity of claims for local self-government. But equally differentiation and interdependence have undermined the centre's capacity to redistribute. An invariant result is not, however, an inevitable one. As Heald (1983, p. 244) argues, the centre can compensate for breaches of interpersonal equity caused by equalization grants. For example, it can use taxes and transfers to offset the effects of discretionary local action on individuals. Any such reforms presupposes explicit preferences and trade-offs between territorial and interpersonal equity in a differentiated and disaggregated polity.

Against this backcloth we can now turn to the consequences of the differentiated polity for interests and classes, and the conclusions should be relatively obvious. Policy networks institutionalize major interests, routinize issues and practise closure to minimize external instabilities; they act to maintain the status quo. At best, therefore, they will foster incremental change in the distribution of resources. The characteristics of SCG foster dynamic conservatism, not innovation, let alone radical change.

The changes in the national government environment along with frequent central intervention have destabilized SCG, and the overall effect on interests and classes has been to render access to services both uncertain and more unequal. The availability of services within and between areas has become uncertain as the volume of resources has been constrained and redistributed within areas. SCG response to resource squeeze has been as variable as its response to service expansion in eras of economic growth. And the simple fact of local variability has virtually guaranteed increased inequality of access across local areas (as in the case of personal social services). These territorial inequalities have been accentuated by central attempts to redistribute resources between services, most notably in the case of educational contraction and revocationalizing the curriculum. These changes run directly counter to equality of opportunity by restricting access to higher levels of education.

The combination of growing territorial and interpersonal inequities has been further accentuated by complexity and policy decline. The effects of the abolition of the GLC and metropolitan counties on service provision remain to be seen, but one objective of the exercise was service contraction. In the case of the inner cities, bypassing partnerships for non-departmental public bodies and the preference for local economic development meant that redistributive or social policies were accorded a low priority. Policy decline has meant, at its simplest, that services were not provided on the scale envisaged. Whether the example is the introduction of housing benefit or implementing care in the community, the level of provision fell below central expectations let alone those of government critics.

In sum, whether talking of territorial or of interpersonal equity, the actual outcome of recent changes has been to make the distribution of services more inequitable, a trend accentuated by instability, complexity and policy decline. There are, however, two important qualifications to this assessment.

First, in a more apparent than real paradox, the characteristics of SCG have served to slow the rate of change. The defensive characteristics of networks are as manifest in an era of resource squeeze as in the competition for incremental growth. Disagreement within the education policy community served to delay the policy of revocationalizing the curriculum. Bypassing this network in favour of the MSC increased expenditure on a redistributive policy and simply delayed (it did not avoid) the need to bargain with the affected parties. If the policy networks institutionalize the existing distribution of power, they also react against efforts to change it. For all their imperfections, policy communities such as education and professionalized networks such as health are examples of dynamic conservatism minimizing increases in inequality.

Second, this discussion has focused on the distribution of resources when, in fact, such inequalities may not be the most important effect of recent changes. Policy networks are structures of resource-dependent organizations which condition the expectations of clients. They generate a national-level ideological structure which includes a set of beliefs about the appropriate form of service provision. The prosaic manifestation of these beliefs includes, for example, the eligibility criteria for services. To the extent that changes in the national government environment have altered the ideology of the networks in the direction of selectivity, as in the case of education, then the inequalities in education will become more marked in the future. Similarly, changes in the national government environment can boost an emergent ideology or reinforce an existing one. For example, the case study of the NI demonstrated that contraction and restructuring did not lead to social policies being given priority but to the reinforcement of beliefs in economic growth, technical efficiency, productivity and profitability. Such ideological changes may be the most important component in the heritage of the era of the 'minimal state'.

The consequences of recent changes are captured in the phrase 'only the strong survive'. The characteristics of SCG have mitigated the distributive effects of recent changes and slowed the rate of increase in territorial and interpersonal equity. Ideological changes may yet accentuate the degree of inequality, but one fact is certain; the networks will change as little as necessary to maintain the position of their dominant interests.

5.4.5 Accountability

More has probably been written on the problems of accountability in British intergovernmental relations than on any other single topic. This section briefly reviews the concept and then concentrates on the defects of accountability in SCG and the consequences for all actors. In contrast to the majority of accounts of this topic, however, relatively little space will be accorded to local autonomy. I will emphasize the importance of designing systems of accountability applicable to the differentiated polity rather than one of its constituent units.

Jones (1977, p. 5) suggests that accountability or responsibility exists when a

> Person or institution is one on whom is laid a task, function or role to perform, together with the capability to carry it out. There is also conferred some discretion and the liability to account for the performance of the duty, which should induce the person or institution to act with concern for the consequences of the decisions made and, in so deciding, to act in conformity with the wishes and needs of those who conferred the authority and receive the account. Accounting should also provide information for the controllers to assess performance. If they are dissatisfied they can withdraw their conferment of authority, and by dismissal break the relationship of responsibility.

As Stanyer (1974, p. 15) has pointed out, rendering an account necessarily involves the specification of its form and substance; a description of the time, place and audience on the occasion of its presentation; and the identification of the consequences of the presentation, especially subsequent actions, if blame is the result. The mechanisms for holding a person or an institution to account are multifarious. Heald (1983, p. 155) distinguishes between political, managerial and legal accountability, and under these headings it is possible to identify nine mechanisms (Smith, 1981, pp. 1163–74).

Without identifying any special problems of accountability in SCG, the first point is that the 'system' of accountability is fragmented, prompting the further suggestion that 'fragmented' inadequately captures the failure of the 'system' – if such it be. At a minimum, it can be argued for SCG that a range of organizations are subject to otiose and ineffective mechanisms of accountability, with the most obvious examples occurring amongst non-departmental public bodies (see Chapter 3, section 3.2.4(ii), pages 136–40). This problem is further compounded by the ambiguous and confused allocation of functions between government bodies. In effect, Chapter 3 is an extended illustration of this point. Not only is it unclear to citizens which organization is responsible for what functions/policies, but it is also difficult to hold any organization to account for policies to which it is but one of many contributors. In effect, there persists a major failure of political accountability: a conclusion which is rendered no less important for either its obviousness or the frequency with which the charge has been made by commentators of 'Left' and 'Right'.[6]

Nor can managerial and legal forms of accountability be viewed as satisfactory substitutes. The tenets of liberal democracy give political accountability pride of place; it is not just a mechanism but *the* mechanism. Managerial and legal accountability are supplements to, not substitutes for, political accountability. Moreover, the evidence does not suggest that these supplementary forms of accountability are conspicuously successful. It would be best to draw a discreet veil over legal accountability. Its restricted scope (Mitchell, 1967) and ideological preoccupations (Griffith, 1981; more reluctantly, Budge *et al.*, 1983, ch. 7) have been noted too often to warrant repetition. Managerial accountability has been a recurrent theme in central administrative reform since the 1960s and it has intensified, rather than abated, in the 1980s. Current standing can be assessed in the following quote from Sir Kenneth Clucas (Permanent Secretary, DT):

> To achieve a least-cost deployment of resources may be only one of a number of objectives, and in any particular case, not a top political priority. Other factors such as compatibility with the ideology of the government of the day, the attitude of important interest groups, acceptability to government backbenchers, effect on individual geographical areas, are all perfectly proper considerations for

Ministers to take into account when deciding for or against any particular step.

There will thus frequently be a clash between considerations of efficiency and other political priorities. Indeed it can be said that the more possible it is in any area of work to set an attainable objective, and realistically allocate a budget to it, the further away this is likely to be from current political interest and sensitivity. There may equally be a clash between accountable management and political control. If a civil servant is to be made individually answerable for a particular area of work then it follows that he must be given the power of decision. If the exercise of that power is subject to ministerial or parliamentary direction then the individual ceases to be responsible. There are large areas over which Parliament would be unwilling to surrender control in this way, and this effectively limits the extent to which management principles can be applied.

(Clucas, 1982, p. 35)

In sum, the fashion will fade, and managerial accountability will always be subordinated to political accountability.

Most important, professional accountability (or self-regulation by reference to a code of ethics) has to be allied to political accountability if the tendency to 'closure' (or the monopoly of policy expertise) is to be counteracted. In British government, secrecy is commonly seen as a major obstacle to accountability (Heald, 1983, pp. 168–9; Cockerell, Hennessy and Walker, 1984). The alliance of official secrecy and professionalized networks is, therefore, an unholy one, reinforcing the insulation of policy from citizens and their elected representatives. It was argued earlier (see Chapter 2, section 2.5.1(iv)) that the claimed benefits of policy networks – namely, expertise, jurisdictional competition, deconcentration and social responsibility – would be realized only to the extent that their boundaries were indeterminate and there was openness of communication. It should be clear that networks rarely meet these conditions. Closure prevails over indeterminacy, secrecy over openness, and in consequence the professionalization of policy networks serves primarily to weaken accountability.

The bulk of these comments are standard fare in discussions of accountability. The references to indeterminacy and openness of communication point to a further defect in the 'system' of accountability which has received considerably less attention; it is focused upon institutions and their processes of decision-making and implementation. Here lies the fundamental problem; to call one institution to account for how it has operated is to disregard key features of the differentiated polity. Policy is the responsibility of no one institution but emerges from the interactions of several. Criticizing the processes of one institution is to disregard the major process, inter-organizational conflict and bargaining. The point at which the several institutions and interorganizational processes come together (at least in theory) is at the point of service delivery. By focusing on the evaluation of policy impact these various institutions and processes can be integrated, if only to show that the impact was diminished by the weaknesses of interorganizational linkages.

The defects of the institutional-process foci of the current mechanisms of accountability can be all too easily illustrated by the national local government system. It is a source of, and sets the limits to, much policy innovation and yet there is no means whereby it can be held to account. In the same way, policy communities are national ideological structures and an important influence on client perceptions of their interests in, and expectations of, policies. And yet each actor in the communities is held to account by different mechanisms, for different facets of the policy at different times. A plethora of evaluations is not intrinsically undesirable. It is their insulation from each other, the weaknesses of the specific mechanisms of accountability and the relative disregard of policy impact which render the 'system' of accountability nugatory. It is a moot point whether or not attenuated mechanisms of accountability are preferable to the absence of accountability. It seems reasonable to presume that 'who gets what public services, when and how' is of concern to the deliverer of policy as well as to the recipient. If so, the attenuated accountability of policy networks is equivalent to no accountability at all.

The failure of accountability in the differentiated polity can also be judged by the rise of sectoral protest. Increasingly such protest focuses on the impact of policy, irrespective of the unit or level of government involved. Sectoral groups switch between levels of government and types of SCG out of necessity, for the policy is the product of no one institution (see Chapter 3, section 3.7.2(ii)). This strategic constraint may serve to dissipate conflict (see Chapter 3, section 2.5.1(v)) but it also demonstrates that sectoral groups are adjusting to the realities of the differentiated polity rather than sticking to its increasingly outmoded mechanisms of accountability.

Accountability in the differentiated polity requires, therefore, indeterminate domains, openness of communication and the evaluation of policy impact. On all these grounds, and from whatever standpoint, the current system has to be adjudged defective. It is as much a problem for the centre *vis-à-vis* SCG (and vice versa) as it is for citizens whether they are simply 'concerned' or consumers of services. Indeed, recent changes in metropolitan government, by increasing complexity, have compounded the problem, and ironically the Conservative government now considers local accountability to be 'of crucial importance' (HMSO, 1986b, p. 21) in its projected reform of local government finance. Unfortunately, importance and an accurate appreciation of 'the problem' do not go hand in hand. Yet again the 'problem' has been defined in terms of one institution (local government) and one process (financing of same). Myopia and blindness have become synonyms. Divorced from questions of functional allocation and institutional complexity, accountability (local or otherwise) will remain a mirage, reform or no reform.

If local autonomy has been conspicuous for its absence in this discussion, it is not because it is irrelevant. It is because the criteria of an effective system of accountability – indeterminacy, openness and evaluation – apply equally to local authorities as to non-departmental public bodies or the system of SCG as a whole. The question of how to design an effective system of accountability is logically prior to the question of whether or not local government/autonomy can be the fulcrum of such a system. In short, this discussion has tried to identify the conditions under which accountability can be effectively enforced in a differentiated polity. The criteria discussed do not replace the traditional yardsticks of accountability discussed at the beginning of this section but they are a necessary revision and extension. For anyone seeking to 'revive' local autonomy, this discussion suggests that the reforms must include reform of the centre to constrain its capacities for both unilateral constitutional change and interventions; encompass the range of sub-central units; and forswear tinkering with the traditional mechanisms of accountability for the evaluation of policy impacts. This reform agenda is of daunting proportions but it does no more than reflect the scale of the problem of accountability in the differentiated, disaggregated and interdependent system of government in Britain.

5.5   Contradictions in the Centreless Society: Unitary State versus Differentiated Polity

In Chapter 1 I said this book aimed to correct a persistent imbalance by showing that sub-central governments, differentiation, disaggregation and interdependence were of equivalent importance to the Prime Minister, the Cabinet and Parliament in the study of British government. I have attempted to substantiate this contention through a description of the actors, an analysis of policy networks and an explanation of changing relationships and of variations in policy outcomes. I have presented a picture of Britain as a differentiated society and argued that the centre's map of British government is inadequate, contributing to the policy mess that is SCG. By way of conclusion I propose to contrast as sharply as possible the images of the unitary state and the differentiated policy. The dichotomies listed in Table 5.3 serve not only as a summary of much of the foregoing but, because they encapsulate the defects of the unitary state model, also identify the continuing contradictions of British government. The

Table 5.3   *The Contradictions of the Centreless Society*

Unitary state	*versus*	*Differentiated polity*
(1) *Authority*		Interdependence
Ideology		Domain consensus
Partisanship		Logic of negotiation
Accountability		Ambiguity
(2) *Bureaucracy*		Differentiation
Co-ordination		Fragmentation
Command		Disaggregation
Direction		Inertia
Control		Intervention
(3) *Territory* (dual polity)		Function
Factorizing		Nationalization
Autonomy		Professionalization
Localism		Institutionalization
Insulation		Politicization

table provides both a critique of the conventional portrait of British government and an explanation for the policy decline of the last decade.

The first point illustrated by Table 5.3 is the range of contradictions in the differentiated polity. Changes in SCG in the postwar period were not caused by any one process, e.g. economic decline, or any simple combination of processes, e.g. economic decline and the resurgence of ideology. To understand the twists and turns of policy, especially over the past decade, it is necessary to explore the tensions between authority and interdependence, bureaucracy and differentiation (and disaggregation) and territory and function. And even this summary is an oversimplification, for each of these tensions can be decomposed into more specific contradictions.

SCG operates in a system characterized by a strong executive tradition and can be no more divorced from the effects of the larger system than any other facet of British politics. The relationship between the centre and SCG is one of 'asymmetric' interdependence, but, equally, the combination of differentiated service delivery systems and the hands-off tradition of central departments has fostered complex patterns of interdependence. Central to any understanding of central–SCG relations is the recurrent tension between interdependence of centre and locality on the one hand and authoritative decision-making by central government on the other. If the centre determines unilaterally the parameters of local action, then SCG can delay and frustrate the impact of central intervention. At the end of this road lies abolition, but the journey is tortuous and exacts high political and administrative costs; for all its much vaunted determination, the Conservative government was no nearer to resolving the tension between authority and interdependence than any of its predecessors.

Partisanship and ideology are crucial to understanding the *form* of the centre's response to the contradiction between authority and interdependence. The two-party system processes issues on a national stage and in an adversarial style which disrupts the logic of negotiation. It encourages the imposition of policies and strategies rather than permitting co-operation to emerge from the interplay of network interests and a sense of mutual advantage. The sheer visibility of issues encourages network participants to 'stand up and be counted', working against circumlocution and indirection, the avoidance of 'difficult' problems and the focus on means (rather than ends) necessary for compromise to emerge. The resurgence of party ideology has accentuated these effects. It both major parties have sought to control local expenditure, only the Conservative Party, with its social-market liberalism, has sought to privatize parts of the public sector. Ideology has been the grit in the well-oiled machinery of the policy networks which has disrupted domain consensus and challenged not only the assumption of inevitable incremental growth but also existing values and associated policies.

The result of these contradictions has been to undermine further the effectiveness of the traditional mechanisms of accountability. Their focus on specific institutions and their processes does not 'fit' the messy reality of a policy-making process which spans interdependent organizations. Confusion and ambiguity remain pre-eminent characteristics of IGR. The doctrines of ministerial accountability to Parliament and of collective Cabinet responsibility belong to a simpler era when the 'Mace' did not confront 'Maze' of the interdependent, differentiated polity. Yet these constitutional myths continue to be acted out as successive governments confront massive policy slippage with no means for calling to account those actors delivering the services, as they are called to account for their 'promises'. Accountability is confounded by ambiguity, breeding frustration and further bouts of speculative if not ineffective action.

If the national political élite is bemused by these constraints on its capacity to realize its goals, the administrative élite concerned to give effect to these goals has to confront the contradiction between bureaucracy and differentiation. The picture of the centre as a co-ordinated machine able to translate intentions into facts disintegrates in the face not only of disaggregated service delivery systems but also of fragmentation at the centre. Historically, the Army and the Roman Catholic Church have been the exemplars of organization and management theory: the efficient line bureaucracies. Whether or not this characterization is (or ever was) accurate, it has exercised a pervasive influence over conceptions of bureaucracy; to the extent that the analogy with 'tools' and 'machines' is commonplace, even 'natural'. It is a profoundly misleading view of bureaucracy in British government. As Vickers (1965, p. 33) has repeatedly emphasized, the bulk of activity in government is not 'goal seeking' but consists of regulating changes in our relations by setting and resetting norms (or standards). The bureaucratic model is a narrow appreciation of relations in SCG which has imposed a succession of specific goals and stuck rigidly to a set of control norms. The failure to reset norms, to appreciate SCG as a set of relations to be regulated over time, is another way of describing the centre's territorial operating code as faulty.

The paradox of British government is that the tradition of 'leaders know best' coexists with a weakness at the centre. As noted in Chapter 3 (section 3.2.2) co-ordination by the Treasury and the Cabinet Office is confounded by government by committee: ministers defend departmental turfs in Cabinet. Underlying the twists and turns of central policy is the simple fact that central government has many interests. Intervention may serve the interests of the Treasury (and even the DoE) but not other spending departments, whose ministers are each embedded in a network which is not only a constraint but also a support in the struggles against central co-ordination. Policy co-ordination is confronted not simply by a determined minister but by the *structure* of the centre with its diversity of interests enshrined in discrete networks.

Just as co-ordination has to overcome central fragmentation, so central commands have to overcome disaggregation. The weakness at the centre is re-enacted in relations with SCG. A centre with 'hands-off' controls attempts to regulate a plethora of organizations which have 'hands-on' controls over services of key importance to the centre. The combination of 'hands-off' central controls with disaggregation has fostered complex patterns of interdependence. The roots of this contradiction lie in the inception of the welfare state. The use of local government as the vehicle for delivering services, coupled with the predilection for 'ad-hocracy', created a range of disaggregated service delivery systems. The bureaucratic notion of command, with its corollary of a line hierarchy of superiors and subordinates, is ineffective in a context where there is no clear 'line'. Disaggregation calls for structures of incentives and sanctions tailored to particular policies and the structures of their networks. In a disaggregated context, command becomes a euphemism for policy slippage.

Policy slippage is increased to the degree that the centre seeks to be the source of policy innovation and to direct SCG. As the Treasury has found to its cost, some policy networks have fought a rearguard action of consequence against 'cuts'. It has had to confront the unwelcome fact of life that the alliance of professions and spending departments in policy networks has generated substantial inertia. Dynamic conservatism results in inertia and frustrated expectations. Innovation is possible – for example, by action at the boundaries of networks and by occupying new policy space – but not through the direction of existing networks without considerable costs in terms of delay.

The combination of central fragmentation, disaggregation and inertia leads to the contradiction between control and intervention. As J. D. Stewart (1983, pp. 60–2) points out, the concept of control is underpinned by a model of the purposive organization in which the centre has clear aims and control exists to the degree that these aims are achieved. But the fragmented centre has multiple goals, and 'its' actions are better described as interventions which impinge on SCG but do not necessarily achieve central purposes. Moreover, viewing central action as intervention leads inevitably to a discussion of unintended consequences; to the state of affairs in which central action does not achieve its stated purposes, proliferates unintended consequences and thereby intensifies the problem of control which the initial central actions were designed to resolve. The resultant policy mess stands as testament to the inefficiency of a bureaucratic model of action in a differentiated polity: a consequence exacerbated by the demise of the dual polity.

For the bulk of the postwar period, the centre's territorial operating code sought to maximize central autonomy by insulating the national political élite from territorial politics. The problem of territorial management was less resolved than avoided. This dual polity was undermined initially by the tensions between territorial and functional politics and subsequently by the direct action of the national political élite.

To reinforce central autonomy and maintain the dual polity, the problem of SCG was factorized, with separate policies for Scotland, Wales and Northern Ireland. Separate treatment can be interpreted as reinforcing national identities but, in the UK context, it facilitated the pre-eminence of Westminster and Whitehall. By accommodating nationalist demands, the dominance of the centre was perpetuated. There was no single problem of territorial protest but a series of discrete or factorized problems to be managed by institutional change and the redistribution of public expenditure. Conflict was diffused, a conclusion which applies equally to the modernization of SCG in England. But if it had low visibility, the tension between territorial and functional policies remained ubiquitous. With the creation of the welfare state came not only differentiation but also the presumption that territorial justice required national or uniform stands. The expectation of equality of access for all to services of equivalent standard through the country required the coexistence of fragmentation between networks and centralization within them, of factorized treatment with national standards.

The resulting tensions were manifested in the contradictions between autonomy and professionalization and between localism and institutionalization. Differentiation and professionalized policy systems grew hand in hand. The traditional conception of local authorities making and adapting policy for local needs and problems had a rival in the professional acting on the national stage and looking to shared notions of best professional practice for policy guidance and innovation. The professions are an early example of non-local sources of 'local' policy but they were followed by local politicians, especially after the reorganization of local government. The burgeoning role of the national community of local government saw the institutionalization of some local politicians at the national level. Indeed, the contradiction between localism, of local policies to meet local needs, and the generalizing of local authority experience by its national representative bodies to meet the legislative needs of the centre has plagued the national community over the past decade.

The combination of nationalization, professionalization and institutionalization served to undermine the mutual insulation of centre and locality which lay at the heart of the dual polity. The decline was accelerated by the actions of the centre. The onset of intensive intervention led to the adoption of a command operating code at variance with the differentiated polity. Not only did the centre lack the capacity to control SCG, but its reliance on bureaucratic strategies multiplied unintended consequences and accelerated the politicization of SCG. This faulty operating code may have its roots in the centre's 'culture of disdain' (Greenwood, 1982, p. 72) but it is more plausibly a product of the dual polity – in which the two levels of government are insulated from each other. When structure imposes blinkers, cultural explanations are embellishment and detail. The command code represents a failure to comprehend that British government is differentiated and disaggregated; the unitary state is a multiform maze of interdependencies. To operate a code at variance with this reality is to build failure into the initial policy design.

The clearest indicator of the demise of the dual polity and the collapse of insulation is the politicization of IGR. Since 1979 this process has proceeded apace, and the government's determination to control individual local authorities has brought ministers into face-to-face conflict with local leaders. Perhaps the most significant feature of the refusal of Liverpool City Council to make a legal budget was the *bargaining* between the secretary of state and local leaders. Rate capping is, potentially, a catalyst to such interaction between national and local élites. And this politicization also demonstrates that IGR are no longer government and politics 'beyond Whitehall' but they are part and parcel of the politics of Whitehall. These changes are probably the most important ones in the British system of IGR during the 1980s, and their full weight remains to be felt.

It is obvious that national economic management problems have dominated the practice and reform of intergovernmental relations. Local expenditure decisions were increasingly determined by central government's public expenditure survey system and the attendant Cabinet decisions throughout the 1970s. Many of the rapid changes in the expenditure targets of local authorities can be attributed directly to the decline of the British economy. Intergovernmental relations have become inextricably entwined with economic management whether the government of the day is Labour or Conservative. The analysis of SCG does not proceed very far, however, if the explanation of changes since 1945 remains confined to their economic context. Any understanding of developments in SCG has to be rooted in an analysis of the range of sub-central organizations and the evolution of their relationship with the national government environment. From this perspective it is possible to explain the demise of the dual polity, why the Conservatives sought control and why their search experienced so many problems. Developments over the past decade suggest that control strategies are at variance with the dual polity, and, when preferred, the outcome will be unintended consequences, recalcitrance, uncertainty, ambiguity and confusion. To a considerable degree, the government has been and remains a prisoner of the interests it seeks to regulate, for those interests are part of the structure of government. And in seeking to escape, government actions have politicized SCG, further eroded the dual polity without finding a substitute territorial operating code and intensified the problem of control. The economic context imposes constraints, it may even generate imperatives for action, but it does not dictate the form of action. Political traditions and choices determine courses of action, even if, once chosen, they constrain future options. The history of SCG is compounded of multiple contradictions – economic, political and organizational. Mono-causal explanations, whether propounded by politician or academic, are doomed to inadequacy. Policy-making for SCG has generated a policy mess because of the failure to appreciate that disaggregation, differentiation, interdependence and policy networks are central characteristics of the British polity which can be no more disregarded than the executive authority of the Prime Minister and the Cabinet or the role of Parliament.

The history of SCG in the postwar period makes gloomy reading – 'a squalid and politically corrupt process' (Jack Straw, *Hansard*, 25 February 1985). Forsaking the literal meaning of this phrase, and interpreting it as an indictment of the selfish pursuit of narrow partisan interests, the history of SCG is a story of central selfishness. If intervention has not been corrupt, it has served the centre's political interests whether the example is the creation of the welfare state, the modernization of SCG, or the containment of public expenditure. If central actions have not been squalid, their results have been a policy mess rooted in the failure to comprehend the differentiated nature of the system. Whatever one's views on the merits of local self-government, it is clear that it has not been the pre-eminent or even a major value to be sustained by central action. If the arguments of this book contain only a kernel of truth, none the less the prospects for SCG are bleak because the challenges and problems it confronts are not the product of a particular set of economic conditions or of a particular political ideology but of trends throughout the postwar period.

Notes

1 This section draws upon material in Rhodes, 1985c, and I would like to thank the publishers, Charles Knight, and the editor, Peter Saunders, for permission to use the material.
2 I found Landau, 1968, and Wildavsky, 1980 (pp. 131–4 and chs. 6 and 9) helpful in developing the idea that indeterminacy is a positive virtue in complex service delivery systems.
3 MINIS refers to the management information system for ministers introduced at the DoE by Michael Heseltine. FMI is the Financial Management Initiative introduced for all government departments in 1982. Raynor scrutinies looked for savings and improved efficiency in specific policies. All three are described and evaluated in Gray and Jenkins, 1985 (ch. 5).
4 There is a voluminous literature on policy evaluation and its methods, which will not be touched on here. For a useful introduction see Weiss, 1972, and for more case studies than you dreamt existed see *Evaluation Studies Annual Review*.
5 The discussion has viewed equality as a question of distributive justice. Such a conception is narrow; see, for example, Tawney, 1931 and Terrill, 1974 (ch. 5). However, it accords with the frequently implicit notion of equality underpinning government policy and it will suffice for present purposes.
6 The list of relevant references is potentially enormous but see Jones, 1977, which provides many additional citations, and compare Hailsham, 1978, and Johnson, 1977, with Benn, 1980, and Sedgemore, 1980, for the views of 'Right' and 'Left' respectively. The concern with accountability is also manifest in recent government publications on non-departmental public bodies (Cabinet Office (MPO) and HM Treasury, 1985) and on local government finance (HMSO, 1986b).

References and Bibliography

Albrow, M. (1968), 'The study of organizations – objectivity or bias?', in J. Gould (ed), *Penguin Social Science Survey* (Harmondsworth: Penguin), pp. 146–67.

Alexander, A. (1982), *Local Government in Britain since Reorganization* (London: Allen & Unwin).

Alexander, A. (1985), 'Structure, centralization and the position of local government', in Loughlin, Gelfand and Young, op. cit., pp. 50–76.

Alford, R. (1975), *Health Care Politics* (Chicago: University of Chicago Press).

Alford, R. R., and Friedland, R. (1985), *Powers of Theory: Capitalism, the State, and Democracy* (London: Cambridge University Press).

Allsop, J. (1984), *Health Policy and the National Health Service* (London: Longmans).

Alt, J. (1971), 'Some social and political correlates of county borough expenditures', *British Journal of Political Science*, vol. 1, pp. 49–62.

Anderson D. *et al.* (1980), *Town Hall Power or Whitehall Pawn?* (London: Institute of Economic Affairs, IEA Readings 25).

Anderson, W. (1960), *Intergovernmental Relations in Review* (Minneapolis, Minn.: University of Minnesota Press).

Armstrong, Sir William (1971), 'The Civil Service Department and its tasks', in R. A. Chapman and A. Dunsire (eds.), *Style in Administration* (London: Allen & Unwin), pp. 314–33.

Arthur, P. (1984), *Government and Politics of Northern Ireland*, 2nd edn (London: Longmans).

Ascher, K. J. (1987), *The Politics of Privatization: Contracting out Public Services* (London: Macmillan).

Ashford, D. (1975), 'Resources, spending and party politics in British local government', *Administration and Society*, vol. 7, no. 3, pp. 286–311.

Ashford, D. (1976), 'Territory vs function: toward a policy-based theory of subnational government', paper to the annual meeting of the American Political Science Association, Chicago, 2–5 September.

Ashford, D. (1982), *British Dogmatism and French Pragmatism: Central–Local Policy-Making in the Welfare State* (London: Allen & Unwin).

Audit Commission for Local Authorities in England and Wales (1984), *The Impact on Local Authorities' Economy, Efficiency and Effectiveness of the Block Grant Distribution System* (London: HMSO).

Axelrod, R. (1976), *Structure of Decision* (Princeton, NJ: Princeton University Press).

BASW (British Association of Social Workers) (n.d.), *A Code of Ethics for Social Work* (London: BASW, Discussion Paper No. 2).

BASW (British Association of Social Workers) (1983), *Social Workers: their Role and Tasks, a BASW Review of the Barclay Report* (London: BASW).

Bacon, R., and Eltis, W. (1978), *Britain's Economic Problems: Too Few Producers*, 2nd edn (London: Macmillan).

Bains Report (Department of the Environment) (1972), *The New Local Authorities: Management and Structure* (London: HMSO).

Barclay Report (1982), *Social Workers, their Role and Tasks* (London: National Institute for Social Work/Bedford Square Press).

Barker, A. (ed.) (1982a), *Quangos in Britain* (London: Macmillan).

Barker, A. (1982b), 'Quango: a word and a campaign', in Barker (1982a), pp. 219–31.

Barker, A., and Couper, M. (1984), 'The art of quasi-judicial administration: the planning appeal and inquiry systems in England', *Urban Law and Policy*, vol. 6, pp. 363–476.

Barnett, J. (1982), *Inside the Treasury* (London: Deutsch).

Barnhouse, L. P. (1972), 'The impact of local authority associations on local government reorganization in England, 1966–71', MA thesis, University of West Virginia.

Barrett, S. (1981), 'Local authorities and the community land scheme', in S. Barrett and C. Fudge (eds.), *Policy and Action* (London: Methuen), pp. 65–86.

Barry, B. (1970), *Sociologists, Economists and Democracy* (London: Collier–Macmillan).

Beer, S. H. (1973), 'The modernization of American federalism', *Publius*, vol. 3, no. 2, pp. 49–95.

Beer, S. H. (1976), 'The adoption of general revenue sharing: a case study in public sector politics', *Public Policy*, vol. 24, pp. 127–95.

Beer, S. H. (1978), 'Federalism, nationalism and democracy in America', *American Political Science Review*, vol. 72, pp. 9–21.

Beer, S. H. (1982), *Britain Against Itself* (London: Faber & Faber).

Bell, D. (1976), *The Coming of Post Industrial Society* (Harmondsworth: Penguin).

Benn, Tony (1980), *Arguments for Socialism* (Harmondsworth: Penguin).

Benson, J. K. (1975), 'The interorganizational network as a political economy', *Administrative Science Quarterly*, vol. 20, pp. 229–49.

Benson, J. K. (1982), 'A framework for policy analysis', in D. Rogers, D. Whitten and Associates, *Interorganizational Coordination* (Ames, Iowa: Iowa State University Press), pp. 137–76.

Berlin, I. (1969), *Four Essays on Liberty* (Oxford: Clarendon Press).

Birch, A. H. (1964), *Representative and Responsible Government* (London: Allen & Unwin).

Birch, A. H. (1977), *Political Integration and Disintegration in the British Isles* (Allen & Unwin).

Birch Committee (1979), *Report of the Committee on Manpower and Training in the Personal Social Services* (London: HMSO).

Birrell, D., and Murie, A. (1980), *Policy and Government in Northern Ireland* (Dublin: Gill & Macmillan).

Bish, R. L. (1971), *The Public Economy of Metropolitan Areas* (Chicago: Markham).

Blackaby, F. T. (ed.) (1978a), *British Economic Policy 1960–74* (Cambridge: Cambridge University Press).

Blackaby, F. T. (1978b), 'General appraisal', in Blackaby, op. cit., pp. 619–55.

Blackaby, F. (ed.) (1979), *De-industrialization* (London: Heinemann).

Blackstone, T. (1971), *A Fair Start: The Provision of Pre-School Education* (Harmondsworth: Allen Lane/Penguin Press).

Blau, P. M., and Scott, W. R. (1963), *Formal Organizations* (London: Routledge & Kegan Paul).

Blowers, A. (1982), 'The perils of being hung', *Local Government Studies*, vol. 8, pp. 13–20.

Boaden, N. (1971), *Urban Policy Making* (London: Cambridge University Press).

Boddy, M., and Fudge, C. (1984), 'Labour councils and the new Left alternative', in M. Boddy and C. Fudge (eds.), *Local Socialism?* (London: Macmillan), pp. 1–21.

Bogdanor, V. (1979), 'Power and participation', *Oxford Review of Education*, vol. 5, no. 2, pp. 157–68.

Booth, T. A. (1981), 'Collaboration between Health and Social Services: part I, a case study of joint care planning, part II, a case study of joint finance', *Policy and Politics*, vol. 9, pp. 23–49 and 205–26.

Bowen, G. (1978), *Survey of Fringe Bodies* (London: Civil Service Department).

Bramley, G. (1984), 'Grant related expenditure and the inner city', *Local Government Studies*, vol. 10, no. 3, pp. 15–37.

Bramley, G., and Evans, A. (1981), 'Block Grant: some unresolved issues', *Policy and Politics*, vol. 9, pp. 173–204.

Bramley, G., and Stewart, M. (1981), 'Implementing public expenditure cuts', in S. Barrett and C. Fudge (eds.), *Policy and Action* (London: Methuen), pp. 39–63.

Bramley, G., Evans, A., Leather, P., and Lambert, C. (1983), *Grant Related Expenditure: A Review of the System* (University of Bristol, School for Advanced Urban Studies, Working Paper No. 29).

Brand, J. A. (1974), *Local Government Reform in England* (London: Croom Helm).

Bridges, Sir Edward (1971), 'Portrait of a profession', in R. A. Chapman and A. Dunsire (eds.), *Style in Administration* (London: Allen & Unwin), pp. 44–60.

Bridges, L., and Vielba, C. (1976), *Structure Plan Examinations in Public: A Descriptive Analysis* (University of Birmingham, Institute of Judicial Administration).

Bristow, S. (1978), 'Local politics after re-organization: the homogenization of local government in England and Wales', *Public Administration Bulletin*, no. 28, December, pp. 17–33.

Brittan, S. (1969), *Steering the Economy* (London: Secker & Warburg).

Broadfoot, P. (ed.) (1984), *Selection, Certification and Control: Social Issues in Educational Assessment* (Brighton: Harvester).

Brown, R. G. S. (1979), *Reorganizing the National Health Service* (Oxford: Blackwell/Robertson).

Budge, I. *et al.* (1983), *The New British Political System* (London: Longmans).

Bulpitt, J. (1975), *The Problem of 'The North Parts'* (University of Warwick, Department of Politics, Working Paper No. 6, November).

Bulpitt, J. (1976), 'English local politics: the collapse of the *ancien régime*', paper to the annual conference of the Political Studies Association, University of Nottingham, March.

Bulpitt, J. (1980), 'Territorial politics in the United Kingdom: an analytical prospectus', mimeo, University of Warwick, Department of Politics, March.

Bulpitt, J. (1982), 'Conservatism, unionism and the problem of territorial management', in Madgwick and Rose, op. cit., pp. 139–76.

Bulpitt, J. (1983), *Territory and Power in the United Kingdom* (Manchester: Manchester University Press).

Bulpitt, J. (1986), 'The discipline of the New Democracy: Mrs Thatcher's domestic statecraft', *Political Studies*, vol. 34, pp. 19–39.

Burns, T. (1966), 'On the plurality of social systems', in T. Burns (ed.), *Industrial Man* (Harmondsworth: Penguin), pp. 232–49.

Buxton, M. J., and Klein, R. E. (1978), *Allocating Health Resources: A Commentary on the Report of the Resource Allocation Working Party* (London: HMSO, Royal Commission on the NHS, Research Paper No. 3).

CCCS (Centre for Contemporary Cultural Studies) (1981), *Unpopular Education: Schooling and Social Democracy in England since 1944* (London: Hutchinson).

CDP (Community Development Project) (1974), *Inter-Project Report* (London: Community Development Project Information and Intelligence Unit).

CHAC (Central Housing Advisory Council) (1969), *Council Housing: Purposes, Procedures and Priorities* (London: HMSO).

CPRS (Central Policy Review Staff) (1977), *Relations between Central Government and Local Authorities* (London: HMSO).

CSD (Civil Service Department) (1981), *Non-Departmental Public Bodies: A Guide for Departments* (London: HMSO). (See also Cabinet Office (MPO) and HM Treasury, 1985.)

Cabinet Office (MPO) and HM Treasury (1985), *Non-Departmental Public Bodies: A Guide for Departments* (London: HMSO). (See also: CSD, 1981.)

Cairncross, A. (1979), 'What is de-industrialization?', in Blackaby, op. cit., pp. 5–17.

Cawson, A. (1978), 'Pluralism, corporatism and the role of the state', *Government and Opposition*, vol. 13, pp. 178–98.

Cawson, A. (1982), *Corporatism and Welfare* (London: Heinemann).

Cawson, A. (1986a), *Corporatism and Political Theory* (Oxford: Blackwell).

Cawson, A. (1986b), *Organized Interests and the State* (London: Sage).

Cawson, A., and Saunders, P. (1983), 'Corporatism, competitive politics and the class struggle', in King, op. cit., pp. 8–27.

Chandler, J. A., and Lawless, P. (1985), *Local Authorities and the Creation of Employment* (Aldershot: Gower).

Chester, D. N. (1951), *Central and Local Government* (London: Macmillan).

Chester, D. N. (1952), 'Machinery of government and planning', in G. Worswick and P. Ady (eds.), *The British Economy 1945–50* (London: Oxford University Press), pp. 336–64.

Chester, Sir Norman (1981), *The English Administrative System 1790–1870* (Oxford: Clarendon Press).

Clarke, Sir Richard (1971), *New Trends in Government* (London: HMSO).

Clegg, S. (1975), *Power, Rule and Domination* (London: Routledge & Kegan Paul).

Clegg, T. (1982), 'Social consumption, social investment and the dual state: the case of transport policy in the Paris region', paper to the annual conference of the Political Studies Association, University of Kent, April.

Clucas, Sir Kenneth (1982), 'Parliament and the civil service', in J. A. G. Griffith, Sir Kenneth Clucas, F. Field and Sir Cecil Clothier, *Parliament and the Executive* (London: RIPA), pp. 23–41.

Coates, D. (1980), *Labour in Power? A Study of the Labour Government 1974–9* (London: Longman).

Cockburn, C. (1979), *The Local State* (London: Pluto).

Cockerell, M., Hennessy, P., and Walker, D. (1984), *Sources Close to the Prime Minister* (London: Macmillan).

Cohen, D., and Lindblom, C. E. (1979), *Usable Knowledge: Social Science and Social Problem Solving* (New Haven, Conn.: Yale University Press).

Committee of Public Accounts (1981), *Financial Control and Accountability in the National Health Service* (17th Report, Session 1980–1, HC255, London: HMSO).

Committee of Public Accounts (1983), *Departments of Industry, Transport and Energy. The Monitoring and Control Activities of Sponsor Departments of Nationalized Industries* (7th Report, Session 1983–4, HC139, London: HMSO).

Committee of Public Accounts (1985), *Operation of the Rate Support Grant System* (7th Report, Session 1985–6, HC47, London: HMSO).

Connolly, M. (1983), *Central–Local Relations in Northern Ireland* (Final Report to the SSRC).

Connolly, M., and Knox, C. (1986), 'A review of the 1985 local government election in Northern Ireland', *Local Government Studies*, vol. 12, no. 2, pp. 15–29.

Conservative Party (1979), *The Conservative Manifesto* (London: Conservative Party).

Cooper, J. (1983), *The Creation of the British Personal Social Services, 1962–1974* (London: Heinemann).

Coopers and Lybrand Associates (1984), *Streamlining the Cities: Summary Report and Updated Analysis of Costs* (London: Coopers & Lybrand Associates, November).

Cousins, P. F. (1982), 'Quasi-official bodies in local government', in Barker, op. cit., pp. 152–63.

Cox, A. (1981), 'Corporatism as reductionism: the analytic limits of the corporatist thesis', *Government and Opposition*, vol. 16, pp. 78–95.

Craig, C. (1980), 'COSLA: a silent voice for local government', in H. M. and N. L. Drucker (eds.), *The Scottish Government Yearbook, 1981* (Edinburgh: Paul Harris), pp. 106–41.

Crewe, I. (1983), 'The electorate: partisan dealignment ten years on', *West European Politics*, vol. 6, pp. 183–215.

Crewe, I., Särlvik, B., and Alt, J. (1977), 'Partisan dealignment in Britain 1964–74', *British Journal of Political Science*, vol. 7, pp. 129–90.

Crispin, A., and Marslen-Wilson, F. (1984), *Education and the New Block Grant* (Final Report to the ESRC).

Crispin, A., and Marslen-Wilson, F. (1986), 'Local responses to block grant: the case of education', in Goldsmith, op. cit., pp. 225–47.

Crossman, R. H. S. (1975), *The Diaries of a Cabinet Minister, Volume 1: Minister of Housing* (London: Cape/Hamilton).

Cullingworth, J. B. (1985), *Town and Country Planning in Britain*, 9th edn (London: Allen & Unwin).

Curwen, P. J. (1986), *Public Enterprise: A Modern Approach* (Brighton: Wheatsheaf).

DHSS (Department of Health and Social Security) (1972), *Management Arrangements for the Reorganized National Health Service* (London: HMSO).

DHSS (Department of Health and Social Security) (1976a), *Sharing Resources for Health in England: Report of the Resource Allocation Working Party* (London: HMSO).

DHSS (Department of Health and Social Security) (1976b), *Priorities for Health and Personal Social Services. A Consultative Document* (London: HMSO).

DHSS (Department of Health and Social Security) (1977), *Priorities in the Health and Social Services: The Way Forward* (London: HMSO).

DHSS (Department of Health and Social Security) (1980), *Mental Handicap: Progress, Problems and Priorities. A Review of Mental Handicap Services in England since the 1971 White Paper* (London: DHSS).

DHSS (Department of Health and Social Security) (1981), *Care in the Community: A Consultative Document on Moving Resources for Care in England* (London: DHSS).

DHSS (Department of Health and Social Security) (1983), *Health Service Development. Care in the Community and Joint Finance* (London: DHSS HC(86)6).

DoE (Department of the Environment) (1985), *Competition in the Provision of Local Authority Services* (London: DoE Consultative Paper, February).

Darke, R., and Walker, R. (eds.) (1977), *Local Government and the Public* (London: Leonard Hill).

Davies, E. M., Gibson, J. G., Game, C. H., and Stewart, J. D. (1983), *Grant Characteristics and Central–Local Relations* (Final Report to the SSRC).

Davies, J. G. (1972), *The Evangelistic Bureaucrat* (London: Tavistock).

Davies, T., and Mason, C. (1981a), *Central–Local Relations in the Implementation of Labour Market Policy. Three Case Studies* (Vol. 1, Redundancies in a small labour market; Vol. 2, Restructuring: training for high technology industry in Swindon; Vol. 3, Redistribution: the case of 'Wider opportunities for Women' in Bath) (Final Report to the SSRC).

Davies, T., and Mason, C. (1981b), 'Local government – a minimal response to labour market restructuring – a case study', *Local Government Studies*, vol. 7, no. 4, pp. 67–82.

Davies, T., Mason, C., with Davies, Liz (1984), *Government and Local Labour Market Policy Implementation* (Aldershot: Gower).

Dearlove, J. (1973), *The Politics of Policy in Local Government* (London: Cambridge University Press).

Dearlove, J. (1979), *The Reorganization of British Local Government* (Cambridge: Cambridge University Press).

Dearlove, J., and Saunders, P. (1984), *Introduction to British Politics* (Oxford/Cambridge: Blackwell/Polity).

Dennis, N. (1972), *Public Participation and Planning Blight* (London: Faber).

de Smith, S. A. (1980), *Judicial Review of Administrative Action*, 4th edn (London: Stevens).

Donnison, D. V. (1973), 'The micro-politics of the City', in D. V. Donnison and D. Eversley (eds.), *London: Urban Patterns, Problems and Policies* (London: Heinemann), pp. 383–404.

Dow, J. C. R. (1964), *The Management of the British Economy, 1945–60* (London: Cambridge University Press).

Dror, Y. (1968), *Public Policymaking Reexamined* (Scranton, Pa.: Chandler).

Drucker, H., Dunleavy, P., Gamble, A., and Peele, G. (eds), (1983) *Developments in British Politics* (London: Macmillan).

Drummond, J. M. (1952), *The Finance of Local Government* (London: Allen & Unwin).

Drummond, J. M., and Kitching, W. A. C. (1962), *The Finance of Local Government* (London: Allen & Unwin).

Dudley, G. (1983), 'The road lobby: a declining force?', in D. Marsh (ed), *Pressure Politics* (London: Junction Books), pp. 104–28.

Duncan, S. S., and Goodwin, M. (1982), 'The local state and restructuring social relations: theory and practice', *International Journal of Urban Regional Research*, vol. 6, pp. 157–85.

Dunleavy, P. (1977), 'Protest and quiescence in urban politics: a critique of pluralist and structuralist Marxist views', *International Journal of Urban and Regional Research*, vol. 1, pp. 193–218.

Dunleavy, P. (1979), 'The urban basis of political alignment', *British Journal of Political Science*, vol. 9, pp. 409–43.

Dunleavy, P. (1980a), *Urban Political Analysis* (London: Macmillan).

Dunleavy, P. (1980b), 'Social and political theory and the issues in central–local relations', in Jones, op. cit., pp. 116–36.

Dunleavy, P. (1980c), 'The political implications of sectoral cleavages and the growth of state employment, part I: the analysis of production cleavages', *Political Studies*, vol. 28, pp. 364–83.

Dunleavy, P. (1980d), 'The political implications of sectoral cleavages and the growth of state employment, part II: cleavage structures and political alignment', *Political Studies*, vol. 28, pp. 527–49.

Dunleavy, P. (1981a), 'Professions and policy change: notes towards a model of ideological corporatism', *Public Administration Bulletin*, no. 36, pp. 3–16.

Dunleavy, P. (1981b), *The Politics of Mass Housing in Britain, 1945–75* (Oxford: Clarendon Press).

Dunleavy, P. (1982a), 'Is there a radical approach to public administration?', *Public Administration*, vol. 60, pp. 215–33.

Dunleavy, P. (1982b), 'Quasi-governmental sector professionalism: some implications for public policy-making in Britain', in Barker, op. cit., pp. 181–205.

Dunleavy, P. (1984), 'The limits to local government', in M. Boddy and C. Fudge (eds.), *Local Socialism?* (London: Macmillan), pp. 49–81.

Dunleavy, P., and Husbands, C. (1985), *British Democracy at the Crossroads* (London: Allen & Unwin).

Dunleavy, P., and Rhodes, R. A. W. (1983), 'Beyond Whitehall', in

Drucker, Dunleavy, Gamble and Peele, op. cit., pp. 106–33.

Dunleavy, P., and Rhodes, R. A. W. (1986), 'Government Beyond Whitehall', in H. Drucker, P. Dunleavy, A. Gamble and G. Peele (eds.), *Developments in British Politics 2* (London: Macmillan), pp. 107–43.

Dunsire, A. (1973), *Administration: The Word and the Science* (London: Martin Robertson).

Dyson, K. (1980), *The State Tradition in Western Europe* (Oxford: Martin Robertson).

ESRC (Economic and Social Research Council) (1984), *Evaluation of the ESRC's Research Initiative on the Relations between Central and Local Government* (London: ESRC, mimeo, December).

Eckstein, H. H. (1958), *The English Health Service* (Cambridge, Mass.: Harvard University Press).

Eckstein, H. H. (1960), *Pressure Group Politics* (London: Allen & Unwin).

Edwards, J., and Batley, R. (1978), *The Politics of Positive Discrimination* (London: Tavistock).

Elcock, H., and Haywood, S. (1980), *The Buck Stops Where? Accountability and Control in the National Health Service* (University of Hull, Institute of Health Studies).

Eldersveld, S. (1964), *Political Parties: A Behavioural Analysis* (Chicago: Rand McNally).

Elgin, D. S., and Bushnell, R. A. (1977), 'The limits to complexity: are bureaucracies becoming unmanageable?', *The Futurist*, December, pp. 337–49.

Elkin, S. (1975), 'Comparative urban politics and interorganizational behaviour', in K. Young (ed.), *Essays in the Study of Urban Politics* (London: Macmillan), pp. 158–84.

Elliott, M. J. (1981), *The Role of Law in Central–Local Relations* (London: SSRC).

Else, P. K., and Marshall, G. P. (1979), *The Management of Public Expenditure* (London: Policy Studies Institute).

Else, P. K., and Marshall, G. P. (1981), 'The unplanning of public expenditure: recent problems in expenditure planning and the consequences of cash limits', *Public Administration*, vol. 59, pp. 253–78.

Elster, J. (1979), *Ulysses and Sirens* (Cambridge: Cambridge University Press).

Elster, J. (1983), *Explaining Technical Change* (Cambridge: Cambridge University Press).

Etzioni, A. (1968), *The Active Society* (New York: Free Press).

Faludi, A. (1973), *Planning Theory* (Oxford: Pergamon).

Farrell, M. (1976), *Northern Ireland: The Orange State* (London: Pluto).

Finer, S. E. (1957), *The Life and Times of Sir Edwin Chadwick* (London: Methuen).

Flynn, N. (1985), 'Direct labour organization', in Ranson, Jones and Walsh, op. cit., pp. 119–34.

Flynn, N., and Leach, S. (1984), *Joint Boards and Joint Committees: An Evaluation* (University of Birmingham, Institute of Local Government Studies).

Flynn, N., Leach, S., and Vielba, C. (1985), *Abolition or Reform? The GLC and the Metropolitan County Councils* (London: Allen & Unwin).

Flynn, R. (1983), 'Co-optation and strategic planning in the local state', in King, op. cit., pp. 85–106.

Foley, D. (1960), 'British town planning: one ideology or three?', in A. Faludi (ed.), *A Reader in Planning Theory* (Oxford: Pergamon), pp. 69–93.

Forrester, A., Lansley, S., and Pauley, R. (1985), *Beyond Our Ken* (London: Fourth Estate).

Forsythe, G. (1973), *Doctors and State Medicine*, 2nd edn (London: Pitman).

Foster, C. D. (1971), *Politics, Finance and the Role of Economics* (London: Allen & Unwin).

Foster, C. D., Jackman, R., and Perlman, M. (1980), *Local Government Finance in a Unitary State* (London: Allen & Unwin).

Fox, D. (1983), 'Central control and local capacity in the housing field', in K. Young (ed.), *National Interests and Local Government* (London: Heinemann), pp. 82–100.

Franklin, M., and Page, E. (1984), 'A critique of the consumption cleavage approach in British voting studies', *Political Studies*, vol. 32, pp. 521–36.

Friend, J., Power, J. M., and Yewlett, C. J. L. (1974), *Public Planning: The Inter-Corporate Dimension* (London: Tavistock).

Fry, G. K. (1985), *The Changing Civil Service* (London: Allen & Unwin).

Fulton Committee (1968), *Report of the Committee on the Civil Service 1966–68* (Cmnd 3638, London: HMSO).

Galbraith, J. K. (1962), *The Affluent Society* (Harmondsworth: Penguin).

Galbraith, J. K. (1969), *The New Industrial State* (Harmondsworth: Penguin).

Garner, J. F. (1970), 'Public corporations in the United Kingdom', in W. Friedmann and J. F. Garner (eds.), *Government Enterprise: A Comparative Study* (London: Stevens), pp. 3–25.

Garner, J. F. (1974), *Administrative Law*, 4th edn (London: Butterworths).

Garner, J. F., and Jones, B. L. (1985), *Garner's Administrative Law*, 6th edn (London: Butterworths).

Garner, M. R. (1982), 'Auditing the efficiency of nationalized industries: enter the Monopolies and Mergers Commission', *Public Administration*, vol. 60, pp. 409–28.

Garner, M. R. (1985), 'The governmental control of public corporations in Britain: a history and an evaluation', paper to the thirteenth world congress of the International Political Science Association, Paris, July.

Gibson, J. (1985), 'Why block grant failed', in Ranson, Jones and Walsh, op. cit., pp. 58–80.

Glennerster, H. (with N. Korman and F. Marslen-Wilson) (1983), *Planning for Priority Groups* (Oxford: Martin Robertson).

Godley, W. (1975), Oral evidence to the Select Committee on Expenditure, 1st Report, Session 1975–6, *The Financing of Public Expenditure*, vol. 2, HC69–11, pp. 212–23 (London: HMSO).

Goldman, S. (1973), *The Developing System of Public Expenditure Management and Control* (London: HMSO).

Goldsmith, M. (1984), *Project Report* (Final Report to the SSRC).

Goldsmith, M. J. (1986a), 'Managing the periphery in a period of fiscal stress', in Goldsmith, op. cit., pp. 152–72.

Goldsmith, M. J. (ed.) (1986b), *New Research in Central–Local Relations* (Aldershot: Gower).

Goldsmith, M., and Rhodes, R. A. W. (1986), *Research Register and Research Digest on Central–Local Relations in Britain* (London: ESRC).

Goldthorpe, J. H. (1980), *Social Mobility and Class Structure in Modern Britain* (Oxford: Clarendon Press).

Goodin, R. E. (1982a), 'Freedom and the welfare state: theoretical foundations', *Journal of Social Policy*, vol. 11, pp. 149–76.

Goodin, R. E. (1982b), *Political Theory and Public Policy* (Chicago: Chicago University Press).

Goodin, R. E. (1982c), 'Rational politicians and rational bureaucrats in Washington and Whitehall', *Public Administration*, vol. 60, pp. 23–41.

Goodwin, M. (1982), 'The local state and the local provision of welfare', paper to the annual conference of the Political Studies Association, University of Kent, April.

Gouldner, A. W. (1970), 'Cosmopolitans and locals: toward an analysis of latent social roles', in O. S. Grusky and G. A. Miller (eds.), *The Sociology of Organizations: Basic Studies* (New York: Free Press), pp. 477–82.

Grant, M. (1984), *Rate Capping and the Law* (London: Association of Metropolitan Authorities).

Grant, M. (1986), *Rate Capping and the Law*, 2nd edn (London: Association of Metropolitan Authorities).

Grant, W. P. (1977), *Independent Local Politics in England and Wales* (Aldershot: Saxon House).

Grant, W. P. (1982), *The Political Economy of Industrial Policy* (London: Butterworths)

Grant, W. P., and Marsh, D. (1977), *The CBI* (London: Hodder & Stoughton).

Gray, A., and Jenkins, W. I. (1982), 'Policy analysis in British central government: the experience of PAR', *Public Administration*, vol. 60, pp. 429–50.

Gray, A., and Jenkins, W. I. (1985), *Administrative Politics in British Government* (Brighton: Wheatsheaf).

Gray, C. (1982), 'The regional water authorities', in B. Hogwood and M. Keating (eds.), *Regional Government in England* (Oxford: Clarendon Press), pp. 143–67.

Gray, V. (1978), 'Accountability in the policy process: an alternative perspective', in Greer, Hedlund and Gibson, op. cit., pp. 169–78.

Green, A. J. (1979), 'Devolution and public finance: Stormont from 1921–1972', *Studies in Public Policy*, no. 49 (University of Strathclyde; Centre for the Study of Public Policy).

Greenwood, R. (1982), 'Pressure from Whitehall', in R. Rose and E. Page (eds.), *Fiscal Stress in the Cities* (London: Cambridge University Press), pp. 44–76.

Greenwood, R. (1983), 'Changing patterns of budgeting in English local government', *Public Administration*, vol. 61, pp. 149–68.

Greenwood, R., Walsh, K., Hinings, C. R., and Ranson, S. (1980), *Patterns of Management in Local Government* (Oxford: Martin Robertson).

Greer, S., Hedlund, R. D. and Gibson, J. L. (eds.) (1978), *Accountability in Urban Society* (London: Sage).

Gregory, R. (1967), 'The minister's line: or the M4 comes to Berkshire', *Public Administration*, vol. 45, pp. 113–28 and 269–86.

Griffith, J. A. G. (1966), *Central Departments and Local Authorities* (London: Allen & Unwin).

Griffith, J. A. G. (1981), *The Politics of the Judiciary*, 2nd edn (Glasgow: Fontana/Collins).

Griffiths Report (1983), *NHS Management Inquiry* (London: DHSS).

Grove, J. W. (1962), *Government and Industry* (London: Longmans).

Gyford, J. (1976), *Local Politics in Britain* (London: Croom Helm).

Gyford, J. (1983a), 'The implications of local socialism', *Local Government Studies*, vol. 9, no. 1, pp. 13–17.

Gyford, J. (1983b), 'The new urban Left: a local road to socialism?', *New Society*, 21 April, pp. 91–3.

Gyford, J. (1984), 'From community action to local socialism', *Local Government Studies*, vol. 10, no. 4, pp. 5–10.

Gyford, J. (1985a), 'The politicization of local government', in Loughlin, Gelfand and Young, op. cit., pp. 77–97.

Gyford, J. (1985b), *The Politics of Local Socialism* (London: Allen & Unwin).

Gyford, J., and James, M. (1983), *National Parties and Local Politics* (London: Allen & Unwin).

HMSO (1961), *The Financial and Economic Obligations of the Nationalized Industries* (Cmnd 1337, London: HMSO).

HMSO (1967), *Nationalized Industries: A Review of Economic and Financial Control* (Cmnd 3437, London: HMSO).

HMSO (1969), *Public Expenditure: A New Presentation* (Cmnd 4017, London: HMSO).

HMSO (1971), *Better Services for the Mentally Handicapped* (Cmnd 4683, London: HMSO).

HMSO (1975), *Capital Investment Procedures* (Cmnd 6106, London: HMSO).

HMSO (1976), *Cash Limits on Public Expenditure* (Cmnd 6440, London: HMSO).

HMSO (1977a), *Education in Schools: A Consultative Document* (Cmnd 6869, London: HMSO).

HMSO (1977b), *Policy for the Inner Cities* (Cmnd 6845, London: HMSO).

HMSO (1978), *The Nationalized Industries* (Cmnd 7131, London: HMSO).

HMSO (1979), *Organic Change in Local Government* (Cmnd 7457, London: HMSO).

HMSO (1983a), *Rates* (Cmnd 9008, London: HMSO).

HMSO (1983b), *Streamlining the Cities* (Cmnd 9063, London: HMSO).

HMSO (1983c), *The Government's Expenditure Plans 1983–84 to 1985–86* (Cmnd 8789, London: HMSO).

HMSO (1986a), *Privatization of the Water Authorities in England and Wales* (Cmnd 9734, London: HMSO).

HMSO (1986b), *Paying for Local Government* (Cmnd 9714, London: HMSO).

Hague, D. C., Mackenzie, W. J. M., and Barker, A. (eds.) (1975), *Public Policy and Private Interests: The Institutions of Compromise* (London: Macmillan).

Haigh, N. (1984), 'Devolved responsibility and centralization: effects of EEC environmental policy', paper to the RIPA conference on 'The Shifting State: Rules, Roles and Boundaries', University of Aston, September.

Hailsham, Lord (1978), *The Dilemmas of Democracy* (London: Collins).

Hall, P., Gracey, H., Drewett, R., and Thomas, R. (1973), *The Containment of Urban England. Volume 2: The Planning System* (London: Allen & Unwin).

Hall, P., and Diamond, D. (1981), 'A research agenda', in P. Hall (ed.), *The Inner City in Context* (London: Heinemann), pp. 132–52.

Halmos, P. (1965), *The Faith of Counsellors* (London: Constable).

Halmos, P. (1970), *The Personal Service Society* (London: Constable).

Halsey, A. H. (1978), 'Government against poverty in school and community', in M. Bulmer (ed.), *Social Policy Research* (London: Macmillan), pp. 139–59.

Halsey, A. H. (ed.) (1972), *Educational Priority*, vol. 1, *EPA Problems and Priorities* (London: HMSO).

Halsey, A. H., Heath, A. F., and Ridge, J. M. (1980), *Origins and Destinations: Family, Class and Education in Modern Britain* (Oxford: Clarendon Press).

Ham, C. (1981), *Policy-Making in the National Health Service* (London: Macmillan).

Ham, C. (1985), *Health Policy in Britain*, 2nd edn (London: Macmillan).

Hambleton, R. (1983), 'Planning systems and policy implementation', *Journal of Public Policy*, vol. 3, pp. 397–418.

Hampton, W. A. (1970), *Democracy and Community* (London: Oxford University Press).

Hanf, K. (1978), 'Introduction', in K. Hanf and F. W. Scharpf (eds.), *Interorganizational Policy Making* (London: Sage), pp. 1–15.

Hardingham, S. (1983), 'LGC surveys privatisation over the last year', *Local Government Chronicle*, 17 June, pp. 655–62.

Hardingham, S. (1984), 'Privatization gets close examination but interest fades', *Local Government Chronicle*, 22 June, pp. 703–8 and 711.

Harris, R., and Seldon, A. (1976), *Pricing or Taxing?* (London: Institute of Economic Affairs, Hobart Paper No. 71).

Hartley, D. (1971), 'The relationship between central and local authorities', *Public Administration*, vol. 49, pp. 439–56.

Hayek, F. (1960), *The Constitution of Liberty* (London: Routledge & Kegan Paul).

Hayward, J. E. S., and Watson, M. (eds.) (1975), *Planning, Politics and Public Policy* (Cambridge: Cambridge University Press).

Haywood, S., and Alaszewski, A. (1980), *Crisis in the Health Service* (London: Croom Helm).

Haywood, S., and Hunter, D. J. (1982), 'Consultative processes in health policy in the United Kingdom: a view from the centre', *Public Administration*, vol. 60, pp. 143–62.

Heald, D. (1980a), 'The economic and financial control of UK nationalized industries', *Economic Journal*, vol. 90, pp. 243–65.

Heald, D. (1980b), 'The Scottish Rate Support Grant: how different from the English and Welsh?', *Public Administration*, vol. 58, pp. 25–46.

Heald, D. (1981), 'UK energy policy: the economic and financial control of the nationalized energy industries', *Energy Policy*, vol. 8, pp. 99–112.

Heald, D. (1982), 'Using Scottish instruments in pursuit of UK objectives', *Local Government Studies*, vol. 8, no. 3, pp. 33–46.

Heald, D. (1983), *Public Expenditure* (Oxford: Martin Robertson).

Heald, D. (1984), 'Privatization and public money', in Steel and Heald, op. cit., pp. 21–43.

Heald, D. (1985), 'Will the privatization of public enterprises solve the problem of control?', *Public Administration*, vol. 63, pp. 7–22.

Heald, D., and Steel, D. R. (1981), 'Nationalized industries: the search for control', *Public Money*, vol. 1, June, pp. 13–19.

Heald, D., and Steel, D. (1982), 'Privatizing public enterprise: an analysis of the government's case', *Political Quarterly*, vol. 53, pp. 333–49.

Hechter, M. (1975), *Internal Colonialism: The Celtic Fringe in British National Development, 1536–1966* (London: Routledge & Kegan Paul).

Heclo, H. (1978), 'Issue networks and the executive establishment', in A. King (ed.), *The New American Political System* (Washington, DC: American Enterprise Inc.), pp. 87–124.

Heclo, H., and Wildavsky, A. (1974), *The Private Government of Public Money* (London: Macmillan).

Henney, A. (1984), *Inside Local Government* (London: Sinclair Browne).

Hepworth, N. P. (1970), *The Finance of Local Government*, 1st edn, 7th edn 1984 (London: Allen & Unwin).

Herbert Committee (1956), *Report of the Committee of Inquiry into the Electricity Supply Industry* (Cmnd 9672, London: HMSO).

Hill, M. J. (1972), *The Sociology of Public Administration* (London: Weidenfeld & Nicolson).

Hinings, C. R., Leach, S., Ranson, S., Skelcher, C. K. (1982), *Policy Planning Systems in Central–Local Relations* (Appendices: A, Transport Policies and Programmes (TPPs); B, Inner City Partnerships and Programmes; C, Central–Local Planning in Education) (Final Report to the SSRC).

Hogwood, B. (1979a), 'The tartan fringe: quangos and other assorted animals in Scotland', *Studies in Public Policy*, no. 34 (Glasgow: University of Strathclyde, Centre for the Study of Public Policy).

Hogwood, B. (1979b), *Government and Shipbuilding* (Aldershot: Saxon House).

Hogwood, B. (1979c), 'Analysing industrial policy: a multi-perspective approach', *Public Administration Bulletin*, no. 29, April, pp. 18–42.

Hogwood, B. (1982a), 'The regional dimension of industrial policy', in Madgwick and Rose, op. cit., pp. 34–66.

Hogwood, B. (1982b), 'Quasi-government in Scotland: Scottish forms within a British setting', in Barker, op. cit., pp. 69–87.

Hogwood, B. and Keating, M. (eds.) (1982), *Regional Government in England* (Oxford: Clarendon Press).

Hogwood, B. and Lindley, P. (1982), 'Variations in regional boundaries', in Hogwood and Keating, op. cit., pp. 21–49.

Holland, P. (1979), *Quango, Quango, Quango: The Full Dossier on Patronage in Britain* (London: Adam Smith Institute).

Hollis, F. (1967), 'Principles and assumptions underlying social work practice', in E. Younghusband (ed.), *Social Work and Social Values* (London: Allen & Unwin), pp. 22–38.

Holroyd Committee (1970), *Report of the Departmental Committee on the Fire Service* (Cmnd 4371, London: HMSO).

Home Office (1978), 'Note on Fire Service responsibilities from the Home Office to the local authority associations', mimeo, 22 June.

Hood, C. C. (1976), *The Limits of Administration* (London: Wiley).

Hood, C. C. (1978), 'Keeping the centre small: explanations of agency type', *Political Studies*, vol. 26, pp. 30–46.

Hood, C. C. (1982a), 'Governmental bodies and government growth', in Barker, op. cit., pp. 44–68.

Hood, C. C. (1982b), 'Review' of S. Barrett and C. Fudge (eds.), *Policy and Action: Essays on the Implementation of Public Policy* (Methuen, 1981), *Public Administration*, vol. 60, pp. 368–9.

Hood, C. C. (1983), *The Tools of Government* (London: Macmillan).

Hood, C. C., and Bradshaw, J. R. (1977), 'The family fund: implications of an unorthodox agency', *Public Administration*, vol. 55, pp. 447–64.

Houlihan, B. (1983a), 'Conceptualizing central–local relations', paper to the annual conference of the Political Studies Association, Newcastle University, April.

Houlihan, B. (1983b), 'The professionalization of housing policy making: the impact of housing investment programmes and professionals', *Public Administration Bulletin*, no. 41, March, pp. 14–31.

Houlihan, B. (1984), 'The regional offices of the DoE – policemen or mediators? A study of local housing policy', *Public Administration*, vol. 62, pp. 401–21.

Hull, C., and Rhodes, R. A. W. (1977), *Intergovernmental Relations in the European Community* (Aldershot: Saxon House).

Hunt, L. (1978), 'Social work and ideology', in N. Timms and D. Watson (eds.), *Philosophy in Social Work* (London: Routledge & Kegan Paul), pp. 7–25.

Isaac-Henry, K. (1975), 'Local authority associations and local government reform', *Local Government Studies*, vol. 1, no. 3, pp. 1–12.

Isaac-Henry, K. (1980a), 'The English local authority associations', *Public Administration Bulletin*, no. 33, August, pp. 21–41.

Isaac-Henry, K. (1980b), 'The Association of Municipal Corporations and the County Councils' Association: a study of influences and pressures on the reorganization of local government 1945–72', PhD thesis, University of London.

Jackman, R. (1985), 'Local government finance', in Loughlin, Gelford and Young, op. cit., pp. 144–68.

Jackson, P. M. (1982a), *The Political Economy of Bureaucracy* (London: Philip Allan).

Jackson, P. M. (1982b), 'The impact of economic theories on local government finance', *Local Government Studies*, vol. 8, no. 1, pp. 21–34.

Jackson, P. M. (1983), 'Public sector labour markets – part I: the evidence', *Economic Review*, vol. 1, no. 2, November, pp. 8–11.

Jackson, P. M. (1984), *Macroeconomic Activity and Local Government Behaviour* (Final Report to the ESRC Panel on Central–Local Government Relations).

Jackson, P. M. (ed.) (1985a), *Implementing Government Policy Initiatives. The Thatcher Administration 1979–1983* (London: RIPA).

Jackson, P. M. (1985b), 'Policy implementation and monetarism: two primers', in Jackson, op. cit., pp. 11–31.

Jackson, P. M. (1985c), 'Perspectives on practical monetarism', in Jackson, op. cit., pp. 33–67.

James, M. (1982), 'The Welsh local authority associations', paper to the conference of the Political Studies Association UK Politics Group, Queen's University, Belfast, September.

James, M. (1983), 'Central–local government relations in Wales', paper to the conference of the Political Studies Association UK Politics Group, Oxford Polytechnic, August.

James, P. H. (1980), *The Reorganization of Secondary Education* (Windsor: NFER).

Jay Committee (1979), *Report of the Committee of Inquiry into Mental Handicap Nursing and Care* (Cmnd 7468, London: HMSO).

Jenkins, S. (1985), 'The Star Chamber, PESC and the Cabinet', *Political Quarterly*, vol. 56, no. 2, pp. 113–21.

Jessop, R. (1978), 'Corporatism, parliamentarism and social democracy', in Schmitter and Lehmbruch, op. cit., pp. 185–212.

Johnson, N. (1977), *In Search of the Constitution* (Oxford: Pergamon).

Johnson, N. (1978), 'The public corporation: an ambiguous species', in D. Butler and A. H. Halsey (eds.), *Policy and Politics: Essays in Honour of Norman Chester* (London: Macmillan), pp. 122–39.

Johnson, N. (1979), 'Editorial: quangos and the structure of government', *Public Administration*, vol. 57, pp. 379–95.

Jones, G. W. (1969), *Borough Politics* (London: Macmillan).

Jones, G. W. (1975), 'Varieties of local politics', *Local Government Studies*, vol. 1, no. 2, pp. 17–32.

Jones, G. W. (1977), *Responsibility and Government* (London: London School of Economics and Political Science).

Jones, G. W. (1980), *New Approaches to the Study of Central-Local Government Relationships* (Aldershot: Gower: SSRC).

Jones, G. W., and Stewart, J. D. (1982), 'The value of local autonomy – a rejoinder', *Local Government Studies*, vol. 8, no. 5, pp. 10–15.

Jones, G. W., and Stewart, J. D. (1983), *The Case for Local Government* (London: Allen & Unwin).

Jones, K. (1978), 'Policy towards the nationalized industries', in Blackaby, op. cit., pp. 484–514.

Jones, P. (1983), 'The British Medical Association: public good or private interest?', in Marsh, op. cit., pp. 83–103.

Jordan, G. (1981), 'Iron triangles, woolly corporatism and elastic nets: images of the policy process', *Journal of Public Policy*, vol. 1, pp. 95–123.

Jordan, G., and Richardson, J. J. (1982), 'The British policy style or the logic of negotiation', in Richardson, op. cit., pp. 80–110.

Jordan, G., Richardson, J. J., and Kimber, R. H. (1977), 'The origins of the Water Act 1973', *Public Administration*, vol. 55, pp. 317–34.

Justice (1980), *The Local Ombudsman: A Review of the First Five Years* (London: Justice).

Karram, T. (1984), 'The local government workforce – public sector paragon or private sector parasite?', *Local Government Studies*, vol. 10, no. 4, pp. 39–58.

Keating, M. (1984), 'Labour's territorial strategy', in I. McAllister and R. Rose (eds.), *The Nationwide Competition for Votes* (London: Frances Pinter), pp. 64–76.

Keating, M., and Midwinter, A. (1983), *The Government of Scotland* (Edinburgh: Mainstream).

Keating, M., and Midwinter, A. (1984), 'The area project approach to economic development in Scotland', *Public Administration*, vol. 62, pp. 108–12.

Keating, M., Midwinter, A., and Taylor, P. (1983), '"Excessive and unreasonable": the politics of the Scottish hit list', *Political Studies*, vol. 31, no. 3, pp. 394–417.

Keating, M., Midwinter, A., and Taylor, P. (1984), 'Implementing the unworkable: Enterprise Zones', *Political Quarterly*, vol. 55, pp. 78–84.

Keating, M., and Rhodes, M. (1981), 'Politics or technocracy? The regional water authorities', *Political Quarterly*, vol. 52, pp. 487–90.

Keating, M., and Rhodes, M. (1982), 'The status of regional government: an analysis of the West Midlands', in Hogwood and Keating, op. cit., pp. 51–73.

Keegan, W., and Pennant-Rea, R. (1979), *Who Runs the Economy?* (London: Temple Smith).

Keith-Lucas, B. (1962), 'Poplarism', *Public Law*, Spring, pp. 52–80.

Keith-Lucas, B., and Richards, P. G. (1978), *A History of Local Government in the Twentieth Century* (London: Allen & Unwin).

Kellas, J. (1973), *The Scottish Political System*, 2nd edn 1975, 3rd edn 1984 (London: Cambridge University Press).

Kellas, J. G., and Madgwick, P. (1982), 'Territorial ministries: the Scottish and Welsh Offices', in Madgwick and Rose, op. cit., pp. 9–33.

Kermode, D. G. (1979), *Devolution at Work: A Case Study of the Isle of Man* (Aldershot: Saxon House).

Kilbrandon Commission (1970), *Commission on the Constitution, Minutes of Evidence, II Scotland* (London: HMSO).

Kilbrandon Commission (1973), *Report of the Royal Commission on the Constitution, 1969–73* (Cmnd 5460, London: HMSO).

Kimber, R. H., and Richardson, J. J. (1974), *Campaigning for the Environment* (London: Routledge & Kegan Paul).

King, D. N. (1973), *Financial and Economic Aspects of Regionalism and Separatism*, Commission on the Constitution, Research Paper 10 (London: HMSO).

King, R. (ed.) (1983a), *Capital and Politics* (London: Routledge & Kegan Paul).

King, R. (1983b), 'The political practice of local capitalist associations', in King, op. cit., pp. 107–31.

Kirby, A. M. (1979), '"Managerialism" and local authority housing: a review', *Public Administration Bulletin*, no. 30, August, pp. 47–60.

Klein, R. (1982), 'Performance, evaluation and the NHS: a case study in conceptual perplexity and organizational complexity', *Public Administration*, vol. 60, pp. 385–407.

Klein, R. (1983), *The Politics of the National Health Service* (London: Longmans).

Kleinberg, B. S. (1973), *American Society in the Postindustrial Age* (Columbus, Ohio: Merrill).

Kogan, M. (1971), *The Politics of Education* (Harmondsworth: Penguin).

Kogan, M. (1975), *Educational Policy Making* (London: Allen & Unwin).

Kogan, M. (1978), *The Politics of Educational Change* (London: Fontana).

Kogan, M., and Van der Eyken, W. (1973), *County Hall* (Harmondsworth: Penguin).

Labour Party (1975), *Devolution and Regional Government in England: A Discussion Document for the Labour Party* (London: Labour Party, November).

Laffin, M. (1982), *Professionalism in Central–Local Government Relations* (Final Report to the SSRC).

Laffin, M. (1985), 'Professionalism in crisis', paper to the annual conference of the Political Studies Association, University of Manchester, April.

Laffin, M. (1986), *Professionalism and Policy: The Role of the Professions in the Central–Local Government Relationship* (Aldershot: Gower).

Laffin, M., and Young, K. (1985), 'The changing roles and responsibilities of local authority chief officers', *Public Administration*, vol. 63, pp. 41–59.

Landau, M. (1969), 'Redundancy, rationality and the problem of duplication and overlap', *Public Administration Review*, vol. 39, pp. 346–58.

Landau, M. (1979), *Political Theory and Political Science* (Brighton: Harvester).

LaPorte, T. (ed.) (1975), *Organized Social Complexity* (Princeton, NJ: Princeton University Press).

Lawless, P. (1979), *Urban Deprivation and Government Initiatives* (London: Faber).

Lawrence, R. J. (1965), *The Government of Northern Ireland: Public Finance and Public Services, 1921–1964* (London: Oxford University Press).

Lawton, D. (1980), *The Politics of the School Curriculum* (London: Routledge & Kegan Paul).

Layfield Committee (1976), *Report of the Committee of Inquiry into Local Government Finance* (Cmnd 6453, London: HMSO).

Leach, S. N. (1982a), 'Inner city partnerships and programmes', in Hinings, Leach, Ranson and Sketcher, op. cit., appendix B.

Leach, S. N. (1982b), 'The politics of the inner city partnerships and programmes', *Local Government Policy Making*, vol. 8, no. 3, pp. 21–39.

Leach, S., Hinings, C. R., Ranson, S., and Skelcher, C. (1983), 'Uses and abuses of policy planning systems', *Local Government Studies*, vol. 9, no. 1, pp. 23–37.

Leach, S., and Stewart, J. D. (1986), *The Hung Counties* (Luton: Local Government Training Board, mimeo).

Lee, J. M. (1963), *Social Leaders and Public Persons* (Oxford: Clarendon Press).

Le Grand, J. (1982), *The Strategy of Equality* (London: Allen & Unwin).

Leibenstein, H. (1966), 'Allocative efficiency versus "X-efficiency"', *American Economic Review*, vol. LV, pp. 392–415.

Levin, P. H. (1979), 'Highway inquiries: a study in governmental responsiveness', *Public Administration*, vol. 57, pp. 21–49.

Levitt, R., and Wall, A. (1984), *The Reorganized National Health Service*, 3rd edn (London: Croom Helm).

Lijphart, A. (1968), *The Politics of Accommodation: Pluralism and Democracy in the Netherlands* (Berkeley, Calif.: University of California Press).

Lindblom, C. E. (1977), *Politics and Markets* (New York: Basic Books).

Lindblom, C. E. (1979), 'Still muddling, not yet through', *Public Administration Review*, vol. 39, pp. 517–26.

Lindley, P. (1982), 'The framework of regional planning 1964–80', in Hogwood and Keating, op. cit., pp. 169–90.

Lipsky, M. (1978), 'The assault on human services: street-level bureaucrats, accountability and the fiscal crisis', in Greer, Hedlund and Gibson, op. cit., pp. 15–38.

Littlechild, S. C. *et al.* (1979a), *The Taming of Government* (London: Institute of Economic Affairs, IEA Readings No. 21).

Littlechild, S. C. (1979b), 'What should government do?', in Littlechild, op. cit., pp. 1–15.

Littlechild, S. C. (1986), *Economic Regulation of Privatized Water Authorities* (London: HMSO).

Lodge, P., and Blackstone, T. (1982), *Educational Policy and Educational Inequality* (Oxford: Martin Robertson).

Lomas, O. (1985), 'Law', in Ranson, Jones and Walsh, op. cit., pp. 81–99.

Lomer, M. (1977), 'The chief executive in local government 1974–76', *Local Government Studies*, vol. 3, no. 4, pp. 17–40.

Loney, M. (1983), *Community against Itself* (London: Heinemann).

Loughlin, M. (1985), 'The restructuring of central–local government legal relations', *Local Government Studies*, vol. 11, no. 6, pp. 59–74.

Loughlin, M. (1986), *Local Government in the Modern State* (London: Sweet & Maxwell).

Loughlin, M., Gelfaud, M. D. and Young, K. (1985), *Half a Century of Municipal Decline 1935–85* (London: Allen & Unwin).

Lowe, P., and Goyder, J. (1983), *Environmental Groups in Politics* (London: Allen & Unwin).

Lowi, T. J. (1969), *The End of Liberalism* (New York: Norton).

Lowi, T. J. (1972), 'Four systems of policy, politics and choice', *Public Administration Review*, vol. 32, pp. 298–310.

Luhmann, N. (1982), *The Differentiation of Society* (New York: Columbia University Press).

Lukes, S. (1974), *Power: A Radical View* (London: Macmillan).

McAllister, I., and Rose, R. (1984), *The Nationwide Competition for Votes* (London: Frances Pinter).

McCrone, D. (ed.) (1983), *The Scottish Government Yearbook 1984* (University of Edinburgh, Unit for the Study of Government in Scotland).

McKay, D., and Cox, A. (1978), 'Confusion and reality in public policy: the case of the British urban programme', *Political Studies*, vol. 26, pp. 491–506.

McKay, D., and Cox, A. (1979), *The Politics of Urban Change* (London: Croom Helm).

Mackenzie, W. J. M. (1969), 'Pressure groups in British government', in R. Rose (ed.), *Studies in British Politics*, 2nd edn (London: Macmillan), pp. 258–75.

Mackenzie, W. J. M., and Grove, J. W. (1957), *Central Administration in Britain* (London: Longmans).

McKeown, T. (1976), *The Role of Medicine* (London: Nuffield Provincial Hospitals Trust).

McFarland, A. (1979), 'Recent social movements and theories of power in America', paper to the annual meeting of the American Political Science Association, Washington, DC, August.

Macfarlane Report (1980), *Education for 16–19 Year Olds* (London: Department of Education and Science).

Macrory Report (1970), *Review Body on Local Government in Northern Ireland* (Cmd 546, Belfast: HMSO).

Madgwick, P. (1986), 'Prime ministerial power revisited', *Social Studies Review*, vol. 1, no. 5, pp. 28–35.

Madgwick, P. J., and James, M. (1980), 'The network of consultative government in Wales' in Jones, op. cit., pp. 101–15.

Madgwick, P., and Rose, R. (eds.) (1982), *The Territorial Dimension in United Kingdom Politics* (London: Macmillan).

Malpass, P. N. (1975), 'Professionalism and the role of architects in local authority housing', *Royal Institute of British Architects Journal*, vol. 82, no. 6, pp. 6–29.

Manzer, R. A. (1970), *Teachers and Politics* (Manchester: Manchester University Press).

March, J. G., and Olsen, J. P. (1984), 'The new institutionalism: organizational factors in political life', *American Political Science Review*, vol. 78, pp. 734–49.

Marsh, D. (ed.), (1983a), *Pressure Politics* (London: Junction Books).

Marsh, D. (1983b), 'Introduction', in Marsh, op. cit., pp. 1–19.

Marsh, D., and Grant, W. P. (1982), 'Tripartism: myth or reality?', in A. G. McGrew and M. J. Wilson (eds.), *Decision Making: Approaches and Analysis* (Manchester: Manchester University Press for the Open University), pp. 291–302.

Marsh, D., and Locksley, G. (1983), 'Capital: the neglected face of power?', in Marsh, op. cit., pp. 21–52.

Martin, J. P. (1984), *Hospitals in Trouble* (Oxford: Blackwell).

Martlew, C. (1983), 'The state and local government finance', *Public Administration*, vol. 61, pp. 127–47.

Mason, C. (1984), 'YTS and local education authorities – a context', *Local Government Studies*, vol. 10, no. 1, pp. 63–73.

Massey, A. (1986), 'Professional élites and BNFL', *Politics*, vol. 6, no. 1, pp. 9–17.

Mellors, C. (1978), *The British MP* (Aldershot: Saxon House).

The Merrison Commission (1979), *Report of the Royal Commission on the National Health Service* (Cmnd 7615, London: HMSO).

Middlemas, K. (1979), *Politics in Industrial Society* (London: Deutsch).

Midwinter, A. (1980), 'The Scottish Office and local authority financial planning', *Public Administration Bulletin*, no. 34, December, pp. 21–43.

Midwinter, A. (1984), *The Politics of Local Spending* (Edinburgh: Mainstream).

Midwinter, A. (1985), 'Setting the rate – Liverpool style', *Local Government Studies*, vol. 11, no. 3, pp. 25–33.

Midwinter, A., and Franklin, M. (1982), *Current Expenditure Guidelines – 1982/83. An Evaluation of the Client Group Method of Assessing Local Authorities' Expenditure Need* (Glasgow: University of Strathclyde, report prepared for Highland Regional Council.)

Midwinter, A., Keating, M., and Taylor, P. (1984), 'Current expenditure guidelines: a failure of indicative planning', *Local Government Studies*, vol. 10, no. 2, pp. 21–31.

Midwinter, A., and Page, E. (1981), 'Cutting local spending – the Scottish experience 1976–80', in C. Hood and M. Wright (eds.), *Big Government in Hard Times* (Oxford: Martin Robertson), pp. 56–76.

Miliband, R. (1973), *The State in Capitalist Society* (London: Quartet).

Mill, J. S. (1910), *Utilitarianism, Liberty and Representative Government* (London: Dent).

Miller, W. L. (1981), *The End of British Politics?* (Oxford: Clarendon Press).

Miller, W. L. (1983), 'The de-nationalization of British politics: the re-emergence of the periphery', *West European Politics*, vol. 6, pp. 103–29.

Milner-Holland Committee (1965), *Report of the Committee on Housing in Greater London* (Cmnd 2605, London: HMSO).

Minns, R. (1974), 'The significance of Clay Cross: another look at district audit', *Policy and Politics*, vol. 2, pp. 309–24.

Mitchell, A. (1974), 'Clay Cross', *Political Quarterly*, vol. 45, pp. 165–79.

Mitchell, J. D. B. (1967), 'Administrative law and parliamentary control', *Political Quarterly*, vol. 38, pp. 360–74.

Moon, J. (n.d.), 'Radical government, neocorporatist structures and policy change: reflections on the Thatcher government's unemployment and new technology policies' (University of Western Australia, Department of Politics, mimeo.)

Moon, J. (1984), 'The response of British governments to unemployment', in Richardson and Henning, op. cit., pp. 15–39.

Moon, J., and Richardson, J. J. (1984), 'Policy-making with a difference? The Technical and Vocational Education Initiative', *Public Administration*, vol. 62, pp. 23–33.

Moon, J., and Richardson, J. J. (1985), *Unemployment in the UK: Politics and Policies* (Aldershot: Gower).

Morrison, H. (1964), *Government and Parliament*, 3rd edn (London: Oxford University Press).

Morton, J. (1970), *The Best Laid Schemes?* (London: Charles Knight).

Mottershead, P. (1978), 'Industrial policy', in Blackaby, op. cit., pp. 418–83.

Muchnick, D. M. (1970), *Urban Renewal in Liverpool* (London: G. Bell & Sons).

Mueller, D. C. (1979), *Public Choice* (Cambridge: Cambridge University Press).

NEDO (National Economic Development Office) (1976), *A Study of UK Nationalized Industries, their Role in the Economy and Control in the Future* (Vol. 1, *Report*; Vol. 2, *Appendix Volume*) (London: HMSO).

Nairn, T. (1977), *The Break-Up of Britain* (London: New Left Books).

Newton, K. (1976), *Second City Politics* (Oxford: Clarendon Press).

Newton, K. (1980), *Balancing the Books* (London: Sage).

Newton, K., and Karran, T. J. (1985), *The Politics of Local Expenditure* (London: Macmillan).

Niskanen, W. A. (1971), *Bureaucracy: Servant or Master?* (London: Institute of Economic Affairs, Hobart Paper No. 5).

Niskanen, W. A. (1973), *Bureaucracy and Representative Government* (Chicago: Aldine-Atherton).

Nordlinger, E. (1981), *On the Autonomy of the Democratic State* (Cambridge, Mass.: Harvard University Press).

Norton, A. L., and Rogers, S. (1981), 'The health service and local government', in G. McLachlan (ed.), *Matters of Moment* (Oxford: Oxford University Press), pp. 107–52.

OECD (Organization for Economic Cooperation and Development) (1975),

Reviews of National Policies for Education: Education Development Strategy in England and Wales (Paris: OECD).

Offe, C. (1975), 'The theory of the capitalist state and the problem of policy formation', in L. Lindberg, R. Alford, C. Crouch, and C. Offe (eds.), *Stress and Contradiction in Modern Capitalism* (London: Lexington), pp. 125–44.

Ogden Report (Department of the Environment) (1973), *New Water Industry* (London: HMSO).

O'Leary, B. (1985a), 'Is there a radical public administration?', *Public Administration*, vol. 83, pp. 345–52.

O'Leary, B. (1985b), 'The execution of the GLC: theories and a policy folly' (London School of Economics and Political Science, Department of Government, mimeo, August).

Oliver, J. (1978), *Working at Stormont* (Dublin: Institute of Public Administration).

Page, E. (1978a), 'Michael Hechter's internal colonial thesis: some theoretical and methodological problems', *European Journal of Political Research*, vol. 6, pp. 295–317.

Page, E. (1978b), 'Why should central–local relations in Scotland be different to those in England?', *Public Administration Bulletin*, no. 28, December, pp. 51–72.

Page, E. (1981), 'Grant consolidation and the development of intergovernmental relations in the United States and the United Kingdom', *Politics*, vol. 1, no. 1, pp. 19–24.

Page, E. (1982), 'The value of local autonomy', *Local Government Studies*, vol. 8, no. 4, pp. 21–42.

Page, E. (1984), *Political Authority and Bureaucratic Power* (Brighton: Wheatsheaf).

Page, E. (1985), 'State development and local government: a comparative study', paper to the thirteenth world congress of the International Political Science Association, Paris, July.

Pahl, R. (1978), 'Will the inner city problems ever go away?', *New Society*, 28 September, pp. 678–81.

Painter, M. (1980), 'Whitehall and roads: a case study of sectoral politics', *Policy and Politics*, vol. 8, pp. 163–86.

Panitch, L. (1980), 'Recent theorizations of corporatism: reflections on a growth industry', *British Journal of Sociology*, vol. 31, pp. 159–87.

Parker, D. J., and Penning-Rowsell, E. C. (1980), *Water Planning in Britain* (London: Allen & Unwin).

Parkin, F. (1979), *Marxism and Class Theory: A Bourgeoise Critique* (London: Tavistock).

Parkinson, M. (1985), *Liverpool on the Brink* (Hermitage, Berks.: Policy Journals).

Parkinson, M., Penny, J., Roberts, V., and Wilks, S. (1982), 'Politics, policies and partnerships: a progress report', paper to the conference of the Political Studies Association, University of Kent, April.

Parkinson, M. H., and Wilks, S. R. M. (1983a), *Inner City Partnership in Liverpool* (Final Report to the SSRC, mimeo).

Parkinson M. H., and Wilks, S. R. M. (1983b), 'Managing urban decline – the case of the inner city partnerships', *Local Government Studies*, vol. 9, no. 5, pp. 23–39.

Parry, R. (1980), 'The territorial dimension in United Kingdom public employment', *Studies in Public Policy*, no. 65 (Glasgow: University of Strathclyde, Centre for the Study of Public Policy).

Parry, R. (1981), 'Scotland as a laboratory for public administration, paper to the conference of the PSA UK Politics Group, Glasgow, September.

Parry, R. (1982), 'Public expenditure in Scotland', in D. McCrone (ed.), *The Scottish Government Yearbook 1983* (University of Edinburgh, Unit for the Study of Government in Scotland), pp. 98–120.

Parsons, T. (1947), 'Introduction', in M. Weber, *The Theory of Social and Economic Organization* (New York: Free Press), pp. 3–86.

Pater, T. E. (1981), *The Making of the National Health Service* (London: King Edward's Hospital Fund).

Pattison, M. (1980), 'Intergovernmental relations and the limitations of central control: reconstructing the politics of comprehensive education', *Oxford Review of Education*, vol. 6, no. 1, pp. 63–89.

Pearce, C. (1980), *The Machinery of Change in Local Government 1888–1974* (London: Allen & Unwin).

Perrow, C. (1979), *Complex Organizations*, 2nd edn (Glencoe, Ill.: Scott, Foresman).

Peston, M. H. (1984), *The British Economy*, 2nd edn (Oxford: Philip Allan).

Pickvance, C. (1976), 'On the study of urban social movements', in C. Pickvance (ed.), *Urban Sociology* (London: Tavistock), pp. 198–218.

Plant, R. (1983), 'The resurgence of ideology', in Drucker, Dunleavy, Gamble and Peele, op. cit., pp. 7–29.

Pliatzky Report (1980), *Report on Non-Departmental Public Bodies* (Cmnd 7797, London: HMSO).

Pliatzky, Sir Leo (1982), *Getting and Spending* (Oxford: Blackwell).

Plowden Committee (1967), *Children and their Primary Schools: A Report of the Central Advisory Council for Education* (HMSO).

Pollitt, C. (1977), 'The public expenditure survey', *Public Administration*, vol. 55, pp. 127–42.

Pollitt, C. (1984), 'Professionals and public policy', *Public Administration Bulletin*, no. 44, April, pp. 29–46.

Pollitt, C. (1985), '"Performance" in government and the public services: the impoverishment of a concept', paper to the fifteenth annual conference of the Public Administration Committee, University of York, September.

Pollock, L., and McAllister, I. (1980), 'A bibliography of United Kingdom politics: Scotland, Wales and Northern Ireland', *Studies in Public Policy*, vol. III (Glasgow: University of Strathclyde, Centre for the Study of Public Policy).

Powell, J. Enoch (1966), *A New Look at Medicine and Politics* (London: Pitman).

Preston, C. (1984), 'The politics of implementation: the European Regional Development Fund and EC Regional Aid to the UK 1975–81', PhD thesis, University of Essex.

Pryke, R. (1981), *The Nationalized Industries* (Oxford: Martin Robertson).

Pulzer, P. (1972), *Political Representation and Elections in Britain*, 2nd edn (London: Allen & Unwin).

Raab, C. D. (1982), 'The quasi-government of Scottish education' in Barker (1982a), pp. 91–107.

Rallings, C., and Thrasher, M. (1986), *The 1985 County Council Election Results in England: A Statistical Digest*, 2 vols. (Plymouth Polytechnic, Centre for the Study of Local Elections).

Ranson, S. (1980), 'Changing relations between centre and locality in education', *Local Government Studies*, vol. 6, no. 6, pp. 3–23.

Ranson, S. (1982), 'Central–local planning in education', in Hinings, Leach, Ranson and Skelcher, op. cit., appendix C.

Ranson, S. (1984), 'Towards a tertiary tri-partism: new codes of social control and the 17+', in Broadfoot, op. cit., pp. 221–44.

Ranson, S. (1985), 'Contradictions in the government of educational change', *Political Studies*, vol. 33, pp. 56–72.

Ranson, S., Jones, G. W. and Walsh, K., (eds), *Between Centre and Locality* (London: Allen & Unwin).

Redcliffe-Maud Commission (1967a), *Royal Commission on Local Government in England: Written Evidence of the Association of Municipal Corporations* (London: HMSO).

Redcliffe-Maud Commission (1967b), *Royal Commission on Local Government in England: Written Evidence of the Department of Education and Science* (London: HMSO).

Redcliffe-Maud Commission (1967c), *Royal Commission on Local Government in England: Written Evidence of the Ministry of Health* (London: HMSO).

Redcliffe-Maud Commission (1968), *Royal Commission on Local Government in England: Written Evidence of Professional Associations* (London: HMSO).

Redcliffe-Maud Commission (1969), *Report of the Royal Commission on Local Government in England 1966–1969* (Cmnd 4040, London: HMSO).

Redwood, J., and Hatch, J. (1982), *Controlling Public Industries* (Oxford: Blackwell).

Regan, D. E. (1966), 'The expert and the administrator: recent changes at the Ministry of Transport', *Public Administration*, vol. 44, pp. 149–67.

Regan, D. (1979), *Local Government and Education* (London: Allen & Unwin).

Regan, D. (1980), 'A headless state: the unaccountable executive in British local government', inaugural lecture, University of Nottingham, 2 May.

Rhodes, G. (1976), 'Local government finance, 1918–1966', in Committee of Inquiry into Local Government Finance (Layfield), appendix 6, *The Relationship between Central and Local Government* (London: HMSO), pp. 102–73.

Rhodes, G. (1981), *Inspectorates in British Government* (London: Allen & Unwin).

Rhodes, R. A. W. (1975a), 'The changing political-management system of local government', paper to the ECPR London Joint Sessions, European Urbanism: Policy and Planning Workshop, London School of Economics and Political Science, April.

Rhodes, R. A. W. (1975b), 'A comparative study of the decision making process within Oxford City and Oxfordshire County Councils, 1963–1968', B.Litt. thesis, University of Oxford.

Rhodes, R. A. W. (1975c), 'The lost world of British local politics', *Local Government Studies*, vol. 1, no. 3, pp. 39–59.

Rhodes, R. A. W. (1976), 'Centre–local relations', in Committee of Inquiry into Local Government Finance (Layfield), Appendix 6, *The Relationship between Central and Local Government* (London: HMSO), pp. 174–202.

Rhodes, R. A. W. (1979), 'Ordering urban change: corporate planning in the government of English cities', in J. Lagroye and V. Wright (eds.), *Local Government in Britain and France* (London: Allen & Unwin), pp. 127–49.

Rhodes, R. A. W. (1981a), *Control and Power in Central–Local Government Relations* (Aldershot: Gower).

Rhodes, R. A. W. (1981b), 'The changing pattern of local government in England: reform or reorganization?', in A. B. Gunlicks (ed.), *Local Government Reform and Reorganization: An International Perspective* (London: Kennikat Press), pp. 93–111.

Rhodes, R. A. W. (1982), *Final Report on the Local Authority Associations in Central–Local Relationships* (Final Report to the SSRC).

Rhodes, R. A. W. (1983), 'Can there be a national community of local government?', *Local Government Studies*, vol. 6, no. 6, pp. 17–37.

Rhodes, R. A. W. (1984), '"Continuity and change in British central–local relations: the "Conservative threat", 1979–83', *British Journal of Political Science*, vol. 14, pp. 311–33.

Rhodes, R. A. W. (1985a), 'Corporatism, pay negotiations and local government', *Public Administration*, vol. 63, pp. 287–307.

Rhodes, R. A. W. (1985b), 'Power-dependence, policy communities and intergovernmental networks', *Public Administration Bulletin*, no. 49, December, pp. 4–31.

Rhodes, R. A. W. (1985c), '"A squalid and politically corrupt process"? Intergovernmental relations in the post-war period', *Local Government Studies*, vol. 11, no. 6, pp. 35–57.

Rhodes, R. A. W. (1986a), *The National World of Local Government* (London: Allen & Unwin).

Rhodes, R. A. W. (1986b), '"Power-dependence" theories of central–local relations: a critical assessment', in Goldsmith, op. cit., pp. 1–33.

Rhodes, R. A. W. (1986c), 'The changing relationships of the national community of local government, 1970–83', in Goldsmith, op. cit., pp. 122–51.

Rhodes, R. A. W. (1986d), *European Policy Making, Implementation and Sub-Central Governments: A Survey* (Maastricht: European Institute of Public Administration).

Rhodes, R. A. W., Hardy, B., and Pudney, K. (1983), *The Reorganization of Local Government and the National Community of Local Government. A Case Study of 'Organic Change'* (Colchester: University of Essex, Department of Government, SSRC Central–Local Relations Project, Discussion Paper No. 4).

Rhodes, R. A. W., and Page, E. (1983), 'The other governments of Britain', in Budge, *et al.*, op. cit., pp. 104–35.

Rhodes, R. A. W., and Wright, V. (eds.) (1987), *Tensions in the Territorial Politics of Western Europe* (London: Frank Cass).

Richards, P. G. (1975), *The Local Government Act 1972: Problems of Implementation* (London: Allen & Unwin).

Richardson, J. J. (ed.) (1982), *Policy Styles in Western Europe* (London: Allen & Unwin).

Richardson, J. J., and Henning, R. (eds.) (1984), *Unemployment: Policy Responses of Western Democracies* (London: Sage).

Richardson, J. J., and Jordan, G. (1979), *Governing under Pressure* (Oxford: Martin Robertson).

Richardson, J. J., Jordan, A. G., and Kimber, R. H. (1978), 'Lobbying, administrative reform and policy styles: the case of land drainage', *Political Studies*, vol. 26, pp. 47–64.

Riddell, P. (1983), *The Thatcher Government* (Oxford: Martin Robertson).

Roberts, L., and Hodgson, P. (1978), 'Local authority associations', *County Councils Gazette*, November, pp. 231–4.

Robson, W. A. (1948), *The Development of Local Government* (London: Allen & Unwin).

Robson, W. A. (1962), *Nationalized Industries and Public Ownership*, 2nd edn (London: Allen & Unwin).

Robson, W. A. (1966), *Local Government in Crisis* (London: Allen & Unwin).

Rogow, A. A., and Shore, P. (1955), *The Labour Government and British Industry, 1945–51* (Oxford: Blackwell).

Rokkan, S. (1970), *Citizens, Electors and Parties* (Oslo: Universitets-forlaget).

Rose, R. (1971), *Governing Without Consensus: An Irish Perspective* (London: Faber).

Rose, R. (1974), *The Problem of Party Government* (London: Macmillan).

Rose, R. (1976), 'The United Kingdom as a multi-national state', in R. Rose (ed.), *Studies in British Politics*, 3rd edn (London: Macmillan), pp. 115–50.

Rose, R. (1982), *Understanding the United Kingdom* (London: Longmans).

Rose, R. (1984), *Understanding Big Government: The Programme Approach* (London: Sage).

Rose, R., and McAllister, I. (1982), *United Kingdom Facts* (London: Macmillan).

Rosenberg, D. (1984), 'The politics of role in local government – perspectives on the role set of treasurers in their relationships to chief executives', *Local Government Studies*, vol. 10, no. 1, pp. 47–62.

Rowley, C. K. (1979), 'Buying out the obstructors?', in Littlechild op. cit., pp. 107–18.

Salaman, G. (1979), *Work Organization* (London: Longmans).

Sampson, A. (1974), *The Sovereign State: The Secret History of ITT* (London: Coronet).

Sancton, A. (1976), 'British socialist theory of the division of power by area', *Political Studies*, vol. 24, pp. 158–70.

Saunders, P. (1980), *Urban Politics* (Harmondsworth: Penguin).

Saunders, P. (1981), *Social Theory and the Urban Question* (London: Hutchinson).

Saunders, P. (1982), 'Why study central–local relations?', *Local Government Studies*, vol. 8, no. 2, pp. 55–66.

Saunders, P. (1983), 'The "regional state": a review of literature and agenda for research', paper to the SSRC conference on Political Theory and Intergovernmental Relations, Nuffield College, Oxford, September.

Saunders, P. (1984), *'We Can't Afford Democracy Too Much': Findings from a Study of Regional State Institutions in South-East England* (University of Sussex, Urban and Regional Studies, Working Paper No. 43, November).

Scarrow, H. (1971), 'Policy pressures by British local government: the case of regulation in the "public interest"', *Comparative Politics*, vol. 4, pp. 1–28.

Schmitter, P. C. and Lehmbruch, G. (eds.) (1979a), *Trends towards Corporatist Intermediation* (London: Sage).

Schmitter, P. C. (1979b), 'Still the century of corporatism?', in Schmitter and Lehmbruch, op. cit., pp. 7–52.

Schon, D. A. (1973), *Beyond the Stable State* (Harmondsworth, Penguin).

School for Advanced Urban Studies (1977), *Planning Systems Research Project: Final Report* (University of Bristol, SAUS, mimeo).

Scott, J. (1979), *Corporations, Classes and Capitalism* (London: Hutchinson).

Sedgemore, B. (1980), *The Secret Constitution* (London: Hodder & Stoughton).

Seebohm Committee (1968), *Report of the Committee on Local Authority and Allied Personal Social Services* (Cmnd 3703, London: HMSO).

Select Committee on Nationalized Industries (1968a), *Ministerial Control of the Nationalized Industries: Vol. I, Report and Proceedings of the Committee* (First Report, Session 1967–8, HC371–I, London: HMSO).

Select Committee on Nationalized Industries (1968b), *Ministerial Control of the Nationalized Industries: Vol. II, Minutes of Evidence* (First Report, Session 1967–8, HC371–II, London: HMSO).

Select Committee on Nationalized Industries (1973), *Capital Investment Procedures* (First Report, Session 1973–4, HC65, London: HMSO).

Self, P. (1971), *Metropolitan Planning: The Planning System of Greater London* (London School of Economics and Political Science, Greater London Papers No. 14).

Self, P., and Storing, H. (1971), *The State and the Farmer* (London: Allen & Unwin).

Sharpe, L. J. (1972), 'British politics and the two regionalisms', in W. D. C. Wright and D. H. Stewart (eds.), *The Exploding City* (Edinburgh: Edinburgh University Press), pp. 131–46.

Sharpe, L. J. (1976), 'Instrumental participation and urban government', in J. A. G. Griffith (ed.), *From Policy to Administration* (London: Allen & Unwin), pp. 115–38.

Sharpe, L. J. (1977), 'Whitehall: structure and people', in D. Kavanagh and R. Rose (eds.), *New Trends in British Politics* (London: Sage), pp. 53–81.

Sharpe, L. J. (1978), 'Reforming the grass roots: an alternative analysis', in D. E. Butler and A. H. Halsey (eds.), *Policy and Politics* (London: Macmillan), pp. 82–110.

Sharpe, L. J. (1979a), 'Decentralist trends in Western democracies: a first appraisal', in L. J. Sharpe (ed.), *Decentralist Trends in Western Democracies* (London: Sage), pp. 9–79.

Sharpe, L. J. (1979b), 'Modernizing the localities: local government in Britain and some comparisons with France', in J. Lagroye and V. Wright (eds.), *Local Government in Britain and France* (London: Allen & Unwin), pp. 42–73.

Sharpe, L. J. (1980), 'Does politics matter? A summary', paper to European Consortium for Political Research (ECPR) Joint Sessions, Workshop on Urban Policy and Expenditure Patterns, Florence, March.

Sharpe, L. J. (1981), 'Is there a fiscal crisis in Western European local government? A first appraisal', in L. J. Sharpe (ed.), *The Local Fiscal Crisis in Western Europe* (London: Sage), pp. 5–28.

Sharpe, L. J. (1985), 'Central co-ordination and the policy network', *Political Studies*, vol. 33, pp. 361–81.

Sharpe, L. J., and Newton, K. (1984), *Does Politics Matter?* (Oxford: Clarendon Press).

Short, P. (1981), *Public Expenditure and Taxation in the UK Regions* (Aldershot: Gower).

Simeon, R. (1972), *Federal–Provincial Diplomacy* (Toronto: University of Toronto Press).

Simon, H. A. (1969), *The Sciences of the Artificial* (Cambridge, Mass.: MIT Press).

Singh, A. (1977), 'UK industry and the world economy: a case of de-industrialization?', *Cambridge Journal of Economics*, vol. 1, pp. 113–36.

Skelcher, C. (1980), 'The changing shape of regional planning', *Town Planning Review*, vol. 51, pp. 324–9.

Skinner, D., and Langdon, J. (1974), *The Story of Clay Cross* (Nottingham: Spokesman).

Smith, B. (1964), *Regionalism in England. 1: Regional Institutions – a Guide* (London: Acton Society Trust).

Smith, B. (1981), 'Control in government: a problem of accountability', *Policy Studies Journal*, vol. 9, pp. 1163–74.

Smith, B. C., and Stanyer, J. (1976), *Administering Britain* (Glasgow: Fontana/Collins).

Smith, T. (1975), 'Britain', in J. E. S. Hayward and M. Watson (eds.), *Planning Politics and Public Policy* (London: Cambridge University Press), pp. 52–69.

Smith, T. (1979), *The Politics of the Corporate Economy* (Oxford: Martin Robertson).

Social Services Committee (1984), *Public Expenditure on the Social Services* (Fourth Report, Session 1983–4, HC395, London: HMSO).

Social Services Committee (1985), *Community Care with Special Reference to Adult Mentally Ill and Mentally Handicapped People* (Second Report, Session 1984–5, HC13–1, London: HMSO).

Stanyer, J. (1974), 'Divided responsibilities: accountability in decentralized government', *Public Administration Bulletin*, no. 17, December, pp. 14–30.

Stanyer, J. (1976), *Understanding Local Government* (Glasgow: Fontana/Collins).

Steed, M. (1969), 'Politics: more balance?', *New Society*, 19 June, pp. 951–2.

Steel, D., and Heald, D. (eds.) (1984), *Privatizing Public Enterprises* (London: RIPA).

Steel, D., and Heald, D. (1985), 'The privatization of public enterprise 1979–83', in Jackson, op. cit., pp. 69–91.

Stevens, R. (1966), *Medical Practice in Modern England* (New Haven, Conn.: Yale University Press).

Stewart, J. D. (1958), *British Pressure Groups* (Oxford: Clarendon Press).

Stewart, J. D. (1971), *Management in Local Government: A Viewpoint* (London: Charles Knight).

Stewart, J. D. (1977), *Management in an Era of Restraint and Central and Local Government Relationships* (London: Municipal Group).

Stewart, J. D. (1980), 'From growth to standstill' in Wright, op. cit., pp. 9–24.

Stewart, J. D. (1983), *Local Government: The Conditions of Choice* (London: Allen & Unwin).

Stewart, J. D. (1986), 'A local service', in S. Ranson and J. Tomlinson (eds.),

The Changing Government of Education (London: Allen & Unwin), pp. 180–90.

Stewart, J. D., Leach, S., and Skelcher, C. (1978), *Organic Change: A Report on Constitutional, Management and Financial Problems* (Birmingham University, Institute of Local Government Studies).

Stewart, Michael (1977), *The Jekyll and Hyde Years: Politics and Economic Policy since 1964* (London: Dent).

Stewart, M. (1983a), 'The inner area planning system', *Policy and Politics*, vol. 11, no. 2, pp. 203–14.

Stewart, M. (1983b), 'The role of central government in local economic development', in K. Young (ed.), *National Interests and Local Government* (London: Heinemann), pp. 105–29.

Stewart, M., and Underwood, J. (1982), 'Inner cities: a multi-agency planning and implementation process', in P. Healey, G. McDougall and M. J. Thomas (eds.), *Planning Theory. Prospects for the 1980s* (Oxford: Pergamon), pp. 211–24.

Stewart, M., and Underwood, J. (1983), 'New relationships in the inner city', in K. Young and C. Mason (eds.), *Urban Economic Development: New Roles and Relationships* (London: Macmillan), pp. 131–51.

Stewart, M., Whitting, G., and Underwood, J. (1983), *Inner Cities Policy: The Principles and Practice of Partnership* (Final Report to the SSRC).

Stringer, J., and Richardson, J. J. (1982), 'Policy stability and policy change: industrial training 1964–82', *Public Administration Bulletin*, no. 39, pp. 22–39.

Tarrow, S. (1977), *Between Centre and Periphery: Grassroot Politicians in Italy and France* (New Haven, Conn.: Yale University Press).

Tarrow, S. (1978), 'Introduction', in S. Tarrow, P. J. Katzenstein and L. Graziano (eds.), *Territorial Politics in Industrial Nations* (London: Praegar), pp. 1–27.

Tawney, R. (1931), *Equality* (London: Allen & Unwin); page references are to the reprinted 4th edition with a new introduction by Richard M. Titmuss, 1964.

Tawney, R. H. (1966), *The Radical Tradition* (Harmondsworth: Penguin).

Taylor, W., and Simon, B. (eds.) (1981), *Education in the Eighties – the Central Issues* (London: Batsford).

Terrill, R. (1974), *R. H. Tawney and his Times* (London: Deutsch).

Thompson, J. D. (1967), *Organization in Action* (New York: McGraw-Hill).

Tivey, L. (1978), *The Politics of the Firm* (Oxford: Martin Robertson).

Tivey, L. (1982a), 'Nationalized industries as organized interests', *Public Administration*, vol. 60, pp. 42–55.

Tivey, L. (1982b), 'Quasi-government for consumers', in Barker, op. cit., pp. 137–51.

Townsend, P., and Davidson, N. (1982), *Inequalities in Health* (Harmondsworth: Penguin).

Travers, T. (1986), 'More accountability or just more paperwork?', *Local Government Chronicle*, 18 April, p. 428.

Travis, A. S., Veal, A. J., Duesbury, K., and White, J. (1978), *The Role of Central Government in Relation to the Provision of Leisure Services in England and Wales* (Birmingham University, Centre for Urban and Regional Studies, Research Memorandum 86).

HM Treasury (1971), 'Public expenditure survey system', Memorandum to the Expenditure Committee, Third Report, *Command Papers on Public Expenditure* (HC549, Session 1970–1, London: HMSO), pp. 17–22.

HM Treasury (1976), 'Evidence by HM Treasury', in Committee of Inquiry into Local Government Finance (Layfield), appendix 1, *Evidence by Government Departments* (London: HMSO), pp. 277–375.

HM Treasury (1979), *Needs Assessment Study – Report* (London: HMSO).

Treasury and Civil Service Committee (1981), *Financing of the Nationalized Industries* (Vol. I, *Report*; Vol. II, *Minutes of Evidence*; Vol. III, *Appendices*) (Eighth Report, Session 1980–1, HC348 I–III, London: HMSO).

Truman, D. B. (1951), *The Governmental Process* (New York: Knopf).

Tudor-Hart, J. (1971), 'The inverse care law', *The Lancet*, 27 February, pp. 405–12.

Tullock, G. (1979), 'Bureaucracy and the growth of government', in Littlechild, op. cit., pp. 21–38.

Urwin, D. W. (1982), 'Territorial structures and political developments in the United Kingdom', in S. Rokkan and D. W. Urwin (eds.), *The Politics of Territorial Identity* (London: Sage), pp. 19–73.

Vickers, Sir Geoffrey (1965), *The Art of Judgement* (London: Chapman & Hall); page references are to the Methuen paperback edition, 1968.

Walker, A. (1982), 'The meaning and social division of community care', in A. Walker (ed.), *Community Care: The Family, the State and Social Policy* (Oxford: Blackwell/Robertson), pp. 13–39.

Walker, D. (1983), *Municipal Empire: The Town Halls and their Beneficiaries* (London: Temple Smith).

Walsh, K., Dunne, R., Stoten, B., and Stewart, J. D. (1984), *Falling School Rolls and the Management of the Teaching Profession* (Windsor: NFER-Nelson).

Ward, H. (1983), 'The anti-nuclear lobby: an unequal struggle?', in Marsh, op. cit., pp. 182–211.

Ward, T. (1984), 'Memorandum by Mr Terry Ward, specialist adviser to the committee', in Treasury and Civil Service Committee, Third Report, *The Government's Expenditure Plans 1984–85 to 1986–87* (Session 1983–4, HC285, London: HMSO), Appendix 1.

Warren, J. H. (1952), *The Municipal Service* (London: Allen & Unwin).

Weaver, Sir Toby (1979), *Department of Education and Science: Central Control of Education* (Milton Keynes: The Open University, E222, Unit 2).

Webb, A., and Wistow, G. (1980), 'Implementation, central–local relations and the personal social services', in Jones, op. cit., pp. 69–83.

Webb, A., and Wistow, G. (1981), 'The personal social services', in P. M. Jackson (ed.), *Government Policy Initiatives 1979–80: Some Case Studies in Public Administration* (London: RIPA), pp. 200–24.

Webb, A., and Wistow, G. (1982a), *Whither State Welfare: Policy and Implementation in the Personal Social Services, 1979–80* (London: RIPA Studies 8).

Webb, A., and Wistow, G. (1982b), 'The personal social services: incrementalism, expediency or systematic social planning', in A. Walker (ed.), *Public Expenditure and Social Priorities* (London: Heinemann), pp. 137–64.

Webb, A., and Wistow, G. (1983), 'Public expenditure and policy implementation: the case of community care', *Public Administration*, vol. 61, pp. 21–44.

Webb, A., and Wistow, G. (1985a), 'Social services', in Ranson, Jones and Walsh, op. cit., pp. 207–24.

Webb, A., and Wistow, G. (1985b), 'Monitoring policy initiatives: the personal social services 1979–83', in Jackson, op. cit., pp. 209–28.

Webb, A., Wistow, G., and Hardy, B. (1986), *Structuring Local Policy Environments: Central-Local Relations in the Health and Personal Social Services* (Final Report to the ESRC, May).

Weber, M. (1947), *The Theory of Social and Economic Organization* (London: Collier-Macmillan).

Weber, M. (1948), *From Max Weber: Essays in Sociology* (London: Routledge & Kegan Paul).

Weiss, C. (1972), *Evaluation Research* (Englewood Cliffs, NJ: Prentice-Hall).

West Midlands Study Group (1956), *Local Government and Central Control* (London: Routledge & Kegan Paul).

Wheatley Commission (1969), *Report of the Royal Commission on Local Government in Scotland 1966–1969* (Cmnd 4150, Edinburgh: HMSO).

Widdicombe Committee (1986a), *Report of the Committee of Inquiry into the Conduct of Local Authority Business* (Cmnd 9797, London: HMSO).

Widdicombe Committee (1986b), *Research Volume I: The Political Organization of Local Authorities* (Cmnd 9798, London: HMSO).

Wildavsky, A. (1969), 'Rescuing policy analysis from PPBS', *Public Administration Review*, vol. 29, pp. 189–202.

Wildavsky, A. (1975), *Budgeting: A Comparative Theory of the Budgetary Process* (Boston: Little, Brown).

Wildavsky, A. (1980), *The Art and Craft of Policy Analysis* (London: Macmillan).

Wilkinson, G., and Jackson, P. M. (1981), *Public Sector Employment in the UK* (University of Leicester, Public Sector Economics Research Centre, mimeo, July).

Willcocks, A. J. (1967), *The Creation of the National Health Service* (London: Routledge & Kegan Paul).

Wistow, G. (1982), 'Collaboration between health and local authorities: why is it necessary?', *Social Policy and Administration*, vol. 16, no. 1, pp. 44–62.

Wistow, G. (1983), 'Joint finance and care in the community: have the incentives worked?', *Public Money*, vol. 3, no. 2, pp. 33–7.

Wistow, G. (1985), 'Community care for the mentally handicapped: disappointing progress', in A. Harrison and J. Gretton (eds.), *Health Care UK, 1985* (Hermitage, Berks.: Policy Journals), pp. 69–78.

Wistow, G., and Fuller, S. (1986), *Joint Planning Since Restructuring: The 1984 Survey of Joint Planning and Joint Finance* (Loughborough: Centre for Research in Social Policy/National Association of Health Authorities).

Wistow, G., and Hardy, B. (1985), 'Transferring care: can financial incentives work?', *Public Money*, vol. 5, no. 4, pp. 31–6.

Wistow, G., and Hardy, B. (1986), 'Transferring care: can financial incentives work?', in A. Harrison and J. Gretton (eds.), *Health Care UK, 1986* (Hermitage, Berks.: Policy Journals), pp. 103–10.

Wolin, S. (1960), *Politics and Vision* (Boston: Little, Brown).

Wood, B. (1976), *The Process of Local Government Reform 1966–1974* (London: Allen & Unwin).

World in Action (1976), 'Chrysler and the Cabinet: how the deal was done' (transcript of Granada Television programme).

Worswick, G. D. N. (1962), 'The British economy 1950–1959', in Worswick and Ady, op. cit., pp. 1–75.

Worswick, G. D. N., and Ady, P. H. (eds.) (1962), *The British Economy in the Nineteen Fifties* (Oxford: Clarendon Press).

Wright, D. S. (1974), 'Intergovernmental relations: an analytical overview', *The Annals*, no. 416, November, pp. 1–16.

Wright, M. (1977), 'Public expenditure in Britain: the crisis of control', *Public Administration*, vol. 55, pp. 143–69.

Wright, M. (ed.) (1980), *Public Spending Decisions* (London: Allen & Unwin).

Wright, M., and Young, S. (1975), 'Regional planning in Britain', in Hayward and Watson, op. cit., pp. 237–68.

Yin, R. K. (1984), *Case Study Research: Design and Methods* (London: Sage).

Young, K. (1975), *Local Politics and the Rise of Party* (Leicester: Leicester University Press).

Young, K. (1977), '"Values" in the policy process', *Policy and Politics*, vol. 5, pp. 1–22.

Young, K., and Mills, Liz (1980), *Public Policy Research: A Review of Qualitative Methods* (London: SSRC).

Young, S. (1982), 'Regional offices of the Department of the Environment: their roles and influences in the 1970s', in Hogwood and Keating, op. cit., pp. 75–95.

Young, S., and Lowe, A. V. (1974), *Intervention in a Mixed Economy* (London: Croom Helm).

Young, S. C. (1984), *An Annotated Bibliography on Relations between Government and Industry in Britain 1960–82*, 2 vols. (London: ESRC).

Younghusband, E. (1978), *Social Work in Britain: 1950–1975*, 2 vols. (London: Allen & Unwin).

Author/Name Index

Subject Index

See 'Analytical Contents' for a guide to the major theories and types of sub-central government discussed in the text. See 'Author/Name Index' for a guide to the discussion of particular authors. This 'Subject Index' concentrates on specific institutions, policies and concepts which are mentioned more than once but not covered in the foregoing.

local education authority 3, 9, 106, 248,
256, 257, 258, 261, 262, 263, 264,
265, 266, 267, 269, 270, 271, 394
Local government, (*passim*); *but see*
180–207 and 306–27; *see also*
Northern Ireland, Scotland, Wales
Local Government Act 1933 117
Local Government Act 1958 118
Local Government Act 1966 344
Local Government Act 1972 117, 135,
140, 307, 316, 317, 320
Local Government Act 1974 119, 136
Local Government Act 1986 135
Local Government (Access to
Information) Act 1985 135
Local Government and Planning
(Scotland) Act 1982 278
Local Government Finance Act 1982 119
Local Government Grants (Social Need)
Act 1969 344
Local Government (Miscellaneous
Provision) (Scotland) Act 1981 277
Local Government, Planning and Land
Act (1980) 118, 135
local government reorganization 9, 34,
72–3, 151, 220, 236, 306–21, 366n,
368, 374–5, 378
Local Government Training Board 222,
306
logic of negotiation 82, 242, 266, 326,
394, 396, 408
London Boroughs Association 193, 312
Lothian Regional Council 278, 279

Manchester 262, 274, 347, 357
Manpower Services Commission 9, 53,
89, 106, 129, 130, 164, 165, 167,
176, 178, 187, 236, 262, 263, 264–6,
334, 336, 339, 358, 394, 401
medical profession 78, 170, 179, 224,
300, 301, 305–6
and ideology 295–6, 300, 305; *see also*
British Medical Association
medium term financial strategy 108, 110,
142, 237, 238, 239, 242, 253
mentally handicapped people 149, 187,
287, 288–98 (*passim*)
Metropolitan County Council 29, 130,
180, 192, 203, 234n, 247, 249, 252,
308–9, 312, 317, 383, 393, 395, 401
Ministry of Agriculture, Fisheries and
Food 112, 156, 160–1, 338
Ministry of Housing and Local
Government 117, 153
Monopolies and Mergers Commission
125, 166

National Advisory Committee on Local
Government 209–10
National Association of Local
Government Officers 223, 317
National Coal Board 112, 121, 123, 124,
125, 176
national community of local government
58, 59, 79, 80, 83, 192, 199–200,
205, 232, 241, 253, 306, 307, 309–10,
310–17 (*passim*), 379, 385, 411
resources of 312–13, 324–5
National Development Team 295, 297
National Economic Development
Council 166, 331, 339
National Economic Development Office
122, 165
National Enterprise Board 329, 331
National Executive Committee, *see*
Labour Party
National Health Service 7, 9, 39, 57, 67,
70, 78, 87, 88, 89, 105, 106, 112,
115, 128–9, 138–9, 150, 164, 170,
175, 177, 179, 187, 204, 215, 218,
224, 231, 347, 348, 349, 355, 358,
363, 368, 370, 372, 375, 390, 392,
394, 395
and community care 287–306 (*passim*)
expenditure of 53, 85–6, 125, 300, 358,
399
and National Association of Health
Authorities 171
in Northern Ireland 169
in Scotland 167
National Health Service Act 1946 112
national local government system 80,
190, 205–6, 232, 258, 326, 327, 371,
405
nationalism 2, 30, 50, 56, 64–6, 69–70,
84, 375–6, 410; *see also* internal
colonialism
nationalization 8, 84, 192, 201, 208, 213,
225, 232, 233, 411
nationalized industries 6, 9, 13, 50, 53,
57, 70, 88, 105, 111–12, 114, 115,
120–8, 136–8, 164, 169, 174–5,
175–6, 177–8, 233n, 236, 237, 328,
330, 332, 333, 342, 374, 375, 379,
385, 392, 393
and consumer councils 137; *see also*
privatization
Nationalized Industries Chairmen's
Group 80, 115, 166, 171, 331, 339
neo-pluralism 48–9, 59, 94, 98–9n, 101n
network, *see* policy network
New Towns Development Corporation
53, 129

non-departmental public bodies 7, 9, 15,
53, 57, 87, 88, 95, 100n, 114, 115,
163, 164–80 (*passim*), 204, 207, 230,
231, 233n, 283–4, 309, 339, 368,
372, 381, 383, 403, 413n
and professions 170, 173, 178–9, 214,
215, 225
Northern Ireland 2, 15, 64, 65, 66, 70,
79, 143–53 (*passim*), 164, 185,
226–7, 228, 231, 282–4, 285, 340,
365, 372, 374, 380, 381, 383, 410
local government in 148, 152, 168,
181, 182, 184, 185, 194, 195, 196,
197, 198, 200, 204, 375; *see also*
nationalism, Northern Ireland
Office, territorial ministries
Northern Ireland Housing Executive
168, 178, 283, 285
Northern Ireland Office (Stormont) 7,
65, 70, 143–53 (*passim*), 168–9, 169,
178, 282, 381

ombudsman
local government 135–6, 205
health services 139
Orange Order 226, 228
organic change 307–8, 311, 313–15,
317–18, 319, 320, 380
Organization for Economic Cooperation
and Development 255–6

Parliament 15, 78, 112, 113, 121, 130,
313, 380
sovereignty 69, 110–11, 115, 209, 408,
412
links with local government 71, 73
party system 70–1, 208–14 (*passim*),
230–1, 379, 386, 408
central-local linkages of 71, 73, 199,
208–14 (*passim*), 231, 315–16, 375
in local government 191–2, 196–8, 354
and local government reorganization
311, 312, 319–21
and policy networks 83, 213, 327
performance indicators 123, 129
personal social services 9, 106, 133, 151,
152, 188–90, 201, 222, 223, 231, 236,
286–306 (*passim*), 307, 370, 401
Plaid Cymru 225, 226
planning – land use 82, 132, 151, 155,
159, 188, 190, 222, 307, 308, 318,
343, 348, 355
police service 83, 104, 130, 133, 204, 309
policy community 9, 78, 95, 236, 237–55,
323–4, 327, 331, 338, 361, 368, 390,
401, 405

expenditure 237–55 (*passim*), 399
education 255–74 (*passim*)
policy impact/outcomes, *see* equity,
evaluation
policy mess 8, 87, 96, 242, 386, 393, 396,
412–13
policy network 3, 4, 9, 48, 56, 60, 67–8,
77–87 (*passim*), 95, 96, 100n, 157,
158, 159, 214, 232, 235–6, 367,
370–1, 385, 389, 400
defined 77
characteristics of 77–8, 95, 284, 301–3,
321–5, 338–43, 343, 361–4, 368–9,
370; *see also* intergovernmental
network, issue network, policy
community, producer network,
professionalized network, territorial
community
Policy planning system 117, 134–5, 137,
138–9, 157, 158, 161, 203, 276, 351,
357
politicization 73, 74, 75, 84, 85, 96,
250–1, 321, 378, 385, 386, 411
and the 'culture of apolitisme' 71, 371,
372, 373
and local government reorganization
181, 320–1; *see also* dual polity
Post Office 123, 124, 126
power-dependence theory 42, 43, 88
pressure groups 43–4, 84, 208, 227–8,
229–31 (*passim*), 231–2, 312, 315,
316, 325, 326; *see also* sectoral
cleavages
privatization 22–3, 85, 125–7, 138, 243,
330, 381, 383, 395
and local government 204; *see also*
contracting-out
producer network 9, 80–1, 95, 236,
330–43 (*passim*), 368, 391, 399
professionalized network 9, 78–9, 95,
219–20, 224, 286–306 (*passim*), 361,
368, 399, 401
professions 23, 28, 35, 36, 38, 45, 47, 81,
96, 158, 170, 173, 178–9, 187–91,
192, 208, 232, 299–300, 301, 302,
303, 304, 305, 316, 361, 372–3, 375,
396, 404
central-local linkages 214–25, 231
and closure 60, 62, 273
and ideology 79, 179, 188–90, 295–6,
300, 305, 318–19, 365–6n
and local government 187–91, 201, 207
and non-departmental public bodies
170, 173, 178–9
and professionalization 8, 41, 58, 59,
411